BUSINESS RESEARCH METHODS

FIFTH EDITION

BUSINESS RESEARCH METHODS

Donald R. Cooper
Florida Atlantic University

C. William Emory
Professor Emeritus
Washington University

IRWIN

Chicago • Bogota • Boston • Buenos Aires • Caracas
London • Madrid • Mexico City • Sydney • Toronto

Senior sponsoring editor: Richard T. Hercher, Jr.
Editorial assistant: Gail Centner
Marketing manager: Brian Kibby
Project editor: Waivah Clement
Project manager: Jon Christopher
Cover designer: Annette Spandoni
Cover illustrator: Jeff Brice
Interior designer: Keith McPherson
Art coordinator: Heather Burbridge
Compositor: The Clarinda Company
Typeface: 10/12 Times Roman
Printer: R. R. Donnelley & Sons Company

Library of Congress Cataloging-in-Publication Data

Cooper, Donald E.
    Business research methods / Donald R. Cooper, C. William Emory.—
5th ed.
        p.   cm.
    Revised ed. of : Business research methods / C. William Emory.
    Includes bibliographical references and index.
    ISBN 0-256-13777-3
    1. Industrial management—Research.   I. Emory, William.
II. Emory, William.   Business research methods.   III. Title.
HD30.4.E47   1995
658′.0072—dc20   94–5000

Printed in the United States of America
1   2   3   4   5   6   7   8   9   0   DO   1   0   9   8   7   6   5   4

To our families

PREFACE

The test of a singularly versatile textbook comes with time, years of use and years of thorough, reliable coverage of the field. In 1976, when *Business Research Methods* was first published, it was a pioneer methodology text in business. The world has witnessed extraordinary change in two decades. Our field has changed too. Advances in technology have revolutionized the way information is processed and research is conducted. Secondary data searches, data collection, data entry and analysis, graphical visualization, reporting, and many related areas have been transformed.

Amidst all these changes, our book has kept pace and remained a favorite. As we approach the third decade of writing *Business Research Methods,* we pledge to continue fulfilling students' learning needs, exceeding professors' instructional requirements, and becoming more relevant to practicing managers. We can accomplish this only by listening to you. Over 70 of our colleagues recently told us what was important to them in teaching research and how we could better serve them. We believe that our responsiveness to their feedback, to the in-depth advice of our reviewers, and to students' expectations distinguishes the leaders of a textbook tradition from the imitators.

Changes to the Fifth Edition

Let us tell you what careful listening has taught us and how that has improved this edition. You asked that *Business Research Methods* maintain its comprehensive coverage of the research process in the business setting. By doing this, we fulfill your need for a text that spans the disciplines of business, providing breadth and depth, and serving as a valuable reference. Many also wanted the topical versatility that has made it suitable for managers and future managers of nonprofit and government organizations—especially those where the functions are similar to business and decisions are based on research information.

We have worked hard to respond to your requests for specific changes. The layout and graphics were again redesigned to make the text more readable and appealing. Icons now identify key components of each chapter for ease of use. Visual images were given a fresh look to accelerate understanding, simplify the explanation of difficult ideas, and promote synthesis. Each chapter was rewritten until it met literary standards for consistent comprehension and reading level.

Special Sections A preview called *Finding Your Way* appears at the beginning of each chapter to outline the scope and organization of topics. An exciting new series of vignettes, *Bringing Research to Life,* creates a sense of continuity and replaces standard chapter introductions. To most students' relief, they highlight the human side of research. True to life, they sometimes show conflict, usually reveal wit and humor, and always deal with practical issues for students and managers. Readers identify with the central characters in this continuing set of short stories. The interactions make for frequent page turning. Gender and multicultural themes are also given tactful treatment with this device. Our more jaded student readers tell us that the vignettes "breathe life into research."

New chapter *Close-Ups* illustrate critical learning points. They have been carefully connected to the content and tone of each chapter. With these auxiliary components, we have enhanced comprehension of each chapter's learning objectives. The synergy of *Bringing Research to Life* and *the Close-Ups* transports the reader through the research process. Starting with an amorphous management concern and working their way to the final report, students develop the skills necessary to produce and report research findings.

The summary section that completes each chapter benefits from a new *Key Terms* feature. Key terms are also bolded in the text. An expanded summary, key terms, discussion questions, reference notes, and revised suggestions for additional reading and reference improve closure for students.

Content Improvements   We think that business research should be more than a slimmed-down, repackaged version of marketing research. Thus, our changes strive to include diverse topical applications: human resource management, sales/sales managment, organizational culture, product development, finance, labor issues, customer satisfaction, retailing, advertising, corporate image—to name just a few.

Besides the new special sections, there are several noteworthy improvements to the chapters. "The Research Process," Chapter 3, was revised to give exploration a more prominent role in problem definition and the research process model. The question hierarchy is better connected to other parts of the text. The topic of valuing research information now receives special treatment in Appendix B. Chapter 4, "The Research Proposal," has rewritten sections on development and evaluation and offers a sample proposal that is connected with the vignette series. Appendix C outlines the construction of an RFP and examines its variations.

A chapter-length special section on "Ethics in Business Research" is introduced in the beginning of the text to stimulate an ongoing exchange about values and practical constraints throughout the chapters that follow. It contains a new guide to resource materials on ethical awareness and three new case studies. "Sampling Design," Chapter 8, has completely rewritten coverage that simplifies this subject for students. Liberal use of examples unifies theory and practice.

"Secondary Data Sources," Chapter 9, and Appendix A on "Business Reference Tools," offer the most comprehensive coverage of this topic you will find. Global communication is stressed by other texts but connectivity is often neglected. We tell you about Internet and provide you with the resources to get connected. Online databases, CD-ROM, e-mail sources, and more traditional search methods are fully explored.

The four statistical chapters have been pared down but retain their high example and graphics count. A special section on nonparametric hypothesis tests is now found in Appendix E. The Irwin *Software Series* for SPSS, SAS, and Minitab is available to supplement these chapters. It is cross-referenced to the chapter examples and discussion questions.

Chapter 18, "Presenting Results: Written and Oral Reports," has a revised section on the most effective graphic presentation aids and a sample research report. This report is the culmination of the project described in *Bringing Research to Life* and several *Close-Ups.* Appendix D contains a sample student project on a different topic.

Features of the Fifth Edition

If you are an existing user of this text, we think you will be delighted with the blending of new and old features. If you are contemplating adopting this text, consider the many features and benefits we offer you and your students.

Professors Will Appreciate:

- A balanced presentation of practical applications and fundamental concepts.
- Timely coverage of ethics in business research, electronic searches, exploratory data analysis, presentation of statistics, charts, and graphics, and communicating research findings.
- A focus on managerial decisions, emphasizing the need for sound reasoning, problem identification and formulation, and testing.
- Methods covered in depth, not a cursory review under the guise of simplicity.
- A process model that guides research question development and the study's sequence yet promotes flexibility in matching methods to problems.
- Topics that receive meager attention in other texts—reasoning and inference, research proposals, designing experiments, observational studies, content analysis, data preparation, statistical diagnostics and assumptions, and many more.
- Software options for data entry, analysis, complex table construction, and presentation layout.
- The availability of Irwin's *Software Series: SPSS, SAS,* and *Minitab Guides* and *Computerized Business Statistics,* diskette and manual.
- An *Instructor's Manual* containing course design ideas, student projects, learning objectives, transparency masters, class discussion suggestions, end-of-chapter and case answers, and test questions.

Students Will Enjoy:

- A crisp style with a readability level that does not talk down—equivalent to a *Business Week* editorial.
- Opening vignettes that offer a humanizing view of the topic with interesting characters, situations, and chapter-to-chapter continuity.
- Extensive learning aids: icons for quick section identification, chapter *Close-Ups* to illustrate important concepts, *Key Terms* boldfaced in the text and summarized, extended chapter summaries, discussion and computer questions, and suggested references for reports and papers.
- Practical examples and skill building techniques for a solid grounding in how to do research.
- Attractive graphics that illustrate learning points, not substitute for content.
- Informative appendices that speed the planning and execution of a research project.
- Exercises that build evaluation skills for assessing the worth of research designs and data handling procedures.
- A comprehensive reference for use beyond the course.

Target Audience and Organization

Over the years, we have taught research and data analysis for MBAs, executive MBAs, doctoral students, and public managers. *Business Research Methods* was originally written with MBAs in mind, although it supports other applications well. When used with undergraduate students, prior exposure to elementary statistics is recommended.

The book consists of four parts that parallel the research process. Part I introduces business research. Its chapters define and characterize the nature of business research, provide a foundation for thinking and reasoning scientifically, develop a step-by-step overview of the research process, explain how to propose a research project, and set the stage for ethical awareness and responsible decision making.

There are four chapters in Part II on the design of research studies. Starting with design strategies and their relative advantages, we go on to the role of measurement, the design of scales for various objectives, and the selection of a sampling design. Part III consists of five chapters on the sources and collection of data. The most frequently used methods and procedures in business research are described: secondary data search procedures, the types and uses of survey methods, instrument development, observational research, and experimentation.

Five chapters comprise Part IV on the analysis and presentation of data. A chapter on how to prepare data, explore it, and complete a preliminary analysis begins the unit. It is convenient for some course designs to skip from this chapter to the final one on reports. However, more advanced students will want the statistical overview of the next three chapters: hypothesis testing and statistical tests for different types of data (Chapter 15), correlation, bivariate regression, and nonparametric association (Chapter 16), and multivariate methods (Chapter 17). The presentation of research results completes Part IV. Appendices offer extensive reference materials and specialized information for advanced students.

Acknowledgments

We are grateful to the survey respondents and reviewers who helped us prepare the fifth edition. Our reviewers were Thomas J. Dudley, Pepperdine University; Hamid Falatoon, University of Redlands; Ralph J. Melaragno, Sonoma State University; Elizabeth E. Regimbal, Cardinal Stritch College; and Pamela Schindler, Wittenberg University. We attempted to make the many changes you sought and retain the features you endorsed. Thank you for your insightful contributions.

A few people deserve a special word of thanks. Jay S. Mendell, Florida Atlantic University, created the vignettes for this edition. He is a gifted storyteller whose colorful characters helped us make practical points about the confluence of quantitative and qualitative research. Darlene A. Parrish did the research and a splendid first draft for Chapter 9 and Appendix A. She has been a business reference librarian for many years and is currently a doctoral student in library science at Florida State University. Pamela R. Cooper cheerfully read many drafts and improved the exposition of difficult concepts. The original cover design was created by Paul D. Cooper, a graphic design student at Arizona State University. To these talented individuals, our gratitude.

We remain indebted to those who helped with the first four editions of the book. Robert Fetter, Claude McMillan, and Alexander Voloatta read the original manuscript and suggested improvements. Constructive critiques were provided by J. K. Bandyopedyay, Phillip Beukema, Alan D. Carey, Francis Connelly, William J. Evans, Stewart E. Fleige, Hamid Noori, Walter Nord, J. Paul Peter, Harold R. Rahmlow, Perri J. Stinson, and Richard A. Wald.

It was a pleasure to work with Heidi Buehre and Richard T. Hercher, Jr., at Irwin. We appreciate their enthusiasm and guidance throughout the project. We also thank the highly professional team that brought the book to completion—in particular, Keith J. McPherson, Waivah Clement, Nancy Dietz, and Gail Centner.

Comments about your successes with the text and suggestions for improvement are highly valued. We earnestly solicit them. You may contact us through our universities or in care of Richard D. Irwin, Inc., 1333 Burr Ridge Parkway, Burr Ridge, IL 60521.

Donald R. Cooper

Contents in Brief

CONTENTS

4   The Research Proposal   76

Special Section: Ethics in Business Research   97

PART II

THE DESIGN OF RESEARCH

5   Design Strategies   112

6 Measurement 138

7 Scaling Design 166

8 Sampling Design 198

PART I

INTRODUCTION TO BUSINESS RESEARCH

 **FINDING YOUR WAY**

BRINGING RESEARCH TO LIFE

"Jason Henry? I'm Myra Wines."

"Yes, come in, Ms. Wines. Sit in the living room. Over here on the sofa. Watch your step around the cables, though."

The silver-haired woman found her way among several crates of partially unpacked computer systems, stepped over a strip of duct tape that held several cables securely in place on the carpet, pushed aside a pile of accounting books that had been stacked on the sofa, and seated herself as gracefully as she could among the heap of textbooks, electronic gear, and unopened paper boxes, then snapped open a briefcase to produce a miniature cassette recorder that she clicked on. "If this makes you nervous, I'll turn it off," she said. "I was a TV investigative reporter for 25 years, and my rule was to run a recording until they told me to turn it off. Old habits die hard . . . especially ones that have gotten you out of a dozen jams."

"Turn it off then," said the younger man, curtly. "It doesn't make me nervous, but I fail to see the need of it. How long have you been out of TV? Were you in TV down here? You must have been on local, not network, because I don't recognize you. We are new here, not even unpacked. You can see that." All this came out in one breath.

"You moved here from Ottawa where you and your wife were employed by the United Nations. Your wife is a doctor in public health. You are an accountant turned business economist. You both graduated from college in California. You have already opened several corporations here in Florida—to do auditing, economic analysis, epidemiological consulting, and diversified business research. I don't know why you need four separate corporations, but that's your business . . . What have I missed?"

"My wife did a weekly public service TV program for distribution by the United Nations. She speaks four languages."

"I knew that. A TV producer for United Nations TV alerted me to your move to Florida."

"Then that covers everything, doesn't it," he said with asperity, "except a birthmark above my knee."

"Your right knee," she said positively. Panic flickered in his eyes and quickly she added, "Just a guess. Fifty-fifty chance of being right, you know."

That broke the tension. He laughed heartily. "I have a gold filling in one of my teeth. Can you tell me which one?"

Now she laughed. "I never bluff against such high odds as 32-to-1."

Then they both laughed. And then he killed the merriment by adding, "The odds would be 31-to-1, by the way, not 32-to-1. There would be one right answer and 31 wrong. Obviously, that makes the odds 31-to-1."

"How many computers do you have," she asked, changing the subject.

"Counting the portables, five, plus several dumb terminals. Plus three printers and one fax for incoming and one for outgoing. And a voice mail system and a pager. I am networking all of this together, as you can see. I have had six phone lines run in here, though I only need four right now. I took two extra, because I don't want the phone company coming in once I am all set up. We can't afford a big apartment, so I'm afraid I'll keep it all here in the living room. I have clients lined up in Phoenix, Butte, and Ottawa, people who will never see this apartment, and as far as they know, I am working out of the classiest suite in this city's best office building, because faxes and phone calls and electronic mail are all they will receive from me."

"Well . . .," she said.

"Yes, that's quite a few computers. But I'm your basic unapologetic computer jockey. I believe that you find the truth by crunching the numbers. I believe that. I really do."

"I don't agree. I'm your basic ex-TV reporter. I believe you get the truth by staying in touch with people, watching world events, seeing the big picture, and digging for revealing details. I have four

(continued)

phone lines—one each for a fax and answering machine, one for a computer that I use to dial into commercial online databases, and two additional phones so I can talk to two people at the same time. I have my own domestic incoming/outgoing 800 number, and if I don't run up a long distance bill of $1,000 a month for international calls, I know I am not living right."

"Really? I find it impossible to believe that being an ex-reporter is so very lucrative?"

"No, it isn't," she said with a chuckle. "When these wrinkles popped out on my face and my hair turned gray, the station fired me. After 25 years they told me I needed a face-lift, and when I said no, they canned me. Just like that. I got the scariest lawyer in town—someone so vicious I had once run a one-week exposé of him—and he got me a terrific settlement.

"I pick up a few thousand every month by giving lectures to conventions. One of my topics is 'The Angry Consumer.' It is very factually based material and absolutely up to date, because I am in daily touch with consumer advocates in every state capital, plus D.C., Ottawa, and even Tokyo and London."

"Is it all opinion and anecdote, or do you have some substantiating statistics?"

"My phone bill is astronomic."

"So it's anecdotal, that's what you're saying."

"If that's what you want to call it," she declared with a tinge of crankiness. "Anyway, to make a long story into a brief audio bite, after one of my particularly hard-hitting talks, one member of the audience approached me, asked a lot of questions about my laptop computer, which I used to control my slide show, and revealed she was the product manager for the very brand of computer that I use, the MindWriter."

"I know the brand. It's good equipment at a good price, but if it breaks down, you are in trouble, according to the computer magazines. However, I have no firsthand evidence the magazines are accurate."

"Well, she was an ex-reporter herself, turned product manager, and she is worried about customer satisfaction, especially in product service. She asked me to fly down to Austin, Texas, to meet with her and her people and to bring my 'numbers cruncher,' as she put it."

"And who would that be?"

"You I hope. I'll level with you. I am not a numbers person."

"I know that. You miscounted your telephone lines a minute ago. 'Fax.' 'Answering machine.' 'Dial-up databases.' 'Two for personal.' That makes five. You said four."

She flushed and counted slowly to 10 under her breath. This young man was not a gracious host. "Then you know what I am talking about," she bit out sharply. "Well, I would really like to do business with these folks in Texas, because my settlement with the TV station runs out in a year, but I cannot go in there without a 'numbers cruncher.' "

"I know something about customer research, and you are right to be nervous . . ."

"Not nervous. Concerned."

"Concerned then. Have it your way. You are right to be concerned. The first step will be to listen carefully and discover exactly what it is the client is concerned about, what the problem is from their point of view, what the problem really is at various levels of abstraction . . ."

"Listening to people. Discussing. Looking at things from different viewpoints. The kind of thing I am good at . . ."

"Right. And then we come to what I am good at. Measurement. Scaling. Survey design. Sampling the customers. Finally we would have to collaborate on reporting the results . . ."

"To which we would each contribute. Right?"

"Right."

"I have two tickets to Austin for next Wednesday. Can you break away from all of this unpacking and cabling and fly down with me."

"Sure. We will work out the money details later, OK?"

"OK. My sources in Toronto say you are intelligent, prickly and pigheaded, inclined to be overly left-brained and intolerant, but respectful of your elders. I think we will get along OK."

"I am willing to proceed on that hypothesis. We'll know when we have returned from Texas."

WHY STUDY RESEARCH?

Research methods provide you with the knowledge and skills you need to solve the problems and meet the challenges of a fast-paced decision-making environment. Business research courses are a recognition that students in business, not-for-profit, and public organizations—in all functional areas—need training in the scientific method and its application to decision making. Two factors stimulate an interest in more scientific decision making: (1) the manager's increased need for more and better information and (2) the availability of improved techniques and tools to meet this need.

During the last two decades, we have witnessed dramatic changes in the business environment. Emerging from a historically economic role, the business organization has evolved in response to the social and political mandates of national public policy, explosive technology growth, and continuing innovations in global communications. These changes have created new knowledge needs for the manager. Other knowledge demands have arisen from problems with mergers, trade policies, protected markets, technology transfers, and macroeconomic savings—investment issues.

The trend toward complexity has increased the risks associated with business decisions, making it more important to have a sound information base. Increased complexity means there are more variables to consider. The competition is more vigorous, with many businesses downsizing to make competitive gains. Workers, shareholders, customers, and the public are better informed and more sensitive to their self-interest. Government continues to show concern with all aspects of society. Each of these factors demands that managers have more and better information upon which to base decisions.

To do well in such an environment, you will need to be equipped with an understanding of scientific methods and a means of incorporating them into decision making. You will need to know how to identify good research and how to conduct it. This book addresses these needs.

As the complexity of the business environment has increased, there has been a commensurate increase in the number and power of the tools to conduct research. There is vastly more knowledge in all fields of management. We have begun to build better theories. The computer has given us a quantum leap in the ability to deal with problems. New techniques of quantitative analysis take advantage of this power. Communication and measurement techniques have also been enhanced. These trends reinforce each other and are having a massive impact on business management.

The Value of Acquiring Skills

Even if your major interest is in other aspects of management, there are at least four situations in which you can profit by having research skills. First, a manager often needs more information before making certain decisions. Your options are limited if there is no one to whom you can delegate this task; you either do not gather the information or gather it yourself with some reasonable level of skill. It is obvious which option is the better.

In a second instance, you may be called upon to do a research study for a higher-level executive. Such an opportunity is especially likely to occur early in your career; it can be just the chance you need to make a favorable impression on that executive. A third reason for having research skills is that you may need to buy research services from others, or at least evaluate research done by others. If you can understand the research design used and adequately judge its quality, your decisions will be better for it.

A fourth reason for you to study research methods is that you may find a career position as a research specialist. As a specialized function, it offers attractive career opportunities, especially in financial analysis, marketing research, and operations research. Job opportunities for researchers in other fields of management also exist.

WHAT IS RESEARCH?

Textbook writers are usually eager to supply definitions. Let's try a different approach. Instead of giving you a template-like definition of research in the managerial setting, let's begin with a few examples of management problems in which information gathering is involved. From these illustrations (see the cases), we can abstract the essence of research. How is it carried out? What can it do? And what should it not be expected to do? As you read these cases, be thinking about the possible range of situations for conducting business research and try to answer the following questions: *What is the purpose of the study? Is research always problem based?*

CASE 1

You work for a corporation that is considering the acquisition of a toy manufacturer. The senior vice president for development asks you to head a task force to investigate six companies that are potential candidates. You assemble a team composed of representatives from the relevant functional areas. Pertinent data are collected from public sources due to the sensitive nature of the project. You examine all of the following: company annual reports, articles in business journals, trade magazines, newspapers, financial analysts' assessments, and company advertisements. The team members then develop summary profiles of the candidate firms based on the characteristics gleaned from the sources. The final report highlights the opportunities and problems that acquisition of the target firm would bring to all areas of the business.

(continued)

CASE 2

You are the office manager for a group of physicians specializing in nuclear medicine and imaging. A prominent health insurance organization has contacted you to promote a new cost containment program. The doctors' committee to whom you will make a recommendation will have a narrow enrollment window for their decision. If they choose to join, they will agree to a reduced fee schedule in exchange for easier filing procedures, quicker reimbursement, and listing on a physicians' referral network. If they decline, they will continue to deal with the patients and the insurance carrier in the current manner. You begin your investigation in the patient files to learn how many are using this carrier. You then consult insurance industry data to discover how many potential patients in your area use this care plan and the likelihood of a patient choosing or switching doctors to find one that subscribes to the program. You attempt to confirm your data with information from professional and association journals. Based on this information, you develop a profile that details the number of patients, overhead, and potential revenue realized by choosing to join the plan.

CASE 3

A paint manufacturer is having trouble maintaining profits. The owner believes inventory management is a weak area of the company's operations. In this industry, the many paint colors, types of paint, and container sizes make it easy for a firm to accumulate large inventories and still be unable to fill customer orders. He asks you to make recommendations. You look into the present warehousing and shipping operations and find excessive sales losses and delivery delays because of out-of-stock conditions. An informal poll of customers confirms your impression. You suspect the present inventory reporting system does not provide the prompt, usable information needed for appropriate production decisions.

Based on this supposition, you familiarize yourself with the latest inventory management techniques in a local college library. You ask the warehouse manager to take an accurate inventory, and you review the incoming orders for the last year. In addition, the owner shows you the production runs of the last year and his method for assessing the need for a particular color or paint type.

Having modeled the last year of business using production, order, and inventory management techniques, you choose the one that provided the best theoretical profit. You run a pilot line using the new control methodology. After two months, the data show a much lower inventory and a higher order fulfillment rate. You recommend that the owner adopt the new inventory method.

(continued)

CASE 4

You work for the alumni association of a private university. The university is eager to develop closer ties with its aging alumni, to provide strong stimuli to encourage increased donations, and to induce older students to return to the university to supplement enrollment. The president's office is considering starting a retirement community geared toward university alumni and asks your association to assess the attractiveness of the proposal from an alumni viewpoint.

Your director asks you to divide the study into four parts. First you are to *report* on the number of alumni who are in the appropriate age bracket, the rate of new entries per year, and the actuarial statistics for the group. This allows the director to assess if the project is worth continuing.

Your early results reveal there are sufficient alumni to make the project feasible. The next step in the study is to *describe* the social and economic characteristics of the target alumni group. You review gift statistics, analyze job titles, and assess home location values. In addition, you review files from the last five years where alumni were asked about their income bracket. You are able to describe the alumni group for your director when you finish.

It is evident that the target alumni can easily afford a retirement community as proposed. The third phase of the study is to *explain* the characteristics of alumni who would be interested in a university-related retirement community. For this phase, you engage the American Association of Retired Persons (AARP) and a retirement community developer. In addition, you search for information on senior citizens from the federal government. From the developer, you learn what characteristics of retirement community planning and construction are most attractive to retirees. From AARP, you learn the main services and features that potential retirees look for in a retirement community.

From the government publications, you learn regulations and recommendations for operating retirement communities and a full range of descriptive information on the typical retirement community dweller. You make an extensive report to both the alumni director and the university president. The report covers the number of eligible alumni, their social and economic standings, and the characteristics of those who would be attracted by the retirement community.

The report excites the university president. She asks for one additional phase to be completed. She needs to *predict* the number of alumni who would be attracted to the project so she can adequately plan the size of the community. At this point, you call on the business college's research methods class for help in designing a questionnaire for the alumni. By providing telephones and funding, you arrange for the class to conduct a survey among a random sample of the eligible alumni population. In addition, you have the class devise a second questionnaire for alumni who will become eligible in the next 10 years. Using the data collected, you can predict the initial demand for the community and estimate the growth in the demand over the next 10 years. You submit your final report to the director and the president.

What Is the Purpose of the Study?

These four cases can be classified by their objectives. Case 1 and the first phase of Case 4 illustrate **reporting.** At the most elementary level, an inquiry may be made only to provide an account or summation of some data, perhaps statistics. The task may be quite simple and the data readily available. At other times, the information may be difficult to find and the assignment calls for knowledge and skill with information sources. Usually there is little inference or conclusion drawing. Purists claim this is not research, although carefully gathered data can have great value. Other researchers argue that at least one form, investigative reporting, has a great deal in common with widely accepted qualitative and clinical research.[1] The design does not have to be complex and require inferences for a project to be called research.

Case 2 and the second phase of Case 4 illustrate a descriptive study. **Description** tries to discover answers to the questions of who, what, when, where, and sometimes how. At this level, the researcher attempts to describe or define a subject, often by creating a profile of a group of problems, people, or events. Such studies may be a distribution of the number of times we observe a single variable or they may involve two or more related variables. They may or may not have the potential for drawing powerful inferences. They do not answer the question why. The descriptive study is popular in business research because of its versatility across disciplines. In not-for-profit corporations and organizations, descriptive investigations have a broad appeal to the administrator and policy analyst for planning, monitoring, and evaluating. In this context, "how" questions address such issues as quantity, cost, efficiency, effectiveness, and adequacy.[2]

Academics have debated the relationship between the next two levels of investigation, explanation and prediction, in terms of which precedes the other. Both types of investigation are grounded in theory, and theory is created to answer why and how questions. For our purposes, **explanation** goes beyond description and attempts to explain the reasons for the phenomenon that the descriptive study only observed. Case 3 and the third phase of Case 4 represent explanation. Here the researcher used theories or at least hypotheses to account for the forces that caused a certain phenomenon to occur.

Take another example. The aviation industry may be interested in explaining the radiation risks for flight crews and passengers from the sun and stars. The variables might include altitude, proximity of air routes to the poles, time of year, and aircraft shielding. Perhaps the relations among the four variables explain the radiation risk variable. This type of study often calls for a high order of inference making.

If we can provide a plausible explanation for an event after it has occurred, it is desirable to be able to predict when it will occur. **Prediction,** the fourth level of investigation, is just as rooted in theory as explanation. Why, for example, would a flight at a specified altitude at one time of year not produce as great a radiation risk to the airliner's occupants as the same flight in another season? The answer to such a question would be valuable in planning air routes. It would also contribute to the development of a better theory of the phenomenon. In business research, prediction is found in studies conducted to evaluate specific courses of action or to forecast current and future values. The final phase of Case 4 is an example of prediction.

Finally, we would like to be able to control the phenomenon once we can explain and predict it. **Control** is a logical outcome of prediction. Success in this endeavor, however, is largely decided by the complexity of the phenomenon and the adequacy of the theory. Using the earlier example, it may not be possible to make substantial changes in altitude and pole proximity variables for airliner routes because of weather, fuel, maintenance, and design limitations of the airplane. However, knowledge of risks associated with specific routes and further study of more controllable variables could reduce the radiation risks to certain occupants, particularly pregnant passengers and crew members.

Is Research Always Problem Based?

In the four cases, studies responded to problems that needed solving. **Applied research** has a practical problem-solving emphasis. It is conducted to reveal answers to specific questions related to action, performance, or policy needs. In this respect, all four examples appear to qualify as applied research. **Pure** or **basic research** is also problem solving, but in a different sense. It aims to solve perplexing questions (that is, problems) of a theoretical nature that have little direct impact on action, performance, or policy decisions. Thus, both applied and pure research are problem based, but applied research is directed much more to making decisions.

Some authorities equate research with basic or scientific investigations and would reject all four examples. History shows, however, that science typically has its beginnings in pragmatic problems of real life. Interest in basic research comes much later, after development of a field's knowledge. Research is too narrowly defined if restricted to the basic variety.

One respected author defines scientific research as a "systematic, controlled, empirical, and critical investigation of natural phenomena guided by theory and hypotheses about the presumed relations among such phenomena."[3] The terms *systematic* and *controlled* in this definition refer to the degree to which the observations are controlled and alternative explanations of the outcome are ruled out. The terms *empirical* and *critical* point to the requirements for the researcher to test subjective beliefs against objective reality and have the findings open to further scrutiny and testing. These qualities are what this author means by "scientific." Whether all research needs to be this stringent and should be "guided by theory and hypotheses about presumed relations" is debatable.

The classical concept of basic research does call for a hypothesis, but in applied research, such a narrow definition omits at least two types of investigations that are highly valued.[4] First is the exploratory study in which the investigators know so little about the area of study that hypotheses have not yet emerged.[5] An equally important area of study is that which purists call merely descriptive. The importance of descriptive research to business should be reinforced:[6]

There is no more devastating condemnation that the self designated theorist makes of the researcher than to label his work purely descriptive. There is an implication that associates "purely descriptive" research with empty-headedness; the label also implies that as a bare minimum every healthy researcher has at least an hypothesis to test, and preferably a whole model. This is nonsense.

In every discipline, but particularly in its early stages of development, purely descriptive research is indispensable. Descriptive research is the stuff out of which the mind of man, the theorist, develops the units that compose his theories. The very essence of description is to name the properties of things: you may do more, but you cannot do less and still have description. The more adequate the description, the greater is the likelihood that the units derived from the description will be useful in subsequent theory building.

In answer to the question posed at the beginning of this section, "Is research always problem based?" the answer is yes. Whether basic or applied, simple or complex, all research should provide an answer to some question.

Business Research Defined

Any of the four types of studies—reporting, description, explanation, or prediction—can properly be called research. We can also conclude from the various examples that *research is a systematic inquiry aimed at providing information to solve problems.* This defines the bare minimum that an effort must meet to be called research. We define **business research** as a systematic inquiry that provides information to guide business decisions.

All the case histories meet this definition, but they suggest different stages of scientific development. A rough measure of the development of science in any field is the degree to which explanation and prediction have replaced reporting and description as research objectives. By this standard, the development of business research is in a comparatively formative stage.

How Scientific Is Business Research?

The development of scientific method in business research lags behind the physical sciences. Physical scientists have been more rigorous in their concepts and research procedures. They are much more advanced in their theory development than are business scientists. The public domain sponsored much physical research, some of it for hundreds of years. Governments have allocated billions of dollars to support such research, driven by the motivation to overcome disease or to improve the human condition. Nations driven by threat of war and national pride have also played a major role in the advance of physical science. Much of the findings of their research is in the public domain.

Business research is of much more recent origin and is largely supported by business organizations that hope to achieve a competitive advantage. Research methods and findings cannot be patented, and sharing findings often results in a loss of competitive advantage. The more valuable the research result is, the greater the value in keeping it a secret. Under such conditions, access to findings is obviously restricted. Even though there is a growing amount of academic business research, it receives meager support when compared to physical research.

Business research operates in a less favorable environment in other ways, too. Physical research is normally conducted under controlled laboratory conditions while business research seldom is. Business research normally deals with such topics as human attitudes, behavior, and performance. People think they already know a lot about these topics and do not easily accept research findings that differ from their opinions.

Even with these hindrances, business researchers are making great strides in the scientific arena. New techniques are being developed, and rigorous research procedures are advancing rapidly. Computers and powerful analytical methods have contributed to this movement, but a greater understanding of the basic principles of sound research is more important.

One outcome of these trends is that research-based decision making will be more widely used in the future than it has been in the past. Managers who are not prepared for this change will be at a severe disadvantage.

WHAT IS GOOD RESEARCH?

Good research uses the **scientific method.** We list several defining characteristics of the scientific method below. A more thorough discussion occurs in Chapter 2.

1. The purpose of the research, or the problem involved, should be clearly defined and sharply delineated in terms as unambiguous as possible. The statement of the research problem should include analysis into its simplest elements, its scope and limitations, and precise specifications of the meanings of all words significant to the research. Failure of the researcher to do this adequately may raise legitimate doubts in the minds of readers as to whether the researcher has sufficient understanding of the problem to make a sound attack upon it.

2. The research procedures used should be described in sufficient detail to permit another researcher to repeat the research. Excepting when secrecy is imposed in the national interest, research reports should reveal with candor the sources of data and the means by which they were obtained. Omission of significant procedural details makes it difficult or impossible to estimate the validity and reliability of the data and justifiably weakens the confidence of the reader in research.

3. The procedural design of the research should be carefully planned to yield results that are as objective as possible. When a sampling of the population is involved, the report should include evidence concerning the degree of representativeness of the sample. A questionnaire ought not to be used when more reliable evidence is available from documentary sources or by direct observation. Bibliographic searches should be as thorough and complete as possible. Experiments should have satisfactory controls. Direct observations should be recorded in writing as soon as possible after the event. Efforts should be made to minimize the influence of personal bias in selecting and recording data.

4. The researcher should report, with complete frankness, flaws in procedural design and estimate their effect upon the findings. There are very few perfect research designs. Some of the imperfections may have little effect upon the validity and reliability of the data; others may invalidate them entirely. A competent researcher should be sensitive to the effects of imperfect design, and his experience in analyzing the data should give him a basis for estimating their influence.

5. Analysis of the data should be sufficiently adequate to reveal its significance, and the methods of analysis used should be appropriate. The extent to which this criterion is met is frequently a good measure of the competence of the researcher. Twenty years of experience in guiding the research of graduate students leads the writer to conclude that adequate analysis of the data is the most difficult phase of research for the novice. The validity and reliability of data should be checked carefully. The data should be classified in ways that assist the researcher to reach pertinent conclusions. When statistical methods are used, the probability of error should be estimated and the criteria of statistical significance applied.

6. Conclusions should be confined to those justified by the data of the research and limited to those for which the data provide an adequate basis. Researchers are often tempted to broaden the basis of inductions by including personal experiences not subject to the controls under which the research data were gathered. This tends to decrease the objectivity of the research and weakens confidence in the findings. Equally undesirable is the all-too-frequent practice of drawing conclusions from a study of a limited population and applying them universally. Good researchers specify the conditions under which their conclusions seem to be valid. Failure to do so justifiably weakens confidence in the research.

7. Greater confidence in the research is warranted if the researcher is experienced, has a good reputation in research, and is a person of integrity.

Were it possible for the reader of a research report to obtain sufficient information about the researcher, this criterion perhaps would be one of the best bases for judging the degree of confidence a piece of research warrants. For this reason, the research report should be accompanied by more information about the qualification of the researcher than is the usual practice.

Some evidence pertinent to estimates of the competence and integrity of the researcher may be found in the report itself. Language that is restrained, clear, and precise; assertions that are carefully drawn and hedged with appropriate reservations; and an apparent effort to achieve maximum objectivity tend to leave a favorable impression of the researcher. On the other hand, generalizations that outrun the evidence upon which they are based, exaggerations, and unnecessary verbiage tend to leave an unfavorable impression.[7]

These seven criteria provide an excellent summary of what is desirable in scholarly research. They should also be applied in business research, but circumstances require adjustments. Criterion 1 calls for specifying what will be done, but in many exploratory studies, it is not possible to be that precise. It is important, however, to state the nature of the research problem clearly and unambiguously.

Criterion 2 calls for complete disclosure of methods and procedures used in the research study. This also is highly desirable. It enables others to test the findings through replication. Such openness to scrutiny has a positive effect on the quality of research. However, competitive advantage often mitigates against disclosure in business research. Sometimes even the acknowledgment of a study's existence would be considered unwise. For example, firms like J. D. Power and Associates will not provide enough information on their methodology to repeat an automotive market study. Similarly, neither Compaq nor IBM knew of the extensive research the other was engaged in at the time each developed its low-cost line of desktop computers.

Criteria 3 through 7 should guide all research studies. While these criteria use phraseology such as "unambiguous as possible," this only recognizes the realities of research work. The aim is always to be objective, yet we are all subjective. We must also recognize that research designs have flaws, even though calling attention to them in our work may be painful.

The threat of bias is mentioned under criterion 3, but it should be given more emphasis. The business researcher often knows from the beginning what results the sponsor would like to have. To combat this potentially biasing influence, it may be necessary to secure an understanding before you start that the objective is to uncover reality—whatever that may be.

Ethics is the final criterion that we would add to the list. Ethical issues in research reflect important moral concerns about the practice of responsible behavior in society. Researchers frequently find themselves precariously balancing the rights of their subjects against the scientific dictates of their chosen method. When this occurs, they have a responsibility to guard the welfare of the participants in their studies, and also the organizations to which they belong, their clients, colleagues, and themselves. Careful consideration must be given to research situations where there is a possibility for physical or psychological harm, exploitation, invasion of privacy, and loss of dignity. The research need must be weighed against the potential for adverse effects. Typically, you can redesign a study, sometimes you cannot. The researcher should be prepared for this dilemma. As part of that preparation, we will address this topic in a special section starting on page 97. You may wish to turn to it now.

THE MANAGER–RESEARCHER RELATIONSHIP

Information gathering is an integral part of any manager's job. So it is not surprising that many managers do their own research, at least part of the time. When they lack either research time or talent, managers may delegate the task to a staff assistant or a research specialist. This delegation of responsibility can result in more relevant results, especially if the research is decision driven and each party makes a full contribution to the joint venture.

Decision-Driven Research

Business research has an inherent value to the extent that it helps management in making decisions. Interesting information about consumers, employees, or competitors might be pleasant to have, but its value is limited. If a study does not help management select more efficient, less risky, or more profitable alternatives than otherwise would be the case, its use should be questioned. The important point is: Applied research in a business environment finds its justification in the contribution it makes to the decision-maker's task.

Participant Contributions

Both managers and researchers have important obligations in making a research study successful. The obligation of managers is to specify their problems and provide researchers with adequate background information. It is usually more effective if managers state their problems in terms of the decisions they must make rather than specify the information they think they need. If this is done, both manager and researcher can jointly decide what information they need.

Researchers also have obligations. Organizations expect them to develop a creative research design that will provide answers to important business questions. Not only should researchers provide data analyzed in terms of the problem specified, but they should also point out the implications that flow from the results. In the process, conflict may arise between what the decision maker wants and what the researcher can provide. The decision maker wants certainty and simple, explicit recommendations, while the researcher often can offer only probabilities and hedged interpretations. This conflict is inherent in their respective roles and has no simple resolution. However, a workable balance can usually be found if each person is sensitive to the demands and restrictions imposed on the other.

Client Relations Problems

In an organizational setting, the researcher should look on the manager as a client. An effective working relationship between researcher and manager is not achieved unless several critical barriers are overcome. Some are traced to management's limited exposure to research. Managers seldom have had either formal training in research methodology or research expertise gained through experience.

In addition, managers often see research people as threats to their personal status. They still view management as the domain of the "intuitive artist" who is the master in this area. They may believe a request for research assistance implies they are inadequate to the task. These fears are often justified. The researcher's function is to test old ideas and new ones. To the insecure manager, the researcher is a potential rival.

The researcher will inevitably have to consider the political situations that develop in any organization. Members strive to maintain their niches and may seek ascendancy over their colleagues. Coalitions form and people engage in various self-serving activities, both overt and covert. As a result, research is blocked or the findings or objectives of the research are distorted for an individual's self-serving purposes. To allow one's operations to be probed with a critical eye may be to invite trouble from others competing for promotion, resources, or other forms of organizational power.

Another problem reflects the explosive growth of research technology in recent years. A knowledge gap has developed between managers and research specialists as model building and more sophisticated investigative techniques have come into use. The manager must now put his or her faith in the research specialist and hope for the best.

A fifth source of client-related stress for researchers is their frequent isolation from managers. Researchers draw back into their specialty and talk among themselves. Management's lack of understanding compounds this problem. The research department can become isolated. These problems have caused some people to advocate the use of a "research generalist." Such a person would head the research activity, help managers detail their research needs, and translate these needs into research problems. He or she would also facilitate the flow of information between manager and researcher that is so important for bringing the researcher into the decision-making process.

One objective of this text is to address these problems. In the chapters that follow, we discuss scientific research procedures and show their application to the pragmatic problems of the business manager. At a minimum, our objective is to make you a more intelligent consumer of research products.

Summary

The managers of tomorrow will need to know more than any managers in history. Research will be a major contributor to that knowledge. Managers will find knowledge of research methods to be of value in many situations. They may need to conduct research either for themselves or others. As buyers of research services, they will need to be able to judge research quality. Finally, they may become research specialists themselves.

Research is any organized inquiry carried out to provide information for solving problems. Business research is a systematic inquiry that provides information to guide business decisions. This includes reporting, descriptive, explanatory, and predictive studies. We emphasize the last three in this book.

What characterizes good research? Generally, one expects good research to be purposeful, with clearly defined goals, with defensible and repeatable procedures, and with evidence of objectivity. The reporting of procedures—their strengths and weaknesses—should be complete and honest. Appropriate analytical techniques should be used; conclusions drawn should be limited to those clearly justified by the findings. If the investigator has an established reputation for quality work, so much the better. The research objective should be weighed against potentially adverse effects.

The manager–researcher relationship is an important one. Both share the obligation of making a project meaningful. Several factors complicate this relationship. Among these are ethical considerations and the political environment.

Key Terms

applied research   explanation
basic research   prediction
business research   pure research
control   reporting
description   scientific method

Discussion Questions

1. What is research? Why should there be any question about the definition of research?

2. Managers who wish to have information on which to base a decision face a make-or-buy situation. What are the problems they face in selecting either of these alternatives?

3. You are manager of the midwestern division of a major corporation, supervising five animal-feed plants scattered over four states. Corporate headquarters asks you to conduct an investigation to determine whether any of these plants should be closed, expanded, moved, or reduced. Is there a possible conflict between your roles as an investigator and manager? Explain.

4. Advise each of the following persons on a specific research study that he or she might find useful. Classify each proposed study as reporting, description, explanation, or prediction.
   a. Manager of the men's furnishings department at a national chain.
   b. Plant manager at a Ford auto assembly plant.
   c. Director of admissions at a large state university.
   d. Investment analyst at an investment firm.
   e. Director of personnel at a large metropolitan hospital.
   f. Product manager for Crest toothpaste at Procter & Gamble.

5. The new president of an old, established company is facing a problem. The company is currently unprofitable and is, in the president's opinion, operating inefficiently. The company sells a wide line of equipment and supplies to the dairy industry. Some items it manufactures, and many it wholesales to dairies, creameries, and similar plants. Because the industry is changing in several ways, survival will be more difficult in the future. In particular, many equipment companies are bypassing the wholesalers and selling directly to dairies. In addition, many of the independent dairies are being taken over by large food chains. How might research help the new president make the right decisions? In answering this question, consider the areas of marketing and finance as well as the whole company.

6. You have received a research report done by a consultant for your firm—a life insurance company. The study is a survey of morale in the home office and covers the opinions of about 500 secretaries and clerks plus about 100 executives and actuaries. You are asked to comment on its quality. What would you look for?

Reference Notes

1. See, for example, Murray Levine, "Investigative Reporting as a Research Method: An Analysis of Bernstein and Woodward's *All The President's Men,*" *American Psychologist* 35 (1980), pp. 626–38.
2. See, for example, Elizabethann O'Sullivan and Gary R. Rassel, *Research Methods for Public Administrators* (New York: Longman, Inc., 1989), pp. 19–39.
3. Fred N. Kerlinger, *Foundations of Behavioral Research,* 3rd ed. (New York: Holt, Rinehart & Winston, 1986), p. 10.
4. A hypothesis is a statement that is advanced for the purpose of testing its truth or falsity.
5. An exploratory study describes an investigation when the final research problem has not yet been clearly fixed. Its aim is to provide the insights needed by the researcher to develop a more formal research design.
6. Reprinted with permission of Macmillan Publishing Co., Inc., from *Theory Building,* rev. ed. 1978, by Robert Dubin. Copyright © 1969 by The Free Press, a division of the Macmillan Co.
7. James Harold Fox, "Criteria of Good Research," *Phi Delta Kappan* 39 (March 1958), pp. 285–86.

Suggested Readings

1. Foreman, Howard E., and Clarence C. Sherwood. *Social Research and Social Policy.* Englewood Cliffs, N.J.: Prentice Hall, 1970. Chapter 2 discusses the contribution of research to social policy.
2. Random, Matthew. *The Social Scientist in American Industry.* New Brunswick, N.J.: Rutgers University Press, 1970. A research report of experiences of social scientists employed in industry. Chapter 9 presents a summary of findings.
3. Richie, J. R. Brent. "Roles of Research in the Management Process." *MSU Business Topics,* Summer 1976, pp. 13–22. A description of the relationship between research methodology and the management process with a classification scheme.

CHAPTER
2 SCIENTIFIC THINKING

 **FINDING YOUR WAY**

BRINGING RESEARCH TO LIFE

"Every summer," said the silver-haired woman, "I was called up for Army Reserve, as a captain. They never knew what to do with me, a woman and a TV journalist. I think they feared my snoopiness would break out of control.

"One summer I was sent to a firing range to test a cannon.

"The range was several hundred acres that had been strip-mined until it was worse than a moonscape. Nothing in there lived or moved; nothing but craters and trenches existed there. And the nearest town—it was so severely depressed that, for the pitifully few jobs we provided, the folks welcomed us in, to bomb their backyard to flinders. Mining was totally played out. Dead. Yet this had been, in its day, one of the most prosperous mining regions, where the people were known for fearlessly and proudly going out to dig and produce.

"The cannon was impressive. We armed it with 3-inch shells, put on ear protectors and goggles and lobbed shells into the range. There would be a tremendous flash and boom, and the shells would go roaring and soaring out of sight, and then we would hear a tremendous boom coming back to us, and then see dust and ash kicked up several hundred feet. We were all very happy not to be down range, I can tell you. We went down range later. There would be a huge crater and a fused puddle of iron, but nothing recognizable except slag and molten rocks, if you call them recognizable.

"There was this one problem. About every 20th shell would be a dud. It would fly off and land, and maybe kick up some dust, but explode it would not.

"On paper, this was not supposed to be a problem. The duds were supposed to be quite safe. An officious second lieutenant was sent down by the arsenal, and he showed us reports that the Army had dropped such duds from hundred-foot platforms, from helicopters, had applied torches to them—everything—and had discovered them to be completely inert. The only thing to ignite one of these duds would be to drop another, live bomb on it.

"Regrettably, this proved not to be the case, because often in the middle of the night we would hear one of these so-called 'duds' explode. We would rush out at dawn, and sure enough, find a new crater, molten slag, molten rock, and so forth. It was quite a mystery.

"So I did what I am supposed to be good at and nosed around. I sat up one night on a hill overlooking the range, and, sure enough, I saw people with flashlights moving around in there.

"Locals were coming in at night, intending to crack open the bombs and scavenge for copper wire or anything they thought was salvageable. Except, of course, this ignited one of the beauties, in a crime that erased any evidence of its perpetration, so to speak, as the perpetrators were vaporized on the spot.

"I hung around town and mixed with the folks, saw how they occupied themselves. They were involved in auto racing, demolition derbies, every kind of thrill sport. It was not unusual to see a 50-mile race with four ambulances on hand on the edge of the oval, to cart off the carnage to the surgical hospital in the next county. I saw men leap into cars with threadbare tires, loose wheels, malfunctioning brakes, brake fluid and transmission fluid drooling all over the track. Nobody thought anything of this. If I asked, their answer was, 'I'll go when my number is up,' or 'It's not in my hands.'

"These good folk had lost all sense of cause and effect. They could wheel their cars out onto the track on a tire they knew was thin as tissue, and if it blew out and put them in the hospital, their reaction was, 'My time came,' or 'Some days you can't win for losin'.'

"It made sense, from a cultural-economic view. That very nonscientific attitude was what has let their men go down in the mines year after year. Was the fire detection and control system out of commission? 'No big deal, 'cause if your number is not up, you have nothing to worry about and if it's up, nothing you can do 'bout it, brother.'

(continued)

"I begged the sheriff to warn them away from our range. 'What's the big problem, Captain Wines?' he asked. 'They are going to kill themselves,' I said. 'They are going to die anyway,' he said. 'We all are going to die. People died every month who never went out on the range.'

"There is no way to deal with such nonscientific thinking by applying logic. We changed our procedure. We would fire the shells in the morning and spend the afternoon finding the duds, to which we would attach kerosene lanterns. At dusk, a fighter-bomber would fly over the area and bomb the lanterns—and the 'dud'—to a molecular state. It was neat and it worked."

STYLES OF THINKING

At the heart of every research course is the question of perspective: How one sees the world affects the kind of questions asked and the answers that can be accepted as explanations. Of the hundreds of questions about organizations or finance or marketing that could be asked, each would presuppose a normative perspective for that particular question and some would be more productive for obtaining answers.

We open this chapter with a discussion of the ways people think about problems. The method of scientific inquiry is one of them, and as a preferred form, its features are contrasted with other styles of thinking. Next covered are the tools of induction and deduction that are necessary for reasoning throughout the research process. Their relation to scientific problem solving is illustrated. Also explored is the role of the scientific attitude in energizing the conduct of research. Finally, we turn to the terminology of science that has been adopted as a specialized language of research. In that section, the building blocks for constructing theory and designing research studies are defined and explained.

Sources of Knowledge

Sources of knowledge range from untested opinion to highly systematic styles of thinking. We rarely think about how we know something or where this knowledge originated as we go about our daily lives, but this is a significant subject for researchers. From ancient times to the present, there has been a persistent interest in discovering how we know. Researchers depend on an ability to discriminate among knowledge sources to identify those that produce the best results for a given situation.

The philosophy of science provides the classifications that help us with this task. Over the years, there has been considerable discussion about the effectiveness of various sources of knowledge. Thinking styles associated with the scientific method are generally regarded as the preeminent means for securing truth, though that truth may not be permanent. But the scientific method is not the only source of our knowledge as this section will attempt to explain.

Figure 2–1 classifies some of the styles of thinking and locates them from the standpoint of logic.[1] We are oriented by the axes. The horizontal axis ranges from a highly idealistic, interpretational stance on one end to empiricism on the other. **Empiricism** is said "to denote observations and propositions based on sense experience and/or derived from such experience by methods of inductive logic, including mathematics and statistics."² Empiricists attempt to describe, explain, and make predictions through observation. This book is concerned with empiricism—with the design of procedures to collect factual information about hypothesized relationships that can be used to decide if a particular image of a problem is correct.

Scientific knowledge is obtained through inductive, empirical approaches. It is also secured through theoretical means that are based in deductive reasoning. A vertical axis is used to represent this orientation in Figure 2–1. The rationalism end of the continuum is of interest. By **rationalism** we mean that reason is a primary source of knowledge. Rationalism differs from empiricism in that rationalists believe all knowledge can be deduced from known laws or basic truths of nature. This is claimed to be possible because underlying laws structure the world logically. From the time of Sir Frances Bacon to the present, adherents of this view maintain that problems are best understood and resolved through formal

FIGURE   2-1   Styles of Thinking

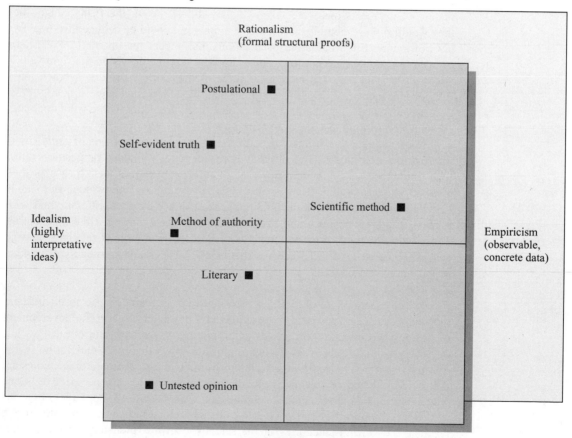

logic or mathematics. Such efforts, of course, operate independently of observation and data collection.

Untested opinion is a form of knowing that people cling to despite contrary evidence. In the indoctrination programs of less enlightened organizations, it is not unusual for new employees to hear, "that's the way we've always done it here," a phrase that confuses entrenchment and habit with efficiency. Most families have an old relative who maintains a conspiracy theory for a memorable world event despite overwhelming evidence. The illogical conclusions of this style are captured by Myra's experience with the locals in the vignette. Myth, superstition, and hunch have been serious competitors for scientific thinking down through time because, as one writer notes, "they have the reassuring feel of certainty before the event they try to predict or control, though seldom afterwards."[3] Business researchers will find little to improve their understanding of reality from this position, though they should be prepared to cope with it on occasion.

A way of knowing often called the method of *self-evident truth* was illustrated by the sheriff in our example. It was self-evident to him that people would die no matter what precautions were taken. If they didn't die on the firing range, then they would from something else. It was inevitable; it could be deduced from known laws of nature. But what about propositions that appear reasonable to one person or even to many but are not true. For example, everyone drives on the right side of the road. That is only self-evident to some of the world's drivers. Women make inferior managers, men of noble birth are natural leaders, or Japanese quality practices are universally applicable to U.S. productivity problems. These were once self-evident propositions that are now dismissed.

Since not all propositions are self-evident, we rely on persons of *authority* to improve our confidence. Too often authority depends on status or position rather than true expertise. Such authorities are often wrong, so it is wise to accept their views cautiously. Authorities serve as important sources of knowledge but should be judged by their integrity, the quality of the evidence they present, and their willingness to present an open and balanced case. Many do not meet these standards. Those who do are often misapplied: Henry Ford on international relations, Lee Iacocca on protected markets, Jack Welch on small business, or John Sculley on brand management.

The *literary* style of thought occupies a viewpoint toward the center of the figure. The literary style of thinking is responsible for many classic case studies in the social sciences. Case studies have played a prominent role in the development of business knowledge. Portions of anthropology, psychiatry, and clinical sociology can also trace their roots to this origin. Maslow's theory of motivation is one example from psychology that is well known in business. Business case studies are a preferred method of teaching in many programs. The literary perspective is one where "a person, a movement, or a whole culture is interpreted, but largely in terms of the specific purposes and perspectives of the actors, rather than in terms of the abstract and general categories of the scientist's own explanatory scheme."[4] Because it is difficult to generalize from individual case studies, our ability to derive principles is restricted.

Figure 2–1 positions the *scientific method* close to the empirical end of the horizontal axis. The essential tenets of science are: (1) direct observation of phenomena, (2) clearly defined variables, methods, and procedures, (3) empirically testable hypotheses, (4) the ability to rule out rival hypotheses, (5) the statistical rather than linguistic justification of conclusions, and (6) the self-correcting process. One author has noted, "Current scientific methods wed the best aspects of the logic of the rational approach with the observational aspects of the empirical orientation into a cohesive, systematic perspective."[5] The application of previously tested and verifiable procedures solved Myra's dilemma with the unexploded bombs. Case 4 in the last chapter is an example of business research that uses the scientific method.

Competing styles of thinking influence research directions in business just as they do throughout the social and behavioral sciences. The *postulational* style can be found in the upper portion of the diagram. Studies in operations research, management science, mathematical modeling, and simulation are postulational. For example, many firms run simulations of their market before a product announcement. These might examine different pricing levels and manufacturing output to optimize profitability. One goal of this perspective is to reduce the object of study to mathematical, formal terms. These terms, called postulates, are used to devise theorems that represent logical proofs. The objective is to deduce a structure that may account for any phenomenon having similar form.

There is no single best perspective from which to view reality or to do science, only preferred ones. The range of available styles of thinking offers many frameworks to confront the diverse problems of business. Some perspectives, such as the postulational style, rely on deductive logical processes. In contrast, the scientific method uses induction; inferences are made about the characteristics of populations based on the observed characteristics of samples. We have also mentioned less desirable ways of thinking that lack a logical foundation and rely on feeling and intuition to understand reality. Useful knowledge abounds; one should simply be aware of the vantage point selected to find it and the strengths and weaknesses of that position.

THE THOUGHT PROCESS: REASONING

Scientific inquiry has been described as a puzzle-solving activity.[6] For the researcher, puzzles are solvable problems that may be clarified or resolved through reasoning. In the opening scene of *The Sign of the Four,* Sir Arthur Conan Doyle uses a conversation between Sherlock Holmes and Dr. Watson to demonstrate the importance of precise reasoning and careful observation in the solving of puzzles and unraveling of mysteries. Watson provides the test by handing Holmes a watch and asking him to venture an opinion on the character or habits of the late owner. Sherlock Holmes's fans are not disappointed in the outcome. After a few moments' examination, Holmes correctly infers the watch belonged to Watson's careless and untidy elder brother, a man who inherited wealth, treated his prospects foolishly, and died a drunkard. The speed of the conclusion is startling, but the trail of his reasoning process from small facts to inductions and on to conclusions, which he confirms with Watson, is a common thought process for detectives, scientists, and puzzle-solvers.

Every day we reason with varying degrees of success and communicate our message, called meaning, in ordinary language or, in special cases, in symbolic, logical form. Our meanings are conveyed through one of two types of discourse: exposition or argument. Exposition consists of descriptive statements that merely state and do not give reasons. Argument, on the other hand, allows us to explain, interpret, defend, challenge, and explore meaning. Two types of argument of great importance to research are deduction and induction.

Deduction
    Deduction is a form of inference that purports to be conclusive—the conclusion must necessarily follow from the reasons given. These reasons are said *to imply the conclusion and to represent a proof.* This is a much stronger and different bond between reasons and conclusions than is found with induction.

For a deduction to be correct, it must be *both true and valid.* That is, the premises (reasons) given for the conclusion must agree with the real world (be true). In addition, the premises must be arranged in a form such that the *conclusion must necessarily follow from the premises.* A deduction is valid if it is impossible for the conclusion to be false if the premises are true. Logicians have established rules by which one can judge whether a deduction is valid. Conclusions are not logically justified if (1) one or more premises are untrue or (2) the argument form is invalid. Yet, the conclusion may still be a true statement, but for reasons other than those given. For example, consider the following simple deduction:

> (Premise 1)—All regular employees can be trusted not to steal.
>
> (Premise 2)—John is a regular employee.
>
> (Conclusion)—John can be trusted not to steal.

If we believe that John can be trusted, we might think this is a sound deduction. But this conclusion cannot be accepted as a sound deduction unless the argument form is valid and the premises true. In this case, the form is valid, and premise 2 can be easily confirmed. However, many may challenge the sweeping premise that "all regular employees can be trusted not to steal." While we may believe John will not steal, such a conclusion is a sound deduction only if both premises are accepted as true. If one premise fails the acceptance test, then the conclusion is not a sound deduction. This is so even if we still have great confidence in John's honesty. Our conclusion, in this case, must be based on our confidence in John as an individual rather than on a general premise that all regular employees are honest.

We may not recognize how much we use deduction to reason out the implications of various acts and conditions. For example, in planning a survey, we might reason as follows:

> (Premise 1)—Inner city household interviewing is especially difficult and expensive.

(Premise 2)—This survey involves substantial inner city household interviewing.

(Conclusion)—The interviewing in this survey will be especially difficult and expensive.

On reflection, it should be apparent that a conclusion that results from deduction is, in a sense, already "contained in" its premises.[7]

Induction

Inductive argument is radically different. There is no such strength of relationship between reasons and conclusions in **induction.** *To induce is to draw a conclusion from one or more particular facts or pieces of evidence.* The conclusion explains the facts, and the facts support the conclusion. To illustrate, suppose you push the light switch in your room and the light fails to go on. This is a fact—the light does not go on when you push the switch. Under such circumstances, we ask, "Why doesn't the light go on?"

One likely answer to this question is a conclusion that the light bulb has burned out. This conclusion is an induction because we know from experience that (1) the light should go on when you push the switch and (2) if the bulb is burned out, the light will not function. The nature of induction, however, is that the conclusion is only a hypothesis. It is one explanation, but there are others that fit the fact just as well. It could be that the electrical power is off in the neighborhood, or it might mean the switch is malfunctioning.

In this example, we see the essential nature of inductive reasoning. The inductive conclusion is an inferential jump beyond the evidence presented. That is, while one conclusion explains the fact of no light, other conclusions can explain the fact also. It may even be that none of the three conclusions we have advanced correctly explains the failure of the light to go on.

For another example, let's consider the situation of Tracy Nelson, a salesperson at the Square Box Company. Tracy has one of the poorest sales records in the company. Her unsatisfactory performance prompts us to ask the question, "Why is she doing so badly?" From our knowledge of Tracy's sales practices, the nature of box selling, and the market, we might conclude (hypothesize) that her problem is that she makes too few sales calls per day to build a good sales record. Other hypotheses might also occur to us on the basis of available evidence. Among them are the following:

1. Tracy's territory does not have the market potential of other territories.
2. Tracy's sales-making skills are so poorly developed that she is not able to close sales effectively.
3. Tracy's territory has been the scene of intense price cutting by local manufacturers, and this has caused her to lose many sales.
4. Some types of people just cannot sell boxes, and Tracy is one of these people.

All of the above hypotheses are inductions we might base on the evidence of Tracy's poor sales record, plus some assumptions or beliefs we hold about her and the selling of boxes. All of them have some chance of being true, but we would probably have more confidence in some than in others. All must be subject to further confirmation before we could hold any of them with much confidence. Confirmation comes with more evidence. The task of research is largely to determine the nature of the evidence needed and to design methods by which to discover and measure this other evidence.

Combining Induction and Deduction

The induction and deduction processes are used in research reasoning in a sequential manner. This has been described by John Dewey as the **double movement of reflective thought.** [8] Induction occurs when we observe a fact and ask, "Why is this?" In answer to this question, we advance a tentative explanation (hypothesis). The hypothesis is plausible if it explains the event or condition (fact) that prompted the question. Deduction is the process by which we test whether the hypothesis is capable of explaining the fact. The process is:

1. You push the light switch and find no light.
2. You ask the question, "Why no light?"
3. You infer a conclusion (hypothesis) to answer the question and explain the fact that the bulb is burned out.
4. You use this hypothesis to conclude (deduce) that the light will not go on when we push the switch. We know from experience that a burned-out bulb will not light.

**FIGURE 2–2
Why Doesn't the
Light Go On?**

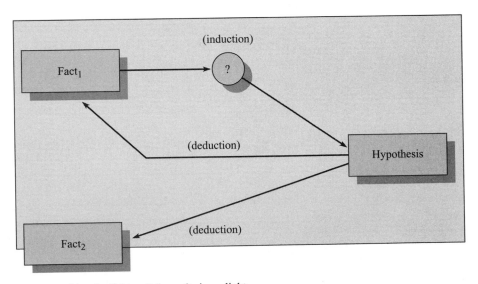

$Fact_1$ = Pushing the light switch results in no light
$Fact_2$ = Inserting a new bulb brings light when switch is pushed

This example is only an exercise in circular reasoning, but it does point out that one must be able to deduce the initiating fact from the hypothesis advanced to explain that fact. This is illustrated in Figure 2–2. A second critical point is also illustrated in this figure. That is, to test a hypothesis, one must be able to deduce other facts from it that can then be investigated. This is what classical research is all about. We must deduce other specific facts or events from the hypothesis and then gather information to see if the deductions are true. In the light example, we deduce:

5. A new bulb put in the lamp will result in light when the switch is pushed.
6. We put in the new bulb and push the switch. The light goes on.

How would the double movement of reflective thought work when applied to Tracy Nelson's problem? The process is illustrated in Figure 2–3. The initial fact$_1$ leads to hypothesis$_1$ that Tracy is lazy. We deduce several other facts from the hypothesis. These are shown as fact$_2$ and fact$_3$. We use research to find out if fact$_2$ and fact$_3$ are true. If they are found to be true, they confirm our hypothesis. If they are not, our hypothesis is not confirmed, and we must look for another explanation.

In most research, the process is more complicated than these simple examples suggest. For instance, we often develop multiple hypotheses by which to explain the phenomenon in question. Then we design a study to test all the hypotheses at once. Not only is this more efficient, but it is also a good way to reduce the attachment (and potential bias) of the researcher for any given hypothesis.

**FIGURE 2–3
Why is Tracy
Nelson's
Performance So
Poor?**

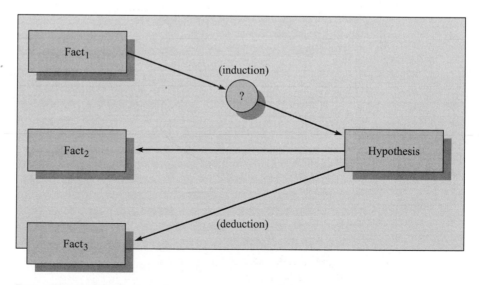

Fact$_1$ = Poor performance record
Fact$_2$ = Late to work regularly
Fact$_3$ = Fewer calls per day than average performance

**Reflective
Thinking and the
Scientific Method**

Induction and deduction, observation, and hypothesis testing can be combined in a systematic way to illustrate the scientific method. The ideas that follow, originally suggested by Dewey and others for problem-solving analysis, represent one approach to assessing the validity of conclusions about observable events; and they are particularly appropriate for researchers whose conclusions depend on empirical data.[9] The researcher:

- Encounters a curiosity, doubt, barrier, suspicion, or obstacle.
- Struggles to state the problem: asks questions, contemplates existing knowledge, gathers facts, and moves from an emotional to an intellectual confrontation with the problem.
- Proposes hypotheses to explain the facts that are believed to be logically related to the problem.
- Deduces outcomes or consequences of the hypotheses: attempts to discover what happens if the results are in the opposite direction of that predicted or if the results support the expectations.
- Formulates several rival hypotheses.
- Devises and conducts a crucial empirical test with various possible outcomes, each of which selectively excludes one or more hypotheses.
- Draws a conclusion, an inductive inference, based on acceptance or rejection of the hypotheses.
- Feeds information back into the original problem, modifying it according to the strength of the evidence.

Eminent scientists who claim there is no such thing as the scientific method, or if it exists, it is not revealed by what they write, caution researchers about using template-like approaches. Their admonitions are well taken, and we would add that the ideas presented here are highly interdependent, are not sequentially fixed, and may be expanded or eliminated based on the nature of the problem and the perspective one has chosen to view it from.[10] Nevertheless, beginning researchers should understand that research, when conducted scientifically, is a process. Chapter 3 is devoted to an elaboration of that process.

THE SCIENTIFIC ATTITUDE

If the tools of thinking are the mind of science, then the scientific attitude is the spirit. The scientific attitude unleashes the creative drive that makes discovery possible. The portraits of scientists involved in some of the most spectacular discoveries of this century—Crick, Watson, Pauling, and others—are the stories of imagination, intuition, curiosity, suspicion, anguish, the rage to know, and self-doubt.[11] But these predispositions are not the exclusive province of the natural scientist. All researchers exercise imagination in the discovery process, in capturing the most essential aspect of the problem, or in selecting a technique that reveals a phenomenon in its most natural state.

Curiosity in its many forms characterized the persistent efforts to understand the relationship between productivity and worker satisfaction. Starting first with the Hawthorne studies, it was thought that employee satisfaction improved productivity.[12] Later research did not bear this out, and the second general conclusion was that satisfaction and productivity were not directly connected since the relationship was affected by a number of other variables. The present state of knowledge suggests satisfaction is sought for reasons not consistently related to work, and productivity varies from simple to challenging tasks. Many contextual variables are now viewed as essential for understanding the original relationship.[13] Over 30 years elapsed while this research was being sorted out. The curiosity to ask questions compounded by the passion not to let go and the discomfort with existing answers sustained these researchers through periods of failure and self-doubt.

Thomas Kuhn, writing in *The Structure of Scientific Revolutions,* has also addressed the question of why scientists attack their problems with such passion and devotion. Scientific inquiry, he says, attracts people for a variety of motives. "Among them are the desire to be useful, the excitement of exploring new territory, the hope of finding order, and the drive to test established knowledge."[14] From applied researchers addressing a manager's need to academicians fascinated with the construction of grand theories, the attitude of science is the enabling spirit of discovery.

UNDERSTANDING THEORY: COMPONENTS AND CONNECTIONS

When we do research, we seek to know "what is" in order to understand, explain, and predict phenomena. We might want to answer the question, "What will be the employee reaction to the new flexible work schedule?" or "Why did the stock market price surge higher when all normal indicators suggested the market would go down?" When dealing with such questions, we must agree on definitions. Which employees? What kind of reaction? What are the major indicators? These questions require the use of concepts, constructs, and definitions. Later we will use variables and hypotheses to make statements and propose tests for the relationships that our questions express. These components or building blocks of theory are reviewed in the next few sections.

Concepts

If one is to understand and communicate information about objects and events, there must be a common ground on which to do it. Concepts are used for this purpose. A **concept** is a bundle of meanings or characteristics associated with certain events, objects, conditions, situations, and the like. Concepts are created by classifying and categorizing objects or events that have common characteristics beyond the single observation. When you think of a spreadsheet or a warranty card, it is not of a single instance but of collected memories of all spreadsheets and warranty cards abstracted to a set of specific and definable characteristics.

We abstract such meanings from reality and use words as labels to designate them. For example, we see a man passing and think, he is running, walking, skipping, crawling, or hopping. These movements all represent concepts. We also have abstracted certain visual elements by which we identified that the moving object was a he not a she or a truck or a horse. We obviously use large numbers of concepts daily in our thinking, conversing, and other activities.

Sources of Concepts   Concepts that are in frequent and general use have been developed over time through shared usage. We have acquired them through personal experience. If we lived in another society, we would hold many of the same concepts (although in a different language). Some concepts, however, are unique to a particular culture and are not readily translated into another language.

Ordinary concepts make up the bulk of communication even in research, but we can often run into difficulty trying to deal with an uncommon concept or a newly advanced idea. One way to handle this problem is to borrow from other languages (for example, *gestalt*) or to borrow from other fields. The concept of gravitation is borrowed from physics and used in marketing in an attempt to explain why people shop where they do. The concept of distance is used in attitude measurement to describe degrees of difference between the attitudes of two or more persons. Threshold is used effectively to describe a concept in perception studies, while velocity is a term borrowed by the economist from the physicist.

Borrowing is not always practical, so we need to (1) adopt new meanings for words (make a word cover a different concept) or (2) develop new labels (words) for concepts. The recent broadening of the meaning of model is an example of the first instance, while the development of concepts such as sibling and status stress are examples of the second. When we adopt new meanings or develop new labels, we begin to develop a specialized jargon or terminology. Researchers in medicine, the physical sciences, and related fields frequently use terms that are unintelligible to outsiders. Jargon no doubt contributes to efficiency of communication among specialists, but excludes everyone else.

Importance to Research   Concepts are basic to all thought and communication, yet we pay little attention to what they are and the problems encountered in their use. In research, special problems grow out of the need for concept precision and inventiveness. We design hypotheses using concepts. We devise measurement concepts by which to test these hypothetical statements. We gather data using these measurement concepts. We may even invent new concepts to express ideas. The success of research hinges on (1) how clearly we conceptualize and (2) how well others understand the concepts we use. For example, when we survey people on the question of tax equity, the questions we use need to tap faithfully the attitudes of the respondents. Attitudes are abstract, yet we must attempt to measure them using carefully selected concepts.

The challenge is to develop concepts that others will clearly understand. We might, for example, ask respondents for an estimate of their family's total income. This may seem to be a simple, unambiguous concept, but we will receive varying and confusing answers unless we restrict or narrow the concept by specifying

(1) time period, such as weekly, monthly, or annually; (2) before or after income taxes; (3) for head of family only or for all family members; and (4) for salary and wages only, or also for dividends, interest, and capital gains. (How about income in kind such as free rent, employee discounts, or food stamps?)

Problems in Concept Use   The use of concepts presents difficulties that are accentuated in a research setting. First, people differ in the meanings they include under the particular label. This problem is so great in normal human communication that we often see cases where people use the same language but do not understand each other. We might all agree to the meaning of such concepts as dog, table, electric light, money, employee, and wife. We may encounter more difficulties, however, when we communicate concepts such as household, retail transaction, dwelling unit, regular user, debit, and wash sale. Still more challenging are concepts that are familiar but not well understood, such as leadership, motivation, personality, social class, and fiscal policy. For example, personality has been defined in the research literature in more than 400 ways.[15] Although this may seem extreme, writers are not able to express the complexity of the determinants of personality and its attributes (e.g., authoritarianism, risk taking, locus of control, achievement orientation, dogmatism, and so forth) in a fashion that produces agreement.

The concepts described represent progressive levels of abstraction, that is, the degree to which the concept does or does not have objective referents. Table is an objective concept in that we can point to tables and we can conjure up in our mind images of tables. An abstraction like personality is much more difficult to visualize. Such abstract concepts are often called constructs.

Constructs

As used in research in the social sciences, a **construct** is an image or idea specifically invented for a given research and/or theory-building purpose. We build constructs by combining the simpler concepts, especially when the idea or image we intend to convey is not directly subject to observation.

Concepts and constructs are easily confused. Here's an example to clarify the differences. A human resource analyst in a software company that employs technical writers is analyzing task attributes of a job in need of redesign. She knows the job description for technical writers consists of three components: presentation quality, language skill, and job interest. Her job analysis reveals more specific characteristics.

Figure 2–4 illustrates some of the concepts and constructs she is dealing with. The concepts at the bottom of the figure (format accuracy, manuscript errors, and typing speed) are the most concrete and easily measured. We can observe typing speed, for example, and even with crude measures agree on what constitutes slow and fast typists. Typing speed is one concept in the group that defines a construct called "presentation quality." Presentation quality is a nonexistent entity, a "constructed type." It is used to communicate the combination of meanings of the three concepts. The analyst uses it as a label for the concepts she has found empirically to be related.

**FIGURE 2–4
Constructs
Composed of
Concepts in a Job
Redesign Example**

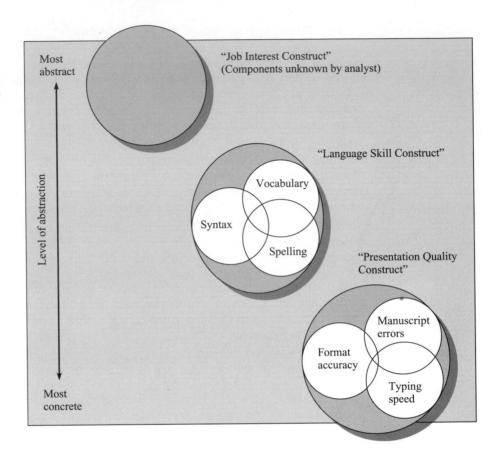

Concepts in the next level in the figure are vocabulary, syntax, and spelling. They were also found by the analyst to be related. They form a construct she called "language skill." She chose this term because these three concepts together defined the language requirement in the job description. Language skill is placed at a higher level of abstraction in the figure because the concepts that comprise it are more difficult to observe and their measures are more complex.

The analyst has not yet measured the last construct, "job interest." It is the least observable and most complex to measure. It will likely be composed of numerous concepts—many of which will be quite abstract. Researchers sometimes refer to such entities as *hypothetical constructs* because they can be inferred only from the data; thus, they are presumed to exist but must await further testing. If research ultimately shows the concepts and constructs in this example to be interrelated, and if the propositions that specify the connections can be supported, the researcher will have the beginning of a **conceptual scheme** to depict the relationships among the knowledge and skill requirements that will clarify the job redesign effort.

Definitions   Confusion about the meaning of the concepts can destroy a research study's value without the researcher or client even knowing it. If words have different meanings to the parties involved, then they are not communicating on the same wavelength. Definitions are one way to reduce this danger.

While there are various types of definitions, the most familiar are dictionary definitions. In these, a concept is defined with a synonym. For example, a customer is defined as a patron; a patron, in turn, is defined as a customer or client of an establishment; a client is defined as one who employs the services of any professional . . ., also, loosely, a patron of any shop.[16] Circular definitions such as these may be adequate for general communication but not for research. Here we must measure concepts, and this requires a more rigorous definition.

Operational Definitions   An **operational definition** is one stated in terms of specific testing criteria or operations. These terms must have empirical referents (that is, we must be able to count, measure, or in some other way gather the information through our senses). Whether the object to be defined is physical (e.g., a machine tool) or highly abstract (e.g., achievement motivation), the definition must specify the characteristics to study and how they are to be observed. The specifications and procedures must be so clear that any competent person using them would classify the objects in the same way.

Suppose college undergraduates are to be classified by class. No one has much trouble understanding such terms as freshman, sophomore, and so forth. The task may not be that simple if you must determine which students fall in each class. To do this, you need an operational definition.

Operational definitions may vary depending on your purpose and the way you choose to measure them. Here are two different situations requiring different definitions of the same concepts.

1. You conduct a survey among students and wish to classify their answers by their class levels. You merely ask them to report their class status and you record it. In this case, class is freshman, sophomore, junior, or senior, and you accept the answer each respondent gives as correct. This is a rather casual definition process but nonetheless an operational definition. It is probably adequate in this case even though some of the respondents report inaccurately.

2. You make a tabulation of the class level of students for the university registrar's annual report. The measurement task here is more critical so your operational definition needs to be more precise. You decide to define class levels in terms of semester hours of credit completed and recorded in each student's record in the registrar's office. Thus:

Freshman	—less than 30 hours credit
Sophomore	—30 to 59 hours credit
Junior	—60 to 89 hours credit
Senior	—over 90 hours credit

These examples deal with relatively concrete concepts, but operational definitions are even more critical for treating abstract ideas. Suppose one tries to measure the construct of "organizational commitment." We may intuitively understand what this means, but to attempt to measure it among workers is difficult. We would probably develop a commitment scale or we may use a scale that has already been developed and validated by someone else. The scale then operationally defines the construct.

While operational definitions are needed in research, they also present some problems. There is the ever-present danger of thinking that a concept and the operational definition are the same thing. We forget that our definitions provide only limited insight into what a concept or construct really is. In fact, the operational definition may be quite narrow and not at all similar to what someone else would use when researching the same topic. When measurements by two different definitions correlate well, it supports the view that they are measuring the same concept.

The problems of operational definitions are particularly difficult when dealing with constructs. In this case, there are few empirical referents by which to confirm that an operational definition really measures what we hope it does. In this case, correlation between two different definition formulations strengthens the belief that you are measuring the same thing. On the other hand, if there is little or no correlation, it may mean we are tapping several different partial meanings of a construct. It may also mean one or both of the definitions are not true labels.

Whatever the form of definition, its purpose in research is basically the same—to provide an understanding and measurement of concepts. We may need to provide operational definitions for only a few critical concepts, but these will almost always be the ones used to develop the relationships found in hypotheses and theories.

Variables

Scientists operate at both theoretical and empirical levels. At the theoretical level, there is a preoccupation with identifying constructs and their relations to propositions and theory. At this level, constructs cannot, as we've said before, be observed. At the empirical level where the propositions are converted to hypotheses and testing occurs, the scientist is likely to be dealing with variables. In actual practice, the term **variable** is used by scientists and researchers as a synonym for construct or the property being studied. In this context, a variable "is a symbol to which numerals or values are assigned."[17]

The numerical value assigned to a variable is based on the variable's properties. For example, some variables, referred to as being *dichotomous,* have only two values reflecting the presence or absence of a property: employed–unemployed or male–female have two values, generally 0 and 1. Variables also take on values representing added categories such as the demographic variables of race or religion. All such variables that produce data that fit into categories are said to be *discrete* since only certain values are possible. A religion variable, for example, where "catholic" is assigned a 5 and "other" is assigned a 6, provides no option for a 5.5.

Independent Variable	*Dependent Variable*
Presumed cause	Presumed effect
Stimulus	Response
Predicted from . . .	Predicted to . . .
Antecedent	Consequence
Manipulated	Measured outcome

Income, temperature, age, or a test score are examples of *continuous* variables. These variables may take on values within a given range or, in some cases, an infinite set. Your test score may range from 0 to 100, your age may be 23.5, and your present income could be $35,000.

Independent and Dependent Variables   Researchers are most interested in relationships among variables. For example, does a participative leadership style (independent variable) influence job satisfaction or performance (dependent variables) or can a superior's modeling of ethical behavior influence the behavior of the subordinate? Figure 2–5 lists some terms that have become synonyms for **independent** and **dependent variables.** It is important to remember there are no preordained variables waiting to be discovered "out there" that are automatically assigned to one category or the other. As one writer notes:

> There's nothing very tricky about the notion of independence and dependence. But there is something tricky about the fact that the relationship of independence and dependence is a figment of the researcher's imagination until demonstrated convincingly. Researchers *hypothesize* relationships of independence and dependence: they invent them, and then they try by reality testing to see if the relationships actually work out that way.[18]

Moderating Variables   There is at least one independent variable (IV) and a dependent variable (DV) in each relationship. It is normally hypothesized that in some way the IV "causes" the DV to occur. For simple relationships, all other variables are considered extraneous and are ignored. Thus, we might be interested in a study of the effect of the four-day workweek on office productivity and hypothesize the following:

> The introduction of the four-day workweek (IV) will lead to increased office productivity per worker-hour (DV).

In actual study situations, however, such a simple one-on-one relationship needs to be conditioned or revised to take other variables into account. Often one uses another type of explanatory variable of value here—the moderating variable (MV). A **moderating variable** is a second independent variable that is included because it is believed to have a significant contributory or contingent effect on the originally stated IV-DV relationship. For example, one might hypothesize that:

INTERACTION EFFECT   CONTINGENT UPON

The introduction of the four-day workweek (IV) will lead to higher productivity (DV), especially among younger workers (MV).

In this case, there is a differential pattern of relationship between the four-day week and productivity that is the result of age differences among the workers.

Whether a given variable is treated as an independent or a moderating variable depends on the hypothesis. If you are interested in studying the impact of length of workweek, you would make the length of week the IV. If you were focusing on the relationship of age of worker and productivity, you might use workweek length as a moderating variable.

Extraneous Variables   An almost infinite number of **extraneous variables** exists that might conceivably affect a given relationship. Some can be treated as independent or moderating variables, but most must either be assumed or excluded from the study. Fortunately, the infinite number of variables has little or no effect on a given situation. Most can be safely ignored. Others may be important, but their impact occurs in such a random fashion as to have little effect.

Using the example of the effect of the four-day workweek, one would normally think the imposition of a local sales tax, the election of a new mayor, a three-day rainy spell, and thousands of similar events and conditions would have little effect on workweek and office productivity.

However, there may be other extraneous variables to consider as possible confounding variables to our hypothesized IV-DV relationship between length of workweek and office productivity. For example, one might think that the kind of work being done would have an effect on any workweek length impact on office productivity. This might lead to our introducing a **control** as follows:

In routine office work (control), the introduction of a four-day workweek (IV) will lead to higher productivity (DV), especially among younger workers (MV).

In this example, we attempt to control for type of work by studying the effects of the four-day week within groups performing different types of work.

Intervening Variables   The variables mentioned with regard to causal relationships are concrete, clearly measurable, and can be seen, counted, or observed in some way. Sometimes, however, one may not be completely satisfied by the explanations they give. Thus, while we may recognize that a four-day workweek results in higher productivity, one might think this is not the full explanation—that workweek length affects some intervening variable, which, in turn, results in higher productivity. An intervening variable is a conceptual mechanism through which the IV and MV might affect the DV. The **intervening variable** may be defined as "that factor which theoretically affects the observed phenomenon but cannot be seen, measured, or manipulated; its effect must be inferred from the effects of the independent and moderator variables on the observed phenomenon."[19]

In the case of the workweek hypothesis, one might view the intervening variable (IVV) to be job satisfaction, giving a hypothesis such as:

Pure intervening variable = partial or full mediation [Same]

The introduction of a four-day workweek will lead to higher productivity by increasing job satisfaction (IVV).

Here are additional examples illustrating the relationships involving independent, moderating, controlled extraneous, and dependent variables. The management of a bank wishes to study the effect of promotion on savings. It might advance the following hypothesis:

A promotion campaign (IV) will increase savings activity (DV), especially when free prizes are offered (MV), but chiefly among smaller savers (control). The results come from enhancing the motivation to save (IVV)

Or suppose you are studying a situation involving the causes of defective parts production. You might hypothesize the following:

Changing to worker self-inspection (IV) will reduce the number of defective parts (DV), when the part can be identified with its producer (MV), in electronic assembly work (control), by stimulating the worker's sense of responsibility (IVV).

Propositions and Hypotheses

The research literature contains disagreements about the meanings of the terms *proposition* and *hypothesis*. We define a **proposition** as a statement about concepts that may be judged as true or false if it refers to observable phenomena. When a proposition is formulated for empirical testing, we call it a **hypothesis.** As a declarative statement, a hypothesis is of a tentative and conjectural nature.

Hypotheses have also been described as statements in which we assign variables to cases. A **case** is defined in this sense as the entity or thing the hypothesis talks about. The variable is the characteristic, trait, or attribute that, in the hypothesis, is imputed to the case.[20] For example, we might form the hypothesis, "Executive Jones (case) has a higher than average achievement motivation (variable)." If our hypothesis was based on more than one case, it would be a *generalization*. For example, "Executives in Company Z (cases) have a higher than average achievement motivation (variable)." Both of these hypotheses are examples of *descriptive hypotheses.*

Descriptive Hypotheses   *These are propositions that typically state the existence, size, form, or distribution of some variable.* For example, "The current unemployment rate in Detroit exceeds 6 percent of the labor force." In this example, the case is Detroit and the variable is unemployment. Examples of other simple descriptive hypotheses are: "American cities are experiencing budget difficulties," and "Eighty percent of Company Z stockholders favor increasing the company's cash dividend." In the first illustration, "city" is the case and "budget problem" is the variable. In the second example, "Company Z" is the case and "stockholder attitude toward increased dividends" is the variable.

Researchers will often use a research question rather than a descriptive hypothesis. Thus, in place of the above hypotheses, we might use the following questions: "What is the unemployment rate in Detroit?" "Are American cities experiencing budget difficulties?" "Do stockholders of Company Z favor an increased cash dividend?" Either format is acceptable, but the hypothesis has several advantages. It encourages researchers to crystallize their thinking about the likely relationships to be found; it further encourages them to think about the implications of a supported or rejected finding. Finally, hypotheses are especially useful for testing statistical significance. Research questions are less frequently used with the next type of situation—one calling for *relational hypotheses*.

Relational Hypotheses   *These are statements that describe a relationship between two variables with respect to some case.* For example, "Foreign cars are perceived by American consumers to be of better quality than domestic cars." In this instance, the case is "consumer" and the variables are "country of origin" and "perceived quality." The nature of the relationship between the two variables is not specified. Is there only an implication that the variables occur in some predictable relationship, or is one variable somehow responsible for the other? The first interpretation indicates a *correlational* relationship while the second indicates an *explanatory,* or *causal,* relationship.

Correlational relationships state merely that the variables occur together in some specified manner without implying that one causes the other. Such weak claims are often made when we believe there are more basic causal forces that affect both variables or when we have not developed enough evidence to claim a stronger linkage. Sample correlational hypotheses are: (1) young machinists (under 35 years of age) are less productive than those who are 35 years or older; (2) the height of women's hemlines varies directly with the level of the business cycle; or (3) people in Atlanta give the president a more favorable rating than do people in St. Louis.

By labeling these as correlational hypotheses, we make no claim that one variable causes the other to change or take on different values. Other persons, however, may view one or more of these hypotheses as reflecting cause-and-effect relationships.

With explanatory or causal hypotheses, there is an implication that the existence of, or a change in, one variable causes or leads to an effect on the other variable. As we noted previously, the causal variable is typically called the independent variable (IV) and the other the dependent variable (DV). "Cause" means roughly to "help make happen." That is, the IV need not be the sole reason for the existence of, or change in, the DV. Examples of explanatory hypotheses are:

1. An increase in family income leads to an increase in the percentage of income saved.
2. Exposure to the company's messages concerning industry problems leads to more favorable attitudes by production workers toward the company.
3. Loyalty to a particular grocery store increases the probability of purchasing the private brands sponsored by that store.

In proposing or interpreting causal hypotheses, the researcher must consider the direction of influence. In many cases, the direction is obvious from the nature of the variables. Thus, in example 1, one would assume that family income influences savings rate rather than the reverse case. In example 2, our ability to identify the direction of influence depends on the research design. If the message clearly precedes the attitude measurement, then the direction of exposure to attitude seems clear; if information about both exposure and attitude were collected at the same time, there might be justification for saying that different attitudes led to selective message exposure or nonexposure. Loyalty to a store may increase the probability of buying the store's private brands, but the use of private brands may also lead to greater store loyalty. In example 3, the variables appear to be interdependent.

The Role of the Hypothesis In research, a hypothesis serves several important functions. The most important is that it guides the direction of the study. A frequent problem in research is the proliferation of interesting information. Unless the urge to include additional elements is curbed, a study can be diluted by trivial concerns that do not answer the basic questions posed. The virtue of the hypothesis is that, if taken seriously, it limits what shall be studied and what shall not. It identifies facts that are relevant and those that are not; in so doing, it suggests which form of research design is likely to be most appropriate. A final role of the hypothesis is to provide a framework for organizing the conclusions that result.

To consider specifically the role of the hypothesis in determining the direction of the research, suppose we use this: "Husbands and wives agree in their perceptions of their respective roles in purchase decisions." The hypothesis specifies who shall be studied, in what context they shall be studied (their consumer decision making), and what shall be studied (their individual perceptions of their roles).

The nature of this hypothesis and the implications of the statement suggest that the best research design is probably a survey. We have at this time no other practical means to ascertain perceptions of people except to ask about them in one way or another. In addition, we are interested only in the roles that are assumed in the purchase or consumer decision-making situation. The study should not, therefore, involve itself in seeking information about other types of roles husband and wife might play. Reflection upon this hypothesis might also reveal that husbands and wives disagree on their perceptions of roles but these differences may be explained in terms of additional variables, such as age, social class, background, personality differences, and other factors not associated with their differences of sex.

What Is a Good Hypothesis? A good hypothesis should fulfill three conditions. The most elementary requirement is that it be *adequate for its purpose*. For a descriptive hypothesis, this means it clearly states the condition, size, or distribution of some variable in terms of values meaningful to the research task. If it is an explanatory hypothesis, it must explain the facts that gave rise to the need for explanation. Using the hypothesis, plus other known and accepted generalizations, one should be able to deduce the original problem condition.

A second major condition is that the hypothesis must be *testable*. A hypothesis is not testable if it calls for techniques that are not available with the present state of the art. A hypothesis is also untestable if it calls for an explanation that defies known physical or psychological laws. Explanatory hypotheses are also untestable if there are no consequences or derivatives that can be deduced for testing purposes.

For explanatory hypotheses, there is another major condition: The hypothesis must be *better than its rivals*. Generally, the better hypothesis has a greater range; it explains more facts and a greater variety of facts than do others. The better hypothesis is also the one that informed judges accept as being the most likely. Their opinions can be highly subjective but depend chiefly on their judgment of which hypothesis fits best with other information. Finally, the better hypothesis is the simple one requiring few conditions or assumptions.

Hypotheses play an important role in the development of theory. While theory development has not historically been an important aspect of business research, it is becoming more so.

Theory

The term *theory* is often used by the layman to express the opposite of fact. In this sense, theory is viewed as being speculative or ivory-tower. One hears that Professor X is too theoretical, that managers need to be practical, or that some idea will not work because it is too theoretical. This is an incorrect picture of the relationship between fact and theory.

When you are too theoretical, your basis of explanation or decision is not sufficiently attuned to specific empirical conditions. This may be so, but it does not prove that theory and fact are opposites. The truth is that fact and theory are each necessary for the other to be of value. Our ability to make rational decisions, as well as to develop scientific knowledge, is measured by the degree to which we combine fact and theory.

We all operate on the basis of theories we hold. In one sense, theories are the generalizations we make about variables and the relationship among them. We use these generalizations to make decisions and predict outcomes. For example, it is midday and you note that the outside natural light is dimming, dark clouds are moving rapidly in from the west, the breeze is freshening, and the air temperature is cooling. Would your understanding of the relationship among these variables (your weather theory) lead you to a prediction of what else will probably occur in a short time?

Consider another situation where you are called on to interview two persons for possible promotion to the position of department manager. Do you have a theory about what characteristics such a person should have? Suppose you interview Ms. A and observe that she answers your questions well, openly, and apparently sincerely. She also expresses thoughtful ideas about how to improve departmental functioning and is articulate in stating her views. Ms. B, on the other hand, is guarded in her comments and reluctant to advance ideas for improvements. She answers questions by saying what "Mr. General Manager wants." She is also less articulate and seems less sincere than Ms. A. You would probably choose A, based upon the way you combine the concepts, definitions, and propositions mentioned into a theory of managerial effectiveness. It may not be a good theory because of the variables we have ignored, but it illustrates the point that we all use theory to guide our decisions, predictions, and explanations.

A **theory** is a set of systematically interrelated concepts, definitions, and propositions that are advanced to explain and predict phenomena (facts). In this sense, we have many theories and use them continually to explain or predict what goes on around us. To the degree that our theories are sound, and fit the situation, we are successful in our explanations and predictions. Thus, while a given theory and a set of facts may not fit, they are not opposites. Our challenge is to build a better theory and to be more skillful in fitting theory and fact together.

A point that may also cause some confusion is that of how theory differs from hypothesis. One person may advance an explanation and call it a theory, while another may call it a hypothesis. It may be difficult to distinguish one from the other since both involve concepts, definitions, and relationships among variables. The basic differences are in the level of complexity and abstraction. Theories tend to be abstract and involve multiple variables, while hypotheses tend to be simple, two-variable propositions involving concrete instances.

In this book, we make the general distinction that the difference between theory and hypothesis is one of degree of complexity and abstraction. At times these may be confused, but it should not make much practical research difference.

Theory and Research   It is important for researchers to recognize the pervasiveness and value of theory. Theory serves us in many useful ways. First, as orientation, it narrows the range of facts we need to study. Any problem may be studied in a number of different ways, and theory suggests which ways are likely to yield the greatest meaning. Theory may also suggest a system for the researcher to impose on data in order to classify them in the most meaningful way. Theory also summarizes what is known about an object of study and states the uniformities that lie beyond the immediate observation; when it does so, theory can also be used to predict further facts that should be found.

Models

The term *model* is used throughout the various fields of business and allied disciplines with little agreement as to definition. This may be because of the numerous functions, structures, and types of models. However, most definitions agree that models represent phenomena through the use of analogy. A **model** is defined here as a representation of a system that is constructed to study some aspect of that system or the system as a whole. Models differ from theories in that a theory's role is explanation whereas a model's role is representation:

> A model is not an explanation; it is only the structure and/or function of a second object or process. A model is the result of taking the structure or function of one object or process and using that as a model for the second. When the substance, either physical or conceptual, of the second object or process has been projected onto the first, a model has been constructed.[21]

Many of our ideas about new product adoption, for example, can be traced to rural sociology models that described how information and innovations spread throughout communities or cultures. Those models were constructed using the analogues of more established medical theories of epidemiology because of the inadequacy of social science theories at the time.

Models may be used for applied or highly theoretical purposes. Almost everyone is familiar with queuing models of services: banks, post offices, telephone switchboards, or airport security stations. Other models that consider assembly lines, transportation, and inventory also attempt to solve immediate practical needs. A model to advance a theory of quality of work life, for example, could target employee behavior under conditions of flextime, permanent part-time, job sharing, and compressed workweek.

Description, explication, and simulation are the three major functions of modeling. Each of these functions is appropriate for applied research or theory building. Descriptive models seek to describe the behavior of elements in a system where theory is inadequate or nonexistent. Explicative models are used to extend the application of well-developed theories or improve our understanding of their key concepts. Simulation models go beyond the goal of clarifying the structural relations of concepts and attempt to reveal the process relations among them.[22] Monte Carlo simulation models are examples of static simulations that represent a system at one point in time. They simulate probabilistic processes using random numbers. Simulations that represent the evolution of a system over time are called dynamic. Redistribution of market share, brand-switching, and prediction of future values are examples that benefit from dynamic modeling.

Summary

Styles of thinking are perspectives or filters for determining how we view and understand reality. They affect what we accept as truth and specify how rigorously we test the information we receive before endorsing it. Although the scientific method is the preeminent means by which we secure empirical information, it is not the only source of truth. Other styles of thinking also have an apparent and often useful influence on business disciplines and place their imprimatur on the theory-building and problem-solving approaches of those fields.

Scientific inquiry is grounded in the inference process. This process is used for the development and testing of various propositions largely through the double movement of reflective thinking. Reflective thinking consists of sequencing induction and deduction in order to explain inductively (by hypothesis) a puzzling condition. In turn, the hypothesis is used in a deduction of further facts that can be sought to confirm or deny the truth of the hypothesis.

Researchers think of the doing of science (rather than the inspiration for discovery or the scientific attitude) as an orderly process that combines induction, deduction, observation, and hypothesis testing into a set of reflective thinking activities. Although the scientific method consists of neither sequential nor independent stages, the problem-solving process that it reveals provides insight into the way research is conducted.

Scientific methods and scientific thinking are based on concepts, the symbols we attach to bundles of meaning that we hold and share with others. We invent concepts to think about and communicate abstractions. We also use higher-level concepts—constructs—for specialized scientific explanatory purposes that are not directly observable. Concepts, constructs, and variables may be defined descriptively or operationally. Operational definitions, which are essential in research, must specify adequately the empirical information needed and how it will be collected. In addition, they must have the proper scope or fit for the research problem at hand.

Concepts and constructs are used at the theoretical levels; variables are used at the empirical level. Variables accept numerals or values for the purpose of testing and measurement. They may be classified as explanatory (independent, dependent, or moderating), extraneous, and intervening.

Propositions are of great interest in research because they may be used to assess the truth or falsity of relationships among observable phenomena. When we advance a proposition for testing, we are hypothesizing. A hypothesis describes the relationships between or among variables. A good hypothesis is one that can explain what it claims to explain, is testable, and has greater range, probability, and simplicity than its rivals.

Sets of interrelated concepts, definitions, and propositions that are advanced to explain and predict phenomena are theories. Models differ from theories in that models are analogies or representations of some aspect of a system or of the system as a whole. Models are used for description, explication, and simulation.

Key Terms

case(s)	model
concept	operational definition
conceptual scheme	proposition
construct	rationalism
deduction	theory
double movement of reflective thought	variable(s)
empiricism	control
hypothesis	dependent
descriptive	extraneous
relational	independent
induction	intervening
	moderating

Discussion Questions

1. Distinguish among the following sets of items and suggest the significance of each in a research context.
   a. Concept and construct.
   b. Deduction and induction.
   c. Operational definition and dictionary definition.
   d. Concept and variable.

    e. Hypothesis and proposition.

    f. Theory and model.

    g. Scientific method and scientific attitude.

2. Describe the characteristics of the scientific method.

3. Find the inductions and deductions in the following. If there are gaps, supply what is needed to make them complete arguments.

    a. Repeated studies indicate that economic conditions vary with—and lag 6 to 12 months behind—the changes in the national money supply. Therefore, we may conclude the money supply is the basic economic variable.

    b. Research studies show that heavy smokers have a higher rate of lung cancer than do nonsmokers; therefore, heavy smoking causes lung cancer.

    c. Show me a person who goes to church regularly, and I will show you a reliable worker.

4. What are the differences among the research approaches (and thinking styles) that guide the predominant kinds of studies done in operations research, marketing, finance, or organizational behavior?

5. Here are some terms commonly found in a management setting. Are they concepts or constructs? Give two different operational definitions for each.

    first-line supervisor   leadership

    employee morale   price-earnings ratio

    assembly line   union democracy

    overdue account   ethical standards

    line management

6. In your company's management-development program, there was a heated discussion between some people who claimed "theory is impractical and thus no good" and others who claimed "good theory is the most practical approach to problems." What position would you take and why?

7. You wish to study a condition that you have observed to the effect that, "Some workers seem to be much more diligent than others."

    a. Propose at least three concepts and three constructs you might use in such a study.

    b. How might any of these concepts and/or constructs be related to explanatory hypotheses?

8. In a metal stamping plant, the production manager has suddenly been faced with a quality problem. The production process forms large sheets of metal into auto fenders using large stamping machines. Suddenly, yesterday, the quality of the stamped fenders deteriorated. This problem began in department A but quickly spread to the other departments. At a meeting to deal with this problem, the assistant plant manager reported that yesterday on the first shift, the foreman in department A caught a worker drinking on the job and summarily fired him. This man had been a problem in the past, and it was reported that he and the foreman had often argued. The workers in department A were angered by this treatment of one of their popular co-workers. The

shop steward claimed the firing was unfair and violated the union contract. As a result, there was considerable negative reaction among the workers.

a. Propose several hypotheses that might account for the sudden surge in poor quality output.

b. Using the double movement of reflective thought, show how you would test these hypotheses.

Reference Notes

1. The title of the figure, and the section, Styles of Thinking, is borrowed from Abraham Kaplan, *The Conduct of Inquiry* (San Francisco: Chandler, 1964), pp. 259–62. The axes and the positions of Churchman's inquiring systems are based on the work of I. I. Mitroff and R. O. Mason, "Business Policy and Metaphysics; Some Philosophical Considerations," *Academy of Management Review 7* (1982), pp. 361–71. The locations of the other philosophical viewpoints in the figure are approximations.
2. P. McC. Miller and M. J. Wilson, eds., *A Dictionary of Social Sciences Methods* (New York: John Wiley & Sons, 1983), p. 27. Also see Benjamin B. Wolman, ed., *Dictionary of Behavioral Science,* 2nd ed. (New York: Academic Press, 1989).
3. Kenneth R. Hoover, *The Elements of Social Scientific Thinking,* 5th ed. (New York: St. Martin's Press, Inc., 1991), p. 5.
4. A. Kaplan, *The Conduct of Inquiry.*
5. George S. Howard, *Methods in the Social Sciences* (Glenview, Ill.: Scott, Foresman, and Co., 1985), p. 7.
6. Thomas S. Kuhn, *The Structure of Scientific Revolutions* (Chicago: University of Chicago Press, 1970).
7. Howard Kahane, *Logic and Philosophy,* 2nd ed. (Belmont, Calif.: Wadsworth Publishing Company, Inc., 1973), p. 3.
8. John Dewey, *How We Think* (Boston: D. C. Heath, 1910), p. 79.
9. This section is based on John Dewey, *How We Think;* Robert J. Kibler, "Basic Communication Research Considerations," in *Methods of Research in Communication,* Philip Emmert and William D. Brooks, eds., (Boston: Houghton Mifflin, 1970); and John R. Platt, "Strong Inference," *Science,* October 16, 1964, pp. 347–53.
10. See, for example, C. Wright Mills, *The Sociological Imagination* (London: Oxford University Press, 1959); and Peter B. Medawar, *The Art of the Soluable* (London: Methuen & Co., 1967).
11. See, for example, Horace F. Judson, *The Eighth Day of Creation: Makers of the Revolution in Biology* (New York: Simon & Schuster, 1979).
12. F. J. Roethlisberger and W. J. Dickson, *Management and the Worker* (Cambridge, Mass.: Harvard University Press, 1939).
13. Paul R. Lawrence, "Historical Development of Organizational Behavior," in *Handbook of Organizational Behavior,* ed. Jay W. Lorsch (Englewood Cliffs, N.J.: Prentice Hall, Inc., 1987), p. 6.
14. Kuhn, *The Structure of Scientific Revolutions,* p. 37.
15. Hoover, *The Elements of Social Scientific Thinking,* p. 21.
16. *Webster's New Collegiate Dictionary* (Springfield, Mass.: G & C Merriam, 1961), pp. 205, 617, and 154.
17. Fred N. Kerlinger, *Foundations of Behavioral Research,* 3rd ed. (New York: Holt, Rinehart & Winston, 1986), p. 27.

18. Hoover, *The Elements of Social Scientific Thinking,* p. 71.
19. Bruce Tuckman, *Conducting Educational Research* (New York: Harcourt Brace Jovanovich, 1972), p. 45.
20. William N. Stephens, *Hypotheses and Evidence* (New York: Thomas Y. Crowell, 1968), p. 5.
21. Leonard C. Hawes, *Pragmatics of Analoguing: Theory and Model Construction in Communication* (Reading, Mass.: Addison-Wesley Publishing Company, 1975), p. 111.
22. Ibid., pp. 116–22.

Suggested Readings

1. Beardsley, Monroe. *Practical Logic.* Englewood Cliffs, N.J.: Prentice Hall, 1969. A lucid discussion of deduction and induction as well as an excellent coverage of argument analysis.
2. Churchman, C. W. *The Design of Inquiring Systems.* New York: Basic Books, 1971. An essential work for understanding the connections between philosophy, science, and the nature of inquiry.
3. Hawes, Leonard C. *Pragmatics of Analoguing: Theory and Model Construction in Communication.* Reading, Mass.: Addison-Wesley Publishing, 1975. A splendid discussion on theory and model building with behavioral science examples.
4. Hoover, Kenneth R. *The Elements of Social Scientific Thinking,* 5th ed. New York: St. Martin's Press, 1991. A brief but highly readable treatise on the elements of science and scientific thinking.
5. Kaplan, Abraham. *The Conduct of Inquiry.* San Francisco: Chandler, 1964. A classic source for the philosophy of science and logical reasoning.
6. Kerlinger, Fred N. *Foundations of Behavioral Research,* 3rd ed. New York: Holt, Rinehart & Winston, 1986. Comprehensive coverage of the scientific concepts and ways of knowing.

3 THE RESEARCH PROCESS

 **FINDING
YOUR WAY**

BRINGING RESEARCH TO LIFE

On the return flight from Austin, Jason and Myra were euphoric.."That went really well," he said. "Better even than I hoped for."

"Yes. Terrific," she said. "Just fine. You handled yourself very well, Jason. You were so patient. Of course, we are not home free. We have lots of work ahead before we line up MindWriter as our client. But it was a good start. Definitely."

"Definitely."

They toasted each other and their visit with the MindWriter product people, especially Gracie Uhura, the product manager. They sat and sipped their drinks, enjoying a feeling of accomplishment.

"On the other hand," said Jason, by and by, "there are going to be a few problems."

"Aren't there always?"

"Gracie wants the sun, the sky, and the moon. She wants everything. Wants to know the demographic characteristics of her users . . . their job descriptions . . . their salaries . . . their ethnicities . . . their educations. Wants to know their perception of her company . . . of the quality of the MindWriter's specific models. Wants to know their satisfaction with the purchase channel and with the service department, too."

"What's wrong with wanting all that, if she can pay?"

"You and I may perceive the company as hugely profitable and a bottomless source of research dollars, but you can bet there is a bean counter somewhere who will want to know how Gracie can justify asking all these questions. What is going to be the payoff in knowing the ethnicity of customers, they will ask of Gracie? And if Gracie cannot explain the justification for needing the information, if Gracie cannot establish that the dollar benefit of knowing is at least as great as the dollar cost of finding out, Mr. Bean Counter is going to strike the question off the list they're willing to pay for."

"Is there no way she can justify this?"

"Oh, sure there is. Or at least there may be. We can do a pilot study for her of a few hundred customers and see if the ethnic background, or the salary level, or any other nonattitudinal item that Gracie cares about, is a good indicator of satisfaction, willingness to make a repeat purchase, and so forth. If it is, maybe more extensive measurement can be justified."

"Clever!"

"Well, that's why we do exploratory research."

"So, am I right in believing you'd want to sell an exploratory contract for that problem first, and propose a larger study later?"

"That would be standard practice. There are questions that have to be resolved before each side can commit to a major study. We want to minimize the risks to both sides. For example, Gracie wants to know the customers' perception of MindWriter's overall quality. But we have to ask ourselves, 'Are these customers really qualified to form independent opinions, or will they simply be parroting what they have read in the computer magazines or what a dealer told them.' We will have to do a pilot study of a few hundred users to determine if it is really useful to ask them their overall impression of the product."

"I follow you!"

"On the other hand, the repair problem really interests me. We can be reasonably sure that the customers know their own minds when it comes to evaluating their firsthand experience with Gracie's service department. This business of returning a computer for service is something you experience firsthand, not something in a magazine, and it's worth studying. Look at these letters."

He went into his briefcase and extracted a sheaf of photocopies. "Here are letters the service department received about MindWriter. And here are notes on phone conversations. One person writes, 'My MindWriter was badly damaged on arrival. I could not believe its condition when I unpacked it.' And here is 'The service technicians seemed to be unable to understand my complaint, but once they understood it, they performed immediate repairs. 'We are going to have to boil these down to a

(continued)

couple of dozen representative questions that can be pilot tested for clarity, reliability, and validity . . . . I'll explain these terms later. The point is, Gracie is going to have to pay us to find out what she really wants, what she wants that has a payoff, what she wants that has a payoff and is researchable . . . . We are going to be very busy in the next few weeks."

"I understand what you are saying, believe it or not. Yes, you are starting to make good sense. I think we are going to get along, dear boy."

"You know what, Myra? I'm starting to think you are right."

THE ORIGIN OF A RESEARCH NEED

Writers usually treat the research task as a sequential process involving several clearly defined steps. Variations are suggested for different situations, but there is much similarity among the sequences proposed. No one claims that research requires completion of each step before going to the next. Recycling, circumventing, and skipping occur. Some steps are begun out of sequence, some are carried out simultaneously, and some may be omitted. Despite these variations, the idea of a sequence is useful when we try to develop a project and keep it orderly as it unfolds.

Figure 3–1 models the sequence of the **research process.** We refer back to it often as we discuss each step. Our discussion of the questions that guide project planning and data gathering are incorporated into the model (compare Figure 3–2 with 3–1). The model also organizes the chapter and introduces the remainder of the book.

The research process begins much like the vignette suggests. A management question or decision triggers the need for information. In other situations, a controversy arises, a major commitment of resources is called for, or conditions in the environment signal the need for a decision. Such events cause managers to reconsider their purposes or objectives, define a problem for solution, or develop strategies for solutions they have identified.

In our view of the research process, the problem—its origin, selection, statement, exploration, and refinement—is the predominant activity in the sequence. Throughout the chapter we emphasize problem-related steps. A familiar quotation from Albert Einstein, no less apt today than when it was written, supports this view:

> The formulation of a problem is far more often essential than its solution, which may be merely a matter of mathematical or experimental skill. To raise new questions, new possibilities, to regard old problems from a new angle requires creative imagination and marks real advance in science.[1]

Whether the researcher is involved in basic or applied research, a thorough understanding of the problem is fundamental to success in the research enterprise.

FIGURE   3–1   The Research Process

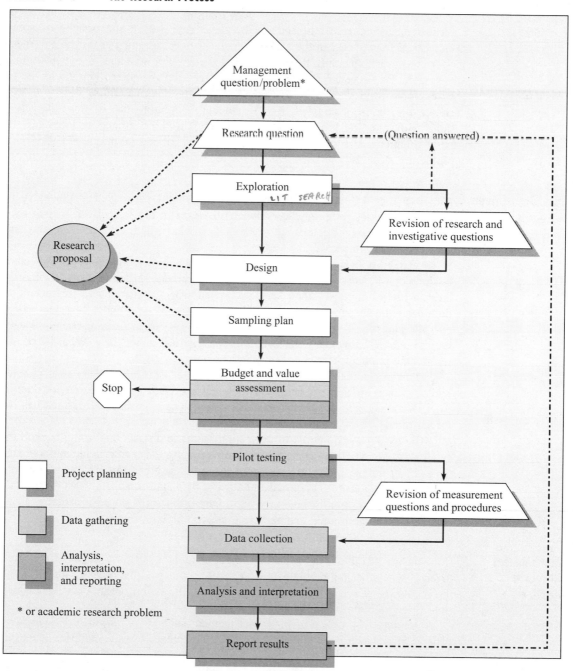

Academic Research Problems

In an academic setting, a particular study may grow out of little more than a student's need to select some research topic for a class assignment. More serious academic research tends to be developed within the bounds of some theoretical framework. In the classical sense, it may be aimed at testing an aspect of a theory or expanding the domain of a theory. For scholars of organizational behavior, the question to be resolved might be whether their field is to be explored from the perspective or organizational determinism or organizational choice or a loosely coupled fit. The student's research may address the question, "How do first-year students and seniors differ on ethical orientation?" In both situations, the researcher's objective is to answer a question or solve a problem.

Tool/Data-Driven Research Problems

Although it is desirable for research to be thoroughly grounded in management decision priorities, often studies wander off target or are less effective than they should be. Two major causes are researcher obsession with certain techniques and an attractive database.

Availability of technique is an important factor in deciding how research shall be done or whether a given study can be done. Persons skilled in given techniques are too often blinded by their special competencies. Their concern for technique dominates the decisions concerning what will be studied and how. In recent years, operations researchers have frequently been accused of approaching problems with the attitude of "How can I use OR techniques here?" rather than "What is the nature of the problem, and how can it best be approached?"

Many researchers are method-bound. They recast their problem so it is amenable to a survey. Some emphasize the case study, while others seldom consider it. The past reluctance of most social scientists to use experimental designs has retarded the development of scientific research in their fields.

The existence of a pool of information seems to distract one from the need for other research. Modern management information systems can provide massive volumes of data. One frequently hears, "We should use all of this information before we do anything else." The provision and use of management information extends beyond what is normally called research. Our emphasis is on information projects that tend to be nonroutine, nonrecurring, and complex in nature.

Management Research Problems

In a business context, the research project originates with the needs of the manager. It would be impossible here to recount all the possible types of management problems for which research is useful. We can, however, define decision making into three problem types.

One type of problem involves management's *choice of purposes or objectives.* The general question is, "What do we want to achieve?" At the company level this might be, "Should we reconsider our basic corporate objectives as they concern our public image?" In a more narrow sense, we might see a management question on objectives that asks, "What goals should we try to achieve in our next labor negotiations?"

A specific question can lead to many studies. Concern for the company's image might lead to a survey among various groups to discover their attitudes toward the company. One question might suggest research into what other companies are doing in this regard; another question might call for a forecast of expected changes in social attitudes. The question concerning labor negotiation objectives might prompt research into what recent settlements in the industry have been. Alternatively, it might involve a survey among workers to find out how well management has met their concerns about quality of work life.

Another set of management decisions involves the *generation and evaluation of solutions*. The general question is, "How can we achieve the ends we seek?" Research projects in this group usually deal with concrete problems that managers quickly recognize as useful. Such projects can involve such strategic questions as, "How can we achieve our five-year goal of doubled sales and net profits?" At a more tactical level, the questions may be as specific as, "Which of three approaches is the most effective way to organize the shipping department?"

A final class of management problems concerns the *trouble/shooting or control situation*. The problem usually involves monitoring or diagnosing various ways in which an organization was failing to achieve its established goals. This group includes such questions as, "Why does our department incur the highest costs?" and "How well is our program meeting its goals?"

The business researcher also finds substantial opportunity in the environment in which an organization functions. These external concerns include such topics as prospective acquisition candidates, the nature and trend of government regulations, cultural changes, and new technology developments.

No matter how the management question is defined, many research directions can be taken. It is the joint responsibility of the researcher and the manager to choose the most productive project.

FORMULATING THE RESEARCH PROBLEM

Is It Researchable?

Not all questions are researchable, and not all research questions are answerable. To be researchable, a question must be one for which observation or other data collection can provide the answer. Many questions cannot be answered based on information alone.

Questions of value and policy must often be weighed in management decisions. Management may be asking, "Should we hold out for a liberalization of the seniority rules in our new labor negotiations?" While information can be brought to bear on this question, such additional considerations as "fairness to the workers" or "management's right to manage" may be important in the decision. It may be possible for many of these questions of value to be transformed into questions of fact. Concerning "fairness to the workers," one might first gather information from which to estimate the extent and degree to which workers will be affected by a rule change; second, one could gather opinion statements of the workers about the fairness of seniority rules. Even so, substantial value elements remain. Left unanswered are such questions as "Should we argue for a policy that will adversely affect the security and well-being of older workers who are least well equipped to cope with this adversity?" Even if a question can be answered by facts alone, it might not be researchable because our procedures or techniques are inadequate.

Ill-Defined Problems   Some categories of problems are so complex, value-laden, and bound by constraints that they prove to be intractable to traditional forms of analysis. These ill-defined or ill-structured problems have characteristics that are virtually opposite those of well-defined problems. One author describes the differences like this:

> To the extent that a problem situation evokes a high level of agreement over a specified community of problem solvers regarding the referents of the attributes in which it is given, the operations that are permitted, and the consequences of those operations, it may be termed unambiguous or well defined with respect to that community. On the other hand, to the extent that a problem evokes a highly variable set of responses concerning referents of attributes, permissible operations, and their consequences, it may be considered ill-defined or ambiguous with respect to that community.[2]

One author pointed out that ill-defined problems are least susceptible to attack from quantitative research methods because such problems have too many interrelated facets for measurement to handle with accuracy.[3] Another authority suggested there are some problems of this type for which methods do not presently exist or, if the methods were to be invented, they might still not provide the data necessary to solve them.[4] Novice researchers should avoid ill-defined problems. Even seasoned researchers will want to conduct a thorough exploratory study before proceeding and consider the latest approaches.

The Question Hierarchy

A useful way to approach the research process is to state the basic problem that prompts the research. From this, try to develop other questions by progressively breaking down the original question into more specific ones. We can think of this as the **hierarchy of questions** (see Figure 3–2).

The process begins at the most general level with the management question. The **management question** represents a decision that a manager must make and is the problem prompting the research. Since the definition of the management problem sets the research task, a poorly defined management problem or question will misdirect research efforts.

For example, a research consultant was asked to help the new management of a bank. The president was concerned about erosion of the bank's profitability and wanted to turn this situation around. The Center City Bank was the oldest and largest of three banks in a city of about 50,000 population. Profits had stagnated in recent years. The president and the consultant discussed the problem facing the organization and settled on the management question as "How can we improve our profit picture?"

Note that the management question does not specify what kind of research is to be done. This question is strictly managerial in thrust. It implies that the bank's management faces the task of developing a strategy for increasing deposits and therefore profits. The question is broad. As a starting point, this is good, although we may want to break such a broad question down into more specific subquestions.

Further discussion between the bank president and the research consultant showed there were really two questions to be answered. The problem of low deposit growth was linked to concerns of a competitive nature. While lowered deposits directly affected profits, another part of the profit weakness was associated with negative factors within the organization. This separation of the management problem into two subproblems may not have occurred without the discussion between the consultant and the manager.

The Research Question   Once the researcher has a clear statement of a manager's question, she must translate it into a research question: a fact-oriented, information-gathering question. As pointed out above, there are probably many different ways to address any management problem. This is the point at which the insight and expertise of the researcher come into play. It is also the point at which the manager's decision is most important. A choice of wrong research for the right problem can be dangerous.

It is important to remember, however, that a manager's motivations for seeking research are not always obvious. Managers might express a genuine need for specific information on which to base a decision. This is the ideal. Sometimes, however, a research study may not really be desirable but is authorized anyway, chiefly because its presence may win approval for a certain manager's pet idea. At other times, research may be authorized as a measure of personal protection for a decision maker in case he or she is criticized later. In these less-than-ideal cases, the researcher may find it more difficult to win the client's interest and support for a sound study design.

**FIGURE   3–2
The Question
Hierarchy**

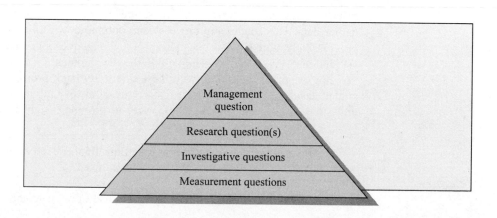

Let's assume, however, the manager's needs for sound research are sincere. Our task then is to formulate a research question that fits this need. A **research question** is the single question or hypothesis that best states the objective of the research study. On occasion, it may be more than one question, but often, it is just one. A study that answers the question provides the manager with the desired information.

For example, the Center City Bank, mentioned earlier, had done no research in the past. It had little specific information about competitors or customers and had not analyzed its internal operations. The client and consultant agreed there were two research subquestions that should be addressed simultaneously. They were:

1. What are the major factors contributing to the bank's failure to achieve a stronger growth rate in deposits?
2. How well is the bank doing regarding
   a. Quality of its work climate?
   b. Efficiency of operations compared to industry norms?
   c. Financial condition compared to industry norms?

The research consultant took on the responsibilities of conducting a study of the competition and the bank's market structure and also a climate survey of its employees. Other studies were undertaken by the bank's accounting firm. Our discussion, however, is concerned only with the consultant's assignment.

Investigative Questions   Once the general research question(s) has been selected, the thinking moves to a more specific level, that of investigative questions. This is where Figure 3–1 offers the option of a detour. When the characteristics of the problem are well defined and the research question is clearly stated, it is possible to deduce the essential subquestions that will guide the project planning stages of the research process. However, if the research question is not well defined, or even somewhat ill defined, the research will need to go on to the exploration and question revision stages to refine the original question and generate the material for constructing investigative questions.

Investigative questions are those the researcher must answer to satisfactorily respond to the general research question. Our purpose is to take a more general research question and break it into more specific questions about which we need to gather data. This fractioning process can continue down through several levels of progressively more specific questions. These are all questions that a researcher must ask and answer for herself. They guide the development of the research direction.

For example, continuing with the Center City bank project, the research consultant developed two major investigative questions for studying the market and several subquestions under each. These were to provide insight into the lack of deposit growth. They were as follows:

1. What is the public's position regarding financial services and their use?
   a. What specific financial services are used?
   b. How attractive are various services?
   c. What factors influence a person's use of a particular service?

2. What is the bank's competitive position?
   a. What are the geographic patterns of our customers and of our competitors' customers?
   b. What is shown by demographic differences among our customers and those of our competitors?
   c. How aware is the public of the bank's promotional efforts?
   d. What opinions does the public hold of the bank and our competitors?
   e. How does growth in services compare among competing institutions?

Investigative questions similarly were developed to guide the second research question for the bank.

Measurement Questions   Measurement questions should be outlined by completion of the project planning stage (see Figure 3–1) but may await pilot testing for refinement. Some studies lend themselves to readily available measurement devices. In such cases, measurement questions have been formulated and tested by previous researchers and are recorded in the literature. More often, the measurement questions should be devised and tailored to parallel the investigative questions. The resources for this task will be the collective insights from all the stages completed to this point but particularly from exploration and pilot testing.

Measurement questions constitute the fourth and final level of the hierarchy. In surveys, the **measurement questions** are those we actually ask the respondents. They appear on the questionnaire. In an observation study, measurement questions are those observers must answer about each subject studied. With the Center City Bank, a survey was conducted among local residents. The questionnaire contained many measurement questions seeking information that provided answers to the investigative questions. Interviews were completed with about 200 residents, and the information collected was used to guide a reorientation of the bank's strategy.

How one structures the research sets the direction of the project. Using the research question hierarchy is a good way to do this. Think of the hierarchy as four sequential stages moving from the general to the specific. While this suggests four discrete levels, it is actually more of a continuum. The investigative question stage, in particular, may involve several levels of questioning before you reach satisfactory measurement questions.

EXPLORATION

An **exploration** typically begins with a search of published data. In addition, the researchers often seek out well-informed people on the topic, especially those who have clearly stated positions on controversial aspects of the problem. Take the case of a company interested in enhancing its position in a given technology that appears to hold potential for future growth. This interest or need might quickly elicit a number of questions:

1. How fast might this technology develop?
2. What are the likely applications of this technology?

3. What companies now possess it and which ones are likely to make a major effort to get it?
4. How much will it take in resources?
5. What are the likely payoffs?

In the above investigation of opportunities, the researchers would probably begin with specific books and periodicals. They would be looking for only certain aspects in this literature, such as (1) recent developments, (2) predictions by informed figures about the prospects of the technology, (3) identification of those involved in the area, and (4) accounts of successful ventures and failures by others in the field.

After familiarization with the literature, they might seek interviews with scientists, engineers, and product developers who are well known in the field. They would give special attention to those who stand at the extremes of opinion about the prospects of the technology. If possible, they would talk with persons having information on particularly thorny problems in development and application. Of course, much of the information will be confidential and competitive. However, skillful investigation can uncover many useful indicators.

An unstructured exploration allows the researcher to revise the research problem and determine what is needed to secure answers to the proposed questions. With some problems, exploration may answer the question and terminate the project (Figure 3–1). If not, the problem chosen should be doable within the constraints that have been imposed. The usefulness of a literature search, experience survey, and focus groups in exploration are discussed in Chapter 5.

QUESTION REVISION: FINE-TUNING

The term *fine-tuning* might seem like rather odd usage for research, but it creates an image that most researchers come to recognize. Fine-tuning the question is precisely what a skillful practitioner must do after the exploration stage. At this point, a clearer picture of the problem begins to emerge. After a preliminary review of the literature, a brief exploratory study, or both, the project begins to crystallize in one of two ways: (1) it is apparent the question has been answered and the process is finished or (2) a different question has appeared than the one originally addressed. The research question does not have to be materially different, but it will have evolved in some fashion. This is not cause for discouragement. A refined question will have better focus and move the research forward with more clarity than the old one.

In addition to fine-tuning the original question, other problem-related activities should be addressed in this phase to enhance the direction of the project:

1. Examine the concepts and constructs to be used in the study. Are they satisfactorily defined? Have operational definitions been employed where appropriate?

2. Review the investigative questions with the intent of breaking them down into specific second- and third-level questions.

3. If hypotheses are used, be certain they meet the quality tests mentioned in the last chapter.

4. Determine what evidence must be collected to answer the various questions and hypotheses.

5. Set the limitations of your study by stating what is not a part of the problem. This will establish a boundary to separate contiguous problems from your primary objective.

DESIGNING THE STUDY

The **design** of the study is the blueprint for fulfilling objectives and answering questions. Selecting a design may be complicated by the availability of a large variety of methods, techniques, procedures, protocols, and sampling plans. For example, you may decide on a secondary data study,[5] case study, survey, experiment, or simulation. If a survey is selected, should it be administered by mail, computer, telephone, oral personal interview? Should all relevant data be collected at one time or at regular intervals? What kind of structure will the questionnaire or interview guide possess? What question wording should be employed? Should the responses be scaled or open-ended? How will reliability and validity be achieved? Will characteristics of the interviewer influence responses to the measurement questions? What kind of training should the data collectors receive? Is a sample or a census to be taken? What types of sampling should be considered? These questions represent only a few of the decisions that have to be made when just one method is chosen.

The creative researcher may benefit from this confusing array of options. The numerous combinations spawned by the abundance of tools may be used to construct alternative perspectives on the same problem. By creating a design using diverse methodologies, researchers are able to achieve greater insight than if they followed the most frequent method encountered in the literature or suggested by a disciplinary bias. Although it must be conceded that students or managers rarely have the resources to pursue a single problem from a multimethod, multistudy strategy, the advantages of several competing designs should be considered before settling on a final one. Chapter 5 discusses the ways in which various research designs may be identified and classified, and Part III of the book provides information on specific methodologies.

SAMPLING

Another step in planning the design is to identify the target population and select the sample. We must determine how many people to interview and who they will be; what events to observe and how many there will be; or how many records to inspect and which ones. A **sample** is a part of the whole population carefully selected to represent that population. When researchers undertake sampling studies, they are interested in estimating one or more population values and/or testing one or more statistical hypotheses.

If a study's objective is to examine the attitudes of U.S. automobile assemblers about quality improvement, the population may be defined as the entire adult population of auto assemblers employed by the auto industry in the United States. Definition of the terms *adult* and *assembler* and the relevant job descriptions included under assembly and "auto industry" may further limit the population under study. The investigator may also want to restrict the research to readily identifiable companies in the market, vehicle types, or assembly processes. The sampling process must then give every person within the definitional structure a known nonzero chance of selection if probability sampling is used. If there is no feasible alternative, a nonprobability approach may be used. Chapter 8 describes both types of samples and the determination of sample size.

RESOURCE ALLOCATION AND BUDGETS

General notions about research budgets have a tendency to single out data collection as the most costly activity. Data collection requires substantial resources but perhaps not as big a part of the budget as clients would expect. Employees must be paid, training and travel must be provided, and other expenses are incurred, but this phase of the project often takes no more than one-third of the total research budget. The geographic scope and the number of observations required do affect the cost, but much of the cost is relatively independent of the size of the data gathering effort. Thus, a guide might be that (1) project planning, (2) data gathering, and (3) analysis, interpretation, and reporting each share about equally in the budget.

Without budgetary approval, many research efforts are terminated for lack of resources. A budget may require significant development and documentation as in grant and contract research or may require less attention as in some in-house projects or investigations funded out of the researcher's own resources. The researcher who seeks funding must be able not only to persuasively justify the costs of the project but also to identify the sources and methods of funding. One author identifies three types of budgets in organizations where research is purchased and cost containment is crucial. (1) Rule-of-thumb budgeting involves taking a fixed percentage of some criterion. For example, a percentage of the prior year's sales revenues may be the basis for determining marketing research for a manufacturer. (2) Departmental or functional area budgeting allocates a portion of total expenditures in the unit to research activities. Government agencies, not-for-profits, and the private sector alike will frequently manage research activities out of functional budgets. Units such as human resources, marketing, or engineering then have the authority to approve their own projects. (3) Task budgeting selects specific projects to support on an ad hoc basis. This is the least proactive but does permit definitive cost-benefit analysis.[6]

There is a great deal of interplay between budgeting and value assessment in any management decision to conduct research. While this is more prevalent in applied research, even low-cost academic studies should be able to demonstrate value to their intended consumers.

VALUING RESEARCH INFORMATION

Managers' motivations for seeking research help vary, and may not always be fully evident. They may feel a real need for specific information by which to guide a decision. At other times, the study may be authorized chiefly because its presence may promote approval for a decision the managers are willing to make without research. At other times, research may be authorized as a measure of personal protection for the decision makers in case the decision is criticized later.

An appropriate research study can help managers avoid losses and increase profits, or it can be a waste. The decision makers usually must face this evaluation question. Typically, they want a firm cost estimate for a project and an equally precise assurance that useful information will result from the study. Even if the researcher can give good cost and information estimates, the managers still must judge whether the benefits outweigh the costs.

Conceptually, the value of applied research is not difficult to determine. In a business situation, the research should produce added revenues or reduce expenses in much the same way as any other investment of resources. One source suggests that the value of research information may be judged in terms of "the difference between the result of decisions made with the information and the result that would be made without it."[7] While such a criterion is simple to state, its actual use presents difficult measurement problems.

Evaluation Methods

Ex Post Facto Evaluation
If there is any measurement of the value of research, it is usually an after-the-fact event. Twedt reported on one such effort, an evaluation of marketing research done at a major corporation.[8] He secured "an objective estimate of the contribution of each project to corporate profitability." He reported that most studies were intended to help management determine which one of two (or more) alternatives was preferable. He guessed that in 60 percent of the decision situations, the correct decision would have been made *without* the benefit of the research information. In the remaining 40 percent of the cases, the research led to the correct decision. Using these data, he estimated that the return on investment in marketing research in this company was 351 percent for the year studied. However, he acknowledges the return on investment figure was inflated because only the direct research costs had been included.

This effort at cost-benefit analysis is commendable even though the results come too late to guide current research decision. Such analysis may sharpen the manager's ability to make judgments about future research proposals. However, the critical problem remains, that of project evaluation *before the study is done.*

Prior Evaluation   A proposal to conduct a thorough management audit of operations in a company may be a worthy one, but neither its costs nor its benefits are easily estimated in advance. Such projects are sufficiently unique that managerial experience seldom provides much aid in evaluating such a proposal either.

Even in these situations, managers can make some useful judgments. They may determine that a management audit is needed because the company is in dire straits and management does not understand the scope of its problems. The management information need may be so great as to assure that the research is approved. In such cases, they may decide to control the research expenditure risk by doing a study in stages. They can then review costs and benefits at the end of each step and give or withhold further authorization. Typical of this approach is the two-stage study discussed in Chapter 5.

Option Analysis   Some progress has been made in the development of methods for assessing the value of research when management has a choice between well-defined options. Each alternative can be judged in terms of estimated costs and benefits associated with it, and a formal analysis can be conducted, but managerial judgment still plays a major role.

While both costs and benefits present major estimating problems, the development of the cost side of the equation is normally the easiest. If the research design can be stated clearly, one can estimate an approximate cost. The critical task is to quantify the benefits from the research. At best, estimates of benefits are crude and largely reflect a more orderly way to estimate outcomes under uncertain conditions. To illustrate how the contribution of research is evaluated in such a decision situation, we must digress briefly into the rudiments of decision theory.

Decision Theory   To compare two or more alternatives, a manager must estimate the expected outcome of each alternative. The case of two choices will be discussed here, although the same approach can be used with more than two choices. Two possible actions (A_1 and A_2) may represent two different ways to organize a company, to provide financing, to produce a product, and so forth. We need not specify the nature of the alternatives in order to describe the approach.

When there are alternatives from which to choose, a rational way to approach the decision is to try to assess the outcomes of each action; then one can choose the outcome that best meets the criterion established for judging alternatives. This criterion is a combination of a *decision rule* and a *decision variable.* For example, the decision variable might be "direct dollar savings," "contribution to overhead and profits," "time required for completion of the project," and so forth.

Usually the decision variable is expressed in dollars, representing sales, costs, or some form of profits or contribution. The decision rule may be "choose the course of action with the lowest loss possibility" or perhaps "choose the alternative that provides the greatest annual net profit." The alternative selected depends on the decision variable chosen and the decision rule used. The evaluation of alternatives requires that (1) they may be explicitly stated, (2) a decision variable be defined by the outcome that may be measured, and (3) a decision rule be determined by which outcomes may be compared. An example of this approach is provided in Appendix B.

THE RESEARCH PROPOSAL

Figure 3–1 depicts the research proposal as an activity that develops concurrently with the project planning phases of the study. The proposal thus incorporates the choices the investigator has made in the preliminary steps.

A written proposal is often required when a study is being suggested. It assures that the parties understand the project's purpose and proposed methods of investigation. Time and budgets are often spelled out, as are other responsibilities and obligations. Depending upon the needs and desires of the client, there may also be substantial background detail and elaboration of proposed techniques.

The length and complexity of research proposals range widely. A graduate student may present a doctoral dissertation proposal that runs 50 pages or more. Applicants for foundation or government research grants typically file a proposal request of a few pages, often in a standardized format specified by the granting agency. Business research proposals normally range from one to ten pages.

Proposal Contents

Every proposal, regardless of length, should include two basic sections. First is the problem statement. In the brief memo type of proposal, the problem statement may be a paragraph setting out the situation and stating the specific task the research will undertake.

Examples of such problem statements are:

1. The Center City Bank is currently the leading bank in the city but recently has not been growing as fast as its major competitors. Before developing a long-range plan to enhance the bank's competitive position, it is important to determine the bank's present competitive status, its advantages and opportunities, and its major deficiencies. The primary objective of this proposed research is to develop a body of benchmark information about the Center City Bank, its major competitors, and the Center City metropolitan area as a market for banking services.

2. Management is faced with a problem of locating a new plant to serve eastern markets. Before this location decision is made, it is proposed that a feasibility study be conducted to determine, for each of five sites, the estimated:

   a. Costs of serving existing customers.

   b. Building, relocation, tax, and operating costs.

     c. Availability of local labor in the six major crafts used in production.

     d. Attractiveness of the living environment for professional and management personnel.

The above statements give the problem facing the respective managements and point out the nature of the research that will be undertaken. Other problem statements might begin with issues raised by behavioral or other theories and state several hypotheses for testing.

A second section includes a statement of what will be done. In the bank example cited, the researcher might propose:

> Personal interviews will be conducted with a minimum of 200 residents of the area to determine their knowledge of, use of, and attitudes toward local banks. In addition, information will be gathered about their banking and financing practices and preferences. Other information of an economic or demographic nature will also be gathered from published sources and public agencies.

Often proposals are much more detailed and include specific measurement devices that will be used, time and cost budgets, sampling plans, and many other details. Chapter 4 describes the construction of research proposals.

PILOT TESTING

The data gathering phase of the research process typically begins with pilot testing. Often pilot testing is skipped when the researcher tries to condense the project (see Figure 3–1).

A **pilot test** is conducted to detect weaknesses in design and instrumentation and provide proxy data for selection of a probability sample. It should therefore draw subjects from the target population and simulate the procedures and protocols that have been designated for data collection. If the study is a survey to be executed by mail, the pilot questionnaire should also be mailed. If the design calls for observation by an unobtrusive researcher, this behavior should be practiced. The size of the pilot group may range from 25 to 100 subjects depending on the method to be tested, but the respondents do not have to be statistically selected. In very small populations or special applications, pilot testing runs the risk of exhausting the supply of respondents and sensitizing them to the purpose of the study. This risk is generally overshadowed by the improvements made to the design by a trial run.

There are a number of variations on pilot testing of which some are intentionally restricted to data collection activities. One form, pretesting, may rely on colleagues, respondent surrogates, or actual respondents for the purpose of refining a measuring instrument. This important activity has saved countless survey studies from disaster by using the suggestions of the respondents to identify and change confusing, awkward, or offensive questions and techniques. An interview study in which one of the authors participated had been designed by a group of college professors for an educational television consortium. In the pilot test, it was discovered that the wording of nearly two-thirds of the questions was unintelligible to the target group, later found to have a median eighth-grade education. The revised instrument incorporated the respondents' language and was successful. Pretesting may be repeated several times to refine instruments and procedures.

DATA COLLECTION

The gathering of data may range from relatively simple observation at one location to a grandiose survey of multinational corporations at sites in different parts of the world. The method selected will largely determine how the data are collected. Questionnaires, standardized tests, observational forms, laboratory notes, and instrument calibration logs are among the devices used to record raw data.

But what are data? One writer defines **data** as the facts presented to the researcher from the study's environment. Data may be further characterized by their: (1) abstractness, (2) verifiability, (3) elusiveness, and (4) closeness to the phenomenon.[9] As abstractions, data are more metaphorical than real; for example, the growth in GNP cannot be observed directly; only the effects of it may be recorded. Second, data are processed by our senses—often limited in comparison to other living organisms. When sensory experiences consistently produce the same result, our data are said to be trustworthy because they may be verified. Third, capturing data is complicated by the speed at which events occur and the time-bound nature of observation. Opinions, preferences, and attitudes vary from one milieu to another and by the passage of time. For example, attitudes about spending during the 1980s differ dramatically one decade later in the same population. Finally, data classify their verity by closeness to the phenomena. Secondary data have had at least one level of interpretation inserted between the event and its recording. Primary data are sought for their proximity to the truth and control over error. These cautions remind us to use care in designing data collection procedures and generalizing from results.

Data are edited to ensure consistency across respondents and to locate emissions. In the case of survey methods, editing reduces errors in the recording, improves legibility, and clarifies unclear and inappropriate responses. Edited data are then put into a form that makes analysis possible. Because it is impractical to place raw data into a report, alphanumeric codes are used to reduce the responses to a more manageable system for storage and future processing. The codes follow various decision rules that the researcher has devised to assist with sorting, tabulating, and analyzing. Personal computers have made it possible to merge editing, coding, and data entry into fewer steps even when the final analysis may be run on a mainframe. Data collection is addressed in more detail in Part III of this book.

ANALYSIS AND INTERPRETATION

After collecting the data, we still need to analyze it. **Data analysis** usually involves reducing accumulated data to a manageable size, developing summaries, looking for patterns, and applying statistical techniques. Scaled responses on questionnaires and experimental instruments often require the analyst to derive various functions, and relationships among variables are frequently explored after that. Further, we must interpret these findings in light of the client's question or, with theory-building research, determine if the results are consistent with our hypotheses and theories.

A modest example involves a market research firm that polls 2,000 people in its test group for a new generation of wallet-sized portable telephones. Each respondent might be asked four questions. "Do you prefer the convenience of Pocket-Phone over wired telephones?" "Are there transmission problems with Pocket-Phone?" "Is Pocket-Phone better suited to transmission from your car than a cellular phone?" "Would cost alone persuade you to purchase Pocket-Phone?" The answers would produce 8,000 pieces of data. Reducing the data to a workable size would yield eight statistics: the percentage of yes and no answers to each question. If a half dozen demographic questions about the respondents were added, the total amount of data could easily triple. And if the questions had been scaled, the analysis would likely require more powerful statistical analysis. Chapters 14 through 17 deal with these topics in more depth.

REPORTING THE RESULTS

Finally, it is necessary to prepare a report and transmit the findings and recommendations to the client for the intended purpose of decision making. The style and organization of the report will differ according to the target audience, the occasion, and the purpose of the research. In applied research, communication of the results may cover a range of actions from a conference call, a letter, a written report, or an oral presentation—and sometimes all of them. Reports should be developed from the client's perspective. The sophistication of the design and sampling plan or the esoteric software used to analyze the data may have helped to establish the researcher's credibility, but in the end, solving the problem is foremost on the manager's mind. Thus, the researcher must accurately assess the manager's needs throughout the research process and incorporate this understanding into the final product.

Research is occasionally shelved without action. Inferior communication of results is a primary contributor. Insightful adaptation to the client's needs and carefully executed work are the prescribed remedies. Occasionally, organizational and environmental forces beyond the researcher's control auger against the implementation of results. Such was the case in a study conducted for the Association of American Publishers, which needed an ad campaign to get people to read more books. The project, costing $125,000, found that only 13 percent of Americans buy general-interest books in stores. When the time came to commit $14 million to the campaign to raise book sales, the membership's interest faded and the project died.[10]

At a minimum, the research report should contain an *executive summary* consisting of a synopsis of the problem, findings, and recommendations; an *overview of the research:* the problem's background, literature summary, methods and procedures, conclusions, and a special section on implementation strategies for the recommendations; and a *technical appendix* with all the materials necessary to replicate the project. Chapter 18 covers this topic in more detail.

CLOSE-UP

The next morning, at 7 A.M. sharp, Myra appeared at Jason's apartment. As she pushed the doorbell, she heard furniture being wrestled across the floor.

"It's open," hollered Jason.

Inside, Jason had cleared furniture and pictures from the south wall and had leaned a slab of plywood against that wall. "There's coffee and doughnuts," he said. "But first give me a hand with this."

"This" was a roll of brown wrapping paper. The two of them worked together and unrolled the hard-to-handle paper left to right across the top two feet of plywood, cut it, and tacked down its corners so it covered the top half of the plywood. Then they started on the lower left side of the slab and tacked down paper on the plywood.

They now had a 4-by-4-foot chart.

Across the top of the first sheet, Myra wrote, "Satisfaction with the Service Department." Today they would focus on the easiest task and leave the customer profile pilot for later. Besides, Gracie was pressed for answers on how the CompleteCare repair program was being received. If they were responsive on the smaller project, they were sure they'd get the OK for the more ambitious one.

Then they helped themselves to coffee and doughnuts, pulled two chairs in front of the chart, and for five minutes stared in silence at its awful blankness.

*   *   *   *   *   *

Myra and Jason had learned a lot about Mind-Writer. First with a trip to the local library before their visit and then the meetings in Austin, they knew the product was sold through computer superstores and independent mail order companies. Myra had gotten hers from PC Express. They also learned that MindWriter ships about 5,000 portable/laptop computers per month. The product is successful yet constrained from the same supply shortages as the rest of the industry. Personal computer magazines were consulted for their annual surveys on service, repair, and technical support. Overall customer satisfaction comparisons were obtained from published sources.

The exploratory sessions in Austin had revealed much about the CompleteCare process. Myra summarized the information under the label "CC Process."

When customers experience a malfunction, they call an 800 number. The call center answers service, support, and ordering questions. Technical line operators are trained to:

- Take the name, phone, address, and Mindwriter model number.
- Detect the nature of the problem.
- Attempt to resolve the problem if they can walk the customer through corrective steps.

If not, the tech-line provides a return authorization code and dispatches a package courier to pick up the unit before 5 P.M. The unit is delivered to Austin for service the next morning. The CompleteCare repair facility calls the customer if the repair information is incomplete. The unit is repaired by the end of that day and picked up by the courier. The call center then updates its database with service record information. If all goes well, the customer receives the repaired unit by 10 A.M. the following morning and about 48 hours have elapsed.

When Myra finished, Jason began to rough out the known "Problems." There were employee shortages at the call center and difficulties getting the new tech-line operators trained. The courier was uneven in executing its pickup and delivery contract. MindWriter was experiencing parts availability problems for some models. And, of course, occasional units were sent back to the

(continued)

customer either not fixed or damaged in some way. Jason believed this meant the service area was not doing an adequate job. But Myra asserted that problems could be in the original packing, in handling, or even from sources related to taking the boxes on and off the shipping pallets.

Because of their brainstorming, they were able to restate management's question, "How do customers like the new repair program?" as a research question and investigative questions.

Research question: What are the satisfaction levels with the CompleteCare service program?

Investigative questions:

    a. How well is the call center helping the customers? Are they helping the customer with instructions? What percentage of customers' technical problems are they solving without callbacks? How long do customers wait on the phone?

    b. How good is the transportation company? Did they pick up and deliver the system responsively? How long do customers wait for them? Was the system damaged due to the package handling?

    c. How good is the repair group? Is the repair complete? Are customers' problems resolved? Are there new problems?

    d. Are customers' expectations being met by the time it takes to repair the systems?

    e. What is customers' overall satisfaction with CompleteCare, and with the MindWriter product?

Jason and Myra now had enough information to go back to MindWriter. In particular, they wanted to know from Gracie whether they had translated her management question in a way that would adequately fulfill her need for information. They also wanted to do in-depth interviews with the service manager, the call center manager, and with the independent package company's account executive. Some investigative questions could be answered by these people. The rest of the questions would need to be translated into measurement questions to ask customers. They were comfortable that with the additional insight from their interviews (and customer letters), they could develop a questionnaire for CompleteCare customers.

Jason planned to test the questionnaire with a limited number of customers, revise the questions, set up the logistics, and then roll out the research program. Sampling would be a critical matter. If Gracie's budget were large, they could use a probability sample from the customer list that MindWriter provides every week. This would make telephone interviews possible. There was a need for a less expensive alternative, however. They decided to propose the questionnaire as a postcard survey to be included with every system as it is returned to the customer. They would also do random sampling from the list of customers who do not respond. The nonresponders would be interviewed on the telephone. This way they could be assured of a cost-effective questionnaire with correction for nonresponse bias.

A tentative schedule was devised before calling Gracie for the follow-up interviews (see Figure 3–3). They wanted to give her target dates for completion of the exploratory phase, completion of the instrument and pilot test, and a deadline for the first month's results.

FIGURE   3–3   A Gantt Chart of the MindWriter Project

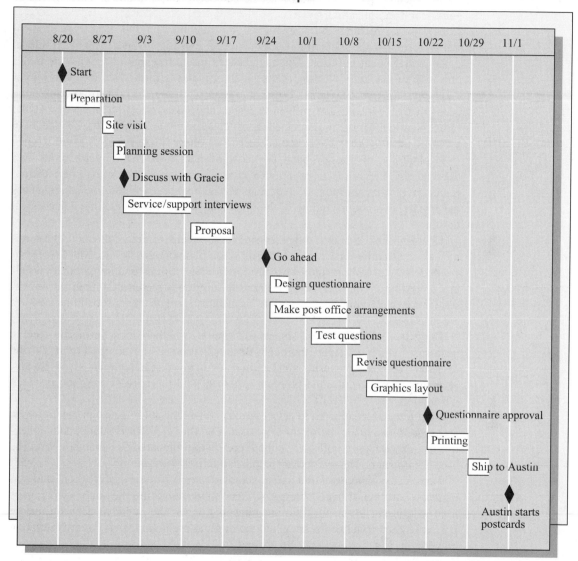

Summary

Research originates in the decision process. A manager needs specific information for setting objectives, defining tasks, finding the best strategy by which to carry out the tasks, or judging how well the strategy is being implemented.

A problem-centered emphasis—the problem's origin, selection, statement, exploration, and refinement—dominates the sequence of the research process. A problem can originate in the arenas of academic or applied management research or may be inappropriately driven by the availability of coveted tools and databases.

To be researchable, a problem must be subject to observation or other forms of empirical data collection.

How one structures the problem sets the direction for the project. A problem can be formulated as a hierarchical sequence of questions. At the most general level is the management question. This is translated into a research question—the major objective of the study. In turn, the research question is further reduced into one or more investigative questions. These questions represent the various facets of the problem to be solved and influence design and data collection planning. At the most specific level are measurement questions that are answered by respondents in a survey or answered about each subject in an observational study.

Exploration of the problem is accomplished through familiarization with the available literature, an experience survey, focus group, or some combination. Revision of the question is a desirable outcome of exploration and enhances the researcher's understanding of the options available for developing a successful design.

Decisions concerning the type of study, the means of data collection, measurement, and sampling plans must be made when planning the design. Most researchers undertake sampling studies because of an interest in estimating population values or testing a statistical hypothesis. Carefully constructed delimitations are essential for specifying an appropriate probability sample. Nonprobability samples are also used.

Budgets and value assessments determine whether most projects receive necessary funding. Their thorough documentation is an integral part of the research proposal. Proposals are required for many research projects and should, at a minimum, describe the problem statement and the specific task the research will undertake.

Pilot tests are conducted to detect weaknesses in the study's design, instruments, and procedures. Once the researcher is satisfied that the plan is sound, data collection begins. Data are collected, edited, coded, and prepared for analysis. With the use of computers, this can be accomplished in a few steps.

Data analysis involves reduction, summarization, pattern examination, and statistical evaluation of hypotheses. A written report describing the study's findings is used to transmit the results and recommendations to the intended decision maker. By cycling the conclusions back into the original problem, a new research iteration may begin, and findings may be applied.

Key Terms

data	management question
data analysis	measurement question(s)
dcsign	pilot test
exploration	research process
hierarchy of questions	research question(s)
investigative question(s)	sample

Discussion Questions

1. What are some management and accompanying research questions that might be useful to the following executives?
   a. The production manager of a shoe factory.
   b. The president of First National Bank.
   c. The vice president of labor relations for an auto manufacturer.
   d. The chief of police in a major city.

2. What are some of the important reasons a research project will fail to make an adequate contribution to the solution of management problems?

3. The vice president of administration calls you into her office and states that the computer programming department is not functioning well because there is excessive turnover among the programmers. She suggests you conduct a survey among other major companies in the region to learn how they handle the problem of high programmer turnover.
   a. What do you think of this problem assessment and research suggestion?
   b. How, if at all, could you improve on the vice president's formulation of the research problem?

4. What are the major problems in the valuation of a research study?

5. Some questions are answerable by research and others are not. Distinguish between them using some management problems of your choosing.

6. You have been approached by the editor of *Gentlemen's Magazine* to carry out a research study. The magazine has been unsuccessful in attracting shoe manufacturers as advertisers. When the sales force tried to secure advertising from shoe manufacturers, they were told men's clothing stores are a small and dying segment of their business. Since *Gentlemen's Magazine* goes chiefly to men's clothing stores, the manufacturers reasoned that it was, therefore, not a good vehicle for their advertising.

   The editor believes that a survey (via mail questionnaire) of men's clothing stores in the United States will probably show that these stores are important outlets for men's shoes and that they are not declining in importance as shoe outlets. He asks you to develop a proposal for the study and submit it to him. Develop research questions or hypotheses of various levels that will enable you to develop a specific proposal.

7. Discuss the problems of trading off exploration and pilot testing under tight budgetary constraints. What are the immediate and long-term effects?

Reference Notes

1. Albert Einstein and L. Infeld, *The Evolution of Physics* (New York: Simon & Schuster, 1938), p. 95.
2. Walter B. Reitman, "Heuristic Decision Procedures, Open Constraints, and the Structure of Ill-Defined Problems" in *Human Judgments and Optimality*, ed. Maynard W. Shelly II and Glenn L. Bryan (New York: John Wiley & Sons, 1964), p. 285.

3. Carl M. Moore, *Group Techniques for Idea Building,* 2nd ed. (Thousand Oaks, Calif.: Sage Publications, 1994).

4. Fred N. Kerlinger, *Foundations of Behavioral Research,* 3rd ed. (New York: Holt, Rinehart & Winston, 1986), pp. 436–37.

5. We have discussed literature review or secondary data studies previously under the heading of Exploration. The option to select secondary data collection as a principal methodology—as an in-depth, critical examination—should be distinguished from the use of published data to enhance one's preliminary knowledge of the problem in the initial stages of research.

6. Walter B. Wentz, *Marketing Research: Management, Method, and Cases* (New York: Harper & Row, 1979), p. 35.

7. Robert D. Buzzell, Donald F. Cox, and Rex V. Brown, *Marketing Research and Information Systems* (New York: McGraw-Hill, 1969), p. 595.

8. Dik Warren Twedt, "What Is the 'Return on Investment' in Marketing Research?" *Journal of Marketing* 30 (January 1966), pp. 62–63.

9. Paul D. Leedy, *How to Read Research and Understand It* (New York: Macmillan, 1981), pp. 67–70.

10. Roger Cohen, "For U.S. Publishers, Awash in Red Ink, the Moment of Truth Looms," *International Herald Tribune,* March 6, 1990, p. 6.

Suggested Readings

1. Fox, David J. *The Research Process in Education,* New York: Holt, Rinehart & Winston, 1969. Chapter 2 includes a research process model to compare with the one in this chapter.

2. Leedy, Paul D. *Practical Research: Planning & Design,* 5th ed. New York: Macmillan, 1992. Practical and readable sections guide students through the research process.

3. Murdick, Robert G., and Donald R. Cooper. *Business Research: Concepts and Guides.* Columbus, Ohio: Grid Publishing, 1982. A supplementary text with a strong emphasis on problem identification and formulation.

4. Selltiz, Claire; Lawrence S. Wrightsman; and Stuart M. Cook. *Research Methods in Social Relations,* 3rd ed. New York: Holt, Rinehart & Winston, 1976. Chapters 1 and 2 present a good research process example and discussion of formulating a research problem.

5. Tull, Donald S., and Del I. Hawkins. *Marketing Research: Meaning, Measurement, and Method.* 6th ed. New York: Macmillan, 1992. The authors provide good coverage of the valuation of research information through a Bayesian decision theory approach.

THE RESEARCH PROPOSAL

 **FINDING
YOUR WAY**

BRINGING
RESEARCH TO LIFE

"Come on over here and meet Robert Buffet." The president of the Economic Development Council seized Myra Wines by the elbow and propelled her across the dining room to meet a tall young man suited in navy-blue pinstripes. She recognized his name: He was local manager of a national accounting firm.

"Hello, Robert," she said. She studied him carefully, sweeping her eyes from his brightly shined black shoes to his razor cut hair. He was about the same age as her new consulting partner, Jason Henry, but something in the way he held himself suggested a self-assurance that Jason had not yet developed. This young man dressed like a banker, while Jason suggested a librarian, a sincere yet somehow impatient librarian.

"And what a pleasure it is to meet you," he said in a ripe baritone voice, smiling with his lips, but not his eyes, which had wandered to a prominent banker who was chatting with a competing CPA.

"Here's the situation, Myra," said the president. "The state commerce secretary has been concerned for some time about the extent to which entrepreneurial companies, which are popping up all over the state, are actually investing in job-building technology. They have contracted with Robert's firm to study the situation in five counties, to assess job creation and the like, and report this back to Tallahassee."

Myra asked, "Am I right in suspecting that the governor is worried that these start-up companies are investing in robotics and computers and not creating new manufacturing jobs?"

"Basically, that is the concern, Ms. Wines," said the tall young man. "We have already cut the contract, you see, in Tallahassee, and so we have the green light to select our five sites and commence the interviewing."

"The thing is, Myra," said the president, "before their task force can come into a county and start interviewing and collecting data, they have got to have the auspices, the sponsorship, so to speak, of a business group. In this county, it is our council that has to look over their proposal and assure the business community it is in their best interests to cooperate."

"And you want me to critically examine the plan and let you know what I think."

"By two weeks from Friday, please," said the president, "as a favor."

"Here is a copy of our proposal," said the tall young man. How awfully nice chatting with you." He grasped her hand, gave it one shake, patted the council president on the shoulder, and headed for the refreshment table, where a local auto dealer presented an easy target for a sales pitch.

THE PURPOSE OF PROPOSALS

A proposal is an individual's or company's offer to produce a product or render a service to a potential buyer or sponsor. The purpose of the research proposal is:

1. To present the problem to be researched and its importance.
2. To discuss the research efforts of others who have worked on related problems.
3. To suggest the data necessary for solving the problem and how the data will be gathered, treated, and interpreted.

In addition, the proposal of a contract researcher must present its plan, services, and credentials in the best possible way to encourage its selection over competitors. In contract research, the survival of companies depends on their ability to develop winning proposals.[1] A **proposal** is also known as a work plan, prospectus, outline, statement of intent, or draft plan.[2] It tells us (1) what will be done, (2) why it will be done, (3) how it will be done, (4) where it will be done, (5) to whom it will be done, and (6) what is the benefit of doing it.[3]

Many students and beginning researchers view the proposal as unnecessary work. In actuality, the more inexperienced a researcher is, the more important it is to have a well-planned and adequately documented proposal. The research proposal is essentially a road map, showing clearly the location from which a journey begins, the destination to be reached, and the method of getting there. Well-prepared proposals include potential problems that may be encountered along the way and methods for avoiding or working around them, much like a road map includes alternate routes for a detour.

SPONSOR USES

All research has a sponsor in one form or another. The student researcher is responsible to the class instructor. The doctoral candidate reports to a dissertation committee. In a corporate setting, whether the research is being done in-house by a research department or under contract to an external research firm, management sponsors the research. University, government, or corporate-sponsored (grant) research use grant committees to evaluate the work.

A research proposal is the first step in the evaluation process. It allows the sponsor to assess the sincerity of your purpose, the clarity of your design, the extent of your background material, and your fitness for undertaking the project. The proposal displays your discipline, organization, and logic. A poorly planned, poorly written, or poorly organized proposal damages your reputation more than the decision not to submit one. Depending on the type of research and the sponsor you have, various aspects of a standard proposal design are emphasized. The proposal, then, provides a document the sponsor can evaluate based upon the current organizational, scholastic, or scientific needs. It allows the research sponsor to assess both the researcher and the proposed design, to compare them against competing proposals, and to make the best selection for the project.

The proposal also provides a basis for the sponsor to evaluate the results of a project. By comparing the final product with the stated objectives, it is easy to decide if the research goals have been achieved.

Another benefit of the proposal is the discipline it brings to the sponsor. Many managers, requesting an in-house, departmental research project, do not adequately define the problem they are addressing. The research proposal acts as a catalyst for discussion between the person conducting the research and the manager. The researcher translates the management question, as described by the manager, into the research question and outlines the objectives of the study. Upon review, the manager may discover that the interpretation of the problem does not encompass all the original symptoms. The proposal, then, serves as the basis for additional discussion between the manager and the researcher until all aspects of the management question are understood. Parts of the problem may not be researchable, or at least not subject to empirical study. An alternate design, such as a qualitative or policy analytic study may need to be proposed. Upon completion of the discussions, a carefully worded research question should emerge. Figure 4–1 reveals how this can work in an iterative fashion until authorization to proceed is granted.

For an outside contract, the process is different. Proposals are usually submitted in response to a request for bid or **request for proposal (RFP).** The

FIGURE   4–1   Proposal Development

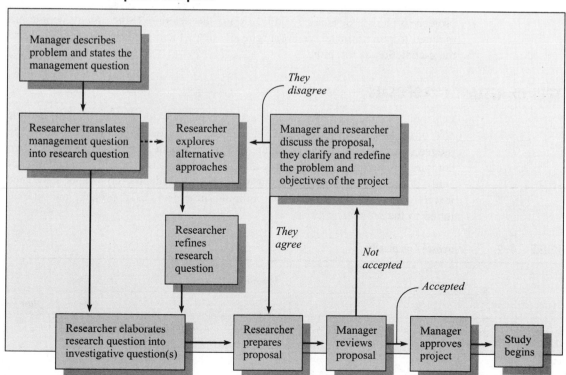

researchers may wish to convince the sponsor that their approach to the research question differs from the problem (management question) specified in the initial RFP. In this way, the researchers can show superior understanding of the problem over competing proposals. Appendix C provides further information on RFPs.

RESEARCHER BENEFITS

A proposal is more beneficial for the beginning researcher than for the sponsor. This does not diminish its relevance to the sponsor. But it is imperative for the beginner researcher to have a tentative work plan that charts the logical steps needed to accomplish the stated goals.

The process of writing a proposal allows the researcher to plan and review the project's steps. Related literature should be examined, thus prompting the researcher to assess previous approaches to the problem and revise the plan accordingly. Additionally, there is the opportunity to spot flaws in the logic, errors in assumptions, or even problems that are not adequately addressed by the objectives and design.

After acceptance of the proposal, the document serves as a guide for the researcher throughout the investigation. Progress can be monitored and milestones noted. At completion, the proposal contains everything needed, outlining the final research report.[4]

A final benefit, especially for the beginning researcher, is that the proposal forces time and budget estimates. These estimates allow researchers to plan the project so work progresses steadily toward the deadline. Since many people are inclined to procrastinate, having a schedule helps them work methodically toward the completion of the project.

TYPES OF RESEARCH PROPOSALS

Depending on the type of project, the sponsoring individual or institution, and the cost of the project, different levels of complexity are required for a proposal to be judged complete. As shown in Figure 4–2, government agencies demand the most complex proposals for their funding analyses. On the other extreme, an exploratory study done within a firm's research division or a student's term paper may need merely a one- to three-page memo outlining the objectives, approach, and time allotted to the project.

FIGURE   4–2   Proposal Complexity

| *Type* | Complexity | | | |
	Least			*Most*
Student	Term paper	Master's thesis	Doctoral thesis	
Internal	Exploratory study	Small-scale study	Large-scale study	
External	Exploratory contract research	Small-scale contract research	Large-scale contract research	Government sponsored

In general, business proposals can be divided between those generated internally and externally. A third category is student proposals. An internal proposal is done for the corporation by the research department of the firm or by staff specialists. External proposals are either solicited or unsolicited. Sponsors can be university grant committees, government agencies, government contractors, corporations, and so forth. With few exceptions, the larger the project, the more complex the proposal. In public sector work, the complexity is generally greater than a comparable private sector proposal.

In terms of complexity, there are three general levels. The exploratory study, which fits between a student term paper and a master's thesis in complexity, is the first, most simple business proposal. More complex and common in business is the small-scale study—either an internal or external contract research project. The large-scale professional study, worth up to several million dollars, will be the highest level of proposals we deal with. Government agency proposals, running several hundred pages, use the same modules that we will discuss below. However, each agency has unique requirements, making generalized coverage beyond the scope of this text.

Figure 4–3 displays a set of modules for building a proposal. Based on the type of proposal you are writing, you may choose the appropriate modules for inclusion. This is a *general guide,* and sometimes more or less than what is shown here is appropriate for a specific purpose. (Your instructor will provide you with requirements unique to your program.) For example, most small-scale studies do not require a glossary of terms. Terms are defined within the body of the proposal. However, if the proposal deals with an esoteric subject that is not familiar to management, it is appropriate to add a glossary. Note the differences between the proposal types in Figure 4–3.

Internal Proposals

Internal proposals are more succinct than external ones. At the least complex end of the continuum, a memo from the researcher to management outlining the problem statement, study objectives, research design, and schedule is enough to start an exploratory study. Privately and publicly held firms are concerned with how to solve a particular problem, make a decision, or improve an aspect of their business. Seldom do businesses begin research studies for other reasons. In the small-scale proposal, the literature review and bibliography are consequently not stressed and can often be stated briefly in the research design.

Since management insists on brevity, an executive summary is mandatory on all but the most simple of proposals (projects that can be proposed in a two-page memo do not need an executive summary). Schedules and budgets are necessary for funds to be committed. For the smaller-scale projects, descriptions are not required for facilities and special resources nor is there a need for a glossary. Since small projects are sponsored by managers familiar with the problem, the associated jargon, requirements, and definitions would be included directly in the text. Also, the measuring instrument and project management modules are not required. Managers will typically leave this detail for the research department.

FIGURE 4–3   When to Include a Proposal Module

Proposal Modules	Student			Internal			External			
	Term Paper	Master's Thesis	Doctoral Thesis	Exploratory Study	Small-Scale Study	Large-Scale Study	Exploratory Study	Small-Scale Contract	Large-Scale Contract	Government Grant or Contract
Executive summary					✔	✔	✔	✔	✔	✔
Problem statement	✔	✔	✔	✔	✔	✔	✔	✔	✔	✔
Research objectives	✔	✔	✔	✔	✔	✔	✔	✔	✔	✔
Literature review		✔	✔			✔			✔	✔
Importance/ benefits of study			✔			✔	✔	✔	✔	✔
Research design		✔	✔	✔	✔	✔	✔	✔	✔	✔
Data analysis			✔						✔	✔
Nature and form of results		✔	✔		✔	✔		✔	✔	✔
Qualification of researchers							✔	✔	✔	✔
Budget					✔	✔	✔	✔	✔	✔
Schedule			✔	✔	✔	✔	✔	✔	✔	✔
Facilities and special resources		✔	✔			✔	✔	✔	✔	✔
Project management						✔			✔	✔
Bibliography	✔	✔	✔			✔			✔	✔
Appendixes Glossary of terms		✔	✔			✔			✔	✔
Measurement instrument			✔			✔			✔	✔

External Proposals

An external proposal is either solicited or unsolicited. A solicited proposal is often in response to an RFP. The proposal is likely competing against several others for a contract or grant. An unsolicited proposal has the advantage of not competing against others but the disadvantage of having to speculate on the ramifications of a problem facing the firm's management. Even more difficult, the writer of an unsolicited proposal must decide to whom the document should be sent.

The most important sections of the external proposal are the objectives, design, qualifications, schedule and budget. The executive summary of an external proposal may be included within the letter of transmittal. As the complexity of the project increases, more information is required about project management and the facilities and special resources. In contract research, the results and objectives sections are the standards against which the completed project is measured. As we move toward government-sponsored research, particular attention must be paid to each specification in the RFP. To ignore or not meet any specification is to disqualify automatically your proposal as "nonresponsive."[5]

STRUCTURING THE RESEARCH PROPOSAL

Consider again Figure 4–3. Using this reference, you can put together a set of modules that tailor your proposal to the intended audience. Each of the following modules is also flexible internally so its content and length may be adapted to specific needs.

Executive Summary

The **executive summary** allows a busy manager or sponsor to understand quickly the thrust of the proposal. It is essentially an informative abstract, giving executives the chance to grasp the essentials of the proposal without having to read the details.[6] The goal of the summary is to secure a positive evaluation by the executive who will pass it on to the staff for a full evaluation. As such, it should include a brief statement of the problem, the research objectives/research question(s), and the benefits of your approach. If it is an unsolicited proposal, a brief description of your qualifications is also appropriate.

Problem Statement

This section convinces the sponsor to continue reading the proposal. You should capture the reader's attention by stating the problem, its background, and consequences. As discussed in Chapter 3, the problem can be represented by the management question. This is the question that starts the research task. The importance of the problem should be emphasized here if a separate module on the importance/benefits of study is not included later in the proposal. In addition, the problem statement will include any restrictions or areas of the problem that will not be addressed.

A problem too broadly stated cannot be addressed adequately by one study. It is important that the problem is distinct from related problems and that the sponsor can see the delimitations clearly. Be sure your problem is clearly stated without the use of idioms or cliches. After reading this section, the potential sponsor should know the problem, its significance, and why something should be done to change the status quo.[7]

Research Objectives

This module addresses the purpose of the investigation. It is here that you lay out exactly what is being planned by the proposed research. In a descriptive study, the objectives can be stated as the research question(s). Recall that the research question can be further broken down into investigative questions. If the proposal is for a causal study, then the objectives can be restated as a hypothesis.

The objectives module flows naturally from the problem statement, giving the sponsor specific, concrete, and achievable goals. It is best to list the objectives either in order of importance or in general terms first, moving to specific terms (i.e., research question followed by underlying investigative questions). The research questions (or hypotheses, if appropriate) should be set off from the flow of the text so they can be found easily.

The research objectives section is the basis for judging the remainder of the proposal and, ultimately, the final report. Verify the consistency of the proposal by checking to see that each objective is discussed in the research design, data analysis, and results sections.

Literature Review

The literature review section examines recent (or historically significant) research studies, company data, or industry reports that act as a basis for the proposed study. Begin your discussion of the related literature and relevant secondary data from a comprehensive perspective, moving to more specific studies that are associated with your problem. If the problem has a historical background, begin with the earliest references.

Avoid the extraneous details of the literature; do a brief review of the information, not a comprehensive report. Emphasize the important results and conclusions of other studies, the relevant data and trends from previous research, and particular methods or designs that could be duplicated or should be avoided. Discuss how the literature applies to the study you are proposing; show the weaknesses or faults in the design, discussing how you would avoid similar problems. If your proposal deals solely with secondary data, discuss the relevance of the data and the bias or lack of bias inherent in it.

Always refer to the original source. If you find something of interest in a quotation, find the original publication and ensure you understand it. In this way, you will avoid any errors of interpretation or transcription.

Close the literature review section by summarizing the important aspects of the literature and interpreting them in terms of your problem. Refine the problem as necessary in light of your findings. For more on the literature review, see Chapter 9, "Secondary Data Sources."

Importance/ Benefits of the Study

This section allows you to describe explicit benefits that will accrue from your study. The importance of "doing the study now" should be emphasized. Usually, this section is not more than a few paragraphs. If you find it difficult to write, then you have probably not understood the problem adequately. Return to the analysis of the problem and ensure, through additional discussions with your sponsor, your research team, or by a re-examination of the literature, that you have captured the essence of the problem.

This section also requires you to understand what is most troubling to your sponsor. If it is a potential union activity, you cannot promise that an employee survey will prevent unionization. You can, however, show the importance of this information and its implications. This benefit may allow management to respond to employee concerns and forge a linkage between those concerns and unionization.

The importance/benefits section is particularly important to the unsolicited external proposal. You must convince the sponsoring organization that your plan will meet its needs.

Literature Search

Research Design

Up to now, you have told the sponsor what the problem is, what your study goals are, and why it is important for you to do the study. The proposal has presented the study's value and benefits. The design module describes what you are going to do in technical terms. This section should include as many subsections as needed to show the phases of the project. Provide information on your proposed design for such tasks as sample selection and size, data collection method, instrumentation, procedures, and ethical requirements. When more than one way exists to approach the design, discuss the methods you rejected and why your selected approach is superior.

Refer to Chapter 5, "Design Strategies," for additional information on research design.

Data Analysis

A brief section on the methods used for analyzing the data is appropriate for large-scale contract research projects and doctoral theses. With smaller projects, the proposed data analysis would be included within the research design section. Describe your proposed treatment and the theoretical basis for using the selected techniques. The object of this section is to assure the sponsor you are following correct assumptions and using theoretically sound data analysis procedures.

This is often an arduous section to write. By use of sample charts and dummy tables, you can make it easier to understand your data analysis. This will make the section easier to write and easier to read. The data analysis section is important enough to contract research that you should contact an expert to review the latest techniques available for your use. If there is no statistical or analytical expertise within your company, be prepared to hire a professional to help with this activity.

Nature and Form of Results

Upon finishing this section, the sponsor should be able to go back to the problem statement and research objectives and discover that each goal of the study has been covered. One should also specify the types of data to be obtained and the interpretations that will be made in the analysis. If the data are to be turned over to the sponsor for proprietary reasons, make sure this is reflected. Alternatively, if the report will go to more than one sponsor, that should be noted.

This section also contains the contractual statement telling the sponsor exactly what types of information will be received. Statistical conclusions, applied findings, recommendations, action plans, models, strategic plans, and so forth are examples of the forms of results.

Qualification of Researchers

This section should begin with the principal investigator. It is also customary to begin qualifications with the highest academic degree held. Experience in carrying out previous research is important, especially in the corporate marketplace, so a concise description of similar projects should be included. Also important to business sponsors is experience as an executive or employee of an organization involved in a related field. Often businesses are reluctant to hire individuals to solve operational problems if they do not have practical experience. Finally, relevant business and technical societies to which the researcher belongs can be included where it is particularly relevant to the research project.[8]

The entire curriculum vitae of each researcher should not be included unless required by the RFP. Instead, refer to the relevant areas of experience and expertise that make the researchers the best selection for the task. Complete vitae information is often placed in an appendix for review by interested sponsors.

Budget

The budget should be presented in the form the sponsor requests. For example, some organizations require secretarial assistance to be individually budgeted, whereas others insist it be included in the research director's fees or the overhead of the operation. In addition, limitations on travel, per diem rates, and capital equipment purchases can change the way in which you prepare a budget.

Typically, the budget should be no more than one to two pages. Figure 4–4 shows a format that can be used for small contract research projects. Additional information, backup details, quotes from vendors, and hourly time and payment calculations should be put into an appendix if required or kept in the researcher's file for future reference.

It is extremely important that you retain all information you use to generate your budget. If you use quotes from external contractors, get the quotation in writing for your file. If you estimate time for interviews, keep explicit notes on how you made the estimate. When the time comes to do the work, you should know exactly how much money is budgeted for each particular task.[9]

Some costs are more elusive than others. Do not forget to build the cost of proposal writing into your fee. Publication and delivery of final reports can be a last-minute expense that can easily be overlooked in preliminary budgets.

Schedule

Your schedule should include the major phases of the project, their timetables, and the milestones that signify completion of a phase. For example, major phases may

FIGURE   4–4   Budget Example

Research Program Budget

Budget Items	Rate	Total Days	Charge
A. Salaries			
1. Research director, Myra Wines	$150/hr	20 hours	$ 3,000
2. Associate, Jason Henry	$100/hr	20 hours	$ 2,000
3. Research assistants (2)	$20/hr	300 hours	$ 6,000
4. Secretarial support (1)	$12/hr	100 hours	$ 1,200
Subtotal			$ 12,200
B. Other costs			
5. Employee services and benefits			
6. Travel			$ 2,500
7. Office supplies			$ 100
8. Telephone			$ 800
9. Rent			
10. Other equipment			
11. Publication and storage costs			$ 100
Subtotal			$ 3,500
C. Total of direct costs			$ 15,700
D. Overhead support			$ 5,480
E. Total funding requested			$ 21,180

be (1) exploratory interviews, (2) final research proposal, (3) questionnaire revision, (4) field interviews, (5) editing and coding, (6) data analysis, and (7) report generation. Each of these phases should have an estimated time schedule and people assigned to the work.

It may be helpful to you and your sponsor if you chart your schedule. You can use a Gantt chart, shown in Chapter 3, Figure 3–3. Alternatively, if the project is large and complex, a critical path method (CPM) of scheduling may be included.[10] In a CPM chart, the nodes represent major milestones, and the arrows suggest the work needed to get to the milestone. More than one arrow pointing to a node indicates all those tasks must be completed before the milestone has been met. Usually a number is placed along the arrow showing the number of days or weeks required for that task to be completed. The pathway from start to end that takes the longest time to complete is called the critical path. This is because any delay in an activity along that path will delay the end of the entire project. An example of a CPM chart is shown in Figure 4–5.[11] Software programs designed for project management will simplify scheduling and charting the schedule. Most are available for personal computers.

Facilities and Special Resources

Often, projects will require special facilities or resources that should be described in detail. For example, a contract exploratory study may need

FIGURE   4–5   CPM Schedule   [PERT CHART]

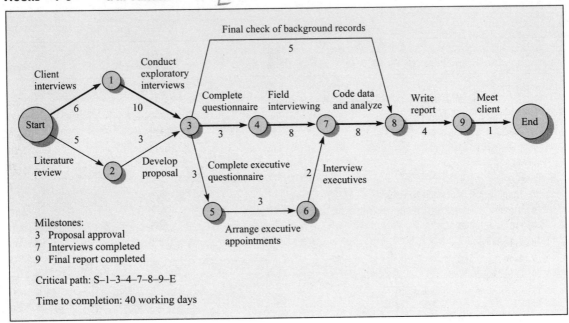

specialized facilities for focus group sessions. Computer-assisted telephone or other interviewing facilities may be required. Alternatively, your proposed data analysis may require sophisticated computer algorithms, and therefore, you need access to an adequate system. These requirements will vary from study to study. The proposal should carefully list the relevant facilities and resources that will be used.

Project Management

The purpose of the project management section is to show the sponsor the research team is organized in a way to do the project efficiently. A master plan is required for complex projects to show how the phases will all be brought together. More than the schedule section, described earlier, the plan includes:

1. The research team's organization.
2. Management procedures and controls for executing the research plan.
3. Examples of management and technical reports.
4. Research team relationship with the sponsor.
5. Financial and legal responsibility.
6. Management competence.

Tables and charts are most helpful in presenting the master plan.

The relationships between researchers and assistants need to be shown when several researchers are part of the team. Sponsors must know that the director is an individual capable of leading the team and being a useful liaison to the sponsor. In addition, procedures for information processing, record control, and expense control are critical to large operations and should be shown as part of the management procedures.

The type and frequency of progress reports should be recorded so the sponsor can expect to be kept up to date and the researchers can expect to be left alone to do research. The sponsor's limits on control during the process should be delineated.

Details such as printing facilities, clerical help, or information processing capabilities that are to be provided by the sponsor are discussed. In addition, rights to the data, the results, and authority to speak for the researcher and for the sponsor are included.

Payment frequency and timing are also covered in the master plan. Finally, proof of financial responsibility and overall management competence are provided.[12]

Bibliography

For all projects that require literature review, a bibliography is necessary. Use the bibliographic format required by the sponsor. If none is specified, a standard style manual (e.g., Kate L. Turabian, *A Manual for Writers of Term Papers, Theses, and Dissertations;* Joseph Gibaldi and Walter S. Achtert, *MLA Handbook for Writers of Research Papers;* or the *Publication Manual of the American Psychological Association*) will provide the details necessary to prepare the bibliography. Many of these sources also make suggestions for successful proposal writing.

Appendices

Glossary   A glossary of terms should be included whenever there are many words unique to the research topic and not understood by the general management community. This is a simple section consisting of terms and definitions. Also, define any acronyms that you use, even if they are defined within the text.

Measurement Instrument   For large projects, it is appropriate to include samples of the measurement instruments if they are available when you assemble the proposal. This allows the sponsor to discuss particular changes in one or more of the instruments. If exploratory work precedes the selection of the measurement instruments, you will not use this appendix section.

Other   Any detail that reinforces the body of the proposal can be included in an appendix. This includes researcher vitae, budget details, and lengthy descriptions of special facilities or resources.

EVALUATING THE RESEARCH PROPOSAL

Proposals are subjected to formal and informal reviews. The formal method has some variations, but its essence is described as follows. Criteria are established before the proposal is received and given weights or points. The proposal is evaluated with a checklist of criteria in hand. Points are recorded for each category reflecting the sponsor's assessment of how well the proposal meets the category's established criteria. Long and complex proposals are typically reviewed by several people with each reviewer responsible for a particular section. After the review, the category scores are added to provide a cumulative total. The proposal with the highest number of points will win the contract. The formal method is most likely to be used for competitive government, university, or public sector grants and also for large-scale contracts.

Small-scale contracts are more prone to informal evaluation. With informal evaluation, the project needs, and thus the criteria, are well understood but not usually well documented. In contrast to the formal method, a system of points is not used and the criteria are not ranked. The process is more qualitative and impressionistic in nature. Figure 4–6 shows an informal review of the proposal discussed in the opening vignette.

In practice, many items contribute to a proposal's acceptance and funding. Primarily, the content discussed above must be included to the level of detail required by the sponsor. Beyond the required modules, there are factors that can quickly eliminate a proposal from consideration and factors that improve the sponsor's reception of the proposal.

First, the proposal must be neatly presented. Although a proposal produced on a word processor and bound with an expensive cover will not overcome design or analysis deficiencies, a poorly presented, unclear, or disorganized proposal will not get serious attention from the reviewing sponsors. Second, the proposal's major topics should be easily found and logically organized. The reviewer should be able to page through the proposal to any section of interest. The proposal also must meet specific guidelines set by the sponsoring company or agency. This includes budgetary restrictions and schedule deadlines.[13]

A fourth important aspect is the technical writing style of the proposal. The problem statement must be easily understood. The research design should be clearly outlined and the methodology explained. The importance/benefits of the study must allow the sponsor to see why the research should be funded. The objectives and results sections should communicate exactly the goals and concrete results that will come from the study. Finally, budget and schedule considerations must be kept in mind. A late proposal will not be reviewed. A schedule that does not meet the expected deadlines will disqualify the proposal. A budget that is too high for the allocated funds will be rejected. Conversely, a budget that is very low compared to competing proposal budgets suggest that either something is missing or there is something wrong with the researchers.

FIGURE 4–6   **Informal Proposal Review**

Wines and Henry Associates
Research Services
200 ShellPoint Tower
Palm Beach, Florida 33480

The President
Economic Development Council
1800 ShellPoint Tower
Palm Beach, Florida 33480

Dear Harry,

I have reviewed Robert Buffet's proposal for an investigation of the job creation practices of local companies, and, in short, I am very much concerned with several aspects of the "proposal." It is not really a proposal at all, as it lacks sufficient detail.

First let me mention that I have diversified my consulting services by taking Mr. Jason Henry as a partner, so that Mr. Buffet and his organization may one day represent competition for me, and you must therefore be aware of a potential conflict of interest and perhaps discount my stated opinions. Since I am delivering this letter to you in two days rather than two weeks (as you requested) you might wish to share my comments and discuss them with other people.

What you and Mr. Buffet gave me is an abbreviated research plan for our county, but since it lacks many features found in a comprehensive proposal, I immediately saw it was not the full proposal that had been funded by the state Commerce Secretary. I called Tallahassee and reached a young woman who hemmed and hawed and refused to say if she was authorized to mail me the full proposal. Finally I gave up arguing and gave her your address and told her she could mail it to you if she experienced an outbreak of belief in government-in-the-sunshine.

I then made several calls to people in Tallahassee whom I know from my days in TV. Did you know that this research ideal is being floated by our senior U. S. senator, who is eager to throw a monkey wrench into the president's tax incentives plan? The senator whispered it to the governor and the governor whispered it to her commerce secretary, and here we are.

The problem statement is rather long and convoluted, but, in short, it poses the questions, "Are new high-tech companies creating jobs for residents of our county? Or are they bringing technical and manufacturing workers from outside the state and by-passing the local work force? Or are they doing research in these companies with a low level of manufacturing job creation? Or are they investing in 'smart' capital equipment that does not create jobs?" If you cut through the verbiage, I think you can see the project is right dead on the mark with its questions.

The research objectives section is fairly straightforward. Buffet's people are going to identify all the companies in this county in the SIC code groups associated with "high tech," and collect information on the number of locally hired employees in various job categories, chiefly in production, and also collect data on capital investment, debt, and other financial data, which my new partner says makes good sense to collect and ought to be easy to do.

There is a section called Importance of the Study, which is full of platitudes and does not get around to mentioning the pending tax legislation. But at least the platitudes are brief.

I become nervous in the Design section. It calls for Mr. Buffet's group to go on site with a "team" and conduct in-depth interviews of the chief operating officer (COO), treasurer, and comptroller of each company, and enter the data into a spreadsheet. I have double-checked this with my partner and also with a banker friend, and both of them assure me that a simple questionnaire might be mailed to the COO. There is no need whatever to send in a team to conduct open-ended interviews. While there might be a noncompliance problem associated with filling out a form, this might appropriately be attended to by pointing out the auspices—the state Commerce Secretary and your Economic Development Council—with an interview request as a last resort.

The proposal contains no budget and no specific list of researchers who will comprise the team. The firm would have carte blanche to go in with anyone on their payroll and try to induce the subjects to stray beyond the stated research objectives to talk about anything at all. Obviously such license would be a marketing tool and might allow the researchers to collect a list of researchable problems not related to the Secretary's needs, as stated in the problem section.

I strongly advise you to tell Mr. Buffet to collect the information through a simple mail survey. Offer to send it out under your Council's letterhead, or see if you can get the Commerce office or even the Governor's office to send it out. But do not subject your local business community to unstructured, free-ranging visits, which are clearly not justified by the research objectives.

Sincerely,

Myra Wines

CLOSE-UP

The focus of this Close-up is a sample proposal. When we checked in on them last, Myra and Jason were planning a proposal for Gracie Uhura at the MindWriter Corporation.

Myra decided to exclude the "executive summary" for two reasons: the proposal is short and the essentials will be contained in their cover letter. The proposal follows the components discussed in this chapter. It is an appropriate adaptation for an external, small-scale study. The module "qualification of researcher" was not needed because the proposal was solicited by MindWriter and the firm had prejudged the researchers' competence before requesting their submission.

Repair Process Satisfaction Proposal MindWriter Corporation CompleteCare Program

Problem Statement

MindWriter Corporation has recently created a service and repair program, CompleteCare, for its portable/laptop/notebook computers. This program promises to provide a rapid response to customers' service problems. Management desires information on the program's effectiveness and its impact on customer satisfaction.

MindWriter is currently experiencing a shortage of trained technical operators in its telephone center. The package courier, contracted to pick up and deliver customers' machines to CompleteCare, has provided irregular execution. MindWriter has also experienced parts' availability problems for some machine types.

Recent phone logs at the call center show complaints about CompleteCare; it is unknown how representative these complaints are and what implications they may have for satisfaction with MindWriter products.

Research Objectives

The purpose of this research is to discover the level of satisfaction with the CompleteCare service program. Specifically, we intend to identify the *component and overall levels of satisfaction* with CompleteCare. Components of the repair process are important targets for investigation because they reveal: (1) how customer tolerance levels for repair performance affect overall satisfaction, and (2) which process components should be immediately improved to elevate overall satisfaction of MindWriter customers experiencing product failures.

We also propose to discover the importance of *types of product failure* on customer satisfaction levels.

Importance/Benefits

High levels of user satisfaction translate into positive word-of-mouth product endorsements. These endorsements influence the purchase outcomes for (1) friends and relatives and (2) business associates.

Critical incidents, such as product failures, have the potential to either *undermine* existing satisfaction levels or *preserve and even increase* the resulting levels of product satisfaction. The outcome of the episode depends on the quality of the manufacturer's response.

An extraordinary response by the manufacturer to such incidents will preserve and enhance user satisfaction levels to the point that direct and indirect benefits derived from such programs will justify their costs.

(continued)

This research has the potential for connecting to ongoing MindWriter customer satisfaction programs and measuring the *long-term effects* of CompleteCare (and product failure incidents) on customer satisfaction.

Research Design

Exploration: Qualitative We will augment our knowledge of CompleteCare by interviewing the service manager, the call center manager, and the independent package company's account executive. Based on a thorough inventory of CompleteCare's internal and external processes, we propose to develop a mail survey.

Questionnaire Design A self-administered questionnaire (postcard size) offers the most cost-effective method for securing feedback on the effectiveness of CompleteCare. The introduction on the postcard will be a variation of MindWriter's current advertising campaign.

Some questions for this instrument will be based on the investigative questions we presented to you previously and others will be from the executive interviews. We anticipate a maximum of 10 questions. A new five-point expectation scale, compatible with your existing customer satisfaction scales, is being designed.

Although we are not convinced that open-ended questions are appropriate for postcard questionnaires, we understand that you and Mr. Malraison like them. A comments/suggestions question will be included. In addition, we will work out a code block that captures the call center's reference number, model, and item(s) serviced.

Logistics The postal arrangements are as follows: box rental, permit, and "business reply" privileges

may be arranged in a few days. The approval for a reduced postage rate will take one to two weeks. The budget section itemizes these costs.

Pilot Test We propose to test the questionnaire with a small sample of customers using your tech-line operators. This will contain your costs. We will then revise the questions and forward them to our graphics designer for layout. The instrument will then be submitted to you for final approval.

Evaluation of Nonresponse Bias We propose to select a random sample of 100 from the list of customers who do not return the questionnaire. Call center records will be used for establishing the sampling frame. Nonresponders will be interviewed on the telephone and their responses compared statistically to responders.

Data Analysis

We will review the postcards that are returned and send you a weekly report listing customers who are either dissatisfied (score a "1" or "2") with any item of the questionnaire or submit a negative comment. This will improve your timeliness in resolving customer complaints. Each month, we will provide you with a report consisting of frequencies and category percentages for each question. Visual displays of the data will be in bar chart/histogram form. We propose to include at least one question dealing with overall satisfaction (of CompleteCare and/or MindWriter). This overall question would be regressed on the individual items to determine each item's importance. A performance grid will identify items needing improvement with an evaluation of priority. Other analyses can be prepared on request.

(continued.)

The open-ended questions will be summarized and reported by model code. If you wish, we can also provide content analysis of these questions.

Results: Deliverables

1. Development and production of a postcard survey. The questionnaire will be packaged with the returned merchandise by MindWriter employees.
2. Weekly exception reports (faxed) listing customers who meet the dissatisfied customer criteria.
3. Monthly reports as described in the data analysis section.
4. An ASCII diskette with each month's data shipped to Austin by the fifth working day of each month.

Budget

Card Layout and Printing   Based on your card estimate, our designer will lay out and print 2,000 cards in the first run ($500.00). The specifications are as follows: 7 point Williamsburg offset hi-bulk with one-over-one black ink. A gray-scale layer with a MindWriter logo or CompleteCare can be positioned under the printed material at a nominal charge. The two-sided cards are 4¼ by 5½.

This allows us to print four cards per page. The opposite side will have the business reply logo, postage paid symbol, and address.

Cost Summary

Interviews	$1,550.00
Travel costs	$2,500.00
Questionnaire development	$1,850.00
Equipment/supplies	$1,325.00
Graphics design	$800.00
Permit fee (annual)	$75.00
Business reply fee (annual)	$185.00
Box rental (annual)	$35.00
Printing costs	$500.00
Data entry (monthly)	$130.00
Monthly data files (each)	$50.00
Monthly reports (each)	$850.00
Total start-up costs	$8,820.00
Monthly run costs	$1,030.00*

*An additional fee of $0.21 per card will be assessed by the post office for business reply mail. At approximately a 30% return rate, we estimate the monthly cost to be less than $50.

Summary   A proposal is an offer to produce a product or render a service to the potential buyer or sponsor. The research proposal presents a problem, discusses related research efforts, outlines the data needed for solving the problem, and shows the design used to gather and analyze the data.

Proposals are valuable to both the research sponsor and the researcher. The sponsor uses the proposal to evaluate a research idea. The proposal is also a useful tool to ensure the sponsor and investigator agree upon the research question. For the beginning researcher, the proposal enables learning from other researchers. In addition, the completed proposal provides a logical guide for the investigation.

We discuss two types of proposals, internal and external. In contrast, student proposals are unique since they focus on learning. Internal and external proposals are more problem-solving oriented. Internal proposals are generated by the staff of a company. External proposals are prepared by an outside firm to obtain contract research. External proposals emphasize qualifications of the researcher, special facilities and resources, and project management aspects such as budgets and schedules. Within each type of proposal there are varying degrees of complexity; a proposal can vary in length between a 2-page memo and more than 100 pages.

Proposals can be written with a set of sections or modules. The difference in the type of proposal and the level of complexity of the project determines what modules should be included.

Proposals can be evaluated formally or informally. The formal process uses a list of criteria and an associated point scale. The informal process is more qualitative. Important aspects beyond content include presentation style, timeliness, and credibility.

Key Terms

executive summary
proposal
request for proposal (RFP)

Discussion Questions

1. What, if any, are the differences between solicited and unsolicited proposals?
2. Select a research report from a business journal. Outline a proposal for the research as if it had not yet been performed. Make estimates of time and costs.
3. You are the new manager of market intelligence in a rapidly expanding software firm. Many product managers and corporate officers have requested market surveys from you on various products. Design a form for a research proposal that can be completed easily by your research staff and the sponsoring manager. Discuss how your form improves communication of the research objectives between the manager and the researcher.
4. What modules would you suggest be included in a proposal for each of the following cases:
   a. The president of your company has asked for a study of the company's health benefits plan and for a comparison of it to other firms' plans.
   b. You are competing for a university-sponsored student research grant, awarded to seniors and graduate students.
   c. A bank is interested in understanding the population trends by location so that it can plan its new branch locations for the next five years. They contacted you for a proposal.
   d. You are interested in starting a new research service, providing monthly information about the use of recyclable items in your state. The proposal will go to several city and county planning agencies, independent waste service providers, and independent and government landfill providers.
5. Consider the new trends in desktop publishing, multimedia computer

authoring and display capabilities, and inexpensive video taping and playback possibilities. How might these be used to enhance research proposals. Give several examples of appropriate use.

6. You are the manager of a research department in a large department store chain. Develop a list of criteria for evaluating the types of research activities listed below. Include a point scale and weighting algorithm.

   a. Market research.

   b. Advertising effectiveness.

   c. Employee opinion surveys.

   d. Credit card operations.

   e. Computer service effectiveness at the individual store level.

Reference Notes

1. Charles T. Brusaw, Gerald J. Alred, and Walter E. Oliu, *Handbook of Technical Writing* 4th ed. (New York: St. Martin's Press, 1992), p. 375.

2. Paul D. Leedy, *Practical Research: Planning and Design,* 2nd ed. (New York: Macmillan, 1980), p. 79.

3. Philip V. Lewis and William H. Baker, *Business Report Writing* (Columbus, Ohio: Grid, 1978), p. 58.

4. Ibid., p. 51.

5. William J. Roetzheim, *Proposal Writing for the Data Processing Consultant* (Englewood Cliffs, N.J.: Prentice Hall, 1986), p. 106.

6. Brusaw, Alred, and Oliu, *Handbook,* p. 11.

7. Lewis and Baker, *Business Report Writing,* p. 58.

8. Robert G. Murdick and Donald R. Cooper, *Business Research: Concepts and Guides* (Columbus, Ohio: Grid, 1982), p. 112.

9. Roetzheim, *Proposal Writing,* pp. 67–68.

10. Many texts cover project management and network analysis. These include details of scheduling and charting techniques such as Gantt charts and CPM charts, which are beyond the scope of this text. See, for example, Chapter 3, "Network Analysis," in Don T. Philips, A. Ravindran, and James J. Solberg, *Operations Research: Principles and Practice* (New York: John Wiley & Sons, 1976); or Chapter 6, "Network Models," in K. Roscoe Davis and Patrick G. McKeon, *Quantitative Models for Management* (Boston: Kent Publishing, 1981).

11. Murdick and Cooper, *Business Research,* p. 114.

12. Ibid., pp. 114–16.

13. Ibid., p. 117.

Suggested Readings

1. Krathwohl, David R. *How to Prepare a Research Proposal.* 3rd ed. Syracuse, N.Y.: Syracuse University Press, 1988. A practical guide and framework for student projects.

2. Leedy, Paul D. *Practical Research: Planning and Design.* 5th ed. New York: Macmillan, 1992. Good coverage of all aspects of planning and design of research projects.

3. Locke, Lawrence F.; Waneen Wyrick Spiduso; and Stephen J. Silverman. *Proposals that Work: A Guide to Planning Dissertations and Grant Proposals.* 3rd ed. Thousand Oaks, Calif.: Sage Publications, 1993. An excellent guide for students and faculty advisors.

ETHICS IN BUSINESS RESEARCH

Like other aspects of business, research demands ethical behavior from its participants. *Ethics* are norms or standards of behavior that guide moral choices about our behavior and our relationships with others. The goal of ethics in research is to ensure that no one is harmed or suffers adverse consequences from research activities. This objective is usually achieved. However, unethical activities are pervasive and include violating nondisclosure agreements, breaking respondent confidentiality, misrepresenting results, deceiving people, invoicing irregularities, avoiding legal liability, and more.

The recognition of ethics as a problem for economic organizations was shown in a recent survey where 80 percent of organizations reported the adoption of an ethical code. Surprisingly, the evidence that this effort has improved ethical practices is questionable. The same study reports limited success for codes that attempt to restrain improper behavior.[1]

There is no single approach to ethical issues. Advocating strict adherence to a set of laws is difficult because of the unforeseen constraints put on researchers. Because of Germany's war history, the government forbids many types of medical research. Consequently, the German people are not able to benefit from the advances in biotechnology and may be unable to use genetically altered drugs in the future. Alternatively, relying on each individual's personal sense of morality is equally problematic. Consider the clash between those who believe death is deliverance from a life of suffering and those who value life to the point of preserving it indefinitely through mechanical means. Each value system claims superior knowledge of moral correctness.

Clearly, a middle ground between being completely code-governed and ethical relativism is necessary. The foundation for that middle ground is an emerging consensus on ethical standards for researchers. Codes and regulations guide researchers and clients. Review boards and peer groups help researchers examine their research proposals for ethical dilemmas. Many design-based ethical problems can be eliminated by careful planning and constant vigilance. In the end, responsible research anticipates ethical dilemmas and attempts to adjust the design, procedures, and protocols during the planning process rather than treating them as an afterthought. Ethical research requires personal integrity from the researcher and the client.

Because of this emphasis, we are discussing ethical behavior in this special section that concludes Part I, "Introduction to Business Research." Our objective is to stimulate an ongoing exchange about values and practical research constraints throughout the chapters that follow. Our coverage is organized around the theme of ethical treatment of respondents, clients, and other researchers. We also highlight appropriate laws and codes, resources for ethical awareness, and cases for application.

ETHICAL TREATMENT OF RESPONDENTS AND SUBJECTS

When ethics are discussed in research design, we often think first about protecting the rights of the respondent or subject. Whether data are gathered in an experiment, interview, observation, or survey, the respondent has many rights to be safeguarded. In general, research must be designed so a respondent does not suffer physical harm, discomfort, pain, embarrassment, or loss of privacy. To safeguard these, the researcher should follow three guidelines:[2]

1. Begin data collection by explaining to the respondent the benefits expected from the research. Neither overstate nor understate the benefits so the respondent is not inclined to exaggerate answers.

2. Explain to the respondents that their rights and well-being will be adequately protected and say how that will be done. This may be accomplished by maintaining confidentiality of the responses or by destroying the names and addresses of the respondents.

3. Be certain that interviewers obtain the informed consent of the respondent. Also, require that the method of getting the consent be appropriate and adequate. When questionnaires contain sensitive questions about family income, it is inadequate to obtain a blanket consent for the questionnaire. Instead, the researcher should explain that the questionnaire contains some sensitive questions and the respondents are free not to answer any question that makes them uncomfortable.

Benefits

Whenever direct contact is made with a respondent, the research benefits should be discussed. An interviewer should begin an introduction with his or her name, the name of the research organization, and a brief description of the purpose and benefit of the research. This puts respondents at ease, they know to whom they are speaking, and it motivates them to answer questions truthfully. In short, knowing why one is being asked questions improves cooperation through honest disclosure of purpose.

Sometimes the actual purpose and benefits of your study or experiment must be concealed from the respondent to avoid introducing bias. The need for concealing objectives leads directly to the problem of deception.

Deception

Deception occurs when the respondent is told only part of the truth or when the truth is fully compromised. Some believe this should never occur. Others suggest two reasons to legitimate deception: (1) to prevent biasing the respondents before the survey or experiment and (2) to protect the confidentiality of a third party (e.g., the client). Deception should not be used in an attempt to improve response rates.

The benefits to be gained by deception should be balanced against the risks to the respondents. When possible, an experiment or interview should be redesigned to reduce reliance on deception. In addition, the respondents' rights and well-being must be adequately protected. In instances where deception in an experiment could produce anxiety, a subject's medical condition should be checked to ensure that no adverse physical harm follows. And finally, the respondent must have given his or her informed consent before participating in the research.

Informed Consent

Securing *informed consent* from respondents is a matter of fully disclosing the procedures of the proposed survey or other research design before requesting permission to proceed with the study. There are exceptions that argue for a signed consent form. When dealing with children, it is wise to have a parent sign a consent form. When doing research with medical or psychological ramifications, it is also wise to have a consent form. If there is a chance the data could harm the respondent or if the researchers offer only limited protection of confidentiality, a signed form detailing the types of limits should be obtained. For most of business research, verbal consent is sufficient. Once the research is completed, the subjects who were deceived should be debriefed.

Debriefing Respondents

Debriefing explains the truth to the participants and describes the major goals of the study and the reasons for using deception. In cases where severe reactions occur, follow-up medical or psychological attention should be provided to continue to ensure the participants remain unharmed by the research.

Even when research does not deceive the respondents, it is a good practice to offer them follow-up information. For surveys and interviews, respondents can be offered a report of the findings. Usually, they will not request additional information. Occasionally, however, the research will be of particular interest to a respondent. A simple set of descriptive charts can be generated for such an individual. This retains the goodwill of the respondent, providing an incentive to participate in future research projects.

For experiments, all subjects should be debriefed. As mentioned previously, this corrects any deception that occurred and it allows subjects to put the experiment into context. Debriefing usually includes a description of the hypothesis being tested and the purpose of the study. Subjects who were not deceived still benefit from the debriefing session. They will be able to understand why the experiment was created. The researchers also gain important insight into what the subjects thought about during and after the experiment. This may lead to modifications in future research designs. Like survey and interview respondents, subjects in experiments and observational studies should be offered a report of the findings.

To what extent do debriefing and informed consent reduce the effects of deception? Research suggests that the majority of subjects do not resent temporary deception and may have more positive feelings about the value of the research after debriefing than those who didn't participate in the study.[3] Nevertheless, this is an ethically thorny issue and should be addressed with sensitivity and concern for research participants.

Rights to Privacy

Privacy laws in the United States are taken seriously. All individuals have a right to privacy, and researchers must respect that right. The importance of the right to privacy is illustrated with an example.

An employee of a large video rental company is also a student at the local university. For a research project, this student and his team members decide to compare the video viewing habits of a sample of customers. Using telephone interviews, the students begin their research. After inquiring about people's viewing habits and the frequency of rentals versus purchases, the students move on to the types of films people watch. They find that most respondents answer questions about their preferences for children's shows, classics, best-sellers, mysteries, and science fiction. But the cooperation ceases when the students question the viewing frequency of pornographic movies. Without the guarantee of privacy, most people would not answer truthfully these kinds of questions, if at all. The study then loses key data.

The privacy guarantee is important not only to retain validity in the research, but also to protect respondents. In the previous example, imagine the harm that could be caused by releasing information on the viewing habits of certain citizens. Clearly, the confidentiality of survey answers is an important aspect of the respondents' right to privacy.

Once the guarantee of *confidentiality* is given, protecting that confidentiality is essential. Researchers should restrict access to information that reveals names, telephone numbers, addresses, or other identifying features. Only researchers who have signed nondisclosure, confidentiality forms should be allowed access to the data. Links between the data or database and the identifying information file should be weakened. Individual interview response sheets should be inaccessible to everyone except the editors and data entry personnel. Occasionally, data collection instruments should be destroyed once the data are in a data file. Data files that make it easy to reconstruct the profiles or identification of individual respondents should be carefully controlled. For very small groups, data should not be made available because it is often easy to pinpoint a person within the group. Employee-satisfaction survey feedback in small units can be easily used to identify an individual through descriptive statistics alone. These last two protections are particularly important in personnel research.[4]

But privacy is more than confidentiality. A *right to privacy* means one has the right to refuse to be interviewed or to refuse to answer any question in an interview. Potential participants have a right to privacy in their own homes, including not admitting researchers and not answering telephones. And they have the right to engage in private behavior in private places without fear of observation. To address these rights, ethical researchers ask permission to interview respondents. They inform respondents of their right to refuse to answer any question. They only schedule field interviews during daylight (and not at meal time), or they will call in advance to set an appointment for an interview. Telephone interviews are limited in time and occur only during reasonable hours. Observation is restricted to public behavior.

ETHICS AND THE CLIENT

There are also ethical considerations to keep in mind when dealing with the research client. Whether undertaking new product, market, personnel, financial, or other research, a client has the right to receive ethically conducted research.

Confidentiality

Two primary types of confidentiality are required by some clients. Many clients wish to undertake research without revealing themselves. This is one reason for hiring outside consulting firms to complete research projects. When a company is testing a new product idea, it may not want consumers to be influenced by the company image. If a company is contemplating entering a new market, it may not wish to have competitors aware of its plans. For these and other reasons, corporations have a right to dissociate themselves from the sponsorship of the project. It is the responsibility of the research firm to respect that desire and devise a plan that safeguards the identity of the client.

The second reason for confidentiality involves the purpose of the study or its details. A client may be testing a new idea that is not yet patented and does not want the competition to know of its plans. It may be investigating employee complaints and does not want to spark union activity. Or a new marketing strategy may be tested. For whatever reason, clients have the right to demand and receive confidentiality between themselves and the researchers.

Right to Quality Research

An important ethical consideration for the researcher and the client is the client's right to quality research. From the proposal through the design to data analysis and final reporting, the researcher guides the client on the proper techniques and interpretations. Ethical researchers provide the client with the type of study he or she needs to solve the managerial question. Often clients will have heard about a sophisticated data handling technique and will want it used even when it is inappropriate for the problem at hand. The researcher should guide the client so this does not occur. The design of the project should be suitable for the problem; it should not be designed so maximum revenue is achieved at the client's expense.

The second aspect of quality research lies in the reporting techniques. We have all heard the phrase, "you can lie with statistics." It is the researcher's task to prevent that from occurring. As you learn about research design, sampling, statistics, and reporting techniques, you'll see that various conditions must be met for results to be valid. The ethical researcher always follows the rules and meets these conditions. The ethical researcher reports findings in ways that minimize the drawing of false conclusions. The ethical researcher also uses charts, graphs, and tables to show the data objectively, despite the client's preferred outcomes.

Client's Ethics

Occasionally, researchers may be asked by clients to identify respondents or their groups, change the data, interpret the data in a favorable light, omit sections of data analysis and conclusions, or change the research findings. Each of these are examples of unethical client behavior. Compliance by the researcher would be a breach of ethical standards.

Let's examine the types of coercion that may occur. A client may offer future contracts or a larger payment for the existing research contract, or the client may threaten to fire or tarnish the researcher's reputation. For some, the request may seem trivial and the reward high. But image, for a moment, what will happen to the researcher who changes research results. Although promised future research contracts, that researcher can never be trusted by the client again. If ethics are for sale, who might be the highest bidder next time? Although the promise of future contracts is enticing, it is unlikely to occur. Each type of coercive reward or punishment has an equally poor outcome. The "greater than" contracted payment is a payoff. The threats to one's professional reputation cannot be carried out effectively by a client who has tried to purchase you. So the rewards for behaving unethically are illusory. What's the best course? Often, it requires confronting the client's demand. Educate the client to the purpose of research and the researcher's role in fact-finding versus the client's role in decision making. Explain how distorting the truth or breaking faith with respondents leads to future problems. Failing moral suasion, terminate the relationship with the client.

RESEARCHERS AND ASSISTANTS

Another ethical responsibility of researchers is their assistants' safety and their own. In addition, the responsibility for ethical behavior rests with the researcher who, along with assistants, is charged with protecting the anonymity of both the client and the respondent.

Safety

It is the researcher's responsibility to design a project so the safety of all interviewers, surveyors, experimenters, or observers is protected. Several factors may be important in these situations. Some urban areas and undeveloped rural areas may be unsafe for research assistants. If, for example, the researcher must personally interview people in a high-crime district, it is reasonable to provide a second team member to protect the researcher. Alternatively, if an assistant feels unsafe after visiting a neighborhood by car, an alternate researcher should be assigned to the destination.[5] It is unethical to require staff members to enter an area where they feel physically threatened. Researchers who are insensitive to these concerns face both research and legal risks—the least of which involves having interviewers falsify instruments.

Ethical Behavior   Researchers should require ethical compliance from team members just as clients expect ethical behavior from the researcher. Assistants are expected to carry out the sampling plan, to interview or observe respondents without bias, and to accurately record all necessary data. Unethical behavior, such as filling in an interview sheet without having asked the respondent the questions, cannot be tolerated. The behavior of the assistants is under the direct control of the responsible researcher or field supervisor. If an assistant behaves improperly in an interview or shares a respondent's interview sheet with an unauthorized person, it is the researcher's responsibility. Consequently, all assistants should be well trained and supervised.

Protection of   As discussed previously, researchers and assistants protect the confidentiality of
Anonymity   the client's information and the anonymity of the respondents. Each person handling data should have signed a confidentiality statement.

PROFESSIONAL STANDARDS

Various standards of ethics exist for the professional researcher. Most corporations and research firms have adopted a code of ethics. Professional societies have codes of ethics that serve as the basis for individual and corporate codes. Federal, state, and local governments also have laws, policies, and procedures in place to regulate research on human beings.

The U.S. government began a process that covers all research having federal support. Initially implemented in 1966, the Institutional Review Boards (IRBs) engage in a risk assessment–benefit analysis review of proposed research. The federal regulations were developed into policy by the Department of Health and Human Services (HHS). Most other federal and state agencies follow the HHS-developed guidelines. Since 1981, the review requirement has been relaxed so routine research no longer needs to go through the complete process.[6] Each institution receiving funding from HHS or doing research for HHS is required to have its own IRB to review research proposals. Many institutions require all research, funded and unfunded, to undergo review by the local IRB. The IRBs concentrate on two areas. First is the guarantee of obtaining complete, informed consent from participants. This can be traced to the first of 10 points in the Nuremberg Code.[7] Complete informed consent has four characteristics:

1. The respondent must be competent to give consent.
2. Consent must be voluntary, free from coercion, force, requirements, and so forth.
3. Respondents must be adequately informed to make a decision.
4. Respondents should know the possible risks or outcomes associated with the research.

The second item of interest to the IRB is the risk assessment–benefit analysis review. In the review, risks are considered when they add to the normal risk of daily life. Significantly, the only benefit considered is the immediate importance of the knowledge to be gained. Possible long-term benefits from applying the knowledge that may be gained in the research are not considered.[8]

Other federal legislation that governs, or influences, the ways in which research is carried out are the Right to Privacy laws. Public Law 95-38 is the Privacy Act of 1974. This was the first law guaranteeing Americans the right to privacy. Public Law 96-440, the Privacy Protection Act of 1980, carries the right to privacy further. These two laws are the basis for protecting the privacy and confidentiality of the respondents and the data.

In an attempt to provide guidelines for their members, several professional associations have adopted a code of ethics that include ethics for research. Effective codes: (1) are regulative in nature, (2) protect the public interest and the interests of the profession served by the code, (3) are behavior specific, and (4) are enforceable.

Among those that are used for business-related research are: the American Association for Public Opinion Research, the American Marketing Association, the American Political Science Association, the American Psychological Association, and the American Sociological Association. These associations update their codes frequently.

While we commend professional societies and business organizations for developing standards, standards without enforcement are ineffectual. A study that assessed the effects of personal and professional values on ethical consulting behavior concluded:

> The findings of this study cast some doubt on the effectiveness of professional codes of ethics and corporate policies that attempt to deal with ethical dilemmas faced by business consultants. A mere codification of ethical values of the profession or organization may not counteract ethical ambivalence created and maintained through reward systems. The results suggest that unless ethical codes and policies are consistently reinforced with a significant reward and punishment structure and truly integrated into the business culture, these mechanisms would be of limited value in actually regulating unethical conduct.[9]

RESOURCES FOR ETHICAL AWARENESS

There is optimism for improving ethical awareness. According to the Center for Business Ethics at Bentley College, a third of the Fortune 500 have ethics officers, a substantial rise since the late 80s. Almost 90 percent of business schools have ethics programs, up from a handful 15 years ago.[10] Diverse resources are available to business students, researchers, and managers for improving awareness and making sound ethical choices. Some of them are listed in the accompanying exhibit.[11]

Books

Chappell, Tom	*The Soul of a Business*	New York: Bantam, 1993.
Hosmer, LaRue	*The Ethics of Management*	Burr Ridge, IL: Irwin Professional, 1991.
Nash, Laura	*Good Intentions Aside*	Cambridge, MA: HBS Press, 1993.
O'Toole, James	*The Executive's Compass*	Oxford, England: Oxford University Press, 1993.
Scott, Mary and Howard Rothman	*Companies with a Conscience*	New York: Birch Lane Press, 1992.
Shaw, W.H.	*Business Ethics*	Los Angeles, CA: Wadsworth Publishing, 1991.
Velasquez, Manuel	*Business Ethics: Concepts and Cases*	New York: Prentice Hall, 1992.

Journals and Magazines

Business Ethics, a magazine with six issues yearly, Minneapolis, MN

Ethikos, a journal on business ethics and compliance issues, Mamaroneck, NY

Journal of Business Ethics, an academic journal from Kluwer Academic Publishers, The Netherlands

Research, Training, and Conferences

Business ethics conferences hosted by The Conference Board, New York, NY (212-759-0900)

Ethics Resource Center, Washington, D.C. (202-737-2258)

Josephson Institute of Ethics, Los Angeles, CA (310-306-1868)

The Center for Business Ethics, Bentley College, Waltham, MA (617-891-2000)

DISCUSSION CASES

The cases below cover a broad range of ethical decisions. You may have experienced similar circumstances or expect to encounter research situations like these. Consider the material in this section and your own standards of conduct as you offer advice to the individuals in these cases. What are the most prudent decisions they can make about their responsibilities to themselves and others? What are the implications of those decisions even if there is no violation of law or regulation?

CASE 1   ## A COMPETITIVE COUP IN THE IN-FLIGHT MAGAZINE

When the manager for market intelligence of a major automotive manufacturer boarded the plane in Chicago, her mind was on shrinking market share and late product announcements. As she settled back to enjoy the remains of a hectic day, she reached for the in-flight magazine. It was jammed into the seat pocket in front of her.

Crammed into this already tiny space was a report with a competitor's logo, marked "Confidential-Restricted Circulation." It contained a description of new product announcements for the next two years. Not only was it intended for a small circle of senior executives but it also answered the questions she had recently proposed to an external research firm.

The proposal for the solicited research could be canceled. Her research budget, already savaged, could be saved. She was home free, legally and career-wise.

She foresaw only one problem. In the last few months, the company's newly hired ethicist had revised the Business Conduct Guidelines. They now required company employees in possession of a competitor's information to return it or face dismissal. But it was still a draft and not formally approved. She had the rest of the flight to decide whether to return the document to the airline or slip it into her briefcase.

CASE 2   ## FREE WATERS IN MIRO BEACH: BOATERS INC. VERSUS CITY GOVERNMENT

In 1989, the city commissioners of Miro Beach proposed limits on boaters who anchor offshore in waterfront areas of the St. Lucinda River adjoining the city. Residents had complained of pollution from the live-aboarders and of a boat parking lot from absentee boaters.

The city based its proposed ordinance on research done by the staff. The staff did not hold graduate degrees in either public or business administration and it was not known if staff members were competent to conduct research. The staff requested a proposal from a team of local university professors who had conducted similar work in the past. The research cost was $10,000. After receiving the proposal, the staff chose to do the work itself and not expend resources for the project. Through an unidentified source, the professors later learned their proposal contained enough information to guide the city's staff and suggested data collection areas that might provide information that could justify the boaters' claims.

(continued)

Based on the staff's one-time survey of waterfront litter, "pump-out" samples, and a weekly frequency count of boats, an ordinance was drafted and a public workshop was held. Shortly after, a group of concerned boat owners formed Boaters, Inc., an association to promote boating, raise funds, and lobby the commission. The group's claim was that the boaters spent thousands of dollars on community goods and services, did not create the litter, and the commission's fact-finding was flawed.

With the latter claim in mind, the boaters flooded the city with public records requests. The clerks reported that some weeks the requests were one per day. Under continued pressure, the city attorney hired a private investigator (PI) to infiltrate Boaters, Inc., to collect information. He rationalized this on the grounds that the boaters had challenged the city's grant applications in order to "blackmail the city into dropping plans to regulate the boaters."

The PI posed as a college student and worked for a time in the home of the boater organization's sponsor while helping with mailings. Despite the PI's inability to corroborate the city attorney's theory, he recommended conducting a background investigation on the organization's principal, an employee of a tabloid newspaper. (Background investigations are generally performed by the FBI on request of city or county police organizations.)

The PI was not a boating enthusiast and soon drew suspicion. Simultaneously, the organization turned up the heat on the city by requesting what amounted to 5,000 pages of information—"studies and all related documents containing the word 'boat.'" Failing to get a response from Miro Beach, the boaters filed suit under the Florida Public Records Act. By this time, the city had spent $20,000.

The case stalled, went to appeal, and was settled in favor of the boaters. A year later, the organization's principal filed an invasion of privacy and slander suit against the city attorney, the PI, and the PI's firm. After six months, the suit was amended to include the city itself and sought $1 million in punitive damages.

Source: adapted from stories in the *Palm Beach Post* during September 1992.

CASE 3   THE HIGH COST OF ORGANIZATIONAL CHANGE

It was his first summer after graduate school, and there were no summer teaching assignments for new hires. But the university was kind enough to steer him to an aviation firm that needed help creating an organizational assessment survey. The assignment was to last five weeks, but it paid about the same as teaching all summer. The work was just about as perfect as it gets for an organizational behavior specialist.

(continued)

The vice president who met him the first day was cordial and smooth. The researcher would report to a senior manager who was coordinating the project with the personnel and legal departments. It was soon apparent that in the 25-year history of the organization, there had never been an employee survey. This was ultimately understandable given management's lack of concern for employee complaints. Working conditions had deteriorated without management intervention, and government inspectors counted the number of heads down at desks as an index of performance. To make matters worse, the engineers were so disgruntled that word of unionization had spread like wildfire. A serious organizing effort was planned before the survey could be approved by the VP.

Personnel at headquarters dispatched nervous staffers to monitor this situation and generally involve themselves with every aspect of the questionnaire. Shadowed, the young researcher began to feel his apprehension turn to paranoia. He consoled himself, however, with the goodwill of 500 enthusiastic, cooperative employees who had tied their hopes for a better working environment to this project.

The data collection was textbook smooth. No one had asked to preview the findings or had showed any particular interest. In the fifth week, he boarded the corporate jet with the VP and senior manager to make a presentation at headquarters. Respondents at that location were invited to attend. Management was intent on heading off unionization by showing their confidence in the isolated nature of "a few engineers' complaints" and legitimizing the results. They had also promised to engage the participants in action planning over the next few days.

An hour into the flight, the VP turned from his reading to the young researcher and said, "We have seen your results, you know. And we would like you to change two key findings. They are not all that critical to this round of fixing the 'bone orchard,' and you'll have another crack at it as a *real consultant* in the fall."

"But that would mean breaking faith with your employees, people who trusted me to present the results objectively. It's what I thought you wanted . . ."

"Yes, well, look at it this way," replied the VP. "All of your findings we can live with, except these two. They're an embarrassment to senior management. Let me put it plainly. We have government contracts into the foreseeable future. You could retire early with consulting income from this place. We'll be met on the runway by someone with new slides. Whadda you say?"

Reference Notes

1. C. S. Benson, "Codes of Ethics," *Journal of Business Ethics,* 1989, pp. 305–9.
2. Elizabethann O'Sullivan and Gary R. Rassel, *Research Methods for Public Administrators* (New York: Longman Inc., 1989), pp. 209–10.
3. Robert A. Baron and Donn Byrne, *Social Psychology: Understanding Human Interaction* (Boston: Allyn and Bacon, 1991), p. 36.
4. Floyd J. Fowler, Jr., *Survey Research Methods,* rev. ed. (Beverly Hills, Calif.: Sage Publications, 1988), p. 138.
5. Ibid., p. 139.
6. Paul Davidson Reynolds, *Ethics and Social Science Research* (Englewood Cliffs, N.J.: Prentice Hall, 1982), pp. 103–8.
7. The Nuremberg Code is a set of 10 moral, ethical, and legal principles for medical experimentation on humans. It comes from the judgment of the Nuremberg Military Tribunal against doctors and scientists who committed World War II Nazi atrocities. For a full listing of the Nuremberg Code, see Jay Katz, *Experimentation with Human Beings* (New York: Russell Sage Foundation, 1972), pp. 305–6. See also Allan J. Kimmel, *Ethics and Values in Applied Social Research* (Newbury Park, Calif.: Sage Publications, 1988), pp. 54–56.
8. Reynolds, *Ethics,* pp. 103–8.
9. Jeff Allen and Duane Davis, "Assessing Some Determinant Effects of Ethical Consulting Behavior: The Case of Personal and Professional Values," *Journal of Business Ethics,* 1993, p. 449.
10. The Center for Business Ethics, Bentley College (Waltham, Mass.); syndicated news release: Daniel Fisher, Bloomberg Financial News, November 2, 1993.
11. Adapted from "The *Inc.* Network," *Inc.,* December 1993, pp. 184–85.

II THE DESIGN
OF RESEARCH

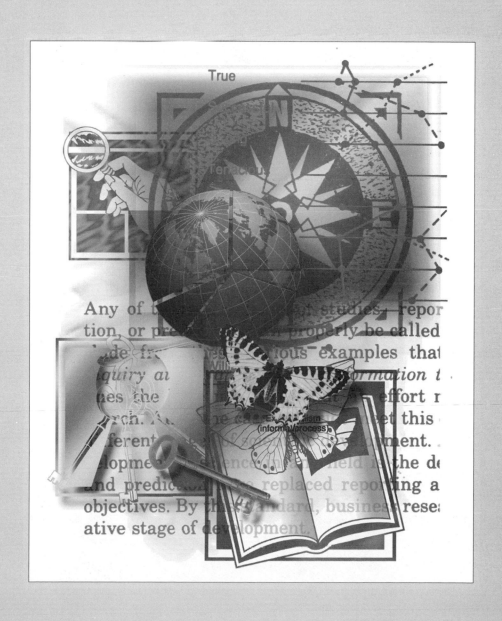

CHAPTER

5 DESIGN STRATEGIES

 FINDING
YOUR WAY

BRINGING RESEARCH TO LIFE

"Arghh!"

Jason Henry leaped up and tossed a paper cup full of coffee at his TV. It hit the set and bounced off, leaving coffee dripping down the screen.

"What's wrong? Is one of you hurt? I'M A DOCTOR!" hollered Dorrie from the bedroom. "And what time is it anyway?"

"Go back to sleep, Dorrie, dear," replied Jason's consulting partner, Myra Wines. "It's 2:30 A.M., and your husband just chose to throw his coffee at the TV, rather than drink it, because he doesn't care for the anchor on cable news."

"She's totally unscientific, you know," grumped Jason.

"She's an inexperienced kid getting her first break on the network," stated Myra, "at an hour when no sane person is watching TV anyway, let alone subjecting it to scientific criticism. So chill out, lad."

To Dorrie she shouted, "We are almost finished here, and soon you will have your husband back."

"It is terrifically unscientific," he said, "to make unsubstantiated conclusions as she did."

"I thought she did a fine job interviewing that psychiatrist—terribly amusing" said Myra. "He was a beautiful choice, with his accent and a beard that reminded me of Freud himself."

"That's not the issue, Myra, and you know it. The fact is, she should not have claimed that when the recent hurricane brushed Galveston, it caused a rash of complaints against auto dealerships."

"I thought she did a moderately good job in the interviews. That was an adorable young couple she found picketing the Mercedes dealership—the girl in a mink jacket and her husband in Gucci loafers, and both of them complaining they were powerless against big business—and you already know how effective I thought the shrink was in presenting his theory of hurricane-induced anger causing people to lash out at business."

"Not the point, again. As entertainment it was admirable. But it was rotten science. She had no before-after comparison. I want to know how many people had complaints against dealerships before the hurricane hit. Pretty clearly, she not only had no file footage of before the hurricane, but she also had no statistics. For all I know the complaint behavior has not changed."

"Do you really believe, Jason, that anyone would have the foresight to collect such information?"

"Why not? The newspapers and TV stations on the Gulf are continually hyping the threat of hurricanes. They must make a fortune selling commercial time at inflated rates during hurricane season. So, yes, they knew a hurricane was due sometime in the near future, or at least possible, and if they were responsible they would have done baseline measurements . . ."

"Not really feasible . . ."

". . . or at least refrain from such pseudoscientific bunkum."

"Is that it? Is that your complaint?"

"That's part of it. The other part is that the hurricane brushed Galveston then skittered out into the Gulf. Forty miles away, Houston was barely touched. Did she bother to check if complaint behavior in Houston was also elevated? Because if it was, that would debunk her theory that the hurricane caused the complaint behavior. You can't blame something that occurred in one location and not in the other for causing behavior seen in both locations. Can you?"

"I guess not."

"So, what did you learn, Myra?" he asked with a touch of condescension."

She laughed heartily. "I learned not to pick a fight with you after hours of steady proposal writing. I learned that after 13 cups of coffee you become humorless, pedantic, and compulsively left-brained. I learned it is time for you to join your infinitely patient wife, while I catch a few winks of sleep on this sofa . . . Sweet dreams, my dear boy! See you for breakfast."

WHAT IS RESEARCH DESIGN?

There are many definitions of "research design," but no one definition imparts the full range of important aspects. Several examples from leading authors can be cited:

> The research design constitutes the blueprint for the collection, measurement, and analysis of data. It aids the scientist in the allocation of his limited resources by posing crucial choices: Is the blueprint to include experiments, interviews, observation, the analysis of records, simulation, or some combination of these? Are the methods of data collection and the research situation to be highly structured? Is an intensive study of a small sample more effective than a less intensive study of a large sample? Should the analysis be primarily quantitative or qualitative?[1]

> Research design is the plan and structure of investigation so conceived as to obtain answers to research questions. The plan is the overall scheme or program of the research. It includes an outline of what the investigator will do from writing hypotheses and their operational implications to the final analysis of data. A structure is the framework, organization, or configuration of . . . the relations among variables of a study. A research design expresses both the structure of the research problem and the plan of investigation used to obtain empirical evidence on relations of the problem.[2]

These definitions differ in detail, but together they give the essentials of **research design.** First, the design is a plan for selecting the sources and types of information used to answer the research question. Second, it is a framework for specifying the relationships among the study's variables. Third, it is a blueprint that outlines each procedure from the hypotheses to the analysis of data. The design provides answers for such questions as: What techniques will be used to gather data? What kind of sampling will be used? How will time and cost constraints be dealt with?

Classification of Designs

Early in any research study, one faces the task of selecting the specific design to use. A number of different design approaches exist, but unfortunately, no simple classification system defines all the variations that must be considered. We can classify research design using at least eight different perspectives.[3]

1. The degree to which the research problem has been crystallized (the study may be either exploratory or formal).
2. The method of data collection (studies may be observational or survey).
3. The power of the researcher to produce effects in the variables under study (the two major types of research are the experimental and the ex post facto).
4. The purpose of the study (research studies may be descriptive or causal).
5. The time dimension (research may be cross-sectional or longitudinal).
6. The topical scope—breadth and depth—of the study (a case or statistical study).
7. The research environment (most business research is conducted in a field setting, although laboratory research is not unusual; simulation is another category).

8. The subjects' perceptions of the research (do they perceive deviations from their everyday routines).

A brief discussion of these perspectives illustrates their nature and contribution to research.

Degree of Problem Crystallization   A study may be viewed as exploratory or formal. The essential distinction between these two is the degree of structure and the immediate objective of the study. **Exploratory studies** tend toward loose structures with the objective of discovering future research tasks. The immediate purpose of exploration is usually to develop hypotheses or questions for further research. The **formal study** begins where the exploration leaves off—it begins with a hypothesis or question and involves precise procedures and data source specifications. The goal of a formal research design is to test the hypotheses or answer the research questions posed.

The exploratory-formalized dichotomy is less precise than some other classifications. All studies have elements of exploration in them and few studies are completely uncharted. Recall that the general project sequence, discussed in Chapter 3, suggests that more formalized studies contain at least an element of exploration before the final choice of design. More detailed consideration of exploratory research is found later in this chapter.

Method of Data Collection   This classification distinguishes between monitoring and interrogation (survey) processes. The former includes **observational studies,** in which the researcher inspects the activities of a subject or the nature of some material without attempting to elicit responses from anyone. A traffic count at an intersection, a search of the library collection, an observation of the actions of a group of decision makers—all are examples of monitoring. In each case the researcher notes and records the information available from observations.

In the **survey** mode, the researcher questions the subjects and collects their responses by personal or impersonal means. The data may result from (1) interview or telephone conversations, (2) self-administered or self-report instruments sent through the mail, left in convenient locations, or transmitted electronically or through another means, or (3) instruments presented before and/or after a treatment or stimulus condition in an experiment.

Researcher Control of Variables   In terms of the researcher's ability to manipulate variables, we differentiate between experimental and ex post facto designs. In an **experiment,** the researcher attempts to control and/or manipulate the variables in the study. It is enough that we can cause variables to be changed or held constant in keeping with our research objectives. Experimental design is appropriate when one wishes to discover whether certain variables produce effects in other variables. Experimentation provides the most powerful support possible for a hypothesis of causation.

With an **ex post facto design,** investigators have no control over the variables in the sense of being able to manipulate them. They can only report what has happened or what is happening. It is important that the researchers using this design not influence the variables; to do so introduces bias. The researcher is limited to holding factors constant by judicious selection of subjects according to strict sampling procedures and by statistical manipulation of findings.

The Purpose of the Study   The essential difference between descriptive and causal studies lies in their objectives. If the research is concerned with finding out who, what, where, when, or how much, then the study is **descriptive.** If it is concerned with learning why, that is, how one variable produces changes in another, it is causal. Research on crime is descriptive when it measures the types of crime committed, how often, when, where, and by whom. In a **causal study,** we try to explain relationships among variables—for instance, why the crime rate is higher in city A than in city B.

The Time Dimension   **Cross-sectional** studies are carried out once and represent a "snapshot" of one point in time. **Longitudinal** studies are repeated over an extended period. The advantage of a longitudinal study is that it can track changes over time.

In longitudinal studies of the *panel* variety, the researcher may study the same people over time. In marketing, panels are set up to report consumption data on a variety of products. These data, collected from national samples, provide a major data bank on relative market share, consumer response to new products, and new promotional methods. Other longitudinal studies, such as *cohort groups,* use different subjects for each sequenced measurement. The service industry might have looked at the needs of aging "baby boomers" by sampling 40-to-45-year-olds in 1990 and 50 to 55 year-olds in 2000. Although each sample would be different, the population of 1945 to 1950 cohort survivors would remain the same.

Some types of information once collected cannot be collected a second time from the same person without the risks of bias. The study of public awareness of an advertising campaign over a six-month period would require different samples for each measurement.

While longitudinal research is important, the constraints of budget and time impose the need for cross-sectional analysis. Some benefits of a longitudinal study can be assured by adroit questioning about past attitudes, history, and future expectations. Responses to these kinds of questions should be interpreted with care, however.

The Topical Scope   The **statistical study** differs from the case study in several ways. Statistical studies are designed for breadth rather than depth. They attempt to capture a population's characteristics by making inferences from a sample's characteristics. Hypotheses are tested quantitatively. Generalizations about findings are presented based on the representativeness of the sample and the validity of the design.

Case studies place more emphasis on a full contextual analysis of fewer events or conditions and their interrelations. Although hypotheses are often used, the reliance on qualitative data makes support or rejection more difficult. An emphasis on detail provides valuable insight for problem solving, evaluation, and strategy. This detail is secured from multiple sources of information. It allows evidence to be verified and avoids missing data.

Although case studies have been maligned as "scientifically worthless" because they do not meet minimal design requirements for comparison,[4] they nonetheless have a significant scientific role. It has been observed that "important scientific propositions have the form of universals, and a universal can be falsified by a single counter-instance."[5] Thus, a single, well-designed case study can provide a major challenge to a theory and provide a source of new hypotheses and constructs simultaneously.

The Research Environment   Designs also differ as to whether they occur under actual environmental conditions or under other conditions. These are called **field** and **laboratory conditions,** respectively.

To simulate is to replicate the essence of a system or process. **Simulations** are being used more in research, especially in operations research. The major characteristics of various conditions and relationships in actual situations are often represented in mathematical models. Role playing and other behavioral activities may also be viewed as simulations.

Subjects' Perceptions   The usefulness of a design may be reduced when people in the study perceive that research is being conducted. **Subjects' perceptions** influence the outcomes of the research in subtle ways or more dramatically as we learned from the pivotal Western Electric Studies of the late 1920s. Although there is no widespread evidence of attempts to please researchers through successful hypothesis guessing nor evidence of the prevalence of sabotage, when subjects believe that something out of the ordinary is happening, they may behave less naturally. There are three levels of perception:

1. Subjects perceive no deviations from everyday routines.
2. Subjects perceive deviations, but as unrelated to the researcher.
3. Subjects perceive deviations as researcher induced.[6]

In all research environments and control situations, researchers need to be vigilant to effects that may alter their conclusions. These serve as a reminder to classify one's study by type, examine validation strength and weaknesses, and be prepared to qualify results accordingly.

Exploratory, descriptive, and causal research designs are discussed in the sections to follow. Other aspects of design are covered in later chapters after sufficient groundwork has been laid for those topics.

EXPLORATORY STUDIES

Exploration is particularly useful when researchers lack a clear idea of the problems they will meet during the study. Through **exploration** the researchers develop the concepts more clearly, establish priorities, and improve the final research design. Exploration may also save time and money if it is decided the problem is not as important as first thought.

Exploration serves other purposes. The area of investigation may be so new or so vague that a researcher needs to do an exploration just to learn something about the problem. Important variables may not be known or thoroughly defined. Hypotheses for the research may be needed. Also, the researcher may explore to be sure it is practical to do a study in the area. A federal government agency proposed that research be done on how executives in a given industry made decisions about raw material purchases. Questions were planned asking how (and at what price spreads) one raw material was substituted for another in certain manufactured products. An exploration to discover if industry executives would divulge adequate information about their decision making on this topic was essential for the study's success.

Despite its obvious value, researchers and managers alike give exploration less attention than it deserves. There are strong pressures for quick answers. And, exploration is sometimes linked to old biases about qualitative research: subjectiveness, nonrepresentativeness, and nonsystematic design. A wiser view is that exploration saves time and money and should not be slighted.

Means of Exploration

The objectives of exploration may be accomplished with several data collection techniques. Both qualitative and quantitative techniques are applicable although exploration relies more heavily on **qualitative techniques.** One author creates a verbal picture to differentiate the two:

> Quality is the essential character or nature of something; quantity is the amount. Quality is the what; quantity the how much. Qualitative refers to the meaning, the definition or analogy or model or metaphor characterizing something, while quantitative assumes the meaning and refers to a measure of it . . . . The difference lies in Steinbeck's [1941] description of the Mexican Sierra, a fish from the Sea of Cortez. One can count the spines on the dorsal fin of a pickled Sierra, 17 plus 15 plus 9. "But," says Steinbeck, "if the Sierra strikes hard on the line so that our hands are burned, if the fish sounds and nearly escapes and finally comes in over the rail, his colors pulsing and his tail beating the air, a whole new relational externality has come into being." Qualitative research would define the being of fishing, the ambiance of a city, the mood of a citizen, or the unifying tradition of a group.[7]

When we consider the scope of qualitative research, several approaches are adaptable for exploratory investigations of management questions:

1. Indepth-interviewing (usually conversational rather than structured).
2. Participant observation (to perceive firsthand what that participants in the setting experience).
3. Films, photographs, and videotape (to capture the life of the group under study).
4. Projective techniques and psychological testing (such as a Thematic Apperception Test, projective measures, games, or role-play).

5. Case studies (for an indepth contextual analysis of a few events or conditions).

6. Street ethnography (to discover how a cultural subgroup describes and structures its world at the street level).

7. Elite interviewing (for information from influential or well-informed people in an organization or community).

8. Document analysis (to evaluate historical or contemporary confidential or public records, reports, government documents, and opinions).

9. Proxemics and kinesics (to study of the use of space and body motion communication, respectively).[8]

By combining these approaches, four exploratory techniques emerge with wide applicability for the business researcher: (1) secondary data analysis, (2) experience surveys, (3) focus groups, and (4) two-stage designs.

Secondary Data Analysis   The first step in an exploratory study is a search of the secondary literature. Studies made by others for their own purposes represent **secondary data.** It is inefficient to discover anew through **primary data** collection or original research what has already been done. There are tens of thousands of periodicals and hundreds of thousands of books on all aspects of business. Data from secondary sources help us decide what needs to be done, and can be a rich source of hypotheses. Special catalogs, subject guides, and electronic indices are available in most libraries that will help in this search. In many cases you can conduct a secondary search from your home or office using a computer, an on-line service, or an Internet gateway. We provide a detailed description of secondary data resources in Chapter 9 and Appendix A.

A search of secondary sources provides an excellent background and will supply many good leads if one is creative. If we confine the investigation to obvious subjects in bibliographic sources, we will often miss much of the best information. Suppose we are interested in estimating the outlook for the copper industry over the next 10 years. We could search through the literature under the headings of copper production and consumption. However, a search restricted to these two topics would miss more than it finds. When a creative search of the copper industry was undertaken, useful information turned up under the following reference headings: mines and minerals; nonferrous metals; forecasting; planning; econometrics; consuming industries such as automotive and communications; countries where copper is produced, such as Chile; and companies prominent in the industry, such as Anaconda and Kennecott.

Experience Survey   While published data are a valuable resource, seldom is more than a fraction of the existing knowledge in a field put into writing. Thus, we will profit by seeking information from persons experienced in the area of study.

When we interview persons in an **experience survey,** we should seek their ideas about important issues or aspects of the subject and discover what is important across the subject's range. The investigative format we use should be flexible enough so that we can explore various avenues that emerge during the interview. What is being done? What has been tried in the past without success? How have things changed? What are the change-producing elements of the situation? Who is involved in decisions, and what roles do they play? What problem areas and barriers can be seen? What are the costs of the processes under study? Who can we count on to assist and/or participate in the research? What are the priority areas?

The product of such questioning may be a new hypothesis, the discarding of an old one, or information about the practicality of doing the study. Probing may show whether certain facilities are available, what factors need to be controlled and how, and who will cooperate in the study.

Discovery is more easily carried out if the researcher can analyze cases that provide special insight. Typical of exploration, we are less interested in getting a representative cross-section than getting information from sources that might be insightful. Assume we are called to study an automobile assembly plant. It has a history of declining productivity, increasing costs, and growing numbers of quality defects. People who might provide insightful information include:

1. Newcomers to the scene—new employees or personnel who may have recently been transferred to this plant from similar plants.
2. Marginal or peripheral individuals—persons whose jobs place them on the margin between contending groups. First-line supervisors and lead workers are often neither management nor workers but something in between.
3. Individuals in transition—recently promoted employees who have been transferred to new departments.
4. Deviants and isolates—those in a given group who hold a different position from the majority—workers who are happy with the present situation, highly productive departments and workers, loners of one sort or another.
5. "Pure" cases or cases that show extreme examples of the conditions under study—the most unproductive departments, the most antagonistic workers, and so forth.
6. Those who fit well and those who do not—the workers who are well established in their organizations versus those who are not, those executives who fully reflect management views and those who do not.
7. Those who represent different positions in the system—unskilled workers, assemblers, superintendents, and so forth.[9]

Focus Groups   With origins in sociology, focus groups became widely used in market research during the 1980s and are used for more diverse research applications in the 90s.[10] A **focus group** is a panel of 8 to 12 respondents led by a trained moderator. The moderator uses group dynamics principles to focus or guide the group in an exchange of ideas, feelings, and experiences on a clearly understood topic. The topical objective is often a new product or product concept. The output of the session is a list of ideas and behavioral observations with recommendations of the moderator. These are later used for quantitative testing. As a group interview tool, focus groups have applied research potential for other functional areas of business, particularly where the generation and evaluation of ideas or assessment of needs are indispensable. In exploratory research, the qualitative data that focus groups produce may be used for enriching all levels of research questions and hypotheses and comparing the effectiveness of design options.

Two-Stage Design   A useful way to design a research study is as a **two-stage design.** With this approach, exploration becomes a separate first stage with limited objectives: (1) clearly defining the research problem and (2) developing the research design. Thus, exploration can be a preliminary study of limited scope and budget.

In arguing for a two-stage approach, we recognize that much about the problem is not known but should be before effort and resources are committed. In these circumstances, one is operating in unknown areas, where it is difficult to predict the problems and costs of the study. Proposals that acknowledge the practicality of this approach are particularly useful when the research budget is inflexible. A limited exploration for a specific, modest cost carries little risk for both parties and often uncovers information that reduces the total research cost. Sometimes the evidence uncovered in the exploration suggests that a major study is unnecessary.

The end of an exploratory study comes when the researchers are convinced they have found the major dimensions of the research task. They may have defined a set of subsidiary investigative questions that can be used as guides to a detailed research design. Or they may have developed several hypotheses about possible causes of a problem situation. They may also have learned that certain other hypotheses are such remote possibilities they can be safely ignored in any subsequent study. Finally, researchers end exploration because they believe additional research is not needed or is not feasible.

In contrast to exploratory studies, formal studies are typically structured with clearly stated hypotheses or investigative questions. Formal studies serve a variety of research objectives: (1) descriptions of phenomena or characteristics associated with a subject population, (2) estimates of the proportions of a population that have these characteristics, (3) discovery of associations among different variables, and finally, (4) discovery and measurement of cause-and-effect relationships among variables. The first three objectives are normally associated with descriptive studies, while the fourth calls for studies of causal relationships.

DESCRIPTIVE STUDIES

The objective of a descriptive study is to learn the who, what, when, where, and how of a topic. The study may be simple or complex; it may be done in many settings. Whatever the form, a descriptive study can be just as demanding of research skills as the causal study, and we should insist upon the same high standards for design and execution.

The simplest **descriptive study** concerns a univariate question or hypothesis in which we ask about, or state something about, the size, form, distribution, or existence of a variable. In an account analysis at a savings and loan association, we might be interested in developing a profile of savers. We may want first to locate them in relation to the association office. The question might be, "What percent of the savers live within a two-mile radius of the office?" Using the hypothesis format, we might predict, "60 percent or more of the savers live within a two-mile radius of the office."

We may also be interested in securing information about other variables:

1. The relative size of accounts.
2. The number of accounts for minors.
3. The number of accounts opened within the last six months.
4. The amount of activity (number of deposits and withdrawals per year) in accounts.

Data on each of these variables, by themselves, may have value for management decisions. Bivariate relationships between these or other variables may be of even greater interest. Cross-tabulations between the distance from the branch and account activity may suggest that differential rates of activity are related to account location. A cross-tabulation of account size and gender of account owner may also show interrelation. Such correlative relationships may not necessarily imply a causal relationship.

Descriptive studies are often much more complex than this example. One study of savers began as described and then went into much greater depth. Part of the study included an observation of account records that revealed a concentration of nearby savers. Their accounts were typically larger and more active than those whose owners lived at a distance. A sample survey of savers provided information on stages in the family life cycle, attitudes toward savings, family income levels, and other matters. Correlation of this information with known savings data showed that larger accounts were owned by women. Further investigation suggested that women with larger accounts were often widowed or working single women who were older than the average account holder. Information about their attitudes and savings practices led to revised business strategies at the savings and loan association.

Some evidence collected suggested causal relationships. The correlation between nearness to the office and the probability of having an account at the office suggested the question, "Why would people who live far from the office have an account there?" In this type of question a hypothesis makes its greatest contribution by pointing out directions that the research might follow. It might be hypothesized that:

1. Distant savers (operationally defined as those with addresses more than two miles from the office) have accounts at the office because they once lived near the office; they were "near" when the account decision was made.

2. Distant savers actually live near the office, but the address on the account is outside the two-mile radius; they are "near," but the records do not show this.

3. Distant savers work near the office; they are "near" by virtue of their work location.

4. Distant savers are not normally near to the office but responded to a promotion that encouraged savers to bank via computer; this is another form of "nearness" in which this concept is transformed into one of "convenience."

When these hypotheses were tested, it was learned that a substantial portion of the distant savers could be accounted for by hypotheses 1 and 3. Conclusion: Location was closely related to saving at a given association. The determination of cause is not so simple, however.

CAUSAL STUDIES

The correlation between location and probability of account holding at the savings and loan association looks like strong evidence to many, but the researcher with scientific training will argue that correlation is not causation. Who is right? The essence of the disagreement seems to lie in the concept of "cause."

The Concept of Cause

One writer asserts, *"There appears to be an inherent gap between the language of theory and research* which can never be bridged in a completely satisfactory way. One *thinks* in terms of theoretical language that contains notions such as causes, forces, systems, and properties. But one's tests are made in terms of covariations, operations, and pointer readings."[11] The essential element of **causation** is that A "produces" B or A "forces" B to occur. But that is an artifact of language, not what happens. Empirically, we can never demonstrate an A–B causality with certainty. This is because we do not "demonstrate" such causal linkages deductively nor use the form or validation of premises that deduction requires for conclusiveness. Unlike deductive syllogisms, empirical conclusions are inferences—inductive conclusions. As such, they are probabilistic statements based on what we observe and measure. But we cannot observe and measure all the processes that may account for the A–B relationship.

In Chapter 2 we discussed the example of a light failing to go on as the switch was pushed. Having ruled out other causes for the light's failure, we were left with one inference that was probably but not certainly the cause.

To meet the ideal standard of causation would require that one variable always caused another and no other variable had the same causal effect. The *method of agreement,* proposed by John Stuart Mill in the 19th century, states "When two or more cases of a given phenomenon have one and only one condition in common, then that condition may be regarded as the cause (or effect) of the phenomenon."[12] Thus, if we can find Z and only Z in every case where we find C, and no others

FIGURE 5–1
Mill's Method
of Agreement

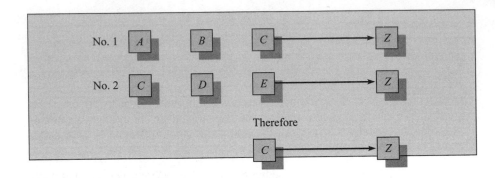

FIGURE 5–2
Mill's Method
of Difference

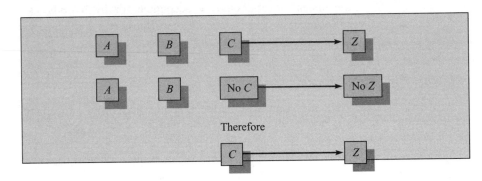

(A, B, D, or *E)* are found with *Z,* then we can conclude that *C* and *Z* are causally related. Figure 5–1 illustrates this method.

An example of the method of agreement might be the problem of occasional high absenteeism on Mondays in a factory. A study of two groups with high absenteeism (No. 1 and No. 2 in Figure 5–1) shows no common job, department, demographic, or personal characteristics *(A, B, D,* and *E)*. However, membership in a camping club *(C)* is common across both groups. The conclusion is that club membership is associated with high absenteeism *(Z)*.

The method of agreement helps rule out some variables as irrelevant. In Figure 5–1, *A, B, D,* and *E* are unlikely to be causes of *Z*. However, there is an implicit assumption that there are no variables to consider other than *A, B, C, D,* and *E*. One can never accept this supposition with certainty because the number of potential variables is infinite. In addition, while *C* may be the cause, it may instead function only in the presence of some other variable not included.

The *negative canon of agreement* states that where the absence of *C* is associated with the absence of *Z,* there is evidence of a causal relationship between *C* and *Z*. Together with the method of agreement, this forms the basis for the *method of difference:* "if there are two or more cases, and in one of them observation *Z* can be made, while in the other it cannot; and if variable *C* occurs when observation *Z* is made, and does not occur when observation *Z* is not made; then it can be asserted that there is a causal relationship between *C* and *Z*.[13] This method is illustrated in Figure 5–2. Although these methods neither assure discovery of all

**FIGURE 5–3
Possible Causal
Models of
Improved Sales
Performance
and Feedback**

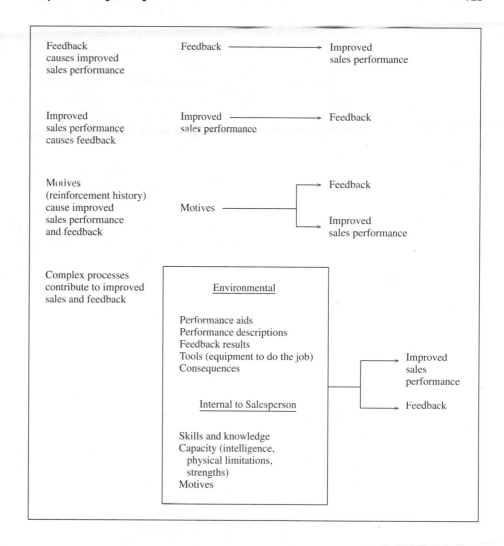

relevant variables nor provide certain proof of causation, they help advance our understanding of causality by eliminating inadequate causal arguments.[14]

A more refined cause-and-effect model proposes individual variables are not the cause of specific effects, but processes are the cause of processes.[15] Evidence for this position is illustrated in Figure 5–3.

Here various cause-and-effect relationships between sales performance and feedback clarify the differences between simple and more complex notions of causality.[16] In the first model, we contend that feedback causes an increase in sales performance. An equally plausible explanation is shown in the second model: Improvement in sales performance causes the salesperson to behave in a proactive way, seeking more feedback to apply to the next experience. A third possibility suggests the reinforcement history of the salesperson is the cause of both initiation of self-administered feedback and working harder to improve performance. In the last example, we suggest that complex processes contribute to changes in feedback and performance. They are in the salesperson's environment and unique to the person. Other examples could show how positive versus negative reinforcement could create upward or downward sequences that would affect both feedback and performance. Yet, all of them make predictions about presumed causal relationships among the variables. Contemporary authors describe the way researchers substitute "prediction" for "causation."

> When scientists speak of "causation," they are often referring to a kind of prediction. Predictions can be considered to reflect cause only when *all* the relevant information is considered. Of course, we can never know *all* the relevant information, so our predictions are consequentially presumptive. Hence the disillusionment in science with the concept of *cause*. Scientists do use the word "cause" from time to time, but do not be misled into thinking that they mean "cause" in the absolute sense.[17]

Causal inferences are going to be made. Although they are not permanent nor universal, they allow us to build knowledge of presumed causes over time. Such empirical conclusions provide us with successive approximations to the truth. Recognizing this caveat, let's look further at the types of causal relationships of interest to business researchers.

Causal Relationships

Our concern in causal analysis is with how one variable affects, or is "responsible for," changes in another variable. The stricter interpretation of "causation," found in experimentation, is that some external factor "produces" a change in the dependent variable. In business research, we often find that the cause-effect relationship is less explicit. We are more interested in understanding, explaining, predicting, and controlling relationships between variables than we are with discerning causes.

If we consider the possible relationships that can occur between two variables, we can conclude there are three possibilities. The relationships may be reciprocal, symmetrical, or asymmetrical.[18] A symmetrical relationship is one in which two variables fluctuate together, but we assume the changes in neither variable are due to changes in the other. Symmetrical conditions are most often found when two variables are alternate indicators of another cause or independent variable. We might conclude that a correlation between low work attendance and active participation in a company camping club is the result of (dependent on) another factor such as a lifestyle preference.

A reciprocal relationship exists when two variables mutually influence or reinforce each other. This could occur if the reading of an advertisement leads to the use of a brand of product. The usage, in turn, sensitizes the person to notice and read more of the advertising of that particular brand.

Asymmetrical Relationships   The major relationships of interest to the research analyst are **asymmetrical.** With these relationships we postulate that changes in one variable (the independent variable, or *IV*) are responsible for changes in another variable (the dependent variable, or *DV*). The identification of the *IV* and *DV* is often obvious, but sometimes the choice is not clear. In these latter cases we evaluate them on the basis of (1) the degree to which they may be altered and (2) the time order between them. Since age, social class, climate, world events, and present manufacturing technology, are relatively unalterable, we normally choose them as independent variables. In addition, when we can detect a time order, we usually find that the *IV* precedes the *DV*.

In business research, the types of asymmetrical relationships of most interest are:

1. *Stimulus-response relationship.* This represents an event or force that results in a response from some object. A price rise results in fewer unit sales; a change in work rules leads to a higher level of worker output; or a change in government economic policy restricts corporate financial decisions. Experiments usually involve stimulus-response relationships.

2. *Property-disposition relationship.* A property is an enduring characteristic of a subject that does not depend upon circumstances for its activation. Age, gender, family status, religious affiliation, ethnic group, and physical condition are personal properties.

   A disposition is a tendency to respond in a certain way under certain circumstances. Dispositions include attitudes, opinions, habits, values, and drives. Examples of property-disposition relationships are the effect of age on attitudes about saving, gender and its effect on attitudes toward social issues, or social class and opinions about taxation. Properties and dispositions are major concepts used in business and social science research.

3. *Disposition-behavior relationship.* Behavior responses include consumption practices, work performance, interpersonal acts, and other kinds of performance. Examples of relationships between dispositions and behavior include opinions about a brand and its purchase, job satisfaction and work output, and moral values and tax cheating. Much of ex post facto causal research involves relationships between properties, dispositions, and behaviors.

4. *Property-behavior relationship.* Examples include such relationships as the stage of the family life cycle and purchases of furniture, social class and family savings patterns, and age and sports participation.

   When thinking about possible causal relationships or proposing causal hypotheses, one must state the positional relationship, cause, and effect.

Testing Causal Hypotheses

While no one can ever be certain that variable *A* causes variable *B* to occur, one can gather some evidence that increases the belief that *A* leads to *B*. We seek three types of evidence, listed on the following page.

1. Is there a predicted covariation between *A* and *B?* That is, do we find that *A* and *B* occur together in the way hypothesized? When *A* does not occur, is there also an absence of *B?* Or, when there is less of *A*, does one also find more or less of *B?* When such conditions of covariation exist, it is an indication of a possible causal connection.

2. Is the time order of events moving in the hypothesized direction? That is, does *A* occur before *B?* If we find that *B* occurs before *A,* we can have little confidence that *A* causes *B.*

3. Is it possible to eliminate other possible causes of *B?* That is, can one determine that *C, D, E,* and so forth do not covary with *B* in a way that suggests possible causal connections?

Causation and Experimental Design   In addition to these three conditions, successful inference making from experimental designs must meet two other requirements. The first is referred to as **control.** All factors with the exception of the independent variable must be held constant and not confounded with another variable that is not part of the study. Second, each person in the study must have an equal chance for exposure to each level of the independent variable. This is **random assignment** of subjects to groups. Here is a demonstration of how these factors are used to detect causation. Assume you wish to conduct a survey of a university's alumni to enlist their support for a new program. There are two different appeals, one largely emotional in nature and the other much more logical in its approach. Before mailing out appeal letters to 50,000 alumni, you decide to conduct an experiment to see whether the emotional or the rational appeal will draw the greater response.

You choose a sample of 300 names from the alumni list and divide them into three groups of 100 each. Two of these groups are designated as the experimental groups. One gets the emotional appeal and the other gets the logical appeal. The third group is the **control group** and it receives no appeal.

Covariation in this case is expressed by the percentage of alumni who respond in relation to the appeal used. Suppose 50 percent of those who receive the emotional appeal respond, while only 35 percent of those receiving the logical appeal respond. Control group members, unaware of the experiment, respond at a 5 percent rate. We would conclude that response probability is enhanced by using the emotional appeal.

The sequence of events was not a problem. There could be no chance that the alumni support led to sending the letter requesting support. However, have other variables confounded the results? That is, could some factor other than the appeal have produced the same results? One can anticipate that certain factors are particularly likely to confound the results. One can control some of these to assure they do not have this confounding effect. If the question studied is of concern only to alumni who attended the university as undergraduates, those who came only to graduate school are not involved. Thus, you would want to be sure the answers from the latter group did not distort the results. Control would be achieved by excluding graduate students.

A second approach to control uses a **matching** process. With alumni, there might be reason to believe that different ratios of support will come from various age groups. To control by matching, we need to be sure the age distribution of alumni is the same in both groups. In a similar way, control could be achieved by matching alumni from engineering, liberal arts, business, and other schools.

Even after using such controls, however, there are other possible confounding variables that one cannot match or exclude. These are dealt with through random assignment.

Randomization is the basic method by which equivalence between experimental and control groups is determined. Experimental and control groups must be established so that they are equal. Matching and controlling are useful, but they do not account for all unknowns. It is best to assign subjects either to experimental or control groups at random (this is not to say haphazardly—randomness must be secured in a carefully controlled fashion according to strict rules of assignment). If the assignments are made randomly, each group should receive its fair share of different factors. The only deviation from this fair share would be that which results from random variation (luck of the draw). The possible impact of these unknown extraneous variables on the dependent variables should also vary at random. The researcher, using tests of statistical significance, can estimate the probable effect of these chance variations on the *DV* and can then compare this estimated effect of extraneous variation to the actual differences found in the *DV* in the experimental and control groups.

We emphasize that random assignment of subjects to experimental and control groups is the *basic technique* by which the two groups can be made equivalent. Matching and other control forms are supplemental ways of improving the quality of measurement. In a sense, matching and controls reduce the extraneous "noise" in the measurement system and in this way improve the sensitivity of measurement of the hypothesized relationship.

Causation and Ex Post Facto Design   Most research studies cannot be carried out experimentally by manipulating variables. Yet we still are interested in the question of causation. Instead of manipulating and/or controlling exposure to an experimental variable, we study subjects who have been exposed to the independent factor and those who have not.

Consider the situation in which several workers in a plant have developed a pattern of absenteeism on Mondays. In searching for hypotheses to explain this phenomenon, we discover that some of these workers are members of a camping club formed a few months ago. Could it be that membership in the club caused increased absenteeism? It is not practical to set up an experiment. This would require us to assign persons to join the club and then determine whether this affected their work attendance.

The better approach would be to get the list of the club's membership and review the absence record of workers, concentrating on their record of work attendance on the Mondays after a camping event. We would also take a sample of

TABLE 5–1   Data on Employee Absenteeism

	Camping Club Member?	
Absences	*Yes*	*No*
High	40	70
Low	10	280

employees who are not members of the club and calculate their Monday absence rates. The results might look something like those found in Table 5–1. The data suggest that membership in the camping club might be a cause of higher Monday absenteeism. Certainly the covariation evidence is consistent with this conclusion; but what other evidence will give us an even greater confidence in our conclusion?

We would like some evidence of time order of events. It is logical to expect that if club membership causes higher absenteeism, there will be a temporal relationship. If the high absenteeism was found only on the Monday immediately following a camping trip, it would be good evidence in support of our hypothesis. If absences from work occur before the camping trip, the time order does not support our hypothesis as well.

Of course, many other factors could be causing the high absenteeism among the club members. Here again, use control techniques to improve the ability to draw firm conclusions. First, in drawing a sample of nonmembers of the club, a random sample should be chosen from the files of all employees. In this way, one can be more confident of a fair representation of average worker absence experiences.

We cannot use assignment of subjects in ex post facto research as we did in experimentation. However, we can gather information about potentially confounding factors and use these data to make cross-classification comparisons. This way we determine whether there is a relationship between club membership, absenteeism, and other factors. Assume we also gather age data on the employees under study and introduce this as a cross-classification variable; the results might look like those in Table 5–2. These data suggest age is also a factor. Younger people are more likely to be among the high absentees. Part of the high absenteeism rate among club members seems to be associated with the fact that most club members are under 30 years of age. Within age groups, it is also apparent that club members have a higher incidence of excessive absenteeism than nonclub members of the same age. More will be said about the analysis of crossbreak data and the interpretation of relationships in later chapters.

The Post Hoc Fallacy   While researchers must necessarily use ex post facto research designs to address causal questions, a word of warning is in order. Club membership among persons with high absentee records is weak evidence for claiming a causal relationship. Similarly, the covariation found between variables must be interpreted carefully when the relationship is based on ex post facto analysis. The term *post hoc fallacy* has been used to describe these frequently unwarranted conclusions.

TABLE 5–2   Data on Employee Absenteeism

	Club Member		Nonclub Member	
Age	High Absentee	Low Absentee	High Absentee	Low Absentee
Under 30 years	36	6	30	48
30 to 45	4	4	35	117
45 and over	0	0	5	115

Ex post facto design is widely used in business research and often is the only approach feasible. In particular, one seeks causal explanations between variables that are impossible to manipulate. Not only can the variables not be manipulated, but the subjects usually cannot be assigned to treatment and control groups in advance. We often find that there are multiple causes rather than one. Be careful using the ex post facto design with causal reasoning. Thorough testing, validating of multiple hypotheses, and controlling for confounding variables are essential.

CLOSE-UP

This chapter Close-Up is an exercise in analyzing research designs. Its objectives are to help you (1) apply the design classifications and distinctions you have just learned to actual studies and (2) "reinvent" a selected study using the design information presented. We abstracted three studies to give you a flavor for the types of research reports that are appropriate for this exercise. You may choose from any of these or perhaps from a readings list for another course.

Directions:

1. Select a study from one of the following abstracts (or one suggested by your instructor) and secure a copy from your library.
2. Using the eight design categories, identify the characteristics of the selected study.

3. Suggest alternative designs that the researchers could have used (use four or more categories).
   a. How would the design look with your changes?
   b. In what ways would it be stronger? Weaker?
   c. Predict the effects on the results using your changes.

Abbreviated Abstracts*
Study 1. This study argues the need to identify in advance those entrepreneurs who will create high-growth firms. The psychodynamics of successful entrepreneurs remain elusive despite considerable research. However, using task motivation theory, in contrast to hierarchic motivation, identification and prediction may be aided. The study's subjects were

(continued)

applicants for development grants under NSF Small Business Innovation Research Program. Data were obtained from 118 entrepreneurs who had founded firms and a comparison group of 41 manager/scientists who had applied but were not founders. Task motivation exhibited a substantial relationship to growth and differentiated entrepreneurs from nonentrepreneurs. Benefits to venture capitalists, investors, and improvement of the speed by which technological innovation could be brought to the marketplace through early identification of talent were cited as practical benefits.

John B. Miner and Norman R. Smith, "Role of Entrepreneurial Task Motivation in the Growth of Technologically Innovative Firms." *Journal of Applied Psychology* 74, no. 4 (1989), pp. 554–60.

Study 2.   Human resource managers have a difficult task balancing the employee's rights to fair treatment and due process against the employer's rights to manage the size and composition of the work force. This study examines the effects of employment at will versus due process personnel policies on organizational efforts to attract new employees. Using 101 undergraduate business students who had read fictitious company brochures, the findings indicated that future job applicants view companies that express employment at will policies significantly less attractive than those who adhere to due process policies; but that may not discourage them from gathering more information and pursuing further employment op-

portunities with the companies who have less favored policies. The hypothesis that employers may be able to offset potential negative effects of employment at will by substantial compensation and benefits was partially supported.

Catherine Schwoerer and Benson Rosen, "Effects of Employment-at-Will Policies and Compensation Policies on Corporate Image and Job Pursuit Intentions," *Journal of Applied Psychology* 74, no. 4 (1989), pp. 653–56.

Study 3.   The self-fulfilling prophecy in interpersonal relationships is often referred to as the *Pygmalion* effect. Studied in a retail setting over a three-month period using newly hired salespeople and their first-level sales managers, this investigation examined the relationships between supervisor's expectations for a subordinate and the resulting performance. Little evidence of the Pygmalion effect was found in the overall sample although it was more operative in men than women. The study's lack of significant findings in contrast to military and educational settings suggest that the process may be more complex than previously thought.

Charlotte D. Sutton and Richard W. Woodman, "Pygmalion Goes to Work: The Effects of Supervisor Expectations in a Retail Setting," *Journal of Applied Psychology* 74, no. 6 (1989), pp. 943–50.

---

*These abstracts differ slightly from those found in the articles. Certain terminology was deleted for the purpose of the exercise. The authors' language in those cases is from the article.

Summary

If the direction of a research project is not clear, it is often wise to follow a two-step research procedure. The first stage is exploratory, aimed at formulating hypotheses and developing the specific research design. The general research process contains three major stages:

1. Exploration of the situation.
2. Collection of data.
3. Analysis and interpretation of results.

A research design is the strategy for a study and the plan by which the strategy is to be carried out. It specifies the methods and procedures for the collection, measurement, and analysis of data. Unfortunately, there is no simple classification of research designs that cover the variations found in practice. Some major perspectives on designs are:

Exploratory versus formalized.

Observational versus survey.

Experimental versus ex post facto.

Descriptive versus causal.

Cross-sectional versus longitudinal.

Case versus statistical.

Field versus laboratory versus simulation.

Subjects perceive no deviations, some deviations, or researcher-induced deviations.

Exploratory research is appropriate for the total study in topic areas where the developed data are limited. In most other studies, exploration is the first stage of a project and is used to orient the researcher and the study. The objective of exploration is the development of hypotheses, not testing.

Formalized studies, including descriptive and causal, are those with substantial structure, specific hypotheses to be tested, or research questions to be answered. Descriptive studies are those used to describe phenomena associated with a subject population or to estimate proportions of the population that have certain characteristics.

Causal studies seek to discover the effect that a variable(s) has on another (or others) or why certain outcomes are obtained. The concept of causality is grounded in the logic of hypothesis testing, which, in turn, produces inductive conclusions. Such conclusions are probabilistic and thus can never be demonstrated with certainty. Current ideas about causality as complex processes improve our understanding over Mill's canons though we can never know all the relevant information necessary to prove causal linkages beyond doubt.

The relationships that occur between two variables may be reciprocal, symmetrical, or asymmetrical. The form of greatest interest to the research analyst, the asymmetrical, takes one of the following forms:

1. Stimulus-response.
2. Property-disposition.
3. Disposition-behavior.
4. Property-behavior.

We test causal hypotheses by seeking to do three things. We *(a)* measure the covariation among variables; *(b)* determine the time order relationships among variables; and *(c)* assure that other factors do not confound the explanatory relationships.

The problems of achieving these aims differ somewhat in experimental and ex post facto studies. Where possible, we try to achieve the ideal of the experimental design with random assignment of subjects, matching of subject characteristics, and manipulation and control of variables. Using these methods and techniques, we measure relationships as accurately and objectively as possible.

Key Terms

asymmetrical relationships	laboratory conditions
case study	longitudinal
causal study (causation)	matching
control	observational study
control group	primary data
cross-sectional	qualitative techniques
descriptive study	random assignment
ex post facto design	research design
experience survey	secondary data
experiment	simulations
exploratory study (exploration)	statistical study
field conditions	subjects' perception
focus group	survey
formal study	two-stage design

Discussion Questions

1. Distinguish between the following:
   a. Exploratory and formalized.
   b. Experimental and ex post facto.
   c. Descriptive and causal
2. What kinds of problems are likely to occur when ascribing cause to inductive conclusions?
3. You have been asked to determine how large corporations prepare for contract negotiations with labor unions. Since you know relatively little about this subject, how would you find out? Be as specific as possible.

4. You are the administrative assistant of a division chief in a large manufacturing organization. You and the division chief have just come from the general manager's office where you were informed that the assemblers' performance was unsatisfactory. You had sensed the tension among the workers but had not considered it unusual. The division chief calls you into the office after the meeting and instructs you to investigate. Suggest at least three different types of research that might be appropriate in this situation.

5. Using yourself as the subject, give an example of each of the following asymmetrical relationships:
   a. Stimulus-response.
   b. Property-disposition.
   c. Disposition-behavior.
   d. Property-behavior.

6. Why not use more control variables rather than depend on randomization as the means of controlling extraneous variables?

7. Propose one or more hypotheses for each of the following variable pairs, specifying which is the *IV* and which the *DV.* Then elaborate the basic hypothesis to include at least one moderating variable or intervening variable.
   a. The Index of Consumer Confidence and the business cycle.
   b. Level of worker output and closeness of supervision of the worker.
   c. Degree of personal friendship between customer and salesperson and the frequency of sales calls on the customer.

8. Researchers seek causal relationships by either experimental or ex post facto research designs.
   a. In what ways are these two approaches similar?
   b. In what ways are they different?

Reference Notes

1. Reprinted with permission of Macmillan Publishing from *Social Research Strategy and Tactics,* 2nd ed., by Bernard S. Phillips, p. 93. Copyright © 1971 by Bernard S. Phillips.
2. Fred N. Kerlinger, *Foundations of Behavioral Research,* 3rd ed. (New York: Holt, Rinehart & Winston, 1986), p. 279.
3. The complexity of research design tends to confuse students as well as writers. The latter respond by forcing order on the vast array of design types through the use of classification schemes or taxonomies. Generally, this is helpful, but because the world defies neat categories, this scheme, like others, may either include or exclude too much.
4. Kerlinger, *Foundations of Behavioral Research,* p. 295.
5. Abraham Kaplan, *The Conduct of Inquiry* (San Francisco: Chandler, 1964), p. 37.
6. W. Charles Redding, "Research Setting: Field Studies," in *Methods of Research in Communication,* ed. Philip Emmert and William D. Brooks (Boston: Houghton Mifflin, 1970), pp. 140–42.
7. John Van Maanen, James M. Dabbs, Jr., and Robert R. Faulkner, *Varieties of Qualitative Research* (Beverly Hills: Calif.: Sage Publications, 1982), p. 32.

8. Catherine Marshall and Gretchen B. Rossman, *Designing Qualitative Research,* (Newbury Park, Calif.: Sage Publications, 1989), pp. 78–108.

9. This classification is suggested in Claire Selltiz, Lawrence S. Wrightsman, and Stuart W. Cook, *Research Methods in Social Relations,* 3rd ed. (New York: Holt, Rinehart & Winston, 1976), pp. 99–101.

10. A comprehensive and detailed presentation may be found in Richard A. Krueger, *Focus Groups: A Practical Guide for Applied Research,* 2nd ed. (Thousand Oaks, Calif.: Sage Publications, 1994); and David L. Morgan, *Successful Focus Groups: Advancing the State of the Art* (Thousand Oaks, Calif.: Sage Publications, 1993). Also see Thomas L. Greenbaum, "Focus Group Spurt Predicted for the '90s," *Marketing News* 24, no. 1 (January 8, 1990), pp. 21–22.

11. Hubert M. Blalock, Jr., *Causal Inferences in Nonexperimental Research* (Chapel Hill, N.C.: University of North Carolina Press, 1964), p. 5.

12. As stated in William J. Goode and Paul K. Hatt, *Methods in Social Research* (New York: McGraw-Hill, 1952), p. 75.

13. From *Methods in Social Research* by William J. Goode and Paul K. Hatt. Copyright © 1952, McGraw-Hill Book Company. Used with permission of McGraw-Hill Book Company.

14. Morris R. Cohen and Ernest Nagel, *An Introduction to Logic and Scientific Method* (New York: Harcourt, Brace, 1934), chap. 13; and Blalock, *Causal Inferences in Nonexperimental Research,* p. 14.

15. R. Carnap, *An Introduction to the Philosophy of Science* (New York: Basic Books, 1966).

16. Content adapted from Thomas F. Gilbert, *Human Competence* (New York: McGraw-Hill, 1978). Tabular concept based on Emanuel J. Mason and William J. Bramble, *Understanding and Conducting Research,* 2nd ed. (New York: McGraw-Hill, 1989), p. 13.

17. Mason and Bramble, *Understanding and Conducting Research,* p. 14.

18. Morris Rosenberg, *The Logic of Survey Analysis* (New York: Basic Books, 1968), p. 3.

Suggested Readings

1. Babbie, Earl R. *The Practice of Social Research.* 6th ed. Belmont, Calif.: Wadsworth, 1992. Chapter 4 is a clear and thorough encapsulation of design.

2. Krathwohl, David R. *Social and Behavioral Science Research: A New Framework for Conceptualizing, Implementing, and Evaluating Research Studies.* San Francisco: Jossey-Bass, 1985. Chapter 9 on causality is insightful, well reasoned, and highly recommended.

3. Mason, Emanuel J., and William J. Bramble. *Understanding and Conducting Research.* 2nd ed. New York: McGraw-Hill, 1989. Chapter 1 has an excellent section on causation; chapter 2 provides an alternative classification of the types of research.

4. Selltiz, Claire; Lawrence S. Wrightsman; and Stuart M. Cook. *Research Methods in Social Relations.* 3rd ed. New York: Holt, Rinehart & Winston, 1976. Chapters 4 and 5 discuss various types of research designs.

FINDING YOUR WAY

BRINGING RESEARCH TO LIFE

"I was a tourist here when the previous executive director, who had served for 15 years, ran off to Vancouver with a violinist. He said he could not endure another year of our claustrophobic winters." The executive director gestured broadly at the still-snow-capped Canadian Rockies that enveloped the White Ice Compound and discouraged casual visitation for most of the year. "Being a recent mugging victim—they took my wallet and broke my wrist—I was happy to stay for a while. And it has been three very happy years, though not easy on my ego since I let corporate North America intrude on our idyllic existence. Not that I blame them for my shortcomings."

"You mean the MindWriter people?" prompted Myra. "The ones who flew us up here? Our clients?"

The executive director propelled Myra and Jason straight across a manicured lawn toward the refreshment tent, where her faculty and paying guests were basking in post-concert euphoria, following a stirring performance of Beethoven by the White Ice Summer Festival Orchestra.

"Please, don't misunderstand," said the executive director. "They have been fine tenants . . . good corporate citizens . . . generous contributors to our little community. When I rented them a part of our compound for use in corporate education, they were quite generously insistent that I avail myself of some of their training for mid-level managers. And I have to admit, now, that their managerial style makes me feel like an inadequate cellist with a stiff wrist, not an executive director evolving toward competence."

"Well, if we are going to help you," ventured Jason, "you had better tell us quickly what you do here. We have a 4 P.M. flight out."

"Surely. And I do appreciate this advice, especially as you have an insider's view of the MindWriter people. We in White Ice have a simple, never varying rhythm of activity. By the middle of September, the paying guests, the visiting artists, the musicians, and the tourists have left White Ice, and I bring in artisans for two weeks of intensive repairs and renovations. Then I prepare financial and artistic reports for the three foundations who have endowed us and also draw up an agenda for capital improvements and special events, which become the basis for frantic proposal writing during the weeks preceding Christmas. From January to April, I am on the phone to travel agents from Mexico City to Juneau to arrange a tight reservation and scheduling process, so that we maximize the use of the facilities during our season. I have developed the ability to keep track of the cash flow, which is not easy, with the Canadian and U. S. dollars mingled.

"During the winter my artistic directors, Frances Braun and Igor Starvinsky—they have been Mr. and Mrs. Braun-Starvinsky for 30 years, which will astonish you when you meet them—prepare the program and hire the musicians, coordinating closely with me on the budget. This is quite complicated, as most of the performing artists spend only two weeks with us, so that fully 600 artists are part of this orchestra over the course of a summer.

"Then in the early spring I hear from the colleges in British Columbia, who send me their music scholarship students for summer employment as dishwashers, waiters, cleaners, and the like."

"Sounds as if you are right on top of the finances," said Myra, "and I suppose in your seminars with the MindWriter people they told you their theory of what to measure in any enterprise . . . and that cash flow is one of three things that must be watched most carefully."

"Oh, yes indeed," the executive director laughed. "Gauging cash flow is not the problem. I descend from a line of genteel poverty. Measuring customer satisfaction—one of the other critical three factors for the MindWriter folks—now that was a problem for me—at first. I was dumbfounded by the care and frequency with which they measure customer satisfaction in the MindWriter seminars. Halfway through a seminar, morning, afternoon, or evening, everyone breaks for coffee and is required to fill out a critique of the speaker. The results are tabulated by the time the last coffee cup has been picked up, and the seminar leader has been given

(continued)

feedback. Is he or she presenting material too slowly? Too quickly? Are there too many jokes or not enough? Are concrete examples beingh used often enough? do the parcipiants want hard copy of the slides? Really is is remarkable. They measure attitudinal data six times a day and even query you about the meals, including taste, appearance, cleanliness and speed, friendliness, and accuracy of service.

"We have a North American association of artistic and executive directors, and since experiencing the MindWriter seminars, I have every year hosted the fall subcommittee meeting on audience development. I take it right out of my budget, and show everyone a fine time—skiing, skating, and a frank exchange of ideas on measuring the customer."

"Smart," said Myra and Jason together.

"My remaining problem is employee commitment, specifically commitment of the orchestral performers to the White Ice Festival. None of the other directors in my association has nearly the rapid turnover of performers we have here, so they are not much help in measuring commitment."

"Then the Braun-Starvinskys will have to be your eyes and ears. You must ask them to listen carefully to the performers. Employee satisfaction is the third leg of the three-legged stool on which performance is based. I'm quoting the MindWriter standard line, by the way," said Myra.

The executive director laughed ironically. "Myra," she said, "look over my shoulder. Directly behind me is a couple in their mid 60s. Please describe as exactly as you can the behavior you observe. But lean forward and whisper, since they have the eyes of a hawk and the hearing of a lark."

"You mean the fellow in the sweatshirt and the woman with her hair in a bun?" whispered Myra. "I've been watching them all afternoon. They are remarkable, horrid, really. You say they are married? Why, he is sleeping. And the woman is nevertheless talking to him nonstop and every 30 seconds shaking him awake. Except he falls right back to sleep. And she does not stop talking, but simply chats a while longer and wakes him again."

"Yes, Myra, there you have them—my artistic directors. He stays up all night composing, and all day, when he is not conducting, he snoozes. And she never stops expressing her opinions, be they lifelong prejudices or vagrant musings, and therefore she never listens well enough to later give a coherent report of anything she has heard or been told. If I have to rely on them for feedback, everything would be filtered and distorted beyond recognition. I might as well query the statue of Chief White Ice."

"Personally, I find untrained observers highly unreliable and inaccurate in measuring and reporting behavior," said Jason.

"He thinks humans are no darned good for anything," apologized Myra. "Have you tried a suggestion box?"

"No, but I do send a letter to each visiting performer soliciting bouquets and brickbats. Do you want to know what some of the performers have written?"

"Shoot," said Jason. "but, quickly, please. Don't want to fly through these mountains at night."

"They write, 'Starvinsky never listens to our ideas.' They write, 'A day under Braun feels like a week on a Los Angeles freeway.' They write, 'We are all highly trained college teachers of music, but we are treated like children.'

"And clearly our performers aren't our only concern. The restaurant employees, the hospitality staff, the stage carpenters, the . . ."

"Hold on," said Jason, scribbling furiously on a napkin. "I can see you have a problem. I'm making a note to send you Patchen's Work Innovation Index and his Job Motivation Index. In fact, I'll send you all his indexes, because he identifies and measures five different dimensions of worker attitudes. You'll find it interesting and maybe it is something you can use. Meanwhile, will you send me your customer satisfaction instrument for concertgoers?"

"Of course, Jason. And be sure I shall act quickly on your suggestions. The Vancouver Sun has commented on our inability to sustain a steady tempo and tonation. When a businessperson fouls up, the mistake may not be evident for days or weeks. But when our orchestra strikes a sour note, 600 audience members—guests, we call them, but they are potentially repeat customers—receive the message at the speed of sound."

THE NATURE OF MEASUREMENT

In everyday usage, measurement occurs when an established yardstick is used to verify the height, weight, or another feature of a physical object. How well you like a song, a painting, or the personality of a friend is also a measurement. In a dictionary sense, to measure is to discover the extent, dimensions, quantity, or capacity of something, especially by comparison with a standard. We measure casually in daily life, but in research, the requirements are rigorous.

Measurement in research consists of assigning numbers to empirical events in compliance with a set of rules. This definition implies that measurement is a three-part process: (1) selecting observable empirical events, (2) using numbers or symbols to represent aspects of the events, and (3) applying a mapping rule to connect the observation to the symbol.[1] Figure 6–1 illustrates the components.

Assume you are studying people who attend an auto show where all of the year's new models are on display. You are interested in learning the male-to-female ratio among attendees. You observe those who enter the show area. If a person is a female, you record an f, and if male, an m. Any other symbols such as 0 and 1 or # and % could be used if you know what group the symbol identifies. Researchers might also want to measure the desirability of the styling of the new Espace van. They interview a sample of visitors and (with a different mapping rule) assign their opinions to the following scale.

FIGURE   6–1   Characteristics of Measurement

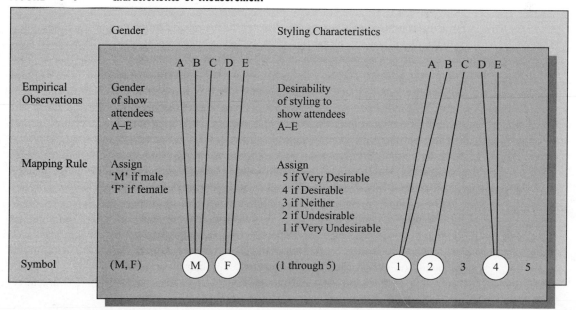

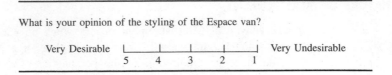

What is your opinion of the styling of the Espace van?

Very Desirable |___|___|___|___|___| Very Undesirable
                 5   4   3   2   1

All measurement theorists would call the opinion rating scale above a form of measurement, but some would challenge the male–female classification. Their argument is that measurement must involve quantification, that is, "the assignment of numbers to objects to represent amounts or degrees of a property possessed by all of the objects."[2] Our discussion endorses the more general view that numbers reflect qualitative and quantitative concepts.

Researchers deduce from a hypothesis that certain conditions should exist in the real world; then they measure for these conditions. If found, they lend support to the hypothesis; if not, they conclude the hypothesis is faulty. An important question at this point is, "Just what does one measure?"

What Is Measured?

Concepts used in research may be classified as objects or as properties. **Objects** include the things of ordinary experience, such as tables, people, books, and automobiles. Objects also include things that are not as concrete, such as genes, attitudes, neutrons, and peer-group pressures. **Properties,** on the other hand, are the characteristics of the objects. A person's physical properties may be stated in terms of weight, height, posture. Psychological properties include attitudes and intelligence. Social properties include leadership ability, class affiliation, or status. These and many other properties of an individual can be measured in a research study.

In a literal sense, researchers do not measure objects or properties. They measure indicants of the properties.[2] Thus, they measure indicants of the properties of objects. It is easy to observe that *A* is taller than *B* and that *C* participates more than *D* in a group process. Or, suppose you are analyzing members of a sales force of several hundred people to learn what personal properties contribute to sales success. The properties are age, years of experience, and number of calls made per week. The indicants in these cases are so accepted that one considers the properties to be observed directly.

In contrast, it is not easy to measure properties like motivation to succeed, ability to stand stress, problem-solving ability, and persuasiveness. Since they cannot be measured directly, one must infer their presence or absence by observing some indicant or pointer measurement. When you begin to make these inferences, there is often disagreement about how to operationalize the indicants.

Not only is it a challenge to measure such constructs, but a study's quality depends on what measures are selected or constructed, and how they fit the circumstances. The nature of measurement scales, sources of error, and characteristics of sound measurement are considered next.

MEASUREMENT SCALES

In measuring, one devises some form of scale and then transfers the observation of property indicants onto this scale. Several types of scales are possible; the appropriate choice depends on what you assume about the mapping rules. Each scale has its own set of underlying assumptions about how the numerals correspond to real world observations.

Scale classifications employ the real numbers system. The most accepted basis for scaling has three characteristics:

1. Numbers are ordered. One number is greater than, less than, or equal to another number.
2. Differences between numbers are ordered. The difference between any pair of numbers is greater than, less than, or equal to the difference between any other pair of numbers.
3. The number series has a unique origin indicated by the number zero.

Combinations of these characteristics of order, distance, and origin provide the following widely used classification of measurement scales:

Type of Scale	Characteristics of Scale	Basic Empirical Operation
Nominal	No order, distance, or origin	Determination of equality
Ordinal	Order but no distance or unique origin	Determination of greater or lesser values
Interval	Both order and distance but no unique origin	Determination of equality of intervals or differences
Ratio	Order, distance, and unique origin	Determination of equality of ratios

Nominal Scales

In the social sciences and business research, nominal scales are probably more widely used than any others. When you use a **nominal scale,** you partition a set into categories that are mutually exclusive and collectively exhaustive. In the camping club illustration used in the last chapter (Table 5–1), persons were classified into four unique categories through cross-classification of club membership and degree of absenteeism. Each employee could be placed in one and only one of the four cells.

The counting of members in each group is the only possible arithmetic operation when a nominal scale is employed. If we use numbers to identify categories, they are recognized as labels only and have no quantitative value. Nominal classifications may consist of any number of separate groups if the groups are mutually exclusive and collectively exhaustive. Thus, one might classify the residents of a city according to their expressed religious preferences. Classification set *A* given in the accompanying table is not a sound nominal scale because it is not collectively exhaustive. Set *B* meets the minimum requirements, although this classification may be more useful for some research purposes than others.

Religious Preferences	
A	*B*
Baptist	Catholic
Catholic	Jewish
Jewish	Protestant
Lutheran	Other
Methodist	None
Presbyterian	
Protestant	

Nominal scales are the least powerful of the four types. They suggest no order or distance relationship and have no arithmetic origin. The scale wastes any information about varying degrees of the property being measured.

Since the only quantification is the number count of cases in each category, the researcher is restricted to the use of the mode as the measure of central tendency.[3] You can conclude which class has the most members, but that is all. There is no generally used measure of dispersion for nominal scales. Several tests for statistical significance may be utilized; the most common is the chi-square test. For measures of association, phi, lambda, or other measures may be appropriate. Significance tests and measures of association are presented in Chapters 15, 16, and Appendix E.

While nominal scales are weak, they are still useful. If no other scale can be used, one can almost always classify one set of properties into a set of equivalent classes. Nominal measures are especially valuable in exploratory work where the objective is to uncover relationships rather than secure precise measurements. These scales are also widely used in survey and other ex post facto research when data are classified by major subgroups of the population. Classifications such as respondents' marital status, gender, political persuasion, and exposure to a certain experience abound. Cross-partitions of these and other variables provide insight into important data patterns.

Ordinal Scales

Ordinal scales include the characteristics of the nominal scale plus an indicator of order. Ordinal scales are possible if the transitivity postulate is fulfilled. This postulate states: If *a* is greater than *b* and *b* is greater than *c,* then *a* is greater than *c.*[4] The use of an ordinal scale implies a statement of "greater than" or "less than" (an equality statement is also acceptable) without stating how much greater or less. Like a rubber yardstick, it can stretch varying amounts at different places along its length. Thus, the real difference between ranks 1 and 2 may be more or less than the difference between ranks 2 and 3.

An ordinal concept can be generalized beyond the simple illustration of $a > b > c$. Any number of cases can be ranked. While ordinal measurement speaks of "greater than" and "less than" measurements, other relationships may be used—

"superior to," "happier than," or "above." A third extension of the ordinal concept occurs when more than one property is of interest. We may ask a taster to rank varieties of carbonated soft drinks by flavor, color, carbonation, and a combination of these characteristics. We can secure the combined ranking either by asking the respondent to make such a ranking or by doing our own combining of the individual rankings. To develop an overall index, the researcher typically adds and averages ranks for each of the three dimensions. This procedure is technically incorrect and, especially for a given respondent, may yield misleading results. When the number of respondents is large, however, these errors average out. A more sophisticated way to combine a number of dimensions into a total index is to use a multidimensional scale (see Chapter 17).

The researcher faces another difficulty when combining the rankings of several respondents. Here again, it is not uncommon to use weighted sums of rank values for a combined index. If there are many observations, this approach will probably give adequate results, though it is not theoretically correct. A better way is to convert the ordinal scale into an interval scale, the values of which can then be added and averaged. One well-known example is Thurstone's *Law of Comparative Judgment*.[5] In its simplest form, Thurstone's procedure says the distance between scale positions of two objects, *A* and *B,* depends on the percentage of judgments in which *A* is preferred to *B.*

Examples of ordinal scales include opinion and preference scales. The widely used paired-comparison technique uses an ordinal scale. Because the numbers of this scale have only a rank meaning, the appropriate measure of central tendency is the median. A percentile or quartile measure reveals the dispersion. Correlations are restricted to various rank-order methods. Measures of statistical significance are technically confined to that body of methods known as nonparametric methods.[6]

Researchers in the behavioral sciences differ about the belief that more powerful parametric significance tests are appropriate with ordinal measures. One position is that this use of parametric tests is incorrect on both theoretical and practical grounds.

> If the measurement is weaker than that of an interval scale, by using parametric methods tests the researcher would "add information" and thereby create distortions . . . .[7]

At the other extreme, some behavioral scientists argue that parametric tests are usually acceptable for ordinal scales.

> . . . the difference between parametric and rank-order tests were not great insofar as significance level and power were concerned.[8]

A view between these extremes recognizes that there are risks in using parametric procedures on ordinal data, but these risks are usually not great.

> The best procedure would seem to be to treat ordinal measurements as though they were interval measurements but to be constantly alert to the possibility of *gross* inequality of intervals.[9]

Because nonparametric tests are abundant, simple to calculate, have good power efficiencies, and do not force the researcher to accept the assumptions of parametric testing, we advise their use with nominal and ordinal scales. It is understandable, however, that because parametric tests (such as t-tests or analysis of variance) are so versatile, accepted, and understood, they will continue to be used with ordinal data when the data approach interval scale characteristics.

Interval Scales

The **interval scale** has the powers of nominal and ordinal scales plus one additional strength: It incorporates the concept of equality of interval (the distance between 1 and 2 equals the distance between 2 and 3). Calendar time is such a scale. For example, the elapsed time between 3 and 6 A.M. equals the time between 4 and 7 A.M. One cannot say, however, 6 A.M. is twice as late as 3 A.M. because "zero time" is an arbitrary origin. Centigrade and Fahrenheit temperature scales are other examples of classical interval scales. Both have an arbitrarily determined zero point.

Many attitude scales are presumed to be interval. Thurstone's differential scale was an early effort to develop such a scale.[10] Users also treat intelligence scores, semantic differential scales, and many other multipoint scales as interval.

When a scale is interval, you use the arithmetic mean as the measure of central tendency. You can compute the average time of first arrival of trucks at a warehouse or the average attitude value for union workers versus nonunion workers on an election. The standard deviation is the measure of dispersion for arrival times or worker opinions. Product moment correlation, *t*-tests, and *F*-tests and other parametric tests are the statistical procedures of choice.[11]

Ratio Scales

Ratio scales incorporate all of the powers of the previous ones plus the provision for absolute zero or origin. The ratio scale represents the actual amounts of a variable. Measures of physical dimensions such as weight, height, distance, and area are examples. In the behavioral sciences, few situations satisfy the requirements of the ratio scale—the area of psychophysics offering some exceptions. In business research, we find ratio scales in many areas. There are money values, population counts, distances, return rates, and amounts of time in a time-period sense.

All statistical techniques mentioned up to this point are usable with ratio scales. Other manipulations carried out with real numbers may be done with ratio-scale values. Thus, multiplication and division can be used with this scale but not with the others mentioned. Geometric and harmonic means are measures of central tendency, and coefficients of variation may also be calculated.

Researchers often encounter the problem of evaluating variables that have been measured at different scale levels. The possession of a CPA by an accountant is a nominal, dichotomous variable, and salary is a ratio variable. Certain statistical techniques require the measurement levels to be the same. Since the nominal variable does not have the characteristics of order, distance, or point of origin, we cannot create them artificially after the fact. The ratio-based salary variable, on the other hand, can be reduced. Rescaling salary downward into high-low, high-medium-low, or another set of categories simplifies the comparison of nominal data. This example is generalizable to other measurement situations. That is, conversion or rescaling of a variable is unidirectional from the more powerful and robust measurement level to the lesser one, not the reverse.[12] The loss of measurement power accompanying such decisions is sometimes costly in that only nonparametric statistics can then be used in data analysis. Thus, the design of the measurement plan should anticipate such problems and avoid them when possible.

SOURCES OF MEASUREMENT DIFFERENCES

The ideal study should be designed and controlled for precise and unambiguous measurement of the variables. Since attainment of this ideal is unlikely, we must recognize the sources of potential error and try to eliminate, neutralize, or otherwise deal with them. Much potential error is systematic (results from a bias) while the remainder is random (occurs erratically). One authority has pointed out several sources from which measured differences can come.[13]

Assume you are conducting an ex post factor survey of the residents of a major city. The study concerns the Prince Corporation, a large manufacturer with headquarters and several major plants located in the city. The objective of the study is to discover the public's opinions about the company and the origin of any generally held adverse opinions.

Ideally, any variation of scores among the respondents would reflect true differences in their opinions about the company. Attitudes toward the firm as an employer, as an ecologically sensitive organization, or as a progressive corporate citizen would be accurately expressed. However, four major error sources may contaminate the results. These sources are the respondent, the situation, the measurer, and the instrument.

Error Sources

The Respondent as an Error Source   Opinion differences will come from relatively stable characteristics of the respondent that affect the scores. Typical of these are employee status, ethnic group membership, social class, and nearness to plants. Many of these dimensions will be anticipated in the design, but others of a less obvious nature will not be. The latter variety might be a traumatic experience a given respondent had with the Prince Corporation or its personnel. The respondent may be reluctant to express strong negative feelings or may have little knowledge about Prince but be reluctant to admit ignorance. This reluctance can lead to an interview of "guesses."

Respondents may also suffer from temporary factors like fatigue, boredom, anxiety, or another distraction; these limit the ability to respond accurately and fully. Hunger, impatience, or general variations in mood may also have an impact.

Situational Factors   These potential problem areas are legion. Any condition that places a strain on the interview can have serious effects on the interviewer–

respondent rapport. If another person is present, that person can distort responses by joining in, by distracting, or merely by being present. If the respondents believe anonymity is not assured, they may be reluctant to express certain feelings. Curbside or intercept interviews are unlikely to elicit elaborate responses while in-home interviews more often do.

The Measurer as an Error Source   The interviewer can distort responses by rewording, paraphrasing, or reordering questions. Stereotypes in appearance and action introduce bias Inflections of voice and conscious or unconscious prompting with smiles, nods, and so forth may encourage or discourage certain replies. Careless mechanical processing—checking of the wrong response or failure to record full replies—will obviously distort findings. In the data analysis stage, further errors may be introduced by incorrect coding, careless tabulation, and faulty statistical calculation.

Instrument as an Error Source   A defective instrument can cause distortion in two major ways. First, it can be too confusing and ambiguous. The use of complex words and syntax beyond respondent comprehension is typical. Leading questions, ambiguous meanings, mechanical defects (inadequate space for replies, response choice omissions, and poor printing) suggest the range of problems.

A more elusive type of instrument deficiency is poor sampling of the universe of content items. Seldom does the instrument explore all the potentially important issues. The Prince Corporation study might treat company image in areas of employment and ecology but omit the company management's civic leadership, its support of local education programs, or its position on minority issues. Even if the general issues are studied, the questions may not cover enough aspects of each area of concern. While we might study the Prince Corporation's image as an employer in terms of salary and wage scales, promotion opportunities, and work stability, perhaps such topics as working conditions, company management relations with organized labor, and retirement and other benefit programs should also be included.

THE CHARACTERISTICS OF SOUND MEASUREMENT

What are the characteristics of a good measurement tool? An intuitive answer to this question is that the tool should be an accurate counter or indicator of what we are interested in measuring. In addition, it should be easy and efficient to use. There are three major criteria for evaluating a measurement tool. They are *validity, reliability,* and *practicality:*

> Validity refers to the extent to which a test measures what we actually wish to measure. Reliability has to do with the accuracy and precision of a measurement procedure . . . Practicality is concerned with a wide range of factors of economy, convenience, and interpretability.[14]

In the following sections, we discuss the nature of these qualities and how researchers can achieve them in their measurement procedures.

Validity   Many forms of validity are mentioned in the research literature, and the number grows as we expand the concern for more scientific measurement. This text features two major forms: external and internal validity.[15] The external validity of research findings refers to their ability to be generalized across persons, settings, and times; more will be said about this in Chapters 8 and 13.[16] In this chapter, we discuss only internal validity. Internal validity is further limited in this discussion to the ability of a research instrument to measure what it is purported to measure. That is, does the instrument really measure what its designer claims it does?

Validity in this context is the extent to which differences found with a measuring tool reflect true differences among respondents being tested. The difficulty in meeting this test is that usually one does not know what the true differences are; if one did, one would not do the measuring. Without direct knowledge of the dimension being studied, you must face the question, "How can one discover validity without direct confirming knowledge?" A quick answer is to seek other relevant evidence that confirms the answers found with the measurement device, but this leads to a second question, "What constitutes relevant evidence?" There is no quick answer this time. What is relevant depends on the nature of the research problem and the researcher's judgment. One way to approach this question is to organize the answer according to measure-relevant types. One widely accepted classification consists of three major forms: **content, criterion-related,** and **construct.**[17]

Content Validity   The content validity of a measuring instrument is the extent to which it provides adequate coverage of the topic under study. If the instrument contains a representative sample of the universe of subject matter of interest, then content validity is good. To evaluate the content validity of an instrument, one must first agree on what elements constitute adequate coverage of the problem. In the Prince Corporation study, one must decide what knowledge, attitudes, and opinions are relevant to the measurement of corporate public image and then decide which forms of these opinions are relevant positions on these topics. If the questionnaire adequately covers the topics that have been defined as the relevant dimensions, we conclude the instrument has good content validity.

Determination of content validity is judgmental and can be approached in several ways. First, the designer may determine it through a careful definition of the topic of concern, the items to be scaled, and the scales to be used. This logical process is often intuitive and unique to each research designer. The research question hierarchy discussed in Chapter 3 helps to reduce research questions into specific questions that have content validity. A second way to determine content validity is to use a panel of persons to judge how well the instrument meets the standards.

An operational example of how an instrument is content validated comes from the employment setting. A panel independently assesses the test items for a performance test. They judge each item to be essential, useful but not essential, or not necessary in assessing performance of a relevant behavior. The "essential" responses on each item from each panelist are evaluated by a Content Validity Ratio, and those meeting a statistical significance value are retained. In both informal judgments and in this systematic process, "content validity is primarily concerned with inferences about test *construction* rather than inferences about test *scores*."[18]

It is important *not* to define "content" too narrowly. If you secure only superficial expressions of opinion in the Prince Corporation public opinion survey, it would probably not have adequate content coverage. The research should delve into the processes by which these opinions came about. How did the respondents come to feel as they did, and what is the intensity of feeling?

Criterion-Related Validity   This form of validity reflects the success of measures used for prediction or estimation. You may want to predict an outcome or estimate the existence of a current behavior or condition. This is *predictive and concurrent validity,* respectively. They differ only in a time perspective. An opinion questionnaire that correctly forecasts the outcome of a union election has predictive validity. An observational method that correctly categorizes families by current income class has concurrent validity. While these examples appear to have simple and unambiguous validity criteria, there are difficulties in estimating validity. Consider the problem of estimating family income. There clearly is a knowable true income for every family. However, we may find it difficult to secure this figure. Thus, while the criterion is conceptually clear, it may be unavailable.

In other cases, there may be several criteria, none of which is completely satisfactory. Consider again the problem of judging success in a sales force. A researcher may want to develop a preemployment test that will predict sales success. There may be several possible criteria, none of which tells the full story. Total sales per salesperson may not adequately reflect territory market potential, competitive conditions, or the different profitability rates of various products. One might rely on the sales manager's overall evaluation, but how unbiased and accurate are those impressions? The researcher must assure that the validity criterion used is itself "valid." One source suggests that any criterion measure must be judged in terms of four qualities: relevance, freedom from bias, reliability, and availability.[19]

A criterion is *relevant* if it is defined and scored in the terms we judge to be the proper measures of salesperson success. If you believe sales success is adequately measured by dollar sales volume achieved per year, then it is the relevant criterion. If you believe success should include a high level of penetration of large accounts, then sales volume alone is not fully relevant. In making this decision, you must rely on your judgment in deciding what partial criteria are appropriate indicants of salesperson success.

Freedom from bias is attained when the criterion gives each salesperson an equal opportunity to score well. The sales criterion would be biased if it did not show adjustments for differences in territory potential and competitive conditions.

A *reliable* criterion is stable or reproducible. An erratic criterion (highly variable sales performances from month to month) can hardly be considered a reliable standard by which to judge performances on a sales employment test. Yet an unreliable criterion is often relevant for the study's purpose because it is the only one available. In such a case, it is possible to use a *correction for attenuation* formula that lets you see what the correlation between the test and the criterion would be if they were made perfectly reliable.[20]

Finally, the information specified by the criterion must be *available*. If not available, how much will it cost and how difficult will it be to secure? The amount of money and effort that should be spent on development of a criterion depends on the importance of the problem for which the test is used.

Once there are test and criterion scores, they must be compared in some way. The usual approach is to correlate them. For example, you might correlate test scores of 40 new salespeople with first-year sales achievements adjusted to reflect differences in territorial selling conditions.

Construct Validity   One may also wish to measure or infer the presence of abstract characteristics for which no empirical validation seems possible. Attitude scales and aptitude and personality tests generally concern concepts that fall in this category. Although this situation is much more difficult, some assurance is still needed that the measurement has an acceptable degree of validity.

In attempting to evaluate construct validity, we consider both the theory and the measuring instrument being used. If we were interested in measuring the effect of ceremony on organizational culture, the way in which ceremony was operationally defined would have to correspond to an empirically grounded theory. Once assured that the construct was meaningful in a theoretical sense, we would next investigate the adequacy of the instrument. If a known measure of ceremony in organizational culture was available, we might correlate the results obtained using this measure with those derived from our new instrument. Such an approach would provide us with preliminary indications of *convergent* validity. Another method of validating the ceremony construct would be to separate it from other constructs in the theory or related theories. To the extent that ceremony could be separated from stories or symbols, we would have completed the first steps toward *discriminant* validity. Established statistical tools such as factor analysis and multitrait-multimethod analysis help determine the construct adequacy of a measuring device.[21]

In the Prince Corporation study, you may be interested in securing a judgment of "how good a citizen" the corporation is. Variations in respondent ratings may be drastically affected if the respondents have substantial differences in opinion about what constitutes proper corporate citizenship. One respondent may believe that any company is an economic organization designed to make profits for its stockholders. She sees relatively little role for corporations in the wide-ranging social issues of the day. Another respondent, at the other end of the continuum, views the corporation as a leader in solving social problems, even at the cost of profits.

Each of these respondents might understand Prince's role in the community but judge it quite differently in light of their views about what the role should be. If these different views are held, you would theorize that other information about these respondents would be logically compatible with their judgments. You might expect the first respondent to oppose high corporate taxes, to be critical of increased involvement of government in family affairs, and to believe that a corporation's major responsibility is to its stockholders. The second respondent would be more likely to favor high corporate income taxes, to opt for more governmental involvement in daily life, and to believe that a corporation's major responsibility is a social one.

Respondents may not be consistent on all questions because the measurements may be crude and the "theory" may be deficient. When hypothesized tests do not confirm the measurement scale, you are faced with a two-edged question: Is your measurement instrument invalid, or is your theory invalid? Answers require more information or the exercise of judgment.

The three forms of validity have been discussed separately, but they are interrelated, both theoretically and operationally. Predictive validity is important for a test designed to predict employee success. In developing such a test, you would probably first postulate the factors (constructs) that provide the basis for useful prediction. That is, you would advance a theory about the variable in employee success—an area for construct validity. Finally, in developing the specific items for inclusion in the success prediction test, you would be concerned with how well the specific items sample the full range of each construct (a matter of content validity).

In the corporate image study for the Prince Corporation, both content and construct validity considerations have been discussed, but what about criterion-related validity? The criteria are less obvious than in the employee success prediction, but there will be judgments made of the quality of evidence about the company's image. The criteria used may be subjective (does the evidence agree with what we believe?) and objective (does the evidence agree with other research findings?). (See Figure 6–2.)

FIGURE   6–2   Summary of Validity Estimates

Type	*What Is Measured*	*Methods*
Content	Degree to which the content of the items adequately represents the universe of all relevant items under study	Judgmental or panel evaluation with Content Validity Ratio
Criterion-related	Degree to which the predictor is adequate in capturing the relevant aspects of the criterion	Correlation
Concurrent	Description of the present; criterion data is available at same time as predictor scores	
Predictive	Prediction of the future; criterion is measured after the passage of time	
Construct	Answers the question, "What accounts for the variance in the measure?" Attempts to identify the underlying construct(s) being measured and determine how well the test represents them.	Judgmental Correlation of proposed test with established one Convergent-discriminant techniques Factor analysis Multitrait-multimethod analysis

Reliability

Test / retest
- includes systematic
  bias
- minimizes random
  error

Reliability means many things to many people, but in most contexts, the notion of consistency emerges. A measure is reliable to the degree that it supplies consistent results. **Reliability** is a contributor to validity and is a necessary but not sufficient condition for validity. The relationship between reliability and validity can be simply illustrated with the use of a bathroom scale. If the scale measures your weight correctly (using a concurrent criterion such as a scale known to be accurate), then it is both reliable and valid. If it consistently overweighs you by six pounds, then the scale is reliable but not valid. If the scale measures erratically from time to time, then it is not reliable and therefore cannot be valid.

Reliability is concerned with estimates of the degree to which a measurement is free of random or unstable error. It is not as valuable as validity determination, but it is much easier to assess. Reliable instruments can be used with confidence that transient and situational factors are not interfering. Reliable instruments are robust; they work well at different times under different conditions. This distinction of time and condition is the basis for frequently used perspectives on reliability—**stability, equivalence,** and **internal consistency.**

Stability   A measure is said to be stable if you can secure consistent results with repeated measurements of the same person with the same instrument. An observation procedure would be stable if it gives the same reading on a particular person when repeated one or more times. It is often possible to repeat observations on a subject and to compare them for consistency. When there is much time between measurements, there is a chance for situational factors to change, thereby affecting the observations. This would appear incorrectly as a drop in reliability of the measurement process.

Stability measurement in survey situations is more difficult and less attractive than for observation studies. While you can observe a certain action repeatedly, you usually can resurvey only once. This leads to a test-retest arrangement—with comparisons between the two tests to learn how reliable they are. Difficulties occur beyond the time delay mentioned with the observation study. If the retest is given too quickly, the respondent will remember the answers already given and repeat them. This results in biased reliability indicators. The test-retest process may introduce bias if the respondent becomes savvy to the testing purpose. Or, the first test sensitizes the respondent to the topic, who may then go on to learn more or form new and different opinions before the retest. Finally, opinions change from situational influences between the tests. In these cases, there is a downward bias in the stability scores.

A suggested remedy is to extend the interval between test and retest (from two weeks to a month). While this may help, the researcher must be alert to the chance an outside factor will contaminate the measurement and distort the stability score. Consequently, stability measurement through the test-retest approach has limited applications. More interest has centered on equivalence.

Equivalence   A second perspective on reliability considers how much error may be introduced by different investigators (in observation) or different samples of items being studied (in questioning or scales). Thus, while stability is concerned with personal and situational fluctuations from one time to another, equivalence is concerned with variations at one point in time among observers and samples of items. A good way to test for the equivalence of measurements by different observers is to compare their scoring of the same event.

In studies where a consensus among experts or observers is required, the similarity of the judge's perceptions is sometimes questioned. How does a panel of supervisors render a judgment on merit raises, a new product's packaging, or future business trends? *Interrater* reliability may be used in these cases to correlate the observations or scores of the judges and render an index of how consistent their ratings are.

The major interest with equivalence is typically not how respondents differ from item to item but how well a given set of items will categorize individuals. That is, there may be many differences in response between two samples of items, but if a person is classified the same way by each test, then the tests have good equivalency.

One tests for item sample equivalence by using alternative or *parallel forms* of the same test administered to the same persons simultaneously. The results of the two tests are then correlated. Under this condition, the length of the testing process is likely to affect the subjects' responses through fatigue, and the inferred reliability of the parallel form will be reduced accordingly. Some measurement theorists recommend an interval between administrations to compensate for this problem. This approach, called *delayed* equivalent forms, is a composite of test-retest and the equivalence method. As in test-retest, one would administer form X followed by form Y to half the examinees and form Y followed by form X to the other half to prevent "order-of-presentation" effects.[22]

The test items to be included in any instrument are limited in number. This limitation implies that a sample of items from a content domain has been chosen and another sample producing a similar number will need to be drawn. It is frequently difficult to create this second set. Yet, if the pool is initially large enough, the items may be randomly selected for each instrument. Even with more sophisticated procedures used by publishers of standardized tests, it is rare to find fully equivalent and interchangeable forms.[23]

Internal Consistency   A third approach to reliability uses only one administration of an instrument or test to assess consistency or homogeneity among the items. The *split-half* technique can be used when the measuring tool has many similar questions or statements to which the subject can respond. The instrument is administered and the results are separated by item into even and odd numbers or into two randomly selected halves. If the results of the correlation are high, the instrument is said to have high reliability in an internal consistency sense; however, the longer the length of the test, the higher the reliability. The Spearman–Brown correction formula is used to adjust for the effect of test length and to estimate reliability of the whole test.

A problem with this approach is that the way the test is split may influence the internal consistency coefficient. To remedy this, other indexes are used to secure reliability estimates without splitting the test's items. The Kuder–Richardson Formula 20 and Cronbach's Coefficient Alpha are two frequently used examples. Cronbach's alpha has the most utility for multi-item scales at the interval level of measurement. The KR20 is the method from which alpha was generalized and is used to estimate reliability for dichotomous items. (See Figure 6–3.)

Improving Reliability   One can improve reliability if external sources of variation are minimized and the conditions under which the measurement occurs are standardized. You can achieve enhanced equivalence through improved investigator consistency by using only well-trained, supervised, and motivated persons to conduct the research. Much can be done to improve equivalence by broadening the sample of items used. You can do this by adding similar questions to the questionnaire or adding more observers or occasions to an observation study.

With measurement instruments such as achievement, attitude, or employment tests, we can often increase equivalence by improving the internal consistency of the test. This approach requires the assumption that a high total score reflects high performance and a low total score, low performance. One selects the extreme scorers, say the top 20 percent and bottom 20 percent, for individual analysis. By this process, you can distinguish those items that differentiate high and low scorers. Items that have little discriminatory power can then be dropped from the test.

FIGURE 6–3   Summary of Reliability Estimates

Type	Coefficient	What Is Measured	Methods
Test-retest	Stability	Reliability of a test or instrument inferred from examinee scores. Same test is administered twice to same subjects over an interval of less than six months.	Correlation
Parallel forms	Equivalence	Degree to which alternative forms of the same measure produce same or similar results. Administered simultaneously or with a delay. Interrater estimates of the similarity of judges' observations or scores.	Correlation
Internal consistency	Split-half KR20 Cronbach's alpha	Degree to which instrument items are homogeneous and reflect the same underlying construct(s).	Specialized correlational formulas

Practicality

The scientific requirements of a project call for the measurement process to be reliable and valid, while the operational requirements call for it to be practical. Practicality has been defined as economy, convenience, and interpretability.[24] While this definition refers to the development of educational and psychological tests, it is meaningful for business measurements as well.

Economy   Some trade-off is usually needed between the ideal research project and the budget. Instrument length is one area where economic pressures are quickly felt. More items give more reliability, but in the interest of limiting the interview or observation time (therefore costs), we hold the item number down. The choice of data collection method is also often dictated by economic factors. The use of long distance telephone surveys has been strongly influenced by the rising costs of personal interviewing. In standardized tests, the cost of test materials alone can be such a significant expense that it encourages multiple reuse. Add to this the need for fast and economical scoring, and we see why computer scoring and scanning are attractive.

Convenience   A measuring device passes the *convenience* test if it is easy to administer. A questionnaire with a set of detailed but clear instructions, with examples, is easier to complete correctly than one that lacks these features. In a well-prepared study, it is not uncommon for the interviewer instructions to be several times longer than the interview questions. Naturally, the more complex the concepts, the greater the need for clear and complete instructions. We can also make the instrument easier to administer by giving close attention to its design and layout. Crowding of material, poor reproductions of illustrations, and the carry over of items from one page to the next make completion of the instrument more difficult.

Interpretability   This aspect of practicality is relevant when persons other than the test designers must interpret the results. It is usually but not exclusively found with standardized tests. In such cases, several key pieces of information make interpretation possible:

1. A statement of the functions the test was designed to measure and the procedures by which it was developed.
2. Detailed instructions for administration.
3. Scoring keys and scoring instructions.
4. Norms for appropriate reference groups.
5. Evidence about reliability.
6. Evidence on the intercorrelations of subscores.
7. Evidence on the relationship of the test to other measures.
8. Guides for test use.

THE DEVELOPMENT OF MEASUREMENT TOOLS

Many concepts in business are easy to measure. For example, if you study wages and worker-benefit payments, you find they are stated in dollar amounts and accurate records are kept. In other instances, researchers want to measure concepts such as motivation, sales effectiveness, or market potential. These constructs must be operationally defined by developing a special measurement procedure. One authority suggests that this process involves four steps: (1) concept development, (2) concept specification, (3) selection of indicators, and (4) formation of indexes.[25]

1. **Concept Development:** The first task is to develop the concepts (constructs). When thinking about the Prince Corporation's image, researchers will have some notion that it concerns the company's reputation among various groups. But what aspects might make up such an image? In developing these ideas, one must enumerate the specific ways the corporation may be involved with various groups and what the nature of each of these involvements is.

2. **Concept Specification:** The second task is to break down the original image into its various components. For the Prince Corporation study, the concept of "corporate image" might be divided into four parts:

1. The corporate citizen—how well Prince is thought of as a contributor to the communities in which it has establishments.

2. Ecological responsibility—how well Prince disposes of its waste products and protects the environment.

3. The employer—how well Prince is regarded as a place in which to work.

4. The supplier of consumer needs—how Prince products and services are viewed by consumers.

In place of this intuitive approach, statistical techniques can be used to determine if these concepts and constructs are part of the image. One such study, using cluster analysis, concluded there are six major dimensions of company image: product reputation, employer role, customer treatment, corporate leadership, defense contribution, and concern for individuals.[26]

3. **Indicator Selection:** Once the dimensions have been set, the indicators to measure each concept must be developed. Since there is seldom a perfect or absolute measure, several possibilities should be considered. Indicators can be questions, statistical measures, or other scoring devices.

With the Prince Corporation, measurement of "corporate citizenship" could be achieved by asking a cross section of the public a single question such as:

Which of the following best describes the reputation of the Prince Corporation as a corporate citizen in our community? (Please check one)

____ The company is a leader in these activities.

____ The company is a strong supporter but not a leader in these activities.

____ The company is an average supporter of these activities.

____ The company is a below average supporter of these activities.

This question is a single-scale index of Prince's corporate citizenship. Single-scale indexes are criticized as less reliable than multiple-factor indexes; one item may not capture the variety of dimensions that could be included in a term. Even when the total concept of "corporate citizenship" is in the question, it is not unusual to find people thinking of one dimension or another; for example, charity support or political activity. It is more desirable to specify the number of dimensions to be included in "corporate citizenship" and then combine them into a summary index.

A summary index involves constructing scales to measure each aspect of corporate citizenship. Ask a cross section of the public to rate the Prince Corporation on the following:

How would you rate the Prince Corporation as a:	Good		(please check)		Poor
1. Supporter of civic fund drives	___	___	___	___	___
2. Supporter of higher education	___	___	___	___	___
3. Supporter of good local government	___	___	___	___	___
4. Supporter of civic development projects	___	___	___	___	___

4. **Formation of Indexes:** When there are several dimensions of a concept, or different measures for each dimension, it may be desirable to combine them into a single index. It is reasonable to believe that each "individual indicator has only a probability relation to what we really want to know."[27] Any single indicator may not be a fair representation of what is being measured. Use of more than one indicator lends stability to the scores and improves their validity.

A simple way to achieve such improvements is to assign scale values to the responses and then combine the scores. By combining the four scale items on the Prince Corporation as a corporate citizen, a single index is created. Assigning a value to each response, ranging from 1 for a poor evaluation to a 5 for a good one, then averaging the scores gives a more reliable measure of the company's citizenship image than does a single question.

Additional sets of scales can be devised to measure how the Prince Corporation is viewed on ecological responsibility and employer image and as a supplier of consumer needs. These sets of scales could also be combined into summary scores. Finally, summary measures for the four dimensions of corporate image might be again combined, and even weighted, to arrive at an overall score that could be called the corporate image index. This index, and its various subscores, might be compared to indices of other corporations that have been similarly measured.

CLOSE-UP

Earlier, Jason Henry had agreed to send the executive director at White Ice some useful tools for measuring job satisfaction and motivation. In reviewing his files, he found the publication:

> Martin Patchen, *Some Questionnaire Measures of Employee Motivation and Morale*, Monograph No. 41 (Ann Arbor, Mich.: Institute for Social Research, University of Michigan, 1965).

The table of contents showed that the monograph included indices on:

Interest in Work Innovation

Job Motivation.

Acceptance of Job Changes.

Willingness to Disagree with Supervisors.

Identification with the Work Organization.

Patchen's study had been conducted at five geographically separate units of the Tennessee Valley Authority, three divisions of an electronics company, and five departments of an appliance manufacturing company. The procedure for developing the measures was first to hold a number of informal interviews with supervisory and nonsupervisory employees. From the knowledge acquired, the researchers constructed the questions. These were then pretested and revised twice on separate groups of TVA employees. Out of this process came a six-item questionnaire on interest in work innovation shown in Figure 6–4. This instrument and the others were completed by employees of the three companies. Reliability of the Index of Interest in Work Innovation was measured by a test-retest of individual questions. The retest was done one month after the first test. Correlating the test-retest scores question by question gave the follow-

ing results (See Chapter 16 for more information on computing a correlation coefficient):

Question	r
Q1	.72
Q2	.72
Q3	.64
Q4	.67
Q5	.54
Q6	.85

The researchers measured criterion-based validity by comparing worker scores on the six questions to ratings of the same workers by their supervisors. Supervisors were asked to "think of specific instances where employees in their units had suggested new or better ways of doing the job. They then ranked employees they personally knew on 'looking out for new ideas.' "[28] The median correlation between index scores and the supervisor ratings was about .35. At TVA, where there was an active suggestion system in operation, they also found that the index scores of suggestors were significantly higher than those of nonsuggestors.

Construct validity was evaluated by comparing scores on the Interest in Work Innovation Index to other job-related variables. Group mean scores on the index were computed for 90 work groups at TVA. These means were then correlated with group scores on other variables that were hypothesized to relate to interest in innovation. The results are shown in Table 6–1.

The researchers concluded, "The Index of Interest in Work Innovation, while a rough one, shows adequate reliability and sufficient evidence of validity to warrant its use in making rough distinctions among groups of people (or among units)."[29] In addition, they tested a short version of the index (items 1, 5, and 6) and found its validity to be almost equal to that of the longer form.

Having reviewed Patchen's research study with its derived indices, Jason forwarded what he

(continued)

FIGURE   6–4   Interest in Work Innovation Index*

1. In your kind of work, if a person tries to change his usual way of doing things, how does it generally turn out?
   (1) ___ Usually turns out worse; the tried and true methods work best in my work.
   (3) ___ Usually doesn't make much difference.
   (5) ___ Usually turns out better; our methods need improvement.

2. Some people prefer doing a job in pretty much the same way because this way they can count on always doing a good job. Others like to go out of their way in order to think up new ways of doing things. How is it with you on your job?
   (1) ___ I always prefer doing things pretty much in the same way.
   (2) ___ I mostly prefer doing things pretty much in the same way.
   (4) ___ I mostly prefer doing things in new and different ways.
   (5) ___ I always prefer doing things in new and different ways.

3. How often do you try out, on your own, a better or faster way of doing something on the job?
   (5) ___ Once a week or more often.
   (4) ___ Two or three times a month.
   (3) ___ About once a month.
   (2) ___ Every few months.
   (1) ___ Rarely or never.

4. How often do you get chances to try out your own ideas on the job, either before or after checking with your supervisor?
   (5) ___ Several times a week or more.
   (4) ___ About once a week.
   (3) ___ Several times a month.
   (2) ___ About once a month.
   (1) ___ Less than once a month.

5. In my kind of job, it's usually better to let your supervisor worry about new or better ways of doing things.
   (1) ___ Strongly agree.
   (2) ___ Mostly agree.
   (4) ___ Mostly disagree.
   (5) ___ Strongly disagree.

6. How many times in the past year have you suggested to your supervisor a different or better way of doing something on the job?
   (1) ___ Never had occasion to do this during the past year.
   (2) ___ Once or twice.
   (3) ___ About three times.
   (4) ___ About five times.
   (5) ___ Six to ten times.
   (6) ___ More than ten times had occasion to do this during the past year.

*Numbers in parentheses preceding each response category indicate the score assigned to each response.
SOURCE: Martin Patchen, *Some Questionnaire Measures of Employee Motivation and Morale,* Monograph No. 41 (Ann Arbor, Mich.: Institute for Social Research, The University of Michigan, 1965), pp. 15–16.

(continued)

TABLE 6–1   **Relation of Scores on Interest in Work Innovation Index* to Scores on Other Job-Related Variables† for 90 Work Groups at TVA (Pearson product-moment correlation coefficient, *r*)**

Variable Name	
1. Job difficulty	.44‡
2. Identification with own occupation	.39‡
3. Control over work methods	.29‡
4. Perceived opportunity for achievement	.28‡
5. Feedback on performance	.19
6. Control over goals in work	.13
7. Need for achievement§	.06
8. Pressure from peers to do a good job	−.05
9. General job motivation	.36‡
10. Willingness to disagree with supervisors	.36‡
11. Acceptance of changes in work situation	.12
12. Identification with TVA	.00
13. Overall satisfaction (with pay, promotion, supervisors, and peers)	.21‖

*The shorter three-item Index B was used for these correlations.

†Variables listed are all indices; each index is composed of several specific questions.

‡$p < .01$, 2-tailed t-test.

§This is the Achievement Risk Preference Scale developed by P. O'Conner and J. W. Atkinson (1960).

‖$p < .05$, 2-tailed t-test.

SOURCE: Martin Patchen, *Some Questionnaire Measures of Employee Motivation and Morale,* Monograph No. 41 (North Ann Arbor, Mich.: Institute for Social Research, The University of Michigan, 1965), p. 24.

found to the symphony director. She would decide if it was adaptable or if she should develop her own instrument. Managers and researchers frequently assume they need a device tailored to their unique situation. This decision can be costly and time-consuming. Reliability testing may be ignored and validity assessments may be confined to impressions about content. Typically, there is no comparable evidence from other studies by which to calibrate the findings.

If Jason's recommendation proves to be inadequate, a further search of existing measures will reveal many established ones that might fit the director's needs. Most are copyrighted but available from commercial sources.

Summary   While people measure things casually in daily life, research measurement is more precise and controlled. In measurement, one settles for measuring properties of the objects rather than the objects themselves. An event is measured in terms of its duration. What happened during it, who was involved, where it occurred, and so forth are all properties of the event. To be more precise, what are measured are indicants of the properties. Thus, for duration, one measures the number of hours and minutes recorded. For what happened, one uses some system to classify types of activities that occurred. Measurement typically uses some sort of scale to classify or quantify the data collected.

There are four scale types. In increasing order of power, they are nominal, ordinal, interval, and ratio. Nominal scales classify without indicating order, distance, or unique origin. Ordinal scales show magnitude relationships of more than and less than but have no distance or unique origin. Interval scales have both order and distance but no unique origin. Ratio scales possess all features.

Instruments may yield incorrect readings of an indicant for many reasons. These may be classified according to error sources: (1) the respondent or subject, (2) situational factors, (3) the measurer, and (4) the instrument.

Sound measurement must meet the tests of validity, reliability, and practicality. Validity is the most critical and reveals the degree to which an instrument measures what it is supposed to measure. Three forms of validity are used to evaluate measurement scales. Content validity exists to the degree that a measure provides an adequate reflection of the topic under study. Its determination is primarily judgmental and intuitive. Criterion-related validity relates to our ability to predict some outcome or estimate the existence of some current condition. Construct validity is the most complex and abstract. A measure has construct validity to the degree that it conforms to predicted correlations of other theoretical propositions.

A measure is reliable if it provides consistent results. Reliability is a partial contributor to validity, but a measurement tool may be reliable without being valid. Three forms of reliability are stability, equivalence, and internal consistency. A measure meets the fourth criterion, practicality, if it is economical, convenient, and interpretable.

Development of measurement tools can be viewed as a four-stage process: (1) concept development, (2) concept specification, (3) selection of observable indicators, and (4) formation of indicators into indices.

Key Terms	interval scales	reliability
	measurement	equivalence
	nominal scales	internal consistency
	objects	stability
	ordinal scales	validity
	properties	construct
	ratio scales	content
		criterion-related

Discussion Questions

1. What can we measure about the four objects listed below? Be as specific as possible.
    a. Laundry detergent.
    b. Employees.
    c. Factory output.
    d. Job satisfaction.

2. *a.* What are the essential differences among nominal, ordinal, interval, and ratio scales?

   b. How do these differences affect the statistical analysis techniques we can use?

3. Below are listed some objects of varying degrees of abstraction. Suggest properties of each of these objects that can be measured by each of the four basic types of scales.

   a. Store customers.

   b. Voter attitudes.

   c. Hardness of steel alloys.

   d. Preference for a particular common stock.

   e. Profitability of various divisions in a company.

4. What are the four major sources of measurement error? Illustrate by example how each of these might affect measurement results in a face-to-face interview situation.

5. Do you agree or disagree with the following statements? Explain.

   a. Validity is more critical to measurement than is reliability.

   b. Content validity is the most difficult type of validity to determine.

   c. A valid measurement is reliable, but a reliable measurement may not be valid.

   d. Stability and equivalence are essentially the same thing.

6. You have been asked to design an instrument by which students can evaluate the quality and value of their various courses. How might you try to assure that your instrument has:

   a. Stability.

   b. Equivalence.

   c. Internal consistency.

   d. Content validity.

   e. Predictive validity.

   f. Construct validity.

7. A book titled *The 100 Best Companies to Work for in America* has just been published. In their study of companies, the authors chose five dimensions and rated each company on them, giving one to five stars to a firm on each dimension. What five dimensions would you use if you had designed their rating system?

8. You have been asked to develop an index of student morale at your school.

   a. What constructs or concepts might you employ?

   b. Choose several of the major concepts and specify their dimensions.

   c. Select observable indicators that you might use to measure these dimensions.

   d. How would you compile these various dimensions into a single index?

   e. How would you judge the reliability and/or validity of these measurements?

Reference Notes

1. Fred N. Kerlinger, *Foundations of Behavioral Research,* 3rd ed. (New York: Holt, Rinehart & Winston, 1986), p. 396; and S. Stevens, "Measurement, Statistics, and the Schemapiric View," *Science,* August 1968, p. 3844.

2. W. S. Torgerson, *Theory and Method of Scaling* (New York: John Wiley & Sons, 1958), p. 19.

3. We assume the reader has had an introductory statistics course in which measures of central tendency such as arithmetic mean, median, and mode have been treated. Similarly, we assume familiarity with measures of dispersion such as the standard deviation, range, and interquartile range. For a brief review of these concepts, refer to Chapter 14 or see an introductory statistics text.

4. While this might intuitively seem to be the case, consider that one might prefer *a* over *b, b* over *c,* yet *c* over *a.* These results cannot be scaled ordinally because there is apparently more than one dimension involved.

5. L. L. Thurstone, *The Measurement of Values* (Chicago: University of Chicago Press, 1959).

6. Parametric tests are appropriate when the measurement is interval or ratio and when we can accept certain assumptions about the underlying distributions of the data with which we are working. Nonparametric tests usually involve much weaker assumptions about measurement scales (nominal and ordinal), and the assumptions about the underlying distribution of the population are fewer and less restrictive. More on these tests is found in Chapters 14, 15, 16, and Appendix E.

7. Sidney Siegel, *Nonparametric Statistics for the Behavioral Sciences* (New York: McGraw-Hill, 1956), p. 32.

8. Norman A. Anderson, "Scales and Statistics: Parametric and Nonparametric," *Psychological Bulletin* 58, no. 4, pp. 315–16.

9. Kerlinger, *Foundations,* p. 403.

10. See Chapter 7 for a discussion of the differential scale.

11. See Chapters 15 and 16 for a discussion of these procedures.

12. The exception involves the creation of a dummy variable for use in regression or discriminant equation. A nonmetric variable is transformed into a metric variable through the assignment of a 0 or 1 and used in a predictive equation.

13. Claire Selltiz, Lawrence S. Wrightsman, and Stuart W. Cook, *Research Methods in Social Relations,* 3rd ed. (New York: Holt, Rinehart & Winston, 1976), pp. 164–69.

14. Robert L. Thorndike and Elizabeth Hagen, *Measurement and Evaluation in Psychology and Education,* 3rd ed. (New York: John Wiley & Sons, 1969), p. 5.

15. Examples of other conceptualizations of validity are factorial validity, job-analytic validity, synthetic validity, rational validity, and statistical conclusion validity.

16. Thomas D. Cook and Donald T. Campbell, "The Design and Conduct of Quasi Experiments and True Experiments in Field Settings," in *Handbook of Industrial and Organizational Psychology,* ed. Marvin D. Dunnette, (Chicago: Rand McNally, 1976), p. 223.

17. *Standards for Educational and Psychological Tests and Manuals* (Washington, D.C.: American Psychological Association, 1974), p. 26.

18. Wayne F. Cascio, *Applied Psychology in Personnel Management* (Reston, Va.: Reston Publishing, 1982), p. 149.

19. Thorndike and Hagen, *Measurement,* p. 168.

20. See, for example, Cascio, *Applied Psychology,* pp. 146–47; and Edward G. Carmines 1and Richard A. Zeller, *Reliability and Validity Assessment* (Beverly Hills, Calif.: Sage Publications, 1979), pp. 48–50.

21. Emanuel J. Mason and William J. Bramble, *Understanding and Conducting Research* (New York: McGraw-Hill, 1989), pp. 260–63.

22. Cascio, *Applied Psychology,* pp. 135–36.

23. Mason and Bramble, *Understanding and Conducting Research,* p. 268.

24. Thorndike and Hagen, *Measurement,* p. 199.

25. Paul F. Lazarsfeld, "Evidence and Inference in Social Research," in *Evidence and Inference,* ed. David Lerner (Glencoe, Ill.: The Free Press, 1950), pp. 108–17.

26. Reuben Cohen, "The Measurement of Corporate Images," in *The Corporation and its Publics,* ed. John W. Riley, Jr. (New York: John Wiley & Sons, 1963), pp. 48–63.

27. Lazarsfeld, "Evidence and Inference," p. 112.

28. Martin Patchen, *Some Questionnaire Measures of Employee Motivation and Morale,* Monograph No. 41 (Ann Arbor, Mich.: Institute for Social Research, University of Michigan, 1965), p. 17.

29. Ibid., p. 25.

Suggested Readings

1. Cascio, Wayne F. *Applied Psychology in Personnel Management,* 4th ed. Englewood Cliffs, NJ: Prentice Hall, 1990.

2. Cook, Thomas D., and Donald T. Campbell. "The Design and Conduct of Quasi-Experiments and True Experiments in Field Settings." In *Handbook of Industrial and Organizational Psychology,* ed. Marvin D. Dunnette. Chicago: Rand McNally, 1976, chap. 7.

3. Guilford, J. P. *Psychometric Methods.* 2nd ed. New York: McGraw-Hill, 1954.

4. Kerlinger, Fred N. *Foundations of Behavioral Research.* 3rd ed. New York: Holt, Rinehart & Winston, 1986, chaps. 25, 26, and 27.

5. Newmark, C. S. *Major Psychological Assessment Instruments.* Boston: Allyn and Bacon, 1989.

6. Nunnally, J. C. *Psychometric Theory.* 2nd ed. New York: McGraw-Hill, 1978.

7. Thorndike, Robert L., and Elizabeth Hagen. *Measurement and Education in Psychology and Education.* 3rd ed. New York: John Wiley & Sons, 1969.

7 SCALING DESIGN

 FINDING
YOUR WAY

BRINGING RESEARCH TO LIFE

They boarded the sleek corporate jet in Palm Beach and were taken aft to meet with the general manager of MindWriter division, who was seated at a conference table that austerely held one sheaf of papers and a white telephone.

"I'm Jean-Claude Malraison," the general manager said. "Myra, please sit here . . . and you must be Jason Henry. On the flight up from Caracas I read your proposal for the CompleteCare project, and I am going to take my staff's word that it is OK, except maybe I don't like the schedule. Here is your contract, which I intend to sign if you answer one question to my satisfaction about the schedule.

"The rules are, I took marketing research in college and didn't like it, so you talk fast, straight, and plainly unless we both decide we need to get technical. If the phone rings, ignore it and keep talking. When you answer my one question I put you off the plane in the first Florida city that has a commercial flight back to . . . to . . ."

"This is Palm Beach, Jean-Claude," said the steward.

"We'll let you off somewhere you can get home from. Fair enough?"

"Yes," said Jason and Myra.

"What I don't like is that you are going to hold everything up so you can develop a scale for the questionnaire. Scaling is what I didn't like in marketing research. It is complicated and it takes too much time. Why can't you use some of the scales our marketing people have been using? Why do you have to reinvent the wheel?" The manager jabbed a finger toward Myra.

"Your research staff agrees with us that it would be inappropriate to adopt surveys developed for use in your consumer products line," said Myra smoothly.

"OK. Computers are not the same as toaster ovens and VCRs. Gotcha. Jason, so what is going to be different about the scales you intend to develop?"

"When we held focus groups with your custom-ers, they continually referred to the need for your product service to 'meet expectations' or 'exceed expectations.' The hundreth time we heard this we realized . . ."

"It's our division credo, 'Underpromise and exceed expectations.'"

"Well, virtually none of the scales developed for customer satisfaction deal with expectations. We want a scale that ranges in five steps from 'Met few expectations' to 'Exceeded expectations,' but we don't know what to name the in-between intervals so that the psychological spacing is equal between increments. We think 'Met many expectations' and 'Met most expectations' and 'Fully met expectations' will be OK, but we want to be sure."

"You are not being fussy there, are you, Jason?"

"No. Because of the way you are running your service operation, we want great precision and reliability."

"Justify that, please, Myra."

"Well, Jean-Claude, besides setting up your own repair force, you have contracted with an outside organization to provide repairs in certain areas, with the intention after six months of comparing the performance of the inside and outside repair organizations and giving the future work to whomever performs better. We feel that such an important decision, which involves the job security of your employees, must have full credibility."

"I can accept that. Good." The manager scribbled a signature on the contract. "You'll receive this contract in three days, after it has wended its way past the paper-pushers. Meantime, you settle for a handshake. Congratulations."

"We can put them down in Orlando," said the steward.

"No," said Jean-Claude. "We are only five minutes out. Turn the plane around and put these folks out where they got on. They can start working this afternoon . . . Gosh, is that the beach out there? It looks great. I've got to get some sun one of these days."

"You do look pale," said Myra, sympathetically.

"*Fais gaffe, tu m'fais mal!*" he muttered under his breath.

THE NATURE OF SCALING

Business research concepts (constructs) are frequently complex and abstract while the available measurement tools can be crude or imprecise. We want a valid measurement, but we get something between the *true score* and the *test score*. When the object is a concrete concept and the measurement tool is standardized, the variation between the true and test scores will be small. This is like the accuracy you would expect in measuring the length of a table with a yardstick. If the concept is abstract (attitudes toward various institutions) and the measurement tool is not standardized (questions about attitudes), then you will not be confident that the test results reflect true scores. This is comparable to measuring the table using your forearm.

This chapter covers procedures that can help measure abstract concepts more accurately. We concentrate on the problems of measuring attitudes and opinions. Similar principles hold for measuring in the physical, psychological, or organizational realms.

Scaling Defined

assigning #s to properties

Scaling is a "procedure for the assignment of numbers (or other symbols) to a property of objects in order to impart some of the characteristics of numbers to the properties in question."[1] Thus, one assigns a number scale to the various levels of heat and cold and calls it a thermometer.

What Is Scaled?   Procedurally, we assign numbers to *indicants* of the properties of objects. If you want to measure the temperature of the air, you know that a property of temperature is that its variation leads to an expansion or contraction of materials such as mercury. You devise a glass tube arrangement with mercury. It provides an indicant of the temperature by the rise and fall of the mercury column in the tube as temperatures change.

In another context, you might devise a scale to measure the durability (property) of paint. You secure a machine with an attached scrub brush that applies a predetermined amount of pressure as it scrubs. You then count the number of brush strokes that it takes to wear through a 10-mil thickness of paint. The scrub count is the indicant of the paint's durability. Or you may judge a person's supervisory capacity (property) by asking a peer group to rate that person on various questions (indicants) that you devise.

Scale Classification

Scales may be discussed in several ways, but we cover those approaches that are of greatest value for business research.[2] Selection of a scale requires decisions in six key areas.

Study Objective   A scale may be designed to (1) measure the characteristics of the respondents who complete it or (2) use these respondents as judges of the objects or stimuli presented to them. You might present people with a scale on government regulatory programs to capture their approval or disapproval of each program. If the respondents themselves are of primary interest, you might combine each person's answers to form an indicator of that person's conservatism or political orientation. The emphasis here is on measuring attitudinal differences among people. With the second study objective, you use the same data but are interested in how people view different government programs. In this instance, the emphasis is on the differences among regulatory programs.

Response Scales   Scales may be classified as *categorical* and *comparative*. These approaches are also known as *rating* and *ranking*, respectively. **Categorical (rating) scales** are used when respondents score some object without direct reference to other objects. They may be asked to rate the styling of new autos on a five-point scale. In **comparative (ranking) scaling,** the respondents are asked to choose which one of a pair of cars has more attractive styling.

Degree of Preference   Scaling approaches may also involve *preference* measurement or *nonpreference* evaluation. In the former, respondents are asked to choose the object each favors or solution each would prefer. In the latter, they are asked to judge which object has more of some characteristic or which solution takes the most resources, without reflecting any personal preference toward objects or solutions.

Scale Properties   Scaling approaches may also be viewed in terms of the scale properties possessed by each. Chapter 6 said scales may be classified as nominal, ordinal, interval, or ratio. The assumptions underlying each scale determine how the scale may be used statistically.

Number of Dimensions   Scales are either unidimensional or multidimensional. With a **unidimensional scale,** one seeks to measure only one attribute of the respondent or object. One measure of employee potential is promotability. It is a single dimension. Several items may be used to measure this dimension and by combining them into a single measure, employees may be placed along a linear continuum of promotability. **Multidimensional scaling** recognizes that an object might be better described in attribute space of n dimensions rather than on a unidimensional continuum. The employee promotability variable might be better expressed by three distinct dimensions—managerial performance, technical performance, and teamwork.

Scale Construction   We can classify scales by the methods used to build them. According to one view, there are five scale design techniques.[3] One is the *arbitrary* approach in which the scale is developed on an ad hoc basis. Such scales may measure the concepts for which they have been designed, but we have little evidence of this. Nevertheless, this is a pervasive technique.

A second approach is the *consensus* scale. A panel of judges evaluates the items to be included in the instrument based on relevance to the topic area and lack of ambiguity. A third technique is the *item analysis* approach. Individual items are developed for a test that is given to a group of respondents. After administering the tests, total scores are calculated. Individual items are then analyzed to determine which ones discriminate between persons or objects with high total scores and low total scores.

Cumulative scales are chosen for their conformance to a ranking of items with ascending and descending discriminating power. In such a scale, the endorsement of an item representing an extreme position results in the endorsement of all items of less extreme positions. Finally, *factor* scales are constructed from intercorrelations of items. Common factors account for the relationships. The relationships are measured statistically through factor analysis or cluster analysis.

Two of the six issues influencing in scale selection, response methods and scale construction techniques, form the basis for the remainder of the chapter.

RESPONSE METHODS

In the last chapter, we said asking questions is a widely used stimulus for measuring concepts. A manager may be asked his or her views concerning an employee. The respondent replies: "good machinist," "a troublemaker," "union activist," "reliable," or a "fast worker with a poor record of attendance." These answers represent different frames of reference for evaluating the worker. Such variety of response is often of limited research value.

Two approaches improve the usefulness of such replies. First, various properties may be separated out and the respondent asked to judge each specific facet. Here, several questions are substituted for a single one. Second, we substitute structuring devices for the free response reply pattern. To quantify dimensions that are essentially qualitative, rating and/or ranking scales are used.

Rating Scales

One uses rating scales to judge properties of objects without reference to other similar objects. These ratings may be in such forms as "like-dislike," "approve-indifferent-disapprove," or other classifications using even more categories. There is little conclusive support for choosing a three-point scale over scales with five or more points. One argument is that more points on a scale provide an opportunity for greater sensitivity of measurement and extraction of variance. The most widely used scales range from three to seven points, and it does not seem to make much difference which number is used.[4]

The **graphic rating scale** is a common and simple form to use. The rater checks his or her response at any point along a continuum. An example of one element of such a scale is the statement found in an employee evaluation form:

"How well does the employee get along with co-workers?"
(place an X at the position along the line
that best reflects your judgment.)

Always gets along |_____| Never gets along

Usually, the respondent's score is a measure of length (millimeters) from either end point.

The second scale also illustrates the graphic principle but is not a good scale for several reasons. Only three of the four positions are likely to be used. Rarely will the choice "always at odds with someone" be used. Another deficiency concerns the vagueness of "sometimes" and "often." The meaning of these terms depends upon each rater's frame of reference so completely that the statement might be challenged on its equivalency and stability. Then, there is "always," which implies no exceptions. A final problem is the graphics are set up in such a way that respondents may feel constrained to brackets along the line. Other graphic rating scales use pictures, icons, or other visuals to communicate with the rater.

"How well does the employee get along with co-workers?"
(Please check)

|_____|_____|_____|

| Always gets | Sometimes has | Often has | Always at odds |
| along well | trouble | trouble | with someone |

Several other rating scale variants are presented next with various lengths of scales.

Variation 1.   Boxes replace the line and make it more certain that respondents will choose only one of four points.

☐ | ☐ | ☐ | ☐
Always gets	Sometimes	Often has	Always at
along well	has trouble	trouble	odds with
			someone

Variation 2.   Two polar positions shown with a number scale used to show degree of opinion.

Gets along well ☐ ☐ ☐ ☐ ☐ Has trouble
1   2   3   4   5

Other Variations.   Shown on the next page are examples of phrasing used to indicate degrees of judgment in surveys.[5]

Three-Point Scales

Greater _____	Equal _____	Less _____
Yes _____	Depends _____	No _____
Above		Below
average _____	Average _____	average _____

Four-Point Scales

Many _____	Some _____	Few _____	None _____
Excellent _____	Good _____	Fair _____	Poor _____
	Next	Next	
Highest _____	highest _____	lowest _____	Lowest _____

Five-Point Scales

Strongly		Un-	Dis-	Strongly dis-
approve _____	Approve _____	decided _____	approve _____	approve _____
Much	Somewhat		Somewhat	Not
greater _____	greater _____	Equal _____	less _____	at all _____
			Dislike	
Like very	Like some-		some-	Dislike very
much _____	what _____	Neutral _____	what _____	much _____

Longer Scales

(Semantic   Good   _____ : : : : : : _____   Bad
differential)

Modern   _____ : : : : : : _____   Old-fashioned

Stapel Scale   ☐ ☐ ☐   ☐ ☐ ☐
                      −   Taste   +

A second form, the **itemized scale,** presents a series of statements from which respondents select one as best reflecting their evaluation. These judgments are ordered in a progression of a property. It is typical to use five to seven categories, with each being defined or illustrated in words. An example is:

How well does the employee get along with co-workers?
___ Almost always involved in some friction or argument with a co-worker.
___ Often at odds with one or more co-workers. The frequency of involvement is clearly above that of the average worker.
___ Sometimes gets involved in friction. The frequency of involvement is about equal to that of the average worker.
___ Infrequently becomes involved in friction with others, definitely less often than most workers.
___ Almost never gets involved in friction situations with other workers.

This form is more difficult to develop, and the statements may not say exactly what the respondent would like to express. On the other hand, it provides more information and meaning to the rater; itemized scales increase reliability because more detailed statements help respondents develop and hold the same frame of reference while they fill them out.

Even with rating scales, there must be some criterion that the respondent uses to judge one object over another. This criterion is typically not explicit, allowing for each person's subjective judgment. In the *comparative rating scale,* this criterion is made explicit. The subject is asked to compare against some experience standard. Job evaluation rating forms use a standard job as the basis for rating others. Job interview analysis forms sometimes specify that the rater compare the interviewee with the typical recruit that the company has hired in the past.

Problems in Using Rating Scales   The value of rating scales for measurement purposes depends upon the assumption that a person can and will make good judgments. Before accepting respondents' ratings, we should consider their tendencies to make errors. Three of the most common are the errors of leniency, central tendency, and halo effect.[6]

The error of **leniency** occurs when a respondent is either an "easy rater" or a "hard rater." The latter is an error of negative leniency. Raters are inclined to score those people higher whom they know well and with whom they are ego-involved. There is also the opposite of this situation—where one rates acquaintances lower because one is aware of the leniency danger and attempts to counteract it. A way to deal with positive leniency is to design the rating scale to anticipate it. An example might be an asymmetrical graphic scale that has only one unfavorable descriptive term and four favorable terms (poor—fair—good—very good—excellent). The scale designer expects that the mean ratings will be near "good" and that there will be a symmetrical distribution about that point.

Raters are reluctant to give extreme judgments, and this fact accounts for the error of **central tendency.** This is most often seen when the rater does not know the person being rated. Efforts to counteract this error are to (1) adjust the strength of descriptive adjectives, (2) space the intermediate descriptive phrases farther apart in graphic scales, (3) provide smaller differences in meaning between steps near the ends of the scale than between the steps near the center, and (4) use more points in the scale.

The **halo effect** is the systematic bias that the rater introduces by carrying over a generalized impression of the subject from one rating to another. You expect the student who does well on the first question of an examination to do well on the second. You conclude a report is good because you like its form, or you believe someone is intelligent because you agree with them. Halo is a pervasive error. It is especially difficult to avoid when the property being studied is not clearly defined, not easily observed, not frequently discussed, involves reactions with others, or is a trait of high moral importance.[7] One way to counteract the halo effect is to rate one trait at a time for all subjects or to have one trait per page.

Rating scales are widely used in business research and generally deserve their popularity. The results obtained with careful use compare favorably with other methods. Rating scales typically require less time. They are interesting and have a wider range of application than most other methods. In addition, they may be used with several properties or variables.

Ranking Scales

In **ranking scales,** the subject directly compares two or more objects and makes choices among them. Frequently, the respondent is asked to select one as the "best" or the "preferred." When dealing with only two choices, this approach is satisfactory, but it often results in "vote-splitting" when more than two choices are found. For example, respondents are asked to select the most preferred among three or more models of a product. Assume that 40 percent choose model A, 30 percent choose model B, and 30 percent choose model C. The question is, "Which is the preferred model?" The analyst would be taking a risk to suggest that A is most preferred. Perhaps that interpretation is correct, but 60 percent of the respondents chose some model other than A. Perhaps all B and C voters would place A last, preferring either B or C to it. This ambiguity can be avoided by using paired comparisons or rank-ordering techniques.

Method of Paired Comparisons   With this technique, the respondent can express attitudes unambiguously by choosing between two objects. Typical of **paired comparisons** would be a product-testing study where a new flavor of soft drink is tested against an established brand. Another example might be to compare two bargaining proposals available to union negotiators. Generally, there are more than two stimuli to judge, resulting in a potentially tedious task for respondents. The number of judgments required in a paired comparison is

$$N = \frac{n(n-1)}{2}$$

where

N = Number of judgments.
n = Number of stimuli or objects to be judged.

If 15 suggestions for bargaining proposals are available to a union, 105 paired comparisons can be made with them.

Paired comparing runs the risk that respondents will tire to the point that they give ill-considered answers or refuse to continue. Opinions differ about what the upper limit is, but five or six stimuli are not unreasonable when the respondent has other questions to answer. If the interview consists only of comparisons, as many as 15 stimuli may be compared.

Reducing the number of comparisons per respondent without reducing the number of objects being studied can lighten this burden. You can present each respondent with only a sample of the stimuli. In using this method, each pair of objects must be compared an equal number of times. Another procedure is to choose a few objects that are believed to cover the range of attractiveness at equal intervals. All other stimuli are then compared to these few standard objects. If 36 employees are to be judged, 4 may be selected as standards and the others divided into four groups of eight each. Within each group, the eight are compared to each other. Then the 32 are individually compared to each of the 4 standard persons. This reduces the number of comparisons from 630 to 240.

Paired-comparison data may be treated in several ways. If there is substantial consistency, we will find that if *A* is preferred to *B,* and *B* to *C,* then *A* will be

TABLE 7-1   Response Patterns of 200 Union Members' Paired Comparisons of Five Suggestions for Union Bargaining Proposal Priorities

	Suggestion				
	A	B	C	D	E
A	—	164*	138	50	70
B	36	—	54	14	30
C	62	146	—	32	50
D	150	186	168	—	118
E	130	170	150	82	—
Total	378	666	510	178	268
Rank order	3	1	2	5	4
M_p	0.478	0.766	0.610	0.278	0.368
Z_j	−0.060	0.730	0.280	−0.590	−0.340
R_j	0.530	1.320	0.870	0.000	0.250

*Interpret this cell, 164 members preferred suggestion B (column) to suggestion A (row)

consistently preferred to C. This condition of transitivity need not always be true but should occur most of the time. When it does, take the total number of preferences among the comparisons as the score for that stimulus. Assume a union bargaining committee is considering five major demand proposals. The committee would like to know how the union membership ranks these proposals. One option would be to ask a sample of the members to pair-compare the personal suggestions. A sample of 200 members might express the views shown by the hypothetical data found in Table 7–1. With a rough comparison of the total preferences for each option, it is apparent that B is the most popular. The rank order for the suggestions is shown.

While a paired comparison provides ordinal data, there is a method for converting it to an interval scale. Known as the Law of Comparative Judgment, it involves converting the frequencies of preferences (such as in Table 7–1) into a table of proportions that are then transformed into a Z matrix by referring to the table of areas under the normal curve.[8] Guilford's procedure is easier to compute and secures essentially the same results. It is called the *composite-standard* method and is illustrated here.[9]

With the composite-standard method we can develop an interval scale from paired comparisons by the following steps. First, using the data in Table 7–1, we calculate the column means. Using column A data and the equation:

$$M_p = \frac{C + 0.5N}{nN} = \frac{378 + 0.5(200)}{5(200)} = 0.478$$

where

M_p = The mean proportion of the columns.
C = The total number of choices for a given suggestion.

Guilford notes, "The correction $0.5N$ in the numerator is for the assumed number of choices the stimulus would have received if it had been compared with itself . . . It is assumed that the standard is the composite of all the stimuli in the series and that M_p is the proportion of times any given stimulus is chosen in preference to that standard."[10] These calculated means are shown in Table 7–1.

The Z values for M_p are secured from the normal curve tables. When the proportion (M_p) is less than 0.5, the Z value is negative, while all proportions over 0.5 are positive.[11] These values are also shown in Table 7–1 as Z_j. Since this scale is an interval scale, the zero is an arbitrary value. We eliminate negative scale values by giving the value of zero to the lowest scale value and then adding the absolute value of this lowest scale value to all other scale items. This scale (R_j) is shown in Figure 7–1.

Method of Rank Order   Another comparative scaling approach is to ask respondents to **rank order** their choices. This method is faster than paired comparisons and is usually easier and more motivating to the respondent. With 7 items, it takes 21 paired comparisons to complete the task while the simple ranking of 7 is easier. With ranking, there is no transitivity problem where A is preferred to B, B to C, but C preferred to A.

A drawback is the number of stimuli that can be handled by this method. Fewer than 5 objects can be ranked easily, but respondents may grow careless in ranking 10 or more items. In addition, the rank ordering is still an ordinal scale with all of its limitations.

There are several simple ways to combine rankings into an overall index. Means cannot properly be calculated, but it is possible to compute medians. Some suggest that the sum of rank values will probably give the best simple indication of composite ranking of stimuli.[12] If there are many respondents, it is possible to translate ordinal rank data into an interval scale. Two general methods are the *normalized-rank* and the *comparative-judgment*.[13] The latter is similar to scaling from paired comparisons. Guilford suggests a *composite-standard* approach similar to that previously discussed.[14]

A complete ranking is sometimes not needed. We secure more cooperation by asking for the first k ranks. Respondents may be asked to judge 25 automobile designs by ranking only their first five choices. To secure a simple ranking of all designs, we total rank values received by each model. We can also develop an interval scale of these data by using either a paired-comparison or composite-standard solution.[15]

FIGURE 7–1
Interval Scale Derived from Paired-Comparison Data Using the Composite-Standard Method

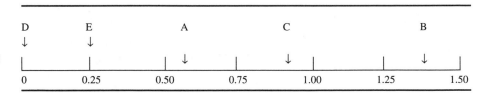

The Method of Successive Intervals   Neither the paired-comparison nor the rank-order method is particularly useful when there are many items. The method of **successive intervals** is sometimes used to sort the items (usually one per card) into piles or groups representing a succession of values. From the sort, an interval scale can be developed.[16]

SCALE CONSTRUCTION TECHNIQUES

Arbitrary Scales   We design **arbitrary scales** by collecting several items that we believe are unambiguous and appropriate to a given topic. Some are chosen for inclusion in the instrument. To illustrate, consider a company image study. We choose a sample of items that we believe are the components of company image. Some are:

How do you regard *(name)* Company's reputation

1. As a place to work?	Bad ___	___	___	___	___ Good
2. As a sponsor of civic projects?	Bad ___	___	___	___	___ Good
3. For ecological concern?	Bad ___	___	___	___	___ Good
4. As an employer of minorities?	Bad ___	___	___	___	___ Good

---

We might score each of these from 1 to 5 depending upon the degree of favorableness reported. The results may be studied in several ways. Totals may be made by individual items, by company, by companies as places to work, for ecological concern, and so on. Totals for each company or for individuals may be calculated to determine how they compare to others. Based on a total for these four items, each company would be scored from 4 to 20 by each respondent. These data may also be analyzed from a respondent-centered point of view. Thus, we might use the attitude scores of each individual to study differences among them.

Arbitrary scales are easy to develop, inexpensive, and can be designed to be highly specific. They provide useful information and are adequate if developed skillfully. There are also weaknesses. The design approach is subjective. If the logic is good, then the scale can be good. The only assurance we have that the items chosen are a representative sample of the universe of content (the totality of what constitutes "company image") is the researcher's insight and ability. We have no evidence that all items will be viewed by respondents from the same frame of reference.

While arbitrary scales are often used, there has been a great effort to develop scale construction techniques that overcome some of their deficiencies. An early attempt was consensus scaling.

Consensus Scaling

Consensus scaling requires that items are selected by a panel of judges who evaluate them on (1) relevance to the topic area, (2) potential for ambiguity, and (3) the level of attitude it represents. A widely known form of this approach is the Thurstone Differential Scale.

Differential scales, also known as the Method of Equal Appearing Intervals, were developed to create an interval rating scale for attitude measurement. Often 50 or more judges evaluate a large number of statements expressing different degrees of favorableness toward an object. There is one statement per card. The judges sort each card into 1 of 11 piles representing their evaluation of the degree of favorableness that the statement expresses. The judge's agreement or disagreement with the statement is not involved. Three of the 11 piles are identified to the judges by labels of "favorable" and "unfavorable" at the extremes and "neutral" at the midpoint. The eight intermediate piles are unlabeled to create the impression of equal-appearing intervals between the three labeled positions.

The scale position for a given statement is found by calculating its median score (placement in the least favorable pile is scored as 1, in the most favorable pile as 11, and in the others according to their place in the order). A measure of dispersion, usually the interquartile range, is calculated for each statement.[17] If a given statement has a large interquartile range, it is judged to be too ambiguous to be used in the final scale. Statements included in the final attitude scale are selected by taking a sample of those with median scores spread evenly from one extreme to the other and with small interquartile ranges. Duplicate scales may be constructed and are sometimes used to provide greater score reliability.

Respondents read approximately 20 statements and select those items with which they agree. The mean or median value of the chosen scale items is then calculated as the measure of the respondent's attitude. Below is part of a classic 50-item scale that was designed to reveal the attitudes of employees toward their employer. The scale values are shown here but would not be on the instrument when it is used.[18]

Scale Value	
10.4	I think this company treats its employees better than any other company does.
8.9	A person can get ahead in this company if he or she tries.
8.5	The company is sincere in wanting to know what its employees think about it.
5.4	I believe accidents will happen no matter what you do about them.
5.1	The workers put as much over on the company as the company puts over on them.
4.1	Soldiering on the job is on the increase.
2.9	My boss gives all the breaks to his lodge and church friends.
2.5	I think the company goes outside to fill good jobs instead of promoting people who are here.
1.5	In the long run this company will "put it over" on you.
1.0	The pay in this company is terrible.

In the instrument, statements are arranged in random order of scale value. If the values are valid and if the questionnaire deals with only one attitude dimension, the typical respondent will choose one or several adjoining items (in terms of scale values). At times, however, divergences occur because a statement appears to tap a different attitude dimension. In the example above, it is possible that the statement, "I believe accidents will happen no matter what you do about them" may evoke a different frame of reference than will "company treatment of its employees," which pervades the other items. A person may honestly select the accident statement (with a 5.4 score) and then choose either lower or higher scored items.

Differential scales are reliable, but they are used more widely in academic studies than in applied business research. Using a panel of judges to evaluate scale items is better than relying on the researcher's opinion, but the method is costly, time-consuming, and ultimately involves decisions of 50 or more individuals.

A different logic underlies the scale construction techniques yet to be discussed. They rely upon the actual responses to the items as the basis for determining item acceptability. The first of these is the item analysis technique.

Item Analysis

The item analysis procedure evaluates an item based on how well it discriminates between those persons whose total score is high and those whose total score is low. The most popular type using this approach is the summated scale.

Summated scales consist of statements that express either a favorable or unfavorable attitude toward the object of interest. The respondent is asked to agree or disagree with each statement. Each response is give a numerical score to reflect its degree of attitude favorableness, and the scores are totaled to measure the respondent's attitude.

The most frequently used form is the **Likert scale.** With this scale the respondent is asked to respond to each statement by choosing one of five agreement choices (three-point and seven-point scales are also used). Below is a modified example from a job satisfaction scale:[19]

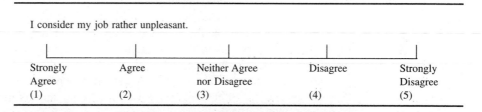

I consider my job rather unpleasant.

| Strongly Agree (1) | Agree (2) | Neither Agree nor Disagree (3) | Disagree (4) | Strongly Disagree (5) |

The numbers indicate the value to be assigned to each possible answer with 1 indicating the least favorable degree of job satisfaction and 5 the most favorable. These values are normally not printed on the instrument but are shown here to indicate the scoring system. The full Brayfield and Rothe Index includes 18 statements, making it possible for a respondent to score from 18 to 90, with 54 points being equivalent to a neutral position. If respondents score near 18, it is clear they hold an unfavorable job attitude; likewise, if the score is quite high, one concludes there is a high degree of job satisfaction. But the interpretation of scores nearer the middle of the scale is less clear. For example, a score of 60 is slightly over in the "favorable" side, but it may actually represent a poor job attitude score when compared to those of other workers.

Summated scales are most useful when it is possible to compare one person's score with a distribution of scores from a well-defined group. They are also very useful when we expect to conduct an experiment or undertake a program of change or improvement. We can use the scales to measure attitudes before and after the experiment, or to judge whether our efforts have had the desired effects. Furthermore, if we wish to correlate scores on the scale to other measures, we can do this without concern for the absolute value of what is "favorable" and what is "unfavorable."

Likert-type scales are relatively easy to develop as compared to the differential scales.[20] The first step is to collect a large number of statements that meet two criteria: (1) each statement is believed to be relevant to the attitude being studied and (2) each is believed to reflect a favorable or unfavorable position on that attitude. People similar to those who are going to be studied are asked to read each statement and to state the level of their agreement with it, using a five-point scale. A scale value of 1 might indicate a strongly unfavorable attitude and 5, a strongly favorable attitude.

Each person's responses are then added to secure a total score. The next step is to array these total scores and select some part of the highest and lowest *total scores,* say, the top 25 percent and the bottom 25 percent. These two extreme groups represent the most favorable and least favorable attitudes toward the topic being studied. They are used as criteria by which to evaluate individual statements. That is, through a comparative analysis of response patterns to each statement by members of these two groups, we learn which statements consistently correlate with low favorability and which with high favorability attitudes.

Item analysis involves calculating the mean scores for each scale item among the low scorers and high scorers. The item means between the high-score group and the low-score group are then tested for significance by calculating *t* values. Finally, the 20 to 25 items that have the greatest *t* values (significant differences between means) are selected for inclusion in the final scale.[21]

This procedure can be illustrated as follows. In evaluating response patterns of the high and low groups to the statement, "I consider my job rather unpleasant," we secure the results shown in Table 7–2.

After finding the *t* values for each statement, we rank order them and select those statements with the highest *t* values. As an approximate indicator of a statement's discrimination power, Edwards suggests using only those statements whose *t* value is 1.75 or greater, provided there are 25 or more subjects in each group.[22] To safeguard against response-set bias, we should word approximately one half of the statements to be favorable and the other half unfavorable.

The Likert scale has many advantages that account for its popularity. It is easy and quick to construct. Each item that is included has met an empirical test for discriminating ability. Since respondents answer each item, it is probably more reliable than the Thurstone scale, and it provides a greater volume of data than does the Thurstone differential scale. It is easy to use this scale both in

TABLE 7-2   Evaluating a Scale Statement by Item Analysis

Response Categories		X	f	fX	fX²	X	f	fX	fX²
				Low Total Score Group				**High Total Score Group**	
Strongly agree		5	3	15	75	5	22	110	550
Agree		4	4	16	64	4	30	120	480
Undecided	①	3	29	87	261	3	15	45	135
Disagree		2	22	44	88	2	4	8	16
Strongly disagree		1	15	15	15	1	2	2	2
Total			73	177	503 ← ② →		73	285	1,183
			n_L	ΣX_L	ΣX_L^2		n_H	ΣX_H	ΣX_H^2

$$\overline{X}_L = \frac{177}{73} = 2.42 \longleftarrow ③ \longrightarrow \overline{X}_H = \frac{285}{73} = 3.90$$

$$\Sigma(X_L - \overline{X}_L)^2 = 503 - \frac{(177)^2}{73} \longleftarrow ④ \longrightarrow \Sigma(X_H - \overline{X}_H)^2 = 1,183 - \frac{(285)^2}{73}$$

$$= 73.84 \qquad\qquad\qquad\qquad = 70.33$$

$$t = \frac{\overline{X}_H - \overline{X}_L}{\sqrt{\dfrac{\Sigma(X_H - \overline{X}_H)^2 + \Sigma(X_L - \overline{X}_L)^2}{n(n-1)}}} \longleftarrow ⑤$$

$$= \frac{3.90 - 2.42}{\sqrt{\dfrac{70.33 + 73.84}{73(73-1)}}}$$

$$= 8.92 \longleftarrow ⑥$$

LEGEND

1. For the statement, "I consider my job rather unpleasant," we select the data from the bottom 25% of the distribution (low total score group) and the top 25% (high total score group). There are 73 people in each group. The remaining 50% in the middle of the distribution is not considered for this analysis. For each of the response categories, the scale's value (X) is multiplied by the frequency or number of respondents (f) who chose that value. These values produce the product (fX). This number is then multiplied by X (fX^2). For example, there are 3 respondents in the low score group who scored a 5 (strongly agreed with the statement): $(fX) = 5 * 3 = 15$; $(fX^2) = 15 * 5 = 75$.

2. The frequencies, products, and squares are summed.

3. A mean score for each group is computed.

4. Deviation scores are computed, squared, and summed as required by the formula.

5. The data are tested in a modified t-test that compares the high and low scoring groups for the item. Notice the mean scores in the numerator of the formula.

6. The calculated value is compared with a criterion, 1.75. If the calculated value (in this case, 8.92) is equal to or exceeds the criterion, the statement is said to be a good discriminator of the measured attitude. (If it is less than the criterion, we would consider it a poor discriminator of the target attitude and delete it from the measuring instrument.) We then select the next item and repeat the process.

respondent-centered and stimulus-centered studies. That is, one can study how responses differ between people and how responses differ between various stimuli. It is also treated as an interval scale.

In these discussions, we implied that the Thurstone and Likert scales can be developed only by using the consensus and item analysis methods, respectively. However, one can develop scales of these types in an arbitrary manner. This is common, especially with the Likert scale. Such scales have the same reliability and validity problems as all arbitrary scales. The safest procedure for developing the Likert and Thurstone scales is as we described it.

Cumulative Scales Total scores on cumulative scales have the same meaning. Given a person's total score, it is possible to estimate which items were answered positively and negatively. The major scale of this type is the **Guttman scalogram.** Scalogram analysis is a procedure for determining whether a set of items forms a unidimensional scale as defined by Guttman.[23] A scale is said to be unidimensional if the responses fall into a pattern in which endorsement of the item reflecting the extreme position results also in endorsing all items that are less extreme.

Assume we are surveying opinions regarding a new style of running shoe. We have developed a preference scale of four items as follows:

1. Style X is good looking.
2. I will insist on style X next time because it is great looking.
3. The appearance of style X is acceptable to me.
4. I prefer style X to other styles.

Respondents are asked to express themselves on each item by indicating whether they agree or disagree. If these items form a unidimensional scale, the response patterns will approach the ideal configuration shown in Table 7–3.

A score of 4 indicates all statements are agreed to and represents the most favorable attitude. Persons with a score of 3 should disagree with item 2 but agree with all others and so on. According to scalogram theory, this pattern confirms that the universe of content (attitude toward the appearance of this running shoe) is scalable.

In developing a scalogram, one first defines the universe of content. Assume you are interested in the attitudes of people toward television advertising. You might define the universe of content as "viewer attitudes toward TV advertising." The second step is to develop items that can be used in a pretest that tell us if this topic is scalable. Guttman suggests that a pretest include 12 or more items, while the final scale may have only 4 to 6 items. Pretest respondent numbers may be small, say 20 or 30, but final scale use should involve 100 or more respondents.[24]

Take the pretest results and order the respondents from top to bottom—from those with the most favorable total score to the least favorable. Then order the

TABLE 7–3   Ideal Scalogram Response Pattern

	Item			
2	*4*	*1*	*3*	*Respondent Score*
X	X	X	X	4
—	X	X	X	3
—	—	X	X	2
—	—	—	X	1
—	—	—	—	0

X = Agree.
— = Disagree.

statements from left to right from the most favorable to the least favorable. The next step is to discard those statements that fail to discriminate well between favorable and unfavorable respondents. Finally, we calculate a Coefficient of Reproducibility (CR).

$$\text{Reproducibility} = 1 - \frac{e}{n(N)}$$

where e is the number of errors, n is the number of items, and N is the number of cases. Reproducibility should be 0.90 or better for a scale to be considered unidimensional.

The scalogram was a pioneering attempt to develop a homogeneous scale. While its claim for unidimensionality has been challenged, the scalogram is useful for assessing behaviors that are highly structured, such as social distance, organizational hierarchies, and evolutionary stages.[25]

Factor Scales

Factor scales include a variety of techniques that have been developed for two problems (1) how to deal with the universe of content that is multidimensional and (2) how to uncover underlying (latent) dimensions that have not been identified.

These techniques are designed to intercorrelate items so their degree of interdependence may be detected. There are many approaches that the advanced student will want to explore, such as latent structure analysis (of which the scalogram is a special case), factor analysis, cluster analysis, and metric and nonmetric multidimensional scaling. We limit the discussion in this section to a major scaling technique, the semantic differential, which is based on factor analysis.[26] Multidimensional scaling is described in Chapter 17.

Semantic Differential (SD)   This scaling method, developed by Osgood and his associates, is an attempt to measure the psychological meanings of an object to an individual.[27] The **semantic differential** is based on the proposition that an object can have several dimensions of connotative meaning. The meanings are located in multidimensional property space, called *semantic space*.

The method consists of a set of bipolar rating scales, usually seven points, by which one or more respondents rate one or more concepts on each scale item. The scale items appear as follows:

Good	_____ :	_____ :	_____ :	_____ :	_____ :	_____ :	_____ Bad
Passive	_____ :	_____ :	_____ :	_____ :	_____ :	_____ :	_____ Active

The technique has been widely used in business for brand image and other marketing studies of institutional images, political issues and personalities, and organizational studies.

The scale developers produced a long list of adjective pairs useful for attitude research. They searched *Roget's Thesaurus* for such adjectives, locating 289 pairs. These were reduced to 76 pairs that were formed into rating scales. They chose 20 concepts with the psychological meaning they wished to probe. The concepts from this historical study illustrate the wide applicability of the technique.

Person concepts—Adlai Stevenson, me, foreigner, my mother.

Abstract concepts—modern art, sin, time, leadership.

Event concepts—debate, birth, dawn, symphony.

Institutions—hospital, America, United Nations, family life.

Physical concepts—knife, boulder, snow, engine.[28]

By factor analyzing the data, they concluded that semantic space is multidimensional rather than unidimensional. Three factors contributed most to meaningful judgments by respondents. While the nature and importance of the factors varied, the major factors that emerged were (1) *evaluation,* (2) *potency* or *power,* and (3) *activity.* The evaluation dimension usually accounted for one-half to three-fourths of the extractable variance. Potency and activity are about equal and together accounted for a little over one-fourth of the extractable variance. Occasionally, the potency and activity dimensions combined to form "dynamism." In other studies they identified lesser dimensions that have been labeled "stability," "tautness," "novelty," and "receptivity." Results of the *Thesaurus* study are shown in Table 7–4.

The SD scale should be adapted to each research problem. The first step in scale development is to select the concepts to be studied. The concepts are nouns, noun phrases, or nonverbal stimuli such as visual sketches. Concepts are chosen by judgment and reflect the nature of the problem under study.

Next, select the original bipolar word pairs or tailor-made scales. If the traditional scale items are used, three criteria should guide their selection. The first is the factor(s) composition. If we use evaluation, potency, and activity, we should use at least three bipolar pairs for each factor. Scores on these individual items should be averaged, by factor, to improve their test reliability. The second selection criterion is the scale's relevance to the concepts being judged. Choose adjectives that allow connotative perceptions to be expressed. Irrelevant concept-scale pairings yield neutral midpoint values that have little information value. A third criterion is that scales should be stable across subjects and concepts. A pair such as "large–small" may be interpreted by some to be denotative when judging a physical object such as "automobile" but be used connotatively in judging abstract concepts such as "quality management." Scales should also be linear between polar opposites and pass through the origin. A pair that fails this test is "rugged–delicate," which is nonlinear on the evaluation dimension. When used separately, both adjectives have favorable meanings.[29] Finally, scales of unknown composition may be used for a particular problem.

To illustrate the SD, assume you are designing a scale to compare four candidates for the leadership position in an industry association. The scale is to be

TABLE 7–4   **Results of *Thesaurus* Study, Unrotated Square Root Factor Analysis**

Evaluation	*Potency*	*Activity*
Good–bad	Hard–soft	Active–passive
Positive–negative	Strong–weak	Fast–slow
Optimistic–pessimistic	Heavy–light	Hot–cold
Complete–incomplete	Masculine–feminine	Excitable–calm
Timely–untimely	Severe–lenient	
	Tenacious–yielding	

Subcategories of Evaluation

Meek Goodness	*Dynamic Goodness*	*Dependable Goodness*	*Hedonistic Goodness*
Clean–dirty	Successful–unsuccessful	True–false	Pleasurable–painful
Kind–cruel	High–low	Reputable–disreputable	Beautiful–ugly
Sociable–unsociable	Meaningful–meaningless	Believing–skeptical	Sociable–unsociable
Light–dark	Important–unimportant	Wise–foolish	Meaningful–meaningless
Altruistic–egotistical	Progressive–regressive	Healthy–sick	
Grateful–ungrateful		Clean–dirty	
Beautiful–ugly			
Harmonious–dissonant			

SOURCE: Adapted from Charles E. Osgood, G. J. Suci, and P. H. Tannenbaum, *The Measurement of Meaning* (Urbana, Ill.: The University of Illinois Press, 1957), Table 5, pp. 52–61.

used by a panel of corporate leaders to rate candidates. The selection of concepts in this case is simple; there are three candidates, plus a fourth—the ideal candidate.

The nature of the problem determines the selection of dimensions and bipolar pairs. Since the person who wins this position must influence business leaders, we decide to use all three factors. The candidate must deal with many people, often in a social setting; must have high integrity; and must take a leadership role in encouraging more progressive policies in the industry. The position will also involve a high degree of personal activity. Based on these requirements, we choose 10 scales to score the candidates from 7 to 1. The negative signs in the original scoring procedure $(-3, -2, -1, 0, +1, +2, +3)$ were found to produce coding errors. Figure 7–2 illustrates the scale used in this situation. The letters along the left side, which show the relevant factor, would be omitted from the actual scale, as would the numeric values shown. Note also that the evaluation, potency, and activity scales are mixed and about half are reversed to minimize the halo effect. To analyze the results, the set of evaluation values are averaged, as are those for the potency and activity dimensions.

The data are displayed in Figure 7–3. Here the adjective pairs are reordered so evaluation, potency, and activity descriptors are grouped together and profiles of three candidates may be compared.

FIGURE 7–2
SD Scale for Analyzing Candidates for an Industry Leadership Position

(E) Sociable	(7): ___:	___:	___:	___:	___:	(1) Unsociable
(P) Weak	(1): ___:	___:	___:	___:	___:	(7) Strong
(A) Active	(7): ___:	___:	___:	___:	___:	(1) Passive
(E) Progressive	(7): ___:	___:	___:	___:	___:	(1) Regressive
(P) Yielding	(1): ___:	___:	___:	___:	___:	(7) Tenacious
(A) Slow	(1): ___:	___:	___:	___:	___:	(7) Fast
(E) True	(7): ___:	___:	___:	___:	___:	(1) False
(P) Heavy	(7): ___:	___:	___:	___:	___:	(1) Light
(A) Hot	(7): ___:	___:	___:	___:	___:	(1) Cold
(E) Unsuccessful	(1): ___:	___:	___:	___:	___:	(7) Successful

FIGURE 7–3
Graphic Representation of SD Analysis

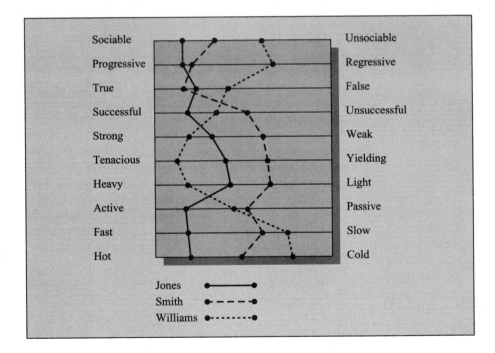

Tailor-Made SD Scales   Many researchers use ad hoc SD scales. One effort explored a retail store image using 35 pairs of words or phrases classified into eight groups. Excerpts from this scale are presented in Figure 7–4.

Other categories of scale items were general characteristics of the company, physical characteristics of the store, prices charged by the store, store personnel, advertising by the store, your friends and the store. Since the scale pairs are closely associated with the characteristics of the store and its use, one could develop image profiles of various stores.

In summary, the SD has several advantages. It produces interval data. It is an efficient and easy way to secure attitudes from a large sample. These attitudes may

FIGURE   7–4   Excerpts from an Ad Hoc Scale for Retail Store Image

---

Convenience of Reaching the Store from Your Location

---

near by ___: ___: ___: ___: ___: ___: ___:	distant
short time required to reach store ___: ___: ___: ___: ___: ___: ___:	long time required to reach store
difficult drive ___: ___: ___: ___: ___: ___: ___:	easy drive
difficult to find parking place ___: ___: ___: ___: ___: ___: ___:	easy to find parking place
convenient to other stores I shop ___: ___: ___: ___: ___: ___: ___:	inconvenient to other stores I shop

Products Offered

---

wide selection of different kinds of products ___: ___: ___: ___: ___: ___: ___:	limited selection of different kinds of products
fully stocked ___: ___: ___: ___: ___: ___: ___:	understocked
undependable products ___: ___: ___: ___: ___: ___: ___:	dependable products
high quality ___: ___: ___: ___: ___: ___: ___:	low quality
numerous brands ___: ___: ___: ___: ___: ___: ___:	few brands
unknown brands ___: ___: ___: ___: ___: ___: ___:	well-known brands

SOURCE: Robert F. Kelly and Ronald Stephenson, "The Semantic Differential: An Information Source for Designing Retail Patronage Appeals," *Journal of Marketing* 31 (October 1967), p. 45.

be measured in both direction and intensity. The total set of responses provides a comprehensive picture of the meaning of an object, and also a measure of the subject doing the rating. It is a standardized technique that is easily repeated but escapes many problems of response distortion found with more direct methods.

Advanced Scaling Techniques

New approaches have removed many deficiencies of traditional scales. Some have evolved to handle specific business research applications. Most techniques mentioned in this section rely on complex computer algorithms and require an understanding of multivariate statistics. *Students interested in further information on these topics should refer to the statistical examples in Chapter 17 and the references.*

Multidimensional scaling (MDS) describes a collection of techniques that deal with property space in a more general manner than the semantic differential. With MDS, one can scale objects, people, or both in ways that provide a visual impression of the relationships among variables. The data-handling characteristics of MDS provide several options: ordinal input (with interval output), and fully metric (interval) and nonmetric modes. The various techniques use proximities as input data. A proximity is an index of perceived similarity or dissimilarity between objects. The objects might be 20 nations (or 10 primary exports) that respondents are asked to judge in pairs of possible combinations as to their similarity. Using a computer program, the ranked or rated relationships are then represented as points on a map in multidimensional space.[30]

We may think of three types of attribute space, each representing a multidimensional map. First, there is objective space in which an object can be positioned in terms of, say, its flavor, weight, and nutritional value. Second, there is subjective space where a person's perceptions of flavor, weight, and nutritional value may be positioned. These maps do not always coincide, but they do provide information about perceptual disparities. Since the subjective maps vary over time, they also provide important trend data. Third, we can describe our preferences for the object's ideal attributes. All objects close to the ideal are more preferred than those farther away. These various configurations are said to reflect the "hidden structure" of the data and make complicated problems much easier to understand.

Another approach, representing a collection of techniques, is **conjoint analysis.** Conjoint analysis is used to measure complex decision making that requires multiattribute judgments. Its primary focus has been the explanation of consumer behavior with numerous applications in product development and marketing.[31]

When discovering and learning about products, consumers define a set of attributes or characteristics they use to compare competing brands or models in a product class. Using these attributes, the product range is evaluated and some brands are eliminated. Then a final set of alternatives (including a nonpurchase or delayed purchase decision) are developed. These evaluations can change if there is new information about additional competitors, or corrections to attribute knowledge, or further thoughts about the attribute. Algebraic theory can be used to model these cognitive processes and develop statistical approximations that reveal the rules the consumer follows in decision making.[32]

For example, a consumer might be considering the purchase of a personal computer. One has a fast processing speed and a high price. The other has a low price and a slower processor. The consumer's choice will be evidence of the utility of the processing speed attribute. Simultaneously, other attributes are being evaluated such as memory, portability, graphics support, user friendliness, and so forth.

Conjoint analysis can produce a scaled value for each attribute as well as a utility value for attributes that have levels (e.g., memory may have a range of 16, 12, or 8 megabytes). Both ranking and rating inputs may be used to evaluate product attributes. Conjoint analysis is not restricted to marketing applications, nor should it be considered a single generalized technique.

Finally, advanced students who are interested in the above techniques may also wish to investigate *magnitude estimation scaling.*[33] Magnitude scales provide access to ratio measurement and open new alternatives to management problems previously addressed through ordinal scales alone. *Rasch models* also offer alternative approaches to a range of traditional measures from dichotomous responses to Likert-type response formats.[34]

CLOSE-UP

Myra and Jason had been working on scaling for the CompleteCare project for a week when the call came to meet MindWriter's general manager at the airport. They had narrowed the choice to three scales: a Likert scale, a conventional rating scale with two verbal anchors, and their hybrid expectations scale. All were five-point scales that were presumed to measure at the interval level.

They needed a statement that could accompany the scale for preliminary evaluation. Return-ing to their list of investigative questions (see Chapter 5 Close-Up), they found a question that seemed to capture the essence of the repair process: "Are customers' problems resolved?" Translated into an assertion for the scale, the statement became, "Resolution of problems that prompted service/repair." They had continued to labor over the wording of the verbal anchors after their meeting with Jean-Claude. It was important that the distance between the numbers would resemble the psychological distance implied by the words.

Appropriate versions of the investigative question were constructed and then the scales were added:

Likert Scale:

The problem that prompted service/repair was resolved.

Strongly Disagree	Disagree	Neither Agree nor Disagree	Agree	Strongly Agree
1	2	3	4	5

Conventional Rating Scale (MindWriter's favorite):

To what extent are you satisfied that the problem that prompted service/repair was resolved?

Very Dissatisfied _____ Very Satisfied

| 1 | 2 | 3 | 4 | 5 |

Expectations Scale:

Resolution of the problem that prompted service/repair

Met **few** expectations	Met **some** expectations	Met **most** expectations	Met **all** expectations	**Exceeded** expectations
1	2	3	4	5

After consulting with MindWriter's research staff, Myra and Jason discussed the advantages of their scale. Myra suggested it was unlikely that CompleteCare would meet none of the customers' expectations. And, with errors of positive leniency, *none* should be replaced by the term *few* so the low end of the scale would be more relevant. Jason had read a *Marketing News* article that said Likert scales and scales similar to MindWriter's frequently produced a heavy concentration of 4s and 5s—a common problem in customer satisfaction research.

They also considered a seven-point scale to remedy this but in the end thought the term *exceeded* on the expectation scale could compensate for scores that clustered on the positive end, making the end point less susceptible to positive leniency.

(continued)

They were ready for a pilot test. They decided to compare their scale with MindWriter's—the Likert scale required that they create more potential items than they had room for on the postcard. Using the CompleteCare database, names, addresses, and phone numbers were selected. Thirty customers were selected at random from those who had recent service. They chose the delayed equivalent forms method for reliability testing (see Chapter 6). Myra administered the expectation scale followed by the satisfaction scale to half of the respondents and the satisfaction scale followed by the expectation scale to the other half. Each half sample experienced a time delay. No "order-of-presentation" effects

were found. Subsequently, they correlated the satisfaction scores with the expectation scores and plotted the results.

Satisfaction and expectation were positively correlated for "problem resolution" (r = .90); reliability based on equivalence was supported. An assessment of test-retest reliability (r = .93) showed that the expectation scale had a higher degree of stability over the one-week interval than the satisfaction scale (r = .75). Their scale also produced linear results (as evidenced by the plot).

The decision was made. Myra and Jason would use their new scale for the CompleteCare project.

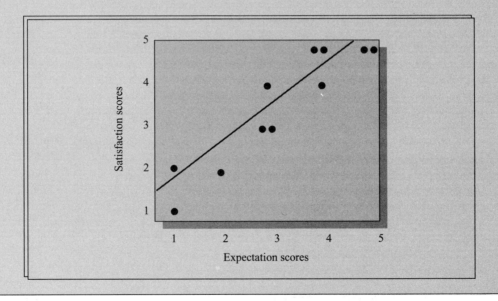

Summary

Scaling describes the procedures by which we assign numbers to opinions, attitudes, and other concepts. Selection of a scale to best meet our needs involves six decisions:

1. Study objective—do we measure the characteristics of the respondent or the stimulus object?
2. Response form—do we measure with a categorical or comparative scale?

3. Degree of preference—do we measure our preferences or make nonpreference judgments?

4. Scale properties—do we measure with nominal, ordinal, interval, or ratio scales?

5. Number of dimensions—do we measure using a unidimensional or multidimensional scale?

6. Scale construction technique—do we develop scales by arbitrary decision, consensus, item analysis, cumulative scaling, or factor analysis?

In this chapter, two classifications—the response form and scale construction techniques—were emphasized.

When using categorical scales, one judges an object in absolute terms against certain specified criteria. You can use either a graphic or an itemized rating scale. When you use comparative or ranking methods, you make relative judgments against other similar objects. Three well-known methods are the paired-comparison, the rank-order, and successive intervals methods.

Arbitrary scales are designed by the researcher's own subjective selection of items. These scales are simple and inexpensive to construct and have a certain face validity for their designer, but it is generally not possible to judge their validity in any other way.

In the consensus method, a panel is used to judge the relevancy, ambiguity, and attitude level of scale items. Those items that are judged best are then included in the final instrument. The Thurstone method of equal-appearing intervals is developed by consensus methods.

With the item analysis approach, one develops many items believed to express either a favorable or an unfavorable attitude toward some general object. These items are then pretested to decide which ones discriminate between persons with high total scores and those with low total scores on the test. Those items that meet this discrimination test are included in the final instrument. Likert scales are often developed using this approach.

With cumulative scales, it is possible to estimate how a respondent has answered individual items by knowing the total score. The items are related to each other, on a particular attitude dimension, so that if one agrees with a more extreme item, one will also agree with items representing less extreme views. Guttman's scalogram is the classic example of this scale.

Factor scales are developed through factor analysis or similar correlation techniques. They are particularly useful in uncovering latent attitude dimensions and approach scaling through the concept of multidimensional attribute space. Semantic differential scales are an example.

Other developments in scaling include multidimensional scaling and conjoint analysis. Each represents a family of related techniques with a variety of applications for handling complex judgments. Magnitude estimation and Rasch models provide methods for reconceptualizing traditional scaling techniques for greater efficiency and freedom from error.

Key Terms

arbitrary scales
categorical (rating) scales
    graphic rating scales
    itemized scales
central tendency (error)
comparative (ranking) scales
    paired comparisons
    rank order
    successive intervals
conjoint analysis
consensus scales (Thurstone)

factor scales
Guttman scalogram
halo effect
item analysis
leniency (error)
Likert/summated scales
multidimensional scaling (MDS)
scaling
semantic differential (SD)
unidimensional scales

Discussion Questions

1. Discuss the relative merits and problems with:
   a. Rating versus ranking scales.
   b. Likert versus differential scales.
   c. Unidimensional versus multidimensional scales.

2. Suppose a researcher gives you a scale to complete on the U.S. economic system. What would the scale look like and how would it be developed if it were a:
   a. Thurstone differential scale.
   b. Likert-type summated scale.
   c. Semantic differential scale.
   d. Scalogram.
   e. Multidimensional scale.

3. This chapter has been partially organized on the basis of five methods of scale construction. What are these methods and how do they differ? Is this difference of real importance? Explain.

4. You receive the results of a paired-comparison preference test of four soft drinks from a sample of 200 persons. The results are as follows:

	Koak	*Zip*	*Pabze*	*Mr. Peepers*
Koak	X	50*	115	35
Zip	150	X	160	70
Pabze	85	40	X	45
Mr. Peepers	165	130	155	X

*Read as 50 persons preferred Zip over Koak.

   a. How do these brands rank in overall preference in this sample?
   b. Develop an interval scale for these four brands.

5. One of the problems in developing rating scales is the choice of response terms to use. Below are samples of some widely used scaling codes. Do you see any problems with them?
   a. Yes ___ Depends ___ No ___
   b. Excellent ___ Good ___ Fair ___ Poor ___
   c. Excellent ___ Good ___ Average ___ Fair ___ Poor ___
   d. Strongly   Un-   Dis-   Strongly Dis-
      Approve ___ Approve ___ certain ___ approve ___ approve ___

6. Assume you are to judge a set of statements that will be used in developing a differential scale for an employee attitude survey. Score each of the below listed statements from 1 to 10, with 10 being the most positive favorable statement and 1 the least favorable. After scoring these statements refer to the section on consensus scaling to compare your judgment with the average judgments made in the actual study. How do you account for differences between your scores and the average scores?

   Score
   _____The pay in this company is terrible.
   _____ I think the company goes outside to fill good jobs instead of promoting people who are here.
   _____ The company is sincere in wanting to know what its employees think about it.
   _____ I think this company treats its employees better than any other company does.
   _____ I believe accidents will happen no matter what you do about them.
   _____ One can get ahead in this company if one tries.
   _____ The workers put as much over on the company as the company puts over on them.
   _____ My boss gives all the breaks to lodge and church friends.
   _____ Soldiering on the job is on the increase.
   _____ In the long run this company will "put it over" on you.

7. Below is a Likert type scale that might be used to evaluate your opinion of the educational program you are in. There are five response categories: Strongly Agree through Neither Agree nor Disagree to Strongly Disagree. If 5 represents the most positive attitude, how would the different items be valued?
   a. This program is not very challenging.
      SA   A   N   D   SD
   b. The general level of teaching is good.
      SA   A   N   D   SD
   c. I really think I am learning a lot from this program.
      SA   A   N   D   SD
   d. Students' suggestions are given little attention here.
      SA   A   N   D   SD
   e. This program does a good job of preparing one for a career.
      SA   A   N   D   SD

n.

l the

   f. This program is below my expectations.

      SA A N D SD

Record your answers to the above items. In what two different ways could such responses be used? What would be the purpose of each?

8. What are the critical differences between a classical SD scale and an ad hoc SD scale? What are the advantages and disadvantages of each?

Reference Notes

1. Bernard S. Phillips, *Social Research Strategy and Tactics,* 2nd ed. (New York: Macmillan, 1971), p. 205.
2. For a discussion of various scale classifications, see W. S. Torgerson, *Theory and Methods of Scaling* (New York: John Wiley & Sons, 1958), chap. 3.
3. E. A. Suchman and R. G. Francis, "Scaling Techniques in Social Research," in *An Introduction to Social Research,* ed. J. T. Doby (Harrisburg, Pa.: The Stackpole Company, 1954), pp. 126–29.
4. A study of research literature in 1940 found that more than three-fourths of the attitude scales used were of the five-point type. A cursory examination of more recent literature suggests that the five-point scale is still common but there also seems to be a growing use of longer scales. For the 1940 study, see Daniel D. Day, "Methods in Attitude Research," *American Sociological Review* 5 (1940), pp. 395–410.
5. Mildred Parten, *Surveys, Polls, and Samples: Practical Procedures* (New York: Harper & Row, 1950), pp. 190–92.
6. J. P. Guilford, *Psychometric Methods* (New York: McGraw-Hill, 1954), pp. 278–79.
7. P. M. Synonds, "Notes on Rating," *Journal of Applied Psychology* 9 (1925), pp. 188–95.
8. See L. L. Thurstone, "A Law of Comparative Judgment," *Psychological Review* 34 (1927), pp. 273–86.
9. From *Psychometric Methods* by J. P. Guilford. Copyright 1954, McGraw-Hill Book Company. Used with permission of McGraw-Hill Book Company.
10. Guilford, *Psychometric Methods,* p. 170.
11. The Z values in this transformation are associated with a given proportion of the *total area* under the normal curve, while Appendix Table F–1 gives the area for one side (or half) of the normal curve. To use Appendix Table F–1 in this calculation we must subtract all M_p values that exceed 0.5 from 1.0 to secure the value with which to enter Table F–1. For example, $1.0 - 0.766 = 0.234$. Entering the body of Table F–1 with this number we find the nearest value is 0.2327, which gives a Z_j of approximately 0.73; recall that all M_p values of less than 0.5 will give Z_j values that are negative.
12. Guilford, *Psychometric Methods,* pp. 179–80.
13. Ibid., p. 180.
14. Ibid., p. 186.
15. For details on these methods see Guilford, *Psychometric Methods,* pp. 188–90.
16. See Milton A. Saffir, "A Comparative Study of Scales Constructed by Three Psychophysical Methods," *Psychometrica* 11, no. 3 (September 1937), pp. 179–98.
17. The interquartile range is a measure of dispersion that includes the middle 50 percent of the items in a distribution.
18. R. S. Uhrbrock, "Attitudes of 4,430 Employees," *Journal of Social Psychology* 5 (1934), pp. 367–68.

19. See A. H. Brayfield and H. F. Rothe, "An Index of Job Satisfaction," *Journal of Applied Psychology* 35 (October 1951), pp. 307–11; the middle label, "undecided," is now often replaced with the phrase, "neither agree nor disagree."

20. One study reported that the construction of a Likert scale took only half the time required to construct a Thurstone scale. See L. L. Thurstone and K. K. Kenney, "A Comparison of the Thurstone and Likert Techniques of Attitude Scale Construction," *Journal of Applied Psychology* 30 (1946), pp. 72–83.

21. Allen L. Edwards, *Techniques of Attitude Scale Construction* (New York: Appleton-Century-Crofts, 1957), pp. 152–54.

22. Ibid., p. 153.

23. Louis Guttman, "A Basis for Scaling Qualitative Data," *American Sociological Review* 9 (1944), pp. 139–50.

24. For details on construction procedure, see Louis Guttman, "The Cornell Technique for Scale and Intensity Analysis," *Educational and Psychological Measurement* 7 (1947), pp. 247–80.

25. John P. Robinson, "Toward a More Appropriate Use of Guttman Scaling," *Public Opinion Quarterly* 37 (Summer 1973), pp. 260–67.

26. For more on the process of factor analysis, see Chapter 17.

27. Charles E. Osgood, G. J. Suci, and P. H. Tannenbaum, *The Measurement of Meaning* (Urbana, Ill.: The University of Illinois Press, 1957).

28. Ibid., p. 49.

29. Ibid., p. 79.

30. See, for example, Joseph B. Kruskal and Myron Wish, *Multidimensional Scaling* (Beverly Hills, Calif.: Sage Publications, 1978); Paul Green and V. R. Rao, *Applied Multidimensional Scaling: A Comparison of Approaches and Algorithms* (New York: Holt, Rinehart, & Winston, 1972); and Paul E. Green and F. J. Carmone, *Multidimensional Scaling in Marketing Analysis* (Boston: Allyn & Bacon, 1970).

31. See P. Cattin and D. R. Wittink, "Commercial Use of Conjoint Analysis: A Survey," *Journal of Marketing* 46 (1982), pp. 44–53; and Cattin and Wittink, "Commercial Use of Conjoint Analysis: An Update" (Paper presented at the ORSA/TIMS Marketing Science Meetings, Richardson, Texas, March 12–15, 1986).

32. Jordan J. Louviere, *Analyzing Decision Making: Metric Conjoint Analysis* (Beverly Hills, Calif.: Sage Publications, 1988), pp. 9–11.

33. See, for example, Milton Lodge, *Magnitude Scaling: Quantitative Measurement of Opinions* (Beverly Hills, Calif.: Sage Publications, 1981); and Donald R. Cooper and Donald A. Clare, "A Magnitude Estimation Scale for Human Values," *Psychological Reports* 49 (1981).

34. David Andrich, *Rasch Models for Measurement* (Beverly Hills, Calif.: Sage Publications, 1988).

Suggested Readings

1. Edwards, Allen L. *Techniques of Attitude Scale Construction.* New York: Appleton-Century-Crofts, 1957. Thorough discussion of basic unidimensional scaling techniques.

2. Kerlinger, Fred N. *Foundations of Behavioral Research.* 3rd ed. New York: Holt, Rinehart & Winston, 1986. Chapters 29, 31, and 32 cover various scaling and other data collection techniques, some of which are not discussed in this text.

3. Miller, Delbert C. *Handbook of Research Design and Social Measurement* 5th ed. Thousand Oaks, Calif.: Sage Publishing, 1991. Presents a large number of existing

sociometric scales and indexes as well as information on their characteristics, validity, and sources.

4. Osgood, Charles E.; George J. Suci; and Percy H. Tannenbaum. *The Measurement of Meaning.* Urbana, Ill.: The University of Illinois Press, 1957. The basic reference on SD scaling.

5. Snider, James G., and Charles E. Osgood, eds. *Semantic Differential Technique.* Chicago: Aldine, 1969. A collection of 52 papers on SD technique plus a semantic atlas for 550 concepts.

6. Summers, Gene F., ed. *Attitude Measurement.* Chicago: Rand McNally, 1970. An excellent collection of papers on various aspects of scaling.

8 SAMPLING DESIGN

 **FINDING YOUR WAY**

BRINGING RESEARCH TO LIFE

"**D**o you know if the post office accepts checks?" asked Audrey, the business manager at the Chevron station.

"Couldn't say," Jason replied.

"Because I am going to spend a *fortune* on stamps and I don't want to carry a lot of cash down there." She waved a thick folio of three-up mailing labels. "I've got to survey our customers. Our banker insists. You know that new loan officer? The MBA? The one named Jasmine, who calls herself 'Jazz'? We asked her for $50,000 so we can open at 5 A.M. and stay open until midnight—we have to put up a fence and some shrubbery, so as not to disturb the apartments in back, and install two new bays—and she told us to survey our customers to find out if many of them are retirees who go to bed early and wake up late and wouldn't use our service. And find out when the others leave for work in the morning and come home at night."

"So you have to do a survey."

"Yes. Three or four questions, maybe—nothing complicated. Like the two I mentioned and 'How long have you been our customer?' "

"How many years have you been our customer," Jason murmured reflexively.

"Oh, yeah, right. More precise, isn't it?" Audrey said. "But the point is, do you know what it costs to write to 1,000 customers?"

He crunched the numbers in his head. Postage to send out the survey. Postage prepaid to have it mailed back. Paper and printing. One envelope outbound and one inbound. Stuffing the outbound and opening and coding the inbound. "Minimum of $1.50 a survey," he said, "if your kids do the stuffing and opening and encoding. Maybe more. You generate labels from your computer, so you don't pay for labels, which saves a mint, maybe 25 cents a name."

"Right. A dollar 50 times 1,000. Plus the kids' time, if I can pry them away from Little League, MTV, and *personal* calls."

"You don't need to survey 1,000 customers you know."

"Whaaat?"

"Pick 100 at random from your customer list. You'll get 10 percent margin of error and save $1,350, plus the kids' time."

"That's hard to believe. Impossible to believe, in fact."

"But it's true," he said. "Look, why don't you take some of the money you save, and instead of just sampling 100 from your existing customer base, also do a separate survey of every 20th person from the Chamber of Commerce directory. You'll have one survey of customers and another of potential customers, and you'll still end up saving over $1,000."

She thought for a moment. "The banker will never believe this," she objected.

"The next time I make a deposit, I'll explain it to her."

"You do that," she said, "and we'll wax your car every three months for the next two years."

THE NATURE OF SAMPLING

Most people intuitively understand the idea of sampling. One taste from a drink tells us whether it is sweet or sour. If we select a few employment records out of a complete set, we usually assume our selection reflects the characteristics of the full set. If some of our staff favors a flexible work schedule, we infer that others will also. These examples vary in their representativeness, but each is a sample.

The basic idea of **sampling** is that by selecting part of the elements in a population, conclusions may be obtained about the entire population. An **element** is the subject on which the measurement is being taken. It is the unit of study. For example, each office worker questioned about a flexible work schedule is a population element, and each business account analyzed is an element of an account population. A **population** is the total collection of elements about which we wish to make some inferences. All office workers in the firm comprise a population of interest; all 4,000 files define a population of interest. A **census** study includes all the elements in the population. If 4,000 files define the population, a census would obtain information from every one of them.

Why Sample?

The economic advantages of taking a sample rather than a census are massive. Consider the cost of taking a census. Why should we spend thousands of dollars interviewing all 4,000 employees in our company if we can find out what we need to know by asking only a few hundred?

Deming argues that the quality of a study is often better with sampling than with a census. He suggests, "Sampling possesses the possibility of better interviewing (testing), more thorough investigation of missing, wrong, or suspicious information, better supervision, and better processing than is possible with complete coverage."[1] Research findings substantiate this opinion. More than 90 percent of the total survey error in one study was from nonsampling sources, and only 10 percent or less was from random sampling error.[2] The U.S. Bureau of the Census shows its confidence in sampling by making sample surveys to check the accuracy of its census.

Sampling also provides much quicker results than does a census. The speed of execution reduces the time between the recognition of a need for information and the availability of that information. Some situations require sampling. When we test the breaking strength of materials, we must destroy them; a census would mean complete destruction of the materials. Sampling is also the only process possible if the population is infinite.

The advantages of sampling over census studies are less compelling when the population is small and the variability is high. Two conditions are appropriate for a census study: (1) a census is *feasible* when the population is small and (2) *necessary* when the elements are quite different from each other.[3] Consider North American manufacturers of stereo components. Fewer than 50 companies design, develop, and manufacture amplifier and loudspeaker products at the high end of the price range. The size of this population suggests a census is feasible. The diversity of their product offerings makes it difficult to accurately sample from this group. Some companies specialize in speakers, some amplifier technology, and others compact disk transports. A census in this situation is appropriate.

Any sample we draw may not be representative of the population from which it is drawn. The result would be that any values we calculate from the sample would be incorrect as estimates of the population values. When the sample is drawn properly, however, some sample elements underestimate the parameters and others overestimate them. Variations in these values counteract each other; this counteraction results in a sample value that is generally close to the population value. For these offsetting effects to occur, however, there must be enough members in the sample and they must be drawn in a way to favor neither overestimation nor underestimation.

What Is a Good Sample?

The ultimate test of a sample design is how well it represents the characteristics of the population it purports to represent. In measurement terms, the sample must be *valid*. Validity of a sample depends upon two considerations.

Accuracy   First is the matter of *accuracy—the degree to which bias is absent from the sample.* An accurate (unbiased) sample is one in which the underestimators and the overestimators are balanced among the members of the sample. There is no **systematic variance** with an accurate sample. Systematic variance has been defined as "the variation in measures due to some known or unknown influences that 'cause' the scores to lean in one direction more than another."[4] It has been observed that homes on the corner of the block are often larger and more valuable than those within blocks. Thus, a sample that selects corner homes only will cause us to overestimate home values in the area.

The classic example of a sample with systematic variance was the *Literary Digest* presidential election poll in 1936 in which more than 2 million persons participated. The poll said Alfred Landon would defeat Franklin Roosevelt for the presidency of the United States. Even the large size of this sample did not counteract its systematic bias. Later evidence showed that the poll drew its sample from the middle and upper classes, while Roosevelt's appeal was heavily among the much larger working class.

Precision   A second criterion of a good sample design is *precision of estimate.* No sample will fully represent its population in all respects. The numerical descriptors that describe samples may be expected to differ from those that describe populations because of random fluctuations inherent in the sampling process. This is called **sampling error** and reflects the influences of chance in drawing the sample members. Sampling error is what is left after all known sources of *systematic variance* have been accounted for. In theory, sampling error consists of random fluctuations only, although some unknown systematic variance may be included when too many or too few sample elements possess a particular characteristic.

Precision is measured by the *standard error of estimate,* a type of standard deviation measurement; the smaller the standard error of estimate, the higher is the precision of the sample. After considering the problems of overcoming bias, it is desirable that the sample design produce a minimum standard error of estimate. However, not all types of sample designs provide estimates of precision, and samples of the same size can produce different amounts of error variance.

TABLE 8-1   Types of Sampling Designs

	Representation Basis	
Element Selection	*Probability*	*Nonprobability*
Unrestricted	Simple random	Convenience
Restricted	Complex random	Purposive
	Systematic	Judgment
	Cluster	Quota
	Stratified	Snowball
	Double	

Types of Sample Design

A variety of sampling techniques is available. The one selected depends on the requirements of the project, its objectives, and funds available. The different approaches may be classified by their representation basis and the element selection techniques, as in Table 8–1.

Representation   The members of a sample are selected either on a probability basis or by another means. **Probability sampling** is based on the concept of *random selection—a controlled procedure that assures that each population element is given a known nonzero chance of selection.*

In contrast, **nonprobability sampling** is nonrandom and subjective. That is, each member does not have a known nonzero chance of being included. Allowing interviewers to choose sample members "at random" (meaning as they wish or wherever they find them) is not random sampling. Only probability samples provide estimates of precision.

Element Selection   Samples may also be classified by whether the elements are selected individually and directly from the population—viewed as a single pool—or whether additional controls are placed on element selection. When each sample element is drawn individually from the population at large, it is an *unrestricted sample. Restricted sampling* covers all other forms of sampling.

PROBABILITY SAMPLING

The unrestricted, simple random sample is the simplest form of probability sampling. Since all probability samples must provide a known nonzero chance of selection for each population element, the **simple random sample** is considered a special case in which each population element has a known and equal chance of selection. In this section, we use the simple random sample and an extended illustration to build a foundation for understanding sampling procedures and choosing probability samples.

The illustration is based on a study conducted by students taking an entrepreneurship class. They are interested in starting a dining club near the campus of

Metro University. Their idea is to make its facilities available on a membership basis. To launch this venture, they will need to make a substantial investment. Research will allow them to reduce many risks. An important research question for their study might be, "Who would patronize the club and on what basis?" Some investigative questions that flow from the larger question are:

1. How many would join the club under various membership and fee arrangements?
2. How much would the average member spend per month?
3. What days would be most popular?
4. What menu and service formats would be most desirable?
5. What lunch times would be most popular?
6. Given the proposed price levels, how often per month would each member have lunch or dinner?
7. What percent of the people in the population say they would join the club, based on the projected rates and services?

We use the last three investigative questions for examples and focus on the last two for assessing the project's risks.

Steps in Sampling Design

There are several decisions to be made in securing a sample. Each requires unique information. While the questions presented here are sequential, an answer to one question often forces a revision to an earlier one. We will consider the following:

1. What is the relevant population?
2. What are the parameters of interest?
3. What is the sampling frame?
4. What is the type of sample?
5. What size sample is needed?
6. How much will it cost?

What Is the Relevant Population?   The definition of the population can be apparent from the management problem or the research objectives but often is not. Is the population for the dining club at Metro University defined as the full-time day students on the main campus of Metro U? Or should the population include all persons employed at Metro U? Or should townspeople who live in the neighborhood be included? Without knowing the service target chosen, it is not obvious which of these is the appropriate population.

There may also be confusion about whether the population consists of individuals, households, or families, or a combination of these. If a study concerns income, then the definition of the population element as individual or household can make quite a difference. Good operational definitions are critical at this point.

Assume the club is to be solely for the students and employees on the main campus. They might define the population as "all currently enrolled students and employees on the main campus of Metro U." However, this does not include family members. They may want to revise the definition to make it "current students, employees, and their families of Metro U, main campus."

What Are the Parameters of Interest?   **Population parameters** are summary descriptors (e.g., mean, variance) of variables of interest *in the population*. **Sample statistics** are descriptors of the relevant variables *computed from sample data*. Sample statistics are estimators of population parameters. They are the basis of our inferences about the population because they are the best estimates of the population.

When the variables of interest in the study are measured on interval or ratio scales, we use the sample mean to estimate the population mean and the sample standard deviation to estimate the population standard deviation. With the investigative questions 5 and 6, the method of determining the sample—including the sample size calculation—is based on interval scale estimators.

Often a study may focus on nominally scaled data. In this event, a population proportion parameter would be of interest. The **population proportion** "is equal to the number of elements in the population belonging to the category of interest, divided by the total number of elements in the population."[5] Proportions measures are necessary for nominal data and are widely used for other measures as well. The most frequent concentration measure is the percentage; the variance equivalent is the *pq* ratio. Examples of data are the proportion of a population that expresses interest in joining the club or the proportion of married students who report they now eat in restaurants at least five times a month. Investigative question 7 would be addressed with a proportions estimator. These procedures are discussed later in this section.

There may also be important subgroups in the population about whom we would like to make estimates. For example, we might want to draw conclusions about the extent of club use that could be expected from married students versus single students, residential students versus commuter students, and so forth. Such questions have a strong impact upon the nature of the sampling frame we accept, the design of the sample, and its size.

What Is the Sampling Frame?   The **sampling frame** is closely related to the population. It is *the list of elements from which the sample is actually drawn.* Ideally, it is a complete and correct list of population members only. As a practical matter, however, the sampling frame often differs from the theoretical population.

The Metro U directory would be the logical choice as a sampling frame. Directories are usually published in the fall, but suppose the study is being done in the spring. The list will be in error because some new people will have come to campus and others will have left since the directory was published. You might use the directory anyway, ignoring the fact that it is not fully current. Just how much inaccuracy one can tolerate in choosing a sampling frame is a matter of judgment. Obviously, if the directory was a year old, the error might be unacceptable. One way to make the frame more representative would be to secure a supplemental list of the new students and employees.

A greater distortion would be introduced if a branch campus population were included in the directory. This would be an example of a too inclusive frame. That is, the frame includes elements other than the ones in which we are interested. (Students and employees who have left since the directory was published are another example.)

Often you have to accept a sampling frame that includes people or cases beyond those in whom you are interested. You may have to use a telephone directory to draw a sample of business telephone numbers. Fortunately, this is easily resolved. You draw a sample from the larger population and screen out those who are not members of the group you wish to study.

The campus dining club survey is an example of a frame problem that is readily solved. Often one finds this task much more of a challenge. Suppose you need to sample the members of an ethnic group, say Asians in Little Rock. There is probably no directory of this population. While you may use the general city directory, sampling from this too inclusive frame would be costly and inefficient. Asians probably represent only a small fraction of Little Rock's population, and the screening task would be monumental. Since ethnic groups frequently cluster in certain neighborhoods, you might identify these areas of concentration and then use a reverse area telephone or city directory to draw a sample. (City directories and reverse telephone directories are organized by street address.)

What Is the Type of Sample?   With personnel records available at a university and a population that is geographically concentrated, a probability sampling method is possible. University directories are generally available, and the costs of using a simple random sample would not be great here. Then, too, since the students are thinking of a major investment in the club, they would like to be confident they have a representative sample.

Choosing a simple random sampling technique has several consequences. With this sample design, the students can make probability-based confidence estimates of various parameters. In using this method they must also give careful attention to the execution of the sampling process. The selection must follow an appropriate procedure in which there is no chance for interviewers or others to modify the selections made. No one other than those selected can be included in the study; strong efforts must be made to include all the elements in the original sampling frame. The students must exclude substitutions except as clearly specified and controlled according to predetermined decision rules.

Despite all this care, the actual sample achieved will not match perfectly the sample that is originally drawn. Some people will refuse to participate and others will be difficult to find. The latter represent the well-known "not-at-home" problem and require that enough callbacks be made to assure they are adequately represented in the sample.

What Size Sample Is Needed?   Much folklore surrounds this question. One false belief is that a sample must be large or it is not representative. This is much less true than most people believe. Recall the *Literary Digest* example. A sample of more than 2 million voters failed to predict correctly a presidential election. In recent years, there has been controversy in congressional hearings about the representativeness of a national sample of TV listeners. Samples of 1,000 or more have been branded as inadequate by many critics but seldom, if ever, by a statistician. Sample size is only one aspect of representativeness. A sample of more than 2 million can be misleading while a sample of 1,000, drawn in the proper manner, can be more than adequate.

Often it is claimed that a sample should bear some proportional relationship to the size of the population from which it is drawn. One hears such views as, "a sample should be at least 10 percent or more of its population if it is to be credible." This is not true. The absolute size of a sample is much more important than its size compared with the population. *How large a sample should be is a function of the variation in the population parameters under study and the estimating precision needed by the researcher.* A sample of 400 may be appropriate sometimes, while more than 2,000 is required in other circumstances; in another case, perhaps only 40 is called for.

The basic formula for calculating sample size in probability sampling assumes an infinite population. Thus, a sample of 100 drawn from a population of 5,000 has roughly the same estimating precision as 100 drawn from a population of 200 million. The only problem with the sample from the larger population is the difficulty of drawing the sample.

The most important factor in determining the size of a sample needed for estimating a population parameter is the size of the population variance. The greater the dispersion or variance in the population, the larger the sample must be to provide estimation precision. If we were asking opinions on a particular topic and everyone in the population held the same view, then a sample of one gives the complete picture of population opinion. If two opinions are possible, it takes a minimum of two in the sample to register them, and it takes a larger sample to estimate the relative frequency of the two views in the population. If a dozen views are possible, an even larger sample is needed to register them and estimate their frequency.

Just how large a sample the students need for their dining club study depends upon how much precision they wish to secure. Since a sample can never reflect its population for certain, the researchers must decide how much precision they need. Precision is measured by (1) the interval range in which they would expect to find the parameter estimate and (2) the degree of confidence they wish to have in the estimate. More on these items later.

The size of the probability sample needed can be affected by the size of the population, but only when the sample size is large compared with the population. This so-called finite adjustment factor enters the calculation when the sample is 5 percent or more of the population. The net effect of the adjustment is to reduce the size of the sample needed to achieve a given level of precision.

Other considerations often weigh heavily upon the sample size decision. The conditions under which the sample is being conducted may suggest that only certain designs are feasible. One type of sample may be the appropriate design because we have no lists of population elements and must therefore sample geographic units. Since various designs have differing statistical and economic efficiencies, the choice of design coupled with the other requirements mentioned above will also affect the size of the sample.

The researcher may also be interested in making estimates concerning various subgroups of the population; then the sample must be large enough for each of these subgroups to meet the desired level. One achieves this in simple random sampling by making the total sample large enough to assure that each critical subgroup meets the minimum size criterion. In more complex sampling procedures, the smaller subgroups are sampled more heavily and then weighted.

How Much Will It Cost?   Cost considerations influence decisions about the size and type of sample and also the data collection methods. Almost all studies have some budgetary constraint, and this can mean a nonprobability sample must be used. Probability sample surveys incur callback costs, listing costs, and a variety of other costs that are not necessary when more haphazard methods are used.

Costs often dictate sample size. If there is a $2,000 budget for interviewing and it costs an estimated $25 to complete a personal interview using a simple random sample, the sample cannot exceed 80 respondents. By changing the design to a geographic cluster sample, we might be able to reduce this to $20 per interview, allowing a sample size of 100. A shift to a self-administered questionnaire might reduce costs to $12 per interview, giving a sample of 167.[6]

Cost factors may also dictate abandoning personal interviewing in favor of either telephone or mail surveys. Thus, telephone interviews might cost $10 each, allowing a sample of 200. In changing the data collection method, the amount and type of data that can be obtained also change.

Sampling Concepts

In this section, we discuss a few concepts that help in understanding probability sampling. Our treatment is largely intuitive using Figures 8–1 and 8–2 and the student project at Metro U.

Figure 8–1 shows a population ($N = 20,000$) consisting of the values of 1, 2, and 3 for the preferred lunch times. The values represent 11:30 A.M., 12:30 P.M., and 1:30 P.M. The values have equal distances representing 60 minutes. The frequency of response *(f)* in the *population distribution,* shown beside the population, is what would be found if a census of the elements was taken. This information is unknowable and we are pretending to be omniscient for the sake of the example. Normally, population data are unavailable or too costly to obtain.

Now assume we sample 10 data points from this population without knowledge of the population's characteristics. We use a table of random numbers, a random number generator, or a sampling procedure from a statistical software program. Our first sample ($n_1 = 10$) provides us with the frequencies shown in Figure 8–1. We also calculate a mean score, $\overline{X}_1 = 1.5$, for this sample. This mean would

FIGURE 8–1   Random Samples of Preferred Lunch Times

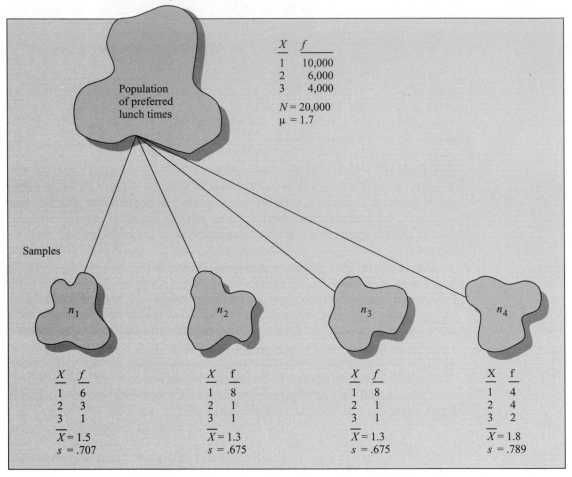

X	f
1	10,000
2	6,000
3	4,000

$N = 20,000$
$\mu = 1.7$

Population of preferred lunch times

Samples

n_1

X	f
1	6
2	3
3	1

$\overline{X} = 1.5$
$s = .707$

n_2

X	f
1	8
2	1
3	1

$\overline{X} = 1.3$
$s = .675$

n_3

X	f
1	8
2	1
3	1

$\overline{X} = 1.3$
$s = .675$

n_4

X	f
1	4
2	4
3	2

$\overline{X} = 1.8$
$s = .789$

Note: The X values 1, 2, 3 are 11:30, 12:30, and 1:30, respectively. The scale has equal intervals of 60 minutes between points.

place the average preferred lunch hour at noon. The mean is a *point estimate* and our best predictor of the unknown population mean, μ (the arithmetic average of the population). Assume further that we return the first sample to the population and draw a second, third, and fourth sample by the same procedure. The frequencies, means, and standard deviations are shown in the figure. The means scores ($\overline{X}_1 = 1.5$, $\overline{X}_2 = 1.3$, $\overline{X}_3 = 1.3$, $\overline{X}_4 = 1.8$) form their own distribution, a *distribution of sample means*—to be used later. As the figure suggests, all the samples share some similarities with the population, but none are perfect duplications because no sample perfectly replicates its population.

We cannot judge which estimate is the true mean. We can say that each of the means is a point estimate of μ although none is likely to be exactly equal to μ. Again, we would know the true population mean with certainty only after completing a census. However, we can estimate the interval in which the true μ will fall by using any of the $\bar{X}$s. This is accomplished through a formula for the **standard error of the mean.** The standard error of the mean is a measure of the distribution of sample means and is the standard deviation of that distribution.

$$\sigma_{\bar{X}} = \frac{s}{\sqrt{n}}$$

where

$\sigma_{\bar{X}}$ = Standard error of the mean.
s = Standard deviation and a measure of dispersion of individual values about the mean.
n = Sample size.

The standard error of the mean varies directly with the standard deviation of the population from which it is drawn. If the population standard deviation were smaller, say .35 instead of .70, the standard error would be only half as large. It also varies inversely with the square root of the sample size. If the square root of the sample size is doubled, the standard error is cut by one-half provided the standard deviation remains constant. These relationships are shown:

	Reducing the Standard Deviation	*Doubling the Square Root of Sample Size*
	$\sigma_{\bar{X}} = \dfrac{.70}{\sqrt{10}} = .22$	$\sigma_{\bar{X}} = \dfrac{.8}{\sqrt{25}} = .16$
$\sigma_{\bar{X}} = \dfrac{s}{\sqrt{n}}$	$\sigma_{\bar{X}} = \dfrac{.35}{\sqrt{10}} = .11$	$\sigma_{\bar{X}} = \dfrac{.8}{\sqrt{100}} = .08$

Let's now examine what happens when we apply sample data (n_1) from Figure 8–1 to the formula.

$$\sigma_{\bar{X}} = \frac{s}{\sqrt{n-1}}$$

where

s = Standard deviation of the sample, n_1.
$n_1 = 10$
$\bar{X}_1 = 1.5$
$s_1 = .707$

Substituting into the equation:

$$\sigma_{\bar{X}} = \frac{.707}{\sqrt{9}} = .236$$

How does this improve our prediction of μ from $\overline{X}$? The standard error creates the *interval range* that brackets the point estimate. In this example, μ is predicted to be 1.5 (the mean of n_1) $\pm$ .24. This range may be visualized on a continuum.

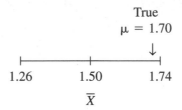

True
$\mu = 1.70$
$\downarrow$

1.26	1.50	1.74

$\overline{X}$

That is, we would expect to find the true μ between 1.26 and 1.74—between 11:46 A.M. and 12:14 P.M. (If 1 = 11:30 and .26 × (60 minutes) = 15.6 minutes, then 1.26 = 11:30 + 15.6 or 11:46.) Since we assume omniscience for this illustration, we know the population average value as 1.7. Further, because standard errors have characteristics like other standard scores, we have 68 percent confidence in this estimate. That is, one standard error encompasses ± 1 Z or 68 percent of the area under the normal curve. Recall that the area under the curve also represents the confidence estimates that we make about our results. The combination of the interval range and the degree of confidence creates the **confidence interval.** To improve our confidence to 95 percent, we would multiply the standard error of .24 by 1.96 *(Z)*, since ± 1.96 Z covers 95 percent of the area under the curve (see Table 8–2). Now, with 95 percent confidence, the interval in which we would find the true mean increases to $\pm$ .47 (from 1.03 to 1.97 or from 11:32 A.M. to 12:28 P.M.).

Parenthetically, if we compute the standard deviation of the *distribution of sample means* {1.5, 1.3, 1.3, 1.8}, we will discover it to be .236. Compare this to the standard error from the formula. The result is consistent with the second

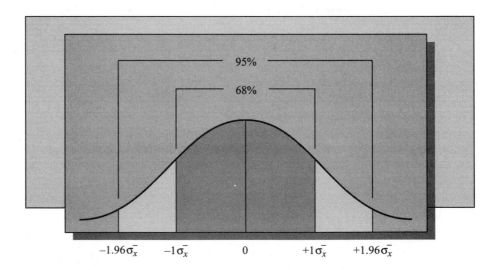

definition of the standard error: *the standard deviation of the distribution of sample means* (n_1, n_2, n_3, and n_4). It is, of course, impractical to draw repeated samples each time we want to generate an interval estimate for μ. Thus, the standard error formula is used. Now let's return to the dining club example and apply some of these concepts to the students' problem.

If the students were to interview *all* the students and employees in the defined population, asking them, "How many times per month would you eat at the club?" they would get a distribution something like that shown in Part A of Figure 8–2. The responses would range from zero to as many as 30 lunches per month with a μ (mu) and σ (sigma).

However, they cannot take a census, so mu and sigma remain unknown. By sampling, they find the mean to be 10.0 and the standard deviation to be 4.1. See Part C of Figure 8–2. Three observations about this sample distribution are consistent with our earlier illustration. First, it is shown as a histogram; it represents a frequency distribution of empirical data, while the smooth curve of Part A is a theoretical distribution. Second, the sample distribution (Part C) is similar in appearance but is not a perfect duplication of the population distribution (Part A). Third, the mean of the sample differs from the mean of the population.

Although the students will not draw repeated samples as we did earlier, if they did, they could plot the mean of each sample to secure the solid line distribution found in B. According to the **central limit theorem,** for sufficiently large samples ($n \geq 30$), the sample means will be distributed around the population mean approximately in a normal distribution. Even if the population is not normally distributed, the distribution of sample means will be normal if there is a large enough set of samples.

Estimating the Interval for the Students' Sample   Any sample mean will fall within the range of the distribution extremes shown in Part B of Figure 8–2. We also know that about 68 percent of the sample means in this distribution will fall between x_3 and x_4. Moving left to x_1 and right to x_2, about 95 percent will fall within this interval.

If we project points x_1 and x_2 up to the population distribution (Part A of Figure 8–2) at points x'_1 and x'_2, we see the interval where any given mean of a random sample of 64 is likely to fall 95 percent of the time. Since we do not know the population mean from which to measure the standard error, we infer that there is also a 95 percent chance that the population mean is within two standard errors of the sample mean (10.0). This inference enables us to find the sample mean, mark off an interval around it, and state a confidence likelihood that the population mean is within this bracket.

Because the students are considering an investment in this project, they would want some assurance that the population mean is close to the figure reported in any sample they take. To find out how close the population mean is to the sample mean, they must calculate the standard error of the mean and estimate an interval range within which the population mean is likely to be.

FIGURE 8–2
A Comparison of the Concepts of Population Distribution, Sample Distribution, and Distribution of Sample Means

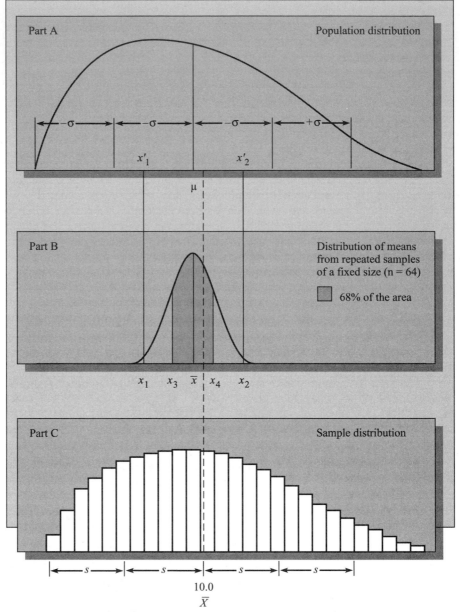

Note: The distributions in these figures are not to scale, but this fact is not critical to an understanding of the dispersion relationships depicted.

Given a sample size of 64, they still need a value for the standard error. Almost never will one have the value for the standard deviation of the population (σ), so we must use a proxy figure. The best proxy for σ is the standard deviation of the sample *(s)*. Here the standard deviation $(s = 4.1)$ was obtained from a pilot sample. As in the earlier example, we adjust the standard error formula for sample data.[7]

$$\sigma_{\overline{X}} = \frac{s}{\sqrt{n-1}} = \frac{4.1}{\sqrt{63}} = \frac{4.1}{7.937} = 0.52$$

If one standard error of the mean is equal to 0.52 visits, then 1.96 standard errors (95 percent) are equal to 1.02 visits. The students can estimate with 95 percent confidence that the population mean of expected visits is within 10.0 ± 1.02 visits, or from 8.98 to 11.02 meal visits per month.

Changing Confidence Intervals   This estimate may not be satisfactory in two ways. First, it may not represent the degree of confidence the students want in the interval estimate considering their risk. They might want a higher degree of confidence than the 95 percent level used here. By referring to a table of areas under the normal curve, various other combinations of probability can be found. Table 8–2 summarizes some of those more commonly used. Thus, if the students want a greater confidence in the probability of including the population mean in the interval range, they can move to a higher standard error, say, $\overline{X} + 3\ \sigma_{\overline{X}}$. Now the population mean lies somewhere between 10.0 ± 3 (0.52) or from 8.44 to 11.56. With 99.73 percent confidence, we can say this interval will include the population mean.

We might wish to have an estimate that will hold for a much smaller range, for example, 10.0 ± 0.2. To secure this smaller interval range, we must either (1) accept a smaller degree of confidence in the results or (2) take a sample large enough to provide this smaller interval with adequate confidence levels.

If one standard error is equal to 0.52 visits, then 0.2 visits would be equal to 0.38 standard errors (0.2/0.52). Referring to a table of area under the normal curve, we find that there is a 29.6 percent chance that the true population mean lies within ± 0.38 standard errors of 10.0.[8] That is, with a sample of 64, the sample mean would be subject to so much error variance that only 30 percent of the time could the students expect to find the population mean between 9.8 and 10.2. This is such a small degree of confidence that the students would normally move to the second alternative; they would increase the sample size until they could secure the desired interval estimate and degree of confidence.

TABLE 8–2   Estimates Associated with Areas under the Curve

Standard Error (Z)	Percent of Area*	Approximate Degree of Confidence	Interval Range
1.00	68.27	68%	μ is between 9.48 and 10.52
1.65	90.10	90%	μ is between 9.14 and 10.86
1.96	95.00	95%	μ is between 8.98 and 11.02
3.00	99.73	>99%	μ is between 8.44 and 11.56

*Includes both tails in a normal distribution.

Calculating the Sample Size for the Frequency of Patronage Question   We are ready to secure a sample size for the first key question in the entrepreneurship project. By way of review, decisions are needed on the following points:

1. The precision desired and how to quantify it:
   —Size of the interval estimate
   —The confidence we want with the estimate
2. The expected dispersion in the population for the question used to measure precision.
3. Whether a finite population adjustment should be used.

The students have selected the investigative question, "frequency of patronage," because they believe it to be critical to the project's risks. Two subjective questions need to be answered to quantify the precision issue. One is how much confidence to place in the population interval estimate; the other is how large the estimating interval should be. The 95 percent confidence level is often used, but more or less confidence may be needed in light of project needs. *The students wanted 95 percent confidence.* This is equal to 1.96 Z.

Similarly, the size of the interval estimate for predicting the population parameter from the sample data should be decided. When a smaller interval is selected, we are saying that precision is vital. On a five-point measurement scale, one-tenth of a point is a very high degree of precision in comparison to a one-point interval. Both the degree of confidence and the desired interval are important determinants of sample size because they determine the standard error of the sample mean. *The students selected ±.5 meals per month per person as the interval estimate most consistent with the project's risks.*

The next factor that affects the size of the sample for a given level of precision is the population dispersion. The smaller the dispersion, the smaller the sample needed to give a representative picture of population members. Suppose we were interested in the age of dining club members. If the population consists of ages ranging from 18 to 25, a smaller sample will give us a better estimate of the population's average age; with a population ranging from 18 to 65 years of age, a larger sample is needed for the same degree of confidence in the estimates. Since the population dispersion is unknowable, the standard deviation of the sample is used as a proxy figure. Typically, this figure is based on previous research on the topic, a pilot test, or a rule of thumb (one-sixth of the range). If the range is from 0 to 30 meals, the rule-of-thumb method would produce a standard deviation of 5 meals. *The students wanted more precision than the rule of thumb method, so they took a pilot sample of 25 and found the standard deviation to be 4.1 meals.*

A final factor affecting the size of a random sample is the size of the population. When the size of the sample exceeds 5 percent of the population, the finite limits of the population constrain the sample size needed. A correction factor is available in that event. *The students computed the sample as an infinite population and then adjusted it for a known 20,000-person population.*

The sample size is computed as:

$$\sigma_{\bar{X}} = \frac{s}{\sqrt{n-1}}$$

$$n = \frac{s^2}{\sigma_{\bar{X}}^2} + 1 = \frac{(4.1)^2}{(.255)^2} + 1$$

$$n = 259$$

where

$$\sigma_{\bar{X}} = 0.255 \text{ from } (0.5/1.96)$$

If the finite population of 20,000 is considered, the sample size is 256 for an interval of $\pm.5$ meals and 95 percent confidence.

$$\sigma_{\bar{X}} = \frac{s}{\sqrt{n-1}} \times \sqrt{\frac{N-n}{N-1}} = 0.255 = \frac{4.1}{\sqrt{n-1}} \times \sqrt{\frac{20,000-n}{20,000-1}}$$

or

$$n = \frac{s^2 N + \sigma_{\bar{X}}^2 (N-1)}{s^2 + \sigma_{\bar{X}}^2 (N-1)}$$

$$n = 256$$

where

$N = $ Size of the population.
$n = $ Size of the sample.

If we are willing to accept a larger interval range (± 1 meal), then $n = 64$.

Calculating the Sample Size for the Proportions Question   Up to this point, sample size has been discussed in terms of interval and ratio variables—measured as arithmetic means, standard deviations, and standard errors of the mean. Just as often, however, we deal with proportions data. An example is a CNN poll that projects the percentage of people who expect to vote for or against a proposition or a candidate. This is usually reported with a margin of error of ± 5 percent.

The second key question concerning the dining club study was: What percentage of the people in the population say they will join the dining club (based on certain projected rates and services)? A sample answers this question using the same general procedure as before. But instead of the arithmetic mean, with proportions, it is p (the proportion of the population that has a given attribute).[9] And instead of the standard deviation, dispersion is measured in terms of $p \times q$ (in which q is the proportion of the population not having the attribute, and $q = 1 - p$). The measure of dispersion of the sample statistic also changes from the standard error of the mean to the standard error of the proportion σ_p.

We calculate a sample size based on this data by making the same two subjective decisions—deciding on an acceptable interval estimate and the degree of confidence. Assume that 30 percent of the students say they will join the club. We decide to estimate the true proportion in the population within 10 percentage points of this figure ($p = 0.30 \pm 0.10$). Assume further that we want to be 95 percent confident that the population parameter is within ± 0.10 of the sample proportion. The calculation of the sample size proceeds as before:

± 0.10 = Desired interval range within which the population proportion is expected (subjective decision).

$1.96\ \sigma_p$ = 95 percent confidence level for estimating the interval within which to expect the population proportion (subjective decision).

$\sigma_p = 0.051$ = Standard error of the proportion (0.10/1.96).

pq = Measure of sample dispersion (used here as an estimate of the population dispersion).

$$\sigma_p = \sqrt{\frac{pq}{n-1}}$$

$$n = \frac{pq}{\sigma_p^2} + 1$$

$$n = \frac{0.3 \times 0.7}{(.051)^2} + 1$$

$$n = 82$$

The sample size of 82 persons is based upon an infinite population assumption. If the sample size is less than 5 percent of the population, there is little to be gained by using a finite population adjustment. The students interpreted the data found with a sample of 82 chosen randomly from the population as: "We can be 95 percent confident that 30 percent of the respondents would say they would join the club with a margin of error of ± 10 percent."

Previously, the students used pilot testing to generate the variance estimate for the calculation. Suppose this is not an option. These data have a feature concerning the variance that is not found with interval or ratio data. The pq ratio can never exceed 0.25. For example, if $p = 0.5$, then $q = 0.5$, and their product is 0.25. If either p or q is greater than 0.5, then their product is smaller than 0.25 (0.4×0.6 = 0.24 and so on). When we have no information regarding the probable p value, we can assume that $p = 0.5$ and solve for the sample size.

$$n = \frac{pq}{\sigma_p^2} + 1$$

$$n = \frac{0.25}{(.051)^2} + 1$$

$$n = 97$$

If we use this maximum variance estimate in the dining club example, we find the sample needs to be 97. Because both investigative questions were of interest, the students would take the larger of the two sample sizes calculated, $n = 256$.

How to Choose a Random Sample   Selecting a random sample is accomplished with the aid of a table of random numbers, a calculator with a random number generator, or computer software. Drawing slips out of a hat or Ping-Pong balls from a drum serve as alternatives if every element in the sampling frame has an equal chance of selection. Mixing the slips (or balls) and returning them between every selection ensures that every element is just as likely to be selected as any other.

A table of random numbers (such as Appendix F, Table F–10) is often a practical mechanism. Random number tables contain digits that have no systematic organization. Whether you look at rows, columns, or diagonals, you will find neither sequence nor order. Appendix F, Table F–10 is arranged into 10 columns of five-digit strings but this is solely for readability.

Assume the students in the entrepreneurship class want a special sample from the population of business school professors (of which there are 95). How would they begin? First the sampling frame is numbered consecutively. Then a random start in the table is found. (Dropping a pencil point-first onto the paper with closed eyes is sufficient.) Let's say the pencil dot lands on the eighth column from the left and 10 numbers down from the top of Appendix F, Table F–10. This would be the five digits 05067. Further, the students agree to read the first two digits in this column downward until 10 faculty members are selected: 05, 27, 69, 94, 18, 61, 36, 85, 71, and 83. The digit 94 appeared twice and the second instance was omitted; 00 was omitted because the sampling frame started with 01. Other approaches to selecting digits are endless: horizontally right to left, bottom to top, diagonally across columns, and so forth. Computer selection would have been more efficient for the larger student project.

CLOSE-UP

Jason was excited by the idea of having his car washed and waxed at no charge. He knew he was trading consulting services cheaply for automotive services, but it *felt* free, so the next day when he went to the bank he approached the new bank officer—the new market development vp, actually—with carefully disguised excitement. This was going to be more fun than working for money.

Gosh, she was a tall woman. Jasmine Rogers. Thirty-five, he guessed, 6 feet 2 inches or even 6 feet 3. Hard to tell when she was sitting. She sat grandly behind a mahogany desk in a cubicle with three glass walls. But the back wall was covered—by sports memorabilia. A basketball shirt said, "Morgan State—African Tour, 1985," and there was another shirt that said, "Harvard B-School Intramurals." There were crossed field hockey sticks, too, and a boomerang, and a picture of her holding the boomerang with small folks he supposed were Australian nationals casting admiring glances at this tall American woman.

(continued)

She came out to greet him and propelled him—almost lifted him—to a seat in her cubicle.

"So, what's up, Jason? Are we taking good care of you? Do you need another dozen computers? What?"

"I wanted to talk to you about the survey you asked Audrey to make. She and Juan own the Chevron station . . ."

"Oh, sure. Audrey and Johnny. Good people . . . Say, if you are thinking of getting a BMW, I can give you a good rate on a loan."

"Well, I'm not in that bracket, Jazz . . . Look, you told Audrey to take a survey of her customers, and that's what I wanted to discuss."

"I didn't intend her to have to hire a high-powered business consultant."

"Well, actually, this is more or less a favor, you see . . ."

She chuckled. He thought she had a nice disposition for a banker. "A favor? By any means did she offer to wax your car about a million times for this favor? I had to turn down that particular offer, being her loan officer. Conflict of interest, you know. But if you want to help her, hey, I say that's great."

"Well, this is no big deal, Jazz. More or less a back-of-the-envelope computation, you see. Except I did it in my head, as there was no envelope handy."

"In your head? Impressive. I was on the math team in high school . . ."

"Here's the thing. Audrey was about to do a census of her customers . . ."

"A census? Surely not a survey of *all* her customers. I wanted just a sample. She must have misunderstood."

"Well, that's the thing . . . I mean, I believe that a sample of maybe 100 customers will do the trick."

"I took marketing research in B-school, Jason, and while I certainly don't want to break Audrey's back, a sample of 100 seems kind of . . . well, thin."

"Maybe I can convince you."

"Maybe." She steepled her fingers thoughtfully and smiled wickedly. "Are you a betting man, Jason?" She placed a tall glass tumbler holding several dozen drinking straws between them. "I am willing to bet you cannot convince me."

"Then let me try. Take the first question you wanted. 'Are you currently retired from work?' This is what we call a proportions question. That is, a certain proportion of people will say they are retired."

"Yes," said the banker. "Suppose 20 percent of the existing customer base says they are retired. I would take that as a very bad omen for a station that opens early and closes late. Why would a retired person want to drop his car off at 6 A.M.?"

"Exactly . . . well, say 20 percent of the people sampled say they are retired. That's a proportion of .20, right? This means that, of the full 1,000-odd customers who comprise the 'population,' the actual proportion falls in a confidence interval centering around .20."

"Let me jump ahead here, Jason, because lunch approaches rapidly. I am willing to settle for a 95 percent chance of correctly locating the population proportion within an interval . . ."

"So you will settle for a 95 percent confidence interval. You remember your statistics, I can see. Well, we need to compute the standard error of the proportion in order to compute the width of the confidence interval. To compute the standard error, we will use the formula . . ."

Jazz leaned forward and grasped Jason's left hand with her right hand, to prevent him from writing formulas in the air, and held up the index finger of her left hand for attention. "One second, Jason. I am willing to bet you this," she extracted one drinking straw from the glass," *this valuable drinking straw*, that I can tell you the formula to use. We take .2 and multiply by .8, and divide by 100 (which is your proposed number of subjects), and take the square root, which is, um . . .,"

(continued)

she rolled her eyes to the ceiling, "which is .04. And we multiply by 2. So the 95 percent confidence interval extends between .20 plus and minus 0.08, from .12 to .28." She laughed merrily and moved the straw closer to her side of the desk. "Come on, Jason, play this game to win. I won't take it out on Audrey."

"That's very good, Jazz, and I'm going to let you keep that straw. But you omitted to consider a significant factor. Would you care to improve your estimate?"

"Hah," she said, "I should have used 99 instead of 100. 'N-1.' Hah!" and she reached for another straw from the tumbler, but Jason snatched the straw from her hands and set it on his side of the desk. Now each of them had a straw.

"That's too small a correction to matter. You lose."

"OK," she said with mock annoyance, "I should have multiplied by 1.96 instead of 2. That's it, isn't it?" And she reached for another straw, but Jason clapped his hand over the tumbler.

"Sorry," he said, "that's true, but again too small a correction to bother with. You should have allowed for the fact that she is sampling 100 out of a population of 1,000. That shrinks the standard error of the mean by the square root of 900/999, which comes to . . ."

"Too small a correction to bother with," shouted Jazz with glee. "Take your hands away from my straws! OK, I'll give that to you, Jason, a sample of 100 will give me all the precision I want for that question. But what about the next question, 'What time do you leave your home in the morning to go to work?' "

"Well, we use a slightly different version of the formula this time. This time we divide the estimated standard deviation of the error by the square root of 100 to get the standard error of the mean."

She reached into the tumbler and withdrew another straw. "Wait just a second, Jason. I will bet you this straw that you don't know the standard error of the sample until after you have taken the sample."

"Well, then you are wrong. Because I happen to know that the morning rush hour extends from about 6:30 to 9:30, a period of 180 minutes, and applying the rule of thumb that the standard deviation is roughly one-sixth of the range, I arrived at a rough value of 30 minutes for the standard deviation, which gives a standard error of the mean of 3 minutes, which is all the precision you could possibly want." He reached for the straw, but this time she pulled it away.

"Wait a second, Mr. Statistician. Where did you get that rule of thumb."

"I don't know," he admitted, "I picked it up during my graduate student days."

"Hah," she exulted. "Keep your straw-pickin' fingers away from my straws!"

"However," he said, "on returning to my office I did have a twinge of doubt about giving this advice to Audrey, so I called the planning department of the local bus company, which keeps enormously detailed statistical records as part of the requirement for their federal transportation subsidy, and they confirmed that the ridership of their number 45 bus through our town, and indeed the ridership of practically every other bus on the system, has a standard deviation of . . . 29 minutes." He extracted the straw. Now he had two, to her one.

"OK, Jason, you win. You have convinced me. If she can retrieve 100 surveys, I'll be satisfied. But I'll bet she will have to send out 200 surveys to get 100 replies."

"Not if her daughter makes follow-up phone calls," said Jason.

"OK, you win, this time. You have two straws to my one, which means I owe you a soda from the sandwich vendor who will pull his cart up outside in about one minute. Let me get my purse."

COMPLEX PROBABILITY SAMPLING

Simple random sampling is often impractical. It requires a population list that is often not available. The design may also be wasteful because it fails to use all the information about a population. In addition, the carrying out of a simple random design may be expensive in time and money. These problems have led to the development of alternate designs that are superior to the simple random design in statistical and/or economic efficiency.

A more efficient sample in a statistical sense is one that provides a given precision (standard error of the mean) with a smaller sample size. A sample that is economically more efficient is one that provides a desired precision at a lower dollar cost. We achieve this with designs that enable us to lower the costs of data collecting, usually through reduced travel expense and interviewer time.

In the discussion that follows, four alternate probability sampling approaches are considered: systematic, stratified, cluster, and double sampling.

Systematic Sampling

A versatile form of probability sampling is **systematic sampling.** In this approach, every kth element in the population is sampled, beginning with a random start of an element in the range of 1 to k. The major advantage of systematic sampling is its simplicity and flexibility. It is easier to instruct field workers to choose the dwelling unit listed on every kth line of a listing sheet than it is to use a random numbers table. With systematic sampling, there is no need to number the cards in a large personnel file before drawing a sample. Merely choose the total number of cards in the file, the sampling ratio, and the random start; then begin drawing a sample by choosing every kth card. Invoices or customer accounts can be sampled by using the last digit or a combination of digits of an invoice or customer account number. Time sampling is also easily accomplished.

While systematic sampling has some theoretical problems, from a practical point of view, it is usually treated as a simple random sample. It is statistically more efficient than a simple random sample when similar population elements are grouped on the list. This might occur if the list elements are ordered chronologically, by size, by class, and so on. Under these conditions, the sample approaches a proportional stratified sample. The effect of this ordering is more pronounced on the results of cluster samples than for element samples and may call for a proportional stratified sampling formula.[10]

A concern with systematic sampling is the possible *periodicity* in the population that parallels the sampling ratio. In sampling days of the week, a one in seven sampling ratio would give biased results. A less obvious case might involve a survey in an area of apartment houses where the typical pattern is eight apartments per building. Many systematic sampling fractions, such as one in eight, could easily oversample some types of apartments and undersample others. The only protection against this is constant vigilance by the researcher.

Another difficulty may arise when there is a *monotonic trend* in the population elements. That is, the population list varies from the smallest to the largest element or vice versa. Even a chronological list may have this effect if a measure has trended in one direction over time. Whether a systematic sample drawn under these conditions provides a biased estimate of the population mean depends upon the initial random draw. Assume that a list of 2,000 commercial banks is created, arrayed from the largest to the smallest, from which a sample of 50 must be drawn for analysis. A sampling ratio of 1 to 20 (begun with a random start at 16) and drawing every 20th bank would exclude the 15 largest banks and would give a downward size bias to the findings. There are ways to deal with this. One might randomize the population before sampling, change the random start several times in the sampling process, or replicate a selection of different samples.

Stratified Sampling

Most populations can be segregated into several mutually exclusive subpopulations, or strata. The process by which the sample is constrained to include elements from each of the segments is called **stratified random sampling.** University students can be divided by their class level, school, gender, and so forth. After a population is divided into the appropriate strata, a simple random sample can be taken within each stratum. The sampling results can then be weighted and combined into appropriate population estimates.

There are three reasons a researcher chooses a stratified random sample. They are (1) to increase a sample's statistical efficiency, (2) to provide adequate data for analyzing the various subpopulations, and (3) to enable different research methods and procedures to be used in different strata.[11]

Stratification is usually more efficient statistically than simple random sampling and at worst is equal to it. With the ideal stratification, each stratum is homogeneous internally and heterogeneous with other strata. This might occur in a sample that includes members of several distinct ethnic groups. In this instance, stratification makes a pronounced improvement in statistical efficiency.

It is also useful when the researcher wants to study the characteristics of certain population subgroups. Thus, if one wishes to draw some conclusions about activities in the different classes of a student body, stratified sampling would be used. Stratification is also called for when different methods of data collection are applied in different parts of the population. This might occur when we survey company employees at the home office with one method but must use a different approach with employees scattered over the country.

If data are available on which to base a stratification decision, how shall we go about it?[12] The ideal stratification would be based on the primary variable under study. If the major concern is to learn how often per month patrons would use the dining club, then one would like to stratify on this expected number of use occasions. The only difficulty with this idea is that if we knew this information, we would not need to do the study. We must, therefore, pick a variable for stratifying that we believe will correlate with the frequency of club use per month.

Researchers often have several important variables about which they want to draw conclusions. A reasonable approach is to seek some basis for stratification that correlates well with the major variables. It might be a single variable (class level) or it might be compound (class by gender). In any event, we will have done a good stratifying job if the stratification base maximizes the difference among strata means and minimizes the within-stratum variances for the variables of major concern.

The more strata used, the closer you come to maximizing interstrata differences and minimizing intrastratum variances. You must base the decision partially on the number of subpopulation groups about which you wish to draw separate conclusions. Costs of stratification also enter the decision. There is little to be gained in estimating population values when the number of strata exceeds six.[13]

The size of the strata samples is calculated with two pieces of information: (1) how large the total sample should be and (2) how the total sample should be allocated among strata. In deciding how to allocate a total sample among various strata, there are proportionate and disproportionate options.

Proportionate versus Disproportionate Sampling   In **proportionate stratified sampling,** each stratum is properly represented so the sample drawn from it is proportionate to the stratum's share of the total population. This approach is more popular than any other stratified sampling procedure. Proportionate sampling will generally have higher statistical efficiency than will a simple random sample. The method is also much easier to carry out than other stratifying methods. A third advantage is that such a sampling procedure provides a self-weighting sample; the population mean can be estimated simply by calculating the mean of all sample cases. On the other hand, proportionate stratified samples will often gain little in statistical efficiency if the strata means and variances are similar for the major variables under study.

Any stratification that departs from the proportionate relationship is **disproportionate.** There are several disproportionate allocation schemes. One type is a judgmentally determined disproportion based upon the idea that each stratum is large enough to secure adequate confidence levels and interval range estimates for individual strata.

Decisions regarding disproportionate sampling, however, are usually made by considering how a sample will be allocated among strata. One author states,

> In a given stratum, take a larger sample if
>
> 1. The stratum is larger.
> 2. The stratum is more variable internally.
> 3. Sampling is cheaper in the stratum.[14]

If one uses these suggestions as a guide, it is possible to develop an optimal stratification scheme. When there is no difference in within-stratum variances and when the costs of sampling among strata are equal, the optimal design is a proportionate sample.

While disproportionate sampling is theoretically superior, there is some question about whether it has wide applicability in a practical sense. If the differences in sampling costs or variances among strata are large, then disproportionate sampling is desirable. It has been suggested that "differences of several-fold are required to make disproportionate sampling worthwhile."[15]

Cluster Sampling   In a simple random sample, each population element is selected individually. The population can also be divided into groups of elements with some groups randomly selected for study. This is **cluster sampling.** An immediate question might be: How does this differ from stratified sampling? They may be compared as follows:

Stratified Sampling	*Cluster Sampling*
1. We divide the population into a few subgroups, each with many elements in it. The subgroups are selected according to some criterion that is related to the variables under study.	1. We divide the population into many subgroups, each with a few elements in it. The subgroups are selected according to some criterion of ease or availability in data collection.
2. We try to secure homogeneity within subgroups and heterogeneity between subgroups.	2. We try to secure heterogeneity within subgroups and homogeneity between subgroups, but we usually get the reverse.
3. We randomly choose elements from within each subgroup.	3. We randomly choose a number of the subgroups, which we then typically study in toto.

When done properly, cluster sampling also provides an unbiased estimate of population parameters. Two conditions foster the use of cluster sampling: (1) the need for more economic efficiency than can be provided by simple random sampling and (2) the frequent unavailability of a practical sampling frame for individual elements.

Statistical efficiency for cluster samples is usually lower than for simple random samples chiefly because clusters are usually homogeneous. Families in the same block (a typical cluster) are often similar in social class, income level, ethnic origin, and so forth.

While statistical efficiency in most cluster sampling may be low, economic efficiency is often great enough to overcome this weakness. The criterion, then, is the net relative efficiency resulting from the trade-off between economic and statistical factors. It may take 690 interviews with a cluster design to give the same precision as 424 simple random interviews. But if it costs only $2 per interview in the cluster situations and $4 in the simple random case, the cluster sample is more attractive.

Area Sampling   Much research involves populations that can be identified with some geographic area. When this occurs, it is possible to use **area sampling,** the most important form of cluster sampling. This method meets both the problems of high sampling cost and the unavailability of a practical sampling frame for individual elements. Area sampling methods have been applied to national populations, county populations, and even smaller areas where there are well-defined political or natural boundaries.

Suppose you want to survey the adult residents of a city. You would seldom be able to secure a listing of such individuals. It would be simple, however, to get a detailed city map that shows the blocks of the city. If you take a sample of these blocks, you are also taking a sample of the adult residents of the city.

Design   In designing cluster samples, including area samples, several questions must be answered.

1. How homogeneous are the clusters?
2. Shall we seek equal or unequal clusters?
3. How large a cluster shall we take?
4. Shall we use a single-stage or multistage cluster?
5. How large a sample is needed?

1. Clusters are homogeneous. This contributes to low statistical efficiency. Sometimes one can improve this efficiency by constructing clusters to increase intracluster variance. In the dining club study, the students might have constructed clusters that included members from all classes. In area sampling, they could combine adjoining blocks that contain different income groups or social classes. Area cluster sections do not have to be contiguous, but the cost savings is lost if they are not near each other.

2. A cluster sample may be composed of clusters of equal or unequal size. The theory of clustering is that the means of sample clusters are unbiased estimates of the population mean. This is more often true when clusters are equal. It is often possible to construct artificial clusters that are approximately equal, but natural clusters, such as households in city blocks, often vary substantially. While one can deal with clusters of unequal size, it may be desirable to reduced or counteract the effects of unequal size. There are several approaches to this.

One way to overcome the variation in cluster size is to combine small clusters and split large clusters until all approximate an average size. A second approach is to stratify clusters by size and choose clusters from each stratum. A third approach is size-stratified subsampling in which clusters are stratified by size and then subsampled, using varying sampling fractions to secure an overall sampling ratio. We may seek an overall sampling fraction of 1/60 and desire that subsamples be about five elements each. One group of clusters might average about 10 elements per cluster. In the "10 elements per cluster" stratum, we might choose 1 in 30 of the clusters and then subsample each chosen cluster at 1/2 rate to secure the overall 1/60 sampling fraction. Among clusters of 120 elements, we might select clusters at a 1/3 rate and then subsample at a 1/20 rate to secure the 1/60 sampling fraction.[16]

3. The third question concerns the size of the cluster. There is no *a priori* answer to this question. Even with single-stage clusters, say, of 5, 20, or 50, it is not clear which size is superior. Some have found that in studies using single-stage clusters, the optimal cluster size is no larger than the typical city block.[17] To compare the efficiency of the above three cluster sizes requires that we discover the different costs for each size and estimate the different variances of the cluster means.

4. The fourth question concerns whether to use a *single-stage* or a *multistage* cluster design. For most area sampling, especially large-scale studies, the tendency is to use multistage methods.

> There are four reasons that justify subsampling, in preference to the direct creation of smaller clusters and their selection in one-stage cluster sampling: (1) *Natural clusters* may exist as convenient sampling units, yet larger than the desired economic size . . . (2) We can *avoid the cost of creating smaller clusters* in the entire population and confine it to the selected sampling units . . . (3) *The effect of clustering* . . . is often less in larger clusters. For example, a compact cluster of four dwellings from a city block may bring into the sample similar dwellings, perhaps from one building; but four dwellings selected separately can be spread around the dissimilar sides of the block. (4) The sampling of *compact clusters may present practical difficulties.* For example, independent interviewing of all members of a household may seem impractical.[18]

5. How large a sample is needed? That is, how many subjects must be interviewed or observed? The answer to this question depends heavily upon the specific cluster design, and these details can be complicated. Unequal clusters and multistage samples are the chief complications and their statistical treatment is beyond the scope of this book.[19] Here we will treat only single-stage samples with equal-size clusters (called simple cluster sampling). It is analogous to simple random sampling.

The simple random sample is really a special case of simple cluster sampling. That is, we can think of a population as consisting of 20,000 clusters of one student each, or 2,000 clusters of 10 students each, and so on. The only difference between a simple random and a simple cluster sample is the size of cluster. Since this is so, we should expect that the calculation of a probability sample size would be the same for both types.

Double Sampling

It may be more convenient or economical to collect some information by sample and then use this information as the basis for selecting a subsample for further study. This procedure is called **double sampling**, *sequential sampling,* or *multiphase sampling.* It is usually found with stratified and/or cluster designs. The calculation procedures are described in more advanced texts.

Double sampling can be illustrated by the dining club example. You might use a telephone survey or another inexpensive survey method to discover who would be interested in joining such a club and the degree of their interest. You might then stratify the interested respondents by degree of interest and subsample among them for intensive interviewing on expected consumption patterns, reactions to various services, and so on. Whether it is more desirable to gather such information by one-stage or two-stage sampling depends largely upon the relative costs of the two methods.

Because of the wide range of sampling designs available, it is often difficult to select an approach that meets the needs of the research question and helps to contain the costs of the project. To help with these choices, Table 8–3 may be used

TABLE 8–3   Comparison of Probability Sampling Designs

Type	Description	Advantages	Disadvantages
Simple random	Each population element has an equal chance of being selected into the sample. Sample drawn using random number table/generator.	Easy to implement with automatic dialing (random digit dialing) and with computerized voice response systems.	Requires a listing of population elements. Takes more time to implement. Uses larger sample sizes. Produces larger errors. Expensive.
Systematic	Selects an element of the population at a beginning with a random start and following the sampling fraction selects every kth element.	Simple to design. Easier to use than the simple random. Easy to determine sampling distribution of mean or proportion. Less expensive than simple random.	Periodicity within the population may skew the sample and results. If the population list has a monotonic trend, a biased estimate will result based on the start point.
Stratified	Divide population into subpopulations or strata and use simple random on each strata. Results may be weighted and combined.	Researcher controls sample size in strata. Increased statistical efficiency. Provides data to represent and analyze subgroups. Enables use of different methods in strata.	Increased error will result if subgroups are selected at different rates. Expensive. Especially expensive if strata on the population have to be created.
Cluster	Population is divided into internally heterogeneous subgroups. Some are randomly selected for further study.	Provides an unbiased estimate of population parameters if properly done. Economically more efficient than simple random. Lowest cost per sample, especially with geographic clusters. Easy to do without a population list.	Often lower statistical efficiency (more error) due to subgroups being homogeneous rather than heterogeneous.
Double (sequential) (multiphase)	Process includes collecting data from a sample using a previously defined technique; based on the information found, selecting a subsample for further study.	May reduce costs if first stage results in enough data to stratify or cluster the population.	If indiscriminately used, it will increase costs.

to compare the various advantages and disadvantages of probability sampling. Non-probability sampling techniques are covered in the next section. They are used frequently and offer the researcher the benefit of low cost. However, they are not based on a theoretical framework and do not operate from statistical theory; consequently, they produce selection bias and nonrepresentative samples. Despite these weaknesses, their widespread use demands their mention here.

NONPROBABILITY SAMPLING

Any discussion of the relative merits of probability versus nonprobability sampling clearly shows the technical superiority of the former. In probability sampling, researchers use a random selection of elements to reduce or eliminate sampling bias. Under such conditions, we can have substantial confidence that the sample is representative of the population from which it is drawn. In addition, with probability sample designs, we can estimate an interval range within which the population parameter is expected to fall. Thus, we not only can reduce the chance for sampling error but also can estimate the range of probable sampling error present.

With a subjective approach like **nonprobability sampling,** the probability of selecting population elements is unknown. There are a variety of ways to choose persons or cases to include in the sample. Often we allow the choice of subjects to be made by field workers on the scene. Under such conditions, there is greater opportunity for bias to enter the sample selection procedure and to distort the findings of the study. Also, we cannot estimate any range within which to expect the population parameter. Given the technical advantages of probability sampling over nonprobability sampling, why would anyone choose the latter? There are some practical reasons for using these less precise methods.

Practical Considerations

We may use nonprobability sampling because such a procedure satisfactorily meets the sampling objectives. While a random sample will give us a true cross section of the population, this may not be the objective of the research. If there is no desire or need to generalize to a population parameter, then there is much less concern about whether the sample fully reflects the population. Often researchers have more limited objectives. They may be looking only for the range of conditions or for examples of dramatic variations. This is especially true in exploratory research where one may wish to contact only certain persons or cases that are clearly nontypical.

A second important reason for choosing nonprobability sampling over probability sample is cost and time. Probability sampling clearly calls for more planning and repeated callbacks to assure that each selected sample member is contacted. These activities are expensive. Carefully controlled nonprobability sampling often seems to give acceptable results, so the investigator may not even consider probability sampling.

Third, while probability sampling may be superior in theory, there are breakdowns in its application. Even carefully stated random sampling procedures may be subject to careless application by the people involved. Thus, the ideal probability sampling may be only partially achieved because of the human element.

It is also possible that nonprobability sampling may be the only feasible alternative. The total population may not be available for study in certain cases. At the scene of a major event, it may be infeasible to even attempt to construct a probability sample. A study of past correspondence between two companies must use an arbitrary sample because the full correspondence is normally not available.

In another sense, those who are included in a sample may select themselves. In mail surveys, those who respond may not represent a true cross section of those who receive the questionnaire. The receivers of the questionnaire decide for themselves whether they will participate. There is some of this self-selection in almost all surveys because every respondent chooses whether to be interviewed.

Methods

Convenience   Nonprobability samples that are unrestricted are called **convenience samples.** They are the least reliable design but normally the cheapest and easiest to conduct. Researchers or field workers have the freedom to choose whomever they find, thus the name *convenience.* Examples include informal pools of friends and neighbors or people responding to a newspaper's invitation for readers to state their positions on some public issue.

While a convenience sample has no controls to ensure precision, it may still be a useful procedure. Often you will take such a sample to test ideas or even to gain ideas about a subject of interest. In the early stages of exploratory research, when you are seeking guidance, you might use this approach. The results may present evidence that is so overwhelming that a more sophisticated sampling procedure is unnecessary. In an interview with students concerning some issue of campus concern, you might talk to 25 students selected sequentially. You discover that the responses are so overwhelmingly one-sided that there is no incentive to interview further.

Purposive Sampling   A nonprobability sample that conforms to certain criteria is called purposive sampling. There are two major types—judgment sampling and quota sampling.

Judgment sampling occurs when a researcher selects sample members to conform to some criterion. In a study of labor problems, you may want to talk only with those who have experienced on-the-job discrimination. Another example of judgment sampling occurs when election results are predicted from only a few selected precincts that have been chosen because of their predictive record in past elections.

When used in the early stages of an exploratory study, a judgment sample is appropriate. When one wishes to select a biased group for screening purposes, this sampling method is also a good choice. Companies often try out new product ideas on their employees. The rationale is that one would expect the firm's employees to be more favorably disposed toward a new product idea than the public. If the product does not pass this group, it does not have prospects for success in the general market.

Quota sampling is the second type of purposive sampling. We use it to improve representativeness. The logic behind quota sampling is that certain relevant characteristics describe the dimensions of the population. If a sample has the same distribution on these characteristics, then it is likely to be representative of the population regarding other variables on which we have no control. Suppose the student body of Metro U is 55 percent female and 45 percent male. The sampling quota would call for sampling students at a 55-45 percent ratio. This would eliminate distortions due to a nonrepresentative gender ratio.

In most quota samples, researchers specify more than one control dimension. Each should meet two tests: (1) It should have a distribution in the population that we can estimate and (2) it should be pertinent to the topic studied. We may believe that responses to a question should vary, depending upon the gender of the respondent. If so, we should seek proportional responses from both men and women. We may also feel that undergraduates differ from graduate students, so this would be a dimension. Other dimensions such as the student's academic discipline, ethnic group, religious affiliation, and social group affiliation may be chosen. Only a few of these controls can be used. To illustrate, suppose we consider the following:

Gender—two categories—male, female.

Class level—two categories—graduate and undergraduate.

College—six categories—Arts and Science, Agriculture, Architecture, Business, Engineering, other.

Religion—four categories—Protestant, Catholic, Jewish, other.

Fraternal affiliation—two categories—member, nonmember.

Family social-economic class—three categories—upper, middle, lower.

In an extreme case, we might ask an interviewer to find a male undergraduate business student, who is Catholic, a fraternity member, and from an upper-class home. All combinations of these five factors would call for 288 such cells to consider. This type of control is known as *precision control*. It gives greater assurance that a sample will be representative of the population. However, it is costly and too difficult to carry out with more than three variables.

When we wish to use more than three control dimensions, we should depend on *frequency control*. With this form of control, the overall percentage of those with each characteristic in the sample should match the percentage holding the same characteristic in the population. No attempt is made to find a combination of specific characteristics in a single person. In frequency control, we would probably find that the accompanying sample array is an adequate reflection of the population.

	Population	Sample
Male	65%	67%
Married	15	14
Undergraduate	70	72
Campus resident	30	28
Independent	75	73
Protestant	39	42
White	90	89

Quota sampling has several weaknesses. First, the idea that quotas on some variables assume a representativeness on others is argument by analogy. It gives no assurance that the sample is representative on the variables being studied. Often, the data used to provide controls may also be dated or inaccurate. There is also a practical limit on the number of simultaneous controls that can be applied to ensure precision. Finally, the choice of subjects is left to field workers to make on a judgmental basis. They may choose only friendly looking people, people who are convenient to them, and so forth.

Despite the problems with quota sampling, it is widely used by opinion pollsters and marketing and other researchers. Probability sampling is usually much more costly and time-consuming. Advocates of quota sampling argue that while there is some danger of systematic bias, the risks are usually not that great. Where predictive validity has been checked (e.g., in election polls), quota sampling has been generally satisfactory.

Snowball   This design has found a niche in recent years in applications where respondents are difficult to identify and are best located through referral networks. In the initial stage of **snowball sampling,** individuals are discovered and may or may not be selected through probability methods. This group is then used to locate others who possess similar characteristics and who, in turn, identify others. Similar to a reverse search for bibliographic sources, the "snowball" gathers subjects as it rolls along. Various techniques are available for selecting a probability snowball with provisions for error identification and statistical testing. Let's consider a brief example.

The high end of the U.S. audio market is composed of several small firms that produce ultra expensive components used in recording and playback of live performances. A risky new technology for improving digital signal processing is being contemplated by one firm. Through their contacts with a select group of recording engineers and electronics designers, the first-stage sample may be identified for interviewing. Subsequent interviewees are likely to reveal critical information for product development and marketing.

Variations on snowball sampling have been used to study drug cultures, teenage gang activities, power elites, community relations, insider trading, and other applications where respondents are difficult to identify and contact.

Summary

Sampling is based on two premises. One is that there is enough similarity among the elements in a population that a few of these elements will adequately represent the characteristics of the total population. The second premise is that while some elements in a sample underestimate a population value, others overestimate this value. The result of these tendencies is that a sample statistic such as the arithmetic mean is generally a good estimate of a population mean.

A good sample has both accuracy and precision. An accurate sample is one in which there is little or no bias or systematic variance. A sample with adequate precision is one that has a sampling error that is within acceptable limits for the study's purpose.

A variety of sampling techniques is available. They may be classified by their representation basis and element selection techniques as shown in the accompanying table.

	Representation Basis	
Element Selection	*Probability*	*Nonprobability*
Unrestricted	Simple random	Convenience
Restricted	Complex random	Purposive
	Systematic	Judgment
	Cluster	Quota
	Stratified	Snowball
	Double	

Probability sampling is based on random selection—a controlled procedure that assures that each population element is given a known nonzero chance of selection. In contrast, nonprobability selection is "not random." When each sample element is drawn individually from the population at large, it is unrestricted sampling. Restricted sampling covers those forms of sampling in which the selection process follows more complex rules.

The simplest type of probability approach is simple random sampling. In this design, each member of the population has an equal chance of being included in a sample. In developing a probability sample, five procedural questions need to be answered:

1. What is the relevant population?
2. What type of sample shall we draw?
3. What sampling frame shall we use?
4. What are the parameters of interest?
5. What size sample is needed?

Two kinds of estimates of a population parameter are made in probability sampling. First we make a point estimate that is the single best estimate of the population value. Then we make an interval estimate that covers the range of values within which we expect the population value to occur, with a given degree of confidence. All sample-based estimates of population parameters should be stated in terms of a confidence interval.

The size of a probability sample is determined by the specifications of the researcher and the nature of the population. These requirements are largely expressed in the following four questions:

1. What is the degree of confidence we want in our parameter estimate?
2. How large an interval range will we accept?
3. What is the degree of variance in the population?
4. Is the population small enough that the sample should be adjusted for finite population?

Cost considerations are also often incorporated into the sample size decision.

Complex sampling is used when conditions make simple random samples impractical or uneconomical. The four major types of complex random sampling discussed in this chapter are: systematic, stratified, cluster, and double sampling. Systematic sampling involves the selection of every kth element in the population by beginning with a random start between elements from 1 to k. Its simplicity in certain cases is its greatest value.

Stratified sampling is based on dividing a population into subpopulations and then randomly sampling from each of these strata. This method usually results in a smaller total sample size than would a simple random design. Stratified samples may be proportionate or disproportionate.

In cluster sampling, we divide the population into convenient groups and then randomly choose the groups to study. It is typically less efficient from a statistical viewpoint than the simple random because of the high degree of homogeneity within the clusters. Its great advantage is the cost savings if the population is dispersed geographically or in time. The most widely used form of clustering is area sampling in which geographic areas are the selection elements.

At times it may be more convenient or economical to collect some information by sample and then use it as a basis for selecting a subsample for further study. This procedure is called double sampling.

Nonprobability sampling also has some compelling practical advantages that account for its widespread use. Often probability sampling is not feasible because the population is not available. Then, too, frequent breakdowns in the application of probability sampling discount its technical advantages. You find also that a true cross section is often not the aim of the researcher. Here the goal may be the discovery of the range or extent of conditions. Finally, nonprobability sampling is usually less expensive to conduct than is probability sampling.

Convenience samples are the simplest and least reliable forms of sampling. Their primary virtue is low cost. One type of purposive sample is the judgmental sample in which one is interested in studying only selected types of subjects. The other type of purposive sampling is the quota sample. Subjects are selected to conform to certain predesignated control measures to secure a representative cross section of the population. Snowball sampling uses a referral approach to reach particularly hard-to-find respondents.

Key Terms

area sampling	quota sampling
census	sample statistics
central limit theorem	sampling
cluster sampling	sampling error
confidence interval	sampling frame
convenience samples	simple random sample
double sampling	snowball sampling
element	standard error of the mean
judgment samples	stratified random sampling
nonprobability sampling	disproportionate
population	proportionate
population parameters	systematic sampling
population proportion	systematic variance
probability sampling	

Discussion Questions

1. Distinguish between:
   a. Statistic and parameter.
   b. Sample frame and population.
   c. Restricted and unrestricted sampling.
   d. Standard deviation and standard error.
   e. Simple random and complex random sampling.
   f. Convenience and purposive sampling.
   g. Sample precision and sample accuracy.
   h. Systematic and error variance.
   i. Variable and attribute parameters.
   j. Point estimate and interval estimate.
   k. Proportionate and disproportionate samples.

2. Under what kind of conditions would you recommend:
   a. A probability sample? A nonprobability sample?
   b. A simple random sample? A cluster sample? A stratified sample?
   c. Using the finite population adjustment factor?
   d. A disproportionate stratified probability sample?

3. You plan to conduct a survey using unrestricted sampling. What are the subjective decisions that you must make?

4. You draw a random sample of 300 employee records from the personnel file and find that the average years of service per employee is 6.3, with a standard deviation of 3.0 years.
   a. What percent of the workers would you expect to have more than 9.3 years service?
   b. What percent would you expect to have more than 5.0 years service?

5. Suppose you needed to interview a representative sample of undergraduate students but had concluded there was no way to use probability sampling methods. You decide to use nonprobability methods. The university registrar can give you counts of the number of students who are freshmen, sophomores, juniors, or seniors, plus how many male and female students are in each class. How would you conduct a reasonably reliable nonprobability sample?

6. You wish to take an unrestricted random sample of undergraduate students at Cranial University to ascertain their levels of spending per month for food purchased off campus and eaten on the premises where purchased. You ask a test sample of nine students about their food expenditures and find that on the average they report spending $20, with two-thirds of them reporting spending from $10 to $30. What size sample do you think you should take? (Assume your universe is infinite.)

7. You wish to adjust your sample calculations to reflect the fact that there are only 2,500 students in your population. How does this additional information affect your estimated sample size in question 6?

8. Suppose you are going to take a sample survey and you want to estimate within a probable plus or minus 5 percent the proportion of people who have made a job change within the past year. What size of sample would you take if it was to be an unrestricted sample?

Reference Notes

1. W. E. Deming, *Sample Design in Business Research* (New York: John Wiley & Sons, 1960), p. 26.
2. Henry Assael and John Keon, "Nonsampling versus Sampling Errors in Survey Research," *Journal of Marketing Research,* Spring 1982, pp. 114–23.
3. A. Parasuraman, *Marketing Research,* 2nd ed. (Reading, Mass.: Addison-Wesley, 1991), p. 477.
4. Fred N. Kerlinger, *Foundations of Behavioral Research,* 3rd ed. (New York: Holt, Rinehart & Winston, 1986), p. 72.
5. Amir D. Aczel, *Complete Business Statistics* (Homewood, Ill.: Richard D. Irwin, 1989), p. 151.
6. All estimates of costs are hypothetical.
7. To make the sample standard deviation an unbiased estimate of the population, it is necessary to divide the sample standard deviation by $\sqrt{n-1}$ rather than $\sqrt{n}$.
8. See Appendix F, Table F–1 at back of book.
9. A proportion is the mean of a dichotomous variable when members of a class receive the value of 1, and nonmembers receive a value of 0.

10. Leslie Kish, *Survey Sampling* (New York: John Wiley & Sons, 1965), p. 188.
11. Ibid., pp. 76–77.
12. Typically, stratification is carried out before the actual sampling, but when this is not possible, it is still possible to poststratify. Ibid., p. 90.
13. W. G. Cochran, *Sampling Techniques,* 2nd ed. (New York: John Wiley & Sons, 1963), p. 134.
14. Ibid., p. 96.
15. Kish, *Survey Sampling,* p. 94.
16. For detailed treatment of these and other cluster sampling methods and problems, see Kish, *Survey Sampling,* pp. 148–247.
17. J. H. Lorie and H. V. Roberts, *Basic Methods of Marketing Research* (New York: McGraw-Hill, 1951), p. 120.
18. Kish, *Survey Sampling,* p. 156.
19. For specifics on these problems and how to solve them, the reader is referred to the many good sampling texts. Two that have already been mentioned are Kish, *Survey Sampling,* chaps. 5, 6, and 7; and Cochran, *Sampling Techniques,* chaps. 9, 10, and 11.

Suggested Readings

1. Deming, W. Edwards. *Sample Design in Business Research.* New York: John Wiley & Sons, 1990. A classic by the late author, an authority on sampling.
2. Kalton, Graham. *Introduction to Survey Sampling.* Beverly Hills, Calif.: Sage Publications, 1983. An overview with particular attention to survey applications.
3. Kish, Leslie. *Survey Sampling.* New York: John Wiley & Sons, 1965. A widely read basic reference on survey sampling.
4. Namias, Jean. *Handbook of Selected Sample Surveys in the Federal Government.* New York: St. John's University Press, 1969. A unique collection of illustrative uses of sampling for surveys carried out by various federal agencies. Of interest both for the sampling designs presented and the information on the methodology used to develop various government statistical data.
5. Yates, F. *Sampling Methods for Censuses and Surveys.* 4th ed. New York: Oxford University Press, 1987. A readable text with emphasis on sampling practices.

III THE SOURCES AND COLLECTION OF DATA

CHAPTER 9 SECONDARY DATA SOURCES

 **FINDING YOUR WAY**

BRINGING
RESEARCH TO LIFE

"Tell me what you know about big banks, Jason," Myra asked her research partner.

"Well, for my master's thesis I wrote an econometric model of the Federal Reserve System . . ."

"Yes, yes. Swell," she said, impatiently. She dropped into a chair and locked her eyes onto his, a gesture that convinced him she was reading his thoughts before his mouth could say them. "Academic economic research, yes. Very impressive, I'm sure. But what do you know practically?" This acerbic remark she sweetened with a wry smile. "And you did some very clever stuff classifying the depositors of a local S&L by using ZIP code demographics. Yes, you did first-rate work there, too, my boy. As a numbers cruncher, you are a prodigy. No doubt about it . . . But do you read the newspapers? What do you know about the political climate for big banks?" He murmured an evasion while he scanned his memory banks, his biocomputer as he called his brain.

Again, she prodded: "The political climate for banks. What do you know, Jason?"

"Well, Myra, it's never good for banks when liberals are running Congress and the White House. Is it?"

"The big banks can feel the eyes of Uncle Sam on them, morning, noon, and night. Which brings us to this." She produced his appointment book from the middle drawer. "While penning myself into your appointment book to work together on your final report for the economic council, I could not help noticing you have an appointment this very noon with a Mr. Armand Croyand of Denver. Do you know who he is, this Mr. Croyand, who has joined us from Denver?"

"No, not really. He identified himself as the principal of Croyand Associates and wanted a few minutes of my time over lunch, as he was swinging through town. I was free, and I said OK."

"Let me help you here. Saying yes to a meeting was a smart move. Leaving for the meeting without discovering in advance who Croyand is . . . well that would be dumb, wouldn't it?

"Since our telephone never sleeps, nor does our computer, nor does the online database of the *Rocky Mountain News,* a few minutes ago I dialed into that online database, and at a cost of maybe $25 learned quite a lot. Want to know what $25 of computer time discovered? It turns out that Mr. Croyand and his associates are the longtime research organization working for InterMountBanc, headquartered out there in Colorado, and he has a reputation for doing fine, deep, imaginative real estate research.

"Further rummaging in the *News's* database reveals that several of the directors recently resigned rather than face scrutiny of their private dealings, and that the new CEO of InterMount and the new directors are all Mr. Clean types who have publicly pledged to stand by the ethical highest standards.

"Now, the plot thickens, doesn't it? I dipped next into the online database of the *Miami Herald,* AND WHAT DO I FIND? I find that InterMount is heavily invested in that new Westridge development in the west county, the one that Ed Byldor is throwing up, the one that is now stopped dead in its tracks while the county commission, in all its wisdom, awaits recommendations from the county planners."

"You are telling me, then, that Mr. Armand Croyand is on town on business and I must treat this as a serious business lunch."

"I am telling you to go to lunch loaded for bear, because this could lead to a very big contract. How are you going to handle Mr. Croyand?"

"Well, first, I will go into the *Herald's* online database and see if the planning commission has taken a public position on Westridge." Myra nodded. "I have to swing by the Chamber of Commerce in an hour to drop off a final report of our aviation study, the one I did on a *pro bono* basis, and that will give me a chance to remind the various staff people there that they owe me a favor and to discover what they have picked up off the record about Westridge, the planning council, and the county commission. If they are sensitive to public opinion, that works in my

(continued)

favor, since I have a political polling background. If they are worried about real estate values, that is harder, but I suppose I can call the library and find out the address of some trade association that can give me a jump start.

"And since the county government center is in walking distance, I'll check the minutes of the county commission for any reports they have received from the planning council."

"Good. What else will you do while you are in the governmental center?"

"Something else?"

"Think."

He thought. "I'll check the bulletin board in the lobby and see when the planning council is due to hold its next public meeting, and I'll see if Westridge is on the agenda of the county commission for this coming Tuesday."

"OK, so far. And suppose you run into one of the commissioners. What will you do?"

"How would I know one if I met one?"

"Their pictures are in the lobby outside their commission chambers. Memorize them. But what if you run into one of the commissioners?"

"I'll say, 'Hello, Commissioner,' and keep going. I'm not a lobbyist: I'm a researcher, and besides I don't have a retainer yet from InterMountBanc."

"When you meet Croyand, concentrate on what he is telling you, and let him discover almost by accident that you are on top of the real estate situation in west county. Make him believe his prowess as a researcher directed him to you, and that he found exactly the right person to help him here in Florida. Let your secondary research scream quietly of your competence."

THE NATURE OF SECONDARY DATA SOURCES

Every study is a search for information about some topic. Researchers can be more confident of their information's integrity by drawing from all relevant sources. This chapter concerns the problems and techniques of finding and using data already collected by others. More specifically, the chapter describes the nature of these data sources and how to use them. While some tools are mentioned here, Appendix A contains a more detailed listing of important indices, guides, and other reference tools for secondary sources.

We classify information sources into primary and secondary types. **Primary data** come from the original sources and are collected especially to answer our research question. Thus, we collect primary data when we observe certain production operations and measure their cost. Studies made by others for their own purposes represent **secondary data.**

Primary and secondary sources each have strengths and weaknesses. With primary sources, researchers can collect precisely the information they want. One usually can specify the operational definitions used and can eliminate, or at least monitor and record, the extraneous influences on the data as they are gathered. However, secondary sources are indispensable.

Uses of Secondary Data

Secondary data are used for three research purposes. First, they fill a need for a specific reference on some point. Examples include the estimated U.S. production of sulfuric acid last year, the population of Atlanta in 1990, or the current rate of return on government bonds. We may also seek reference benchmarks against which to test other findings. From a sample survey, we could estimate the percentage of the population that has certain age and income characteristics. These estimates could then be checked against census data.

Another use of secondary data is as an integral part of a larger research study. Research procedures typically call for some early exploration to learn if the past can contribute to the present study. In essence, the researcher tries to keep from "reinventing the wheel." Data from secondary sources help us decide what further research needs to be done and can be a rich source of hypotheses.

Finally, secondary data may be used as the sole basis for a research study. The historical method is the classic example, but it is hardly the only one. Retrospective research often requires the use of past published data. In many research situations, one cannot conduct primary research because of physical, legal, or cost limitations. The federal government frequently solves this problem with the massive amount of data it publishes each year.

Advantages and Disadvantages of Secondary Data

Secondary sources can usually be found more quickly and cheaply than primary data. Collecting primary data can be so costly and time-consuming as to be impractical. We cannot hope to gather primary information comparable to census reports and industry statistics at any cost. These collections are not only voluminous and detailed, but their collection also is provided for by law. Most research on past events also has to rely on secondary data sources. Similarly, data about distant places often can be collected more cheaply through secondary sources.

The most important limitation with secondary sources is that the information may not meet one's specific needs. This is source material that has been collected by others for their own purpose. Definitions will differ, units of measure are different, and different times may be involved. It is difficult to assess the accuracy of the information because one knows little about the research design or the conditions under which the research occurred. Finally, secondary information is often out of date. A study made five years ago may not be relevant today.

TYPES OF SECONDARY SOURCES

Data sources may be classified as either internal (organizational) or external sources of information.

Internal Sources

Internal sources of organizational data are so varied that it is difficult to provide generalizations about their use. Accounting and management information systems create and store much of the internal data. Research and development, planning, and marketing functions also contribute. Examples are departmental reports, production summaries, financial and accounting reports, and marketing and sales studies. The collection methods used are unique to the specific situation, and collection success depends on knowing just where and how to look. Sometimes the information may exist in central files (i.e., at headquarters), in computer databases, or in departmental chronological files. In other organizations, a central library keeps all relevant information. Systematic searches should be made through exploratory interviews with everyone who handles the information. Often company librarians, MIS, PR/communications, or departmental secretaries can help in pinpointing critical data sources. Internal data sources may be the only source of information for many studies.

External Sources

External sources are created outside the organization and are more varied than internal sources. There are also better defined methods for finding them. This discussion is restricted to published sources, although other sources of information may be useful.

Published sources of data can be classified into five categories. The newest and fastest growing one is computerized databases. They are composed of interrelated data files. The files are sets of records grouped together for storage on some medium. Access may be through online search or CD-ROM. Online databases are often specialized and focus on information about a particular field. At last count, over 3,600 online databases were being offered by some 1,600 producers. Access to these databases was available through 555 online service systems.[1] Access to remote data files is now possible through a worldwide network called Internet. Users can access library catalogs and other computerized files (some of which are full text) from remote locations.

Another major source of secondary data is periodicals. The 32nd edition of *Ulrich's International Periodicals Directory* lists approximately 140,000 periodicals worldwide. The third source is books. It is estimated that over 47,000 book titles are published in the United States annually.[2] A fourth source of materials for secondary research is government documents. *The Monthly Catalog* of U.S. government publications had over 20,000 listings in a recent year, and this represented only a fraction of the total government output.

The last major source of published information consists of diverse materials from special collections. Within this category there are many reference books, each a compendium of a range of information. A second group includes university publications, of which there are master's theses, doctoral dissertations, and research records. A third group includes company publications such as financial reports, company policy statements, speeches by prominent executives, sales literature, product specifications, and many others. There are miscellaneous information sources consisting of the productions of various trade, professional, and other associations. These organizations often publish statistical compilations, research reports, and proceedings of meetings. Finally, there are personal documents. These are used in historical and other social science research, but less frequently in business studies.

SEARCH PROCEDURES

An important resource for collecting secondary data is the library. Assume you are doing an exploratory study or conducting a library research project. First, you seek the appropriate information sources by matching your information needs against the library's indexing systems. When you have matched and listed the sources, you are ready for the second part: to extract the specific information and assemble it into an appropriate form.

Electronic and Traditional Libraries

The library of the future will be one without walls or boundaries. Today, you can access information from your home through a computer network like Internet, collect data throughout the world, and have many materials faxed to you.

In the past, access to Internet was limited to researchers employed by governmental agencies or colleges and universities. This restriction is changing rapidly, and companies throughout the world are coming online.

Although access to Internet is already a reality at many universities, students will still have a need for the "traditional" library. You can use various types of traditional libraries, including public, special, and academic. Public libraries usually develop collections that are very consumer oriented, but are weak in the area of scholarly, research sources. Special libraries, such as corporate libraries, develop a collection (usually more technical) that reflects their business (i.e., engineering, manufacturing) and normally restricts use to employees. Academic (college or university) libraries will have most of the sources you will need for graduate-level research projects.

The first step to conducting research in a library is to decide which sources will provide access (primarily indices and abstracts) to the data you need to collect. The indices to this information will be available either in an electronic format, requiring a computerized search, or in a paper format, requiring a manual search.

Sometimes it helps to do preliminary reading on the topic you would like to research by using encyclopedias or elementary textbooks. You access these sources through a library's catalog holdings. Most university libraries have electronic access to their catalogs, and many are networked with other university catalogs. If you know the names of journals in your subject area, you can narrow your topic by looking at recent issues that discuss current trends.

However, a basic search for information usually progresses from the general to the specific. The exact sequence and importance of individual sources will vary depending upon the subject and your knowledge. One general approach might follow the flow diagram in Figure 9–1.

Search for Bibliographies   If you have some knowledge in the field, you should first develop a bibliography. This makes the entire research project more efficient because you quickly find an inventory of material on the subject. By inspecting titles, authors, dates, and other indexing information, you can select the priority sources for further study. You see the development of the subject over time, discover the authoritative sources, and can be more assured of covering the full range of materials. Every search turns up only a sampling of the available information, but it is important that you secure an adequate sample.

The logical first step is for you to learn whether someone else has already prepared a bibliography on the subject. Bibliographies frequently accompany

FIGURE   9–1   Secondary Data Search

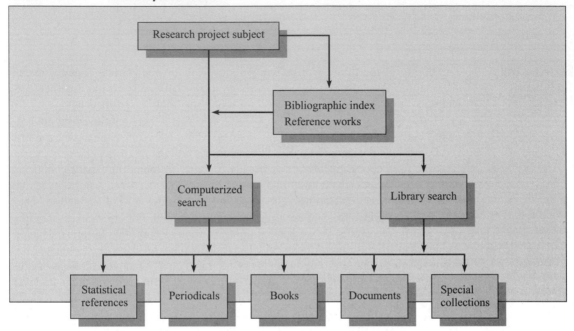

articles and books, and it is wasteful to duplicate such effort. Therefore, the first step may be to go to the *Bibliographic Index: A Cumulative Bibliography of Bibliographies* (New York: H. W. Wilson, 1937 to date). This publication, organized by subject, is an index to books, magazine articles, and other printed materials that include bibliographies. Thus, you may find publications in which the authors have listed their reference sources on the subject.

You can also search a library's catalog for bibliographies, using general business terms such as finance, accounting, marketing, management, and others. Many of these bibliographies have subsections that cover more specific topics.

If no bibliographies are available, you will develop your own by finding references to books, periodical articles (including newspapers, magazines, and journals), documents, and other miscellaneous sources. The indices, which give you references to these sources, can be found through a computerized search or a manual (paper) search.

Computer Search Procedures

Most **computerized searches** can be done at a library, although some academic libraries have catalogs that can be searched from your home or office via a modem. Searches by computer are fast, comprehensive, and effective. Databases are necessary for a search.

A **database** is a large collection of data in a computer, organized so it can be expanded, updated, and retrieved rapidly for various uses.[3] Databases are divided into two broad categories: reference and source. A **reference database** contains

**FIGURE 9–2
Sample Online
Search**

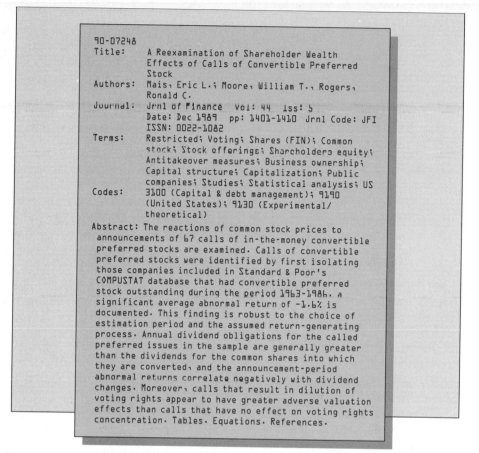

90-07248
Title: A Reexamination of Shareholder Wealth
          Effects of Calls of Convertible Preferred
          Stock
Authors: Mais, Eric L.; Moore, William T., Rogers,
          Ronald C.
Journal: Jrnl of Finance   Vol: 44   Iss: 5
          Date: Dec 1989   pp: 1401-1410   Jrnl Code: JFI
          ISSN: 0022-1082
Terms: Restricted; Voting; Shares (FIN); Common
          stock; Stock offerings; Shareholders equity;
          Antitakeover measures; Business ownership;
          Capital structure; Capitalization; Public
          companies; Studies; Statistical analysis; US
Codes: 3100 (Capital & debt management); 9190
          (United States); 9130 (Experimental/
          theoretical)
Abstract: The reactions of common stock prices to
          announcements of 67 calls of in-the-money convertible
          preferred stocks are examined. Calls of convertible
          preferred stocks were identified by first isolating
          those companies included in Standard & Poor's
          COMPUSTAT database that had convertible preferred
          stock outstanding during the period 1963-1986, a
          significant average abnormal return of -1.6% is
          documented. This finding is robust to the choice of
          estimation period and the assumed return-generating
          process. Annual dividend obligations for the called
          preferred issues in the sample are generally greater
          than the dividends for the common shares into which
          they are converted, and the announcement-period
          abnormal returns correlate negatively with dividend
          changes. Moreover, calls that result in dilution of
          voting rights appear to have greater adverse valuation
          effects than calls that have no effect on voting rights
          concentration. Tables. Equations. References.

SOURCE: Sample search from *Abstracted Business Information ABI/INFORM* (Louisville, Ky.: U.M.I./Data Courier, 1990), Item 90–07248.

citations that require further investigation by the researcher. A source database contains complete information. Reference databases include bibliographic, abstract, and indexing services such as *ABI/INFORM* (Abstracted Business Information, U.M.I./Data Courier, Louisville, Kentucky). These databases contain indices and detailed abstracts on articles gathered from over 400 journals related to business, management, administration, sales, and marketing. Monthly updates keep the database current with the addition of 1,600 citations and abstracts.[4] See Figure 9–2 for an example of an article abstract.

Source databases include everything outside bibliographic, abstract, and indexing services. They may be numeric, where the information is presented in number form, such as census data, or they may be full-text databases, in which every word of the original source can be read or printed for future reference. The *Dow Jones News/Retrieval Service* (Dow Jones, Princeton, New Jersey) is an example of a full-text database. It includes articles from *The Wall Street Journal, Barron's,* and the Dow Jones news wire. It is updated continually throughout the day, and full news stories are available 90 seconds after they come off the wire. These stories are maintained for 90 days.[5] Another example is *Harvard Business Review's* database service. Through either the Data Base Department at HBS Publishing Division or through HBR/Online accessed via BRS, DIALOG, EASYNET, NEXIS or DATASTAR, it is possible to search all previously published materials from the *Harvard Business Review.*

Not all databases are available to everyone; many numeric databases are limited by the high cost of use or by the location of the access terminals. Many are in-house or interdepartmental resources and cannot be used by the public. Information about databases is available from a variety of sources; some are included in Appendix A. Databases may be accessed through Internet, online remote systems, or a CD-ROM.

Internet   The **Internet** is an international network of hundreds of computer networks connecting over 2 million computers and millions of users. It is estimated to be growing by 1,000 computers each day. Funding for Internet is provided by both commercial and government organizations. Loosely run through cooperation, it is guided by three boards, the Internet Society (ISOC), the Internet Engineering Task Force (IETF), and the Internet Architecture Board (IAB). The historic purpose of Internet was to provide basic network services "to support open research and education in and among U.S. research and instructional institutions, plus research arms of for-profit firms when engaged in open scholarly communication and research."[6]

In 1991, the National Science Foundation lifted the ban on commercial use of the Internet. Users can now gain access through their university, their company, a commercial service (such as CompuServe, Prodigy, America Online, and GEnie), or a local bulletin board service (BBS) with an Internet feed. Typically, university librarians have access and act as navigators for Internet. In addition, many departments, colleges, and schools have Internet access and experts.

The seven major features of Internet are (1) electronic mail, (2) file transfer, (3) running programs on other computers, (4) searching for files and databases, (5) information exchange, (6) games, and (7) personal communications. For students involved in research, the most important aspects are the ability to search library catalogs, information databases, news reports, government information, and reference works. In addition, collaboration and discussion with national and international researchers is possible through Internet's electronic mail (e-mail) and discussion groups. Gopher, Veronica, WAIS (Wide Area Information Server), and e-mail are the most common access tools for students. Gophers provide access to over 1,300 online library catalogs, text files, phone books, and databases stored in WAIS, e-mail directories, and news networks. The typical Gopher menu begins by giving the user a choice of the following categories:[7]

1. Electronic books.
2. Electronic journals collection.
3. Information from the U.S. federal government.

4. Library catalogs via Telnet.
5. Library of Congress records.
6. Newspapers, magazines, and newsletters.
7. Reference works.

Veronica is a searching mechanism used with Gophers. WAIS had over 450 data sources in 1993. An Internet user tells of typing in the following question to WAIS: "Tell me about deforestation in the Amazon rain forest." Fifteen articles from various sources in WAIS, ranked in relevance to the question were listed in the returned message.[8] E-mail conversations can occur one on one and in discussion groups. One listing describes 850 groups organized around topics such as motorcycles, Bulgarian society, and tax laws.[9] Some groups of interest to business students are:

Deming: a forum for exchange of ideas and research related to the late W. Edwards Deming's work on quality. Located on the LISTSERV at address: deming-1@uhccvm.

Ethics: a group exchanging views about business ethics. Located on the LISTSERV at address: buseth-1@ubvm.cc.buffalo.edu.

Human Resources: an information listing on training and development of human resources. Located on the LISTSERV at: trdev-1@psuvm.psu.edu.

Industrial Psychology: a forum on organizational behavior and industrial and organization psychology. Located on the LISTSERV at: ioob-1@uga.-bitnet.

MBA Studies: a discussion list devoted to MBA curricula. Located on the LISTSERV at: mba-1@marist.bitnet.

Research Methodologies: a group discussing research methods. Located on the LISTSERV at address: methods@rpitsvm.

TQM: a discussion group on total quality management in manufacturing and service industries. Located on the LISTSERV at address: quality@pucc.princeton.edu.

From the full text of a classic work to international university library catalogs, and from government information to e-mail with experts, the Internet provides endless opportunities for information retrieval. Appendix A contains a list of books that will help the beginner get started with Internet.

Online Databases   The term **online** refers to the process by which a researcher can enter computerized databases on remote computer systems. This is accomplished with a computer terminal, personal and/or portable computer, a direct communication line to the system, or a telephone line with a modem. Appropriate software is necessary to conduct the search. Fees are charged for online databases by vendors and/or publishers. Costs may include:

1. Subscription fees that are paid once or annually.
2. Monthly minimum charges for use of the service.

3. Connect time fees by the hour or minute, which vary by database and the length of the connection.
4. Charges for printed material requested from the system.
5. Charges for the telecommunication network that links the researcher to the computer of the online service.

Public and university libraries may offer online database research services for a fee. Corporate libraries subscribe to various databases for use by employees. Often the actual access to the database is accomplished by a trained librarian after consultation with the primary researcher.

Some widely used online databases are:

1. *ABI/INFORM* (Abstracted Business Information) U.M.I./Data Courier, Louisville, Kentucky.
2. *Dow Jones News/Retrieval Service,* Dow Jones, Princeton, New Jersey.
3. *Lexis,* Mead Data Central, Dayton, Ohio, a full-text legal database.
4. *Compuserve,* H & R Block, Inc., Columbus, Ohio.
5. *The Source,* Reader's Digest Association, Inc., McLean, Virginia.
6. *Prodigy,* Prodigy Services, Co., White Plains, New York.
7. *America Online,* Vienna, Virginia.

The last four databases offer access to a variety of business and financial information, games, electronic mail, and personal computing services.

Overseas, computer terminals for the French MINITEL system, a computer-based information system, are available free to all telephone customers. This service allows access to hundreds of full-text databases on a fee basis. Examples are a news line, a reservation information service, and a cultural biography service. Integrated computer-based services such as MINITEL will become more common.

CD-ROM Databases   **CD-ROM** stands for computer disk/read only memory. It is familiar to the public as the compact disk (CD). Data are stored on CD-ROM disks; to retrieve the data, a disk is placed in a CD-ROM drive attached to a personal computer. The data are read from the CD-ROM and displayed on the computer screen or printed on a local printer. A typical disk can store about 250,000 book pages.[10] The disks are purchased on a subscription basis from a publisher or vendor, and subscribers periodically receive new disks with updated information. Libraries that subscribe to these databases use their personal computers for the search process and update their information as the new disks are received. They can also network these CD-ROM databases on a LAN (local area network), enabling more than one user to reach the same database simultaneously.

Many CD-ROM databases are indexes to periodical literature such as *ABI/INFORM,* published by University Microfilms, Inc. Similar to the online service, *ABI/INFORM* provides search capabilities and abstracts (summaries) of articles on various business topics. The full text of many articles found in *ABI/INFORM* is currently available in *Business Periodicals On-Disc. Infotrac General Business File,* which is published by Information Access Company and organized in three parts, includes references to articles on business topics in *Business Index,* company and industry information in *General Business File,* and financial reports on companies in *Investext.* The full text of some newspapers such as *The Wall Street Journal* and the *New York Times* are also available in CD-ROM databases for recent years. Sample output from a CD-ROM search is shown in Figure 9–3. Additional CD-ROM databases are listed in Appendix A.

Advantages and Disadvantages of a Computerized Search   A computerized search has three major advantages over a manual one. The first is speed. In just seconds, the computer can scan thousands of citations in the computer databases and reduce the amount of error that might occur in a manual search. The computer search also brings added flexibility to the search. A computer search can combine subject items in ways that are not possible in a manual search. Every meaningful word in an

**FIGURE   9–3
Sample
CD-ROM Search**

```
STOCKHOLDERS' DERIVATIVE ACTIONS
   -analysis
   -cases
   -economic aspects
   -legal aspects
   -litigation
   -management
   -Massachusetts
   -planning
   -prevention
   -rules and regulations
STOCKHOLDERS' EQUITY
   see
      Capital stock
STOCKHOLDERS' MEETINGS

                                              General Periodicals Index-A
STOCKHOLDERS' DERIVATIVE ACTIONS
   -analysis

      Your ownership; how to stay out of trouble. il v3
The Business Owner  Oct '89  p. 5(3)

      The unlocking of corporate America. (institutional investors
want more control of companies) by Phyllis Feinberg il
v25 Pension World Feb'89 p14(4)
                                    LIBRARY SUBSCRIBES TO JOURNAL
      Investor waits for AMI response to his request for CEO's ouster.
(M. Lee Pearce, American Medical International Inc., Walter L Weisman)
by Howard Kim il   v18 Modern Healthcare July 29 '88 p2(1)
                                                              39W0417
                                    LIBRARY SUBSCRIBES TO JOURNAL

      Bryan family appears to be winning proxy fight: preliminary count
shows lead for those opposed to election to the board of three
Burt Sugarman-supported directors. by Andrew Radolf   v121
Editor & Publisher  May 28 '88  p11(2)
                                    LIBRARY SUBSCRIBES TO JOURNAL
```

Source: Sample search from *Infotrac: General Periodicals Index-A* (Information Access Company, 1990).

index entry (including full abstracts) can be searched, unwanted aspects of a subject can be eliminated, and the results can be focused on only those citations that fit the research need. Because the computerized versions of familiar print indexes are updated more frequently than the printed copies, a computerized search will often retrieve more current material than is possible in a manual search. One example of this is University Microfilms International's *Dissertation Abstracts.*

There are also some inherent disadvantages with computerized searches. Each of these can be overcome by careful planning and thought. A computerized search uses one or more key words, exactly as typed into the system. As a result, synonyms and alternate spellings are not automatically searched. Careful planning and use of a thesaurus are necessary to ensure the researcher finds all the available citations in the database. At the other extreme, a computerized search will often find many sources that contain the key words the researcher has used, but the citation is not related to the subject being studied. This raises the cost of the search without providing additional benefit to the researcher. A third disadvantage is that the computerized databases are limited in the number of years they cover. It is usually necessary to revert to a traditional library search (manual search) for journal articles written before the mid-70s. The speed, flexibility, and coverage provided by computerized searches usually far outweigh these disadvantages.

Planning a Computerized Search   Preparing for a database search forces the researcher to think through the topic carefully and to plan a research strategy. Doing this early in the research process can help to clarify the topic and highlight possible problem areas so they can be resolved.

Once a strategy is decided, the researcher is ready to begin the search and will move through the following steps, whatever the type of database or retrieval system that is used:

1. Select an appropriate database (this may be changed as the search continues).
2. Type in the search term(s).
3. Examine the number of possible citations—expand or limit that number.
4. Retrieve an initial citation or citations.
5. Review the citations and decide if the search needs modification for additional, fewer, or more precise citations.
6. Investigate the citations (unless the search was conducted on a full-text database).

Although computerized searching may seem very confusing at first, proficiency will increase as the researcher continues to use this valuable research tool.

Library Search Procedure

In contrast to the computerized search, a manual search is more time-consuming. Although computerized searching is now available in most libraries, it is still important to know how to conduct a manual search, using the paper volumes. It is only by doing a thorough search (both computerized and manual), that the researcher knows that all possible sources of secondary data have been investigated.

Periodicals as a Source   Periodicals are often the best single source of information for the business researcher. There are thousands of publications covering almost any subject imaginable. Periodicals are especially useful in providing the most current information.

For those who do not have access to computerized indices, libraries have paper indices by which the investigator may quickly review the contents of many periodicals without physically finding the publications. The most widely known of these is the *Reader's Guide to Periodical Literature.* This is a subject guide to about 180 general-interest magazines such as *Time, Newsweek, Business Week, Fortune, Scientific American,* and others. It is useful for topics of general interest, but it also includes many articles on business and technological matters.

Four widely available paper indices (which are also available in a computerized format) are germane to business topics. They are:

1. *Business Periodicals Index.* New York: H. W. Wilson, 1958 to date.
2. *Applied Science and Technology Index.* New York: H. W. Wilson, 1958 to date.
3. *Public Affairs Information Service Bulletin.* New York: 1915 to date.
4. *Predicasts F & S Index of Corporations and Industries.* Detroit: Funk & Scott, 1960 to date.

The *Business Periodicals Index* (BPI) is a subject index of articles from approximately 260 business and economics periodicals. It is quite useful as a guide to the practical aspects of business operations and for specific industries and businesses. A companion index is the *Applied Science and Technology Index* (ASTI). The ASTI catalogs those periodicals that concentrate on scientific and technological subjects, but many articles on nontechnical subjects are also included in these periodicals. It is organized by subject and covers approximately 300 publications.

The third major index of value to the business researcher is the *Public Affairs Information Service Bulletin* (PAIS). Its coverage overlaps the BPI to some extent, but it also includes a more wide-ranging list of English-language publications from around the world. In addition, many books, government publications, and pamphlets are also indexed by subject. It covers many nonperiodical publications that become available from time to time.

The *Predicasts F & S Index of Corporations and Industries* indexes articles in periodicals and other references on U.S. corporations and industries. Currently, this index covers about 750 publications. Through 1966, coverage also included the same topics for Canada, Great Britain, and Japan. Since 1966, a companion volume, called the *Predicasts F & S Index International,* covers companies, industries, and countries outside the United States.

The *New York Times* and *The Wall Street Journal* also have their own paper indices. The *New York Times Index* can be searched for references back to 1851. *The*

Wall Street Journal Index is divided into two sections, one for corporate news arranged by the name of the firm and one for general news arranged by subject. Both indices are updated monthly. There are many other indices and bibliographies available for researching business topics. Some others include: *Social Science Citations Index* (that has the unique feature of listing the articles citing the referenced work), *Psychological Abstracts, The Accounting & Tax Index,* and *Education Index.*

Be sure to notice the date on the most current index you use. Since publication of indices takes approximately three months, it may be necessary to manually search the most appropriate journals' last few issues to ensure you have found the latest information on your selected topic.[11]

While these periodical indices are invaluable, they may still prove to be inadequate for a specific research study. This may occur because they cover such a small portion of the periodicals published. Many publications with valuable information are not indexed in any of the guides mentioned. Several references identify magazines associated with specific industries. One that lists trade and professional associations and their publication is called the *National Trade and Professional Associations of the United States,* 28th ed. (Washington, D.C.: Columbia Books, 1993). The *Encyclopedia of Associations,* 28th ed. (Detroit: Gale Research Company, 1993) will also give you a listing of national associations around the country.

Another helpful source available in most libraries is *Ayer Directory of Publications* (Philadelphia: Ayer Press, 1980 to date). This is an annual list of American newspapers and periodicals, arranged by state and city of publication; it gives detailed information about each title. It also has an alphabetical list of titles and a classified list of trade, technical, and professional journals.

To locate the nearest library that has copies of magazines found from these sources, refer to *New Serial Titles* (Washington, D.C.: Library of Congress, 1953 to date) and the *Union List of Serials in Libraries of the United States and Canada,* 3rd ed., 5 vols. (New York: H. W. Wilson, 1965). Together, these are the most comprehensive lists of periodicals available.

Books as a Source   As you continue the search along the investigative channels shown in Figure 9–1, you will use a catalog to gain information from books. Using a computerized catalog, the researcher can look up any book using the title, the author, or the general subject heading. Each system is different, but typically the researcher will type in "T=selected title" for a title search, "A=selected author" for an author search, or "S=selected general subject category" for a subject search. The system will respond with a list of books. The researcher can request further information on any book on the list. If you are searching in a traditional card catalog, books are listed by author, title, and subject.

Whether using a computerized catalog or traditional library card catalog, searching by subject headings is usually the easiest, but can also present a confusing problem. If you do not happen to think of the same exact subject heading statement used by the library, you may miss some good sources. One way to prevent this is to refer to U.S. Library of Congress, Cataloging Policy and Support Office, *Library of Congress Subject Headings,* 16th ed. (Washington, D.C.:

Cataloging Distribution Service, Library of Congress, 1993). This reference shows the headings used in any public catalog following the Library of Congress system. In addition, it suggests related subjects. If the subject matter is specialized or narrow in scope, is very new, or if little has been published on it, there may not be a reference in the catalog.

It is often a shock to inexperienced researchers when they find no references to their subject in the library's public catalog. This may result from one of three circumstances: (1) a library can have only a small percentage of the publications that are produced, (2) the topic may be so narrow that it is not the subject of a full book or pamphlet in the library collection, or (3) the material on the subject may be in the library in a collection not listed in the public catalog.

A library's holdings are always restricted by limited funds and by the interests of those who choose books for the library. In a university library, the holdings reflect the perceived importance of various disciplines and the specific interests of faculty members.

Books might have been published on the topic even though they are not available in the library. You can track down these references by going to a guide to published books. One good one is *Cumulative Book Index: World List of Books in the English Language* (New York: II. W. Wilson, 1928 to present). This guide includes books published in the English language in the United States since 1930 and in other parts of the world. Books are recorded by author, title, and subject. Other guides are listed in Appendix A.

The second type of failure to find a reference in the public catalog occurs when the topic is not the subject of a separate publication. However, it may be included in some work that covers a more general topic. Information on executive bonus systems may not be found in a card catalog. A search under the broader subject of management will show many publications that may include coverage of bonus arrangements.

A third possibility is that the library has holdings on subjects that are not listed in the card catalog. This is the case with most U.S. government publications. Many state and local government publications are also not cataloged. In addition, libraries have vertical files with pamphlets, speeches, bulletins, annual reports of companies, bank reports, and similar items that are of interest to the business researcher. Usually these are not recorded in the public catalog.

Documents as a Source   The topics covered in documentary publications range widely. The source for searching U.S. government document publications is the U.S. Superintendent of Documents, *United States Government Publications: Monthly Catalog* (Washington, D.C.: U.S. Government Printing Office, 1893 to date). Materials issued by all branches of the U.S. government are listed by name of the issuing office. There are monthly and annual subject indices that are valuable to the investigator. The *Monthly Catalog* is also available in a CD-ROM database called the Government Documents Catalog Service (GDCS), which is updated monthly. Documents are indexed by title, key word (various combinations), subject, and other access points. However, for retrospective searching the *Monthly Catalog* is still the source to use.

The listings in the *Monthly Catalog* will often have a heavy black dot in the margin next to an entry. The dot identifies that item as a publication that is available to depository libraries. Depository libraries have been designated by the U.S. government to hold a collection of major government documents. This program is designed to assure widespread distribution of government literature. A list of regional depository libraries is given in each issue of the *Monthly Catalog*. Even the largest depository library will not have every depository marked item. A library usually selects only designated publications that fit with the interests of its patrons. A metropolitan library may choose few of the agricultural items. With each entry in the *Monthly Catalog* is a special Superintendent of Documents classification number. Library holdings of documents are often, but not always, shelved by this number.

Government publications are good sources of information in many topic areas. The entire area of economic statistics is one of these areas. There are also important documents concerning many scientific fields, government relations to business, and business operations. The various congressional committee reports frequently have testimony about business operations that is seldom available anyplace else. The documents on the literature of agricultural marketing contain many pioneering field experiment research studies.

Special Collections: Miscellaneous Sources   A final category listed in Figure 9–1 is special collections. Among these are many reference works, some of which have already been mentioned. Others are listed in Appendix A at the back of the book. Data published by business associations may be listed in the public catalog, or the material may be in vertical files kept by the library. The contents of the files are primarily pamphlets. Company annual reports and other similar materials are also more likely to be found in uncataloged collections, especially in microfilm or microfiche collections. Another source of subject files is a local newspaper's "morgue." This area typically contains clippings on every subject ever published in that newspaper. Often the public is able to gain access to the local newspaper's morgue.[12]

Publications from colleges and universities are a major miscellaneous source. Doctoral dissertations are particularly valuable if you are investigating subjects at the frontiers of knowledge. The dissertations of people receiving their doctorates at a given university will usually be cataloged in that university's library only. *American Doctoral Dissertations* (Ann Arbor, Mich.: Xerox University Microfilms, 1957 to date) and *Dissertation Abstracts International* (Ann Arbor, Mich.: Xerox University Microfilms, 1938 to date) offer information about dissertations from other universities. The first publication provides "complete listing of all Ph.D. and other doctoral dissertations accepted by American and Canadian universities." Another excellent reference for tracking down university research publications is Associated University Bureaus of Business and Economic Research, *Index of Publications of Bureaus of Business and Economic Research,* 1950–1956 (Eugene, Ore.: 1957 to date). This is an index to the reports, bulletins, and monographs published by university bureaus of business research. Supplements include some articles appearing in periodicals published by these bureaus.

STATISTICAL REFERENCES

Data are classified as either statistical or nonstatistical in nature. Government documents and company and association publications are often statistical in nature, while periodicals and books are frequently nonstatistical. Here is an outline of some important statistical sources for the business researcher.

Statistical Guides   There are many statistical sources with a wealth of data, yet it is often difficult to find the specific information needed. There are guides, however, that can help locate the major statistical sources or provide descriptions of the various statistical publications. Two such sources are mentioned here, while more are given in Appendix A.

The first is *Statistics Sources,* 15th ed. (Detroit: Gale Research, 1992). This volume identifies primary sources of statistical data, for the United States and other countries, on subjects arranged alphabetically. Another source is *The Guide to U.S. Government Statistics* (McLean, Va.: Documents Index, Inc., 1992/93). This work is a guide to U.S. government statistical publications. Access can be made through the document index cataloging number, agency, area, subject, or title. The guides mentioned above are directories to the location of the various types of statistics and do not themselves present statistical data. Other sources that give references to statistical information found in a collection of articles on microfiche include: *American Statistics Index* (ASI), *Statistical Reference Index* (SRI), and *Index to International Statistics* (IIS). ASI provides access to statistics in federal publications. SRI indexes statistics from state agencies and private organizations. IIS provides access to international statistics, many of which are from United Nations publications. The complete references for these sources are found in Appendix A.

Several widely available reference books simply give various statistical information. The most important of these is U.S. Bureau of the Census, *Statistical Abstract of the United States* (Washington, D.C.: U.S. Government Printing Office, 1879 to date). This is an annual compendium of summary statistics on the political, social, industrial, and economic life of the United States. It should be the starting point in gathering statistical data on most topics. The *Statistical Abstract* has two particular values to the business researcher. First, it is the most comprehensive and up-to-date compilation of statistics covering wide areas of our natural life. Second, even if the specific figures or detail needed are not presented, the source notes for the tables and appended bibliography of sources of statistics are useful guides for further research.

There are several major supplements to the *Statistical Abstract of the United States. The County and City Data Book* provides recent figures for states, counties, cities of 25,000 or more, and places of 2,500 or more. The data include figures on population, vital statistics, industry, elections, and many other items. *The Congressional District Data Book* presents similar variety of information by congressional district. Finally, the *Historical Statistics of the United States* brings together historical series of wide general interest from colonial times to 1970.

Four major monthly governmental periodicals provide most of the current statistics available on our economy and its operation. The *Survey of Current Business* contains about 2,500 statistical series on income, expenditures, production and prices of commodities, and many other aspects of the economy. Historical figures for the statistical data published in the *Survey of Current Business* are available in a supplement titled *Business Statistics,* published in odd-numbered years. A second major statistical source is the *Federal Reserve Bulletin.* It publishes a large volume of national economic data with emphasis upon financial statistics. The third major governmental publication is the *Monthly Labor Review,* which publishes data on such topics as work and labor conditions, wage rates, and consumer price indices. The fourth is the *Business Conditions Digest,* which contains about 600 economic time series in a form convenient for forecasters and business analysts.

Many other government periodicals contain regular statistical information about transportation, agriculture, health, education, welfare, and other areas. Hundreds of privately published periodicals also provide statistical information.

Census Data

The periodic censuses conducted by the U.S. government are a basic statistical datasource in the United States. The oldest of these censuses is the *Census of Population* first taken for the year 1790; it has been taken at 10-year intervals since. Over the years, there have been substantial additions to the type of information collected in this census. Much of the information compiled during the 1990 census is available in a CD-ROM format. Today, one can secure detailed breakdowns of population by ethnic, economic, social, and occupational characteristics. Many of these data are available by state, county, metropolitan area, city, and census tract (a small homogeneous urban area that consists of a few hundred to a few thousand people). In addition, special enumerations of data may be purchased for smaller areas or for special combinations of variables selected for a particular project.

In recent decades, a *Census of Housing* has been conducted with the population census. It provides information about the cost of housing, rental values, quality of housing, size of homes, occupancy rates, and other information. In some metropolitan areas, housing data are available down to as small a geographic unit as a single city block.

Many business and industrial censuses have been taken at varying intervals. One is the *Census of Manufactures,* which was first taken for the year 1809, but has been published at frequent intervals only since 1929. Another major census is the *Census of Business.* It was first published for 1929 and has been published since then at intervals of four or five years. The *Census of Business* is divided into three units, the "Census of Retail Trade," the "Census of Wholesale Trade," and the "Census of Selected Services." Major censuses are also taken in agriculture, transportation, government, construction industries, and mining and mineral industries.

Several useful compilations of economic data for small geographic areas are provided by private sources. *Sales and Marketing Management* magazine publishes annually a "Survey of Buying Power." It provides current estimates of population, income, retail sales, and a variety of other statistics for every county and standard statistical metropolitan area in the United States and for most cities of about 10,000 population or more.

This brief coverage of statistical publications includes only the major sources of the most readily available statistical data. In each case, only those that specialize in statistics are given. In addition, many valuable statistics will be found in publications that are primarily nonstatistical in nature.

EXTRACTING INFORMATION

Gathering and recording information from sources are often viewed as simple chores within the competence of anyone. These tasks are frequently done poorly but may be improved in three ways. First, you must select the information to record. That is, some information will be useful and some will not; some will add to your collection and some will be repetitious. These decisions are guided by the research purpose. Set up an outline of the topic as quickly as possible, even knowing it will probably change as you gather more information. The idea that "I'll gather all of the material and then decide how to organize it" is inefficient. Much interesting information that turns up is diversionary and unproductive.

The second task is to decide how to record what you will extract from the published material. Should you report it verbatim, paraphrase it, or outline it? More often than not, outlining is the most efficient method. For specific important decisions or statements, you will wish to record them verbatim. In a few other instances, a paraphrase statement of the author's position is suitable.

The third task is to develop an orderly recording system. With it, you can have the extracted information available when needed, have a ready reference source for checking, and have maximum flexibility in organizing the information.

A Recording System

The first requirement of a recording system is ease of use. Many researchers use a software program to record both bibliographic references and the notes taken from them. When the results can be imported into word processors, such a system is very efficient. Other researchers use cards. Recording information on cards allows for flexible handling and organizing. Some even advocate putting a single fact or idea on each individual card; this obviously promotes maximum flexibility, but it also fragments the information. The single-idea-per-card concept is probably more desirable in cases where the researcher does not have a clear idea of subject organization.

One method of recording uses two sets of cards and an outline of the key elements or questions regarding the topic. While the outline may change as the researcher gains insight into the subject, it helps in deciding which information is needed and how various bits of information should be related.

One set of cards (probably 3-by-5 cards) is used for bibliographic references, and the second set (probably 5-by-8 cards) is used for the actual note taking. The 3-by-5 cards should be set up in proper bibliographic format, one reference per card, so they can be used later for footnote statements and for the drafting of the bibliography. These cards can be coded by a simple system that may be used to identify specific passages on the note cards. One useful coding system employs a combination letter and number (F1, F2, and so forth) to identify each author whose last name begins with F.

CLOSE-UP

Assume an executive in your organization asks for a review of the technical forecasting function. One member of your team is assigned to find all past forecasts and match them against the actual performances of products in the marketplace. For this she uses internal sources. Another member is charged with evaluating external forecasting organizations whose services can be purchased. He works primarily in direct contact with those external organizations. Your job is to evaluate the theoretical basis on which the forecasting function is based and the way in which it has evolved over the last 20 years. You break your task into two distinct parts: information before mid-1970, when the function began operating in the organization, and information after 1970 showing the evolution of technical forecasting over the last 20 years.

Although you know little about technical forecasting in 1970, you are confident since you know how to use the proper research tools. Your search begins with your company's library. It subscribes to a wide range of computerized databases, so your first step is to meet with the librarian. You learn that most of the databases begin coverage in the early 1980s. However, one source, the UMI *Dissertation Abstracts,* covers information as early as 1861. You order a search based on "technological forecasting," "technological and forecasting," or "technical and forecast" from 1950 to 1970.

Your next step is to continue your search at the library of a local university, and the sequence followed is illustrated in a general way by the flow diagram in Figure 9–1.[13] You check the 1970 versions of the *Encyclopaedia Britannica* and the *International Encyclopedia of the Social Sciences.* These are usually good sources for some quick information about a topic; but here, there is no men-

tion of technological forecasting. This is likely to happen if a topic or its terminology are new.

Next, you try two guides to business reference materials. These provide lists of bibliographies, handbooks, textbooks, and manuals that are often helpful. These sources are Edwin T. Coman, *Sources of Business Information,* and Harvard University, *Selected Business Reference Sources.* In the Coman book, nine books are listed on forecasting, but nothing that specifically mentions technological forecasting. It also lists a bibliography on business forecasting.

While putting Coman back on the shelf, serendipity takes over. Researchers need to cultivate a certain sensitivity that enables them to find things by luck. On the shelf, about two books away from the Coman book, is a 152-page bibliography, dated 1965, titled, *Business Trends and Forecasting,* published as *Management Information Guide No. 9* by the Gale Research Company. This turns out to be an excellent annotated bibliography. The annotations are so complete that a study of the contents shows there was virtually nothing on technological forecasting in business forecasting books up to 1965. While this is negative information, it is useful. You decide to restrict your search to the period since 1965.

With the preliminary steps not paying off, you decide to go directly to the *Bibliographic Index* (BI). In the index for 1966–1968, you find two entries listing bibliographies on technological forecasting. Search of earlier indices back to 1960 turns up nothing further. The BI for 1969 has not mentioned the subject, while the April 1970 index has one reference.

Since the topic includes the word *technological,* you decide first to investigate the *Applied Science and Technology Index.* You review entries from 1963 to June 1970 and find one entry on the subject in the 1966 volume. There are three entries in 1967, five in 1968, four in 1969, and

(continued)

one in 1970. From 1966 to mid-1970, you find a total of 14 entries in ASTI referencing articles about technological forecasting. A search of PAIS for the same period turns up 11 more references to articles on technological forecasting, while BPI produces 19 that do not duplicate any found in the other two indices.

Moving now to the public catalog, you learn the library has only one of the two books mentioned in the BI but does list two other books on technological forecasting and one published proceeding of a conference. Three out of four of these items come from European sources. Their cards in the public catalog show that three books have bibliographies ranging from 3 to 40 pages.

Although finding four books on the subject in the card catalog is encouraging, you search further by going to the *Library of Congress Subject Catalog.* This is rewarded by finding four more books listed there. You now have identified eight English-language books that have been published on technological forecasting from 1967 to 1970. Some of these new discoveries may be in a local library, or you might choose to buy one or more of them.

With an inventory of eight book references and 44 periodical references, there is not much incen

tive to look further, but for the sake of completeness, you search through the annual subject indexes of the *Monthly Catalog* of the U.S. Superintendent of Documents. From 1968 through mid-1970, there are eight references to published government documents on technological forecasting. All of them concern technological forecasting in the Soviet Union. None of them is on the depository list.

You return to the company library and discover the computer search of dissertations reveals there were no dissertations on technical forecasting before 1970. In total, then, after several hours of search, you have bibliography cards that include:

Eight books specifically about technological forecasting, at least four of which have extensive bibliographies to check.

Forty-four periodical references.

Eight government document references.

With this list, the reference search is well launched. The problem now is to find the references, weed out those that do not hold promise, and extract appropriate information from the remainder.

The 5-by-8 note cards (some prefer to use regular 8 ½-by-11 paper) provide more adequate space for writing information. On the note card margins, the bibliography reference codes may be entered to provide a ready source reference for each idea. Allied ideas from different sources may be placed on the same card without losing the ability to track each reference back to its source. The use of this system will enable you to develop a substantial set of notes, easily reorganized, and with each idea referenced to the source. Figure 9–4 illustrates such cards.

EVALUATING SECONDARY DATA

This chapter has stressed the value of secondary data sources, but there is still the task of evaluating the data. This evaluation takes two forms: first, how well do the data fit the research needs; and second, what confidence can you put in the accuracy and legitimacy of the data?

**FIGURE 9–4
A Note Card
Example**

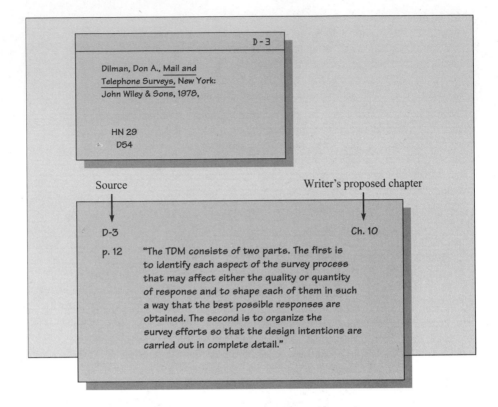

Paramount in any consideration of secondary data is the inescapable fact that the data were not originally collected for our needs. Do you understand the definitions and classifications employed? Are their meanings consistent with your own? The measurements used and the topical coverage and time frame are important.

The question of data quality is, first, a question of data accuracy. It is good research practice to go to the original source of the information rather than use an intermediate source that has quoted from the original. This enables you to avoid any errors in transcription and review the cautionary and other comments that went along with the original data. Finally, you may uncover revisions that have been made in the data since the intermediate source used it.

Another aspect of data accuracy concerns its completeness: How much does the reported material cover? Is it based upon a narrow sample, a large population, or what? Answers to these questions may suggest that the data are not appropriate for the problem. Another aspect of data quality concerns the capability of the source of the data. In this context, there are two concerns: first, are the persons who conducted the study people in whom you can have confidence? Are they highly regarded? Is their organization well regarded? A second aspect of source capability concerns the original source: Could the respondent answer this question? What are the chances that the respondent would know and be willing to give such information under the study conditions?

A concern that any investigator has in studying the quality of secondary data is the degree to which they accurately reflect reality. A confounding factor is that of possible bias. Perhaps the study was conducted for some purpose that may have dictated a particular orientation. Again, the question of who did the research, whether the findings promote a special interest, and how the investigation was conducted are all important clues. One must especially be on guard when a report does not contain the methodology and sampling design. These are of prime concern in determining if the secondary data are adequate for the investigator's research purposes.

Summary

The use of secondary data sources for research presents some unique challenges. The collection of data from within a person's own organization, in particular, defies generalized description. Published data, on the other hand, are cataloged and coded to simplify their use.

Sources may be classed into four major groups and a special collections category. Computerized databases are the newest, most dynamic sources available. Internet, a worldwide access to databases and networks, has revolutionized the way in which we view traditional library research. Some databases are online, accessible through a computer terminal, personal or portable computer. Others have the data stored on CD-ROM; the data can be displayed on a personal computer's screen or printed. These databases cover not only current periodicals and newspapers, but also statistical data. Indices, abstracts, bibliographic listings, and source material are all available through a variety of services to which a company, library, or individual subscribe. Periodicals are especially valuable for current information and for topics of limited scope. Books are usually the basic source for general coverage and for established topics of breadth or depth. Documents from governmental organizations are a fourth major source of secondary data. Finally, there are special collections of materials produced by private research organizations, universities, trade associations, and reference services.

In using secondary data sources, researchers have two jobs. First, they must define their research needs to be able to use coding systems. These systems have been developed to make printed information more accessible and to ensure that the computerized search is exhaustive. This requires the researchers to be knowledgeable about major reference tools and have skills using them. The second task is to secure adequate usable data from the information storage system. This calls for skill in extracting information efficiently and the ability to judge how much confidence to place in the information.

Research based on secondary sources may sometimes answer the research question. Normally, secondary sources serve as either (1) the exploratory phase of a study or (2) the basis for discovery and building upon the work of others. The selection of a design, instruments, and data analysis can be influenced by the quality of the sources selected.

Key Terms

CD-ROM
computerized searches
database
   reference
   source

external source
internal source
Internet
online
primary data
secondary data

Discussion Questions

1. Some researchers find that their sole sources are secondary data. Why might this be? Name some management research situations where secondary data sources are probably the only ones feasible.

2. While card catalogs of libraries are useful, what problems do you see if a researcher depends only on the catalog for information sources?

3. Many managements gather and analyze statistical data for small geographic areas. For what types of businesses do you think these data might be important? For what purposes might they want such information? What types of data might they use? Where might they secure such information from secondary sources?

4. Assume you work for a medium-sized retail clothing chain. Put together a proposal for adding computerized database capability to the company library at central headquarters. What services would you subscribe to? How would employees have access to the information? How can you convince your management that this would be a beneficial move?

5. Assume you are asked to investigate the use of mathematical programming in accounting applications; you decide to depend upon secondary data sources. What search tools might you use? Which do you think would be the most fruitful? Sketch a flow diagram of your search sequence.

6. What are the problems of secondary data quality that researchers must face? How can they deal with them?

7. Secure a recent copy of the *Statistical Abstract* and determine what information is available on the following topics:

   a. Coal mining.
   b. Consumer credit.
   c. Advertising expenditures.
   d. Labor unions.
   e. Social welfare expenditures.
   f. Hospitals in the United States.
   g. Law enforcement.

8. Compare the costs of doing research with and without computerized databases. Assume a research assistant is paid $10 per hour. Check the rates for computerized research at your library. Based on this data, when would you recommend that a researcher use a computerized search?

9. Choose a line of trade and determine what data are available for that line at a state and local level in the *Census of Business.*

10. Choose a two-digit industry classification from the *Census of Manufactures,* and determine the type of information available for it. How much information is available at more detailed (for example, four-digit) levels?

11. While computer databases are very useful and fast, what problems would you anticipate for the researcher who depends solely on a computer search for information?

12. Below are a number of requests that a young staff assistant might receive. What specific tools or services would you expect to use to find the requisite information? (Appendix A may be helpful.)

    a. The president wants a list of six of the best references that have appeared on executive compensation during the last year.

    b. Has the FTC published any recent statements (within the last year) concerning its position regarding quality stabilization?

    c. A man at a western university is said to have completed his Ph.D. dissertation last year on competition problems in our industry. Can we find out whether or not this is true? How can we get a copy?

    d. I need a list of the major companies located in Greensboro, North Carolina.

    e. Please get me a list of the directors of General Motors, Microsoft, and Morgan Stanley & Co.

    f. A new book has recently come out concerning technological forecasting. Can you get the reference for me?

    g. Is there a trade magazine that specializes in the flooring industry?

    h. The Fuji Bank of Tokyo, Japan, has issued a special study in its December 1993 *Fuji Bank Bulletin.* Where can I get a copy?

    i. I would like to track down a study of small-scale service franchising that was recently published by a bureau of business research at one of the southern universities. Can you help me?

Reference Notes

1. *Directory of Online Databases, 9.1* (New York: Cuadra/ Elsevier Associates, January 1988).

2. *The Bowker Annual of Library and Book Trade Information,* 37th ed. (New York: R. R. Bowker, 1992), p. 502.

3. "Database," *Webster's New World Dictionary,* 2nd college ed. (New York: Simon & Schuster, 1984).

4. W. A. Katz, *Introduction to Reference Work, Volume I: Reference Services and Reference Processes,* 5th ed. (New York: McGraw-Hill, 1987), p. 125.

5. Ibid., p. 133.

6. National Science Foundation, *The NSFNET Backbone Services Acceptable Use Policy,* June 1992.

7. Richard J. Smith and Mark Gibbs, *Navigating the Internet* (Carmel, Ind.: Sams Publishing, 1993), p. 142.

8. Adam C. Engst, *Internet Starter Kit for Macintosh* (Indianapolis, Ind: Hayden Books, 1993), p. 12.
9. Ibid., pp. 429–530.
10. Katz, *Introduction to Reference Work,* p. 142.
11. William V. Ruch and Maurice L. Crawford, *Business Reports Written and Oral* (Boston: PWS-KENT Publishing Company, 1988), p. 75.
12. Ibid., p. 76.
13. This example is based on an actual study.

Suggested Readings

1. Barzun, Jacques, and Henry F. Graff. *The Modern Researcher.* 5th ed. Boston: Houghton Mifflin Co., 1992.
2. Daneills, Lorna M. *Business Information Sources.* 3rd ed. Berkeley: University of California Press, 1993.
3. Johnson, H. Webster; Anthony J. Faria; and Ernest L. Maier. *How to Use the Business Library: With Sources of Business Information.* 5th ed. Cincinnati: South-Western Publishing Co., 1984.
4. Katz, W. A. *Introduction to Reference Work.* 6th ed. New York: McGraw-Hill, 1992.

10 SURVEY METHODS

**FINDING
YOUR WAY**

BRINGING RESEARCH TO LIFE

From 100 feet away, Eric Burbidge saw that the number 99 bus was filthy. It would smell on the inside, he was sure. Forty riders were docilely lined up to board—one was a letter carrier, and a collection of other blue-collar men and women comprised the rest. Some were idly thumbing through newspapers—Good! Very good!—some were chatting, and two were ruminating slowly on hero sandwiches, which he supposed they had picked up at the tavern across the street from the bus station.

Burbidge swept past the queued passengers, taking care not to make premature eye contact, and brusquely rapped his clipboard against the bus's folding door. With a whoosh the driver snapped the door open, and Burbidge heaved himself up onto the bus. No one tried to follow him up, which he would not have allowed anyway, as he needed time to interrogate the driver, to see if the man would be of any help.

"Good evening, driver. I am Mr. Burbidge, and I am from headquarters."

"That figures. We don't see many suits on route 99."

"Then you know why I have had to come out here." He'd been with the bus company for three months, and this was the first time he had been required to board and ride a bus. What is that smell? Machine oil . . . sandwich meats . . . what else do the route's demographics suggest would be tracked every day through this bus? Sweat, of course! "I am conducting a scientific survey to determine the newspaper readership, if any, of riders on this route."

"Yessir," murmured the driver, without enthusiasm.

"If you have been reading your employees' newsletter, you must know that the corporation is soon to announce a restructuring of the route system and schedule, pursuant to which we shall have to purchase advertising space in the leading media to reveal our new route structure, maps, and schedules."

"Won't that be a mess," muttered the driver, in the same flat tone. "And, yessir, I read your newsletter. For 15 years I have read it."

"According to our records, you have been a driver on this very route for five years, and so you may have noticed that this route runs north-to-south equidistantly between the twin cities . . ."

"The route runs north-south, with one city on the east and the other on the west, yessir. I caught on to that long ago, sir. It's right there on the route map, sir. Clean splits the line between East City and West City and never gets closer to one than the other. If you want to get to one city or the other, you transfer to another bus. My bus just goes straight north. Right up there on the route map, sir."

"As corporate research director," said Burbidge, gracefully emphasizing his point by pointing a forefinger roofward, "I take nothing for granted, but instead provide scientific methodology, in this instance to test my hypothesis that readership of newspapers on this route would be equally divided between the *East City Gazette* and the *West City Tribune*. To that very end I have prepared this survey of your riders, which with your complete cooperation I have selected to pass out along this route, on this day, at this time."

"Newspapers, you say," said the driver, showing a flicker of involvement. "I could tell you quite a lot about those newspapers . . ."

"Not required! This is a scientific survey of riders on route 99, and anecdotal information is not appropriate. What I require of you is to let the passengers up onto the bus so I may give them these pencils and surveys, and then to refrain from swerving or unnecessarily agitating the bus while they are filling out my surveys. Do you think you can manage that?"

"I'd better turn on the inside lights, don't you think?"

"Well, of course, turn on the lights. That goes without saying."

The passengers boarded slowly, exchanging pleasantries with the driver. They were quite a little clan, Burbidge could see.

(continued)

The bus rolled steadily northward, and Burbidge was pleased to see that riders hunched over his one-page survey, though he was struck by how long it took them to answer the simplest of questions. As each completed the survey, he or she shyly shuffled forward and proffered it to Burbidge without comment.

Just when he sensed everything was going as well as might be expected, two men stood up, one in the front by the driver, one in the rear, and spread their legs and straddled the aisles. A ball of newsprint was tossed into the aisle, and the passengers began whooping and batting the paper forward and back. "What is this, driver?" demanded Burbidge.

"Hockey. They are playing hockey. The idea is to knock the ball between this guy's legs or that guy's in the back."

"Aren't you going to stop them?"

"No harm done. These are a friendly bunch. Big sports fans. In fact," said the driver, whose voice had gained enthusiasm when evading discussion of company business, "the East City club is playing pro hockey tonight, so when I clean out the bus, most of the newspapers will be the *East City Gazette.*" He rattled on, contributing to Burbidge's annoyance, explaining that the riders liked to study the night's pro game in advance, the better to discuss it among themselves, so newsstand sales were brisk in the terminal, but only for the newspaper that did the better job of covering the *sport de jour.* "Of course, tomorrow night there is pro basketball in West City, and most of the riders will pick up the *West City Tribune* at the newsstands."

"That's impossible to accept," shouted Burbidge. "Such behavior would bias my scientific survey, which asks for the paper they most recently purchased!".

"Well, you had better accept it. B'cause I've been cleaning out this bus for five years. It's the *Gazette* before hockey, and the *Trib* before basketball. This is a hockey crowd tonight, which means extra *Gazettes.*"

Burbidge was mortified and hoped he wasn't revealing his distress to the driver. Surely the driver would not understand the consequences of this predicament in biasing the survey. But the driver added, "'Course, in the mornings these folks bring the papers that the newsboys toss on their lawns, so you don't see such a situation."

"That is very difficult to accept, driver. It means that by choosing between sampling this route—morning or evening—I get a systematically different set of results, and by choosing a hockey night or a basketball night, I further incline toward different results." Burbidge was thinking out loud, almost in a trance.

"Naturally," agreed the driver, with irritating enthusiasm.

"Be still, driver. I have to think." Burbidge was shaken.

The driver had now warmed to his exposition of trash can sociological research. "Of course, by reading my newsletter, as I do, I know that by the time you announce the new routes and schedules, we will be finished with hockey and basketball and into the baseball season." Was there irony in the driver's chuckle?

"If you are furnishing me information that is at all reliable, driver, then the generalizability of my survey would be contingent on whether I ride in the morning or evening, on the professional sports schedule on a particular night, and on the season of the year."

"That's part of it, yessir."

"Part of it? Part of it? You mean, there's more? There is something else I haven't thought of?"

"Well, yessir, because, you see, most of these folks on the 5:15 bus are East City folks, and most of the people on the 5:45 bus are West City folks, so your outcomes would naturally depend on whether you took survey on the 5:15 or 5:45 bus."

Burbidge was shaken and no longer able to muster a vigorous "impossible to accept" or even a "difficult to accept."

"How can this be? Tell me."

"Well, you see, the 5:15 bus on this route—the one you are on now—gets to Boght Corners at 5:55,

(continued)

and the East City folks transfer onto the eastbound bus that is waiting there for them. Most of the West City folks hang out in the bar across the street from the terminal, get on the 5:45 bus and rendezvous at 6:25 with the westbound bus at Boght Corners."

"I see. I see." Ho was reconsidering the wisdom of this survey. "AND IS THERE ANYTHING ELSE you would care to share with me?"

"Only that the 5:45 boarders don't read the newspaper much at all, as they have been watching sports on the TV in the bar, are lightly soused,

some of them, and can't read the small print because I don't turn on the inside lights."

"I might as well have stayed home," Burbidge cried in despair.

The driver stopped the bus and swiveled to face Burbidge. "Wouldn't that have been a pity, sir, as I would have been deprived of this excellent lesson in scientific research."

Burbidge studied the driver carefully, struggling to believe this last remark was not the unkindest cut of all. No, he concluded, the bumpkin is too disingenuous to be capable of irony.

CHARACTERISTICS OF SURVEYS

Research designs can be classified by the communication method used to gather primary source data. There are really only two alternatives. We can *observe* conditions, events, people, or processes. Or we can *question* or *survey* people about various topics. We begin this chapter by discussing the characteristics and applications of the survey method. We then examine the strengths and weaknesses of data collection modes—personal interview, telephone interview, and self-administered/mail survey.

To **survey** is to question people and record their responses for analysis. The great strength of questioning as a primary data collecting technique is its versatility. It does not require that there be a visual or other objective perception of the information sought by the researcher. Abstract information of all types can be gathered only by questioning others. We can seldom learn much about opinions and attitudes except by questioning. This is also true for intentions and expectations. Information about past events is often available only through questioning of people who remember the events.

Surveys are more efficient and economical than observation. Information can be gathered by a few well-chosen questions that would take much more time and effort to gather by observation. Surveying, using the telephone or the mail as a medium of communication, can expand geographic coverage at a fraction of the cost and time required by observation.

The questioning technique has its shortcomings, however. The major weakness is that the quality of information secured depends heavily on the ability and willingness of respondents to cooperate. Often, people will refuse an interview or fail to reply to a mail survey. There may be many reasons for this unwillingness to cooperate. Certain people at certain times fail to see any value in participation; they also may fear the interview experience for some personal reason, or they may view the topic as too sensitive.

Even if respondents do participate, they may not have the knowledge sought or even have an opinion on the topic of concern. Under these circumstances, their proper response should be "don't know" or "have no opinion." Too often, respondents feel obliged to express some opinion even if they do not have one. In those cases, it is difficult for researchers to know how true or reliable the answers are.

Respondents may also interpret a question or concept differently from what was intended by the researcher. In this frame of reference, the respondent is answering a question different from the one being asked. Finally, a respondent may intentionally mislead the researcher by giving false information. It is difficult for a researcher to identify these occasions. Thus, survey responses should be accepted for what they are—statements by others that reflect varying degrees of truth. Despite these weaknesses, surveying is widely used in business research.

Applications

The most appropriate applications are those where respondents are uniquely qualified to provide the desired information. We should expect that such facts as age, income, immediate family situation, and so forth would be appropriate topics on which one would expect to get good data. However, if we ask the respondent to report on events that have not been personally experienced, we need to assess the replies carefully. If the purpose is to learn what the respondent understands to be the case, it is legitimate to accept the answers given. But if our intent is to learn what the event or situation was, recognize that the respondent is reporting second-hand data and the accuracy of the information declines. We should not depend on these sources if a more direct source can be found. A family member should be asked about another family member's experience only when there is no other way to get the information directly.

Questions can be used to inquire about subjects that are exclusively internal to the respondent. We include here such items as attitudes, opinions, expectations, and intentions. Such information can be made available to the researcher if the right questions are asked of respondents. It becomes, finally, a matter of whether to ask direct or indirect questions to collect the most meaningful data. More is said about this topic in the next chapter.

Besides the considerations mentioned above, various methods are used to interview respondents. Questioning can be carried out by face-to-face interviewing, by telephone, by mail, or by a combination of these. While there are many commonalities among these approaches, several considerations are unique to each.

PERSONAL INTERVIEWING

A **personal interview** (i.e., face to face) is a two-way conversation initiated by an interviewer to obtain information from a respondent. The differences in roles of interviewer and respondent are pronounced. They are typically strangers, and the interviewer generally controls the topics and patterns of discussion. The consequences of the event are usually insignificant for the respondent. The respondent is asked to provide information with little hope of receiving any immediate or direct benefit from this cooperation. Yet if the interview is carried off successfully, it is an excellent data collection technique.

Evaluation of the Personal Interview

There are real advantages and clear limitations to personal interviewing. The greatest value lies in the depth and detail of information that can be secured. It far exceeds the information secured from telephone and mail surveys. The interviewer can also do more things to improve the quality of the information received than with other methods. Interviewers can note conditions of the interview, probe with additional questions and gather supplemental information through observation.

The interviewers also have more control than with other kinds of interrogation. They can prescreen to assure the correct respondent is replying and can set up and control interviewing conditions. They can use special scoring devices and visual materials. Finally, interviewers can adjust to the language of the interview because they can observe the problems and effects the interview is having on the respondent.

With such advantages, why would anyone want to use any other survey method? Probably the greatest reason is that the method is costly, both in money and time. A personal interview may cost anywhere from a few dollars to $100 or more for an interview with a hard-to-reach person. Costs are particularly high if the study covers a wide geographic area or has stringent sampling requirements. An exception to this is **intercept interviews** that target shoppers in centralized locations such as shopping malls. Intercept interviews reduce costs associated with the need for several interviewers, training, and travel. Product and service demonstrations can also be coordinated, further reducing costs. Their cost-effectiveness, however, is offset when representative sampling is crucial to the study's outcome.

Survey costs have risen rapidly in recent years for most survey methods because changes in the social climate have made personal interviewing more difficult. Many people have become more reluctant to talk with strangers or permit visits in their homes.

Interviewers are reluctant to visit unfamiliar neighborhoods alone, especially for evening interviewing. Finally, results of personal interviews can be affected adversely by interviewers who alter the questions asked or in other ways bias the results. More about this is discussed later in the chapter. If we are to overcome these deficiencies, we must appreciate the conditions necessary for interview success.

Success Requirements   Three broad conditions must be met to have a successful personal interview. They are (1) availability of the needed information from the respondent, (2) an understanding by the respondent of his or her role, and (3) adequate motivation by the respondent to cooperate. The interviewer can do little about the respondent's information level. Screening questions can qualify respondents when there is doubt about their ability to answer. This is the study designer's responsibility.

Interviewers can influence respondents in many ways. An interviewer can explain what kind of answer is sought, how complete it should be, and in what terms it should be expressed. Interviewers even do some coaching in the interview, although this can be a biasing factor.

FIGURE   10–1   Opposing Motivation Levels Affecting a Respondent in an Interview

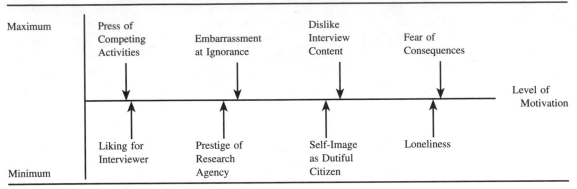

Source: Robert L. Kahn and Charles F. Cannell "Interviewing," David L. Sills, ed., *International Encyclopedia of the Social Sciences,* vol. 8, p. 153. Copyright © 1968 by Crowell Collier and Macmillan, Inc.

Respondent motivation is a responsibility of the interviewer. Studies of reactions to many surveys show that respondents can be motivated to participate in personal interviews and, in fact, can even enjoy the experience. In one study, more than 90 percent of respondents said the interview experience was interesting, and three-fourths reported they were willing to be interviewed again.[1]

Kahn and Cannell point out that a variety of forces affect respondent motivation in an interview. Many of these involve the interviewer. A graphic way to represent these various forces is presented in Figure 10–1.

Interviewing Technique[2]

At first, it may seem easy to question another person about various topics, but research interviewing is not so simple. What we do or say as interviewers can make or break a study. Respondents often react more to their feelings about the interviewer than to the content of the questions. It is also important that the interviewer ask the questions properly, record the responses accurately, and probe meaningfully. To achieve these aims, the interviewer must be trained to carry out those procedures that foster a good interviewing relationship.

Increasing Respondent's Receptiveness   The first goal in an interview is to establish a friendly relationship with the respondent. Three factors will help with respondent receptiveness. The respondent must (1) believe the experience will be pleasant and satisfying, (2) think the survey is important and worthwhile, and (3) have any mental reservations satisfied. Whether the experience will be pleasant and satisfying depends heavily upon the interviewer. Typically, respondents will cooperate with an interviewer whose behavior reveals confidence and engages people on a personal level. Effective interviewers are not differentiated by demographic characteristics but by these interpersonal skills. By confidence, we mean that most respondents are immediately convinced they will want to participate in the study and cooperate fully with the interviewer. An engaging personal style is one where the interviewer instantly establishes credibility by adapting to the individual needs of the respondent.

For the respondent to think that the survey is important and worthwhile, some explanation of the study's purpose is necessary although the amount will vary. It is the interviewer's responsibility to discover what explanation is needed and to supply it. Usually, the interviewer should state the purpose of the study, tell how the information will be used, and suggest what is expected of the respondent. Respondents should feel that their cooperation will be meaningful to themselves and to the survey results. When this is achieved, more respondents will express their views willingly. Respondents often have reservations about being interviewed that must be overcome. They may suspect the interviewer is a disguised salesperson, bill collector, or the like. In addition, they may also feel inadequate or fear they will be embarrassed by the questioning. Techniques for successful interviewing of respondents in their homes follow.

The Introduction   The respondent's first reaction to the request for an interview is at best a guarded one. Interviewer appearance and action are critical in forming a good first impression. Interviewers should immediately identify themselves by name and organization, showing any special identification. Introductory letters or other information confirm the study's legitimacy. In this brief period, the interviewer must display friendly intentions and stimulate the respondent's interest.

The interviewer's introductory explanations should be no more detailed than necessary. Too much information can introduce a bias. However, some respondents will demand more detail. For them, the interviewer might explain the objective of the study, its background, how the respondent was selected, the confidential nature of the interview (if it is such), and the beneficial values of the research findings. Be prepared to deal with questions such as:

"How did you happen to pick me?"

"Who gave you our name?"

"I don't know enough about this. Why don't you go next door?"

"Why are you doing this study?"[3]

The home interview typically involves two stages. The first occurs at the door when the introductory remarks are made, but this is not a satisfactory location for many interviews. In trying to secure entrance, it is considered more effective to suggest the desired action rather than to ask permission. "May I come in?" can be easily countered with a respondent's no, while "I would like to come in and talk with you about X" is more successful.

If the Respondent Is Busy or Away   If it is obvious that the respondent is busy, it may be a good idea to give a general introduction and try to stimulate enough interest to arrange an interview at another time. If the designated respondent is not at home, the interviewer should briefly explain the proposed visit to the person who is contacted. It is desirable to establish good relations with intermediaries since their attitudes can help in contacting the proper respondent.

The Good Interviewing Relationship   The successful interview is based on rapport, meaning a relationship of confidence and understanding exists between interviewer and respondent. Interview situations are often new to respondents, and they need help in defining their roles. The interviewer can help by conveying that the interview is confidential and important and that the respondent can discuss the topics with freedom from censure, coercion, or pressure. Under such conditions, the respondent can obtain much satisfaction in "opening up" without pressure being exerted.

Gathering the Data   To this point, the communication aspects of the interviewing process have been stressed. Having completed the introduction and established initial rapport, the interviewer turns to the technical task of gathering information. The interview centers on the prearranged questioning sequence. The technical task is well defined in studies with a structured questioning procedure (in contrast to an exploratory interview situation). The interviewer should follow the exact wording of the questions, ask them in the order presented, and ask every question that is specified. When questions are misunderstood or misinterpreted, they should be repeated.

A difficult task in interviewing is to make certain the answers adequately satisfy the question's objectives. To do this, the interviewer must learn the objectives of each question from a study of the survey instructions or by asking the project director. It is important to have this information well in mind because many first responses are inadequate even in the best-planned studies.

The technique of stimulating respondents to answer more fully and relevantly is termed **probing.** Since it presents a great potential for bias, a probe should be neutral and appear as a natural part of the conversation. There are different probing styles:

1. A brief assertion of understanding and interest. With comments such as "I see" or "yes" or "uh-huh," the interviewer can tell the respondent that the interviewer is listening and is interested in more.

2. An expectant pause. The simplest way to suggest to the respondent to say more is a pause along with an expectant look or a nod of the head. This approach must be used with caution. Some respondents have nothing more to say, and frequent pausing could give them some embarrassing silences.

3. Repeating the question. This is particularly useful when the respondent appears not to understand the question or has strayed from the subject.

4. Repeating the respondent's reply. This can be done while writing it down and often serves as a good probe. Hearing thoughts restated often promotes revisions or further comments.

5. A neutral question or comment. Such comments make a direct bid for more information. Examples are: "How do you mean?" "Can you tell me more about your thinking on that?" "Why do you think that is so?" "Anything else?"[4]

Another valuable technique is to ask for clarification. This approach is particularly effective when the answer is unclear or is inconsistent with something already said. Here the interviewer suggests he or she failed to understand fully. Typical of such probes is, "I'm not *quite* sure I know what you mean by that—could you tell me a little more?" or "I'm sorry, but I'm not sure I understand. Did you say previously that . . .?" It is important that the interviewer take the blame for failure to understand so as not to appear to be cross-examining the respondent.

A specific type of response that requires persistent probing is the "I don't know." This is a satisfactory response if the respondent does not know. But too often, "I don't know" means the respondent (1) does not understand, (2) says this to get time to think, or (3) is trying to evade the question. The interviewer can best probe this type of reply by using the expectant pause or by some reassuring remark such as, "We are interested in your ideas about this."[5]

Recording the Interview   While the methods used in recording will vary, the interviewer usually writes down the answers of the respondent. Some guidelines can make this task more efficient. First, it is important to record responses as they occur. If you wait until later, you lose much of what is said. If there is a time constraint, the interviewer should use some shorthand system that will preserve the essence of the respondent's replies without converting them into the interviewer's paraphrases. Abbreviating words, leaving out articles and prepositions, and using only key words are good ways to do this.

Another technique is for the interviewer to repeat the response while writing it down. This helps to hold the respondent's interest during the writing and checks the interviewer's understanding of what the respondent has said. Normally the interviewer should start the writing when the respondent begins to reply. The interviewer should also record all probes and other comments on the questionnaire in parentheses to set them off from responses.

Selection and Training   The job requirements for interviewers include some college experience, good communication skills, flexible schedules, willingness to tolerate intermittent work hours, and mobility. This results in an interviewer profile that is largely composed of college-educated white females who have few child-care responsibilities.[6] Little research evidence suggests that other profiles would increase performance or reduce error except in studies where the question directly involves ethnicity or religion or where volunteer interviewers are used. The former would imply that matching for race or religion should be considered, and the latter cautions against the use of volunteers because of attrition, recording error, and training-related problems.

Field interviewers receive varying degrees of training, ranging from brief written instructions to extensive sessions. Commercial market research firms often provide lower levels of training, while governmental, educational, and similar research organizations provide more extensive training.

Written instructions should be provided in all studies. Such instructions should cover at least the general objectives of the study and something on the problems that have been encountered in tests of the interview procedure and how they were solved. In addition, most questions should be discussed separately, giving the interviewer some insight into the purpose of the question, examples of adequate and inadequate responses, and other suggestions such as how to probe for more information. Definitions should be included so the interviewer can explain and interpret in a standardized manner.

Evidence supports the value of training. In one widely cited study, intensive training produced significant improvements in interviewer performance. The training effect was so great that performances of individual interviewers before training were poor predictors of post-training performance.[7]

Several sources suggest an interview training program should do the following:

1. Provide new interviewers with the principles of measurement; give them an intellectual grasp of the data collection function and a basis for evaluating interviewing behavior.
2. Provide practice in introductions and introductory materials.
3. Teach the techniques of interviewing.
4. Teach wording and "skip" instructions to help with a smooth and consistent flow of questions.
5. Teach how to probe.
6. Provide experience in recording answers of different types and on different scales.
7. Provide the opportunity for practice and evaluation by conducting interviews under controlled conditions.
8. Offer careful evaluation of interviews, especially at the beginning of actual data collection. Such evaluation should include review of interview protocols.[8]

Interview Problems

In personal interviewing, the researcher must deal with bias and cost. While each is discussed separately, they are interrelated. Biased results grow out of three types of error: sampling error, nonresponse error, and response error. Sampling error has been previously discussed.

Nonresponse Error   Availability is an important source of error for personal interviews. This **nonresponse error** occurs when you cannot locate whom you are supposed to study. It is an especially difficult problem when using a probability sample of subjects. In such a case, there are predesignated persons to be interviewed; the task is to find these respondents. If you are forced to interview substitutes, an unknown but possibly substantial bias is introduced. One study of nonresponse found that only 31 percent of all first calls (and 20 percent of all first calls in major metropolitan areas) were completed. The best first-call rate of 52 percent was for rural male respondents contacted after 6 P.M. on a weekday.

The most reliable solution to nonresponse problems is to make **callbacks.** If enough attempts are made, it is usually possible to contact most target respondents, although unlimited callbacks are expensive.[9] An original contact plus three callbacks should usually secure about 85 percent of the target respondents. Yet in one study, 36 percent of central city residents still were not contacted after three callbacks.[10]

This problem relates to a second kind of nonresponse error—accessibility. In central cities where getting access to the respondent can be a problem, household access may be complicated by apartment security and locations that produce safety problems for nighttime follow-up.[11] In suburban areas, gated developments prohibit free access to interviewers.

One way to improve the productivity of callbacks is to vary them by time of day and day of the week. Sometimes neighbors can suggest the best time to call. An approach that has been used successfully is to treat all remaining nonrespondents as a new subpopulation after a few callbacks. A random sample is then drawn from this group, and every effort is made to complete this sample with 100 percent response. These findings can then be weighted into the total population estimate.

Another approach is to adjust the results by weighting.[12] In a survey in which central city residents are underrepresented, we can weight the results of interviews that are completed to give them full representation in the results. The weakness of this approach is that weighted returns often differ from those that would be secured if callbacks were made. Weighting for nonresponse after only one contact attempt will probably not overcome nonresponse bias, but respondent characteristics converge on their population values after two to three callbacks.[13]

A third way to deal with this nonresponse problem is to substitute someone else for the missing respondent, but this is dangerous. "At home" respondents are likely to differ from "not at home" persons in systematic ways. One study suggested that "not at home" persons are younger, better educated, more urban and have a higher income than the average.[14]

If one must substitute, it is better for the interviewer to ask others in the household about the designated respondent. This approach has worked well "when questions are objective, when informants have a high degree of observability with respect to respondents, when the population is homogeneous, and when the setting of the interview provides no clear-cut motivation to distort responses in one direction or another."[15]

Response Error   When the data reported differ from the actual data, **response error** occurs. There are many ways such errors can happen. Errors can be made in the processing and tabulating of data. Errors occur when the respondent fails to report fully and accurately. One study found that liquid asset holdings were typically underestimated by as much as 25 to 50 percent. Other data, such as income and purchases of consumer durables, are more accurately reported. Respondents have difficulty in reporting fully and accurately on topics that are sensitive or involve ego matters. Consistent control or elimination of such respondent bias is a problem that has yet to be solved. The best advice is to use trained interviewers who are knowledgeable about such problems.

Interviewer error is also a major source of response bias. From the introduction to the conclusion of the interview, there are many points where the interviewer's control of the process can affect the quality of the data. There are three different kinds of error concerning the interview techniques just discussed:

1. The sample loses credibility and is likely to be biased if interviewers do not do a good job of enlisting respondent cooperation.
2. The precision of survey estimates will be reduced and there will be more error around estimates to the extent that interviewers are inconsistent in ways that influence the data.
3. Answers may be systematically inaccurate or biased when interviewers fail to appropriately train and motivate respondents or fail to establish an appropriate interpersonal setting for reporting what is called for.[16]

Perhaps the most insidious form of interviewer error is cheating. Surveying is difficult work, often done by part-time employees, usually with only limited training and under little direct supervision. Under such conditions, falsification of an answer to an overlooked question is an easy, harmless first step that can be followed by more pervasive forgery. It is not known how much of this occurs, but it should be of constant concern to research directors.

It is also obvious that an interviewer can distort the results of any survey by inappropriate suggestions, word emphasis, tone of voice, and question rephrasing. Such activities, whether premeditated or merely due to carelessness, are widespread. This problem was investigated with a simple structured questionnaire and planted respondents to report on the interviewers. The conclusion was "the high frequency of deviations from instructed behavior are alarming."[17]

Interviewers can influence respondents in many other ways also. Older interviewers are often seen as authority figures by young respondents, who modify their responses accordingly. Some research indicates that perceived social distance between interviewer and respondent has a distorting effect, although the studies do not fully agree on just what this relationship is.[18]

There are many studies on the various aspects of interviewer bias, most of which support the conclusion that it is a problem. However, many findings differ on the exact dimension of this bias and the conditions under which it occurs. In the light of this confusion, the safest course for researchers is to recognize that there is a constant potential for response error.

Costs   While professional interviewers' wage scales are typically not high, interviewing is costly, and these costs continue to rise. Much of the cost results from the substantial interviewer time taken up with administrative and travel tasks. Respondents are often geographically scattered, and this adds to the cost. Repeated contacts (recommended at six to nine per household) are expensive. In recent years, some professional research organizations have attempted to gain control of these spiraling costs. Interviewers have typically been paid on an hourly rate, but this method rewards inefficient interviewers and often results in field costs exceeding budgets.[19] The U.S. Bureau of the Census and the National Opinion Research Center have experimented with production standards and a formula pay system that provide an incentive for efficient interviewers. This approach has cut field costs about 10 percent and has improved the accuracy of the forecasts of field-work costs.

A second approach to the reduction of field costs has been to use the telephone to schedule personal interviews. Telephone calls to set up appointments for interviews are reported to reduce personal calls by 25 percent without reducing cooperation rates.[20] Telephone screening is also valuable when a study is concerned with a rare population. In one such case, where blind persons were sought, it was found that telephone screening of households was only one-third the cost of screening on a face-to-face basis.[21]

A third approach to the problem of high field costs is to use self-administered questionnaires. In one study, a personal interview was conducted in the household with a self-administered questionnaire left for one or more other members of the household to complete. In this study, the cost per complete case was reduced by half when compared to personal interviews. A comparison between a personal interview and a self-administered questionnaire seeking the same data showed that there was generally sufficient similarity of answers to enable them to be combined.[22]

TELEPHONE INTERVIEWING

The telephone can be helpful in setting up personal interviews and screening large populations for unusual types of respondents. Studies have also shown that making prior notification calls can improve the response rates of mail surveys. However, the **telephone interview** makes its greatest contribution in survey work is as a unique mode of communication to collect information from respondents.

Evaluation of the Telephone Interview

Of the advantages that telephone interviewing offers, probably none ranks higher than its moderate cost. One study reports that sampling and data collection costs for telephone surveys can run from 45 to 64 percent lower than comparable personal interviews.[23] Much of the savings comes from cuts in travel costs and administrative savings from training and supervision. All calls are made from a single location, enabling the researcher to use fewer, yet more skilled interviewers. Telephones are especially economical when there are callbacks and respondents are widely scattered. With WATS lines, it is possible to interview nationally at a reasonable cost.

With the widespread use of computers, telephone interviewing can be combined with immediate entry of the responses into a data file using terminals, personal computers, or voice data entry. This brings added savings in time and money. **Computer-assisted telephone interviewing (CATI)** is used in research organizations throughout the world. A CATI facility consists of acoustically isolated interviewing carrels organized around supervisory stations. The telephone interviewer in each carrel has a personal computer or terminal that is networked to the phone system and the central data processing unit. Questioning is driven by a software program that prompts the interviewers with introductory statements, qualifying questions, and precoded questionnaire items. These materials appear on the interviewers' monitors. CATI works with a telephone number management system to select numbers, dial the sample, and enter responses. One facility, the Survey Research Center at the University of Michigan, consists of 60 carrels with 100 interviewers working in shifts from 8 a.m. to midnight (EST) to call nationwide. When fully staffed, they produce more than 10,000 interview hours per month.[24]

Another means of securing immediate response data is the **computer-administered telephone survey.** Unlike CATI, there is no interviewer. A computer calls the phone number, conducts the interview, places data into a file for later tabulation, and terminates. The questions are voice-synthesized and the respondent's answer and computer timing triggers continuation or disconnect. This mode is often compared to the self-administered questionnaire (discussed later in the chapter) and offers the advantage of respondent privacy. One study showed that the *noncontact rate* for the electronic survey mode is similar to other telephone interviews when a random phone list is used. It also found that rejection of this mode of data collection affects the *refusal rate* because people more easily hang up on a computer than a human.[25] The **noncontact rate** is a ratio of potential contacts (no answer, busy, answering machine, and disconnects but not refusals) to all potential contacts. The **refusal rate** refers to eligible sample of contacts where the respondent has declined the interview.

When compared to either personal interviews or mail surveys, the use of telephones brings a faster completion of a study, sometimes taking only a day or so for the fieldwork. When compared to personal interviewing, it is also likely that interviewer bias is reduced by using telephones.

Recent estimates of 'he percentage of U.S. households with at least one telephone are above 95 percent. In 13 states, 99 percent of all households are reported to have phone service.[26] Access to respondents through low-cost, efficient means has made telephone interviewing a very attractive alternative for marketing, public opinion, and academic researchers.

Finally, behavioral norms work to the advantage of telephone interviewing: if someone is present, a ringing phone will usually be answered, and it is the caller who decides the purpose, length, and termination of the call.[27]

Disadvantages   There are also disadvantages to using the telephone for research. Obviously, the respondent must be available by phone. Usage rates are not as high in households composed of single adults, less educated, poorer minorities, and individuals employed as nonprofessional, nonmanagerial workers.[28] These variations can be a source of bias.

Because about 20 percent of American households move each year, there are always many obsolete numbers and new households for which numbers have not yet been published. In addition, it is estimated that about 22 percent of all household phone numbers are unlisted.[29] Another source says the highest incidence of nonlisting is in the West, in large metropolitan areas, among nonwhites, and for persons between 18 and 34 years of age.[30] Several methods have been developed to overcome this deficiency of directories; among them are techniques for choosing phone numbers by using random digit dialing or combinations of directories and random dialing.[31] **Random dialing procedures** normally call for choosing exchanges or exchange blocks and then generating random numbers within these blocks for calling.[32]

A limit on interview length is another disadvantage of the telephone, but the degree of this limitation depends on the respondent's interest in the topic. Ten minutes has generally been thought of as the maximum, but interviews of 20 minutes or more are not uncommon. Interviews ran for 1½ hours in one long-distance survey.[33]

In telephone interviewing, it is not possible to use maps, illustrations, or complex scales. The medium also limits the complexity of the questioning and the use of sorting techniques. One ingenious solution to the scale deficiency, however, has been to employ a nine-point scaling approach and to ask the respondent to visualize this by using the telephone dial or keypad.[34]

Some studies suggest that the response rate in telephone studies is lower than for comparable face-to-face interviews. One reason is that respondents find it easier to terminate an interview. Telemarketing practices may also contribute. Public reaction to investigative reports of wrong doing and unethical behavior places an added burden on the researcher trying to convince a respondent that the interview is not a pretext for soliciting contributions or selling products.

It has also been found that telephone surveys can result in less thorough responses and that those interviewed by phone find the experience to be less rewarding to them than a personal interview. Respondents report less rapport with telephone interviewers than with personal interviewers. Given the growing costs and difficulties of personal interviews, it is likely that an even higher share of surveys will be by telephone in the future. Thus, it behooves the business researcher using telephone surveys to attempt to improve the enjoyment of the interview. One authority suggests:

> We need to experiment with techniques to improve the enjoyment of the interview by the respondent, maximize the overall completion rate, and minimize response error on specific measures. This work might fruitfully begin with efforts at translating into verbal messages the visual cues that fill the interaction in a face-to-face interview: the smiles, frowns, raising of eyebrows, eye contact, etc. All of these cues have informational content and are important parts of the personal interview setting. We can perhaps purposefully choose those cues that are most important to data quality and respondent trust and discard the many that are extraneous to the survey interaction.[35]

Trends   Future trends in telephone interviewing bear watching. These include the effects of answering machines and multi-line households on sampling, the variations among the 60 telephone companies' services and the degree of cooperation that will be extended to researchers, and the ways in which random-digit dialing can be made to deal with nonworking and noneligible numbers.[36]

The answering machine could pose potentially complex response-rate problems since they are conservatively estimated to have 25 percent penetration in American households. A benchmark study discovered a substantial portion of answering machine households are accessible: the subsequent contract rate was greater in answering machine households than in no machine households and about equal with busy households. Other findings suggested that (1) individuals with answering machines were more likely to participate, (2) machine use was more prevalent on weekends than weekday evenings, and (3) they were more commonplace in urban than rural areas. Questions about the sociodemographics of users and nonusers and the relationship the answering machine use to the rapid changes in the wireless market remain to be answered.[37]

SELF-ADMINISTERED QUESTIONNAIRES/MAIL SURVEYS

The **self-administered questionnaire** has become ubiquitous in modern living. Service evaluations of hotels, restaurants, car dealerships, and transportation providers furnish ready examples. Often a short questionnaire is left to be completed by the respondent in a convenient location or is packaged with a product. User registrations, product information requests in magazines, warranty cards, and even the MindWriter repair study illustrated in the text follow the self-administered mode. In this section, we discuss the merits of the **mail survey,** a self-administered questionnaire delivered by the Postal Service or a courier service. It has both special problems and unique advantages.

Evaluation of the Mail Survey

Mail surveys typically cost less than personal interviews. Telephone and mail costs are in the same general range, although in specific cases, either may be lower. The more dispersed the sample, the more likely it is that mail will be the low-cost method. A mail study can cost less because it is often a one-person job. Another value in using mail is that we can contact respondents who might otherwise be inaccessible. People such as major corporate executives are difficult to reach in any other way. When the researcher has no specific person to contact, say in a study of corporations, the mail survey often will be routed to the appropriate respondent.

In a mail survey, the respondent can take more time to collect facts, talk with others, or consider replies at length than is possible with the telephone or personal interview. Finally, mail surveys are typically perceived as more impersonal, providing more anonymity than the other communication modes.

The major weakness of the mail survey is nonresponse. Many studies have shown that the better educated and those more interested in the topic answer mail surveys. A high percentage of those who reply to a given survey have usually replied to others, while a large share of those who do not respond are habitual nonrespondents.[38] Mail surveys with a return of about 30 percent are often considered satisfactory, but there are instances of more than 70 percent response.[39] In either of these cases, there are many nonresponders, and we usually know nothing about how those who answer might differ from those who do not answer.

The second major limitation of mail surveys concerns the type and amount of information that can be secured this way. We normally do not expect to secure large amounts of information and cannot probe deeply into questions. It is generally believed that respondents will refuse to cooperate with a long and/or complex mail questionnaire. Returned mail questionnaires with many questions left unanswered testify to this problem, but there are also many exceptions. One general rule of thumb is that the respondent should be able to answer the questionnaire in no more than 10 minutes. On the other hand, one study reports on a study of the general population found more than a 70 percent response to a questionnaire calling for 158 answers.[40]

Improving Returns

The research literature is filled with studies addressing the problems of improving mail survey returns. Seemingly every possible variable has been studied. One authority reports that well over 200 methodological articles have been published on efforts to improve mail response rates. Two review articles concluded few variables consistently showed positive response rates.[41] Several practical suggestions emerge from the conclusions.[42]

Follow-ups. Follow-ups, or reminders, are very successful in increasing response rates. Since each successive follow-up results in added returns, the very persistent (and well-financed) researcher can potentially achieve an extremely high total response rate. However, the value of additional information thus obtained must be weighed against the costs required for successive contacts.

Preliminary Notification. There is evidence that advance notification, particularly by telephone, is effective in increasing response rates; it also serves to accelerate the rate of return. However, follow-ups are a better investment than preliminary notification.

Concurrent Techniques

1. *Questionnaire Length.* Although common sense suggests that short questionnaires should obtain higher response rates than longer questionnaires, research evidence does not support this view.

2. *Survey Sponsorship.* There is little experimental evidence concerning the influence of survey sponsorship on response rates; however, the sparse evidence that does exist suggests that official or "respected" sponsorship increases response rates.

3. *Return Envelopes.* The study that tested the hypothesis that return envelopes increase response rates suggests that the inclusion of a stamped, return envelope does encourage response because it simplifies questionnaire return.

4. *Postage.* Many tests regarding postage are reported in the literature, but few studies have tested the same variables. The existing evidence shows that special delivery is very effective in increasing response rates. Findings do not show a significant advantage for first class over third class, for commemorative stamps over ordinary postage, for stamped mail over metered mail, or for multiple small denomination stamps over single larger denomination stamps.

5. *Personalization.* Empirical evidence suggests that personalization of the mailing has no clear-cut advantage in terms of improved response rates. Neither personal inside addresses nor individually signed cover letters

significantly increased response rates; personally typed cover letters proved to be somewhat effective in most but not all cases cited. The one study that tested the use of a titled signature versus one without a title did show a significant advantage in favor of the title.

6. *Cover Letters.* The influence of the cover letter on response rates has received almost no experimental attention, although the cover letter is an integral part of the mail survey. It is the most logical vehicle for persuading individuals to respond, yet the few studies that are reported offer no insights as to its formulation.

7. *Anonymity.* Experimental evidence shows that the promise of anonymity to respondents—either explicit or implied—has no significant effect on response rates.

8. *Size, Reproduction, and Color.* The few studies that examined the effects of questionnaire size, method of reproduction, and color found no significant difference in response rates.

9. *Money Incentives.* A monetary incentive sent with the questionnaire is very effective in increasing response rates. Larger sums bring in added response, but at a cost that may exceed the value of the added information.

10. *Deadline Dates.* The few studies that tested the impact of deadline dates found that they did not increase the response rate; however, they did serve to accelerate the rate of questionnaire return.

These suggestions and conclusions are not unequivocal because "the manipulation of one or two techniques independently of all others may do little to stimulate response."[43] Efforts should be directed toward the more important question of maximizing the overall probability of response. The Total Design Method (TDM) is proposed to meet this need. The TDM consists of two parts.[44] First, one must identify the aspects of the survey process that affect the response rate, either qualitatively or quantitatively. Each aspect must be shaped to obtain the best response. The second part consists of organizing the survey efforts so the design intentions are carried out in detail. The results achieved with the TDM in 48 surveys showed response rates of 50 to 94 percent, with a median response rate of 74 percent.[45]

Implementing the Mail Survey

In the TDM approach, explicit attention is given to each point of the survey process at which the response may break down. For example:[46]

1. The wrong address and a low-rate postage can result in nondelivery or nonreturn.

2. The letter may look like junk mail and be discarded without being opened.

3. Lack of proper instructions for completion lead to nonresponse.

4. The wrong person opens the letter and fails to call it to the attention of the right person.

5. A respondent finds no convincing explanation for completing the survey and discards it.

6. A respondent temporarily lays the questionnaire aside and fails to complete it.
7. The return address is lost so the questionnaire cannot be returned.

Efforts to overcome these problems will vary according to the circumstances, but some general suggestions can be made.

The Process   A questionnaire, a cover letter, and a return envelope are sent. Incentives, such as dollar bills and coins, are often attached to the letter in commercial studies. Follow-ups are usually needed to get the maximum response. Opinions differ about how many follow-ups are needed and how they should be timed. Some researchers mail the first follow-up only several days after the original mailing. The TDM approach uses these follow-ups:

1. One week later—a preprinted postcard to all recipients thanking them for returns and reminding others to complete and mail the questionnaire.
2. Three weeks after the original mailing—a new questionnaire plus a letter telling nonrespondents that the questionnaire has not been received and repeating the basic appeal of the original letter.
3. Seven weeks after original mailing—a third cover letter and questionnaire are sent by certified mail to the remaining nonrespondents.

The Appeal   The appeal to make to respondents may be an altruistic one or it may be a more expedient stimulus. The former is often found when the questionnaire is short, easy to complete, and does not require much effort from a respondent. Anonymity may or may not be mentioned. A brief letter emphasizes the "Would you do me a favor?" approach. Often some token is sent to symbolize the researcher's appreciation. This often is not powerful enough. An appeal is needed that tells how important the problem is to a group that the respondent identifies with. The cover letter should also convey that the respondent's help is needed to solve a problem. Researchers are portrayed as reasonable people making a reasonable appeal for help. They are identified as intermediaries between the person asked to help and an important problem.

The TDM approach depends heavily on personalization to convey to respondents that they are important to the study. Such a personalized approach requires much more than just putting the respondent's name on the cover letter and using a real signature. The total effect must be personalized and should include typing of names and addresses on the envelope rather than on labels, signing the researchers' names in a contrasting color, and using first-class mail. Another strong element of personalization is available on the follow-ups when the respondent can be told, "as of today we have not received your questionnaire." Other techniques such as computer printing enables one to make personal references to respondents within the body of the letter. The standard is to make the appeals comparable in appearance and content to what one would expect in a business or professional letter.

Finally, a mixed model can be used to improve response. One study compared the use of "drop-off" delivery of a self-administered questionnaire to a mail survey.[47] Under the drop-off system, a lightly trained survey taker personally delivered the questionnaires to target households and returned in a couple of days for the completed instrument. Response rates for the drop-off system were typically above 70 percent—much higher than for comparable mail surveys. Simultaneously, the cost per completed questionnaire was from 18 to 40 percent lower than the mail surveys.

Beyond a higher response rate and lower cost per response, the drop-off method gives greater control over sample design, permits thorough identification of the respondents' geographic location, and allows the researcher to eliminate those who fall outside a predefined sample frame (persons of the wrong age, income, or other characteristics). Additional information can also be gathered by observation on the visits. However, the cost advantage of this method is probably restricted to studies where respondents can be reached with little travel.

SELECTING AN OPTIMAL METHOD

The choice of a method is not as complicated as it might first appear. By comparing your research objectives with the strengths and weaknesses of each method, it is possible to choose one that is optimally suited to your needs. Table 10–1 presents a summary of the advantages and disadvantages of personal interviews, telephone interviews, and mail surveys that should be useful for making such a comparison.

When your investigative questions call for information from hard-to-reach or inaccessible respondents, the telephone interview or mail survey should be considered. However, if data must be collected very quickly, the mail survey would likely be ruled out because of lack of control over the returns. Alternatively, you may decide your objective requires extensive questioning and probing; then the personal interview should be considered.

If none of the choices turns out to be a particularly good fit, it is possible to combine the best characteristics of two or more alternatives into a *mixed mode*. Although this decision will incur the costs of the combined modes, the flexibility of tailoring a method to your unique needs is often an acceptable trade-off.

Ultimately, all researchers are confronted by the practical realities of cost and deadlines. Table 10–1 suggests that, on the average, personal interviews are the costliest and take the most field time unless a large field team is used. Telephone interviews are moderate in cost and offer the quickest option. Mail surveys are the least expensive and require a longer data collection period. The use of the computer to select respondents and reduce coding and processing time will continue to improve the cost-to-performance profiles of these methods in the future.

SUPPLIERS OF SURVEY SERVICES

The needs of organizations for information often exceed their internal resources. Such factors as specialized expertise, a large field team, unique facilities, or a rapid turnaround prompt managers to seek assistance from research suppliers of survey-related services.

TABLE 10–1   **Comparison of Survey Methods**

	Personal Interviews	*Telephone Interviews*	*Mail Survey*
Description	People selected to be part of the sample are interviewed in person by a trained interviewer.	People selected to be part of the sample are interviewed on the telephone by a trained interviewer.	Questionnaires are mailed to sample to be self-administered. A stamped return envelope is generally included. Incentives may be used to increase response rate.
Advantages	Good cooperation from respondents. Interviewer can answer questions about survey, probe for answers, use follow-up questions, and gather information by observation. Special visual aids and scoring devices can be used. Illiterate and functionally illiterate respondents can be reached. Interviewer can prescreen respondent to ensure he/she fits the population profile. CAPI—Computer-assisted personal interviewing: responses can be entered into a portable microcomputer to reduce error and cost.	Lower costs than personal interview. Expanded geographic coverage without dramatic increase in costs. Uses fewer, more highly skilled interviewers. Reduced interviewer bias. Fastest completion time. Better access to hard-to-reach respondents through repeated callbacks. Can use computerized random digit dialing. CATI—computer-assisted telephone interviewing: responses can be entered directly into a computer file to reduce error and cost.	Often lowest cost option. Expanded geographic coverage without increase in costs. Requires minimal staff. Perceived as more anonymous. Allows respondents time to think about questions. Allows contact with otherwise inaccessible respondents (i.e., CEOs).
Disadvantages	High costs. Need for highly trained interviewers. Longer period needed in the field collecting data. May be wide geographic dispersion. Follow-up is labor intensive. Not all respondents are available or accessible. Some respondents are unwilling to talk to strangers in their homes. Some neighborhoods are difficult to visit. Questions may be altered or respondent coached by interviewers.	Response rate is lower than for personal interview. Higher costs if interviewing geographically dispersed sample. Interview length must be limited. Many phone numbers are unlisted or not working, making directory listings unreliable. Some target groups are not available by phone. Illustrations cannot be used. Responses may be less complete.	Low response rate. No interviewer intervention available (for probing or explanation). Cannot be long/complex. Accurate mailing lists needed. Often respondents returning survey represent extremes of the population (skewed responses).

Commercial suppliers of research services vary from full-service operations to specialty consultants. When confidentiality is likely to affect competitive advantage, the manager or staff will sometimes prefer to bid only a phase of the project. Alternatively, the organization's staff members may possess such unique knowledge of a product or service that they must fulfill a part of the study themselves. Regardless, the exploratory work, design, sampling, data collection, or processing and analysis may be contracted separately or as a whole. [48] Most corporations use a request for proposal (RFP) to describe their requirements and seek competitive bids (see Appendix C).

Research firms also offer special advantages that their clients do not typically maintain in-house. Centralized-location interviewing, focus group facilities, or computer-assisted telephone facilities may be particularly desirable for certain research needs. A professionally trained staff with considerable experience in similar management problems is another benefit. Data processing and statistical analysis capabilities are especially important for some projects. Other vendors have specially designed software for interviewing and data tabulation.[49]

Panel suppliers provide another type of research service with emphasis on longitudinal survey work.[50] By using the same respondents over time, panels can track trends in attitudes toward issues or products, product adoption or consumption behavior, and a myriad of other research interests. Suppliers of panel data can secure information from personal and telephone interviewing techniques as well as the mail and mixed modes. Diaries are a common means of chronicling events of research interest by the panel members. These are mailed back to the research organization. Electronic data collection for panel-type respondent groups is aided by point-of-sale terminals and scanners. And mechanical devices placed in the homes of panel members evaluate media usage.

Summary

The major advantages of personal interviewing are the ability to explore topics in great depth, to achieve a high degree of interviewer control, and to provide maximum interviewer flexibility for meeting unique situations. However, this method is costly and time-consuming, and the flexibility can result in excessive interviewer bias.

A successful interview requires that we seek information the respondent can provide and that the respondent understands the role and is motivated to play this role. Motivation, in particular, is a task for the interviewer. Good rapport with the respondent should be quickly established, and then the technical process of collecting data should begin. The latter often calls for skillful probing to supplement the answers volunteered by the respondent.

Two factors cause bias in interviewing. One is "nonresponse." It is a concern with all types of surveys. Some studies show that first calls will often secure as few as 20 percent of the designated respondents. Various methods are useful for increasing this representation, the most effective being making callbacks until adequate numbers of completed interviews are secured. The second factor is "response error" in which the respondent fails to give a complete answer. The interviewer can contribute to the correction of this problem.

Telephone interviewing has become much more popular in recent years because of the diffusion of telephone service in American households and the low cost of this method compared with personal interviewing. Long-distance telephone interviewing is also growing in use. There are also disadvantages to telephone interviewing. Many phone numbers are unlisted, and directory listings become obsolete quickly; there is also a limit on the length and depth of interviews using the telephone.

Mail surveys are another widely used low-cost method, especially when the population is scattered geographically. Replying to a mail survey calls for some overt action by the respondent. As a result, the response rates for mail surveys are low, although many techniques can be used to motivate respondents to participate.

The optimal survey method is the one that is instrumental for answering your research question and dealing with the constraints imposed by time, budget, and human resources. The opportunity to combine several survey methodologies makes the use of the mixed mode desirable in many projects.

Suppliers of survey services offer special advantages to clients. A professionally trained research staff, centralized-location interviewing, focus group facilities, and computer-assisted facilities are among them. Specialty firms offer software and computer-based assistance for telephone and personal interviewing as well as mail and mixed modes. Panel suppliers produce data for longitudinal studies of all varieties.

KEY TERMS

callbacks
computer-administered telephone
  survey
computer-assisted telephone
  interviewing (CATI)
intercept interview
interviewer error
mail survey
noncontact rate

nonresponse error
personal interview
probing
random dialing procedures
refusal rate
response errors
self-administered questionnaire
survey
telephone interview

Discussion Questions

1. Distinguish among response error, interviewer error, and nonresponse error.

2. Assume you are planning to interview shoppers in a shopping mall about their views on increased food prices and what the federal government should do about them. In what different ways might you try to motivate them to cooperate in your survey?

3. In recent years, in-home personal interviews have grown more costly and more difficult to complete. Suppose, however, you have a project in which you need to talk with people in the home. What might you do to hold down the costs and increase the response rate?

phone 1st - arrange appointments,
determine whether they will cooperate

4. How do environmental factors affect response rates in personal interviews? How can we overcome these environmental problems?

5. In the following situations, would you use a personal interview, telephone survey, or mail survey? Give your reasons.
   a. A survey of the residents of a new subdivision on why they happened to select that area in which to live. You also wish to secure some information about what they like and do not like about life in the subdivision.
   b. A poll of students at Cranial University on their preferences among three candidates who are running for presidency of the student government.
   c. A survey of 58 wholesale grocery companies, scattered over the eastern United States, on their personnel management policies for warehouse personnel.
   d. A survey of financial officers of the Fortune 500 corporations to learn their prediction for the economic outlook in their industries for next year.
   e. A survey of pharmacists in the state of Illinois to secure their opinions concerning a proposed state law to permit the advertising of prescription drugs.

6. You decide to take a telephone survey of 40 families in the 721- exchange area. You want an excellent representation of all subscribers in the exchange area. Explain how you would carry out this study.

7. You plan to conduct a mail survey of the traffic managers of 1,000 major manufacturing companies across the country. The study concerns their company policies regarding the payment of moving expenses for employees who are transferred. What might you do to improve the response rate of such a survey?

Reference Notes

1. Robert L. Kahn and Charles F. Cannell, *The Dynamics of Interviewing* (New York: John Wiley & Sons, 1957), pp. 45–51.
2. One of the top research organizations in the world is the Survey Research Center of the University of Michigan. The material in this section draws heavily upon the *Interviewer's Manual,* rev. ed. (Ann Arbor, Mich.: Survey Research Center, University of Michigan, 1976); and Floyd J. Fowler, Jr., *Survey Research Methods* (Beverly Hills, Calif.: Sage Publications, 1988), chap. 7.
3. Survey Research Center, *Interviewer's Manual,* p. 8.
4. Ibid., pp. 15–16.
5. Ibid., p. 17.
6. Fowler, *Survey Research Methods,* p. 112.
7. S. A. Richardson, B.S. Dohrenwend, and D. Klein, *Interviewing: Its Forms and Functions* (New York: Basic Books, 1965), pp. 328–58.
8. Reprinted by special permission from Charles F. Cannell and Robert L. Kahn, "Interviewing," in *The Handbook of Social Psychology,* 2nd ed., vol. 2, edited by Lindzey-Aronson (Reading, Mass.: Addison Wesley, 1968). See also, Fowler, *Survey Research Methods,* p. 115; and P.J. Guenzel, T.R. Berkmans, and Charles F. Cannell, *General Interviewing Techniques* (Ann Arbor, Mich.: Institute for Social Research, 1983).

9. In one study, 5.5 percent of white respondents and 11 percent of nonwhite respondents were still not contacted after six calls. See W. C. Dunkelberg and G. S. Day, "Nonresponse Bias and Callbacks in Sample Surveys," *Journal of Marketing Research,* may 1974, table 3.

10. Ibid.

11. Fowler, *Survey Research Methods,* p. 50.

12. C. H. Fuller, "Weighting to Adjust for Survey Nonresponse," *Public Opinion Quarterly,* Summer 1974, pp. 239–46.

13. Dunkleberg and Day, "Nonresponse Bias," table 3.

14. Ibid., pp. 160–68.

15. Eleanore Singer, "Agreement between Inaccessible Respondents and Informants," *Public Opinion Quarterly,* Winter 1972–73, pp. 603–11.

16. Fowler, *Survey Research Methods,* p. 111.

17. B. W. Schyberger, "A Study of Interviewer Behavior," *Journal of Marketing Research,* February 1967, p. 35.

18. B. S. Dohrenwend, J. A. Williams, Jr., and C. H. Weiss, "Interviewer Biasing Effects: Toward a Reconciliation of Findings," *Public Opinion Quarterly,* Spring 1969, pp. 121–29.

19. Seymour Sudman, *Reducing the Costs of Surveys* (Chicago: Aldine Publishing, 1967), p. 67.

20. Ibid., p. 59.

21. Ibid., p. 63.

22. Ibid., p. 53.

23. Robert M. Groves and Robert L. Kahn, *Surveys by Telephone* (New York: Academic Press, 1979), p. 223.

24. Institute for Social Research, *ISR Newsletter* (Ann Arbor, Mich.: University of Michigan), 1991–92, p. 3.

25. Michael J. Havice, "Measuring Nonresponse and Refusals to an Electronic Telephone Survey," *Journalism Quarterly,* Fall 1990, pp. 521–30.

26. Paul J. Lavrakas, *Telephone Survey Methods: Sampling, Selection, and Supervision* (Beverly Hills, Calif.: Sage Publications, 1987), pp. 14–15.

27. See, for example, J. H. Frey, Jr., *Survey Research by Telephone* (Beverly Hills, Calif.: Sage Publications, 1983).

28. See, for example, Groves and Kahn, *Surveys by Telephone.*

29. R. W. Graves, "An Empirical Comparison of Two Telephone Sample Designs," *Journal of Marketing Research,* November 1978, p. 622.

30. G. J. Glasser and G. D. Metzger, "National Estimates of Nonlisted Telephone Households and Their Characteristics," *Journal of Marketing Research,* August 1975, p. 360.

31. G. J. Glasser and G. D. Metzger, "Random Digit Dialing as a Method of Telephone Sampling," *Journal of Marketing Research,* February 1972, pp. 59–64; and Seymour Sudman, "The Uses of Telephone Directories for Survey Sampling," *Journal of Marketing Research,* May 1973, pp. 204–7.

32. A block is defined as an exchange group composed of the first four or more digits of a seven-digit number such as 721–0, 721–1, and so forth.

33. Sudman, *Reducing the Costs of Surveys,* p. 65.

34. J. J. Wheatley, "Self-Administered Written Questionnaires or Telephone Interviews," *Journal of Marketing Research,* February 1973, pp. 94–95.

35. Groves and Kahn, *Survey by Telephone,* p. 223.

36. Lavrakas, *Telephone Survey Methods,* p. 16.

37. Peter S. Tuckel and Barry M. Feinberg, "The Answering Machine Poses Many Questions for Telephone Survey Researchers," *Public Opinion Quarterly,* Summer 1991, pp. 200–217.

38. D. Wallace, "A Case for and against Mail Questionnaires," *Public Opinion Quarterly,* Spring 1954, pp. 40–52.

39. Don A. Dillman, "Increasing Mail Questionnaire Response in Large Samples of the General Public," *Public Opinion Quarterly,* Summer 1972, pp. 254–57.

40. Don A. Dillman, *Mail and Telephone Surveys* (New York: John Wiley & Sons, 1978), p. 6.

41. Leslie Kanuk and Conrad Berenson, "Mail Surveys and Response Rates: A Literature Review," *Journal of Marketing Research,* November 1975, pp. 440–53; and Arnold S. Linsky, "Stimulating Responses to Mailed Questionnaires: A Review," *Public Opinion Quarterly* 39 (1975), pp. 82–101.

42. Kanuk and Berenson, "Mail Surveys," p. 450. Reprinted from the *Journal of Marketing Research,* published by the American Marketing Association.

43. Dillman, *Mail and Telephone Surveys,* p. 8.

44. Ibid., p. 12.

45. Ibid., pp. 22–24.

46. Ibid., pp. 160–61.

47. C. H. Lovelock, Ronald Still, David Cullwick, and Ira M. Kaufman, "An Evaluation of the Effectiveness of Drop-Off Questionnaire Delivery," *Journal of Marketing Research,* November 1976, pp. 358–64.

48. For an excellent discussion of the sources and types of research services, see the section on primary data collection and panel vendors in Duane Davis and Robert M. Cosenza, *Business Research for Decision Making,* 2nd ed. (Boston: PWS-Kent, 1988), pp. 280–87.

49. There are a number of sources for research services, some of which are annotated. For current listings, consult the latest edition of the *Marketing Services Guide & The American Marketing Association Membership Directory* (Chicago: American Marketing Association); *Consultants and Consulting Organizations Directory* (Detroit, Mich.: Gale Research Corporation); or the research section of *Marketing News.* Also see "Software for Marketing and Marketing Research," *Marketing News,* February 14, 1986, pp. 9–22.

50. A list of major panel vendors is provided by Davis and Cosenza, *Business Research for Decision Making,* p. 287. For an evaluation of the panel process, see Seymour Sudman and Robert Ferber, *Consumer Panels* (Chicago: American Marketing Association, 1979).

Suggested Readings

1. Barabba, Vincent P. "The Market Research Encyclopedia." *Harvard Business Review* 90, no. 1 (1990), pp. 105–17. A set of reference tables for managers and researchers. Of particular interest is the second table, which compares mail, telephone, personal, and mixed mode interviews on several dimensions including response rates, costs, and probability versus nonprobability sampling decisions.

2. Dexter, Louis A. *Elite and Specialized Interviewing.* Evanston, Ill.: Northwestern University Press, 1970. Discusses the techniques and problems of interviewing "people in important or exposed positions."

3. Dillman, Don A. *Mail and Telephone Surveys.* New York: John Wiley & Sons, 1978. A practical book on mail and telephone survey projects. The entire book is recommended. It includes an extensive bibliography.

4. Fowler, Floyd J., Jr. *Survey Research Methods,* 2nd ed. Thousand Oaks, Calif.: Sage Publications, 1993. An excellent overview of all aspects of the survey process.

5. Groves, R. M., et al. *Telephone Survey Methodology.* New York: John Wiley & Sons, 1988. An important reference on telephone collection techniques.

6. Lavrakas, Paul J. *Telephone Survey Methods: Sampling, Selection, and Supervision.* 2nd ed. Thousand Oaks, Calif.: Sage Publications, 1993. This specialized work takes an applied perspective of interest to students and managers. Chapters 3, 5, and 6 on supervision are particularly useful.

11 SURVEY INSTRUMENTS

 **FINDING YOUR WAY**

BRINGING RESEARCH TO LIFE

"**J**ason, you gotta see this," Myra called to her research partner. She was waving a letter above her head and laughing so hard that Jason could barely understand her.

"You remember me telling you about my Aunt Edna, the not-so-retired attorney in Albany? Well, she sent this for my amusement, I guess. It's just so typical of how people, particularly physicians and even bright businesspeople, design questionnaires."

"Like MindWriter?" he murmured impatiently, looking up from the partially finished questionnaire on his computer screen.

"Come on, Jason, give it a rest. And read this," she prodded.

Edna Koogan, P.A.
Attorney at Law
P. O. Box 5558219-2767
Albany, New York 122212-2767

Dr. Edith Coblenz, M.D.
3456 Barshoot Building
Albany, New York 12212

Dear Edith,

I want you to have my side of this morning's incident at the Albany Outpatient Laser Clinic, Inc. I am sure you have by now heard from the business manager and the admissions director and possibly the anesthesiologist. You are a stockholder in the Center, I know, and as your former lawyer and current patient, I thought I owed you a warning and explanation.

You told me to report to the Center at 7 A.M. for a workup in preparation for eye surgery tomorrow. I caught a cab and was there at 6:55 promptly and was then obliged to stand outside in lightly drifting snow until the doors opened. (Yes, I set my watch by the radio the night before, so there is no possibility of an error. They were late opening the admissions department, and that's that.)

I identified myself as your patient, and at once the receptionist called someone from the back

room and said, "Ms. Koogan's personal physician is Dr. Coblenz," which is, of course, not true, as you are my eye doctor, and my personal physician is Dr. Burke in Troy. But I was too cold to argue and there were people lined up behind me.

The fellow who had scooted in from the back insisted on taking my glasses and medications with him "for a workup," as he said. As soon as he had disappeared with my glasses the first admissions clerk disappeared and a second one appeared and handed me a "questionnaire" to fill out. You are going to think I am exaggerating, but it appeared to be a photocopy of a photocopy of a photocopy and was very faintly printed in small gray type on a light gray sheet. When I pointed out that I was about to be admitted for treatment of glaucoma, a leading cause of blindness, she told me, "Do the best you can." When I objected emphatically, she seemed taken aback. I suppose most of her 80-year-old patients are more compliant, but I guess I am an intractable old woman.

Was I wrong to object to the questionnaire being too faint and the type too small? Am I the first glaucoma patient who has ever been treated at the Laser Center? If I am, they must have opened yesterday, because what do you need the laser for if not eye surgery? If I am not, one would think they would understand you can't ask someone blind in one eye to fill out such a questionnaire. She finally, grudgingly, asked me to sit by her side, so she could help me.

There were several questions about my name, address, age, and occupation (which I had her list as "retired"). Then she wanted to know the name of the admitting physician and then the phone number (but not the name) of the physician who was most familiar with my health. I said the admitting physician was an eye doctor and the physician most familiar with my health was a G.P., and asked, which did she want the phone number for, the eye doctor or the G.P.? She became very angry then and admonished me to try and "get over that bad attitude." Then she told me to go over and sit somewhere and fill out the form as best I could.

A very nice patient (hemorrhoids, no vision problems) heard our conversation and offered to help me. She began reading the questionnaire

(continued)

and came to the item, "Past Medical History: Yes or No." She didn't think this made any sense, and neither did I, because everyone has a past medical history, and no one would answer no; but after a while we decided that it meant I should answer yes or no to all of the questions underneath, such as did I have diabetes? Did I have heart disease? and the like. But I was beginning to have doubts about this questionnaire—or, more specifically, about whoever had written it and what sort of organization would pass out such a form.

But when we came to "Have you ever had or been treated for recent cold or flu?" we could not decide if it meant, have I ever had flu? Or have I had flu recently (I had flu six months ago, but is that "recent"?) so we asked the receptionist, and she became almost speechless and said she would get me some help.

After a while the "help" appeared—a nurse who wanted to measure my blood pressure and induce me to take a blue pill, which she said would be good for my "nerves." I refused and pointed out rather curtly that this was not a gulag but an admissions department a place of business, for crying out loud, where they ought to be able to handle a little criticism from someone trained to elicit accurate information.

I went back to the questionnaire, and by then several nice people had pitched in to help me. But this made it even harder to decide on the answers, because we understood so many of the questions differently and couldn't agree. When we came to "Are all your teeth intact? one man thought it meant, Do you have false teeth? And another thought it meant Do you have any broken dentures? But a woman who assured me her son is a dentist said it meant, Do you have any loose teeth? We decided to settle that by eeny-meany-miney-moe.

Then there was the question, "Do you have limited motion of your neck?" and by then everyone was enjoying the incongruity of these questions. Of course I have limited motion of the neck. Doesn't everyone? We decided to save that question for later clarification.

After all of the yes-no questions there came various other stumpers, such as "Please list your current medications." The problem is, of course, that I have purple eye drops and yellow eye drops, but the young man had taken them away from me "for a workup," so I had no way of accurately answering the questions. I was pretty sure one of them was glucagon, so I guessed and put that down, but then I had second thoughts and scratched it out. (When I got home, I checked and it was betagan, not glucagon.)

There were four of us working on the questionnaire by then, and we were laughing and crowing and having a high time and discharging our anxieties, which got the admissions clerk very flustered and annoyed. So she called the anesthetist, a stuckup young fellow who said he had written the questionnaire himself and had never had any problems at all with it. That is when I told him, if he had not had any problems with this questionnaire, this proved it was better to be lucky than smart.

He said he was going to overlook my "attitude" because he knew I was old and anxious about the coming operation, and I told him I was going to take my business somewhere else because of the bilaterality problem. What is that? he asked, what is the "bilaterality problem"? I said, I have two eyes, and if anyone as dumb as him went after me with a knife, he would probably take the wrong eye.

I caught a cab and sent my neighbor back for my glasses. As your lawyer, I urge you not to involve yourself with such fools.

Lovingly,
Edna

THE INSTRUMENT DEVELOPMENT PROCESS

New researchers often want to draft questions immediately. They are reluctant to go through the preliminaries that make for successful surveys. How we refine a problem and take it through the research process was discussed in Chapter 3, but its importance to instrument development is stressed here.

Question Hierarchy

The process of moving from the general management objective or problem to specific measurement questions goes through four major question levels:

1. The management question—the problem the manager wants answered.
2. The research question(s)—the fact-based translation of the question the researcher must answer to contribute to the solution of the management question.
3. The investigative questions—those specific questions the researcher must ask to provide sufficient detail and coverage of the research question. Within this level, there may be several questions as the researcher moves from the general to the specific.
4. The measurement questions—those questions respondents must answer if the researcher is to gather the needed information.

Procedural Example   Replacing an imprecise management question with specific measurement questions is an exercise in analytical reasoning. We described that process incrementally in the Close-Up sections of Chapters 3, 4, and 7. In Chapter 3, Myra and Jason's fact-finding at MindWriter resulted in their ability to state the problem as management, research, and investigative questions. Adding context to the questions allowed them to construct the proposal described in Chapter 4. In Chapter 7, they returned to the list of investigative questions and selected one question to use in testing their scaling approach. Here is a brief review of the first three steps and the measurement questions that resulted.

The MindWriter Questionnaire

Synopsis of the problem. MindWriter Corporation's new service and repair program, CompleteCare, for portable/laptop/notebook computers was designed to provide a rapid response to customers' service problems. Management needs information on the program's effectiveness and its impact on customer satisfaction. There is also a shortage of trained technical operators in the company's telephone center. The package courier is uneven in executing its pickup and delivery contract. Parts availability problems exist for some machine types. Occasionally, customers receive units that are either not fixed or damaged in some way.

Management question: How do customers like the new repair program?

Research question: What is the level of satisfaction with the CompleteCare service program?

Investigative questions:

a. How well is the call center helping the customers? Are they helping the customer with instructions? What percentage of customers' technical problems are they solving without callbacks? How long do customers wait on the phone?

b. How good is the transportation company? Did they pick up and deliver the system responsively? How long do customers wait for them? Was the system damaged due to the package handling?

c. How good is the repair group? Is the repair complete? Are customers' problems resolved? Are there new problems?

d. Are customers' expectations being met by the time it takes to repair the systems?

e. What is the customers' overall satisfaction with CompleteCare and with the Mindwriter product?

Measurement questions: The measurement questions are shown in Figure 11–1.[1] Of the investigative questions in *a,* the first two are addressed as "responsiveness" and "competence" with telephone assistance in the questionnaire. The second two investigative questions may be answered by accessing the company's database. The questionnaire's three-part question on courier service parallels investigative question *b.* Specific service deficiencies are expected to be recorded in the "Comment/Suggestion" section. Investigative questions under *c* and *d* are covered with questionnaire items 3, 4, and 5. Since deficiencies in item 5 may be attributed to both the repair facility and the courier, the reasons are cross-checked during analysis. Questionnaire item 6 uses

FIGURE 11–1   Measurement Questions for the MindWriter Study

	Met **few** expectations 1	Met **some** expectations 2	Met **most** expectations 3	Met **all** expectations 4	**Exceeded** expectations 5
1. Telephone assistance with your problem:	1	2	3	4	5
a. Responsiveness	1	2	3	4	5
b. Technical competence	1	2	3	4	5
2. The courier service's effectiveness:					
a. Arrangements	1	2	3	4	5
b. Pickup speed	1	2	3	4	5
c. Delivery speed	1	2	3	4	5
3. Speed of the overall repair process.	1	2	3	4	5
4. Resolution of the problem that prompted service/repair.	1	2	3	4	5
5. Condition of your MindWriter on arrival.	1	2	3	4	5
6. Overall impression of CompleteCare's effectiveness.	1	2	3	4	5
7. Likelihood of using CompleteCare on another occasion. (1 = very unlikely 3 = neither likely nor unlikely 5 = very likely)	1	2	3	4	5
8. Likelihood of repurchasing a MindWriter based on: (1 = very unlikely 3 = neither likely nor unlikely 5 = very likely)					
a. Service/repair experience	1	2	3	4	5
b. Product performance	1	2	3	4	5

MindWriter personal computers offer you ease of use and maintenance. When you need service, we want you to rely on *CompeteCare,* wherever you may be. That's why we're asking you to take a moment to tell us how well we've served you.

Comments/Suggestions: _____

How may we contact you to follow up on any problems you have experienced?

(_____) _____

Last Name   First Name   Phone

_____ City   State   Zip

Service Code

the same language as the last investigative question. Questionnaire item 7 is an extension of item 6 but is attempting to secure an impression of behavioral intent to use CompleteCare again. Finally, the last questionnaire item goes beyond the scope of the research and investigative questions to tie repurchase to positive product and service experience. This question was designed to connect this study to ongoing research at MindWriter.

Survey Strategy

In the previous example, we previewed the final questionnaire to show you the direction of this chapter. Normally, once the researcher understands the connection between the investigative questions and the potential measurement questions, a strategy for the survey is the next logical step. This precedes getting down to the particulars of instrument design. Prominent among the strategic concerns are:

1. What communication mode will be used?
2. How much structure should be placed on the question-and-answer processes?
3. Should the questioning approach be disguised and, if so, to what degree?

Communication Mode   Surveys may be conducted by personal interview, telephone, mail, computer, or some combination of these. The decision on which method to use will affect the design of the instrument. In personal interviewing, it is possible to use graphics and other questioning tools more easily than by mail or phone.

Process Structure   Questionnaires and interview schedules can vary from those that have a great deal of structure to those that are essentially unstructured. An **interview schedule** is the questionnaire used in an interview. It contains three types of questions: identification, sociological-demographic, and measurement. The latter may be **structured questions** that present the respondents with a fixed set of choices, often called *closed questions*. **Unstructured questions** do not have a limited set of responses but do provide a frame of reference for respondents' answers. They are sometimes referred to as *open-ended questions*.

At the unstructured extreme, are in-depth interviews where the interviewer's task is to encourage the respondent to talk about a set of topics. The **in-depth interview** encourages respondents to share as much information as possible in an unconstrained environment. The interviewer uses a minimum of prompts and guiding questions.

With more focused in-depth interviews, the researcher provides additional guidance by using a set of questions to promote discussion and elaboration by the respondent. In such interviews, the researcher guides the topical direction and coverage. Whether structured or unstructured, the aim is to provide a relaxed environment in which the respondent will be open to discuss topics in depth. Such questioning is often used in exploratory research or where the investigator is dealing with complex topics that do not lend themselves to structured interviewing. If we were doing case research among various participants in a major event, a substantial portion of the questioning would be unique to each respondent.

Focus group interviews are widely used in marketing research. In this setting, 8 to 12 people are brought together to discuss a certain topic such as new product ideas, reactions to certain consumer problems, and so forth. The interviewer generally has a list of specific points he or she would like to see discussed, and these are used to prompt discussion. When the discussion stays within these bounds, the interviewer lets the group continue their interaction.

Even if the questioning process is quite structured, we must still decide whether to use structured or unstructured response formats.

Objective Disguise   Another consideration in survey instrument design is whether the purpose of the study should be disguised. Some degree of disguise is often present in survey questions, especially to shield the study's sponsor. A **disguised question** is designed to conceal its true purpose. Here we are concerned with the more general problem. Shall we disguise the *objectives* of the questions? The accepted wisdom is that often we must do this or abandon the research. The decision about when to use disguised questioning may be made easier by identifying four situations relevant to this problem.

1. Asking for information from respondents who know it at a conscious level and are willing to provide it. Have they attended the showing of a foreign film in the last six months?

2. Asking for information from respondents who know it at a conscious level but are unwilling to provide it. Ask for an opinion on some topic for which they hold a socially unacceptable view.

3. Asking for information that is knowable at a conscious level but the respondents may not know. For example, ask why their actions differ from those of others when the reason lies outside their knowledge and experience.

4. Asking for information that the respondents do not know at a conscious level although they have the information at some deeper level. For example, seek insight into the basic motivations underlying their consumption practices.

The first situation seldom needs disguised questions, but in the second, respondents may not give their true feelings or may give stereotyped answers. The researcher can encourage more accurate answers by phrasing the questions in a hypothetical way or by asking how "people around here feel about this topic." The assumption is that responses to these questions will indirectly reveal the respondent's opinions.

Respondents frequently reply with stereotypical answers because they have not given the subject much thought. This problem may also be approached indirectly. In one corporate image study, the buyers of control instruments were asked for the "five characteristics which a control manufacturer must have if he wants your business." The 5 highest ranked from a list of more than 20 possible descriptors are given in list A in the accompanying table.[2]

Rank	List A Most Important Characteristics	List B Best Differentiators
1	Quality products	Diversified line
2	Dependable	Leader
3	Cooperative	Pioneer
4	Quality conscious	Dependable
5	Accurate	Accurate

The buyers were also asked to choose the descriptions that best characterized each of the six major suppliers in the industry. These responses were then analyzed to determine which terms best differentiated each buyer's preferred supplier from the others. This quite different ranking is shown in list B. Further interviewing showed that list B descriptions much more accurately reflected the real factors that led to choosing one supplier over another.

Indirect questioning and analysis may often be needed to achieve the research objective in the third situation. A classic example is a study of government bond buying during World War II.[3] A survey sought reasons why some people bought more war bonds than others with equal ability to buy. Frequent buyers had been personally solicited to buy bonds. No direct "why" question to respondents could have provided the answer to this question because respondents did not know they were receiving a different solicitation approach.

The last situation represents an in-depth study that may or may not be disguised. **Projective techniques** (such as sentence completion tests, cartoon or balloon tests, word association tests) thoroughly disguise the study objective, but they are often difficult to interpret.

Schedule Design

The procedure to follow in developing a survey varies from case to case, but a useful approach consists of four major steps.

Information-Need Determination   The research question hierarchy is the first step. In many studies, an exploratory investigation is necessary to assure that one understands the full dimensions of the subject. In the MindWriter project, exploration was limited to several interviews because the concepts were not complicated and the researchers had experience in the industry. In the Prince Corporation image study (Chapter 6), many exploratory interviews were needed to assure all investigative topics were covered.

Researchers are concerned with adequate coverage of the topic and with securing the information in its most usable form. A good way to test how well the study plan meets these needs is to develop "dummy" tables in which to display the data one expects to secure. This serves as a check on whether the plan meets the data needs.

Data Gathering Process Decisions   At this stage, one chooses how to gather the data. First, which communication process or combination of processes is most appropriate? Personal or impersonal? Telephone or face to face? In-home or at other sites? In the *MindWriter* example, this decision was easy. The dispersion of respondents, the necessity of a service experience, and budget limitations all dictated a mail survey. In the Prince Corporation, there was a desire to use telephone interviews because of cost savings. However, the study objectives called for data that could not easily be collected by telephone.

The degree of question and response structure must also be decided. *Question structure is affected largely by the communication mode chosen. Response structure decisions depend more on the content and objectives of specific questions.* In the mail survey, it was necessary to use structured questions. Most of the responses were also structured. In the exploratory stages of the Prince study, both questions and responses were unstructured, but in the final project both were largely structured.

The degree of disguise is the third decision needed. In the MindWriter study, the questions were direct and the specific information sought was undisguised. The purpose of the study and its sponsorship were also undisguised. In the Prince Corporation study, the questions concerned only a few companies, giving the sponsor only a limited disguise. Many questions sought direct answers, but sometimes indirect questioning was used to seek answers on sensitive topics or to reduce stereotypical answers.

Instrument Drafting   You begin actual instrument design by drafting specific measurement questions. In doing this, consider both the subject content and the wording of each question. As the questions are formulated, you need also to establish a logical sequence for the questions. Often the content of one question assumes other questions have been asked. The psychological order of the questions is also important. Questions that are more interesting, easier to answer, and less threatening usually are placed early in the sequence to encourage commitment and promote rapport.

Instrument Testing   Once a draft of the instrument has been developed, it must be tested. The first test can be done by the designers. There will be many differences of opinion and suggestions for improvement. Usually at least two or three drafts can be profitably developed in-house by bringing colleagues into this process. Field testing the questionnaire requires that it be taken or sent to persons typical of the designated target respondents. We discuss pretesting later in the chapter.

QUESTION CONSTRUCTION

Survey instruments normally include three types of information. The most important of these is the *target data:* facts, attitudes, preferences, and expectations about the central topic. A second type concerns the respondent characteristics needed for *classification and analysis.* Gender, age, family life cycle stage, household income, social class, and attitudes toward topics allied to the study's subject are included. Other classification data depend on the particular study and its research objectives. A third type of information is *administrative*. This includes respondent identification, interviewer identification, date, place, and conditions of the interview.

Drafting the questions begins once you decide on the information needed and the collection processes to use. In developing a survey instrument, there are four major decision areas: (1) question content, (2) question wording, (3) response structure, and (4) question sequence. These will be discussed sequentially, although in practice the process is not orderly. For this discussion, we have assumed the questions are structured.

Question Content

Should This Question Be Asked?　Questions that merely produce "interesting information" cannot be justified on either economic or research grounds. Challenge each question's function. Does it contribute significant information toward answering an investigative question? Will it hurt if we do not have it? Can we infer the answer from another question?

Is the Question of Proper Scope and Coverage?　Does it include so much content that it should be broken into two questions? Reducing the number of questions is highly desirable, but don't try to ask **double-barreled questions,** two questions in one. Two related examples are to ask "have you ever had *or* been treated for a recent cold *or* flu?" and, to men's wear retailers, "Are this year's shoe sales *and* gross profits higher than last year's?" The first example has two double-barreled questions. The second one is more typical of this problem. Less obvious complications arise when we ask for a family's TV station preference when a better question would be to ask the station preference of each family member.

Another test of question content is, "Does it ask all that needs to be asked?" We ask for the respondent's income when we really want to know the family's income. We sometimes ask why when this simple question will not adequately cover the range of causal relationships we want to explore. Perhaps two questions on product use by the heavy consumer should be asked while one question would do for the light user.

Questions are also inadequate if they do not provide the information needed to interpret responses fully. If you ask about the Prince Corporation's image as an employer, have you recognized that different levels of employees may have different reactions? Do you need to ask the question about other companies so you can evaluate relative attitudes?

Can the Respondent Answer Adequately?　While the question may cover the territory, does the respondent know the answer? Respondents typically want to cooperate in interviews, but they often assume that giving some answer is more helpful than denying knowledge of a topic. Their desire to impress the interviewer may encourage them to give answers based on no information. A classic illustration of this problem occurred with the following question:[4]

"Which of the following statements most closely coincides with your opinion of the Metallic Metals Act?"

Answers	*Responses*
1. It would be a good move on the part of the United States.	15%
2. It would be a good thing but should be left to the individual states.	41
3. It is all right for foreign countries but should not be required here.	11
4. It is of no value at all.	3
5. Have no opinion.	30

The response pattern shows that 70 percent of those interviewed had a fairly clear opinion of the Metallic Metals Act; however, *there is no such act.* The respondents apparently assumed that if a question is asked, then they should provide an answer. Give them reasonable-sounding choices and they will select one even if they know nothing about the topic.

Assuming that respondents have prior knowledge or understanding may be risky. The risk is getting many answers that have little basis in fact. The Metallic Metals Act illustration may be challenged as unusual, but in another case, a Gallup report revealed that 45 percent of the persons surveyed did not know what a "lobbyist in Washington" was, and 88 percent could not give a correct description of "jurisdictional strike."[5]

To counteract this tendency, **filter questions** are used to qualify the respondent's knowledge. If the *MindWriter* service questionnaire was being given to all recent purchasers of their products, we might ask, "Have you required service for your machine since its purchase?" Only those for whom service was relevant would provide responses.

There is another side to this problem. In some studies, the degree of respondent expertise can be substantial, and simplified explanations are inappropriate. In asking the public about gross margins in menswear stores, be sure the respondent understands the nature of gross margin. When surveying merchants, such explanations are not needed. The question designer should consider the respondent information level when determining the content and appropriateness of a question.

The adequacy problem also occurs when you ask questions that overtax the respondent's recall ability. Most cannot recall much that has happened in the past, unless it was dramatic. You may remember the first brand of cigarette you smoked and the circumstances yet be unable to recall much about later brand changes. If the events surveyed are of incidental interest to respondents, they will probably be unable to recall them correctly even a short time later. An unaided recall question, "What radio programs did you listen to last night?" might locate as little as 10 percent of those who actually listened to a program.[6]

Answering adequacy also depends on the proper balance between generality and specificity. We often ask questions in terms too general and detached from respondent experiences. Asking for average annual consumption may make an unrealistic demand for generalization on people who do not think in these terms. Why not ask how often the product was used last week or last month? Too often respondents are asked to recall individual use experiences over an extended time and to average them for us. This is asking interviewees to do our work and encourages substantial response errors. It may contribute to a higher refusal rate.

There is a danger in being too specific. We may ask about movie attendance for the last week when this is too short a time span on which to base attendance estimates. It may be better to ask about attendance, say, for the last month. There are no firm rules about this generality-specificity problem. Developing the right level of generality depends upon the situation and the art and experience of the question designer.

The ability of respondents to answer adequately is also often distorted by questions whose content is biased by what is included or omitted. The question may explicitly mention only the positive or negative aspects of the topic or make unwarranted assumptions about the respondent's position. Consider an experiment in which the following two forms of a question were asked:

A.   What is your favorite brand of ice cream?_____

B.   Some people have a favorite brand of ice cream while others do not have a favorite brand. In which group are you? (please check)

                          _____ I have a favorite brand of ice cream.
                          _____ I do not have a favorite brand of ice cream.

What is your favorite (if you have a favorite)?_____

Fifty-seven randomly chosen graduate business students answered version A, and 56 answered version B. Their responses are shown in the accompanying table.

Response	*Version A*	*Version B*
Named a favorite brand	77%*	39%*
Named a favorite flavor rather than a brand	19	18
Had no favorite brand	4	43
Total	100%	100%
	n = 57	56

*Significant difference at the 0.001 level.

The probable cause of the difference in brand preference is that A is a **leading question.** It assumes and suggests that everyone has a favorite brand of ice cream and will report it. Version B indicates the respondent need not have a favorite.

A deficiency in both versions is that about one respondent in five misinterpreted the meaning of *brand*. This misinterpretation cannot be attributed to low education, low intelligence, or nonexposure to the topic. The subjects were students who had studied at least one course in marketing in which branding was prominently treated. Word confusion difficulties are discussed in a later section.

Will the Respondents Answer Willingly?   Even if respondents have the information, they may be unwilling to give it. Some topics are considered too sensitive to discuss with strangers. These will vary from person to person, but one study suggests the most sensitive topics concern money matters and family life.[7] More than one-fourth of those interviewed mentioned these as the topics about which they would be "least willing to answer questions." Respondents of lower socioeconomic status also included political matters in this "least willing" list. Respondents may also be unwilling to give correct answers for ego reasons. Many exaggerate their incomes, the number of cars owned, social status, and the amount of high-prestige literature they read. They also minimize their ages and the amount of low-prestige literature they read. Many respondents are reluctant to try to give an adequate response. Often this will occur when they see the topic as irrelevant to their own interests or to their perception of the survey's purpose. They participate halfheartedly, often answer with "don't know," give negative replies, refuse to be interviewed, or give stereotypical responses.

The researcher's challenge is to develop approaches to overcome these troublesome areas. Three approaches can be used to secure thorough and truthful information: (1) motivate the respondent to provide appropriate information, (2) change the design of the questioning process, or (3) use methods other than questioning to secure the data.

Motivation   Build good rapport with the respondent. Most information can be secured by direct undisguised questioning if rapport has been developed. Good rapport is particularly useful in building respondent interest in the project, and the more interest respondents have, the more cooperation they will give. One can also overcome respondent unwillingness by providing some material compensation for cooperation. This approach has been especially successful in mail surveys.

The assurance of confidentiality can also increase respondents' motivations. One approach is to give discrete assurances, both by question wording and interviewer comments and actions, that all types of behavior, attitudes, and positions on controversial or sensitive subjects are acceptable and normal. Where it can be said truthfully, we can *guarantee* the respondents that their answers will be used only in combined statistical totals. If they are convinced that their replies contribute to some important purpose, they are more likely to be candid, even with taboo topics.

Redesign   You can redesign the questioning process to improve the quality of answers. We might show that confidentiality is integral to the administration of the survey by using a group administration of questionnaires, accompanied by a ballot-box collection procedure. Even in face-to-face interviews, the respondent may fill in the part of the questionnaire containing sensitive information and then seal the entire instrument in an envelope. While this approach does not guarantee confidentiality, it does suggest it. We can also develop appropriate questioning sequences that will more adroitly lead a respondent from "safe" questions gradually to those that are more sensitive.

Indirect questioning is a widely used approach for securing opinions on sensitive topics. The respondents are asked how "other people" or "people around here" feel about a topic. It is assumed the respondents will reply in terms of their own attitudes and experiences, but this is hardly certain. It may give a good measure of the majority opinion on a topic but fail either to reflect the views of the respondent or of minority segments.

With certain topics, it is possible to secure answers by using a proxy code. When we seek family income classes we can hand the respondent a card with income brackets like:

A. Under $15,000 per year
B. $15,000 to $24,999 per year
C. $25,000 to $34,999 per year
D. $35,000 and over per year

The respondent is then asked to report the appropriate bracket as either A, B, C, or D. For some reason, respondents are more willing to provide such an obvious proxy measure than to give actual dollar values.

Other Approaches   Sometimes questioning will not secure the information needed. A classic example concerns a survey to discover magazines read by respondents. An unusually high rate was reported for prestigious magazines, and an unusually low rate was reported for tabloid magazines. The study was revised so that instead of being interviewed, the subjects were asked to contribute their old magazines to a charity drive. The collection gave a more realistic estimate of readership of both types of magazines.[8] Another study on the use of similar unobtrusive measures cites many other types of research situations where unique techniques have been used to secure more valid information than was possible from a survey.[9] (See Chapter 12.)

Question Wording

The difficulties caused by question wording exceed most other sources of distortion in surveys. They have led one social scientist to conclude:

> To many who worked in the Research Branch it soon became evident that error or bias attributable to sampling and to methods of questionnaire administration were relatively small as compared with other types of variations—especially variation attributable to different ways of wording questions.[10]

While it is impossible to say which wording of a question is best, we can point out several areas that cause respondent confusion and measurement error. The diligent question designer will put a given question through many revisions before it satisfies these criteria.[11]

1. Is the question stated in terms of a shared vocabulary?
2. Is the question clear?
3. Are there unstated or misleading assumptions?
4. Is there biased wording?
5. Is there the right degree of personalization?
6. Are adequate alternatives presented?

Shared Vocabulary   Because a survey is an exchange of ideas between interviewer and respondent, each must understand what the other says, and this is possible only if the vocabulary used is common to both parties.[12] Two problems arise. First, the words must be simple enough to allow adequate communication with persons of limited education. This is dealt with by reducing the level of word difficulty to simple English words and phrases (more is said about this in the section on word clarity).

Technical language is the second issue. Even highly educated respondents cannot answer questions stated in unfamiliar technical terms. It also poses difficulties for interviewers. In one study of how corporation executives handled various financial problems, interviewers had to be conversant with technical financial terms. This presented the researcher with two alternatives—hire people knowledgeable in finance and teach them interviewing skills or teach financial concepts to experienced interviewers.[13]

Question Clarity   It is frustrating when people misunderstand a question that has been painstakingly written. This is partially a problem of the shared vocabularies already mentioned. Beyond this is the difficulty of understanding long and complex sentences or involved phraseology. The dilemma arises from the requirements of question design (need to be explicit, to present alternatives, and to explain meanings). All contribute to longer and more involved sentences.[14]

A great obstacle to effective question wording is the choice of words. The questions to be asked of the public should be restricted to the most common 2,000 words in the English language.[15] Even the use of simple words is not enough. Many words have vague references or meanings that must be found in their context. In a repair study, technicians were asked, "How many radio sets did you repair last month?" This is an unambiguous question, but respondents interpreted it in two ways. Some viewed it as a question of them alone, while others interpreted it as a more inclusive "you," suggesting the total output of the shop. Typical of the many problem words are *any, could, would, should, fair, near, often,* and *average.* One author recommends that after we have stated a question as precisely as possible, we should test each word with this checklist:

1. Does it mean what we intend?
2. Does it have other meanings?
3. If so, does the context make the intended meaning clear?
4. Does the word have more than one pronunciation?
5. Is there any word or similar pronunciation that might be confused?
6. Is a simpler word or phrase suggested?[16]

Assumptions   Unwarranted assumptions contribute to many problems of question wording. In the Prince Corporation study, what percentage of the population would understand the terms *conglomerate,* or *multinational company?* We cause other problems when we use "blab" words—abstract concepts that have many overtones and emotional qualifications.[17] Without concrete referents, meanings are too vague for the researcher's needs. Examples of such words are *business, government,* and *society.* Suppose that in the Prince Corporation study we asked the question, "How involved is business in the affairs of our society?" What is meant by "involved"? What parts of "society"? Is there such a thing as "business" per se?

Inherent in word meaning problems is also the matter of a frame of reference. Each of us understands concepts, words, and expressions in the light of our own experience. The U.S. Bureau of Census wanted to know how many people were in the labor market. To learn whether a person was employed, it asked, "Did you do any work for pay or profit last week?" The researchers erroneously assumed there would be a common frame of reference between the interviewer and respondents on the meaning of *work.* Unfortunately, many persons viewed themselves primarily as homemakers or students. They failed to report that they also worked at a job during the week. This difference in a frame of reference resulted in a consistent underestimation of the number of people working in the United States.

This question was replaced by two questions, the first of which sought a statement on the respondent's major activity during the week. If the respondent gave a nonwork classification, a second question was asked to determine if he or she had done any work for pay besides this major activity. This revision increased the estimate of total employment by more than 1 million people, with about half of them working 35 hours or more per week.[18]

The frame of reference can be controlled in two ways. First, the interviewer may seek to learn the frame of reference used by the respondent. When asking respondents to evaluate their reasons for judging a labor contract offer, it is necessary to learn the frames of reference they use. Is the labor offer being evaluated in terms of the specific offer being made, the failure of management to respond to other demands, the personalities involved, or the personal economic pressures that have resulted from a long strike?

It can be useful to specify the frame of reference for the respondent. In asking for an opinion about the new labor contract offer, we might specify that the question concerns the size of the wage offer, the sincerity of management's offer, or another frame of reference of interest.

Biased Wording   Bias is the distortion of responses in one direction. It can result from many of the problems already discussed, but word choice is often the major source. Obviously such words or phrases as *politically correct* or *fundamentalist* must be used with great care. Strong adjectives can be particularly distorting. One alleged opinion survey, concerned with the subject of preparation for death, included the following question: "Do you think that decent, low-cost funerals are sensible?" Who could be against anything that is decent or sensible? There is a question about whether this was a legitimate survey or a burial service sales campaign, but it shows how suggestive an adjective can be.

We can also strongly bias the respondent by using prestigious names in a question. In a survey on whether the War and Navy departments should be combined into a single Defense Department, one form said, "General Eisenhower says the Army and Navy should be combined," while the other version omitted his name. In the first version (name included), 49 percent of the respondents approved of having one department, while in the second version, only 29 percent favored one department.[19]

We also can bias response through the use of superlatives, slang expressions, and fad words. These are best excluded unless they are critical to the objective of the question. Ethnic references should also be stated with care.

Personalization   How personalized should a question be? Should we ask, "What would you do about . . .?" Or should we ask, "What would *people* do about . . .?" The effect of personalization is shown in a classic example reported by Cantril.[20] A split test was made of a question concerning attitudes about the expansion of our armed forces in 1940.

Should the United States do aₙy of the following at this time?
A. Increase our armed forces further, even if it means more taxes.
B. Increase our armed forces further, even if you have to pay a special tax.

Eighty-eight percent of those answering question A thought we should increase the army, while only 79 percent of those answering question B favored increasing the army.

These and other examples show that responses are changed by personalizing questions, but it is not clear whether this is for better or for worse. We often cannot tell which answer is superior. Perhaps the best that can be said is that when either form is acceptable, we should choose that which appears to present the issues more realistically. If there are doubts, then split versions should be used.

Adequate Alternatives?   Have we adequately expressed the alternatives with respect to the point of the question? It is usually wise to express each alternative explicitly to avoid bias. This is illustrated well with a pair of questions that were asked of matched samples of respondents.[21] The forms used were:

A. Do you think most manufacturing companies that lay off workers during slack periods could arrange things to avoid layoffs and give steady work right through the year?

B. Do you think most manufacturing companies that lay off workers in slack periods could avoid layoffs and provide steady work right through the year, or do you think layoffs are unavoidable?

	A	B
Company could avoid layoffs	63%	35%
Could not avoid layoffs	22	41
No opinion	15	24

Toward Better Questions There is no substitute for a thorough understanding of question-wording problems. Beyond this, however, several things can be done to help improve survey results. At the original question drafting, try developing positive, negative, and neutral versions of each question. This practice dramatizes the problems of bias. Sometimes use an extreme version. If we ask people about their children, we want our opinion statement to *encourage* the mention of all children.

Once we have developed a set of questions (including some with the same purpose), we then test and revise them. Inexperienced researchers normally underestimate the need for designing—testing—revision. Revising a question five or more times is not unusual. Finally, if there is still doubt about which version is more appropriate, we should use different question versions that go to matched or random selections of the respondents.

Response Structure

A third major decision area in question design is the degree and form of structure imposed on responses. The options range from **open** (free choice of words) to **closed** (specified alternatives). Free responses, in turn, range from those in which the respondents express themselves extensively to those in which their latitude is restricted to choosing one word in a "fill-in" question. Closed responses typically are categorized as dichotomous or multiple choice.

Situational Determinants Five situational factors affect the decision of whether to use open- or closed-response questions.[22] They are:

1. Objectives of the interview.
2. Respondent's level of information about the topic.
3. Degree respondent has thought through the topic.
4. Ease of communication and motivation of respondent to talk.
5. Degree to which the above respondent factors are known to the interviewer.

If the objective of the question is only to classify the respondent on some stated point of view, then the closed form will serve well. Assume you are interested only in whether a respondent approves or disapproves of a certain corporate policy. A closed-response form will provide this answer. This would ignore the full scope of the respondent's opinion and its antecedents. If the objective is to explore a wider territory, then an open-response form would be more desirable.

As mentioned earlier, open-response questions are appropriate when the objective is to discover opinions and degrees of knowledge. They are also appropriate when the interviewer seeks sources of information, dates of events, and suggestions or when probes are used to secure more information.

When the topic of a question is outside the respondent's experience, the open-ended question may be the better way to learn his or her level of information. Open-ended questions also help to uncover certainty of feelings and expressions of intensity, although well-designed closed questions can do the same.

If a respondent has developed a clear opinion on the topic, a closed-response question does well. If an answer has not been thought out, the open-ended question may give the respondent a chance to ponder a reply, then elaborate and revise it.

Experience has shown that closed questions typically require less motivation and answering them is less threatening to respondents. In contrast, the response alternatives sometimes suggest which answer is appropriate; in this sense, they may be biased.

Finally, it may be better to use open-response questions when the interviewer does not have a clear idea of the respondent's frame of reference or level of information. Such conditions are likely to occur in exploratory research or in pilot testing. Closed-response questions are better when there is a clear frame of reference, the respondent's level of information is predictable, and the researcher believes the respondent understands the topic.

Dichotomous Questions   While the open-ended question has many advantages, closed questions are generally preferable in large surveys. They reduce the variability of response, make fewer demands on interviewer skills, are less costly to administer, and are much easier to code and analyze. After adequate exploration and testing, we can often develop closed questions that will perform as effectively as open questions in many situations. Experimental studies suggest that closed questions are equal to or superior to open-response questions in many more applications than is commonly believed.[23]

Should a closed question call for a dichotomous or multiple-choice response? Often this is a simple decision dictated by the nature of the problem. The topic may be clearly **dichotomous.** Something is a fact or it is not; a respondent can either recall or not recall information. In many two-way questions, however, there are potential alternatives beyond the stated two. For example, the respondent may answer "don't know," "no opinion," or even "in-between." In other cases, there are two opposing or complementary choices, but there may also be a qualified choice ("yes, if X doesn't occur," or "sometimes yes and sometimes no," or "about the same"). Thus, two-way questions often become multiple choice and these additional responses should be included.

One may omit the middle response if interested in which direction the respondent is leaning. One may also omit the middle answer when the topic is one where people retreat to a safe middle ground, if it is available. Dichotomous questions suggest opposing responses, but this is not always the best arrangement. One response may be so unlikely that it would be better to adopt the middle ground alternative as one of the two choices. For example, if we ask respondents whether they are underpaid or overpaid, we are not likely to get many agreements with the latter choice. The choices might better be underpaid and paid equitably.

Multiple-Choice Questions   **Multiple-choice questions** are appropriate where there are more than two alternatives or where we seek gradations of preference, interest, or agreement. Multiple-choice questions can be efficient, but they also present unique design problems. When the list of choices is not exhaustive, respondents may want to give an answer that is not an alternative. This occurs when the desired response is one that combines two or more of the listed individual alternatives. We might ask whether mine safety rules should be determined by the (1) mine companies, (2) miners, (3) federal government, or (4) state government. Many people may believe such rules should be set by two or more of these groups acting jointly, but the question does not include this response.

A second problem occurs when some response category has not been anticipated. For example, the union has not been mentioned in the alternatives on mine safety laws. Many respondents would lump this alternative with miners, but others will view it as a separate category. Some respondents may believe certain rules should be set by a federal agency, others by industry–national union negotiation, and still others through local management–worker committees. When the researcher tries to provide for all possible options, the list can become exhausting. We guard against this by discovering the major choices through pretesting. Then we add the category "other (please specify)" to provide for all other options.

Another challenge in alternative selection occurs when the choices are not mutually exclusive (the respondent sees two or more responses as overlapping). In a multiple-choice question that asks students why they went to a certain college, the following response alternatives might be listed about the chosen school:

1. Good academic reputation.
2. Specific program of study desired.
3. Enjoyable campus life.
4. Many friends from home attend.
5. High quality of the faculty.

It is likely that items 1 and 5 will be viewed as overlapping, and some may see items 3 and 4 in the same way.

It is also important to seek a fair balance in choices. One study showed that an off-balance presentation of alternatives biases the results in favor of the more heavily offered side.[24] If four gradations of alternatives are on one side of a question and two on the other side, responses will tend to be biased toward the better represented side.

It is necessary in multiple-choice questions to present reasonable alternatives. This is particularly so when choices are numbers or identifications. If we ask, "Which of the following numbers is closest to the number of students enrolled in American colleges and universities today?" The following choices might be presented:

1. 75,000.
2. 750,000.
3. 7,500,000.
4. 25,000,000.
5. 75,000,000.

It should be obvious to most respondents that at least three of these choices are not reasonable in the light of our general knowledge about the population of the United States.

The order of choices given can also be a problem. Numbers are normally presented in order of magnitude. This practice introduces a bias. The respondent assumes that if there is a list of five numbers, the correct answer will lie somewhere in the middle of the group. Researchers often add a couple of incorrect numbers on each side of the correct one. To counteract this tendency, put the correct number at an extreme more often.

Order bias with nonnumeric data leads to choosing the first or last alternatives over the middle ones. This bias can be counteracted by using the split-ballot technique. To implement this in face-to-face interviews, list the alternatives on a card to be handed to the respondent when asking the question. Cards with different choice orders can be alternated to assure positional balance. Leave the choices unnumbered on the card so respondents reply by giving the choice itself rather than its identifying number. It is a good practice to use cards like this any time there are four or more question alternatives. This saves the interviewer's reading time and assures a more valid answer by keeping the full range of choices in front of the respondent.

In most multiple-choice questions, there is also a problem of assuring that the choices represent a undimensional scale. That is, the alternatives all represent different aspects of the same *conceptual dimension.* In the college selection example, the list included features associated with a college that might be attractive to a student. This list, while not exhaustive, illustrated aspects of the concept of "college attractiveness." But it did not mention other concepts that might affect a school attendance decision. Parents and peer advice, local alumni efforts, and school advisor suggestions may influence the decision, but these represent a conceptual dimension different from "school attractiveness."

All types of response styles have their advantages and disadvantages. All forms are often found in the same questionnaire, and the situational factors mentioned earlier are the major guides in this matter. There is a tendency, however, to use closed-response forms instead of the more flexible open-response type.

Question Sequence

The design of survey questions is influenced by the need to relate each question to the others in the instrument. Question sequencing is particularly important. The basic principle to guide sequence decisions is: *The nature and needs of the respondent must determine the sequence of questions and the organization of the schedule.* A guide may be suggested to implement this principle:

1. The question process must quickly awaken interest and motivate the respondent to participate in the interview.
2. The respondent should not be confronted by early requests for information that might be considered personal or ego threatening.
3. The questioning process should begin with simple items and move to the more complex, and from general items to the more specific.
4. Changes in the frame of reference should be small and should be clearly pointed out.

The first challenge is to awaken the respondent's interest in the study and motivate participation. We try to bring this about by choosing questions that are attention getting and not controversial. If the questions have human interest value, so much the better. It is possible that the early questions will contribute hard data to the major study objective, but their major task is to overcome the motivational barrier.

The second suggestion concerns a request for sensitive information too early in the process. Two forms of this error are common. There is usually a need to ask for personal classification information about respondents. They normally will provide these data, but the request should be made toward the end. If sought immediately, it often causes respondents to feel threatened, dampening their interest and motivation to continue. It is also dangerous to ask any question at the start that is too personal. For example, respondents in one survey were asked whether they suffered from insomnia. When the question was asked immediately after the interviewer's introductory remarks, about 12 percent of those interviewed admitted to having insomnia. When a matched sample was asked the same question after two **buffer questions** (neutral questions designed chiefly to establish rapport with the respondent), 23 percent admitted having insomnia.[25]

A third point is to place simpler questions first and move progressively to more complex ones. Even simple questions that require much thought should be deferred until later. These recommendations can help reduce the number of "don't know" responses that are so prevalent early in interviews.

The procedure of moving from general to more specific questions is sometimes called the **funnel approach.** The objectives of this procedure are to learn the respondent's frame of reference and to extract the full range of desired information while limiting the distortion effect of earlier questions on later ones. This process may be illustrated with the following series of questions:

1. How do you think this country is getting along in its relations with other countries?
2. How do you think we are doing in our relations with Russia?
3. Do you think we ought to be dealing with Russia differently than we are now?
4. *(If yes)* What should we be doing differently?
5. Some people say we should get tougher with Russia and others think we are too tough as it is; how do you feel about it?[26]

The first question introduces the general subject and provides some insight into the respondent's frame of reference. The second question narrows the concern to a single country, while the third and fourth seek views on how the United States should deal with Russia. The fifth question illustrates a specific opinion area and would be asked only if this point of toughness had not been covered in earlier responses.

There is also a risk of interaction whenever two or more questions are related. The two questions shown in the table were asked in a national survey at the start of World War II:[27]

	Percent Answering Yes	
Question	*A Asked First*	*B Asked First*
A. Should the United States permit its citizens to join the French and British Armies?	45%	40%
B. Should the United States permit its citizens to join the German army?	31	22

Apparently, if respondents first endorsed enlistments with the Allies, some felt obliged to extend this privilege to joining the Germans. Where the decision was first made against joining the German army, a percentage of the respondents felt constrained from approving the option to join the Allies.

Finally, questions should be arranged so there is a minimum of shifting in subject matter and frame of reference. Respondents often interpret questions in the light of earlier questions and will miss shifts of perspective or subject unless they are clearly stated. Respondents fail to listen carefully and frequently jump to conclusions about the import of a given question before it is completely stated. Their answers are strongly influenced by their frame of reference. Any change in subject by the interviewer may not register with them unless made strong and obvious.

SOURCES OF EXISTING QUESTIONS

Consistent with the text's orientation, the tools of data collection should be adapted to the problem, not the reverse. Thus, the focus of this chapter has been on crafting an instrument to answer specific investigative questions. But the reality of inventing and refining questions demands considerable time and effort. For some topics, this process can be shortened by a careful review of the related literature and an examination of existing instrument sourcebooks.

A review of literature will reveal instruments used in similar studies that may be obtained by writing the researchers or, if copyrighted, purchased through a clearinghouse. Many instruments are available through compilations and sourcebooks. The latter are a rich source of ideas for tailoring questions to meet the needs of one's project. Several compilations are recommended, and we have added others and consolidated them in Table 11–1.[28]

Borrowing items from existing sources is not without risks. It is quite difficult to generalize the reliability and validity of selected items or portions of a questionnaire that have been taken out of the original context. Retesting is also warranted if it is necessary to report the reliability and validity of the instrument being constructed. Time and situation-specific fluctuations should be scrutinized. Remember that the original estimates are only as good as the sampling and testing procedures, and many researchers you borrow from may not have reported that information.

Language, phrasing, and idioms can also pose problems. Questions tend to age and may not appear (or sound) as relevant to the respondent as freshly worded ones would. Integrating existing and newly constructed questions is problematic. When adjacent questions are relied upon to carry context in one questionnaire and then not selected for the customized application, the newly selected question is left without necessary meaning.[29] Whether an instrument is constructed from scratch or adapted from the ideas of others, pretesting is recommended.

PRETESTING

Pretesting detects weaknesses in the instruments. Designers typically test informally in the initial stages and build more structure into the tests along the way. In this section we discuss field testing of the instrument.

Pretesting relies on colleagues, respondent surrogates, or actual respondents to evaluate and refine a measuring instrument. Most studies use two or more pretests. National projects may use one trial to examine local reaction and another to check for regional differences. Although many researchers try to keep pretest conditions and times close to what they expect for the actual study, personal interview

TABLE 11-1   Sources of Questions

Author(s)	Title	Source
Philip E. Converse, Jean D. Dotson, Wendy J. Hoag, and William H. McGee, III, eds.	*American Social Attitudes Data Sourcebook 1947–1978*	Cambridge, Mass.: Harvard University Press, 1980
George H. Gallup	*The Gallup Poll: 1935–1971*	New York: Random House, 1935–1971; Wilmington, Del.: Scholarly Resources, Inc., 1972–1985
George H. Gallup, Jr., ed.	*The Gallup Poll: Public Opinion* [annual series]	Wilmington, Del.: Scholarly Resources, Inc., 1986–1993
Elizabeth H. Hastings and Philip K. Hastings, eds.	*Index to International Public Opinion 1986–87*	Westport, Conn.: Greenwood Press, 1988
Philip K. Hastings and Jessie C. Southwick, eds.	*Survey Data for Trend Analysis: An Index to Repeated Questions in the U.S. National Surveys Held by the Roper Public Opinion Research Center*	Storrs, Conn.: Roper Center for Public Opinion Research, Inc., 1974
Elizabeth Martin, Diana McDuffee, and Stanley Presser	*Sourcebook of Harris National Surveys: Repeated Questions 1963–1976*	Chapel Hill, N.C.: Institute for Research in Social Science, University of North Carolina Press, 1981
National Opinion Research Center	*General Social Surveys 1972–1985: Cumulative Code Book*	Chicago: NORC, 1985
John P. Robinson, Robert Athanasiou, and Kendra B. Head	*Measures of Occupational Attitudes and Occupational Characteristics*	Ann Arbor, Mich.: Institute for Social Research, 1968
John P. Robinson and Philip R. Shaver	*Measures of Social-Psychological Attitudes,* rev. ed.	Ann Arbor, Mich.: Institute for Social Research, 1973

and telephone limitations make it desirable to test in the evenings or on weekends to interview people who are not available for contact at other times.

Test mailings are useful, but it is often faster to use a substitute procedure. In the MindWriter example, the managers who were interviewed in the exploratory study were later asked to review the pilot questionnaire. The interviewers left and returned later for them. Upon their return, they went over the questions with the manager. They explained that they wanted the manager's reactions to question clarity and ease of answering. After several such interviews, the instrument was revised and the testing process repeated with customers. With minor revision, the questionnaire was reproduced and prepared for inserting into the computer packing material.

Most of what we know about pretesting is prescriptive. According to contemporary authors,

There are no general principles of good pretesting, no systematization of practice, no consensus about expectations, and we rarely leave records for each other. How a pretest was conducted, what investigators learned from it, how they redesigned their questionnaire on the basis of it—these matters are reported only sketchily in research reports, if at all.[30]

Nevertheless, conventional wisdom suggests that pretesting is not only an established practice for discovering errors but also is useful for training the research team. Ironically, professionals who have participated in scores of studies are more likely to pretest an instrument than a beginning researcher hurrying to complete a project.

Methods of Pretesting[31]

Different approaches taken by interviewers and the respondents' awareness of those approaches affect the pretest. If the researcher alerts respondents to their involvement in a preliminary test of the questionnaire, the respondents are essentially being enlisted as collaborators in the refinement process. Under these conditions, detailed probing of the parts of the question, including phrases and words, is appropriate. Because of the time required for probing and discussion, it is likely that only the most critical questions will be reviewed. The respondent group may therefore need to be conscripted from colleagues and friends to secure the additional time and motivation needed to cover an entire questionnaire. If friends or associates are used, experience suggests that they introduce more bias than strangers, argue more about wording, and generally make it more difficult to accomplish other goals of pretesting such as timing the length of questions or sections.

When the researcher does not inform the respondent that the activity is a pretest, it is still possible to probe for reactions but without the cooperation and commitment of time provided by collaborators. The comprehensiveness of the effort also suffers because of flagging cooperation. The virtue of this approach is that the questionnaire can be tested under conditions approaching those of the final study. This realism is similarly useful for training interviewers.

Occasionally, a highly experienced researcher may improvise questions. When this occurs, it is essential to record the interview or take detailed notes so the questionnaire may be reconstructed later. It is more probable that field interviewers would use an interview schedule. Similarly, a team of interviewers would be required to follow the schedule's prearranged sequence of questions. Only experienced investigators should be free to depart from the interview schedule and explore respondents' answers by adding probes.

Purposes of Pretesting

There are abundant reasons for pretesting questionnaires and interview schedules. In this section we discuss several and raise questions to help you plan an effective test of your instrument.

Respondent Interest An important purpose of pretesting is to discover the respondents' reactions to the questions. If respondents do not find the experience stimulating when an interviewer is physically present, how will they react on the phone or in the self-administered mode? Pretesting should help to discover where repetitiveness or redundancy is bothersome or what topics were not covered that the respondent expected. An alert interviewer will look for questions or even sections that were perceived to be sensitive or threatening or topics about which nothing is known.

Meaning   Questions that we borrow or adapt from the work of others carry an authoritativeness that may prompt us to avoid pretesting them, but they are often most in need of examination. Are they still timely? Is the language relevant? Do they need context from adjacent questions? Newly constructed questions should be similarly checked for meaning to the respondent. Does the question evoke the same meaning as that intended by the researcher? How different is the researcher's frame of reference from that of the average respondent? Words and phrases that trigger a "what do you mean?" response from the respondent need to be singled out for further refinement.

Question Transformation   Respondents do not necessarily process every word in the question. They also do not share the same definitions for the terms they hear. When this happens, respondents modify the question to make it fit their own frame of reference or simply change it so it makes sense to them. Probing is necessary to discover how respondents have transformed the question when this is suspected.[32]

Continuity and Flow   In self-administered questionnaires, questions should read effortlessly and flow from one to another and from one section to another. In personal and telephone interviews, the sound of the question and its transition must be fluid as well. A long set of questions with nine-point scales that worked well in a mail instrument would not be effective on the telephone unless you ask respondents to visualize the scale as the touch keys on their phone. Moreover, the types of transitions that may appear redundant in writing may be exactly the ones that need to be heard in personal or telephone interviewing.

Question Sequence   Question arrangement can play a significant role in the success of the instrument. Many authorities recommend starting with stimulating questions and placing sensitive questions last. Since questions concerning income and family life are most likely to be refused, this is often good advice for building trust before getting into a refusal situation. However, stimulating questions need to be tested first to be sure they are stimulating. And when background questions are asked earlier in the interview, some demographic information will be salvaged if questioning is terminated. Pretesting with a large enough group permits some experimentation with alternating these sequences.

Skip Instructions   In interviews and questionnaires, **skip patterns** and their contingency sequences may not work as envisioned on paper. Skip patterns are designed to route or sequence the response to another question contingent on the answer to the previous question. Pretesting in the field helps to identify problems with box-and-arrow schematics that the designers may not have thought of. By correcting them in the revision stage, we also avoid problems with flow and continuity.

Variability   With a small group of respondents, pretesting cannot provide definitive quantitative conclusions but will deliver an early warning about items that may not discriminate among respondents or where meaningful subgrouping may occur in the final sample. With 25 to 100 respondents in the pretest group, statistical data on the proportion of respondents answering yes or no or marking strongly agree to strongly disagree can supplement the qualitative information noted by the interviewers. This information is useful for sample size calculations and getting preliminary indications of reliability problems with scaled questions.

Length and Timing   Most draft questionnaires or interview schedules suffer from lengthiness. By timing each question and section, the researcher is in a better position to make decisions about modifying or cutting material. In personal and telephone interviews, labor is a project expense. Thus, if the budget influences the final length of the questionnaire, an accurate estimate of elapsed time is essential. Video- or audiotaped pretests may also be used for this purpose. Their function in reducing errors in data recording is widely accepted.

Summary

The versatility of the survey method is its greatest strength. It is an exceptionally practical way to gather opinions, knowledge, and behavioral intentions. Its dependency upon the respondent's verbal behavior is its greatest weakness. Not only may intentionally false information be given, but verbal behavior can also be dramatically changed by many factors.

Several choices must be made in designing a survey instrument. Survey research can be a face-to-face interview, or it can be much less personal, using indirect media and self-administered questionnaires. The questioning process can be unstructured as with in-depth interviewing and similar approaches, or the questions can be clearly structured. Responses may be unstructured with open-ended respondent answers or structured with the respondent choosing an answer from a set of listed possibilities. The degree to which the objectives and intent of the questions should be disguised must also be decided.

The development of a survey instrument is often considered unessential by those who believe just about anyone can do it. Question development will be easier if the designer follows the research question hierarchy concept. The logical process begins with the management question then moves on to the research question, the investigative questions, and finally to the measurement questions.

Three general classes of information are generally obtained. The most important is the information of major topical concern. A second class is data concerning respondent characteristics and other information used chiefly for classification and analysis. Finally, certain administrative information is needed.

Question construction has four critical decision areas. They are (1) question content, (2) question wording, (3) response structure, and (4) question sequence. Question content should pass the following tests:

1. Should the question be asked?
2. Is the question of proper scope?
3. Can the respondent answer adequately?
4. Will respondents answer adequately?

Question-wording difficulties exceed most other sources of distortion in surveys. Retention of a question should be confirmed by answering:

1. Is the question stated in terms of a shared vocabulary?
2. Is the question clear?
3. Are there unstated or misleading assumptions?
4. Is there biased wording?
5. Is there the right degree of personalization?
6. Are adequate alternatives presented?

The response structure is influenced by five situational determinants:

1. Objectives of the interview.
2. Respondent's level of information about the topic.
3. Degree respondent has thought through the topic.
4. Ease of communication and motivation of respondent to talk.
5. Degree to which the above respondent factors are known to the interviewer.

Both two-way and multiple-choice questions have their values and their def˙ ˙en-cies, but on balance, the latter are preferred if only because few questions have only two possible answers.

Question sequence can drastically affect resp ndent willingness to cooperate and the quality of responses received. Generally, tne sequence should begin with efforts to awaken the respondent's interest in continuing the interview. Early questions should be simple rather than complex, easy rather than difficult, nonthreatening, and obviously germane to the announced objective of the study. Frame-of-reference changes should be minimal, and questions should be sequenced so earlier questions do not distort the replies of later ones.

A special problem in question design is that of learning the reasons for actions or opinions. A simple "why" question is too often used and almost as often fails to secure the needed information. To measure reasons, the researcher needs first to analyze the research objectives and the type of actions or opinions under study. In this analysis, an accounting scheme should be used. This is an organized list of factors believed to be relevant causes or influences upon the actions, attitudes, or intentions under study. When done in this manner, substantial causal information can be secured.

Sources of existing questions for the construction of questionnaires include the literature of related research and sourcebooks of scales and questionnaires. Borrowing items has attendant risks such as time and situation-specific reliability and validity problems. Incompatibility of language and idiom also needs to be considered.

Pretesting the instrument is recommended to identify problems before the actual collection of data begins. Although the advice on pretesting is not empirical, conventional wisdom is sound in requiring corrective action and revision of newly constructed or adapted questions. Pretesting methods are selected after reviewing the respondent awareness and the degree of structure needed. The amount of probing attempted, the type of respondents selected, and the realism obtained is affected by the combination of these factors.

Insights and ideas for refining instruments result from thoroughness in pretesting. Among the purposes of the pretest are: determining respondent interest, discovering if the questions have meaning for the respondent, checking for respondent modification of a question's intent, examining question continuity and flow, experimenting with question sequencing patterns, evaluating skip instructions for the interviewers, collecting early warning data on item variability, and fixing the length and timing of the instrument.

KEY TERMS

buffer question	interview schedule
closed question	leading question
dichotomous question	multiple-choice question
disguised question	open-ended question
double-barreled question	pretesting
filter question	projective techniques
focus group	skip pattern
funnel approach	structured question/response
in-depth interview	unstructured question/response

Discussion Questions

1. Distinguish between:
   a. Direct and indirect questions
   b. Open and closed questions.
   c. Research, investigative, and measurement questions.
   d. Question and response structure.
2. Why is the survey technique so popular? When is it not appropriate?
3. What special problems do open-ended questions have? How can these be minimized? In what situations is the open-ended question most useful?
4. Why might a researcher wish to disguise the questioning objective of a study?
5. One of the major reasons that survey research may not be effective is because the survey instruments are less useful than they should be. What would you say are the four major faults of the survey instrument designer?

6. Why is it desirable to pretest survey instruments? What information can you secure from such a pretest? How can you find the best wording for a question on a questionnaire?

7. One design problem in the development of survey instruments concerns the sequence of questions. What suggestions would you give to people designing their first questionnaire?

8. One of the major problems facing the designer of a survey instrument is the assumptions made. What are the major "problem assumptions"?

9. Below are six questions that might be found on questionnaires. Comment on each as to whether it is a good question. If not, tell why. (Assume that no lead-in or screening questions are required for these. That is, judge the question on its own merits.)

   a. Do you read the *National Geographic* magazine regularly?

   b. What percent of your time is spent asking for information from others in your organization?

   c. When did you first start chewing gum?

   d. How much discretionary buying power do you have each year?

   e. Why did you decide to attend Big State University?

   f. Do you think the president is doing a good job now?

10. One student class project was to develop a brief self-administered questionnaire by which students might quickly evaluate a professor. One student submitted the following instrument. Evaluate the questions asked and the format of the instrument.

Professor Evaluation Form

1. Overall, how would you rate this professor?

   _____ good; _____ fair, _____ poor.

2. Does this professor:
   a. Have good class delivery? _____
   b. Know the subject? _____
   c. Have a positive attitude toward the subject? _____
   d. Grade fairly? _____
   e. Have a sense of humor? _____
   f. Use audiovisuals, case examples, or other classroom aids? _____
   g. Return exams promptly? _____

3. What is the professor's strongest point? _____

4. What is the professor's weakest point? _____

5. What kind of class does the professor teach? _____

6. Is this course required? _____

7. Would you take another course from this professor? _____

11. Below is a copy of the letter and mail questionnaire received by a professor who is a member of the American Society of Training Directors. Please evaluate the usefulness and tone of the letter and the questions and format of the instrument.

Dear ASTD Member:

In partial fulfillment of master's degree work, I have chosen to do a descriptive study of the industrial trainer in our area. Using the roster of the ASTD as a mailing list, your name came to me. I am enclosing a short questionnaire and a return envelope. I hope you will take a few minutes and fill out the questionnaire as soon as possible, as the sooner the information is returned to me, the better.

Sincerely,

Questionnaire

Directions: Please answer as briefly as possible.

1. With what company did you enter the field of training? _____

2. How long have you been in the field of training? _____

3. How long have you been in the training department of the company with which you are presently employed? _____

4. How long has the training department in your company been in existence? _____

5. Is the training department a subdivision of another department? _____ If so, what department? _____

6. For what functions (other than training) is your department responsible? _____

7. How many people, including yourself, are in the training department of your company? (Local plant or establishment) _____

8. What degrees do you hold and from what institutions? _____ Major _____ Minor _____

9. Why were you chosen for training? What special qualifications do you have that prompted your entry into training? _____ _____ _____

10. What experience would you consider necessary for an individual to enter into the field of training with your company? Include both educational requirements and actual experience. _____ _____ _____ _____

Reference Notes

1. The MindWriter questionnaire used in this example is based on an actual questionnaire copyrighted by Cooper Research Group, Inc., 1993, for an unidentified client who shares the intellectual property rights. No part of the format, question wording, sequence, or scale may be produced or transmitted in any form or by any means, electronic or mechanical, including photocopy, recording, or any information storage and retrieval system, without permission in writing from Cooper Research Group, Inc. Reprinted with permission.

2. Louis Cohen, "The Differentiation Ratio in Corporate Research," *Journal of Advertising Research* 4 (September 1967), pp. 34–35.

3. Dorwin Cartwright, "Some Principles of Mass Persuasion," *Human Relations* 2 (1948), p. 266.

4. Sam Gill, "How Do You Stand on Sin?" *Tide,* March 14, 1947, p. 72.

5. Stanley Payne, *The Art of Asking Questions* (Princeton, N.J.: Princeton University Press, 1951), p. 18.

6. Unaided recall gives respondents no clues as to possible answers, while aided recall gives them a list of radio programs that played last night and then asks them which ones they had heard. See Harper W. Boyd, Jr., and Ralph Westfall, *Marketing Research,* 3rd ed. (Homewood, Ill.: Richard D. Irwin, Inc., 1972), p. 293.

7. Gideon Sjoberg, "A Questionnaire on Questionnaires," *Public Opinion Quarterly* 18 (Winter 1954), p. 425.

8. Perceival White, *Market Analysis* (New York: McGraw-Hill, 1921).

9. Eugene J. Webb, Donald T. Campbell, Richard D. Schwartz, and Lee Sechrest, *Unobtrusive Measures: Nonreactive Research in the Social Sciences* (Chicago: Rand McNally, 1966).

10. S. A. Stouffer et al., *Measurement and Prediction, Studies in Social Psychology in World War II,* vol. 4 (Princeton, N.J.: Princeton University Press, 1950), p. 709.

11. An excellent example of the question revision process is presented in Payne, *The Art of Asking Questions,* pp. 214–25. This example illustrates that a relatively simple question can go through as many as 41 different versions before being judged satisfactory.

12. Robert L. Kahn and Charles F. Cannell, *The Dynamics of Interviewing* (New York: John Wiley & Sons, 1957), p. 108.

13. Ibid., p. 110.

14. More will be said on the general problems of readability in Chapter 18.

15. Payne, *The Art of Asking Questions,* p. 140.

16. Ibid., p. 141.

17. Ibid., p. 149.

18. Gertrude Bancroft and Emmett H. Welch, "Recent Experiences with Problems of Labor Force Measurement," *Journal of the American Statistical Association* 41 (1946), pp. 303–12.

19. National Opinion Research Center, *Proceedings of the Central City Conference on Public Opinion Research* (Denver, Colo.: University of Denver, 1946), p. 73.

20. Hadley Cantril, ed., *Gauging Public Opinion* (Princeton, N.J.: Princeton University Press, 1944), p. 48.

21. Payne, *The Art of Asking Questions,* pp. 7–8.

22. Kahn and Cannell, *Dynamics of Interviewing,* p. 132.

23. Barbara Snell Dohrenwend, "Some Effects of Open and Closed Questions on Respondents' Answers," *Human Organization* 24 (Summer 1965), pp. 175–84.

24. Cantril, *Gauging Public Opinion,* p. 31.

25. Frederick J. Thumin, "Watch for These Unseen Variables," *Journal of Marketing* 26 (July 1962), pp. 58–60.

26. Charles F. Cannell and Robert L. Kahn, "The Collection of Data by Interviewing," in *Research Methods in the Behavioral Sciences,* ed. Leon Festinger and Daniel Katz (New York: Holt, Rinehart & Winston, 1953), p. 349.

27. Cantril, *Gauging Public Opinion,* p. 28.

28. Jean M. Converse and Stanley Presser, *Survey Questions: Handcrafting the Standardized Questionnaire* (Beverly Hills, Calif.: Sage Publications, 1986), pp. 50–51.

29. Ibid., p. 51.
30. Ibid., p. 52.
31. The sections on methods and purposes of pretesting are largely adapted from Converse and Presser, *Survey Questions,* pp. 51–64; and the Survey Research Center, *Interviewer's Manual,* rev. ed. (Ann Arbor, Mich.: Survey Research Center, Institute for Social Research, 1976), pp. 133–34. For an extended discussion of the phases of pretesting, see Converse and Presser, pp. 65–75.
32. W. R. Belson, *The Design and Understanding of Survey Questions* (Aldershot, England: Gower, 1981), pp. 76–86.

Suggested Readings

1. Converse, Jean M., and Stanley Presser. *Survey Questions: Handcrafting the Standardized Questionnaire.* Beverly Hills, Calif.: Sage Publications, 1986. A worthy successor to Stanley Payne's classic. Advice on how to write survey questions based on professional experience and the experimental literature.
2. Dillman, Don A. *Mail and Telephone Surveys.* New York: John Wiley & Sons, 1978. Chapters 3, 4, and 6 are on question construction. Extensive bibliography.
3. Kahn, Robert L., and Charles F. Cannell. *The Dynamics of Interviewing.* New York: John Wiley & Sons, 1957. Chapters 5 and 6 cover questionnaire design.
4. Payne, Stanley L. *The Art of Asking Questions.* Princeton, N.J.: Princeton University Press, 1951. An enjoyable book on the many problems found in developing useful survey questions. A classic resource.
5. Selltiz, Claire; Lawrence S. Wrightsman; and Stuart W. Cook. *Research Methods in Social Relations.* 3rd ed. New York: Holt, Rinehart & Winston, 1976. Appendix B is an especially well-organized set of guides for questionnaire development.
6. Sudman, Seymour, and Norman N. Bradburn. *Asking Questions: A Practical Guide to Questionnaire Design.* San Francisco: Jossey-Bass, 1982. This book covers the major issues in writing individual questions and constructing scales. The emphasis is on structured questions and interview schedules.

12 OBSERVATION

FINDING YOUR WAY

BRINGING
RESEARCH TO LIFE

Their conversation turned to most frightening experiences. Myra took the first turn.

"I was a foreign correspondent," said Myra. "Not a war correspondent, mind you—I hadn't signed on for anything risky—when a coterie of local thugs got their hands on some high-quality plastique and declared themselves freedom fighters. They found my reports unsympathetic and three times in one month, I lost my hotel—just came home and found my digs reduced to rubble—and this happened three times. The funny thing is, I would have stayed on for a fourth or fifth hotel, but I could not afford to replace my typewriters on the local black market."

"That is scary," said Dorrie Madison-Henry. "I have nothing to equal it. During my internship, I had to resuscitate three people in one night. Brought each of them back from clinical death. But that was exciting more than scary. For scariness, nothing matches Jason's experience with Otto Darnell."

"You mean the Otto Darnell, the infamous 'O Darn,' who dropped the winning pass in the Rose Bowl?"

"That Otto, yes," said Jason. "He dropped the pass with 20 seconds to go—and in the end zone—and all he could say was, 'O, darn,' hence his nickname. Otto was tall and broad and fast, and he had huge hands, and he was one of the smartest guys I have met. So on paper he looked like an All-American wide receiver. But he was always dropping things, and if he were here I would not offer him a cup of coffee over Dorrie's white carpet.

"Otto's uncle owned an electronics assembly plant in the northwest part of the state. He made miniature TV cameras for industrial and bank security and such. Right after the Rose Bowl, he asked us up, to maybe take Otto's mind off his football foul-up and also to brainstorm a production problem. Around 5 every afternoon, the quality of assembled cameras deteriorated. Uncle had six women assembling the cameras—good, loyal, hard workers—and

he could not pinpoint the quality problem. If he sat and watched them, they were on their best behavior and followed standard operating procedures, and their quality stayed up. Likewise, if they knew he was spying on them with one of his cameras. But if they suspected that he'd stopped watching, bugs began to creep into quality, and always around 5 P.M.

"Otto and I questioned the women. They denied deviating from the standards, and, of course, they were not going to 'rat out' anybody of their group."

"Wouldn't expect them to."

"So we didn't bother asking them to inform on each other. But Otto was watching carefully and told me later that five of the women took covert glances at a sixth, Bertha, who looked fidgety. She was a huge, good-natured, serious woman, ferociously devoted to an honest day's work, to my uncle, and to the company; but she looked nervous, Otto said, blinking her eyes and twitching her lips, as if she were close to tears from keeping a dirty secret. And she would not look Otto in the eyes. I, myself, didn't notice this behavior . . ."

"Because you were probably reading questions from a clipboard and not looking up," snapped Myra.

"I suppose . . . Well, the window in the assembly room was what you call mirrored glass. Otto got the idea of unscrewing all the 60-watt bulbs inside the room and replacing them with 200-waters, so that after the sun went down, we could look in through the windows and observe the six women, without much likelihood that they would see us, so long as we didn't attract their attention to the window.

"The problem was, this was a fifth-story window, so we could not stand outside and point the camera in. We had to run up to the sixth story, to an empty room, and cable a TV to a video monitor-recorder, and crank open the sixth-floor window and lower the TV camera down to the fifth story on a pole. I was supposed to watch the monitor and tell Otto, 'pan left,' 'pan right,' until we had rolled enough tape to see where the problem was.

(continued)

"No sooner had Otto opened the window than I heard, 'Oh, darn.' He had dropped the camera, and I could see it swinging below the window by its thread of an optical cable. So I leaned way out the window to snare it, knowing that if Otto were to set his hands on it, he would surely make matters worse. Not that they weren't bad enough—as time was flying.

"When I tell you what happened next remember that Otto was very ego-involved in this observation idea and could not stand the thought of letting down his side, not again, not so soon after the bowl game. I felt him grab me by the ankles and he lowered me out the window. In a stage whisper he said, 'Grab it, and hold it, and pan it left and right, very slowly.'

"So there I was upside down and trying not to look down, at the five-and-a-half-story drop into a snowbank.

"Someday I'll show you the video recording. You can see the six women at work, and, in particular, you can see that every now and then Bertha would dip her hand into her left smock pocket and bring her hand up to her mouth and then down to pick up a chip and then press the chip into the circuit board. This was not standard operations.

"This was fairly scary, but was soon to get scarier by far. The camera happened to be pointed toward Bertha when I carelessly let it rap against the window. In the video, you can see Bertha glance up and reach for the switch to stop the assembly line and warily stroll over to the window and crank it open. All of this was against standard procedures, of course—stopping the line, leaving the workstation, opening the window, and I had a very bad feeling about what was going to happen next. And I was dizzy, and nauseous, and cold.

"She sees me, and with the camera pointing straight in her face, you see her reach back into her hair and withdraw a hat pin which is holding her bandanna in place, and thrust out and jam the hat pin toward me. The hat pin goes past the camera and her arm goes past, up to the elbow.

"She stuck the huge pin in Otto's big ham of a hand, and that was when he yelped, 'Oh, darn,' and let go of my left ankle.

"Now the video goes black, as I let go of the camera and it breaks loose from its cable. There I am, swinging around, first looking in the window, looking at the moon, looking at the parking lot, looking down at the snowbank maybe 40 feet below, all at the same time, it seemed.

"I must have grabbed Bertha, because I remember that Otto was pulling up and Bertha was pulling back, and Bertha won, thank goodness! and we fell backward, me on top of Bertha.

"After the scuffling and hollering and then everyone calming down when they recognized me, we had the good wits to check the contents of Bertha's pocket. It was full of greasy, salted peanuts. The poor gal was not able to wait until her 6 P.M. dinner break and was feeding herself secretly and quietly. Then with the greasy fingers she was picking up a chip and pressing the greasy pins into the circuit board.

"Uncle advanced the supper hour to 4:45 and the problem disappeared."

"Quite a triumph of observation," said Myra.

"It was craziness," said Jason. "I was a lunatic to trust Otto to lean out the window and not drop the camera. It took us two guys half an hour the next morning to dig the camera out of a snowbank, and I could not stop thinking, this might be me, buried head down in the snow. And overall, it was no great coup of observation. I mean, ask yourself, why hadn't the people in quality control noticed grease on the circuit boards?"

THE USES OF OBSERVATION

Much of what we know comes from observation. We notice co-workers' reactions to political intrigue, the sounds of the assembly area, the smell of perfume, the taste of office coffee, the smoothness of the vice president's marble desk, and a host of other stimuli. While such observation may be a basis for knowledge, the collection processes are often haphazard.

In research, observation qualifies as scientific inquiry when it is specifically designated to answer a research question, is systematically planned and executed, uses proper controls, and provides a reliable and valid account of what happened. The versatility of observation makes it an indispensable primary source method and a supplement for other methods. Many academics have a limited view of observation, relegating it to a minor technique of field data collection. This ignores its potential for forging business decisions and denies its historic stature as a creative means to obtain primary data.

Besides collecting data visually, observation involves listening, reading, smelling, and touching. Behavioral scientists define observation in terms of animal or human behavior, but this too is limiting. As used in this text, **observation** includes the full range of monitoring behavioral and nonbehavioral activities and conditions, which can be classified roughly as follows:

1. Nonbehavioral observation
   a. Record analysis
   b. Physical condition analysis
   c. Physical process analysis
2. Behavioral observation
   a. Nonverbal analysis
   b. Linguistic analysis
   c. Extralinguistic analysis
   d. Spatial analysis

Nonbehavioral Observation

A prevalent form of observation research is **record analysis.** This may involve historical or current records and public or private records. They may be written, printed, sound-recorded, photographed, or videotaped. Historical statistical data are often the only sources used for a study. Analysis of current financial records and economic data also provides a major data source for studies. Other examples of this type of observation are the content analysis of competitive advertising and the analysis of personnel records.

Physical condition analysis is typified by store audits of merchandise availability, studies of plant safety compliance, analysis of inventory conditions, and analysis of financial statements. **Process** or **activity analysis** includes time/motion studies of manufacturing processes, traffic flows in a distribution system, paperwork flows in an office, and the study of financial flows in our banking system.

Behavioral Observation

The observational study of persons can be classified into four major categories.[1] **Nonverbal behavior** is the most prevalent of these and includes body movement, motor expressions, and even exchanged glances. At the gross body movement level, one might study how a salesperson travels a territory. At a fine level, one can study the body movements of a worker assembling a product or time sample the activity of a department's work force to discover the share of time each spends in various ways. More abstractly, one can study body movement as an indicator of interest or boredom, anger or pleasure in a certain environment. Motor expressions such as facial movements can be observed as a sign of emotional states. Eye blink rates are studied as indicators of interest in advertising messages. Finally, exchanged glances are of interest in studies of interpersonal behavior.

Linguistic behavior is a second frequently used form of behavior observation. One simple type, familiar to most students, is the tally of "ahs" (or other annoying sounds or words) a professor makes during a class. More serious applications are the study of a sales presentation's content or the study of what, how, and how much information is conveyed in a training situation. A third form of linguistic behavior involves interaction processes that occur between two people or in small groups. Bales has proposed one widely used system for classifying such linguistic interactions.[2]

Behavior may also be analyzed on an **extralinguistic** level. Sometimes this is as important a means of communication as the linguistic. One author has suggested there are four dimensions to extralinguistic activity.[3] They are (1) vocal, including pitch, loudness, and timbre; (2) temporal, including the rate of speaking, duration of utterance, and rhythm; (3) interaction, including the tendencies to interrupt, dominate, or inhibit; and (4) verbal stylistic, including vocabulary and pronunciation peculiarities, dialect, and characteristic expressions. These dimensions could add substantial insight to the linguistic content of the interactions between supervisors and subordinates or salespeople and customers.

A fourth type of behavior study involves **spatial relationships,** especially how a person relates physically to others. One form of this study, *proxemics,* concerns how people organize the territory about them and how they maintain discrete distances between themselves and others. A study of how salespeople physically approach customers or a study of the effects of crowding in a workplace are examples of this type of observation.

Often in a study, one will be interested in two or more of these types of information. This will require more than one observer. In these forms of behavior study, it is also important to consider the relationship between observers and subjects.

EVALUATION OF THE OBSERVATIONAL METHOD

Observation is the only method available to gather certain types of information. The study of records, mechanical processes, and lower animals falls into this category. Most small children and illiterate and functionally illiterate people cannot be surveyed effectively or subjected to experimentation.

Another value of observation is that we can collect the original data at the time they occur. We need not depend upon reports by others. Every respondent filters information no matter how well intentioned he or she is. Forgetting occurs, and there are reasons the respondent may not want to report fully and fairly. Observation overcomes many of these deficiencies of questioning.

A third strength is that we can secure information that most participants would ignore either because it is so common and expected or because it is not seen as relevant. For example, if you are observing buying activity in a store, there may be conditions important to the research study that the shopper would not notice or consider important, such as: What is the weather? The day of the week? The time of day? Customer traffic at the time? Promotional activity in competing stores? We can expect to learn only a part of the answers to these questions from most respondents.

The fourth advantage of observation is that it alone can capture the whole event as it occurs in its natural environment. Whereas the environment of an experiment may seem contrived to subjects and the number and types of questions limit the range of responses from respondents, observation is less restrictive than most primary collection methods. Also, the limitations on the length of data collection activities imposed by surveys or experiments are relaxed for observation. You may be interested in all the conditions surrounding a confrontation at a bargaining session between union and management representatives. These sessions may extend over time, and any effort to study the unfolding of the negotiation process is facilitated by observation. Questioning could seldom provide the insight of observation for many aspects of the negotiation process.

Finally, subjects seem to accept an observational intrusion better than questioning. It is less demanding of them and normally has a less biasing effect on their behavior than does questioning. In addition, it is also possible to conduct disguised and unobtrusive observation studies much more easily than disguised questioning.

There are some research limitations of the observational method. The observer normally must be at the scene of the event when it takes place, yet it is often impossible to predict where and when the event will occur. One way to guard against missing an event is to observe for prolonged periods until it does occur, but this brings up a second disadvantage. Observation is a slow and expensive process that requires either human observers or costly surveillance equipment.

A third limitation of observation is that its most reliable results are restricted to information that can be learned by overt action or surface indicators. To go below the surface, the observer must make inferences. Two observers will probably agree on the nature of various surface events, but the inferences they draw from such data are much more variable.

Fourth, the research environment is more likely suited to subjective assessment and recording of data than controls and quantification of events. When control is exercised through active intervention by the researchers, their participation may threaten the validity of what is being assessed. Even with small sample sizes, the observation records can be disproportionately large and difficult to analyze.

Fifth, observation is limited as a way to learn of the past. It is similarly limited as a method by which to learn what is going on in the present at some distant place. It is also difficult to gather information on such topics as intentions, attitudes, opinions, or preferences.

Any consideration of the merits of observation confirms its value when used with care and understanding.

THE OBSERVER–SUBJECT RELATIONSHIP

Interrogation presents a clear opportunity for interviewer bias. The problem is less pronounced with observation but is still real. The relationship between observer and subject may be viewed from three perspectives: (1) whether the observation is direct or indirect, (2) whether the observer's presence is known or unknown to the subject, and (3) what role the observer plays.

Directness of Observation

Direct observation describes the situation in which the observer is physically present and personally monitors what takes place. This approach is very flexible because it allows the observer to react to and report subtle aspects of events and behavior as they occur. He or she is also free to shift places, change the focus of the observation, or concentrate on unexpected events if they should occur. A weakness of this approach is that the observers' perception circuits may become overloaded as events move quickly; they must later try to reconstruct what they were not able to record. Also, observer fatigue, boredom, and distracting events can reduce the accuracy and completeness of such observation.

Indirect observation is the term used to describe studies in which the recording is done by mechanical, photographic, or electronic means. For example, a special camera that takes one frame every second is mounted in a department of a large store to study customer and employee movement. Such methods are less flexible than direct observation, but they are much less biasing and may be less erratic in accuracy. Another advantage of such indirect systems is the permanent record can be reanalyzed to include many different aspects of an event. Electronic recording devices, which have improved in quality and declined in cost, are being used more frequently in observation research.

Concealment

A second factor affecting the observer–subject relationship concerns whether the presence of the observer should be known to the subject. When the observer is known, there is a risk of atypical activity by the subjects. The initial entry of an observer into a situation often upsets activity patterns of the subjects, but this influence can usually be dissipated quickly. This is especially so when subjects are engaged in some absorbing activity or the presence of observers offers no potential threat to the subjects' self-interest. The potential bias from subject awareness of observers is always a matter of concern, however.

Observers use **concealment** to shield themselves from the object of their observation. Often technical means are used such as one-way mirrors, hidden cameras, or microphones. These methods reduce the risk of observer bias but bring up a question of ethics. Hidden observation is a form of spying, and the propriety of this action must be reviewed carefully.

A modified approach involves partial concealment. The presence of the observer is not concealed, but the objectives and subject of interest are. A study of selling methods may be conducted by sending an observer with a salesperson who is making calls on customers. However, the observer's real purpose may be hidden from both the salesperson and the customer (e.g., she may pretend she is analyzing the display and layout characteristics of the stores they are visiting).

Participation

The third observer–subject issue is whether the observer should participate in the situation while observing. A more involved arrangement, **participant observation,** exists when the observer enters the social setting and acts both as an observer and a participant. Sometimes he or she is known as an observer to some or all of the participants, while at other times the true role is concealed. While reducing the potential for bias, this again raises an ethical issue. Often subjects will not have given their consent and will not have knowledge of or access to the findings. After being deceived and having their privacy invaded, what further damage could come to the subjects if the results became public? This needs to be addressed when concealment and covert participation are used.

Participant observation makes a dual demand on the observer. Recording can interfere with participation, and participation can interfere with observation. The observer's role may influence the way others act. Because of these problems, participant observation is less used in business research than, say, in anthropology or sociology. It is typically restricted to cases where nonparticipant observation is not practical; for example, a study of the functioning of a traveling auditing team.

CONDUCTING AN OBSERVATIONAL STUDY

The Type of Study

Observation is found in almost all research studies, at least at the exploratory stage. Such data collection is known as **simple observation.** Its practice is not standardized, as one would expect, because of the discovery nature of exploratory research. The decision to use observation as the major data collection method may be made as early as the moment the researcher moves from research questions to investigative questions. The latter specify the outcomes of the study—the specific questions the researcher must answer with collected data. If the study is to be something other than exploratory, **systematic observation** employs standardized procedures, trained observers, schedules for recording, and other devices for the observer that mirror the scientific procedures of other primary data methods. Systematic studies vary in terms of the emphasis placed on recording and encoding of observational information:

> At one end of the continuum are methods that are unstructured and open-ended. The observer tries to provide as complete and nonselective a description as possible. On the other end of the continuum are more structured and predefined methods that itemize, count, and categorize behavior. Here the investigator decides beforehand which behavior will be recorded and how frequently observations will be made. The investigator using structured observation is much more discriminating in choosing which behavior will be recorded and precisely how they are to be coded.[4]

One author classifies observational studies by the degree of structure in the environmental setting and the amount of structure imposed on the environment by the researcher:[5]

Researcher	Environment
1. Completely unstructured	Natural setting
2. Unstructured	Laboratory
3. Structured	Natural setting
4. Completely structured	Laboratory

The researcher conducting a class 1 observational study would be in a natural or field setting endeavoring to adapt to the culture. A typical example would be an "ethnographic" study in which the researcher, as a participant observer, becomes a part of the culture and describes in great detail everything surrounding the event or activity of interest. Donald Roy, in the widely used case in organizational behavior, "Banana Time," took a punch press job in a factory to describe the rituals that a small work group relied upon to make their highly repetitive, monotonous work bearable.[6] With other purposes in mind, business researchers may use this type of study for hypothesis generation.

Class 4 studies are at the opposite end of the continuum from unstructured field investigations. The research purpose of this category is to test hypotheses; therefore, a definitive plan for observing specific, operationalized behavior is known in advance. This requires a measuring instrument, called an **observational checklist,** analogous to a questionnaire. Checklists should possess a high degree of precision in defining relevant behavior or acts and have mutually exclusive and exhaustive categories. The coding is frequently closed, thereby simplifying data analysis. The subject groups being observed must be comparable and the laboratory conditions identical. The classic example of a class 4 study was Bales's investigation into group interaction.[7] Many team-building, decision-making, and assessment center studies follow this structural pattern.

The two middle classes emphasize the best characteristics of either researcher-imposed controls or setting. In class 2, the researcher uses the facilities of a laboratory—videotape recording, two-way mirrors, props, and stage sets—to introduce more control into the environment while simultaneously reducing the time needed for observation. In contrast, a class 3 study would take advantage of a structured observational instrument in a natural setting.

Content Specification

Specific conditions, events, or activities that we want to observe determine the observational reporting system (and correspond to measurement questions). To specify the observation content, we should include both the major variables of interest and any other variables that may affect them. From this cataloging, we then select those items we plan to observe. For each variable chosen, we must define it operationally if there is any question of concept ambiguity or special meanings.

Even if the concept is a common one, we must make certain that all agree

TABLE 12–1   Content of Observation: Factual versus Inferential

Factual	Inferential
Introduction/identification of salesperson and customer.	Credibility of salesperson. Qualified status of customer.
Time and day of week.	Convenience for the customer. Welcoming attitude of the customer.
Product presented.	Customer interest in product.
Selling points presented per product.	Customer acceptance of selling points per product.
Number of customer objections raised per product.	Customer concerns about features and benefits.
Salesperson's rebuttal of objections.	Effectiveness of salesperson's rebuttal attempts.
Salesperson's attempt to restore control.	Effectiveness of salesperson's control attempt Consequence for customer who prefers interaction.
Length of interview.	Customer's/salesperson's degree of enthusiasm for the interview.
Environmental factors interfering with the interview.	Level of distraction for the customer.
Customer purchase decision.	General evaluation of sales presentation skill.

upon the measurement terms by which to record results. For example, we may agree that variable *W* will be reported by count, while variable *Y* will be counted and the effectiveness of its use judged qualitatively.

Observation may be at either a *factual* or an *inferential* level. Table 12–1 shows how we could separate the factual and inferential components of a salesperson's presentation.

This table is suggestive only. It does not include many other variables that might be of interest, including data on customer purchase history; company, industry, and general economic conditions; the order in which sales arguments are presented; and specific words used to describe certain product characteristics. The particular content of observation will also be affected by the nature of the observation setting.

Observer Training   There are a few general guidelines for selection. The observer must have sufficient concentration powers to function in a setting full of distractions. The ability to remember the details of an experience is also an asset. There is also a need to select people who would be unobtrusive in the situation. An obviously attractive observer would be a distraction in some settings but ideal in others. The same can be said for age or ethnic background.

If observation is at the surface level and involves a simple checklist or coding system, then experience is less important. Inexperience may even be an advantage if there is a risk that experienced observers may bring preset convictions about the topic. Regardless, most observers are subject to fatigue, halo effects, and **observer**

drift, a decay in reliability or validity over time that affects the coding of categories.[8] Only intensive videotaped training relieves these problems.

The observers should be thoroughly versed in the requirements of the specific study. Each observer should be informed of the outcomes sought and the precise content elements to be studied. Observer trials with the instrument and sample videotapes should be used until a high degree of reliability is apparent in their observations. Where there are interpretative differences between observers, they should be reconciled.

Data Collection

The data collection plan specifies the details of the task. In essence it answers the questions of who, what, when, and how.

Who Are the Targets?   What qualifies a subject to be observed? Must each meet a given criterion—those who initiate a specific action? Who are the contacts to gain entry (in an ethnographic study), the intermediaries to help with introductions, the contacts to reach if conditions change or trouble develops? Who has responsibility for the various aspects of the study? Who fulfills the ethical responsibilities to the subjects?

What?   The characteristics of the observation must be set in terms of sampling elements and units of analysis. This is achieved when an event-time dimension and "act" terms are defined. In **event sampling,** the researcher records selected behavior that answer the investigative questions. In **time sampling,** the researcher must choose among a time point sample, continuous real-time measurement, or a time-interval sample. For a time-point sample, recording occurs at fixed points for a specified length. With continuous measurement, behavior or the elapsed time of the behavior is recorded. Like continuous measurement, time-interval sampling records every behavior in real time but only counts the behavior once during the interval.[9]

Assume the observer is instructed to observe a quality control inspection process for 10 minutes out of each hour (a duration of two minutes each for five times). Over a prolonged period, if the samples are drawn randomly, time sampling can give a good estimate of the pattern of activities. In a time-interval sampling of workers in a department, the outcome may be a judgment of how well the department is being supervised. In a study of sales presentations using continuous real-time sampling, the research outcome may be an assessment of a given salesperson's effectiveness or the effectiveness of different types of persuasive messages.

Other important dimensions are defined by *acts*. The concept of an act is established by the needs of the study. It is the basic unit of observation such as (1) a single expressed thought, (2) a physical movement, (3) a facial expression, or (4) a motor skill. Although they may be well defined, they will often continue to present difficulties for the observer. A single statement from a sales presentation may include several thoughts about product advantages, a rebuttal to an objection about a feature, or some remark about a competitor. The observer is hard-pressed to sort out each thought, decide whether it represents a separate unit of observation, and then record it quickly enough to follow continued statements.

When?   Is the time of the study important or can any time be used? In a study of out-of-stock conditions in a supermarket, the exact times of observation may be important. Inventory is shipped to the store on certain days only, and buying peaks occur on other days. The likelihood of a given product being out of stock is a function of both time-related activities.

How?   Shall the data be directly observed? If there is more than one observer, how shall they divide the task? How shall the results be recorded for later analysis? How shall the observers deal with various situations that may occur—when expected actions do not take place or when the observer is challenged by someone in the setting?

Observers face unlimited variations in conditions. Fortunately, most problems do not occur simultaneously. When the plans are thorough and the observers well trained, observational research is quite successful.

UNOBTRUSIVE MEASURES

Up to this point, our discussion has focused on direct observation as a traditional approach to data collection. Like surveys and experiments, some observational studies—particularly participant observation—require the observer to be physically present in the research situation. This contributes to a **reactivity response** or a phenomenon where subjects alter their behavior in response to the researcher. (You are familiar with the historic research at Western Electric and the so-called *Hawthorne effect* and to the reactions interviewers produce in respondents that bias the findings of a study.)

Webb and his colleagues have given us an insight into some very innovative observational procedures that can be both nonreactive and inconspicuously applied. Called **unobtrusive measures,** this set of approaches encourages creative and imaginative forms of indirect observation, archival searches, and variations on simple and contrived observation.[10] Of particular interest are the measures involving indirect observation based on physical traces that include *erosion* (measures of wear) and *accretion* (measures of deposit).

Natural erosion measures are illustrated by the frequency of replacement of vinyl floor tile in front of museum exhibits as an indicator of exhibit popularity. The study of wear and tear on book pages are a measure of library book use or counting the remaining brochures in a car dealer's display rack after a favorable magazine review suggest consumer interest.

Physical traces also include natural accretion such as discovering the advertising listenership of radio stations by observing car radio settings as autos are brought in for service. Another type of unobtrusive study involves estimating liquor and magazine consumption by collecting and analyzing family trash. An interesting application of the former compared beer consumption reports acquired through interviews with the findings of sampled trash. If the interview data were valid, the consumption figures for the area were at 15 percent. However, the validity was questioned when the beer can count from trash supported a 77 percent consumption rate.[11]

William Rathje is a professor of archaeology at the University of Arizona and founder of the Garbage Project in Tucson. His study of trash, refuse, rubbish, and litter resulted in the subdiscipline that the *Oxford English Dictionary* has called *garbology.* By excavating landfills, he has gained insight into human behavior and cultural patterns—sometimes sorting the contents of up to 150 coded categories. His previous studies have shown that "people will describe their behavior to satisfy cultural expectations, like the mothers in Tucson who unanimously claimed they made their baby food from scratch, but whose garbage told a very different tale."[12]

Physical trace methods present a strong argument for use based on their ability to provide low-cost access to frequency, attendance, and incidence data without contamination from other methods or reactivity from subjects. They are excellent "triangulation" devices for cross-validation. Thus, they work well as supplements to other methods. Designing an unobtrusive study can test a researcher's creativity, and one must be especially careful about inferences made from the findings. Erosion results may have occurred because of wear factors not considered, and accretion material may be the result of selective deposit or survival.

CLOSE-UP

The design of an observational study follows the same pattern as other research. Once the researcher has specified the investigative questions, it is often apparent that the best way to conduct the study is through observation. Guidance for conducting an observation and translating the investigative question(s) into an observational checklist are the subject of this section. We first review the procedural steps and then explain how to create a checklist.

Most studies that use the observational method follow a general sequence of steps that parallel the research process. Here we adapt to the terminology of the observational method:

1. Define the content of the study.
2. Develop a data collection plan that identifies subjects, sampling strategy, and *acts* (operationalized as a checklist or coding scheme).
3. Secure and train observers.
4. Collect the data.
5. Analyze the data.

In "Bringing Research to Life," we recounted a humorous incident in a quality control situation that used observation. Assume our concerns are more serious. We have limited resources so the study will be small. Management is concerned about a deterioration of quality in its assembled product, security cameras, toward the end of each day. The management question is, "Why are products failing quality assurance in the afternoon?" The research question might be stated, "What factors affect the quality of assembled cameras?" Although we presume that management is correct about the time, we will allow the data to confirm this. The investigative questions could then include: "What is the variability due to changes in parts vendors? Inventory? Does the manufacturing procedure change during the day? Is it shift dependent? To what extent is the failure rate contingent on time? What is the role of workplace conditions? Is it linked to assembler performance?"

Further assume that through interviewing, we isolate the *content of the study* to assembler behavior in the natural environment. The major variables of interest will be operationalized from the assembler's job description and the environmental conditions of the assembly area.

The *observational targets* will be the assemblers and their *acts* (physical behavior consistent with the job description). We have chosen to sample during the late afternoon, initially, and we will use *time sampling* on a *continuous* basis. This allows us to record all relevant behavior and complete an environmental checklist. The observation will be *direct* and we will operate from *concealment* using the one-way mirror on the door to the assembly area.

A tour of the assembly area revealed a rectangular room with east- and west-facing windows. The workstations run the length of the rectangle, splitting the room in half and facing north. Comfortable chairs are present and parts bins are to the right of each workstation, requiring the assembler to turn westward to select parts. The windows have shades and there is both general and task lighting.

The variables to be measured (measurement questions) were derived from the investigative questions on workplace conditions and assembler performance. Notes taken on the tour improved our understanding of contextual variables. By examining the workplace first, we can assess and begin to rule out environmental variables (lighting, temperature, noise, and other variables controlled by the production facility) before moving on to behavioral characteristics. Both checklists will be revised after pretesting. The *observational checklist* for the assembly environment features a range of measures from graphic rating scales to category scales. It is shown in Figure 12–1.

The assemblers are subject to periodic and unscheduled supervisory visits and normal workplace rules for a drug-free environment. Nevertheless, the foremost ethical concern is restricting the observations to assembly activities. Using the company's cameras, we will run one on wide angle for context and the other zoomed-in to capture individual assembler behavior on a *time interval* sampling. The observation will be videotaped so a consistent stimulus may be used to train observers, pretest and refine the checklists, and have a benchmark for later comparison. The behavioral checklist will be devised after studying the job descriptions and viewing the preliminary videotape.

(continued)

FIGURE   12–1   Environmental Observation Checklist

ProSec Electronics: Assembly Observational Study

Time Stamp: _____   Observer: _____

Lights: General Area ☐ On ☐ Off ☐ Malfunction   **Comments:**

Workstations ☐ On ☐ Off ☐ Malfunction

Lighting (general)

Irregularly Bright	Uniformly Bright	Uniformly Even	Uniformly Dim	Irregularly Dim
☐	☐	☐	☐	☐

(Note locations for discrepancies)

Shades (Estimate and color in)

(West)   (East)

Example
70%

% Used _____   % Used _____

Temperature

Cold   Standard   Hot

65°   70°   75°   80°

Cleanliness (Circle)

Very Clean |———|———|———| Very Dirty
                 1   2   3   4   5
              General Area

Very Clean |———|———|———| Very Dirty
                 1   2   3   4   5
              Workstation
        (Note individual deficiencies below)

Noise Level
(decibels: mark scale per reading)

Quiet   Loud
|————————|————————|
50   75   100

Assemblers at Workstations during Observation

	Yes		No
Virginia	☐		☐
Bertha	☐		☐
Gladys	☐		☐
Maria	☐		☐
Helen	☐		☐
Roberta	☐		☐

Nonassembly Personnel in Room: **Activities of Nonassemblers:**

Comments:

Summary

Observation is one of the few options available for studying records, mechanical processes, lower animals, small children, or complex interactive processes. We can gather data as the event occurs and can come closer to capturing the whole event than with interrogation. On the other hand, we have to be present to catch the event or have some recording device on the scene to do the job.

Observation includes a variety of monitoring situations that cover nonbehavioral and behavioral activities.

The strengths of observation as a data collection method include: (1) securing information about people or activities that cannot be derived from experiments or surveys, (2) avoiding respondent filtering and forgetting, (3) securing environmental context information, (4) optimizing the naturalness of the setting, and (5) reducing obtrusiveness.

Observation may be limited by: (1) the difficulty of waiting for long periods to capture the relevant phenomena, (2) the expense of observer costs and equipment, (3) the reliability of inferences from surface indicators, (4) the problems of quantification and disproportionately large records, and (5) limitations to present activities and inferences about cognitive processes.

We can classify observation in terms of the observer-subject relationship. This relationship may be viewed from three perspectives: (1) Is the observation direct or indirect? (2) Is the observer's presence known or unknown? (3) Is the observer a participant or nonparticipant?

The design of an observational study follows the same general pattern as other research. Observational studies fall into four general types based on the degree of structure and the nature of the observational environment. The researcher must define the content of the study; develop a data collection plan that identifies subjects, sampling strategy, and "acts" (often operationalized as a checklist or coding scheme); secure and train observers; and launch the study.

Unobtrusive measures offer an unusual and creative approach to reducing reactivity in observational research by indirect observation and other methods. Measures of erosion and accretion serve as ways to confirm the findings from other methods or operate as singular data sources.

Key Terms

concealment
event sampling
extralinguistic behavior
linguistic behavior
nonverbal behavior
observation
  direct

indirect
simple
systematic
observational checklist
observer drift
participant observation
physical condition analysis

(continued)

process (activity) analysis   spatial relationships
record analysis   time sampling
reactivity response   unobtrusive measures

**Discussion
Questions**

1. Compare the advantages and disadvantages of the survey to those of observation. Under which circumstances could you make a case for using observation?

2. What ethical risks are involved in observation? Unobtrusive measures?

3. The observer–subject relationship is an important consideration in the design of observational studies. What kind of relationship would you recommend in each of the following cases?
   a. Observation of professional conduct in the classroom by the student author of a course evaluation guide.
   b. Observation of retail shoppers by a researcher who is interested in determining the customer purchase time by type of good purchased.
   c. Observation of a focus group interview by a client.
   d. Effectiveness of individual farm worker organizers in their efforts to organize employees of grape growers.

4. Assume you are to set up an observational study in which you will observe five students engaging in a discussion of the question "How should students organize a network that will be beneficial for postcollege employment connections?
   a. What are the varieties of information that might be observed in such a setting?
   b. Select a limited number of content areas for study and operationally define the observation "acts" that should be measured.

5. Develop a checklist to be used by observers in the previous study.
   a. Determine how many observers you need and assign two or three to a specific observation task.
   b. Compare the results of the group members' checklists for stability of recorded perceptions.

6. Based on present or past work experience, suggest problems that could be resolved using observation-based data.

7. You wish to analyze the pedestrian traffic that passes a given store in a major shopping center. You are interested in determining how many shoppers pass by this store, and you would like to classify these shoppers on various relevant dimensions. Any information you secure should be obtainable from observation alone.
   a. What other information might you find useful to observe?
   b. How would you decide what information to collect?
   c. Devise the operational definitions you would need.

     d. What would you say in the way of instructions to the observers you plan to use?

     e. How might you sample this shopper traffic?

8. Distinguish:

     a. Relative values of questioning and observation.

     b. Nonverbal, linguistic, and extralinguistic analysis.

     c. Factual and inferential observation.

Reference Notes

1. K. E. Weick, "Systematic Observational Methods," in *The Handbook of Social Psychology,* vol. 2, ed. G. Lindzey and E. Aronson (Reading, Mass.: Addison-Wesley Publishing, 1968), p. 360.
2. R. Bales, *Interaction Process Analysis* (Reading, Mass.: Addison-Wesley Publishing, 1950).
3. Weick, "Systematic Observational Methods," p. 381.
4. Louise H. Kidder and Charles M. Judd, *Research Methods in Social Relations,* 5th ed. (New York: Holt, Rinehart & Winston, 1986), p. 292.
5. Kenneth D. Bailey, *Methods of Social Science,* 2nd ed. (New York: Free Press, 1982), pp. 252-54.
6. Excerpted from Donald F. Roy, " 'Banana Time,' Job Satisfaction, and Informal Interaction," *Human Organization* 18, no. 4 (Winter 1959–60), pp. 151–68; cited in Allan R. Cohen, Stephen L. Fink, Herman Gadon, and Robin D. Willits, *Effective Behavior in Organizations,* 5th ed. (Homewood, Ill.: Richard D. Irwin, 1992).
7. Robert F. Bales, *Personality and Interpersonal Behavior* (New York: Holt, Rinehart & Winston, 1970).
8. Kidder and Judd, *Research Methods in Social Relations,* pp. 298–99.
9. Ibid., p. 291.
10. E. J. Webb, D. T. Campbell, R.D. Schwartz, L. Sechrest, and J. B. Grove, *Nonreactive Measures in the Social Sciences,* 2nd ed. (Boston: Houghton Mifflin, 1981).
11. W. L. Rathje and W. W. Hughes, "The Garbage Project as a Nonreactive Approach: Garbage in . . . Garbage Out?" in *Perspectives on Attitude Assessment: Surveys and Their Alternatives,* ed. H. W. Sinaiko and L. A. Broedling (Washington, D.C.: Smithsonian Institution, 1975).
12. William Grimes, "If It's Scientific, It's 'Garbology,' " *International Herald Tribune,* August 15–16, 1992, p. 17.

Suggested Readings

1. Bailey, Kenneth D. *Methods of Social Research,* 4th ed. New York: Free Press, 1994. Includes a thorough discussion of observational strategies.
2. Bales, Robert F. *Personality and Interpersonal Behavior.* New York: Holt, Rinehart & Winston, 1970. From a pioneer in interaction process analysis, a model for structured observation, checklists, and coding schemes.
3. Kidder, Louise H., and Charles M. Judd. *Research Methods in Social Relations,* 5th ed. New York: Holt, Rinehart & Winston, 1986. Chapter 12 gives a fine overview of observational types and sampling plans.
4. Webb, E. J.; D. T. Campbell; R. D. Schwartz; L. Sechrest; and J. B. Grove. *Nonreactive Measures in the Social Sciences,* 2nd ed. Boston: Houghton Mifflin, 1981. The classic source of information on all aspects of unobtrusive measures. Excellent examples and ideas for planning projects.

13 EXPERIMENTATION

 **FINDING YOUR WAY**

BRINGING
RESEARCH TO LIFE

"Let me put my hand on your tummy."

"What?"

"Oh, did I wake you?"

"You know you did."

"I want to put my hand on your tummy."

"Of course, you woke me. What time is it? Midnight? . . . All right. Place your hand on my abdomen." All he felt was arrhythmic pulsating of peristalsis.

"It's not time," she said. "May I go back to sleep?"

"Dorrie, hon', I've been thinking . . ."

"What?"

"I've been thinking . . . we should not wait. We should give them names . . . now."

"How will we know the right names?"

"Suppose we call them Terry and Robin. They don't have to be boys or girls. The names will fit, don't you see? Either way, the names will fit."

They lay side by side in the darkness, in silence. Silence maybe meant he was thinking and would rouse here again. No use fighting to regain sleep. Hear him out. "Why the hurry, Jason?"

"I want you to talk to them. I want you to say, 'Robin, dearest, this is your mommy,' and "Terry, your mommy and daddy love you terrifically much.' "

"Nice. May I go back to sleep?"

Again he was silent in the darkness. Then, "This has possibilities, you know . . ."

"*Possibilities.*" Please, no possibilities. No twilight zone ideas, grasped at in the gray area between conscious and unconscious, wakefulness and asleep, and proposed with utter seriousness.

"Say, you read poetry to Robin. You say, 'Robin, this is for you, and it is by a very famous poet, William Blake . . ."

" 'Tyger, tyger, burning bright . . .' "

"That's the idea. Say you read poetry to Robin and maybe sing to Terry. Well, maybe it is not so

good an idea letting you sing to little Terry, because you do not sing nearly as well as you read poetry. We would want the differential treatments to be delivered with more or less equal efficacy, wouldn't we? So, maybe you should should read Shakespeare to Terry and Blake to Robin, and then in - puberty we will see if one has a preference for Shakespeare over Blake."

She rolled over on an elbow. "I see. You are suggesting, that if the twins are monozygous . . . share the same genetic makeup . . . they will differentially emphasize contrasting environmental stimuli administered during the earliest development of their central nervous systems."

"Yes."

"You woke me for this?"

"Yes, whatever treatment . . . stimuli . . . remarks . . . you direct to them through internal dialogue, such as poetry by Blake and Shakespeare, will fall on almost identically genetically endowed organisms . . . Of course, I would have to trust you to adhere to the experimental protocols we devise."

He did not hear her angry gasp.

When she regained her composure, she ventured, "Following your line of thought, perhaps Blake and Shakespeare would not be good alternative treatments, since they wrote in different styles and were not contemporaries . . . assuming we take all of this seriously . . . which I am certain I do not do."

"I am not sure I have heard you express equal enthusiasm for Blake and Shakespeare, so you will surely bias the administration of the treatment in favor of Blake, your favorite."

"Let me understand this, sweetheart." She was fully awake now and sitting up. "I might not stick to the protocols, and you do not trust me to avoid bias in administering the 'treatments' with equal enthusiasm."

"Well, at the conscious level, I have to trust you, because you are a doctor . . ."

". . . and my wife and life's companion . . . and the parent of our children . . ."

". . . and you understand the importance of nice

(continued)

clean experimentation. But, yes, biases might be present at the subconscious level and remain difficult to control."

She sat up. "Wanting to call the babies by name is a sentimental impulse. My heart says it is sweet of you to want me to talk to them, but my brain says this is a cruel experiment. Nevertheless, let's talk about 'nice clean experimentation,' as you call it.

"Jason, *Tales from the Petri Dish* may have ethicists and the public spinning, but we are talking about *our* children here, not genetically created identical twin embryos, not even gene-spliced tomato experiments. First, you cannot differentially direct treatment to one or the other. Never—no, not in my wildest dreams—should I believe one of my unborn babies knows he is Robin or Terry. Second, when they reach an age when they attend nursery school, we will totally lose our ability to differentially apply stimuli . . ."

"Would you consider home schooling?"

"I'm a public health doctor, Jason. Doctors don't work at home! That's why we have hospitals! And, third, I would have no way, after their birth, to know I am not reading Blake to the very one to whom I was reading Shakespeare to in the womb, and vice versa."

"OK, OK. No need to get huffy."

"Jason," she struggled for self-control, "Jason, I am experiencing the joys and pains of a multiple pregnancy. There are certain hormonal changes . . . yes . . . which I have heard you indelicately call 'gland things', but I am a professional person and am well aware of my responsibilities—to the public, to you, to my unborn children, and to myself—to maintain my emotional equilibrium. So lay off, Jason!"

"I'm sorry I woke you. OK?"

"Waking me is only part of the problem. It's what you woke me for—this lame idea that just popped into your head, this notion to manipulate your own offspring, which you forced on me without any critical thinking in advance."

"Well, I was curious, that's all. I was brainstorming."

"If you were doing research in the university or hospital, you would not float such a lame idea, because a human subjects committee would roast you for such an ethically questionable idea, starting with . . . I don't know . . . starting with whether unborn children are able to give informed consent, whether I am able to give consent on their behalf, and ending up, maybe, by asking what right you have to try to alter the artistic sensibilities of anyone's offspring. You don't get away with crazy ideas like this in business research, do you?"

There was a long silence. "Swell," he said. "Can we get back to sleep, then?"

"Let's hope so. But let me explain something. Experimentation is not about ideas that pop into your head because you cannot sleep." She pulled his face close, so that by the light shining in from a street lamp he could see how rigid her lips were. "Experimentation is about needing to know something so badly that you cannot live without an answer, because others cannot live without an answer.

"This year I am part of a program to administer treatments to 150 mortally ill subjects. They know that 75 of them are receiving an experimental treatment and 75 receiving colored saline solution. It's a double-blind experiment, so I have no idea who is receiving the placebo.

"Do you have an idea what it means to know you are withholding the promise of life from 75 human beings? Do you grasp what it means to look into their eyes and have them look back and maybe cry, so an unspoken message passes—'Don't let me die.'

"This is not what I expected in medical school, Jason. I expected, then, to do my best to save every life. But my fellow doctors are counting on me for proof, Jason, so they may justify the treatment and request funding. I am not playing games with people, Jason. I am letting people die so others may live.

"What experimentation is about is not having a brainstorm, not scratching a mental itch. Experimentation is responsibility."

WHAT IS EXPERIMENTATION?

Why do events occur under some conditions and not under others? Research methods that answer such questions are called "causal" methods. (Recall the discussion of causality in Chapter 5.) Ex post facto research designs, where a researcher interviews respondents or observes what is or what has been, also have the potential for discovering causality. The distinction between these methods and experimentation is that the researcher is required to accept the world as it is found, whereas an experiment allows the researcher to alter systematically the variables of interest and observe what changes follow.

In this chapter we define experimentation and discuss its advantages and disadvantages. An outline for the conduct of an experiment is presented as a vehicle to introduce important concepts. The questions of internal and external validity will also be examined: Does the experimental treatment determine the observed difference or was some extraneous variable responsible? And, how can one generalize the results of the study across times, settings, and persons? The chapter concludes with a review of the most widely accepted designs and a brief example.

Experiments are studies involving intervention by the researcher beyond that required for measurement. The usual intervention is to manipulate some variable in a setting and observe how it affects the subjects being studied (e.g., people or physical entities). The researcher manipulates the independent or explanatory variable and then observes whether the hypothesized dependent variable is affected by the intervention.

An example of such an intervention is the study of bystanders and thieves.[1] In this experiment, students were asked to come to an office where they had an opportunity to see a fellow student steal some money from a receptionist's desk. The stealing, of course, was done by a confederate of the experimenter. The major hypothesis concerned whether people observing a theft would be more likely to report it (1) if they observed the crime alone or (2) if they were in the company of someone else. The independent or explanatory variable, therefore, was the state of either being alone when observing the theft or bring in the company of another person. The dependent variable was whether the subjects reported observing the crime. The results suggested that bystanders were more likely to report the theft if they observed it alone rather than in another person's company.

On what grounds did the researchers conclude that people who were alone were more likely to report crimes observed than people in the company of others? Three types of considerations formed the basis for this conclusion. First, there must be an agreement between independent and dependent variables. The presence or absence of one is associated with the presence or absence of the other. Thus, more reports of the theft (DV) came from lone observers (IV_1) than from paired observers (IV_2).

Beyond this correlation of independent and dependent variables, the time order of the occurrence of the variables must be considered. The dependent variable should not precede the independent variable. They may occur almost simultaneously or the independent variable should occur before the dependent variable. This requirement is of little concern since it is unlikely that people could report a theft before observing it.

The third and important support for the conclusion comes when researchers are confident that *other extraneous variables did not influence the dependent variable.* To assure that these other variables are not the source of influence, we control their ability to confound the planned comparison. Under laboratory conditions, standardized conditions for control can be arranged. The crime observation experiment was carried out in an office set up as a laboratory. The entire event was staged without the observers' knowledge. The receptionist whose money was to be stolen was instructed to speak and act in a specific way. Only the receptionist, observers, and the "criminal" were in the office. The same process was repeated with each run of the experiment.

While such controls are important, further precautions are needed to assure the results achieved reflect the influence of the independent variable alone on the dependent variable.

AN EVALUATION OF EXPERIMENTS

Advantages

When we elaborated on the concept of cause in Chapter 5, we said causality could not be proved with certainty, but the probability of one variable being linked to another could be established convincingly. The experiment comes closer than any primary data collection method to accomplishing this goal. The foremost advantage is the researcher's ability to manipulate the independent variable. The probability that changes in the dependent variable are a function of that manipulation increases consequently. Also, a control group serves as a comparison to assess the existence and potency of the manipulation.

The second advantage of the experiment is that contamination from extraneous variables can be controlled more effectively than with other designs. This helps the researcher isolate experimental variables and evaluate their impact over time. Third, the convenience and cost of experimentation are superior to other methods. These benefits allow the experimenter opportunistic scheduling of data collection and the flexibility to adjust variables and conditions that evoke extremes not observed under routine circumstances. In addition, combinations of variables can be assembled for testing rather than having to search for their fortuitous appearance in business.

Fourth, **replication** or repeating an experiment with different subject groups and conditions leads to the discovery of an average effect of the independent variable across people, situations, and times. Finally, researchers can use naturally occurring events and, to some extent, field experiments to reduce the subjects' perceptions of the researcher as a source of intervention or deviation in their everyday lives.

Disadvantages

The artificiality of the laboratory is arguably a primary disadvantage of the experimental method. However, many subjects' perceptions of a contrived environment can be improved by investment in the facility. Second, generalization from nonprobability samples can pose problems despite random assignment. The extent to which a study can be generalized from college students to managers or executives is open to question. And when an experiment is unsuccessfully disguised, volunteer subjects are often those with the most interest in the topic.

Third, despite the low costs of experimentation, many marked applications of experimentation far outrun the budgets for other primary data collection methods. Fourth, experimentation is most effectively targeted at problems of the present or immediate future. Experimental studies of the past are not feasible, and studies about intentions or predictions are difficult. Finally, business research is often concerned with the study of people. There are limits to the types of manipulation and controls that are ethical.

CONDUCTING AN EXPERIMENT[2]

In a well-executed experiment, researchers must complete a series of activities to carry out their craft successfully. Although the experiment is the premier scientific methodology for establishing causation, the resourcefulness and creativeness of the researcher are needed to make the experiment live up to its potential. In this section, we discuss seven activities the researcher must accomplish to ensure the success of the endeavor:

1. Select relevant variables.
2. Specify the level(s) of the treatment.
3. Control the experimental environment.
4. Choose the experimental design.
5. Select and assign the subjects.
6. Pilot test, revise, and test.
7. Analyze the data.

Selecting Relevant Variables

Throughout the book we have discussed the idea that a research problem can be conceptualized as a hierarchy of questions. Starting with a management problem, the researcher's task was to translate an amorphous problem into question or hypothesis that best stated the objectives of the research. Depending on the complexity of the problem, investigative questions and additional hypotheses could be created to address specific facets of the study or data that needed to be gathered. Further, we mentioned that a hypothesis is a relational statement because it describes a relationship between two or more variables. It must also be **operationalized,** a term we used earlier in discussing how concepts are transformed into variables to make them measurable and subject to testing.

Consider the following research question:

Does a sales presentation that places benefits information in the introduction of the message lead to improved retention of product knowledge?

Since a hypothesis is a tentative statement—a speculation—about the outcome of the study, it might take the form of:

Sales presentations in which the benefits module is placed in the introduction of a 12-minute message produce better retention of product knowledge than those where the benefits module is placed in the conclusion.

The researchers' challenges at this step are to (1) select variables that are the best operational representations of the original concepts, (2) determine how many variables to test, and (3) select or design appropriate measures for them.

In the previous example, the researcher would need to select variables that best operationalized the concepts *sales presentation, product benefits, retention,* and *product knowledge.* The product's classification and the nature of the intended audience should also be defined. In addition, the term *better* could be operationalized statistically by means of a significance test.

The number of variables in an experiment is constrained by the project budget, the time allocated, the availability of appropriate controls, and the number of subjects being tested. For statistical reasons, there must be more subjects than variables.[3]

The selection of measures for testing requires a thorough review of the available literature and instruments. In addition, measures must be adapted to the unique needs of the research situation without compromising their intended purpose or original meaning.

Specifying the Levels of Treatment

The level of the independent variable is the distinction the researcher makes between different aspects of the treatment condition. For example, if salary is hypothesized to have an effect on employees exercising stock purchase options, it might be divided into high, middle, and low ranges to represent three levels of the independent variable.

The levels assigned to an independent variable should be based on simplicity and common sense. In the sales presentation example, the experimenter should not select 8 minutes and 10 minutes as the starting points to represent the two levels if the average message about the product is 12 minutes. Similarly, by placing the benefits module in the first and second minutes of the presentation, observable differences may not occur because the levels are too close together. Thus, in the first trial, the researcher would likely position the midpoint of the benefits module the same interval from the end of the introduction as from the end of the conclusion.

Under an entirely different hypothesis, several levels of the independent variable may be needed to test order of presentation effects. Here we use only two. Alternatively a **control group** could provide a base level for comparison. The control group is composed of subjects who are not exposed to the independent variable(s), in contrast to those who receive the **experimental treatment** (manipulation of the independent variable(s)).

Controlling the Experimental Environment

Chapter 2 discussed the nature of extraneous variables and the need for their control. In our sales presentation experiment, extraneous variables could appear as differences in age, gender, race, dress, communications competence, and many other characteristics of the presenter, the message, or the situation. These have potential for distorting the effect of the treatment on the dependent variable and must be controlled or eliminated. However, at this stage, we are principally concerned with **environmental control,** holding constant the physical environment of the experiment. The introduction of the experiment to the subjects and the instructions would likely be videotaped to assure consistency. The arrangement of the room, the time of administration, the experimenter's contact with the subjects, and so forth must all be consistent across each administration of the experiment.

Other forms of control involve subjects and experimenters. When subjects do not know if they are receiving the experimental treatment, they are said to be blind. When the experimenters do not know if they are giving the treatment to the experimental group or the control, the experiment is **double-blind.** Both approaches control unwanted complications such as subjects' reactions to expected conditions or experimenter influence.

Choosing the Experimental Design

Unlike the general classifications of research design that were discussed in Chapter 5, experimental designs are unique to the experimental method. They serve as positional and statistical plans to designate relationships between experimental treatments and the experimenter's observations or measurement points in the temporal scheme of the study. Many of these designs are diagrammed and described later in the chapter. In the conduct of the experiment, the researchers apply their design knowledge to select one that is best suited to the goals of the research. A judicious selection of the design improves the probability that the observed change in the dependent variable was caused by the manipulation of the independent variable and not by another factor. It simultaneously strengthens generalizability of results beyond the experimental setting.

Selecting and Assigning Subjects

The subjects selected for the experiment should be representative of the population to which the researcher wishes to generalize. This may seem self-evident, but we have witnessed several decades of experimentation with college sophomores that contradict that assumption. In the sales presentation example, corporate buyers, purchasing managers, or others in a decision-making capacity would provide better generalizing power than undergraduate college students *if* the product in question was targeted for industrial use rather than to the consumer.

The procedure for random sampling of experimental subjects is similar in principle to the selection of respondents for a survey. We have also discussed random sampling in Chapter 8. The researcher first prepares a sampling frame, and then the subjects for the experiment are assigned to groups using a table of random numbers/random number generator. Systematic sampling may be used if the sampling frame is free from any form of periodicity that parallels the sampling ratio. Since the sampling frame is often small, experimental subjects are recruited, thus they are a self-selecting sample. However, if randomization is used, those assigned to the experimental group are likely to be similar to those assigned to the control group. **Random assignment** to the groups is required to make the groups as comparable as possible with respect to the dependent variable. Randomization does not guarantee that if a pretest of the groups was conducted before the treatment condition they would be pronounced identical; but it is an assurance that those differences remaining are randomly distributed. In our example, we would need three randomly assigned groups—one for each of the two levels of the independent variable and one for the control group.

When it is not possible to randomly assign subjects to groups, **matching** may be used. Matching employs a nonprobability quota sampling approach. The object of matching is to have each experimental and control subject matched on every characteristic used in the research. This becomes more cumbersome as the number of variables and groups in the study increases. Since the characteristics of concern are only those that are correlated with the treatment condition or the dependent variable, they are easier to identify, control, and match.[4] In the sales presentation experiment, if a large part of the sample was composed of businesswomen who had recently completed communications training, we would not want the characteristics of gender, business experience, and communication training to be disproportionally assigned to one group.

Some authorities suggest a **quota matrix** as the most efficient means of visualizing the matching process.[5] In Figure 13–1, one-third of the subjects from each cell of the matrix would be assigned to each of the three groups. If matching does not alleviate the assignment problem, a combination of matching, randomization, or increasing the sample size would be used.

Pilot Testing, Revising, and Testing

The procedures for this stage are similar to those of other forms of primary data collection. Pilot testing procedure is intended to reveal errors in the design and improper control of extraneous or environmental conditions. Pretesting the instruments permits refinement before the final test. This is the researcher's best opportunity to revise scripts, look for control problems with laboratory conditions, and scan the environment for factors that might confound the results. In field experiments, researchers are sometimes caught off guard by events that have a dramatic effect on subjects: the test marketing of a competitor's product announced before an experiment, or a reduction in force, reorganization, or merger before a crucial organizational intervention. The experiment should be timed so subjects are not sensitized to the independent variable by factors in the environment.

Analyzing the Data

If adequate planning and pretesting have occurred, the experimental data will take an order and structure uncommon to surveys and unstructured observational studies. It is not that data from experiments are easy to analyze; they are simply more conveniently arranged because of the levels of the treatment condition, pretests and posttests, and the group structure. The choice of statistical techniques is commensurately simplified.

FIGURE 13–1   Quota Matrix Example

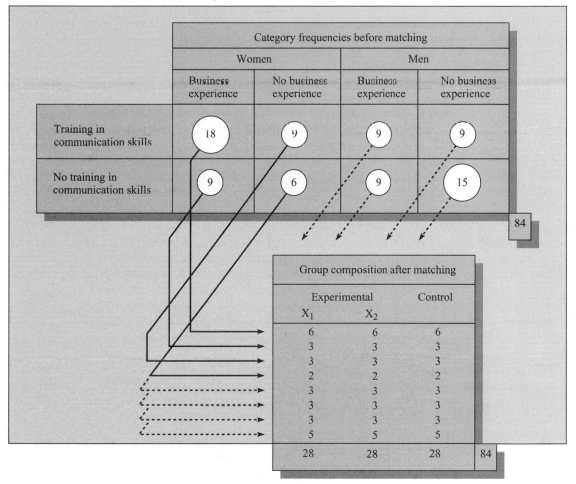

Researchers have several measurement and instrument options with experiments. Among them are: (1) observational techniques and coding schemes, (2) paper-and-pencil tests, (3) self-report instruments with open or closed questions, (4) scaling techniques (e.g., Likert scales, semantic differentials, Q-sort), and (5) physiological measures (e.g., galvanic skin response, EKG, voice pitch analysis, eye dilation).

VALIDITY IN EXPERIMENTATION

Even when an experiment is the ideal research design, it is not without problems. There is always a question about whether the results are true. We have previously defined validity in terms of whether a measure accomplishes its claims. While there are several different types of validity, here only the two major varieties are considered: **Internal validity**—do the conclusions we draw about a demonstrated experimental relationship truly imply cause? **External validity**—does an observed causal relationship generalize across persons, settings, and times?[6] Each of these types of validity has specific threats we need to guard against.

Internal Validity

Among the many threats to internal validity, we consider seven major ones here.

History   During the time that an experiment is taking place, some events may occur that confuse the relationship being studied. In many experimental designs, we take a control measurement (O_1) of the dependent variable before introducing the manipulation *(X)*. After the manipulation, take an after measurement (O_2) of the dependent variable. Then the difference between O_1 and O_2 is the change that the manipulation has caused. A company's management may wish to find the best way to educate its workers about the financial condition of the company before this year's labor negotiations. To assess the value of such an effort, they give employees a test on their knowledge about the company's finances (O_1). Then they present the educational campaign *(X)* to these employees, after which they again measure the knowledge level (O_2). This design, known as a preexperiment because it is not a very strong design, can be diagrammed as follows:

$$O_1 \qquad X \qquad O_2$$

Pretest   Manipulation   Posttest

Between O_1 and O_2, however, many events could occur to confound the effects of the education effort. A newspaper article might appear about companies with financial problems, a union meeting might be held at which this topic is discussed, or another occurrence could distort the effects of the company's education test.

Maturation   Changes may also occur within the subject that are a function of the passage of time and are not specific to any particular event. These are of special concern when the study covers a long time, but may also be factors in tests that are as short as an hour or two. A subject can become hungry, bored, or tired in a short time, and this can affect response results.

Testing   The process of taking a test can affect the scores of a second test. The mere experience of taking the first test can have a learning effect that influences the results of the second test.

Instrumentation   This is a threat to internal validity that results from changes between observations, in measuring instrument or observer. Using different questions at each measurement is an obvious source of potential trouble, but using different observers or interviewers also threaten validity. There can even be an instrumentation problem if the same observer is used for all measurements. Observer boredom, fatigue, experience, or anticipation of results can all distort the results of separate observations.

Selection   An important threat to internal validity is the differential selection of subjects for experimental and control groups. Validity considerations require that the groups be equivalent in every respect. If subjects are randomly assigned to experimental and control groups, this selection problem can be largely overcome. Additionally, the equivalence of the groups can be enhanced by matching the members of the groups on key factors.

Statistical Regression   This factor operates especially when groups have been selected by their extreme scores. Suppose we measure the output of all workers in a department for a few days before an experiment and then conduct the experiment only with those in the top 25 percent and bottom 25 percent of productivity scores. No matter what is done between O_1 and O_2, there is a strong tendency for the average of the high scores at O_1 to decline at O_2 and for the low scores at O_1 to increase. This tendency results from imperfect measurement that, in effect, records some persons abnormally high and abnormally low at O_1. In the second measurement, members of both groups score more closely to their long-run mean scores.

Experiment Mortality   This occurs when the composition of the study groups changes during the test. Attrition is especially likely in the experimental group, and with each dropout, the group changes. Members of the control group, because they are not affected by the testing situation, are less likely to withdraw. In a compensation incentive study, some employees might not like the change in compensation method and withdraw from the test group; this could distort the comparison with the control group that has continued working under the established system, perhaps without knowing a test is under way. All the threats mentioned to this point are generally, but not always, dealt with adequately in experiments by random assignment. However, five added threats to internal validity are independent of whether one randomizes.[7] The first three have the effect of equalizing experimental and control groups.

1. *Diffusion or imitation of treatment*—If people in the experimental and control groups talk, then those in the control group may learn of the treatment, eliminating the difference between the groups.
2. *Compensatory equalization*—Where the experimental treatment is much more desirable, there may be an administrative reluctance to deprive the control group members. Compensatory actions for the control groups may confound the experiment.
3. *Compensatory rivalry*—This may occur when members of the control group know they are the control group. This may generate competitive pressures, causing the control group members to try harder.
4. *Resentful demoralization of the disadvantaged*—When the treatment is desirable and the experiment is obtrusive, control group members may become resentful of their deprivation and lower their cooperation and output.

5. *Local history*—The regular history effect already mentioned impacts both experimental and control groups alike. However, when one assigns all experimental persons to one group session and all control people to another, there is a chance for some idiosyncratic event to confound results. This problem can be handled by administering treatments to individuals or small groups that are randomly assigned to experimental or control sessions.

External Validity

Internal validity factors cause confusion about whether the experimental treatment *(X)* or extraneous factors are the source of observation differences. In contrast, external validity is concerned with the interaction of the experimental treatment with other factors and the resulting impact on abilities to generalize to (and across) times, settings, or persons. Among the major threats to external validity are the following interactive possibilities.

The Reactivity of Testing on *X* The reactive effect is one of sensitizing the subjects by the pretest so they respond to the experimental stimulus in a different way. A before-measurement of the level of knowledge about the ecology programs of a company will often sensitize the subject to the various experimental communication efforts that might then be made about the company. This before-measurement effect can be particularly significant in attitude studies.

Interaction of Selection and *X* The process by which test subjects are selected for an experiment may be a threat to external validity. The population from which one selects subjects may not be the same as the population to which one wishes to generalize results. Suppose you use a selected group of workers in one department for the test of the piecework incentive system, the question may remain about whether you can extrapolate the results to all production workers. Or consider a study in which you ask a cross section of a population to participate in an experiment but a substantial number refuse. If you do the experiment only with those who agree to participate, can the results be generalized to the total population?

Other Reactive Factors The experimental settings themselves may have a biasing effect on a subject's response to *X*. An artificial setting can obviously give results that are not representative of larger populations. Suppose the group of workers that is given the incentive pay is moved to a different work area to separate them from the control group. These new conditions alone could create a strong reactive condition.

If subjects know they are participating in an experiment, there may be a tendency to role-play in a way that distorts the effects of *X*. Another reactive effect is the possible interaction between *X* and subject characteristics. An incentive pay proposal may be more effective with persons in one type of job, with a certain skill level, or with a certain personality trait.

Problems of internal validity can be solved by the careful design of experiments, but this is less true for external validity. External validity is largely a matter of generalization, and in a logical sense, this is an inductive process of extrapolating beyond the data collected. In generalizing, estimate the factors that can be ignored and that will interact with the experimental variable. Assume the closer two events are in time, space, and measurement, the more likely they will follow the same laws. As a rule of thumb first seek internal validity. Try to secure as much external validity as is compatible with the internal validity requirements by making experimental conditions as similar as possible to conditions under which the results will apply.

EXPERIMENTAL RESEARCH DESIGNS

The many experimental designs vary widely in terms of their power to control contamination of the relationship between independent and dependent variables. The most widely accepted designs are based on this characteristic of control: (1) preexperiments, (2) true experiments, and (3) field experiments. (See Figure 13–2.)

Preexperimental Designs

All three preexperimental designs are weak in terms of their scientific measurement power. That is, they fail to control adequately the various threats to internal validity. This is especially the case with the one-shot case study.

One-Shot Case Study   This may be diagramed as follows:

X	*O*	(1)
Treatment or manipulation of independent variable	Observation or measurements of dependent variable	

An example is an employee education campaign about the company's financial condition without a prior measurement of employee knowledge. Results would reveal only how much the employees know after the education campaign, but there is no way to judge the effectiveness of the campaign. How well do you think this design would meet the various threats to internal validity? The lack of a pretest and control group make this design inadequate for establishing causality.

The One-Group Pretest-Posttest Design   This is the design used earlier in the educational example. It meets the various threats to internal validity better than the one-shot case study, but it is still a weak design. How well does it control for history? Maturation? Testing effect? The others?

O	*X*	*O*	(2)
Pretest	Manipulation	Posttest	

FIGURE 13–2
Key to Design
Symbols

X	An X represents the introduction of an experimental stimulus to a group. The effects of this independent variable(s) are of major interest.
O	An O identifies a measurement or observation activity.
R	An R indicates that the group members have been randomly assigned to a group.

The X's and O's in the diagram are read from left to right in temporal order.

$$O \ X \ O \ O$$
Time

X's and O's vertical to each other indicate that the stimulus and/or observation take place simultaneously.

$$X \ O$$
$$O$$
Time
q

Parallel rows that are not separated by dashed lines indicate that comparison groups have been equalized by the randomization process.

$$X \ O$$
$$O$$

Those separated with a dashed line have not been so equalized.

$$O \ X \ O$$
- - - - -
$$O$$

The Static Group Comparison   This design provides for two groups, one of which receives the experimental stimulus while the other serves as a control. In a field setting, imagine this scenario. A forest fire or other natural disaster is the experimental treatment and psychological trauma (or property loss) suffered by the residents is the measured outcome. A pretest before the forest fire would be possible, but not on a large scale (as in the California fires). Moreover, timing of the pretest would be problematic. The control group, receiving the posttest, would consist of residents whose property was spared.

$$X \quad O_1 \qquad\qquad\qquad (3)$$

$$- - - - - - - - -$$

$$O_2$$

The addition of a comparison group makes a substantial improvement over the other two designs. Its chief weakness is that there is no way to assure the two groups are equivalent.

True Experimental Designs

The major deficiency of the previous designs is that they fail to provide comparison groups that are truly equivalent. The way to achieve equivalency is through matching and random assignment. With randomly assigned groups, we can employ tests of statistical significance of the observed differences.

It is common to show an X for the test stimulus and a blank for the existence of a control situation. This is an oversimplification of what really occurs. More precisely, there is an X_1 and an X_2, and sometimes more. The X_1 identifies one specific independent variable while X_2 is another independent variable that has been chosen, often arbitrarily, as the control case. Different levels of the same independent variable may also be used with one level serving as the control.

Pretest-Posttest Control Group Design   This design consists of adding a control group to the design number 2 (one group pretest-posttest) and assigning the subjects to either of the groups by a random procedure. The diagram is:

$$R \quad O_1 \quad X \quad O_2 \qquad\qquad\qquad (4)$$

$$R \quad O_3 \qquad\quad O_4$$

The effect of the experimental variable is

$$E = (O_2 - O_1) - (O_4 - O_3)$$

In this design, the seven major internal validity problems are dealt with fairly well, although there are still some difficulties. Local history may occur in one group and not the other. Also, if communication exists between people in test and control groups, there can be rivalry and other internal validity problems.

Maturation, testing, and regression are handled well because one would expect them to be felt equally in experimental and control groups. Mortality, however, can be a problem if there are different dropout rates in the study groups. Selection is adequately dealt with by random assignment.

The record of this design is not as good on external validity. There is a chance for a reactive effect from testing. This might be a substantial influence in attitude change studies where pretests introduce unusual topics and content. Nor does this design ensure against reaction between selection and the experimental variable. Even random selection may be defeated by a high decline rate by subjects. This would result in using a disproportionate share of people who are essentially volunteers who may not be typical of the population. If this occurs, we will need to replicate the experiment several times with other groups under other conditions before we can be confident of external validity.

Posttest Only Control Group Design   In this design, the pretest measurements are omitted. These pretests are well established in classical research design but are not really necessary when it is possible to randomize. The design is:

$$R \quad X \quad O_1 \tag{5}$$
$$R \qquad O_2$$

The experimental effect is measured by the difference between O_1 and O_2. The simplicity of this design makes it more attractive than the pretest-posttest control group design. Internal validity threats from history, maturation, selection, and statistical regression are adequately controlled by random assignment. Since the subjects are measured only once, the threats of testing and instrumentation are reduced, but different mortality rates between experimental and control groups continue to be a potential problem. In terms of external validity, this design reduces the problem of testing interaction effect, although other problems remain.

Extensions of True Experimental Designs

The true experimental designs have been discussed in their classical forms, but researchers normally use an operational extension of the basic design. These extensions differ from the classical design forms in terms of (1) the number of different experimental stimuli that are considered simultaneously by the experimenter and (2) the extent to which assignment procedures are used to increase precision.

Before considering the types of extensions, some terms that are commonly used in the literature of applied experimentation are introduced. **Factor** is widely used to denote an independent variable. Factors are divided into **treatment levels,** which represent various subgroups. A factor may have two or more levels such as (1) male and female; (2) large, medium, and small; or (3) no training, brief training, and extended training. These levels should be operationally defined.

Factors may also be classified by whether the experimenter can manipulate the levels associated with the subject. **Active factors** are those the experimenter can manipulate by causing a subject to receive one level or another. Treatment is used to denote the different levels of active factors. With the second type, the **blocking factor,** the experimenter can only identify and classify the subject on an existing level. Gender, age group, customer status, and organizational rank are examples of blocking factors because the subject comes to the experiment with a preexisting level of each.

Up to this point, the assumption is that experimental subjects are people, but this is often not so. A better term for subject is **test unit;** it can refer equally well to an individual, organization, geographic market, animal, machine type, mix of materials, and innumerable other entities.

Completely Randomized Design   The basic form of the true experiment is a completely randomized design. To illustrate its use, and that of more complex designs, consider a decision now facing the pricing manager at the Big Top Cannery. He would like to know what the ideal difference in price should be between the Big Top's private brand of canned vegetables and the national brands such as Del Monte and Stokely's.

It is possible to set up an experiment on price differentials for canned green beans. Eighteen company stores and three price spreads (treatment levels) of one cent, three cents, and five cents between the company brand and national brands are used for the study. Six of the stores are assigned randomly to each of the treatment groups. The price differentials are maintained for a period, and then a tally is made of the sales volumes and gross profit of the canned green beans for each group of stores.

This design can be diagramed as follows:

$$R \quad O_1 \quad X_1 \quad O_2 \qquad\qquad (6)$$
$$R \quad O_3 \quad X_3 \quad O_4$$
$$R \quad O_5 \quad X_5 \quad O_6$$

Here, O_1, O_3, and O_5 represent the total gross profits for canned green beans in the treatment stores for the month before the test. X_1, X_3, and X_5 represent the one-cent, three-cent, and five-cent treatments, while O_2, O_4, and O_6 are the gross profits for the month after the test started.

It is assumed that the randomization of stores to the three treatment groups was sufficient to make the three store groups equivalent. Where there is reason to believe this is not so, we must use a more complex design.

Randomized Block Design   When there is a single major extraneous variable, the randomized block design is used. Random assignment is still the basic way to assure equivalency among treatment groups, but something more is needed for two reasons. The more critical reason is that the sample being studied may be so small that it is risky to depend upon random assignment alone to assure equivalency. Small samples, such as the 18 stores, are typical in field experiments because of high costs or because few test units are available. Another reason for blocking is to learn whether treatments bring different results among various groups of subjects.

Consider again the canned green beans pricing experiment. Assume there is reason to believe that lower income families are more sensitive to price differentials than are higher income families. This factor could seriously distort our results unless we stratify the stores by customer income. Each of the 18 stores is assigned to one of three income blocks and randomly assigned, within blocks, to the price difference treatments. The design is shown in the accompanying table.

In this design, one can measure both **main effects** and **interaction effects.** Main effect is the average direct influence that a particular treatment has independent of other factors. Interaction is the influence of one factor on the effect of another. The main effect of each price differential is secured by calculating the impact of each of the three treatments averaged over the different blocks. An interaction effect occurs if you find that different customer income levels have a pronounced influence on the customer reactions to the price differentials. (See Chapter 15.)

		Blocking Factor—Customer Income			
Active Factor—Price Difference		*High*	*Medium*	*Low*	
1 cent	R	X_1	X_1	X_1	
3 cents	R	X_2	X_2	X_2	(7)
5 cents	R	X_3	X_3	X_3	

Note that the *O*s have been omitted. The horizontal rows no longer indicate a time sequence, but various levels of the blocking factor. However, before-and-after measurements are associated with each of the treatments.

Whether this design improves the precision of the experimental measurement depends upon how successfully the design reduces the variance within blocks and maximizes the variance between blocks. That is, if the response patterns are about the same in each block then there is little value to the more complex design. Blocking may be counterproductive.

Latin Square Design   The Latin square may be used when there are two major extraneous factors. To continue with the pricing example, assume we decide to block on the size of store and on customer income. It is convenient to consider these two blocking factors as forming the rows and columns of a table. Each factor is divided into three levels to provide nine groups of stores, each representing a unique combination of the two blocking variables. Treatments are then randomly assigned to these cells so a given treatment appears only once in each row and column. Because of this restriction, a Latin square must have the same number of rows, columns, and treatments. The design looks like the table below.

	Customer Income			
Store Size	*High*	*Medium*	*Low*	
Large	X_3	X_1	X_2	
Medium	X_2	X_3	X_1	
Small	X_1	X_2	X_3	(8)

Treatments can be assigned by using a table of random numbers to set the order of treatment in the first row. For example, the pattern may be 3, 1, 2 as shown above. Following this, the other two cells of the first column are filled similarly, and the remaining treatments are assigned to meet the restriction that there can be no more than one treatment type in each row and column.

The experiment is carried out, sales results are gathered, and the average treatment effect calculated. From this, we can determine the main effect of the various price spreads on the sales of company and national brands. With cost information, we can discover which price differential produces the greatest margin.

A limitation of the Latin square is that we must assume there is no interaction between treatments and blocking factors. Therefore, we cannot determine the interrelationships among store size, customer income, and price spreads. This limitation exits because there is not an exposure of all combinations of treatments, store sizes, and customer income groups. To do so would take a table of 27 cells, while this one has only 9. This can be accomplished by repeating the experiment twice to furnish the number needed to provide for every combination of store size, customer income, and treatment. If one is not especially interested in interaction, the Latin square is much more economical.

Factorial Design   One misconception that many have about experiments is that you can manipulate only one variable at a time. This is not true; with factorial designs, you can deal with more than one treatment simultaneously. Consider again the pricing experiment. The president of the chain might also be interested in finding the effect of posting unit prices on the shelf to aid shopper decision making. The accompanying table can be used to design an experiment to include both the price differentials and the unit pricing.

	Price Spread			
Unit Price Information?	*1 Cent*	*3 Cents*	*5 Cents*	
Yes	X_1Y_1	X_1Y_2	X_1Y_3	
No	X_2Y_1	X_2Y_2	X_2Y_3	(9)

This is known by a 2×3 factorial design in which we use two factors: one with two levels and one with three levels of intensity. The version shown here is completely randomized, with the stores being randomly assigned to one of six treatment combinations. With such a design, it is possible to estimate the main effects of each of the two independent variables and the interactions between them. The results can give answers to the following questions.

1. What are the sales effects of the different price spreads between company and national brands?
2. What are the sales effects of using unit price marking on the shelves?
3. What are the sales effect interrelations between price spread and the presence of unit price information?

Covariance Analysis   Up to this point, we have discussed direct control of extraneous variables through blocking. It is also possible to apply some degree of indirect statistical control on one or more variables through analysis of covariance. Even with randomization, one may find that the "before" measurement shows an average knowledge level difference between experimental and control groups. With covariance analysis, one can adjust statistically for this "before" difference. Another application might occur if the canned green beans pricing experiment was carried out with a completely randomized design, only to find there is a contamination effect from differences in average customer income levels. With covariance analysis, one can still do some "statistical blocking" on average customer income even after the experiment has been run.

Field Experiments: Quasi- or Semi-Experiments[8]

Under field conditions, we often cannot control enough of the extraneous variables or the experimental treatment to use a true experimental design. Because the stimulus condition occurs in a natural environment, a **field experiment** is required.

A modern version of the bystander and thief field experiment, mentioned at the beginning of the chapter, involves the use of electronic article surveillance to prevent shrinkage due to shoplifting. In a proprietary study, a shopper came to the optical counter of an upscale mall store and asked the salesperson to see special designer frames. The salesperson, a confederate of the experimenter, replied that she would get them from a case in the adjoining department and disappeared. The "thief" selected two pairs of sunglasses from an open display, deactivated the security tags at the counter, and walked out of the store.

Thirty-five percent of the subjects (store customers) reported the theft upon the return of the salesperson. Sixty-three percent reported it when the salesperson asked about the shopper. Unlike previous studies, the presence of a second customer did not reduce the willingness to report a theft.

This study was not possible with a control group, a pretest, or randomization of customers, but the information gained was essential and justified a compromise of true experimental designs.

Under such conditions, we use the preexperimental designs previously discussed or quasi-experiments. In a quasi-experiment, we often cannot know when or to whom to expose the experimental treatment. Usually, however, we can decide when and whom to measure. A quasi-experiment is inferior to a true experimental design but is usually superior to preexperimental designs. In this section, we consider a few common ones.

Nonequivalent Control Group Design   This is a strong and widely used quasi-experimental design. It differs from experimental design (4) because the test and control groups are not randomly assigned. The design is diagrammed as follows:

$$O_1 \quad X \quad O_2$$
$$\text{————————} \quad (10)$$
$$O_3 \qquad\quad O_4$$

There are two varieties. One is the *intact equivalent design* in which the membership of the experimental and control groups is naturally assembled. For example, we may use different classes in a school, membership in similar clubs, or customers from similar stores. Ideally, the two groups should be as alike as possible. This design is especially useful when any type of individual selection process would be reactive.

A second variation, the *self-selected experimental group design,* is weaker because volunteers are recruited to form the experimental group, while nonvolunteer subjects are used for control. Such a design is likely when subjects believe it would

Quasi-experiment:
- cannot control internal validity
- cannot control & control
- experiment: Can randomize & control all
- basically equivalent groups - only differences are treatments

VS true experiment

In QUASI, Do NOT HAVE EQUIVALENT GROUPS
- CAN'T RANDOMIZE

be in their interest to be a subject in an experiment—say, an experimental training program.

Comparison of pretest results ($O_1 - O_3$) is one indicator of the degree of equivalency between test and control groups. If the pretest results are significantly different, there is a real question as to the groups' comparability. On the other hand, if pretest observations are similar between groups, there is more reason to believe internal validity of the experiment is good.

Separate Sample Pretest-Posttest Design   This design is most applicable when we cannot know when and to whom to introduce the treatment but can decide when and whom to measure. The basic design is:

$$R \quad O_1 \quad (X) \tag{11}$$

$$R \quad\quad X \quad O_2$$

The bracketed treatment (X) is irrelevant to the purpose of the study but is shown to suggest the experimenter cannot control the treatment.

This is not a strong design because several threats to internal validity are not handled adequately. History can confound the results but can be overcome by repeating the study at other times in other settings. In contrast, it is considered superior to true experiments in external validity. Its strength results from its being a field experiment in which the samples are usually drawn from the population to which we wish to generalize our findings.

We would find this design more appropriate if the population is large, or a before-measurement is reactive, or there is no way to restrict the application of the treatment. Assume a company is planning an intense campaign to change its employees' attitudes toward energy conversation. It might draw two random samples of employees, one of which is interviewed regarding energy use attitudes before the information campaign. After the campaign the other group is interviewed.

Group Time Series Design   A time series introduces repeated observations before and after the treatment and allows subjects to act as their own controls. The single treatment group design has before-after measurements as the only controls. There is also a multiple design with two or more comparison groups as well as the repeated measurements in each treatment group.

The time series format is especially useful where regularly kept records are a natural part of the environment and are unlikely to be reactive. The time series approach is also a good way to study unplanned events in an ex post facto manner. If the federal government would suddenly begin price controls, we could still study the effects of this action later if we had regularly collected records for the period before and after the advent of price control.

The internal validity problem for this design is history. To reduce this risk, we keep a record of possible extraneous factors during the experiment and attempt to adjust the results to reflect their influence.

CLOSE-UP

A JOB ENRICHMENT QUASI-EXPERIMENT[9]

One theory of job attitudes holds that "hygiene" factors, which include working conditions, pay, security, status, interpersonal relationships, and company policy, can be a major source of dissatisfaction among workers but have little positive motivational power. This theory holds that the positive motivator factors are intrinsic to the job; they include achievement, recognition for achievement, the work itself, responsibility, and growth or advancement.[10]

A study of the value of job enrichment as a builder of job satisfaction was carried out with laboratory technicians or "experimental officers" (EOs) in a British chemical company. The project was a multiple group time series quasi-experiment. The project is diagrammed at the bottom of the page.

Two sections of the department acted as experimental groups and two as control groups. It is not clear how these were chosen, but there was no mention of random assignment. One of the experimental groups and one of the control groups worked closely together, while the other two groups were separated geographically and were engaged in different research. Hygiene factors were held constant during the research, and the

studies were kept confidential to avoid the tendency of participants to act in artificial ways.

A before-measurement was made using a job reaction survey instrument. This indicated the EOs typically had low morale, and many wrote of their frustrations. All EOs were asked to write monthly progress reports, and these were used to assess the quality of their work. The assessment was made against eight specifically defined criteria by a panel of three managers who were not members of the department. These assessors were never told which laboratory technicians were in the experimental group and which were in the control group.

The study extended over a year, with the treatments introduced in the experimental groups at the start of the 12-month study period. Changes were made to give experimental group EOs important chances for achievement; these changes also made the work more challenging. Recognition of achievement was given, authority over certain aspects was increased, new managerial responsibilities were assigned to the senior EOs, added advancements were given to others, and the opportunity for self-initiated work was provided. After about six months, these same changes were instituted with one of the control groups, while the remaining group continued for the entire period as a control. Several months of EO progress reports were available as a prior base line for evaluation. The results of this project are shown in Figure 13–3.

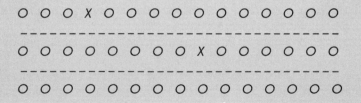

FIGURE   13–3   Assessment of *EOs* Monthly Reports

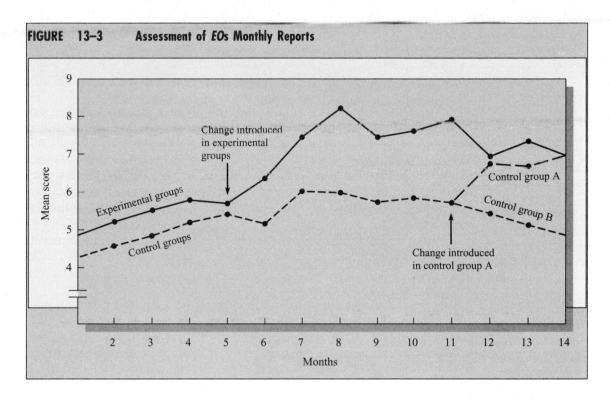

Summary   Experiments are studies involving intervention by the researcher beyond that required for measurement. The usual intervention is to manipulate a variable (the
independent variable) and observe how it affects the subjects being studied (the
dependent variable).

An evaluation of the experimental method reveals several advantages: (1) the
ability to uncover causal relationships, (2) provisions for controlling extraneous and
environmental variables, (3) convenience and low cost of creating test situations
rather than searching for their appearance in business situations (4) replicating findings to rule out idiosyncratic or isolated results and (5) the ability to exploit
naturally occurring events.

Some advantages of other methods are liabilities for the experiment: (1) the artificial setting of the laboratory, (2) generalizability from nonprobability samples,
(3) disproportionate costs in select business situations, (4) a focus restricted to the
present and immediate future, and (5) ethical issues related to manipulation and
control of human subjects.

Consideration of the following activities is essential for the execution of a well-
planned experiment:

1. Select relevant variables for testing.
2. Specify the levels of treatment.

3. Control the environmental and extraneous factors.

4. Choose an experimental design suited to the hypothesis.

5. Select and assign subjects to groups.

6. Pilot test, revise, and conduct the final test.

7. Analyze the data.

We judge various types of experimental research designs by how well they meet the tests of internal and external validity. An experiment has high internal validity if one has confidence that the experimental treatment has been the source of change in the dependent variable. More specifically, a design's internal validity is judged by how well it meets seven threats. These are history, maturation, testing, instrumentation, selection, statistical regression, and experimental mortality.

External validity is high when the results of an experiment are judged to apply to some larger population. Such an experiment is said to have high external validity regarding that population. Three potential threats to external validity are testing reactivity, selection interaction, and other reactive factors.

Experimental research designs include: (1) prexperiments, (2) true experiments, and (3) quasi-experiments. The main distinction among these types is the degree of control that the researcher can exercise over validity problems.

Three preexperimental designs were presented. They represent the crudest form of experimentation and are only undertaken when nothing stronger is possible. Their weakness is the lack of an equivalent comparison group, and as a result, they fail to meet many internal validity criteria. They are the (1) one-shot study, (2) one-group pretest-posttest design, and (3) static-group comparison.

Two forms of the true experiment were also presented. Their central characteristic is that they provide a means by which we can assure equivalence between experimental and control groups through random assignment to the groups. These designs are (1) pretest-posttest control group and (2) posttest-only control group.

The classical two-group experiment can be extended to multigroup designs in which different levels of the test variable are used as controls rather than the classical nontest control. In addition, the true experimental design is extended into more sophisticated forms that use blocking. Two such forms, the randomized block and the Latin square, are discussed. Finally, the factorial design is discussed in which two or more independent variables can be accommodated.

Between the extremes of preexperiments, with little or no control, and true experiments, with random assignment, there is a gray area in which we find quasi-experiments. These are useful designs when some variables can be controlled, but equivalent experimental and control groups usually cannot be established by random assignment. There are many quasi-experimental designs, but only three are discussed in this chapter: (1) nonequivalent control group design, (2) separate sample pretest-posttest design, and (3) group time series design.

Key Terms

active factors
blind
blocking factors
control group
double-blind
environmental control
experimental treatment
experiments
external validity
factor
field experiment

interaction effects
internal validity
main effects
matching
operationalized
quota matrix
random assignment
replication
test unit
treatment level

**Discussion
Questions**

1. Distinguish between:
    a. Internal and external validity.
    b. Preexperiment and quasi-experiment.
    c. History and maturation.
    d. Random sampling, randomization, and matching.
    e. Active and blocking factors.
    f. Environmental variables and extraneous variables.

2. Compare the advantages of experiments with survey and observational methods.

3. Describe how you would operationalize variables for experimental testing in the following research question: What are the performance differences between 10 microcomputers connected in a local area network (LAN) and one minicomputer with 10 terminals?

4. What ethical problems do you see in conducting experiments with human subjects?

5. Why would a noted social science researcher say, "It is essential that we always keep in mind the model of the controlled experiment, even if in practice we have to deviate from an ideal model"?

6. What are the essential characteristics that distinguish a true experiment from other research designs?

7. Suggest at least two specific situations each, in marketing, finance, and production, in which you think an experiment would be an appropriate research design. Which of the various designs would you recommend for each of the situations? What specific internal and/or external validity threats would you face with your suggested designs?

8. You are asked to develop an experiment for a study on the effect that compensation has upon the response rates secured from personal interview subjects. This study will involve 300 people who will be assigned to one of the following conditions: (1) no compensation, (2) $1 compensation, and

(3) $3 compensation. A number of sensitive issues will be explored concerning various social problems, and the 300 people will be drawn from the adult population.

Describe how your design would be set up if it were a completely randomized design, randomized block design, Latin square, factorial (suggest another active variable to use). Which would you use? Why?

9. What type of experimental design would you recommend in each of the following cases? Suggest in some detail how you would design each study:

   a. A test of three methods of compensation of factory workers. The methods are hourly wage, incentive pay, and weekly salary. The dependent variable is direct labor cost per unit of output.

   b. The effects of various levels of advertising effort and price reduction on the sale of specific branded grocery products by a retail grocery chain.

   c. The Ajax Auto Company is expecting to announce soon the largest profits in the company's history and the largest bonuses ever awarded to its executives. Company management is concerned about the effect of these acts on public attitudes toward retaining or dropping quotas on the importation of foreign cars into the United States.

   d. It has been claimed that the use of fast-paced music played over a store's P.A. system will speed the shopping rate of customers without any adverse effect on the amount spent per customer.

Reference Notes

1. Bibb Latane and J. M. Darley, *The Unresponsive Bystander: Why Doesn't He Help?* (New York: Appleton-Century-Crofts, 1970), pp. 69–77. Research into the responses of bystanders who witness crimes was stimulated by an incident in New York City where Kitty Genovese was attacked and killed in the presence of 38 witnesses who refused to come to her aid or summon authorities.

2. This section is largely adapted from Julian L. Simon and Paul Burstein, *Basic Research Methods in Social Science,* 3rd ed. (New York: Random House, 1985), pp. 128–33.

3. For a thorough explanation of this topic, see Helena C. Kraemer and Sue Thiemann, *How Many Subjects? Statistical Power Analysis in Research* (Beverly Hills, Calif.: Sage Publications, 1987).

4. Kenneth D. Bailey, *Methods of Social Research,* 2nd ed. (New York: Free Press, 1982), pp. 230–33.

5. The concept of a quota matrix and the tabular form for Figure 13–1 were adapted from Earl R. Babbie, *The Practice of Social Research,* 5th ed. (Belmont, Calif: Wadsworth Publishing, 1989), pp. 218–19.

6. Donald T. Campbell and Julian C. Stanley, *Experimental and Quasi-Experimental Designs for Research* (Chicago: Rand McNally, 1963), p. 5.

7. Thomas D. Cook and Donald T. Campbell, "The Design and Conduct of Quasi-Experiments and True Experiments in Field Settings," in *Handbook of Industrial and Organizational Psychology,* ed. Marvin D. Dunnette (Chicago: Rand McNally, 1976), p. 223.

8. For an in-depth discussion of many quasi-experiment designs and their internal validity, see Cook and Campbell, "Design and Conduct," pp. 246–98.
9. William J. Paul, Jr., Keith B. Robertson, and Frederick Herzberg, "Job Enrichment Pays Off," *Harvard Business Review,* March–April 1969, pp. 61–78.
10. Frederick J. Herzberg, "One More Time: How Do You Motivate Employees?" *Harvard Business Review,* January–February 1968, pp. 53–62.

Suggested Readings

1. Campbell, Donald T., and Julian C. Stanley. *Experimental and Quasi-Experimental Designs for Research.* Chicago: Rand McNally, 1963. A universally quoted discussion of experimental designs in the social sciences.
2. Cook, Thomas D., and Donald T. Campbell. "The Design and Conduct of Quasi-Experiments and True Experiments in Field Settings." In *Handbook of Industrial and Organizational Psychology,* 2nd ed. eds. Marvin D. Dunnette and Leaetta M. Hough. Palo Alto, Calif.: Consulting Psychologists Press, 1990.
   _____. *Quasi-Experimentation: Design and Analysis Issues for Field Settings.* Chicago: Rand McNally, 1979. Major authoritative works on both true and quasi-experiments and their design. Already classic references.
3. Edwards, Allen. *Experimental Design in Psychological Research.* 4th ed. New York: Holt, Rinehart & Winston, 1972. A complete treatment of experimental design with helpful illustrative examples.
4. Green, Paul E., Donald S. Tull and Gerald Albaum. *Research for Marketing Decisions.* 5th ed. Englewood Cliffs, N.J.: Prentice Hall, 1988. A definitive text with sections on the application of experimentation to marketing research.
5. Kirk, Roger E. *Experimental Design: Procedures for the Behavioral Sciences.* 2nd ed. Belmont, Calif.: Brooks/Cole Publishing, 1982. An advanced text on the statistical aspects of experimental design.
6. Krathwohl, David R. *Social and Behavioral Science Research: A New Framework for Conceptualizing, Implementing, and Evaluating Research Studies.* San Francisco: Jossey-Bas, 1985. Chapters 3, 4, and 5 present a convincing argument for reformulating internal and external validity into broader concepts. A conceptually refreshing approach.

ANALYSIS AND PRESENTATION OF DATA

DATA PREPARATION AND PRELIMINARY ANALYSIS

 **FINDING
YOUR WAY**

INTRODUCTION

Once the data begin to flow in, attention turns to data analysis. If the project has been done correctly, the analysis planning is already done. Back in the research design stage or at least by completion of the proposal or the pilot test, decisions were made about how to analyze the data. Unfortunately, many researchers wait until the analysis stage to decide what to do. This results in the late discovery that some data will not be collected, will be collected in the wrong form, or will exhibit unanticipated characteristics.

This chapter addresses two topics. The first is *data preparation,* which includes editing, coding, and data entry. These activities assure the accuracy of the data and its conversion from raw form to reduced and classified forms that are more appropriate for the analysis. Second, *preliminary data analysis* involves breaking down, inspecting, and rearranging data to start the search for meaningful descriptions, patterns, and relationships.

Before concluding this introduction, we must comment briefly on several assumptions of this part of the book. This book was developed for and with graduate students. It may be used successfully with undergraduates if an elementary statistics course was a prerequisite. Without that grounding, some of the ideas presented here may require remedial study. This chapter describes how to prepare data, explore it, and complete a preliminary analysis. We have tried to make it easy to use. Readers whose research objectives are reporting or basic description will find that this chapter is sufficient for their data analysis needs. Others, whose research goals are explanation or prediction, will want to continue on to hypothesis testing. For them, this chapter is an indispensable prelude to the remainder of the book.

EDITING

The customary first step in analysis is to edit the raw data. **Editing** detects errors and omissions, corrects them when possible, and certifies that minimum data quality standards are achieved. The editor's purpose is to assure that data are (1) accurate, (2) consistent with other information, (3) uniformly entered, (4) complete, and (5) arranged to simplify coding and tabulation.

In the following question asked of military officers, one respondent checked two categories, indicating that he was in the reserves and currently serving on active duty.

Please indicate your current military status:

- ☑ Active duty officer
- ☐ National Guard officer
- ☑ Reserve officer
- ☐ Separated officer
- ☐ Retired officer

The editor's responsibility is to decide which of the responses is consistent with the intent of the question or other information in the survey and is most accurate for this individual respondent.

Field Editing

During the stress of data collection, the researcher often uses ad hoc abbreviations and special symbols. Soon after the interview, experiment, or observation the investigator should review the reporting forms. It is difficult to complete what was abbreviated or written in shorthand or made illegibly if the entry is not caught that day. When gaps are present from interviews, a callback should be made rather than guessing what the respondent "probably would have said." Self-interviewing has no place in quality research.

In large projects, field editing review is a responsibility of the field supervisor. It, too, should be done soon after the data have been gathered. A second important control function of the field supervisor is to validate the field results. This normally means he or she will reinterview some percentage of the respondents, at least on some questions. Many commercial research firms will recontact about 10 percent of the respondents.

Central Editing

At this point, the data should get a thorough editing. For a small study, the use of a single editor assures maximum consistency. In large studies, the tasks may be broken down so each editor can deal with one entire section. This approach will not identify inconsistencies between answers in different sections. However, this problem can be handled by identifying points of possible inconsistency and having one editor check specifically for them.

Sometimes it is obvious that an entry is incorrect, entered in the wrong place, or states time in months when it was requested in weeks. When replies clearly are inappropriate or missing, the editor can sometimes detect the proper answer by reviewing the other information in the schedule. This practice, however, should be limited to those few cases where it is obvious what the correct answer is. It may be better to contact the respondent for correct information, if time and budget allow. Another alternative is for the editor to strike out the answer if it is clearly inappropriate. Here an editing entry of "no answer" or "unknown" is called for.

Another editing problem concerns faking. Armchair interviewing is difficult to spot, but the editor is in the best position to do so. One approach is to check responses to open-ended questions. These are most difficult to fake. Distinctive response patterns in other questions will often emerge if faking is occurring. To uncover this, the editor must analyze the interview schedules by interviewer.

Some useful rules to guide editors in their work are:

1. Be familiar with instructions given to interviewers and coders.
2. Do not destroy, erase, or make illegible the original entry by the interviewer. Original entries should be crossed out with a single line to remain legible.

3. Make all entries on a schedule in some distinctive color and in a standardized form.

4. Initial all answers changed or supplied.

5. Place initials and date of editing on each schedule completed.

CODING

Coding involves assigning numbers or other symbols to answers so the responses can be grouped into a limited number of classes or categories. The classifying of data into limited categories sacrifices some data detail but is necessary for efficient analysis. Instead of entering the word *male* or *female* in response to a question that asks for the identification of one's gender, the codes "M" or "F" could be used. Normally this variable would be coded 1 for male and 2 for female or 0 and 1. If we used M and F, or other letters, in combination with numbers and symbols, the code would be called *alphanumeric*. When numbers are used exclusively, the code is *numeric*.

Coding helps the researcher to reduce several thousand replies to a few categories containing the critical information needed for analysis. In coding, *categories* are the partitioning of a set; and categorization is the process of using rules to partition a body of data.

Coding Rules

Four rules guide the establishment of category sets. The categories should be:

1. Appropriate to the research problem and purpose.
2. Exhaustive.
3. Mutually exclusive.
4. Derived from one classification principle.

Appropriateness   Categories must provide the best partitioning of data for testing hypotheses and showing relationships. Year-by-year age differences may be important to the question being researched. If so, wider age classifications hamper our analysis. If specific income, attitude, or reason categories are critical to the testing relationship, then we must assure that the best groupings are chosen. In particular, choose class boundaries that match those being used for comparisons. It is disheartening, late in a study, to discover that age, income, or other frequency classes do not precisely match those of data with which we wish to make comparisons.

Exhaustiveness   If there are a large number of "other" responses, it suggests our classification set may be too limited. In such cases, we may not be tapping the full range of information in the data. Failure to present an adequate list of alternatives is especially damaging when multiple-choice questions are used. Any answer that is not specified in the set will surely be underrepresented in the tally.

While the exhaustiveness requirement in a single category set may be obvious, a second aspect is less apparent. Does the one set of categories fully capture all the information in the data? For example, responses to an open-ended question about family economic prospects for the next year may originally be classified only in terms of being optimistic or pessimistic. It may also be enlightening to classify responses in terms of other concepts such as the precise nature of these expectations (income or jobs) and variations in responses between family heads and others in the family.

Mutual Exclusivity   Another important rule is that category components should be mutually exclusive. This standard is met when a specific answer can be placed in one and only one cell in a category set. For example, in an occupation survey, the classifications may be (1) professional, (2) managerial, (3) sales, (4) clerical, (5) crafts, (6) operatives, and (7) unemployed. Some respondents will think of themselves as being in more than one of these groups. The person who views selling as a profession and spends time supervising others may fit under three of these categories. A function of operational definitions is to provide categories that are composed of mutually exclusive elements. Here, operational definitions of the occupations to be classified under "professional," "managerial," and "sales" should clarify the situation. The problem of how to handle an unemployed salesperson brings up a fourth rule of category design.

Single Dimension   The need for a category set to follow a single classificatory principle means every class in the category set is defined in terms of one concept. Returning to the occupation survey example, the person in the study might be both a salesperson and unemployed. The "salesperson" label expresses the concept of an *occupation type,* while the response "unemployed" is another dimension concerned with *current employment status* without regard to the respondent's normal occupation. When a category set uses more than one dimension, it will normally not be mutually exclusive unless the cells in the set combine the dimensions (employed manager, unemployed manager, and so on).

Codebook Construction

A **codebook,** or *coding scheme,* contains each variable in the study and specifies the application of coding rules to the variable. It is used by the researcher or research staff as a guide to make data entry less prone to error and more efficient. It is also the definitive source for locating the positions of variables in the data file during analysis. Most codebooks contain the question number, variable name, location of the variable's code on the input medium, descriptors for the response options, and whether the variable is alpha or numeric. An example of a codebook is shown in Figure 14–1. When pilot testing has been conducted, there should be sufficient information about the variables to prepare a codebook. A preliminary codebook used with pilot data may reveal coding problems that will need to be corrected before collecting and processing the data for the final study. Although most codebooks are produced by hand, time-saving computer software is available for this purpose.

FIGURE   14–1   Sample Codebook for Questionnaire Items

Project _____   [ID]

Question Number	Variable Number	Column Location	Code Descriptors	Software Variable Name
_____	_____	1	Record number	RECNUM
_____	_____	2–4	Respondent number	RESPID
1	1	5–9	Zip code 99999 = Missing	ZIP
2	2	10–11	Birth year 99 = Missing	BIRTH
3	3	12	Gender 1 = Male 2 = Female 9 = Missing	SEX
4	4	13	Marital status 1 = Married 2 = Widow(er) 3 = Divorced 4 = Separated 5 = Never married 9 = Missing	MARITAL
5	5	14	Own–Rent 1 = Own 2 = Rent 3 = Provided 9 = Missing	HOUSING
6	6		Purchase reason(s) 1 = Mentioned 0 = Not mentioned	PURCH
6	7	15	Bought home	REASON
		16	Birth of child	
		17	Death of relative or friend	
		18	Promoted	
		19	Changed job/career	
		20	Paid college expenses	
		21	Acquired assets	
		22	Retired	
		23	Changed marital status	
		24	Started business	
		25	Expanded business	
		26	Parent's influence	
		27	Contacted by agent	
		28	Other	

Closed Question Coding

The responses to closed questions include scaled items and others for which answers can be anticipated. When codes are established early in the research process, it is possible to precode the questionnaire. **Precoding** is particularly helpful for data entry because it makes the intermediate step of completing a coding sheet unnecessary. The data are accessible directly from the questionnaire. A respondent, interviewer, field supervisor, or researcher (depending on the data collection method) is able to assign an appropriate numerical response on the instrument by checking, circling, or printing it in the proper coding location.

Figure 14–2 shows questions in the sample codebook. When precoding is used, editing may precede data processing. Note question 4 where the respondent may choose between five characteristics of marital status and enter the number of the

FIGURE 14–2   Sample Questionnaire Items

1. What is the zip code of your current residence?   _ _ _ _ _ (5–9)

2. What is the year of your birth?   19 _ _ (10–11)

3. Sex   (1) Male   Indicate your choice → _ (12)
          (2) Female   by number

4. What is your marital status?

      (1) Married
      (2) Widow(er)   Indicate your choice → _ (13)
      (3) Divorced   by number
      (4) Separated
      (5) Never married

5. Do you own or rent your primary residence?

      (1) Own   Indicate your choice → _ (14)
      (2) Rent   by number
      (3) Living quarters provided

6. What prompted you to purchase your most recent life insurance policy?

      _____
      _____
      _____
      _____
      _____
      _____

item best representing present status in the shaded portion of the questionnaire. This code is later transferred to an input medium for analysis.

Open Question Coding

Closed questions are favored by researchers over open questions for their efficiency and specificity. They are easier to measure, record, code, and analyze. But there are situations where insufficient information or lack of a hypothesis prohibits preparing response categories in advance. Other reasons for using open-ended responses include the need to measure sensitive or disapproved behavior, to discover saliency, or to encourage natural modes of expression.[1]

In Figure 14–2, question 6 illustrates the use of an open question for which advance knowledge of response options was not available. The answer to "What prompted you to purchase your most recent life insurance policy?" was filled in by the respondent, as a short answer essay. After preliminary evaluation, response categories (shown in the codebook, Figure 14–1) were created for that item. Although most responses could be accounted for by the derived categories, an "other" category was established to meet the coding rule of exhaustiveness.

Using Content Analysis for Open Questions

Content analysis measures the semantic content or the "what" aspect of a message. Its breadth makes it a flexible and wide-ranging tool that may be used as a methodology or as a problem-specific technique. Trend-watching organizations like the BrainReserve, the Naisbitt Group, SRI International, and Inferential Focus use variations on content analysis for selected projects, often spotting changes from newspapers or magazine articles before they can be confirmed statistically. The Naisbitt Group's content analysis of 2 million local newspaper articles compiled over a 12-year period resulted in the publication of *Megatrends*. After a brief review of the characteristics of content analysis, we will consider one of its many problem-specific applications, handling open-ended questions.

Content analysis has been described as "a research technique for the objective, systematic, and quantitative description of the manifest content of a communication."[2] Because this definition is sometimes confused with simply counting obvious message aspects such as words or attributes, more recent interpretations have broadened the definition to include latent as well as manifest content, the symbolic meaning of messages, and qualitative analysis. One author states:

> In any single written message, one can count letters, words, or sentences. One can categorize phrases, describe the logical structure of expressions, ascertain associations, connotations, denotations, elocutionary forces, and one can also offer psychiatric, sociological, or political interpretations. All of these may be simultaneously valid. In short, a message may convey a multitude of contents even to a single receiver.[3]

Content analysis follows a systematic process starting with the selection of a unitization scheme. The units may be syntactical, referential, propositional, or thematic. Syntactical units are illustrated by words, which are the smallest and most reliable. Referential units may be objects, events, persons, and so forth to which an expression refers. An advertiser may refer to a product as a "classic," a "power performer," or "ranked first in safety"—each denoting the same object.

Propositional units use several frameworks. One might show the relationships among the actor, the mode of acting, and the object; for example, "subscribers [actor] to this periodical save [mode of acting] $15 [object of the action] over the single issue rate." Thematic units are higher-level abstractions inferred from their connection to a unique structure or pattern in the content. A response to a question about working conditions may reflect a temporal theme: the past ("how good things used to be here"), the present ("the need to talk with management now before production gets worse"), or the future ("employee expectations to be involved in planning and goal-setting").

Other aspects of the methodology include selection of a sampling plan, development of recording and coding instructions, data reduction, inferences about the context, and statistical analysis. Content analysis guards against selective perception of the content, has provision for the rigorous application of reliability and validity criteria, and is amenable to computerization.

The data to be content analyzed include materials of interest to business researchers: books, chapters, historical documents, speeches, interviews, advertisements, promotional brochures, group interactions, paragraphs, and words. Any recorded activity with its own syntax and semantics is subject to measurement and analysis. Thus, content analysis may be used to analyze written, audio, or video data from experiments, observations, surveys, and secondary data studies.

Let's look at an informal application of content analysis to a problematic, open-ended question. In this truncated example, suppose employees in the assembly operation of a unionized manufacturing firm are asked, "How can management–employee relations be improved?" A sample of the responses yields the following:

1. Management should treat the worker with more respect.
2. Managers should stop trying to speed up the assembly line.
3. Working conditions in the shop are terrible. Managers should correct them.
4. The foreman should be fired. He is unfair in his treatment of workers.
5. Managers should form management–worker councils in the department to iron out problems and improve relations.
6. Management should stop trying to undermine union leadership.
7. Management should accept the union's latest proposals on new work rules.

The first step requires that the units developed reflect the objectives for which the data were collected. The research question was concerned with learning what the assemblers thought was the locus of responsibility for improving company–employee relations. The categories selected are key words and referential units. The first pass through the data produced a few general categories shown in Figure 14–3. This set of categories was mutually exclusive and contained only one concept dimension. The use of "other" assured that the category set was exhaustive. If the sample had suggested that many respondents identified the need for action by the public, government, or regulatory bodies, then including all of them in "other" would ignore much of the richness of the data.

Since responses to this type of question often suggest specific actions, the

FIGURE   14–3   Open-Ended Coding Example (before revision)

Question: "How can management–employee relations be improved?"

Locus of Responsibility	*Mentioned*	*Not Mentioned*
A. Management	_____	_____
B. Union	_____	_____
C. Worker (other than union)	_____	_____
D. Joint management–union	_____	_____
E. Joint management–workers	_____	_____
F. Other	_____	_____

second evaluation of the data used propositional units. This identified action objects and the actors previously discovered. Had we used only the set of categories in Figure 14–3, the analysis would have omitted a considerable amount of information. The second analysis produced categories for action planning:

1. Human relations.
2. Production processes.
3. Working conditions.
4. Other action areas.
5. No action area identified.

How could we categorize a response suggesting a combined management–production process suggestion? Figure 14–4 illustrates a combination of alternatives. By taking the categories of the first list with the action areas, it is possible to get an accurate frequency count of the joint classification possibilities for this question.

"Don't Know" Responses

The **"don't know" (DK) response** presents special problems for data preparation. When the DK response group is small, it is not troublesome, but there are times when it is of major concern; and it may even be the most frequent response received. Does this mean the question that elicited this response is useless? The answer is, "It all depends." Most DK answers fall into two categories.[4] First, there is the legitimate DK response when the respondent does not know the answer and this response meets our research objectives (we expect DK responses and consider them to be useful answers).

In the second situation, a DK reply illustrates the researcher's failure to get the appropriate information. Consider the following illustrative questions:

1. Who developed the Managerial Grid concept?
2. Do you believe the new president's fiscal policy is sound?
3. Do you like your present job?
4. Which of the various brands of chewing gum do you believe has the best quality?
5. How often each year do you go to the movies?

FIGURE 14–4
Revised
Open-Ended Coding
Using Combined
Criteria

Question: "How can management-employee relations be improved?"

Locus of Responsibility	Frequency	
	Mentioned	Not Mentioned
A. Management		
1. Human relations	☐	☐
2. Production processes	☐	☐
3. Working conditions	☐	☐
4. Other action area	☐	☐
5. No action area	☐	☐
B.	.	.
C.	.	.
D.	.	.
E.	.	.
F. Other		
1. Human relations	☐	☐
2. Production processes	☐	☐
3. Working conditions	☐	☐
4. Other action areas	☐	☐
5. No action area	☐	☐

It is reasonable to expect that some legitimate DK responses will be made to each of these questions. In the first question, the respondents are asked for a level of information that they often will not have. There seems to be little reason to withhold a correct answer if known. Thus, most DK answers to this question should be considered as legitimate.

DK response in the second question presents a different problem. It is not immediately clear whether the respondent is ignorant of the president's fiscal policy or knows the policy but has not made a judgment about it. The researchers should have asked two questions: In the first, they would have determined the respondent's level of awareness of fiscal policy; if the interviewee passed the awareness test, then a second question would have secured judgment on fiscal policy.

In the remaining three questions, the DK response is more likely to be a failure of the questioning process, although some will surely be legitimate. The respondent may be reluctant to give the information. DK response to question 3 may be a way of saying, "I do not want to answer that question." Question 4 might also elicit a DK response in which the reply translates to, "This is too unimportant to talk about." In question 5, the respondents are being asked to do some calculation about a topic to which they attach little importance. Now the DK may mean, "I do not want to do that work for something that has so little importance."

Dealing with Undesired DK Responses   The best way to deal with undesired DK answers is to design better questions at the beginning. The interviewers, however, must deal with the problem in the field. Before interviewing, they should identify

TABLE 14-1   Handling "Don't Know" Responses

	Do You Like Your Present Job?		
Years of Service	Yes	No	Don't Know
Less than 1 year	10%	40%	38%
1–3 years	30	30	32
4 years or more	60	30	30
Total	100%	100%	100%
n =	650	150	200

the questions for which a DK response is unsatisfactory. Several actions are then possible. First, good interviewer–respondent rapport will motivate respondents to provide more usable answers. When interviewers recognize an evasive DK response, they can repeat the question or probe for a more definite answer. Finally, the interviewer may record verbatim any elaboration by the respondent and buck the problem on to the editor.

If the editor finds many undesired responses, little can be done unless the verbatim comments can be interpreted. Understanding the real meaning relies on clues from the respondent's other questions. One way to do this is to estimate the allocation of DK answers from other data in the questionnaire. The pattern of responses may parallel income, education, or experience levels. Suppose a question concerning whether the employee likes his present job elicited the answers in Table 14–1. The correlation between years of service and the "don't know" answers and the "no" answers would suggest that most of the "don't knows" are disguised "no" answers.

There are several ways to handle "don't know" responses in the tabulations. If there are only a few, it does not make much difference how they are handled, but they will probably be kept as a separate category. If the DK response is legitimate, it should remain as a separate reply category. When we are not sure how to treat it, we should keep it as a separate category and let the reader make the decision.

Another way to treat DK responses is to assume they occur almost randomly. Using this approach, we distribute them among the other answers in the same ratio that the other answers occur. This assumes that those who reply "don't know" are proportionally distributed among all of the groups studied. This can be achieved either by prorating the DK responses or by excluding all DK replies from the tabulation. The latter approach is better since it does not inflate the actual number of other responses.

DATA ENTRY

In the last few years, we have witnessed an explosion in information processing technology. Researchers have profited from new and more efficient ways of speeding up the research process (see Figure 14–5). **Data entry** converts information gathered by secondary or primary methods to a medium for viewing and

FIGURE   14–5   Methods of Data Entry

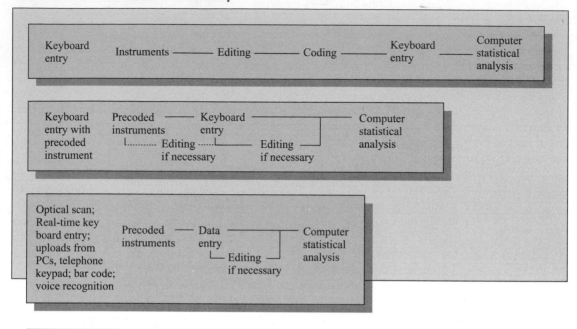

Time required for completion

manipulation. Keyboard entry remains a mainstay for researchers who need to create a data file immediately and store it in a minimal space on a variety of media.

Optical scanning instruments, the ubiquitous choice of testing services, have improved efficiency. Examinees darken small circles, ellipses, or sets of parallel lines to choose a test answer. Optical scanners process the marked-sensed questionnaires and store the answers in a file. This technology has been adopted by questionnaire designers for more routine data collection. It reduces the number of times data are handled, thereby reducing the number of errors that are introduced.

Voting procedures used in several states are another example of direct response entry. With a specially prepared punch card, citizens cast their votes by pressing a pen-shaped instrument against the card next to the preferred candidate. This opens a small hole in a specific column and row of the card. The cards are collected and placed directly into a card reader. This method also removes the coding and entry steps. Another governmental application is the 1040EZ form used by the Internal Revenue Service. These are designed for computerized number and character recognition. Similar character recognition techniques are employed for many forms of data collection. Again, both approaches move the response from the question to data analysis with little handling.

The cost of technology has allowed most researchers access to desktop or portable computers or a terminal linked to a larger computer. This technology enables computer-assisted telephone or personal interviews to be completed with answers entered directly for processing, eliminating intermediate steps and errors.

The increase in computerized random-digit dialing encouraged other data collection innovations. **Voice recognition** and response systems, while still far from mature, are providing some interesting alternatives for the telephone interviewer. Such systems can be used with software that is programmed to call specific three-digit prefixes with randomly generated four-digit numbers, reaching a random sample within a set geographical area. Upon getting a voice response, the computer will branch into a questionnaire routine. Currently, the systems are programmed to record the verbal answers, but voice recognition is improving quickly enough that these systems will soon translate voice responses into data files. Telephone keypad response is another capability made possible by computers linked to telephone lines. Using the telephone keypad (touch tone), the respondent answers questions by pressing the appropriate number. The computer captures the data by "listening," decoding the tone's electrical signal, and storing the numeric or alphabetic answer in a data file.

Field interviewers can use portable computers or electronic notebooks instead of clipboards and pencils. With a built-in communications modem or cellular link, their files can be sent directly to another computer in the field or to a remote site. This lets supervisors inspect data immediately or simplifies processing at a central facility.

Bar code readers are used in several applications: point-of-sale terminals, inventory control, product and brand tracking, and at busy rental car locations to speed the return of cars and generate invoices. This technology can be used to simplify the interviewer's role as a data recorder. Instead of writing (or typing) information about the respondents and their answers by hand, the interviewer can pass a bar code wand over the appropriate codes. The data are recorded in a small, lightweight unit for translation later.

Even with these time reductions between data collection and analysis, continuing innovations in multimedia technology are being developed by the personal computer business. The capability to integrate visual images, audio, and data may soon replace video equipment as the preferred method for recording an experiment, interview, or focus group. A copy of the response data could be extracted for data analysis, but the audio and visual images would remain intact for later evaluation.

Other techniques on the horizon will continue to improve research efficiency and effectiveness. Although technology will never replace researcher judgment, it can reduce data-handling errors, decrease time between data collection and analysis, and help in providing more usable information.

Data Entry Formats

The use of a full screen editor, where an entire data file can be edited or browsed, is a viable means of data entry for statistical packages like SPSS, SYSTAT, SAS, or BMDP.

For large projects, database programs serve as valuable data entry devices. A **database** is a collection of data organized for computerized retrieval. Programs

FIGURE   14–6   Data Fields, Records, Files, and Databases

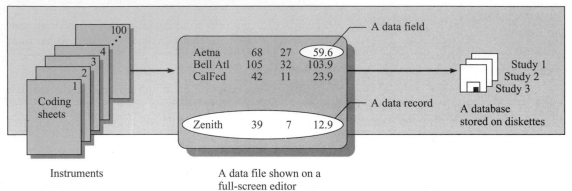

Instruments   A data file shown on a
                               full-screen editor

Data fields represent single elements of information (e.g., an answer to a question, a description, a number, a statement, etc.). Data fields can contain numeric, alphabetic, or symbolic information. A **record** is a set of data fields that are related. Records are the rows of a data file or spreadsheet program worksheet. **Data files** are sets of records that are grouped together for storage on diskettes, disks, tapes, CD-ROM, or optical disks. **Databases** are made up of one or more data files that are interrelated.
SOURCE: Company data: Public domain.

allow users to define data fields and link files so storage, retrieval, and updating are simplified. The relationship between data fields, records, files, and databases is illustrated in Figure 14–6. A company's personnel records serve as an example of a database. Employee information may be kept in several files: salary and position, education, benefits, and home and family. The data are separated so authorized people can see only those parts pertinent to their needs. However, the files may be linked so that when an individual changes her name, the change is entered once and all the files are updated.

Researchers consider database entry when they have large amounts of potentially linked data that will be retrieved and tabulated in different ways over time. Another application of a database program is a "front-end" entry mechanism. A telephone interviewer may ask the question, "How many children live in your home?" The computer's software has been programmed to accept any answer between 0 and 20. If a "P" is accidentally struck, the program will not accept the answer and will return the interviewer to the question. Using a precoded online instrument, much of the editing needed previously is done by the program. In addition, the program can be set for automatic conditional branching. In the example, an answer of 1 or greater causes the program to prompt the questioner to ask the ages of the children. A zero causes the age question to be automatically skipped. Although this option is available whenever interactive computing is used, front-end processing is typically done within the database design. The database will then store the data into a set of linked files that allow the data to be easily sorted. Descriptive statistics and tables are readily generated from within the base.

Another way for entering data found a special niche with personal computers. Spreadsheets were pioneered in the late 1970s as a specialized type of database. For data that need organizing, tabulating, and simple statistics, spreadsheets provide an easy-to-learn mechanism. They also offer some database management, graphics, and presentation capabilities.

Data entry on a **spreadsheet** uses numbered rows and letter columns with a matrix of thousands of cells into which an entry may be placed. Spreadsheets allow you to type numbers, formulas, and text into appropriate cells. Many statistics programs for personal computers and also charting and graphics applications have data editors similar to the spreadsheet format as shown in Figure 14–7. This is a convenient and flexible means for entering and viewing the data.

PRELIMINARY ANALYSIS

The convenience of data entry via spreadsheet or with the data editor of a statistical program makes it tempting to move directly to statistical analysis. Why waste time finding out if the data confirm the hypothesis that motivated the study? Why not begin with statistical summaries and then hypothesis tests?

In Chapter 2, we said research conducted scientifically is a puzzle-solving activity. We also noted that an attitude of curiosity, suspicion, and imagination was essential to the discovery process. It is natural, then, that exploration of the data would be an integral part of our perspective. When the study's purpose is not the production of causal inferences, confirmatory data analysis is not required. When it is, we advocate discovering as much as possible about the data before selecting the appropriate means of confirmation.

An Exploratory Data Analysis Approach

Exploratory data analysis (EDA) is a data analysis perspective and set of techniques.[5] With **exploratory data analysis,** the data guide the choice of analysis—or a revision of the planned analysis—rather than the analysis presuming to overlay its structure on the data without the benefit of the analyst's scrutiny. This is comparable to our position that research should be problem oriented rather than tool driven. The flexibility to respond to the patterns revealed by successive iterations in the discovery process is an important attribute of this approach. By comparison, **confirmatory data analysis** occupies a position closer to classical statistical inference in its use of significance and confidence. But confirmatory analysis may also differ from traditional practices by using information from a closely related data set or by validating findings through the gathering and analyzing of new data.[6]

One authority compared exploratory data analysis to the role of police detectives and other investigators and confirmatory analysis to that of judges and the judicial system. The former are involved in the search for clues and evidence, and the latter are preoccupied with evaluating the strength of what is found. Exploratory data analysis is the first step in the search for evidence without which confirmatory analysis has nothing to evaluate.[7] Consistent with that analogy, EDA shares a commonality with exploratory designs, not formalized ones. Because it doesn't follow a rigid structure, it is free to take many paths in unraveling the mysteries in the data—to sift the unpredictable from the predictable.

FIGURE   14–7   Data Entry Using Spreadsheets and Editors

Spreadsheet Data Entry: Lotus 1-2-3 ®

| File Edit | Worksheet | Range | Graph | Data | Style | Tools | Window |

A:A2: [W4]   @IF(@CELL("type",B2..B17)="l",A1+1,@S(AH2..AH2))

CompleteCare

	A	A	B	C	D	E	F	G	H	I	J	K	L	M	N
1		Card	Received	1a.	1b.	2a.	2b.	2c.	3.	4.	5.	6.	7.	8a.	8b.
2	1	2-20	5	5	4	5	5	5	5	5	5	5	3	5
3	2	2-20	4	4	4	2	5	4	4	4	4	3	5	5
4	3	2-20	4	4	4	4	4	3	5	4	5	5	4	5
5	4	2-20	4	4	3	1	4	5	3	3	4	4	5	5
6	5	2-20	5	4	5	5	5	4	4	5	5	5	4	3
7	6	2-20	3	3	1	3	1	2	4	1	2	5	4	3
8	7	2-20	4	4	4	4	4	5	5	5	5	5	4	3
9	8	2-20	5	5	5	4	5	5	5	1	5	5	5	3
10	9	2-20	5	5	2	5	5	5	5	5	5	4	5	5
11	10	2-20		4	4	4	4	1	3	5	3	5	3	5
12	11	2-21	4	4	1	4	4	4	4	4	5	5	4	5
13	12	2-21	4	5	5			5	4	4	4	5	4	5
14	13	2-21	4	5	3	5	5	4	4	4	3	5	5	
15	14	2-21	3	4	4	4	4	4	4	4	4	5	5	4
16	15	2-21	5	4	4	4	4	3	4	4	4	4	5	5
17	16	2-21	1	4	5	4	4	4	4	2	3	5	3	4
18	17	2-21	5	4	4	5	5	5	5	4	5	4	4	5
19	18	2-21	5	5	4	5	5	5	5	5	5	4	4	5

Statistical Program Data Editor: Data Desk ®

Company	Assets	Sales	Market Value
Rockwell Int'l	9033	12534	5491
Sundstrand	1503	1595	1341
Alco Standard	1546	4207	1290
Comdisco	4293	1758	1091
General Signal	1324	1918	1029
Tecumseh Products	1034	1510	697
Timken	1566	1533	895
FMC	2819	3415	1253

A major contribution of the exploratory approach lies in the emphasis on visual representations and graphical techniques over summary statistics. Summary statistics, as you will see momentarily, may obscure, conceal, or even misrepresent the underlying structure of the data. When numerical summaries are used exclusively and accepted without visual inspection, the selection of confirmatory models may be precipitous, based on flawed assumptions, and may consequently produce erroneous conclusions.[8] For these reasons, preliminary analysis should begin with visual inspection, not numerical summaries. After that it is not only possible but also desirable to cycle between exploratory and confirmatory approaches.

In the following sections, we will survey the fundamentals of EDA with respect to distributions, displays, and techniques. But first, in the Close-Up, we review descriptive statistics and start building a case for doing something wiser than taking a quick look at number summaries and wading into inferential statistics.

CLOSE-UP: DESCRIPTIVE STATISTICS

DESCRIBING DISTRIBUTIONS

In the first part of the chapter, we discussed how responses could be coded and entered. When nominal measurements were involved (e.g., company classifications like high-tech, consumer products, retailing), each category would be represented by its own numerical code. With ordinal data, the item's rank, reflecting a position in the range from the lowest to the highest, would be entered. The same is true with interval-ratio scores. When these data are tabulated, they may be arrayed from the lowest to the highest scores on their scales. Together with the frequency of occurrence, the observations form a **distribution** of values.

Many variables of interest in the business environment have distributions that approximate a **standard normal distribution.** This distribution, shown in Part A of Figure 14–8, is the most significant theoretical distribution in statistics. It is a standard of comparison for describing distributions of sample data and is used with inferential statistics that assume normally distributed variables.

The characteristics of location, spread, and shape describe distributions. Their definitions, applications, and formulas fall under the heading of **descriptive statistics.** Although the definitions will be familiar to most readers, the review takes the following perspective on distributional characteristics:

1. A distribution's shape is just as consequential as its location and spread.
2. Visual representations are superior to numerical ones for discovering a distribution's shape.
3. The choice of summary statistics to describe a single variable is contingent on the appropriateness of those statistics for the shape of the distribution.[9]

MEASURES OF LOCATION (Centrality)

The common **measures of location,** often called **central tendency** or *center,* include the mean, median, and mode.

Mean

The **mean** is the arithmetic average. It is the sum of the observed values in the distribution divided by the number of observations. It is the location measure most frequently used for interval-ratio data but can be misleading when the distribution contains extreme scores, large or

(continued)

FIGURE   14–8   Characteristics of Distributions

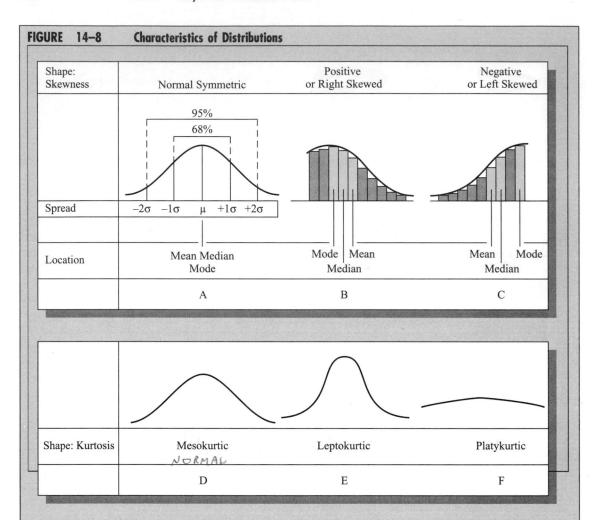

Shape: Skewness	Normal Symmetric	Positive or Right Skewed	Negative or Left Skewed
Spread	-2σ -1σ μ $+1\sigma$ $+2\sigma$		
Location	Mean Median Mode	Mode | Mean Median	Mean | Mode Median
	A	B	C

Shape: Kurtosis	Mesokurtic NORMAL	Leptokurtic	Platykurtic
	D	E	F

small. The symbol for the sample mean is $\bar{X}$. The Greek letter *mu* (μ) is used to represent the population mean.

$$\bar{X} = \sum_{i=1}^{n} \frac{X_i}{n}$$

Median

The **median** is the midpoint of the distribution. Half of the observations in the distribution fall above and the other half fall below the median. When the distribution has an even number of ob-

servations, the median is the average of the two middle scores. The median is the most appropriate locator of center for ordinal data and has resistance to extreme scores, thereby making it a preferred measure for interval-ratio data—particularly those with asymmetric distributions. The median is sometimes symbolized, *M* or *mdn*.

Mode

The **mode** is the most frequently occurring value. When there is more than one score that has the

(continued)

highest yet equal frequency, the distribution is bi-modal or multimodal. When every score has an equal number of observations, there is no mode. The mode is the location measure for nominal data and a point of reference along with the median and mean for examining spread and shape.

MEASURES OF SPREAD

The common **measures of spread,** alternatively referred to as *dispersion* or **variability,** are the variance, standard deviation, range, interquartile range, and quartile deviation. They describe how scores cluster or scatter in a distribution.

Variance

The **variance** is the average of the squared deviation scores from the distribution's mean. It is a measure of score dispersion about the mean. If all the scores are identical, the variance is 0. The greater the dispersion of scores, the greater the variance. Both the variance and the standard deviation are used with interval-ratio data. The symbol for the sample variance is s^2, and the population variance is the Greek letter *sigma* squared (σ^2).

$$s^2 = \sum_{i=1}^{n} \frac{(X_i - \bar{X})^2}{n - 1}$$

Standard Deviation

The **standard deviation** is the positive square root of the variance. It is perhaps the most frequently used measure of spread because it improves interpretability by removing the variance's square and expressing deviations in their original units (e.g., net profits in dollars, not dollars squared). Like the mean, the standard deviation is

affected by extreme scores. The symbol for the sample standard deviation is *s,* and a population standard deviation is σ. Alternatively, it is labeled *std. dev.*

$$s = \sqrt{s^2}$$

Range

The **range** is the difference between the largest and smallest score in the distribution. Unlike the standard deviation, it is computed from only the minimum and maximum scores; thus, it is a very rough measure of spread. Using the range as a point of comparison, it is possible to get an idea of the homogeneity (small std. dev.) or heterogeneity (large std. dev.) of the distribution. For homogeneous distributions, the ratio of the range to the standard deviation should be between 2 and 6. A number above 6 would indicate a high degree of heterogeneity. The range provides useful but limited information for all data. It is mandatory for ordinal data.

Interquartile Range

The **interquartile range** (IQR) is the difference between the first and third quartile of the distribution. It is also called the *midspread*. Ordinal or ranked data use this measure in conjunction with the median. It is also used with interval-ratio data when asymmetrical distributions are suspected or for exploratory analysis. Recall the following relationships: the minimum value of the distribution is the 0th percentile, the maximum, the 100th percentile. The first quartile (Q_1) is the 25th percentile; it is also known as the *lower hinge* when used with boxplots. The median, or Q_2, is the 50th percentile. The third quartile (Q_3) is the 75th percentile; it is also known as the *upper hinge*. The IQR is the distance between the hinges.[10]

(continued)

Quartile Deviation

The **quartile deviation,** or semi-interquartile range, is expressed as:

$$Q = \frac{Q_1 - Q_3}{2}$$

The quartile deviation is always used with the median for ordinal data. It is helpful for interval-ratio data of a skewed nature. In a normal distribution, the median plus one quartile deviation (Q) on either side encompasses 50 percent of the observations. Eight Qs cover approximately the range. Q's relationship with the standard deviation is constant (Q = .6745s) when scores are normally distributed.

MEASURES OF SHAPE

The **measures of shape,** *skewness* and *kurtosis,* describe departures from the symmetry of a distribution and its relative flatness (or peakedness), respectively. They are related to statistics known as *moments,* which use deviation scores $(X - \overline{X})$. The variance, for example, is a second power moment. The measures of shape use third and fourth power deviations for their computations and are often difficult to interpret when extreme scores are in the distribution. Generally, shape is best communicated through visual displays.

Skewness

Skewness is a measure of a distribution's deviation from symmetry. In a symmetrical distribution, the mean, median, and mode are in the same location. A distribution that has cases stretching toward one tail or the other is called skewed. As shown in Figure 14–8, when the tail stretches to

the left, to smaller values, it is negatively skewed. Scores stretching toward the right, toward larger values, skew the distribution positively. Note the relationship between the mean, median, and mode in asymmetrical distributions. The symbol for skewness is *sk*.

$$sk = \frac{m_3}{m_2\sqrt{m_2}} = \frac{\Sigma x^3/N}{(\sqrt{\Sigma x^2/N})^3}$$

When a distribution approaches symmetry, *sk* is approximately 0. With a positive skew, *sk* will be a positive number; with negative skew, *sk* will be negative.

Kurtosis

As illustrated in Figure 14–8, **kurtosis** is a measure of a distribution's peakedness (or flatness). Distributions where scores cluster heavily or pile up in the center (along with more observations than normal in the extreme tails) are peaked or *leptokurtic.* Flat distributions with scores more evenly distributed and tails fatter than a normal distribution are called *platykurtic.* Intermediate or *mesokurtic* distributions are neither too peaked nor too flat. The symbol for kurtosis is *ku*.

$$ku = \frac{m_4}{m_2{}^2} - 3 = \frac{\Sigma x^4/N}{(\Sigma x^2/N)^2} - 3$$

The value of *ku* for a normal or mesokurtic distribution is 0. A leptokurtic distribution will have a positive value and the platykurtic will be negative. As with skewness, the larger the absolute value of the index, the more extreme the characteristic.

TABLE 14–2 **A Frequency Table of Market Sector**

Value Label	Value	Frequency	Percent	Valid Percent	Cum. Percent
Chemical and materials	1	10	10.0	10.0	10.0
Consumer products	2	8	8.0	8.0	18.0
Durables/capital equipment	3	7	7.0	7.0	25.0
Energy	4	13	13.0	13.0	38.0
Financial	5	24	24.0	24.0	62.0
Health	6	4	4.0	4.0	66.0
High-tech	7	11	11.0	11.0	77.0
Insurance	8	6	6.0	6.0	83.0
Retailing	9	7	7.0	7.0	90.0
Other	10	10	10.0	10.0	100.0
Total		100	100.0	100.0	

Valid cases   100   Missing cases   0

TECHNIQUES FOR DISPLAYING AND EXAMINING DISTRIBUTIONS[11]

The techniques for displaying data in this section use examples from the Forbes 500s. There were 783 companies that qualified for one of the four Forbes lists. A proportionate stratified sample (n = 100), with the business sector used as the stratification criterion, represents the first data set. The second set of data (N = 50) is the Forbes Super50. From the top ranked firms, Forbes created the Super50 to represent the most powerful corporations in American.[12]

Frequency Tables, Bar Charts, and Pie Charts

Several useful techniques for displaying data are not new to EDA. They are essential to any preliminary examination of the data. For example, a **frequency table** is a simple device for arraying data. An example is presented in Table 14–2. It arrays data from the lowest value to the highest, with columns for percent, percent adjusted for missing values, and cumulative percent. Sector, the nominal variable that describes the business classifications or markets of the sampled corporations, provides the observations for this table. Although there are 100 observations, the small number of categories makes the variable easily tabled. The same data are presented in Figure 14–9 using a bar chart and a pie chart. The values and percentages are more readily understood in this format, and visualization of the sector categories and their relative sizes is improved.

When the variable of interest is measured on an interval-ratio scale, and is one with many potential values, these techniques are not particularly informative. Table 14–3 is a condensed frequency table of net profits in millions of dollars from the Super50. Only one score, 922, has a frequency greater than one. Thus, the primary contribution of this table is an ordered list of values. If the table were

FIGURE   14–9   Nominal Variable Displays

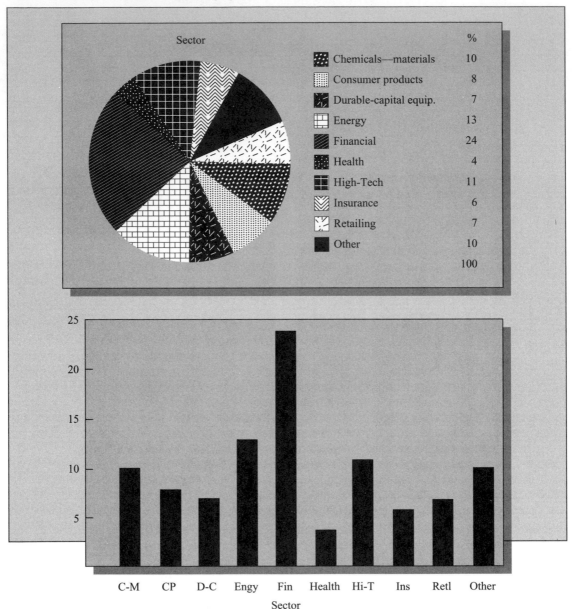

converted to a bar chart, it would have 48 bars of equal length and one bar with two occurrences. And bar charts do not reserve spaces for values where no observations occur within the range. Constructing a pie chart for this variable would also be pointless.

TABLE 14–3   Frequency Table for Net Profits, Forbes Super50 Data (dollars in millions)

Value	Freq.	Pct.	Cum. Pct.	Value	Freq.	Pct.	Cum. Pct.
251.00	1	2	2	1110.70	1	2	54
498.00	1	2	4	1157.00	1	2	56
529.00	1	2	6	1238.20	1	2	58
562.00	1	2	8	1242.00	1	2	60
584.00	1	2	10	1244.00	1	2	62
639.40	1	2	12	1367.50	1	2	64
675.00	1	2	14	1395.00	1	2	66
701.00	1	2	16	1417.30	1	2	68
702.10	1	2	18	1508.50	1	2	70
740.60	1	2	20	1610.00	1	2	72
802.00	1	2	22	1695.00	1	2	74
807.30	1	2	24	1723.80	1	2	76
807.60	1	2	26	1809.00	1	2	78
809.00	1	2	28	1953.00	1	2	80
820.00	1	2	30	2413.00	1	2	82
846.00	1	2	32	2480.00	1	2	84
875.80	1	2	34	2487.00	1	2	86
900.60	1	2	36	2697.00	1	2	88
901.40	1	2	38	2946.00	1	2	90
907.10	1	2	40	2975.00	1	2	92
922.00	2	4	44	3758.00	1	2	94
965.00	1	2	46	3825.00	1	2	96
1074.50	1	2	48	3939.00	1	2	98
1075.90	1	2	50	4224.30	1	2	100
1092.80	1	2	52				
	Valid cases		50		Missing cases		0

Histograms

The histogram is a conventional solution for the display of interval-ratio data. **Histograms** are used when it is possible to group the variable's values into intervals. Histograms are constructed with bars (or asterisks that represent data values) where each value occupies an equal amount of area within the enclosed area. Data analysts find histograms useful for (1) displaying all intervals in a distribution, even those without observed values, and (2) examining the shape of the distribution for skewness, kurtosis, and the modal pattern. When looking at a histogram, one might ask: Is there a single hump (a mode)? Are subgroups identifiable when multiple modes are present? Are straggling data values detached from the central concentration?[13]

The values for net profits in Table 14–3 were measured on a ratio scale and are easily grouped. Other variables possessing an underlying order are similarly appropriate for histograms. A histogram would not be used for a nominal variable like sector (Figure 14–9) that has no order to its categories.

A histogram of net profits from the Super50 is shown in Figure 14–10. The first column, labeled count, lists the number of observations within the interval. The second column records the midpoint of the interval. This histogram was

FIGURE   14–10   Histogram of Net Profits, Forbes Super50 (dollars in millions)

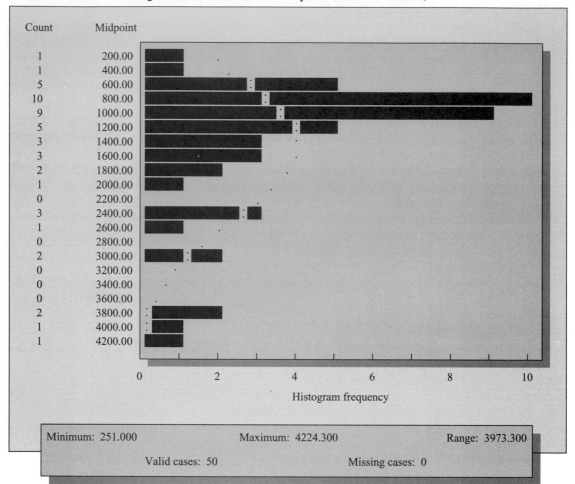

constructed with intervals 200 increments wide, and the first interval contains only one observation, 251. This value is found in the frequency table (Table 14–3). Intervals with 0 counts show gaps in the data and alert the analyst to look for problems with spread. Note that a normal curve was superimposed on the histogram to provide an indication of departures from normality. When the right tail of the distribution is compared with the frequency table, we find four extreme values (3758, 3825, 3939, and 4224.3). Along with the peaked center and reduced number of observations in the left tail, this histogram has warned us of irregularities in the data.

Stem-and-Leaf Displays[14]

The **stem-and-leaf** display is an EDA technique that is closely related to the histogram. It shares some of its features but offers several unique advantages. It is easy to construct by hand for small samples or may be produced by computer programs.

In contrast to histograms, which lose information by grouping data values into intervals, the stem-and-leaf presents actual data values that can be inspected directly without the use of enclosed bars or asterisks as the representation medium. This feature reveals the distribution of values within the interval and preserves their rank order for finding the median, quartiles, and other summary statistics. It also eases linking a specific observation back to the data file and to the subject that produced it.

Visualization is the second advantage of stem-and-leaf displays. The range of values is apparent in a glance, and both shape and spread impressions are immediate. Patterns in the data are easily observed such as gaps where no values exist, areas where values are clustered, or outlying values that differ from the main body of the data.

To construct a simple stem-and-leaf, we will use the net profits data from the high tech sector of the Forbes 500 sample. Table 14–4 lists the data by company.

The creation of a stem-and-leaf follows a few simple steps starting with splitting the observations into a *stem,* the leading digits, and the *leaves,* the trailing digits. The leading digits are written in rank order to the left of a vertical line as shown in Figure 14–11 (A). These form the stems. Data values within the range that might have occurred but are not present are also included. Leaves are then added, dividing each leaf into those trailing digits that will appear in the display and those that will be ignored, as in Figure 14–11 (B). The finished display appears in Part C of the figure.

A column of *depths* to the left of the stem is used to identify the median, quartiles, and other summary values. The depths are determined by counting from each end of the distribution toward the middle and cumulating this count on each line. The middle line of the display in Figure 14–11 (C) *is* the median in this example but may simply *include* the median in other distributions. The middle line has in parentheses the number of leaves on the stem where the median resides. If the distribution has an even number of data points, this notation is omitted.

TABLE 14–4   Data Table for Net Profits, High-Tech Stratum of Forbes 500 Sample (dollars in millions)

Company	Net Profits
Micron Technology	74.0
Cray Research	89.0
Sunstrand	120.8
Automatic Data Processing	196.2
Texas Instruments	291.7
Allied-Signal	528.0
MCI Communications	603.0
Rockwell International	720.7
Hewlett-Packard	809.0
Bell South	1,695.0
AT&T	2,697.0

FIGURE   14–11   Constructing a Stem-and-Leaf Display

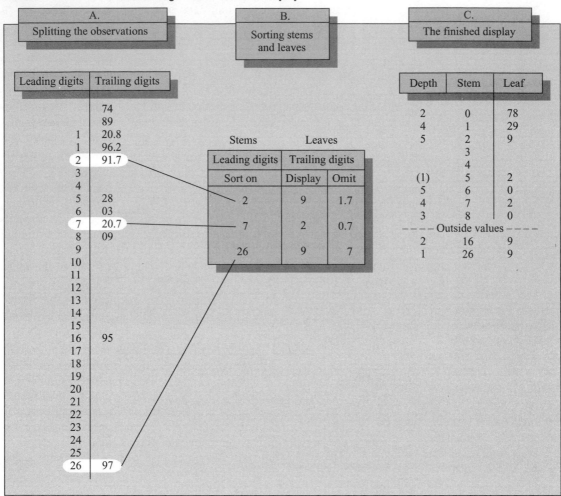

Stem-and-leaf displays are adaptable to a variety of data types that one may encounter. Both expanding or condensing the display may be accomplished based on the detail required by the analyst. Figure 14–11 (C) is a condensed example.

Boxplots[15]

The **boxplot,** or *box-and-whisker plot,* is another technique used frequently in exploratory data analysis.[16] A boxplot reduces the detail of the stem-and-leaf display and provides a different visual image of the distribution's location, spread, shape, tail length, and outliers. Boxplots are extensions of the **five-number summary** of a distribution. This summary consists of the median, upper and lower quartiles, and the largest and smallest observations. The median and quartiles are used because they are particularly **resistant statistics.** Resistance is a characteristic that "provides insensitivity to localized misbehavior in data."[17] Resistant statistics are unaffected by outliers and change only slightly in response to the replacement of small portions of the data set.

Recall the previous discussion of the mean and standard deviation in the Close-Up. Now assume we take the data set {5,6,6,7,7,7,8,8,9}. The mean of the set is 7 and the standard deviation, 1.23. If the 9 is replaced with 90, the mean becomes 16 and the standard deviation increases to 27.78. The mean is now two times larger than most of the numbers in the distribution, and the standard deviation is more than 22 times its original size. By changing only one of nine values, the location and spread summaries have been disturbed to the point where they no longer represent the other eight values. Both the mean and the standard deviation are considered **nonresistant statistics;** they are susceptible to the effects of extreme values in the tails of the distribution and do not represent typical values well under conditions of asymmetry. The standard deviation is particularly problematic because it is computed from the squared deviations from the mean.[18] In contrast, the median and quartiles are highly resistant to change. When we changed the 9 to 90, the median remained at 7 and the lower and upper quartiles stayed at 6 and 8, respectively. Because of the nature of quartiles, up to 25 percent of the data can be made extreme without perturbing the median, the rectangular composition of the plot, or the quartiles themselves. These characteristics of resistance are incorporated into the construction of boxplots.

Boxplots may be constructed easily by hand or by computer programs. The basic ingredients of the plot are the (1) rectangular plot that encompasses 50 percent of the data values, (2) a center line (or other notation) marking the median and going through the width of the box, (3) the edges of the box, called hinges, and (4) the whiskers that extend from the right and left hinges to the largest and smallest values. These values may be found within 1.5 times the interquartile range (IQR) from either edge of the box. These components and their relationships are shown in Figure 14–12.

We can create a boxplot of net profits of the high-tech stratum, from the information provided in Table 14–4. With the five-number summary, we have the basis for a skeletal plot.

Minimum	Lower Hinge	Median	Upper Hinge	Maximum
74	158.5	528	764.85	2679

The plot shown in Figure 14–13 started with these data and the following calculations. Beginning with the box, the ends are drawn using the lower and upper quartiles (hinge) data. The median is drawn in at 528. Then the IQR is calculated $(765 - 159 = 606)$, rounding for the illustration.

From this we can locate the lower and upper fences. The inside fences are -750 and 1674. The lower and upper outside fences are -1659 and 2583. Next, the smallest and largest data values from the distribution within the inner fences

FIGURE   14–12   Boxplot Components

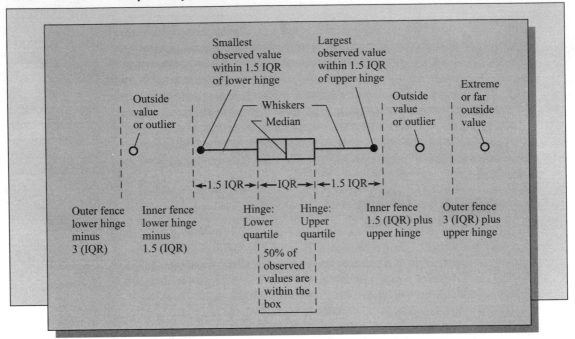

are used to determine the whisker length. These values are 74 and 809. We are now able to see the outliers in relation to the "main body" of the data. **Outliers** are data points that exceed ±1.5 IQRs of a boxplot's hinges. Data values for the outliers are added, and identifiers are provided. The completed boxplot is shown in Figure 14–13.

IQR	Distance to	Inner Fence	
		(−)	(+)
606	* (±1.5) = 909	159 − 909 = −750	1674 = 909 + 765

IQR	Distance to	Outer Fence	
		(−)	(+)
606	*(±3) = 1818	159 − 1818 = −1659	2583 = 1818 + 765

In preliminary analysis, it is important to separate legitimate outliers from errors in measurement, editing, coding, and data entry. Outliers that reflect unusual

**FIGURE   14–13
Boxplot of Net
Profits,
High-Tech
Stratum of
Forbes 500
Sample (dollars
in millions)**

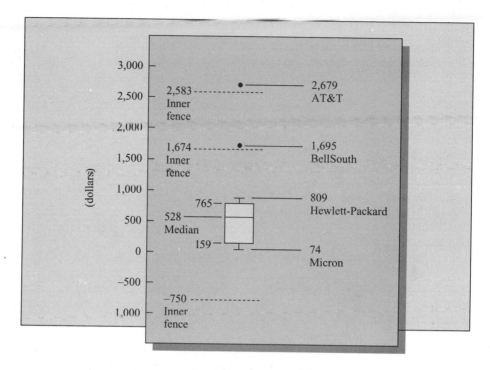

cases are an important source of information for the study. They are displayed, given special statistical treatment, or other portions of the data set are sometimes shielded from their effects. Outliers that are mistakes should be corrected or removed.

Figure 14–14 summarizes several comparisons that are of help to the analyst. Boxplots are an excellent diagnostic tool, especially when graphed on the same scale. The upper two plots in the figure are both symmetric, but one is larger than the other. Larger box widths are sometimes used when the second variable, from the same measurement scale, comes from a larger sample size. The box widths should be proportional to the square root of the sample size, but not all plotting programs account for this.[19] Right and left skewed distributions and those with reduced spread are also presented clearly in the plot comparison. Finally, groups may be compared using multiple plots. One variation, in which a notch at the median marks off a confidence interval to test the equality of group medians, takes us a step closer to hypothesis testing.[20] Here the sides of the box return to full width at the upper and lower confidence intervals. When the intervals do not overlap, we can be confident, at a specified confidence level, that the medians of the two populations are different.

In Figure 14–15, multiple boxplots compare five sectors on the net profits variable. The overall impression is one of potential problems for the analyst: unequal variances, skewness, and extreme outliers. Note the similarities of the profiles of finance and retailing in contrast to high tech and insurance sectors. If hypothesis tests are planned, further examination of this plot for each sector would require a stem-and-leaf display and a five-number summary. From this, we could make

FIGURE   14–14   Diagnostics with Boxplots

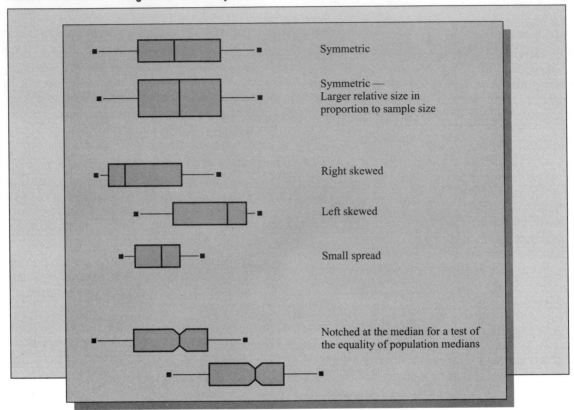

decisions on test selection and whether the data should be transformed or reexpressed before further analysis.

Transformation[21]   Many examples in this section have departed from normality. While this makes for good illustrations, such data pose special problems in preliminary analysis. Transformation is one solution to this problem. **Transformation** is the reexpression of data on a new scale using a single mathematical function for each data point. Although nominal and ordinal data may be transformed, the procedures are beyond the scope of this book. We will consider only interval-ratio scale transformations here.

The fact that data collected on one scale are found to depart from the assumptions of normality and constant variance does not preclude reexpressing them on another scale. What is discovered, of course, must be linked to the original data.

We transform data for several reasons: (1) to improve interpretation and compatibility with other data sets, (2) to enhance symmetry and stabilize spread, and (3) to improve linear relationships between and among variables. We improve interpretation when we find alternate ways to understand the data and discover

FIGURE 14–15
Boxplot Comparison of Sectors on Net Profits

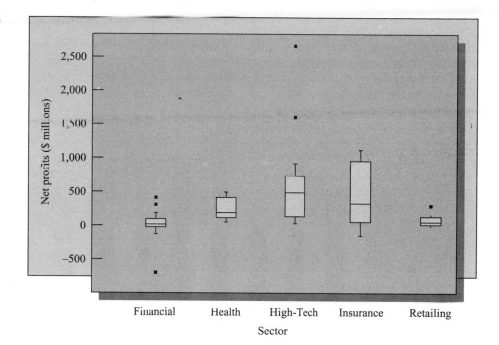

patterns or relationships that may not have been revealed on the original scales. A **standard score,** or Z *score,* may be calculated to improve compatibility among variables that come from different scales and require comparison. Z scores convey distance in standard deviation units with a mean of 0 and a standard deviation of 1. This is accomplished by converting the raw score, X_i, to:

$$Z = \frac{X_i - \overline{X}}{s}$$

Z scores improve interpretation through their reference to the normal curve and our understanding of the areas under it.

Conversion of centimeters to inches, stones to pounds, liters to gallons, or Celsius to Fahrenheit are examples of linear conversions that change the scale but do not change symmetry or spread. Many statisticians consider these data manipulations instead of transformations.

Nonlinear transformations are often needed to satisfy the other two reasons for reexpressing data. Normality and constancy of variance are important assumptions for many parametric statistical techniques. A transformation to reduce skewness and stabilize variance makes it possible to use various confirmatory techniques without violating their assumptions. Analysis of the relationship between variables also benefits from transformation. Improved predictions and better diagnostics of fit and residuals (as in regression analysis) are frequent payoffs.

Transformations are defined with power, *p,* as the reexpression of *x* with x^p.[22] Table 14–5 shows the most frequently used power transformations.

TABLE 14–5   **Frequently Used Power Transformations**

Power	Transformation
3	Cube
2	Square
1	No change: existing data
½	Square root
0	Logarithm (usually Lg_{10})
$-½$	Reciprocal root
-1	Reciprocal
-2	Reciprocal square
-3	Reciprocal cube

We use *spread-and-level* plots to guide our choice of a power transformation. By plotting the log of the median against the log of the interquartile range, we can find the slope of the plot: where *p*, the power we are seeking, is equal to $1 -$ slope. Although ¼ and ⅓ powers often result—and are sometimes preferred, many computer programs require rounding the transformation to the nearest half power.

The asset variable in the Forbes 500 sample illustrates this concept. The data distribution shows a right skew. The five-number summary (data in millions of dollars) reveals an extreme score as the maximum data point:

Minimum	Lower Hinge	Median	Upper Hinge	Maximum
411	1609	3466	7580	107369

The largest observation, 107369, is 17 IQRs beyond the main body of data. There are 12 other values beyond the outer fence.

A quick calculation of the ratio of the largest observation to the smallest (107369/411 = 261.24) serves as the final confirmation that transformation is worthwhile. It is desirable that this informal index is greater than 20; with ratios less than 2, transformation is not practical.[23] From this information, we might conclude that the asset variable is a good candidate for transformation.

The next step is to interpret the computer-generated spread-and-level plot. In Figure 14–16, we have two such plots with sector.[24] The white boxes in the left panel show the slope to be 1.082 and the recommended power (*p* = 1 − slope) is −.082. Consulting Table 14–5, it appears that a logarithmic transformation would be a good choice. Additionally the test for homogeneity of variance across the sector variable was rejected (significance, $p < .05$). This suggests a violation of a statistical requirement that could affect later hypothesis testing. In the right panel of the figure, our transformation has changed the slope and alleviated our concerns about spread (the Levene test for homogeneity of variance was not rejected, $p > .05$). With further trials, we might find a better reexpression. However, the log transformation successfully compressed the larger observations.

FIGURE   14–16   Spread-and-Level Plots: Before and After Transformation

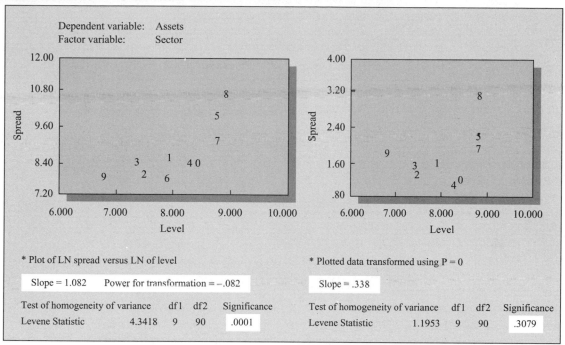

Dependent variable: Assets
Factor variable: Sector

* Plot of LN spread versus LN of level

| Slope = 1.082 | Power for transformation = −.082 |

Test of homogeneity of variance	df1	df2	Significance
Levene Statistic	4.3418	9	90	.0001

* Plotted data transformed using P = 0

| Slope = .338 |

Test of homogeneity of variance	df1	df2	Significance
Levene Statistic	1.1953	9	90	.3079

For researchers who communicate their findings to management, the advantages of reexpression must be balanced against practical considerations. Some transformed scales have no familiar analogies. Logarithmic dollars can be explained, but how about reciprocal root dollars? Attitude and preference scales might be better understood transformed, but the question of interpretation remains.

Throughout this section we have exploited the visual techniques of exploratory data analysis to look beyond numerical summaries and gain insight into the behavior of the data. Few of the approaches have stressed the need for advanced mathematics, and all have an intuitive appeal for the analyst. When the more common ways of summarizing location, spread, and shape have conveyed an inadequate picture of the data, we have used more resistant statistics to protect us from the effects of extreme scores and occasional errors. We have also emphasized the value of transforming the original scale of the data during preliminary analysis rather than at the point of hypothesis testing. The final topic of EDA, residual analysis, we have left for a later section.

CROSSTABULATION

The last section focused primarily on single variable distributions where observations were collected on interval-ratio scales. Frequency tables were introduced for tabulating counts or percentages, and exploratory data analysis techniques were

TABLE 14–6   Sample SPSS Crosstabulation of Gender by Overseas Assignment Opportunity

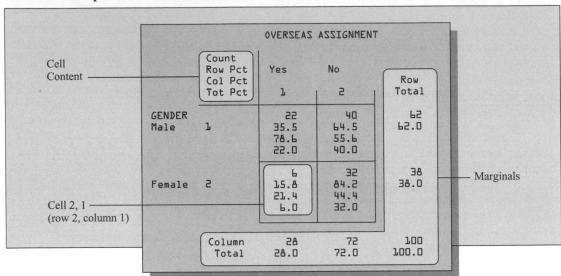

recommended for graphical display and examination of distributions. Many studies would be content to conclude data analysis at this point. Other studies, particularly those with variables composed of category data (frequency counts of nominally scaled variables), may need to inspect the relationships between and among those variables. This analysis is commonly done with crosstabulation.

Crosstabulation is a technique for comparing two classification variables, such as gender and selection by one's company for an overseas assignment. The technique uses tables having rows and columns that correspond to the levels or values of each variable's categories. Table 14–6 is an example of a computer-generated crosstabulation. This table has two rows for gender and two columns for assignment selection. The combination of the variables with their values produces four **cells.** Each cell contains a count of the cases of the joint classification and also the row, column, and total percentages. The number of row cells and column cells is often used to designate the size of the table, as in this 2 × 2 table. The cells are individually identified by their row and column numbers, as illustrated. Row and column totals, called **marginals,** appear at the bottom and right "margins" of the table. They show the counts and percentages of the separate rows and columns.

When tables are constructed for statistical testing, we call them **contingency tables,** and the test determines if the classification variables are independent. Of course, tables may be larger than 2 × 2.

The Use of Percentages

Percentages serve two purposes in data presentation. They simplify by reducing all numbers to a range from 0 to 100. Second, they translate the data into standard

TABLE 14–7   Comparison of Percentages in Crosstabulation Studies of Gender by Overseas Assignment

			Study 1						Study 2		
			OVERSEAS ASSIGNMENT						OVERSEAS ASSIGNMENT		
	Count Row Pct Col Pct Tot Pct		Yes 1	No 2	Row Total		Count Row Pct Col Pct Tot Pct		Yes 1	No 2	Row Total
GENDER Male	1		22 35.5 78.6 22.0	40 64.5 55.6 40.0	62 62.0	GENDER Male	1		225 25.0 62.5 15.0	675 75.0 59.2 45.0	900 60.0
Female	2		6 15.8 21.4 6.0	32 84.2 44.4 32.0	38 38.0	Female	2		135 22.5 37.5 9.0	465 77.5 40.8 31.0	600 40.0
	Column Total		28 28.0	72 72.0	100 100.0		Column Total		360 24.0	1140 76.0	1500 100.0

form, with a base of 100, for relative comparisons. In a sampling situation, the number of cases that fall into a category is meaningless unless it is related to some base. A count of 28 overseas assignees has little meaning unless we know it is from a sample of 100. Using the latter as a base, we conclude that 28 percent of this study's sample has an overseas assignment.

While the above is useful, it is even more useful when the research problem calls for a comparison of several distributions of data. Assume the previously reported data was collected five years ago and the present study had a sample of 1,500, of which 360 were selected for overseas assignments. By using percentages, we can see the relative relationships and shifts in the data (see Table 14–7).

With two-dimension tables, the selection of a row or column will accentuate a particular distribution or comparison. This raises the question about which direction the percentages should be calculated. Most computer programs offer options for presenting percentages in both directions and interchanging the rows and columns of the table. But in situations when one variable is hypothesized to be the presumed cause, is thought to effect or predict a response, or is simply antecedent to the other variable, we label it the independent variable. Percentages should then be computed in the direction of this variable. Thus, if the independent variable is placed on the row, select row percentages; if it is on the column, select column percentages.[25] In which direction should the percentages run in the previous example? If only the column percentages are reported, we imply that assignment status has some effect on gender. This is implausible. When percentages are reported by rows, the implication is that gender influences selection for overseas assignments.

Care should be taken in interpreting percentages from tables. Consider again the data in Table 14–7. From the first to the second study, it is apparent that the percentage of females selected for overseas assignment rose from 6 to 9 percent of their respective samples. This is not to be confused with the percentage of women in the samples who happen to be assignees. Among all *women* eligible for selection in the first study, 15.8 percent were assigned and 84.2 percent were not. Among all *overseas selectees* in the first study, 21.4 percent were women. Similar comparisons can be made for the other categories.

Percentages are used by virtually everyone dealing with numbers and often incorrectly. The following guidelines, if used during analysis, will prevent errors in reporting.[26]

1. *Averaging percentages.* Percentages cannot be averaged unless each is weighted by the size of the group from which it is derived. Thus, a simple average will not suffice, and it is necessary to use a weighted average.

2. *Use of too large percentages.* This often defeats the purpose of percentages—to simplify. A large percentage is difficult to understand and is confusing. If a 1,000 percent increase is experienced, it is better to describe this as a tenfold increase.

3. *Using too small a base.* Percentages hide the base from which they have been computed. A figure of 60 percent when contrasted with 30 percent would appear to suggest a sizable difference. Yet if there are only three cases in the one category and six in the other, the differences would not be as significant as they have been made to appear with percentages.

4. *Percentage decreases can never exceed 100 percent.* This is obvious, but this type of mistake occurs frequently. The higher figure should always be used as the base. For example, if a price was reduced from $1.00 to $.25 the decrease would be 75 percent (75/100).

Elaboration and Control Variables

The recognition of a meaningful relationship between variables generally signals a need for further investigation into the circumstances. Even if one finds a statistically significant relationship, the questions of why and under what conditions remain. The introduction of a third variable to interpret the relationship is often necessary. This is called **elaboration analysis.** A **control variable,** or *test factor,* is an additional variable that is simultaneously evaluated with the original relationship. Contingency tables serve as the framework for elaboration analysis. Elaboration analysis provides the student with a good example of the scientific reasoning process discussed in Chapter 2. The tables in this section use percentages and do not test relationships statistically.

In an earlier chapter, we introduced the example of the manufacturing facility with high absenteeism on Mondays. Observation suggested that many workers who were absent frequently on Mondays were also members of a camping club. Table 14–8 shows the club membership and the Monday absentee pattern. Percentages

TABLE 14–8   Club Membership and Levels of Monday Absenteeism (percent)*

	Club Member?	
Absentee Status	*Yes*	*No*
High	40%	20%
Low	60	80
Total	100%	100%
n =	(60)	(300)

*Data hypothetical.

TABLE 14–9   Club Membership and Levels of Absenteeism by Age of Employee (percent)*

Absentee Status	Young		Old	
	Club Member	*Not a Club Member*	*Club Member*	*Not a Club Member*
High	48%	46%	14%	15%
Low	52	54	86	85
Total	100%	100%	100%	100%
n =	(46)	(50)	(14)	(250)

*Data hypothetical.

are calculated in the likely direction of influence. While one might conclude that club membership is the probable cause of absenteeism, recall our previous discussion of causality and consider other relationships that might be operating.

Our search for other explanations begins in Table 14–9. Here we have introduced a control variable, the age of employees, as a third variable. Club membership and absenteeism are being examined while controlling for or holding constant age. Obviously, age is not literally being held constant, but what is being shown is how the absenteeism-club membership relationship is affected when two distinct age groups are accounted for. Through this elaboration, we investigate the contingent relationships between (1) age and club membership, (2) age and absenteeism, and (3) club membership and absenteeism. We find that there are associations between all three. First, persons classified as "young" are more likely to be club members than are "old" workers. Second, there is clearly a much higher rate of absenteeism among young workers than older ones. Third, as shown in Table 14–8, club members have higher absenteeism rates than do nonclub members. The elaboration shows, however, that inserting age virtually eliminates the effect of club membership on absenteeism. The original club-absenteeism relationship resulted from the higher concentration of young workers in the club rather than from the effect of membership itself.

TABLE 14–10   Levels of Absenteeism and Age of Worker by Worker Skill Level (Percent)

	Unskilled		Skilled	
Absentee Status	*Young*	*Old*	*Young*	*Old*
High	47%	16%	46%	14%
Low	53	84	54	86
Total	100%	100%	100%	100%
n =	(59)	(104)	(37)	(160)

When one analyzes associations through elaboration, there are different ways to logically relate the third variable with the original two. We will review the situations under which the control variable may be considered extraneous, component, intervening, suppressor, or distorter. We will also note briefly the role of conditional relationships.[27]

Extraneous Variables   One may stratify on some third factor and find that the original relationship between two variables disappears. This is evidence that the original *IV-DV* association is a spurious one. For example, in Table 14–9, club membership is *not* an important factor for explaining absenteeism among the workers. Thus, a highly plausible interpretation is misleading.

On the other hand, this process can be used to provide evidence that dubious interpretations are sound. That is, if the introduction of the third variable does not affect the original relationship, then there would be some support for the original relationship. This point is illustrated in Table 14–10 in which the newfound relationship between absenteeism and age is analyzed further by adding a test factor of job skill. This analysis suggests that the absenteeism-age relationship holds up; the skill variable is largely extraneous. Each time a relevant third variable is introduced and the relationship remains, the more confidence one can have in the relationship between age and absenteeism.

Component Variables   In business research, propositions may be true, but the *IV* is so global as to offer little real insight. If we break the *IV* down into its components, we may understand more about the relationship. For example, we might find that blue-collar and white-collar workers react differently to a training exercise. This is less enlightening than to discover that the difference is due more to specific work culture differences between the two groups. Similarly, it is one thing to find that expenditures for wine vary among families at different stages in the family life cycle, but it is more revealing if we can find the component within the family life cycle that controls the expenditure.

To illustrate the nature of the component variable, consider the assumption that successful salespeople have a certain type of personality. To test this hypothesis,

TABLE 14–11   Personality and Sales Success (percent)*

| Sales Success | (A) Personality Test Scores | | (B) Empathy Test | | | |
| | | | High | | Low | |
	High	Low	High	Low	High	Low
Yes	60%	30%	68%	55%	32%	23%
No	40	70	32	45	68	77
Total	100%	100%	100%	100%	100%	100%
n =	(100)	(100)	(78)	(22)	(22)	(78)

*Data hypothetical.

personality tests are given to 200 newly hired salespeople. After some time, we learn which people have been successful and which have not. Then we cross-classify them by their total scores on the personality tests. We may secure results like those found in Part A of Table 14–11. These hypothetical data suggest that scores on the personality battery are helpful predictors. On the other hand, such a global variable tells us little about the specific personality factors that may be operating.

The hypothesis has also been advanced, however, that successful salespeople generally have a high empathy for others. One can test this by using the empathy component of the general personality test, securing the relationships shown in Part B of Table 14–11. This shows that the empathy component of the test battery is an important contributor to the ability to predict which salespeople will be successful.

Intervening Variables   When one attempts to infer cause in social phenomena, an ongoing stream of events proceed serially, and in some complexity, from presumed causes to presumed effects. In such a chain of connections, there is the chance that the original independent variable affects the dependent variable through some intervening factor. Thus, B is a consequence of A and a determinant of C.

To illustrate the nature of this intervention, again consider the case in which younger workers show a much higher absenteeism rate than do older workers. However, it is hard to imagine that age causes absenteeism. There must be something in the relationship that we have yet to see. Much has been made in recent years of the decline of the "work ethic" in society. We surmise that many younger people do not accept this ethic. Therefore, we might hypothesize that the higher absenteeism from younger workers results from their greater rejection of the work ethic.

Change in workers' age → Change in work ethic → Change in absenteeism

TABLE 14-12   **Worker Age and Absenteeism by Work Ethic Attitude (percent)***

Absentee Status	Reject Work Ethic		Accept Work Ethic	
	Young	Old	Young	Old
High	96%	71%	13%	3%
Low	4	29	87	97
Total	100%	100%	100%	100%
n =	(70)	(35)	(15)	(240)

*Data hypothetical.

TABLE 14-13   **Shopper Income Class and Use of Unit Pricing Information by Shopper Education Level (percent)***

Use of Unit Price Information	(A) Income Class		(B)			
			High Education		Low Education	
	Middle Income	Lower Income	Middle Income	Low Income	Middle Income	Low Income
High	30%	30%	34%	50%	18%	23%
Low	70	70	66	50	82	77
Total	100%	100%	100%	100%	100%	100%
n =	(200)	(200)	(150)	(50)	(50)	(150)

*Data hypothetical.

We administer a scale to the workers that measures their attitudes toward work and find the relationships shown in Table 14–12.

Suppressor Variables   When these variables are operative, there is no relationship between two variables while logic suggests there should be one. You may be misled into thinking that an absence of correlation is true when actually the *IV-DV* relationship is blocked out or dampened by the suppressor variable. For example, you might expect that shoppers from lower income families would be more responsive than middle-class shoppers to the introduction of unit pricing in grocery stores. Suppose that you conduct a study and find little difference between lower income and middle-income families in their response to unit pricing (Part A of Table 14–13). You hypothesize that the expected higher responsiveness of lower income families has been suppressed in the statistics because the better educated would respond more to unit pricing, but it is the poorly educated who are concentrated in the lower income group. This revised hypothesis is tested in Part B of Table 14–13. The results show that the lower

Tᴀʙʟᴇ 14–14   **Bank Use and Home-Bank Distance by Distance of Competition (percent)***

Have Account?	(A)		(B) Competition is Farther		Competition is Closer	
	0–1 Miles	*1 + Mile*	*0–1 Miles*	*1 + Miles*	*0–1 Miles*	*1 + Miles*
Yes	35%	40%	60%	52%	27%	22%
No	65	60	40	48	73	73
Total	100%	100%	100%	100%	100%	100%
n =	(200)	(200)	(50)	(120)	(150)	(80)

*Data hypothetical.

income shopper does respond more than the middle-income shopper to unit pricing when education level is held constant.

Distorter Variables   Distorter variables are those that, when accounted for, reveal the correct interpretation is the reverse of that suggested by the original data. It is often argued that families typically use the bank closest to their home. Suppose we conduct a study of 400 households; 200 of which are located within a mile of our client bank, while the other 200 are located more than a mile from the bank. The results show something unusual. It seems that a higher percentage of the more distant families are customers of the bank than are the near-by families. These results are shown in Part A of Table 14–14. Since this does not seem reasonable, we look for further information that might explain this anomaly. A third variable, the comparison of the distance from the family's home to the nearest competing bank, is introduced. Then each family is classi-fied by whether the competing bank is closer or more distant to the family's home than is our bank. The results of this analysis, shown in Part B of Table 14–14, imply that the correct interpretation is the opposite of the original. After adjusting for the nearness of the competing bank, we find that the closer a family's home is to the bank, the more likely the family is to have an account with that bank.

Conditional Relationships   In the elaboration examples used to this point, the intro-duction of a test factor has generally affected various subgroups in approximately the same way. It may be, however, that the impact of the test factor affects one subgroup more than another. These are **conditional relationships** and represent a situation where we wish to specify the conditions under which the original rela-tionship is strengthened or weakened. Assume in the absenteeism study, we used a test variable of worker seniority (rather than age) along with the original club membership-absenteeism relationship. This is illustrated in Table 14–15 on the fol-lowing page and suggests that seniority is an important factor in explaining absen-teeism. However, there is an interaction between seniority and club membership

TABLE 14–15   Club Membership and Levels of Absenteeism by Seniority (percent)

Absentee Status	Less than 3 Years' Seniority		3 Years or More Seniority	
	Club Member	Not a Club Member	Club Member	Not a Club Member
High	51%	35%	7%	17%
Low	49	65	93	83
Total	100%	100%	100%	100%
n =	(45)	(150)	(15)	(249)

and their effects on absenteeism. With low seniority employees, club membership appears to stimulate added absenteeism. Among more senior employees, just the opposite occurs.

In summary, the introduction of test factors can make two contributions. Elaboration may keep us from being misled; we may accept a hypothesis that is false, and we may reject a hypothesis that is true. When we consider extraneous variables, we help avert the acceptance of a false hypothesis. Use of a suppressor variable analysis helps avoid the rejection of hypotheses that are true while the use of distorter variable analysis helps us avoid both cases.

The second contribution is a more precise and specific understanding of a two-variable relationship. By using component variables, we can find out what aspect of a general variable is critical to the relationship. The use of an intervening variable may give a more precise understanding of the temporal and logical process of movement from *IV* to *DV;* the use of an antecedent variable may allow an extension of the causal sequence.

Computer-Generated Tables

Elaboration can be a cumbersome and time-consuming process. However, statistical packages like BMDP, Minitab, SAS, SPSS, and SYSTAT have among their programs many options for the construction of *n*-way tables with provision for multiple control variables.

Now suppose you are interested in creating a crosstabulation of two variables with one control. Whatever the number of values in the primary variables, the control variable with five values determines the number of tables. For some applications, it is appropriate to have five separate tables, and for others, it might be preferable to have adjoining tables or have the values of all the variables in one. Management reports are of the latter variety. Table 14–16 presents an example in which all three variables are handled under the same banner. Programs such as this one can handle far more complex tables and statistical information.[28]

An advanced variation on elaboration analysis is **automatic interaction detection** (AID). AID is a sequential partitioning procedure that begins with a dependent variable and a set of predictors. It searches among up to 300 variables for the

TABLE 14–16   SPSS Crosstabulation with Control and Nested Variables

	Control variable					
	category 1			category 2		
	Nested variable			Nested variable		
	cat 1	cat 2	cat 3	cat 1	cat 2	cat 3
Stub...	Cells...					

	SEX OF EMPLOYEE			
	MALES		FEMALES	
	MINORITY CLASSIFICATION		MINORITY CLASSIFICATION	
	WHITE	NONWHITE	WHITE	NONWHITE
EMPLOYMENT CATEGORY				
CLERICAL	16%	7%	18%	7%
OFFICE TRAINEE	7%	3%	17%	2%
SECURITY OFFICER	3%	3%		
COLLEGE TRAINEE	7%	0%	1%	
EXEMPT EMPLOYEE	6%	0%	0%	
MBA TRAINEE	1%	0%	0%	
TECHNICAL	1%			

best single division according to each predictor variable, chooses one, and splits the sample into two subgroups to maximize the reduction in the unexplained sum of squares of the dependent variable. These two subgroups then become two separate samples for further analysis. The search procedure is repeated to find the variable that, when split into two parts, makes the next largest contribution to the reduction of unexplained variation in each subsample, and so on.

Figure 14–17 illustrates the analysis tree that resulted from an AID study of the do-it-yourself activities of families.[29] The initial dependent variable is the annual hours spent in home production by heads of families and wives. The illustration shows that the best binary split was between married couples and single persons. The latter spent substantially less time in do-it-yourself activities. The married couples sample was then analyzed against the remaining variables, and the best binary split for reducing unexplained variance was the type of family dwelling. Further analysis indicated larger families, with more education, who lived in rural areas and whose youngest child was between two and eight years of age, were the most active do-it-yourselfers, with an average of 1,168 hours per year per family.

FIGURE   14–17   **Automatic Interaction Detection Example (hours of home production by heads of families and wives)***

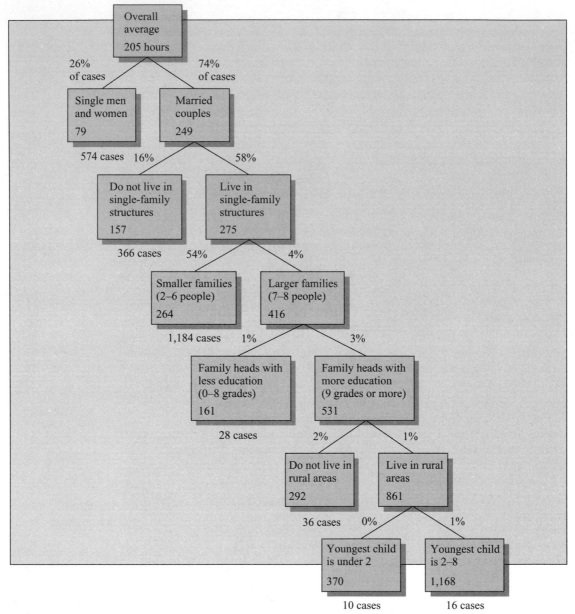

*Home production is unpaid other than housework minus volunteer work, courses, and lessons (data for 2,214 families).

Summary

The first step in data preparation is to edit the collected raw data to detect errors and omissions and to assure quality standards. The editor is responsible for making the data accurate, consistent with other data, uniformly entered, and ready for coding. In survey work, it is common to use both field and central editing.

Coding is the process of assigning numbers and other symbols to answers so we can classify the responses into categories. Categories should be appropriate to the research problem, exhaustive of the data, mutually exclusive, and unidimensional. The reduction of information through coding requires the researcher to design category sets carefully using as much of the data as possible. Codebooks are guides to reduce data entry error and serve as a compendium of variable locations and other information for the analysis stage.

Closed questions include scaled items and other items for which answers are anticipated. Precoding of closed items avoids tedious completion of coding sheets for each response. Open-question coding is more difficult since answers are not prepared in advance, but it does encourage disclosure of complete information. A systematic method to analyze open questions is called content analysis. It uses pre-selected sampling units to produce frequency counts and other insights on data patterns.

"Don't know" replies are evaluated in the light of the question's nature and the respondent. While many DKs are legitimate, some result from questions that are ambiguous or from an interviewing situation that is not motivating. It is better to report DKs as a separate category unless there are compelling reasons to treat them otherwise.

Data entry is accomplished by keyboard entry from precoded instruments, optical scanning, real-time keyboarding, telephone pad data entry, bar codes, voice recognition, and data transfers from electronic notebooks and laptop computers. Full-screen editors, database programs, spreadsheets, and editors in statistical software programs offer flexibility for entering, manipulating, and transferring data.

The objective of preliminary data analysis is to learn as much as possible about the data. Exploratory data analysis (EDA) simplifies this goal by providing a perspective and set of tools to search for clues and patterns. EDA augments rather than supplants traditional statistics. Beyond the numerical summaries of location, spread, and shape, EDA uses visual displays to provide a complete and accurate impression of distributions and variable relationships.

Frequency tables array data from highest to lowest values with counts and percentages. They are most useful for inspecting the range of responses and their repeated occurrence. Bar charts and pie charts are appropriate for relative comparisons of nominal data, while histograms are optimally used with continuous variables where intervals group the responses.

Stem-and-leaf displays and boxplots are EDA techniques that provide visual representations of distributions. The former present actual data values using a histogram-type device that allows inspection of spread and shape. Boxplots use the five-number summary to convey a detailed picture distribution's main body, tails, and outliers. Both rely on resistant statistics to overcome the limitations of descriptive measures that are subject to extreme scores. Transformation may be necessary to reexpress metric data to reduce or remove problems of asymmetry, inequality of variance, or other abnormalities.

Preliminary evaluation of relationships involving nominally scaled variables employs crosstabulation. The tables used for this purpose consist of cells and marginals. The cells contain combinations of count, row, column, and total percentages. The tabular structure is the framework for later statistical testing.

An elaboration model adds one or more control variables to the basic two-variable relationship. This third variable may be related to the primary relationship as extraneous, component, intervening, suppressor, or distorter influences.

Computer software for all types of cross-classification analysis is available.

Key Terms

automatic interaction detection
boxplot
cells
central tendency
codebook
coding
conditional relationships
confirmatory data analysis
content analysis
contingency tables
control variables
   component
   distorter
   extraneous
   intervening
   suppressor
crosstabulation
data entry
   bar code
   database
   optical scanning
   spreadsheet
   voice recognition
data fields
data files
descriptive statistics
distribution
DK (don't know) response

editing
elaboration analysis
exploratory data analysis
five-number summary
frequency table
histogram
marginal
measures of location
   mean
   median
   mode
measures of shape
   kurtosis
   skewness
measures of spread
   interquartile range
   quartile deviation
   range
   standard deviation
   variance
outliers
precoding
record
resistant statistics (nonresistant)
standard normal distribution
standard scores (Z scores)
stem-and-leaf display
transformation
variability

Discussion Questions

1. Define or explain:
   a. Coding rules.
   b. Spreadsheet data entry.
   c. Control or test variables in elaboration.
   d. Alphanumeric variables.
   e. Precoded instruments.
   f. Nonresistant statistics.
   g. Measures of shape.
   h. The five-number summary.
   i. Notched boxplots.
   j. Spread-and-level plots.

2. How should one handle "don't know" responses?

3. A problem facing the shoe store manager is that many shoes must eventually be sold at markdown prices. This prompts us to conduct a mail survey of shoe store managements in which we ask, "What methods have you found most successful for reducing the high markdowns problem?" We are interested in extracting as much information as possible from these answers to better understand the full range of strategies that store managements use. Establish what you think are category sets to code 500 responses similar to the 14 below. Try to develop an integrated set of classifications that reflects your theory of markdown management. After developing the set, use it to code the 14 responses.

   a. Have not found the answer. As long as we buy style shoes, we will have markdowns. We use PMs on slow merchandise, but it does not eliminate markdowns. (PM is "push-money"—special item bonuses for selling a particular style of shoe.)
   b. Using PMs before too old. Also reducing price during season. Holding meetings with salespeople indicating which shoes to push.
   c. By putting PMs on any slow-selling items and promoting same. More careful check of shoes purchased.
   d. Keep a close watch on your stock and markdown when you have to; that is, rather than wait, take a small markdown on a shoe that is not moving at the time.
   e. Using the PM method.
   f. Less advance buying—more dependence on in-stock shoes.
   g. Sales—catch bad guys before it's too late and close out.
   h. Buy as much good merchandise as you can at special prices to help make up some markdowns.
   i. Reducing opening buys and depending on fill-in service. PMs for salespeople.
   j. Buy more frequently, better buying, PM on slow-moving merchandise.
   k. Careful buying at lowest prices. Cash on the buying line. Buying closeouts. FDs (FD—factory discontinued style), overstock, "cancellations."
   l. By buying less "chanceable" shoes. Buy only what you need, watch sizes, don't go overboard on new fads.

    m. Buying more staple merchandise. Buying more from fewer lines. Sticking with better nationally advertised merchandise.

    n. No successful method with the current style situation. Manufacturers are experimenting, the retailer takes the markdowns—cuts gross profit by about 3 percent—keep your stock at lowest level without losing sales.

4. How do the following detect errors in the data?
    a. Histogram.
    b. Stem-and-leaf display.
    c. Boxplot.
    d. Crosstabulation.

5. Use the data in Table 14–3 to construct a stem-and-leaf display.
    a. Where do you find the main body of the distribution?
    b. How many values reside outside the inner fence(s)?

6. Select the sales variable from the accompanying table.
    a. Create a five-number summary.
    b. Construct a boxplot.
    c. Interpret your results in terms of summary measures.

Data Table for Discussion Questions 6–8

	Market Value	Sales	Sector		Market Value	Sales	Sector
1	24983.00	8966.00	2	26	9009.00	17533.00	4
2	31307.00	126932.00	3	27	7842.00	11113.00	2
3	57193.00	54574.00	7	28	5431.00	19671.00	8
4	57676.00	86656.00	4	29	5811.00	11389.00	5
5	60345.00	62710.00	7	30	16257.00	15242.00	2
6	22190.00	96146.00	3	31	16247.00	10211.00	7
7	36566.00	39011.00	2	32	18548.00	9593.00	7
8	44646.00	36112.00	7	33	13620.00	9691.00	7
9	25022.00	50220.00	4	34	10750.00	12844.00	3
10	26043.00	25099.00	1	35	12450.00	18398.00	2
11	13152.00	53794.00	2	36	16729.00	20276.00	7
12	11234.00	25047.00	5	37	16532.00	8730.00	7
13	26666.00	23966.00	4	38	5111.00	17635.00	10
14	20747.00	17424.00	7	39	9116.00	8588.00	4
15	25826.00	13996.00	7	40	26325.00	25922.00	2
16	15423.00	32416.00	4	41	8249.00	16103.00	2
17	15263.00	14150.00	8	42	8407.00	14083.00	3
18	18146.00	17600.00	1	43	18537.00	11990.00	10
19	18739.00	15351.00	4	44	23866.00	29443.00	4
20	23272.00	22605.00	2	45	6872.00	19532.00	7
21	7875.00	37970.00	5	46	4319.00	10018.00	5
22	8122.00	11557.00	5	47	9505.00	12937.00	7
23	18072.00	11449.00	7	48	3891.00	15654.00	8
24	6404.00	20054.00	8	49	8090.00	7492.00	4
25	16056.00	13211.00	7	50	11119.00	12345.00	7

7. Select the market value variable from the data table and construct a histogram with available software.
    a. What is the gain in information with 5,000-, 2,000-, or 1,000-unit intervals?
    b. Which would be the best interval to convey results to management?
    c. Why would this data need reexpression?
    d. What is the optimal power transformation for this data?

8. Recode the sales variable from the data table into five or fewer categories and crosstabulate it with five sectors that you select (sectors are coded 1–10 and rank ordered in Figure 14–9). Display your findings with counts and percentages.

9. Define a small sample of class members, work associates, or friends and ask them to answer the following in a paragraph or two: "What are your career aspirations for the next five years?" Use one of the four basic units of content analysis to analyze their responses. Describe your findings as frequencies for the unit of analysis selected.

10. Suppose you were preparing two-way tables of percentages for the following pairs of variables. How would you run the percentages?
    a. Age and consumption of breakfast cereal.
    b. Family income and confidence about the family's future.
    c. Marital status and sports participation.
    d. Crime rate and unemployment rate.

11. You study the attrition between the students who enter college as freshmen and those who stay to graduate. You find the following relationships between attrition, aid, and distance of home from school.

	Aid		Home Near Aid		Home Far Aid	
	Yes	*No*	*Yes*	*No*	*Yes*	*No*
Drop out	25%	20%	5%	15%	30%	40%
Stay	75	80	95	85	70	60

What is your interpretation? (In your interpretation, consider all variables and relationships.)

12. A local health agency is experimenting with two appeal letters, A and B, by which to raise funds. It sends out 400 of the A appeal and 400 of the B appeal (divided equally among working class and middle-class neighborhoods). The agency secures the following results:

	Appeal A		Appeal B	
	Middle Class	*Working Class*	*Middle Class*	*Working Class*
Contribution	20%	40%	15%	30%
No contribution	80	60	85	70
	100	100	100	100

> *a.* Which appeal is the best?
> *b.* Which class responded better?
> *c.* Is appeal or social class a more powerful independent variable?

13. Assume you have collected data on employees of a large corporation in a major metropolitan area. You analyze the data by type of work classification, education level, and whether the workers were reared in a rural or urban setting. The results are as shown below. How would you interpret them?

Annual Employee Turnover per 100 Employees

	Part A		Part B			
			High Education		Low Education	
	Salaried	*Wage*	*Salaried*	*Wage*	*Salaried*	*Wage*
Rural	8	16	6	14	18	18
Urban	12	16	10	12	19	20

Reference Notes

1. Jean M. Converse and Stanley Presser, *Survey Questions: Handcrafting the Standardized Questionnaire* (Beverly Hills, Calif.: Sage Publications, 1986), pp. 34–35.
2. B. Berelson, *Content Analysis in Communication Research* (New York: Free Press, 1952), p. 18.
3. Klaus Krippendorff, *Content Analysis: An Introduction to Its Methodology* (Beverly Hills, Calif.: Sage Publications, 1980), p. 22.
4. Hans Zeisel, *Say It with Figures,* 6th ed. (New York: Harper & Row, 1985), pp. 48–49.
5. John W. Tukey, *Exploratory Data Analysis* (Reading, Mass.: Addison-Wesley Publishing, 1977).
6. David C. Hoaglin, Frederick Mosteller, and John W. Tukey, eds., *Understanding Robust and Exploratory Data Analysis* (New York: John Wiley & Sons, 1983), p. 2.
7. Tukey, *Exploratory Data Analysis,* pp. 2–3.
8. Frederick Hartwig with Brian E. Dearing, *Exploratory Data Analysis* (Beverly Hills, Calif.: Sage Publications, 1979), pp. 9–12.
9. Ibid., p. 15.
10. Different definitions of quartiles are based on variations in their calculation. We use

Q_1, 25th percentile, and the lower hinge synonymously, and Q_3, 75th percentile, and the upper hinge, similarly. There are technical differences, although they do not make much of a difference in this context.

11. The figures and tables in this section were created with statistical and graphic programs whose modules or subroutines are particularly suited to exploratory data analysis. The authors gratefully acknowledge the following vendors for evaluation and use of their products:

    SPSS Inc.
    444 N. Michigan Ave.
    Chicago, IL 60611

    SPSS® Base System Syntax Reference Guide, Release 6.0 (Chicago: SPSS Inc., 1993). *SPSS® for Windows™, CHAID™, Release 6.0,* Jay Magidson/SPSS Inc. (Chicago: SPSS Inc., 1993). *SPSS® for Windows, Base System User's Guide, Release 6.0,* Marija J. Norusis/SPSS Inc. (Chicago: SPSS Inc., 1993).

    Data Desk 4.0®
    Data Description
    P.O. Box 4555
    Ithaca, NY 14852

    Paul F. Velleman, *Data Desk⁴® Handbook; Statistics Guide,* 2 vols. (Ithaca, N.Y.: Data Description, 1992).

    SYSTAT® for the Macintosh, Version 5.2
    SYSTAT Inc.
    1800 Sherman Ave.
    Evanston, IL 60201

    Leland Wilkinson, Mary Ann Hill, and Erin Vang, *Statistics; Graphics; Data; Version 5.2 Editions* (Evanston, Il.: SYSTAT, Inc., 1992).

12. "The Forbes 500s Annual Directory," *Forbes,* April 30, 1990, pp. 221–434.
13. Paul F. Velleman and David C. Hoaglin, *Applications, Basics, and Computing of Exploratory Data Analysis* (Boston: Duxbury Press, 1981), p. 13.
14. This section is based on John D. Emerson and David C. Hoaglin, "Stem-and-Leaf Displays," in *Understanding Robust and Exploratory Data Analysis,* ed. David C. Hoaglin, Frederick Mosteller, and John W. Tukey (New York: John Wiley & Sons, 1983), pp. 7–31; and Velleman and Hoaglin, *Applications,* pp. 1–13.
15. This section is adapted from the following excellent discussions of boxplots: Velleman and Hoaglin, *Applications,* pp. 65–76; Hartwig, *Exploratory Data Analysis,* pp. 19–25; John D. Emerson and Judith Strenio, "Boxplots and Batch Comparison," in *Understanding Robust and Exploratory Data Analysis,* pp. 59–93; and Amir D. Aczel, *Complete Business Statistics* (Homewood, Ill,: Richard D. Irwin, 1989), pp. 723–28.
16. Tukey, *Exploratory Data Analysis,* pp. 27–55.
17. Hoaglin et al., *Understanding Robust and Exploratory Data Anlaysis,* p. 2.
18. Several robust estimators are suitable replacements for the mean and standard deviation that we do not discuss here. For example, the trimmed mean, trimean, and the M-estimators (such as Huber's, Tukey's, Hampel's, and Andrew's estimators) and the median absolute deviation or MAD. See Hoaglin et al., *Understanding Robust and Exploratory Data Analysis,* chap. 10; and Marija J. Norusis/SPSS, Inc., *SPSS for*

Windows Base System User's Guide, Release 6.0 (Chicago: SPSS, Inc., 1993), chap. 9.

19. R. McGill, J. W. Tukey, and W. A. Larsen, "Variations of Box Plots," *The American Statistician* 32 (1978), pp. 12–16.

20. See J. Chambers, W. Cleveland, B. Kleiner, and P. Tukey, *Graphical Methods for Data Analysis* (Boston: Duxbury Press, 1983).

21. This section is based on the discussion of transformation in John D. Emerson and Michael A. Stoto, "Transforming Data," in *Understanding Robust and Exploratory Data Analysis,* pp. 97–127; and Velleman and Hoaglin, *Applications,* pp. 48–53.

22. Hoaglin et al., *Understanding Robust and Exploratory Data Analysis,* p. 77.

23. Ibid., p. 125.

24. SPSS Release 4.0.5 was used to prepare this analysis.

25. Norusis, *Base System User's Guide,* p. 203.

26. Harper W. Boyd, Jr., and Ralph Westfall, *Marketing Research,* 3rd ed. (Homewood, Ill.: Richard D. Irwin, 1972), p. 540.

27. Morris Rosenberg, *The Logic of Survey Analysis* (New York: Basic Books, 1968). The discussion in this section draws on the concepts advanced by Rosenberg. Also see Earl Babbie, *The Practice of Social Research,* 5th ed. (Belmont, Calif.: Wadsworth Publishing, 1989). Babbie presents an excellent summary of the history, development, and application of the elaboration model.

28. SPSS-X Tables™ software with their systems file: Bank Data.

29. J. Morgan, I. Siageldin, and N. Baerwaldt, *Productive Americans* (Ann Arbor, Mich.: Survey Research Center, University of Michigan, 1965), p. 128. For a more recent review, see Douglas L. MacLachlan and Jonny K. Johansson, "Market Segmentation with Multivariate AID," *Journal of Marketing,* Winter 1981, pp. 74–84.

Suggested Readings

1. Hartwig, Frederick, with Brian E. Dearing, *Exploratory Data Analysis.* Beverly Hills, Calif.: Sage Publications, 1979. Chapter 4 on data transformation is particularly informative.

2. Hoaglin, David C.; Frederick Mosteller; and John W. Tukey, eds. *Understanding Robust and Exploratory Data Analysis.* New York: John Wiley & Sons, 1983. A complete and advanced treatment of the subject. Especially well organized topical coverage.

3. Norusis, Marija J./SPSS, Inc. *SPSS Base System User's Guide, Release 6.0.* Chicago: SPSS, Inc., 1993. Chapter 7 through 10 are most appropriate for preliminary analysis. The style is clear and well suited to managers and nonmathematicians. The control language is illustrated with data examples making this a well-documented reference guide for basic analysis.

4. Rosenberg, Morris. *The Logic of Survey Analysis.* New York: Basic Books, 1968. An excellent treatment of causal analysis using cross-breaks. Highly recommended.

5. Tukey, John W. *Exploratory Data Analysis.* Reading, Mass.: Addison-Wesley Publishing, 1977. The pioneering and widely quoted work on EDA. Presented convincingly and with numerous examples.

6. Velleman, Paul F., and David C. Hoaglin. *Applications, Basics, and Computing of Exploratory Data Analysis.* Boston: Duxbury Press, 1981. The basics of EDA are presented in a straightforward style with helpful examples and excellent connections to computer applications.

7. Zeisel, Hans. *Say It with Figures.* 6th ed. New York: Harper & Row, 1985. The entire book is worth reading for its excellent discussion of numerical presentation.

15 HYPOTHESIS TESTING

**FINDING
YOUR WAY**

INTRODUCTION

In the last chapter, we discussed the procedures for data preparation and preliminary analysis. The next step for many studies is hypothesis testing.

Just as your understanding of scientific reasoning was an important foundation in the last chapter for the elaboration model, recollection of the specific differences between induction and deduction is fundamental to hypothesis testing. Inductive reasoning moves from specific facts to general, but tentative, conclusions. We can never be absolutely sure that inductive conclusions are flawless. With the aid of probability estimates, we can qualify our results and state the degree of confidence we have in them. Statistical inference is an application of inductive reasoning. It allows us to reason from evidence found in the sample to conclusions we wish to make about the population.

Inferential statistics in the second of two major categories of statistical procedures, the other being descriptive statistics. We used descriptive statistics in the last chapter when exploration and description of distributions were emphasized.

Under the heading of **inferential statistics,** two topics are discussed in this book. The first, estimation of population values, was used with sampling in Chapter 8, but we will return to it here briefly. The second, testing statistical hypotheses, is the primary subject of this chapter.

In the next few sections, we will refresh your memory of hypothesis testing and look at selected statistical tests. Many are basic, but they illustrate the diverse types of data and situations a researcher may encounter. A section on nonparametric techniques in Appendix D provides further study for those with a special interest in nominal and ordinal variables.

HYPOTHESIS TESTING

Testing Approaches

There are two approaches to hypothesis testing. The more established is the classical or sampling-theory approach; the second is known as the Bayesian approach. **Classical statistics** are found in all of the major statistics books and are widely used in research applications. This approach represents an objective view of probability in which the decision making rests totally upon an analysis of available sampling data. A hypothesis is established, it is rejected or fails to be rejected, based on the sample data collected.

Bayesian statistics are an extension of the classical approach. They also use sampling data for making decisions, but they go beyond them to consider all other available information. This additional information consists of subjective probability estimates stated in terms of degrees of belief. These subjective estimates are based on general experience rather than on specific collected data. They are expressed as a prior distribution that can be revised after gathering sample information. The revised estimate, known as a posterior distribution, may be further revised by additional information, and so on. Various decision rules are established, cost and other estimates can be introduced, and the expected outcomes of combinations of these elements are used to judge decision alternatives.

The Bayesian approach, based on the centuries-old Bayes theorem, has emerged as an alternative hypothesis-testing procedure since the mid-1950s. An example of Bayesian decision making is presented in Appendix B on the topic of valuing research information. The reader interested in learning more about Bayesian statistics is referred to the suggested readings at the end of this chapter.

Statistical Significance

Following the sampling-theory approach, we accept or reject a hypothesis on the basis of sampling information alone. Since any sample will almost surely vary somewhat from its population, we must judge whether these differences are statistically significant or insignificant. A difference has **statistical significance** if there is good reason to believe the difference does not represent random sampling fluctuations only. For example, the controller of a large retail chain may be concerned about a possible slowdown in payments by the company's customers. She measures the rate of payment in terms of the average number of days receivables outstanding. Generally, the company has maintained an average of about 50 days with a standard deviation of 10 days. Suppose the controller has all of the customer accounts analyzed and finds the average is now 51 days. Is this difference statistically significant from 50? Of course it is because the difference is based on a census of the accounts and there is no sampling involved. It is a fact that the population average has moved from 50 to 51 days. While it is of statistical significance, whether it is of **practical significance** is another question. If the controller judges that this variation has no real importance, then it is of little practical significance.

Since it would be too expensive to analyze all of a company's receivables frequently, we normally resort to sampling. Assume a sample of 25 accounts is randomly selected and the average days outstanding are calculated to be 54. Is this statistically significant? The answer is not obvious. It is significant if there is good reason to believe the average age of the total group of receivables has moved up from 50. Since the evidence consists only of a sample, consider the second possibility, that this is only a random sampling error and thus not significant. The task is to judge whether such a result from this sample is or is not statistically significant. To answer this question, one needs to consider further the logic of hypothesis testing.

The Logic of Hypothesis Testing

In classical tests of significance, two kinds of hypotheses are used. The **null hypothesis** is used for testing. It is a statement that no difference exists between the parameter and the statistic being compared to it. In the controller example, the null hypothesis states that the population parameter of 50 days has not changed. A second, or **alternative hypothesis,** holds that there has been a change in average days outstanding (i.e., the sample statistic of 54 indicates the population value probably is no longer 50). The alternative hypothesis is the logical opposite of the null hypothesis.

The accounts receivable example can be used further to explore how these concepts are used to test for significance. The null hypothesis (H_0) is: There has been no change from the 50 days average age of accounts outstanding. The alternative hypothesis (H_A) may take several forms, depending upon the objective of the researchers. The H_A may be of the "not the same" form. The average age of accounts has changed from 50 days. A second variety may be either "greater than" or "less than." The average age of receivables has increased (decreased) from 50 days.

These types of alternative hypotheses correspond with two-tailed and one-tailed tests. A **two-tailed test,** or nondirectional test, considers two possibilities: the average could be more than 50 days or it could be less than 50 days. To test this hypothesis, the regions of rejection are divided into two tails of the distribution. A **one-tailed,** or directional, **test** places the entire probability of an unlikely outcome into the tail specified by the alternative hypothesis. In Figure 15–1, the first diagram represents a nondirectional hypothesis and the second is a directional hypothesis of the "greater than" variety.

Hypotheses for the example may be expressed in the following form:

Null, H_0: μ (mu) $= 50$ days

Alternative, H_A: μ $\neq 50$ days (not the same case)

or H_A: μ > 50 days (greater than case)

or H_A: μ < 50 days (less than case)

**FIGURE   15–1
One- and
Two-Tailed Tests
at the 5%
Level of
Significance**

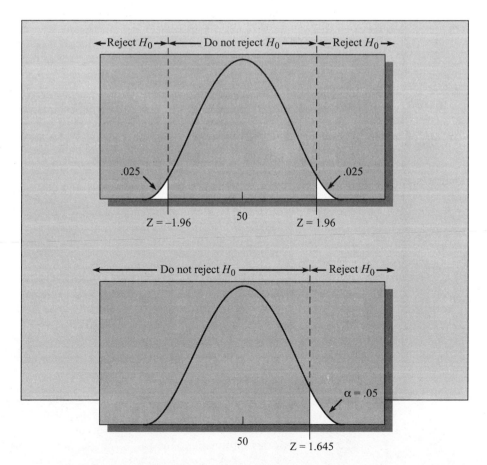

In testing these hypotheses, adopt the decision rule: Take no corrective action if the analysis shows that one cannot reject the null hypothesis. Note "not to reject" rather than "accept" the null hypothesis. It is argued that a null hypothesis can never be proved and therefore cannot be "accepted." Here, again, we see the influence of inductive reasoning. Unlike deduction, where the connections between premises and conclusions provide a legitimate claim of "conclusive proof," inductive conclusions do not possess that advantage. Statistical testing gives only a chance to (1) disprove (reject) or (2) fail to reject the hypothesis. Despite this terminology, it is common to hear "accept the null" rather than the clumsy "fail to reject the null." In this discussion, the less formal "accept" means "fail to reject" the null hypothesis.

If we reject a null hypothesis (finding a statistically significant difference), then we are accepting the alternative hypothesis. In either accepting or rejecting a null hypothesis, incorrect decisions can be made. A null hypothesis can be accepted when it should have been rejected or rejected when it should have been accepted.

These problems are illustrated with an analogy to the American legal system.[1] In our system of justice, the innocence of an indicted person is presumed until proof of guilt beyond a reasonable doubt can be established. In hypothesis testing, this is the null hypothesis; there should be no difference between the presumption and the outcome unless contrary evidence is furnished. Once evidence establishes beyond reasonable doubt that innocence can no longer be maintained, a just conviction is required. This is equivalent to rejecting the null hypothesis and accepting the alternative hypothesis. Incorrect decisions or errors are the other two possible outcomes. We can unjustly convict an innocent person, or we can acquit a guilty person.

Table 15–1 compares the statistical situation to the legal one. One of two conditions exists in nature—either the null hypothesis is true or the alternative hypothesis is true. An indicted person is innocent or guilty. Two decisions can be made about these conditions: one may accept the null hypothesis or reject it (thereby accepting the alternative). Two of these situations result in correct decisions, while the other two lead to decision errors.

When a **Type I error** (α) is committed, a true null hypothesis is rejected; the innocent person is unjustly convicted. The α value is called the *level of significance* and is the probability of rejecting the true null. With a **Type II error** (β), one fails to reject a false null hypothesis resulting in an unjust acquittal with the guilty person going free. Based on our system of justice, it is more important to reduce the probability of convicting the innocent than acquitting the guilty. Similarly, hypothesis testing places a greater emphasis on Type I errors than on Type II. Each of these errors is examined in more detail.

Type I Error   Assume the controller's problem is deciding whether the average age of accounts receivable has changed. Assume the population mean is 50 days, the standard deviation of the population is 10 days, and the size of the sample is 25 accounts. With this information, one can calculate the standard error of the mean

TABLE 15–1   **Comparison of Statistical Decisions to Legal Analogy**

$(\sigma_{\bar{X}})$ (the standard deviation of distribution of sample means). This hypothetical distribution is pictured in Figure 15–2. The standard error of the mean is calculated to be two days.

$$\sigma_{\bar{X}} = \frac{\sigma}{\sqrt{n}} = \frac{10}{\sqrt{25}} = 2$$

If the decision is to reject H_0 with a 95 percent confidence interval ($\alpha = .05$), a Type I error of .025 in each tail is accepted (assumes a two-tailed test). In Part A of Figure 15–2, see the **regions of rejection** indicated by the shaded areas. The area between these two regions is known as the **region of acceptance.** The dividing points between rejection and acceptance areas are called **critical values.** Since the distribution of sample means is normal, the critical values can be computed in terms of the standardized random variable.[2]

where

$Z = 1.96$ (significance level $= .05$).
$\bar{X}_C = $ The critical value of the sample mean.
$\mu = $ The population value stated in $H_0 = 50$.
$\sigma_{\bar{X}} = $ The standard error of a distribution of means of samples of 25.

$$Z = \frac{\overline{X} - \mu}{\sigma_{\overline{X}}}$$

$$-1.96 = \frac{\overline{X}_{C_1} - 50}{2}$$

$$\overline{X}_{C_1} = 46.08$$

$$1.96 = \frac{\overline{X}_{C_2} - 50}{2}$$

$$\overline{X}_{C_2} = 53.92$$

The probability of a Type I error is

$$\alpha = .05, \text{ or } 5\%$$

The probability of a correct decision if the null hypothesis is true is 95 percent. By changing the probability of a Type I error, you move critical values either closer to or farther away from the assumed parameter of 50. This can be done if a smaller or larger α error is desired and critical values are moved to reflect this. One can also change the Type 1 error and the regions of acceptance by changing the size of the sample. For example, if one takes a sample of 100, the critical values that provide a Type I error of .05 are 48.04 and 51.96.

The alternative hypothesis concerned a change in either direction from 50, but the controller may be interested only in increases in the age of receivables. For this, one uses a one-tailed (greater than) H_A and places the entire region of rejection in the upper tail of the distribution. One can accept a 5 percent α risk and compute a new critical value ($\overline{X}_C$). (See Appendix Table F–1 to find the Z value of 1.645 for the area of .05 under the curve.) Substitute this in the Z equation and solve for $\overline{X}_C$.

$$Z = 1.645 = \frac{\overline{X}_C - 50}{2}$$

$$\overline{X}_C = 53.29$$

This new critical value, the boundary between the regions of acceptance and rejection, is pictured in Part B of Figure 15–2.

Type II Error   The controller would commit a Type II error (β) by accepting the null hypothesis ($\mu = 50$) when in truth it had changed. This kind of error is difficult to detect. The probability of committing a β error depends on five factors: (1) the true value of the parameter, (2) the α level we have selected, (3) whether a one- or two-tailed test was used to evaluate the hypothesis, (4) the sample standard deviation, and (5) the size of the sample. We secure a different β error if the new μ moves from 50 to 54 than if it moves only to 52. We must compute separate β error estimates for each of a number of assumed new population parameters and $\overline{X}_C$ values. To illustrate, assume μ has actually moved to 54 from 50. Under these

FIGURE 15–2
Probability of
Making a Type I
Error Given H_0
is True

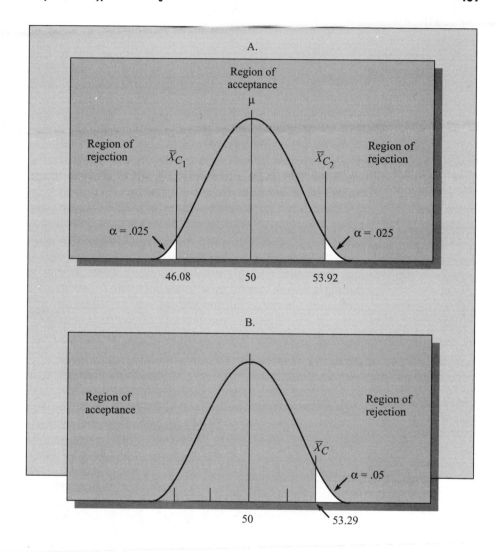

conditions, what is the probability of our making a Type II error if the critical value
is set at 53.29? This may be expressed in the following fashion:

$P(A_2|S_1) = \alpha = .05$ (assume a one-tailed alternative hypothesis)
$P(A_1|S_2) = \beta = ?$

If the new μ is 54, then

$$\sigma_{\bar{X}} = \frac{\sigma}{\sqrt{n}} = \frac{10}{\sqrt{25}} = 2$$

$$Z = \frac{\bar{X} - \mu}{\sigma_{\bar{X}}} = \frac{53.29 - 54}{2} = -.355$$

Using Table F–1 in Appendix F, we interpolate between .35 and .36 Z scores to find the .355 Z score. The area between the mean and Z is .1387. β is the tail area, or the area below the Z, and is calculated as:

$$\beta = .50 - .1387 = .36$$

This condition is shown in Figure 15–3. With an α of .05 and a sample of 25, there is a 36 percent probability of a Type II (β error) if the μ is 54. We also speak of the **power of the test** that is $(1 - \beta)$. For this example, the power of the test equals 64 percent $(1 - .36)$; that is, we will correctly reject the false null hypothesis with a 64 percent probability. A power of 64 percent is less than the 80 percent minimum percentage usually needed.

There are several ways to reduce a Type II error. We can shift the critical value closer to the original μ of 50, but to do this we must accept a bigger α. Whether to take this action depends on the evaluation of the relative α and β risks. It might be desirable to enlarge the acceptable α risk because a worsening of the receivables situation would probably call for increased efforts to stimulate collections. Committing a Type I error would mean only that we engaged in efforts to stimulate collections when the situation had not worsened. This act probably would not have many adverse effects even if the days of credit outstanding had not increased.

A second way to reduce Type II error is to increase sample size. For example, if the sample were increased to 100, the power of the test would be much stronger.

$$\sigma_{\overline{X}} = \frac{\sigma}{\sqrt{n}} = \frac{10}{\sqrt{100}} = 1$$

$$Z = \frac{\overline{X} - \mu}{\sigma_{\overline{X}}} = \frac{53.29 - 54}{1} = -.71$$

$$\beta = .50 - .2612 = .24$$

**FIGURE 15–3
Probability of
Making a Type
II Error (β)**

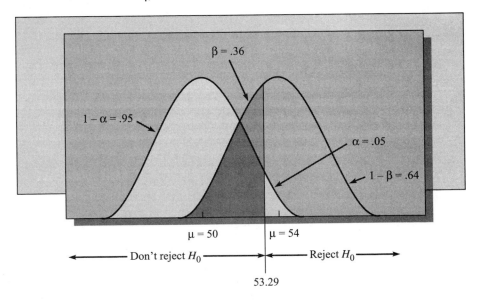

This would reduce the Type II error to 24 percent and increase the power of the test to 76 percent.

A third method seeks to improve both α and β errors simultaneously and is difficult to accomplish. We know that measuring instruments, observations, and recording produce error. By using a better measuring device, tightening the observation and recording processes, or devising a more efficient sample, we can reduce the variability of observations. This diminishes the standard error of estimate that in turn reduces the sampling distributions' spread. The net effect is that there is less tail area in the error regions.

Statistical Testing Procedures

Testing for statistical significance follows a relatively well-defined pattern, although authors differ in the number and sequence of steps. One six-stage sequence is as follows:

1. *State the null hypothesis.* While the researcher is usually interested in testing a hypothesis of change or differences, the null hypothesis is always used for statistical testing purposes.

2. *Choose the statistical test.* To test a hypothesis, one must choose an appropriate statistical test. There are many tests from which to choose, and there are at least four criteria that can be used in choosing a test. One is the power efficiency of the test. A more powerful test provides the same level of significance with a smaller sample than a less powerful test. In addition, in choosing a test, one can consider how the sample is drawn, the nature of the population, and the type of measurement scale used. For instance, some tests are useful only when the sequence of scores is known or when observations are paired. Other tests are appropriate only if the population has certain characteristics; still other tests are useful only if the measurement scale is interval or ratio. More attention is given to test selection in the next section.

3. *Select the desired level of significance.* The choice of the **level of significance** should be made before we collect the data. The most common level is .05, although .01 is also widely used. Other α levels such as .10, .025, or .001 are sometimes chosen. The exact level to choose is largely determined by how much α risk one is willing to accept and the effect that this choice has on β risk. The larger the α, the lower the β.

4. *Compute the calculated difference value.* After the data are collected, use the formula for the appropriate significance test to obtain the calculated value.

5. *Obtain the critical test value.* After we compute the calculated t, χ^2, or other measure, we must look up the critical value in the appropriate table for that distribution. The critical value is the criterion that defines the region of rejection from the region of acceptance of the null hypothesis.

6. *Make the decision.* For most tests if the calculated value is larger than the critical value, we reject the null hypothesis and conclude that the alternative hypothesis is supported (although it is by no means proved). If the critical value is the larger, we conclude we have failed to reject the null.[3]

TESTS OF SIGNIFICANCE

This section provides an overview of statistical tests that are representative of the vast array available to the researcher. After a review of the general types and their assumptions, the procedures for selecting an appropriate test are discussed. The remainder of the section contains examples of parametric and nonparametric tests for one-sample, two-sample, and *k*-sample cases. Readers needing a comprehensive treatment of significance tests are referred to the suggested readings at the end of this chapter.

Types of Tests

There are two general classes of significance tests: parametric and nonparametric. **Parametric tests** are more powerful because their data are derived from interval and ratio measurements. **Nonparametric tests** are used to test hypotheses with nominal and ordinal data. Parametric techniques are the tests of choice if their assumptions are met.

Some assumptions for parametric tests include:

1. The observations must be independent. That is, the selection of any one case should not affect the chances for any other case to be included in the sample.
2. The observations should be drawn from normally distributed populations.
3. These populations should have equal variances.
4. The measurement scales should be at least interval so that arithmetic operations can be used with them.

The researcher is responsible for reviewing the assumptions pertinent to the chosen test and performing diagnostic checks on the data to assure the selection's appropriateness. The normality of a distribution may be checked in several ways. We have previously discussed the measures of location, shape, and spread for preliminary analysis and considered graphic techniques for exploring data patterns and examining distributions.

Another diagnostic tool is the **normal probability plot.** This plot compares the observed values with those expected from a normal distribution.[4] If the data display the characteristics of normality, the points will fall within a narrow band along a straight line. An example is shown in the upper left panel of Figure 15–4.

An alternate way to look at this is to plot the deviations from the straight line. These are shown in a "detrended plot" in the upper right panel of the figure. Here we would expect the points to cluster without pattern around a straight line passing horizontally through 0. In the bottom two panels of Figure 15–4, there is neither a straight line in the normal probability plot nor a random distribution of points about 0 in the detrended plot. Visually, the bottom two plots tell us the variable is not normally distributed. In addition, two separate tests of the hypothesis that the data come from normal distributions are rejected at a significance level of less than .01.[5] If we wished to check another assumption, say one of equal variance, the

FIGURE   15–4   Probability Plots and Tests of Normality

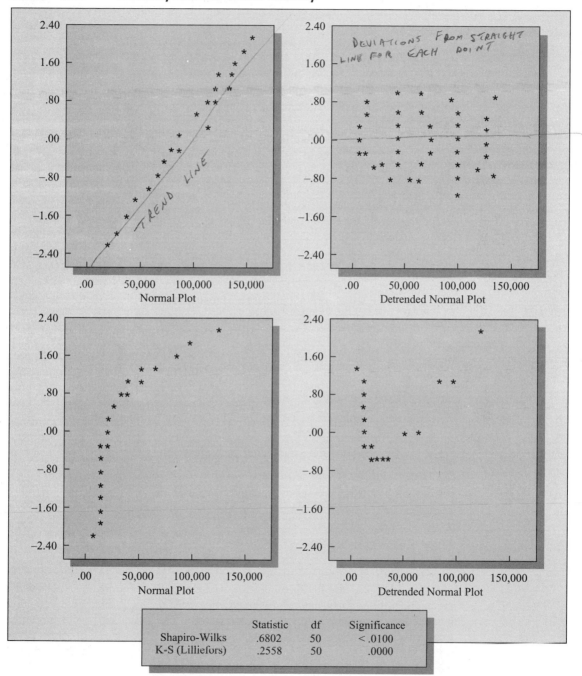

	Statistic	df	Significance
Shapiro-Wilks	.6802	50	< .0100
K-S (Lilliefors)	.2558	50	.0000

spread-and-level plot and Levene test described in Chapter 14 would be appropriate. Statistical software programs often provide diagnostic tools for checking assumptions. These may be nested within a specific statistical procedure, such as analysis of variance or regression, or provided as a general set of tools for examining assumptions.

Parametric tests place different emphasis on the importance of assumptions. Some tests are quite robust and hold up well despite violations. With others, a departure from linearity or equality of variance may threaten the validity of the results.

Nonparametric tests have fewer and less stringent assumptions. They do not specify normally distributed populations or homogeneity of variance. Some tests require independence of cases, while others are expressly designed for situations with related cases. Nonparametric tests are the only ones usable with nominal data; they are the only technically correct tests to use with ordinal data, although parametric tests are sometimes employed in this case. Nonparametric tests may also be used for interval and ratio data although they waste some of the information available. Nonparametric tests are also easy to understand and to use. Parametric tests have greater efficiency when their use is appropriate, but even in such cases, nonparametric tests often achieve an efficiency as high as 95 percent. This means the nonparametric test will provide the same statistical testing power with a sample of 100 as a parametric test with a sample of 95.

How to Select a Test

In attempting to choose a particular significance test, at least three questions should be considered:

1. Does the test involve one sample, two samples, or k samples?
2. If two samples or k samples are involved, are the individual cases independent or related?
3. Is the measurement scale nominal, ordinal, interval, or ratio?

Additional questions may arise once answers to these are known: What is the sample size? If there are several samples, are they of equal size? Have the data been weighted? Have the data been transformed? Often such questions are unique to the selected technique. The answers can complicate the selection, but once a tentative choice is made, most standard statistics textbooks will provide further details.

Decision trees provide a more systematic means of selecting techniques. One widely used guide from the Institute for Social Research starts with questions about the number of variables, nature of the variables (continuous, discrete, dichotomous, independent, dependent, and so forth), and level of measurement. It goes through a tree structure asking detailed questions about the nature of the relationships being searched, compared, or tested. Over 130 solutions to data analysis problems are paired with commonly asked questions.[6]

An expert system offers another approach to choosing appropriate statistics. Capitalizing on the power and convenience of personal computers, expert system

FIGURE   15–5   **Recommended Statistical Techniques by Measurement Level and Testing Situation**

Measurement Level	One-Sample Case	Two-Sample Case		k-Sample Case	
		Related Samples	*Independent Samples*	*Related Samples*	*Independent Samples*
Nominal	Binomial χ^2 one-sample	McNemar	Fisher exact test χ^2 two-sample	Cochran Q	χ^2 for k samples
Ordinal	Kolmogorov-Smirnov one-sample test Runs test	Sign test Wilcoxon matched pairs	Median test Mann-Whitney U test Kolmogorov-Smirnov Wald-Wolfowitz	Friedman two-way ANOVA	Median extension Kruskal-Wallis one-way ANOVA
Interval and ratio	t test Z test	t test for paired samples	t test Z test	Repeated measures ANOVA	One-way ANOVA

programs provide a comprehensive search of the statistical terrain just as a computer search of secondary sources does. Most programs ask about your research objectives, the nature of your data, and the intended audience for your final report. When you are not 100 percent confident of your answers, you can bracket them with an estimate of the degree of your certainty. One such program, Statistical Navigator, covers eight categories of statistics from exploratory data analysis through reliability testing and multivariate data analysis. In response to your answers, a report is printed containing recommendations, rationale for selections, references, and the statistical packages that offer the suggested procedure.[7]

In this chapter, we used the above three criteria to develop a classification of the major parametric and nonparametric tests and measures. This is shown in Figure 15–5.[8] For example, if your testing situation involved two samples, the samples were independent, and the data were interval, the figure suggests the t test of differences as the appropriate choice. The most frequently used tests in Figure 15–5 are covered next with additional examples in Appendix E.

One-Sample Tests

One-sample tests are used when we have a single sample and wish to test the hypothesis that it comes from a specified population. In this case we encounter questions such as:

1. Is there a difference between observed frequencies and the frequencies we would expect, based on some theory?
2. Is there a difference between observed and expected proportions?
3. Is it reasonable to conclude that a sample is drawn from a population with some specified distribution (normal, Poisson, and so forth)?
4. Is there a significant difference between some measures of central tendency ($\overline{X}$) and its population parameter (μ)?

A number of tests may be appropriate in this situation. The parametric test is discussed first.

Parametric Test   The Z or t test is used to determine the statistical significance between a sample distribution mean and a parameter.

The **Z and t distributions** differ with the t having more tail area than that found in the normal distribution. This is a compensation for the lack of information about the population standard deviation. Although the sample standard deviation is used as a proxy figure, the imprecision makes it necessary to go further away from 0 to include the percentage of values in the t distribution necessarily found in the standard normal.

When sample sizes approach 120, the sample standard deviation becomes a very good estimate of σ; beyond 120, the t and Z distributions are virtually identical.

Some typical real world applications of the one-sample test are:

1. Finding the average monthly balance of credit card holders compared to the average monthly balance five years ago.
2. Comparing the failure rate of computers in a 20-hour test of quality specifications.
3. Discovering the proportion of people who would shop in a new district compared to the assumed population proportion.
4. Comparing the average income taxes collected this year to last year's income tax revenues.

Example   To illustrate the application of the t test to the one-sample case, consider again the controller's problem mentioned earlier. With a sample of 100 accounts, she finds that the mean is 52.5 days outstanding receivables, with a standard deviation of 14. Do these results indicate the population mean might still be 50 days?

In this problem, we have only the sample standard deviation (s). This must be used in place of the population standard deviation (σ). When we substitute s for σ, we use the t distribution, especially if the sample size is less than 30. We define t as:

$$ t = \frac{\overline{X} - \mu}{s/\sqrt{n}} $$

This significance test is conducted by following the six-step procedure recommended earlier.

1. *Null hypothesis. H_0:* = 50 days.
   H_A: > 50 days (one-tailed test).
2. *Statistical test.* Choose the t test because the data are ratio measurements. Assume the underlying population is normal and we have randomly selected the sample from the population of customer accounts.
3. *Significance level.* Let $\alpha = .05$, with $n = 100$.

4. *Calculated value.* $t = \dfrac{52.5 - 50}{14/\sqrt{100}} = \dfrac{2.5}{1.4} = 1.786$; d.f. $= n - 1 = 99$.

5. *Critical test value.* We obtain this by entering the table of the *t* distribution (Appendix Table F–2 at back of book) with 99 d.f. and a level of significance value of .05. We secure a critical value of about 1.66 (interpolated between d.f. $= 60$ and d.f. $= 120$).

6. *Decision.* In this case, the calculated value is greater than the critical value (1.786 > 1.66), so we reject the null hypothesis and conclude that the average accounts receivable outstanding has increased.

Nonparametric Test   A variety of nonparametric tests may be used in a one-sample situation, depending upon the measurement scale used and other conditions. If the measurement scale is nominal (classificatory only), it is possible to use either the binomial test or the χ^2 one-sample test. The binomial test is appropriate when the population is viewed as only two classes, such as male and female, buyer and non-buyer, and successful and unsuccessful. Thus, all observations fall into one or the other of these categories. This test is particularly useful when the size of sample is so small that the χ^2 test cannot be used.

Chi-Square (χ^2) Test   Probably the most widely used nonparametric test of significance is the **chi-square test.** It is particularly useful in tests involving nominal data but can be used for higher scales. Typical are cases where persons, events, or objects are grouped in two or more nominal categories such as "yes-no," "favor-undecided-against," or class "A, B, C, or D."

Using this technique we test for significant differences between the *observed* distribution of data among categories and the *expected* distribution based upon the null hypothesis. Chi-square is useful in cases of one-sample analysis, two independent samples, or *k* independent samples. It must be calculated with actual counts rather than percentages.

In the one-sample case, we establish a null hypothesis based on the expected frequency of objects in each category. Then the deviations of the actual frequencies in each category are compared with the hypothesized frequencies. The greater the difference between them, the less the probability that these differences can be attributed to chance. The value of χ^2 is the measure that expresses the extent of this difference. The larger the divergence, the larger the χ^2 value.

The formula by which the χ^2 test is calculated is:

$$\chi^2 = \sum_{i=1}^{k} \frac{(O_i - E_i)^2}{E_i}$$

in which

O_i = Observed number of cases categorized in the *i*th category.
E_i = Expected number of cases in the *i*th category under H_0.
k = The number of categories.

There is a different distribution for χ^2 for each number of degrees of freedom (d.f.), defined as $(k - 1)$ or the number of categories in the classification minus one.

$$\text{d.f.} = k - 1$$

With chi-square contingency tables of the two sample or k-sample variety, we have both rows and columns in the cross-classification table. In that instance, d.f. is defined as rows minus 1 $(r - 1)$ times columns minus 1 $(c - 1)$.

$$\text{d.f.} = (r - 1)(c - 1)$$

In a 2×2 table there is 1 d.f., and in a 3×2 table there are 2 d.f. Depending on the number of degrees of freedom, we must be certain the numbers in each cell are large enough to make the χ^2 test appropriate. When d.f. $= 1$, each expected frequency should be at least 5 in size. If d.f. > 1, then the χ^2 test should not be used if more than 20 percent of the expected frequencies are smaller than 5, or when any expected frequency is less than 1. Expected frequencies can often be increased by combining adjacent categories. Four categories of freshmen, sophomores, juniors, and seniors might be classified into upper class and lower class. If there are only two categories and still there are too few in a given class, it is better to use the binomial test.

Assume a survey of student interest in the dining club that was discussed in Chapter 8 is taken. We have interviewed 200 students and learned of their intentions to join such a club. We would like to analyze the results by living arrangement (type and location of student housing and eating arrangements). The 200 responses are classified into the four categories shown in the accompanying table. Do these variations indicate there is a significant difference among these students or are these sampling variations only? Proceed as follows:

1. *Null hypothesis.* H_0: $O_i = E_i$.
   That is, the proportion in the population who intend to join the club is independent of living arrangement. In H_A: $O_i \neq E_i$, the proportion in the population who intend to join the club is dependent on living arrangement.

2. *Statistical test.* Use the one-sample χ^2 to compare the observed distribution to a hypothesized distribution. The χ^2 test is used because the responses are classified into nominal categories, and there are sufficient observations.

3. *Significance level.* Let $\alpha = .05$.

4. *Calculated value.* $\chi^2 = \sum_{i=1}^{k} \dfrac{(O_i - E_i)^2}{E_i}$

   Calculate the expected distribution by determining what proportion of the 200 students interviewed were in each group. Then apply these proportions to the number who intend to join the club. Then calculate the following:

$$\chi^2 = \frac{(16 - 27)^2}{27} + \frac{(13 - 12)^2}{12} + \frac{(16 - 12)^2}{12} + \frac{(15 - 9)^2}{9}$$

$$= 4.48 + 0.08 + 1.33 + 4.0$$

$$= 9.89$$

$$\text{d.f.} = (4 - 1)(2 - 1) = 3$$

5. *Critical test value.* Enter the table of critical value for χ^2 (Appendix Table F–3) with 3 d.f. and secure a value of 7.82 for $\alpha = .05$.

6. *Decision.* The calculated value is greater than the critical value, so the null hypothesis is rejected.

Living Arrangement	(1) Intend to Join	(2) Number Interviewed	(3) Percent (No. Interviewed/200)	(4) Expected Frequencies (Percent × 60)
Dorm/fraternity	16	90	45	27
Apartment/rooming house, nearby	13	40	20	12
Apartment/rooming house, distant	16	40	20	12
Live at home	15	30	15	9
Total	60	200	100	60

TWO INDEPENDENT SAMPLES TESTS

The need to use **two independent samples tests** is often encountered in business research. We might compare the purchasing predispositions of a sample of subscribers from two magazines to discover if they are from the same population. Similarly, a test of output methods from two production lines or the price movements of common stock from two samples could be compared. A study of worker productivity from two groups or different samples from a public opinion poll would also use this method.

Parametric Test   The Z and t tests are frequently used parametric tests for independent samples although the F test can be used.

The **Z test** is used with large sample sizes (exceeding 30 for both independent samples) or with smaller samples when the data are normally distributed and population variances are known. The formula for the Z test is:

$$Z = \frac{(\overline{X}_1 - \overline{X}_2) - (\mu_1 - \mu_2)0}{\sqrt{\dfrac{S_1^2}{n_1} + \dfrac{S_2^2}{n_2}}}$$

With small sample sizes, normally distributed populations, and assuming equal population variances, the *t* test is appropriate:

$$t = \frac{(\bar{X}_1 - \bar{X}_2) - (\mu_1 - \mu_2)\cancel{0}}{\sqrt{S_p^2 \left(\dfrac{1}{n_1} + \dfrac{1}{n_2}\right)}}$$

where

$(\mu_1 - \mu_2)$ is the difference between the two population means.
S_p^2 is associated with the pooled variance estimate:

$$S_p^2 = \frac{(n_1 - 1)S_1^2 + (n_2 - 1)S_2^2}{n_1 + n_2 - 2}$$

To illustrate this application, consider a problem that might face a manager who wishes to test the effectiveness of two methods for training new salespeople. The company selects 22 sales trainees who are randomly divided into two experimental groups—one receives type A and the other type B training. The salespeople are then assigned and managed without regard to the training they have received. At the year's end, the manager reviews the performances of salespeople in these groups and finds the following results:

	A Group	B Group
Average weekly sales	$\bar{X}_1 = \$1,500$	$\bar{X}_2 = \$1,300$
Standard deviation	$s_1 = 225$	$s_2 = 251$

Following the standard testing procedure, we will determine whether one training method is superior to the other.

1. *Null hypothesis.* H_0: There is no difference in sales results produced by the two training methods.

   H_A: Training method A produces sales results superior to those of method B.

2. *Statistical test.* The *t* test is chosen because the data are at least interval and the samples are independent.

3. *Significance level.* $\alpha = .05$ (one-tailed test).

4. *Calculated value.*

$$t = \frac{(1,500 - 1,300) - 0}{\sqrt{\dfrac{(10)(225)^2 + (10)(251)^2}{20}\left(\dfrac{1}{11} + \dfrac{1}{11}\right)}}$$

$$= \frac{200}{101.63} = 1.97, \text{d.f.} = 20$$

There are $n - 1$ degrees of freedom in each sample, so total d.f. = $(11 - 1) + (11 - 1) = 20$.

5. *Critical test value.* Enter the table of the t distribution with d.f. = 20, one-tailed test, $\alpha = .05$. The critical value is 1.725.

6. *Decision.* Since the calculated value is larger than the critical value (1.97 > 1.725), reject the null hypothesis and conclude that training method A is superior.

Nonparametric Test   The chi-square test χ^2 is appropriate for situations in which a test for differences between samples is required. It is especially valuable for nominal data but can be used with ordinal measurements. When parametric data have been reduced to categories, they are frequently treated with χ^2 although this results in a loss of information. Preparing to solve this problem is the same as presented earlier although the formula differs slightly:

$$\chi^2 = \sum_i \sum_j \frac{(O_{ij} - E_{ij})^2}{E_{ij}}$$

in which

O_{ij} = Observed number of cases categorized in the ijth cell.
E_{ij} = Expected number of cases under H_0 to be categorized in the ijth cell.

Suppose a manager implementing a smoke-free workplace policy is interested in whether smoking affects worker accidents. Since the company has complete reports of on-the-job accidents, she draws a sample of names of workers who were involved in accidents during the last year. A similar sample from among workers who had no reported accidents in the last year is drawn. She interviews members of both groups to determine if they are smokers or not. The results appear in the following table.

Smoker	Count Expected Values	On-the-Job Accident Yes	No	Row Total
Heavy		12	4	16
		8.24	7.75	
Moderate		9	6	15
		7.73	7.27	
Nonsmoker		13	22	35
		18.03	16.97	
Column Total		34	32	66

The expected values have been calculated and are shown. The testing procedure is:

1. *Null hypothesis. H_0:* There is no difference in on-the-job accident occurrences between smokers and nonsmokers.
   H_A: There is a difference in on-the-job accident occurrences between smokers and nonsmokers.
2. *Statistical test.* χ^2 is appropriate but it may waste some of the data because the measurement appears to be ordinal.
3. *Significance level.* $\alpha = .05$, with d.f. $= (3 - 1)(2 - 1) = 2$.
4. *Calculated value.* The expected distribution is provided by the marginal totals of the table. If there is no relationship between accidents and smoking, there will be the same proportion of smokers in both accident and nonaccident classes. The numbers of expected observations in each cell are calculated by multiplying the two marginal totals common to a particular cell and dividing this product by n. For example,

$$\frac{34*16}{66} = 8.24, \text{ the expected value in cell } (1, 1)$$

$$\chi^2 = \frac{(12 - 8.24)^2}{8.24} + \frac{(4 - 7.75)^2}{7.75} + \frac{(9 - 7.73)^2}{7.73} + \frac{(6 - 7.27)^2}{7.27} +$$

$$\frac{(13 - 18.03)^2}{18.03} + \frac{(22 - 16.97)^2}{16.97}$$

$$= 6.86$$

5. *Critical test value.* Enter Appendix Table F–3 and find the critical value 5.99 with $\alpha = .05$ and d.f. $= 2$.
6. *Decision.* Since the calculated value is greater than the critical value, the null hypothesis is rejected.

For chi-square to operate properly, data must come from random samples of multinomial distributions and the expected frequencies should not be too small. We previously noted the traditional caution that expected frequencies below 5 should not comprise more than 20 percent of the cells, and no cell should have an E_i of less than 1. Some research has argued that these restrictions are too severe.[9]

In another type of χ^2, the 2×2 table, a correction known as *Yates' correction for continuity* is often applied when sample sizes are greater than 40 or when the sample is between 20 and 40 and the E_i s are 5 or more. The formula for this correction is:

$$\chi^2 = \frac{n\left(\mid AD - BC \mid - \frac{n}{2}\right)^2}{(A + B)(C + D)(A + C)(B + D)}$$

where the letters represent the cells designated as:

A	B
C	D

When applying the continuity correction to the data shown in Figure 15–6, a χ^2 value of 5.25 is obtained. The observed level of significance for this value is .02192. If the level of significance had been set at .01, we would accept the null hypothesis. However, had we calculated χ^2 without correction, the value would have been 6.25, which has an observed level of significance of .01242. Some researchers may be tempted to reject the null at this level. (But note that the critical value of χ^2 at .01 with 1 d.f. is 6.64. See Appendix Table F–3.) The literature is in conflict regarding the merits of the Yates' correction, but this example suggests one should take care when interpreting 2×2 tables.[10] To err on the conservative side would be in keeping with our prior discussion of Type I errors.

The Mantel-Haenszel test and the Likelihood Ratio also appear in this figure. The former is used with ordinal data, so it does not apply; and the latter, based on maximum likelihood theory, produces results similar to Pearson's chi-square.

FIGURE 15–6 **Comparison of Corrected and Noncorrected Chi-Square Results Using SPSS Procedure Crosstab**

```
        INCOME  Income by CPA Possession of a CPA

                        CPA
                Count
                        Yes      No
                                            Row
                         1        2        Total
        INCOME  ──────────────────────────────

                High 1    30       30         60
                                              60.0

                Low 2     10       30         40
                                              40.0

                Column    40       60        100
                Total    40.0     60.0      100.0


Chi Square                        Value      D.F.     Significance
─────────────────────────────────────────────────────────────────
Pearson                           6.25000      1         .01242
Continuity Correction             5.25174      1         .02192
Lilelihood Ratio                  6.43786      1         .01117
Mantel-Haenszel                   6.18750      1         .01287
Minimum Expected Frequency: 16.000
```

Two Related Samples Tests

The **two related samples tests** concerns those situations in which persons, objects, or events are closely matched or the phenomena are measured twice. One might compare the output of specific workers before and after vacations, the performance of the same stocks at two intervals, or the effects of an experimental stimulus when persons were randomly assigned to groups and given pretests and posttests. Both parametric and nonparametric tests are applicable under these conditions.

Parametric Test   The t test for independent samples would normally be inappropriate for this situation because one of its assumptions is that observations are independent. This problem is solved by a formula where the difference is found between each matched pair of observations, thereby reducing the two samples to the equivalent of a one-sample case. That is, there are now several differences, each independent of the other, for which one can compute various statistics.

In the following formula, the average difference, $\overline{D}$, corresponds to the normal distribution when the σ difference is known and the sample size is sufficient. The statistic t with $(n-1)$ degrees of freedom is defined as:

$$t = \frac{\overline{D}}{S_D/\sqrt{n}}$$

where:

$$\overline{D} = \frac{\Sigma D}{n}$$

$$S_D = \sqrt{\frac{\Sigma D^2 - \frac{(\Sigma D)^2}{n}}{n-1}}$$

To illustrate this application, we use sales data (in millions of dollars) for 1988 and 1989 from 10 companies of the Forbes Super50 found in Table 15–2.

TABLE 15–2   Sales Data for Paired-Samples t Test (dollars in millions)

Company	Sales 1989	Sales 1988	Difference D	D^2
GM	126932	123505	3427	11744329
GE	54574	49662	4912	24127744
Exxon	86656	78944	7712	59474944
IBM	62710	59512	3192	10227204
Ford	96146	92300	3846	14791716
AT&T	36112	35173	939	881721
Mobil	50220	48111	2109	4447881
DuPont	35099	32427	2632	6927424
Sears	53794	49975	3819	14584761
Amoco	23966	20779	3187	10156969
Totals			$\Sigma D = 35781$	$\Sigma D^2 = 157364693$

1. *Null hypothesis.* H_0: $\mu = 0$, there is no difference between the two years' sales records; and H_A: $\mu \neq 0$, there is a difference between sales for 1988 and 1989.
2. *Statistical test.* The matched or paired samples *t* test is chosen because there are repeated measures on each company, the data are not independent, and the measurement is ratio.
3. *Significance level.* Let $\alpha = .01$, with $n = 10$ and d.f. $= n - 1$.
4. *Calculated value.*

$$t = \frac{\overline{D}}{S_D/\sqrt{n}} = \frac{3,578.10}{570.93} = 6.28; \text{d.f.} = 9$$

5. *Critical test value.* Enter the Appendix Table F–2 with d.f. $= 9$, two-tailed test, $\alpha = .01$. The critical value is 3.25.
6. *Decision.* Since the calculated value is greater than the critical value ($6.28 > 3.25$), reject the null hypothesis and conclude there is a statistically significant difference between 1989 and 1988 sales.

A computer solution to the problem is illustrated in Figure 15–7. Notice that an *observed significance level* is printed for the calculated *t* value. With SPSS, this is often rounded and would be interpreted as significant at the .0005 level. The correlation coefficient, to the left of the *t* value, is a measure of the relationship between the two pairs of scores. In situations where matching has occurred (such as husbands' and wives' scores), it reveals the degree to which the matching has been effective in reducing the variability of the mean difference.

Nonparametric Test The McNemar test may be used with either nominal or ordinal data and is especially useful with before-after measurement of the same subjects.

FIGURE 15–7 **Sample SPSS Output for Paired-Samples *t* Test**

```
SPSS Release 4.0 for Macintosh

                    ---t-tests for paired samples---

                   Number                   Standard        Standard
    Variable       of cases      Mean       Deviation        Error

    89 Sales          10       62620.9000   31777.649      10048.975
    88 Sales          10       62620.8000   31072.871       9836.104


    (Difference    Standard    Standard          2-tail   │    t     Degrees of   2-tail
     Mean)         Deviation    Error    Corr.    Prob.   │  Value    Freedom      Prob.

     3582.1000     1803.159    570.209   .999     .000    │  6.28        9          .000
```

Test the significance of any observed change by setting up a fourfold table of frequencies to represent the first and second set of responses:

	After	
Before	*Do Not Favor*	*Favor*
Favor	A	B
Do not favor	C	D

Since $A + D$ represents the total number of people who changed (B and C are no-change responses), the expectation under a null hypothesis is that $\frac{1}{2}(A + D)$ cases change in one direction and the same proportion in the other direction. The McNemar test uses the following transformation of the χ^2 test:

$$\chi^2 = \frac{(|A - D| - 1)^2}{A + D} \text{ with d.f.} = 1$$

The "minus 1" in the equation is a correction for continuity since the χ^2 is a continuous distribution and the observed frequencies represent a discrete distribution.

To illustrate this test's application, we use survey data from a large corporation whose management decided to tell employees of the "values of teamwork" in an internal education campaign. They took a random sample of their employees before the campaign, asking them to complete a questionnaire on their attitudes on this topic. On the basis of their responses, the workers were divided into equal groups as to their favorable or unfavorable views of teamwork. After the campaign, the same 200 employees were asked again to complete the questionnaire. They were again classified as to favorable or unfavorable attitudes. The testing process is:

1. *Null hypothesis.* H_0: $P(A) = P(D)$.
   H_A: $P(A) \neq P(D)$.
2. *Statistical test.* The McNemar test is chosen because nominal data are used, and the study involves before-after measurements of two related samples.
3. *Significance level.* Let $\alpha = .05$, with $n = 200$.
4. *Calculated value.*

$$\chi^2 = \frac{(|10 - 40| - 1)^2}{10 + 40} = \frac{29^2}{50} = 16.82; \text{ d.f.} = 1.$$

	After	
Before	*Unfavorable*	*Favorable*
Favorable	10	90
Unfavorable	60	40

5. *Critical test value.* Enter the table of the χ^2 distribution and find the critical value to be 3.84 with $\alpha = .05$ and d.f. $= 1$.

6. *Decision.* The calculated value is greater than the critical value ($16.82 > 3.84$) indicating one should reject the null hypothesis. In fact, χ^2 is so large that it would have surpassed an α of .001.

k Independent Samples Tests

In business and economic research, we often use *k* **independent samples tests** when three or more samples are involved. Under this condition, we are interested in learning whether the samples might have come from the same or identical populations. When the data are measured on an interval-ratio scale and we can meet the necessary assumptions, analysis of variance and the *F* test are used. If preliminary analysis shows the assumptions cannot be met or if the data were measured on an ordinal or nominal scale, a nonparametric test should be selected.

As with the two-sample case, the samples are assumed to be independent. This is the condition of a completely randomized experiment when subjects are randomly assigned to various treatment groups. It is also common for an ex post facto study to require comparison of more than two independent sample means.

Parametric Test   The statistical method for testing the null hypothesis that the means of several populations are equal is **analysis of variance (ANOVA).** *One-way analysis of variance* is described in this section. It uses a single-factor, fixed-effects model to compare the effects of one factor (brands of coffee, varieties of residential housing, types of retail stores) on a continuous dependent variable. In a fixed-effects model, the levels of the factor are established in advance and the results are not generalizable to other levels of treatment. For example, if coffee were Jamaican grown, Colombian grown, and Honduran grown, we could not extend our inferences to coffee grown in Guatemala or Mexico.

To use ANOVA, certain conditions must be met. The samples must be randomly selected from normal populations and the populations should have equal variances. In addition, the distance from one value to its group's mean should be independent of the distances of other values to that mean (independence of error). ANOVA is reasonably robust, and minor variations from normality and equal variance are tolerable. Nevertheless, the analyst should check the assumptions with the diagnostic techniques previously described.

Analysis of variance, as the name implies, breaks down or partitions total variability into component parts. Unlike the *t* test, which uses sample standard deviations, ANOVA uses squared deviations or the variance so computation of distances of the individual data points from their own mean or from the grand mean can be summed (recall that standard deviations sum to zero).

In an ANOVA model, each group has its own mean and values that deviate from that mean. Similarly, all the data points from all of the groups produced an overall *grand mean*. The total deviation is the sum of the squared differences between each data point and the overall grand mean.

The total deviation of any particular data point may be partitioned into *between-groups variance* and *within-groups variance*. The between-groups variance represents the effect of the **treatment** or factor. The differences of between-group means imply that each group was treated differently and the treatment will appear as deviations of the sample means from the grand mean. Even if this were not so, there would still be some natural variability among subjects and some variability attributable to sampling. The within-groups variance describes the deviations of the data points within each group from the sample mean. This results from variability among subjects and from random variation. It is often called error.

Intuitively, we might conclude that when the variability attributable to the treatment exceeds the variability arising from error and random fluctuations, the viability of the null hypothesis begins to diminish. And this is exactly the way the test statistic for analysis of variance works.

The test statistic for ANOVA if the **F ratio.** It compares the variance from the last two sources:

$$F = \frac{\text{Between-groups variance}}{\text{Within-groups variance}} = \frac{\text{Mean square}_{between}}{\text{Mean square}_{within}}$$

where

$$\text{Mean square}_{between} = \frac{\text{Sum of squares}_{between}}{\text{Degrees of freedom}_{between}}$$

$$\text{Mean square}_{within} = \frac{\text{Sum of squares}_{within}}{\text{Degrees of freedom}_{within}}$$

To compute the *F* ratio, the sum of the squared deviations for the numerator and denominator are divided by their respective degrees of freedom. By dividing, we are computing the variance as an average or mean, thus the term *mean square*. The degrees of freedom for the numerator, the mean square between groups, is one less than the number of groups $(k - 1)$. The degrees of freedom for the denominator, the mean square within groups, is the total number of observations minus the number of groups $(n - k)$.

If the null hypothesis is true, there should be no difference between the populations, and the ratio should be close to 1. If the population means are not equal, the numerator should manifest this difference, and the *F* ratio should be greater than 1. The *F* distribution determines the size of ratio necessary to reject the null hypothesis for a particular sample size and level of significance.

To illustrate one-way ANOVA, consider the travel industry magazine that received several reports from international travelers about the quality of in-flight service on various carriers from the United States to Europe. Before writing a feature story coinciding with a peak travel period, the magazine decided to retain a researcher to secure a more balanced perspective on the reactions of travelers. The researcher selected passengers who had current impressions of meal service, comfort, and friendliness with a major carrier. Three airlines were chosen and 20 passengers were randomly selected for each airline. The data, found in Table 15–3,[11] are used for this and the next two examples. For the one-way analysis of

TABLE 15-3   Data Table: Analysis of Variance Examples

Subject	Flight Service Rating 1	Flight Service Rating 2	Airline	Class	Subject	Flight Service Rating 1	Flight Service Rating 2	Airline	Class
1	40	36	1	1	32	70	80	2	2
2	28	28	1	1	33	73	79	2	2
3	36	30	1	1	34	72	88	2	2
4	32	28	1	1	35	73	89	2	2
5	60	40	1	1	36	71	72	2	2
6	12	14	1	1	37	55	58	2	2
7	32	26	1	1	38	68	67	2	2
8	36	30	1	1	39	81	85	2	2
9	44	38	1	1	40	78	80	2	2
10	36	35	1	1	41	92	95	3	1
11	40	42	1	2	42	56	60	3	1
12	68	49	1	2	43	64	70	3	1
13	20	24	1	2	44	72	78	3	1
14	33	35	1	2	45	48	65	3	1
15	65	40	1	2	46	52	70	3	1
16	40	36	1	2	47	64	79	3	1
17	51	29	1	2	48	68	81	3	1
18	25	24	1	2	49	76	69	3	1
19	37	23	1	2	50	56	78	3	1
20	44	41	1	2	51	88	92	3	2
21	56	67	2	1	52	79	85	3	2
22	48	58	2	1	53	92	94	3	2
23	64	78	2	1	54	88	93	3	2
24	56	68	2	1	55	73	90	3	2
25	28	69	2	1	56	68	67	3	2
26	32	74	2	1	57	81	85	3	2
27	42	55	2	1	58	95	95	3	2
28	40	55	2	1	59	68	67	3	2
29	61	80	2	1	60	78	83	3	2
30	58	78	2	1					
31	52	65	2	2					

Airline 1 = Delta; 2 = Lufthansa; 3 = KLM
Class 1 = Economy; 2 = Business.
All data are hypothetical.

variance problem, we are only concerned with the columns labeled Flight Service Rating 1 and Airline. The factor, airline, is the grouping variable for three carriers. Again, we follow the procedure:

1. *Null hypothesis.* H_0: $\mu_{A1} = \mu_{A2} = \mu_{A3}$.
   H_A: $\mu_{A1} \neq \mu_{A2} \neq \mu_{A3}$.

2. *Statistical test.* The F test is chosen because we have k independent samples, accept the assumptions of analysis of variance, and have interval data.

3. *Significance level.* Let $\alpha = .05$, and d.f. = [numerator $(k - 1) = (3 - 1) = 2$], [denominator $(n - k) = (60 - 3) = 57$] = $(2, 57)$.

4. *Calculated value.*

$$F = \frac{MS_b}{MS_W} = \frac{5822.017}{205.695} = 28.304, \text{ d.f. } (2, 57)$$

See summary in Table 15–4.

5. *Critical test value.* Enter the Appendix Table F–9 with d.f. $(2, 57)$, $\alpha = .05$. The critical value is 3.16.

6. *Decision.* Since the calculated value is greater than the critical value (28.3 > 3.16), we reject the null hypothesis and conclude there are statistically significant differences between two or more pairs of means.

The ANOVA table found in Table 15–4 is a standard way of summarizing the results of analysis of variance. It contains the sources of variation, degrees of freedom, sum of squares, mean squares, and calculated F value. The probability of

TABLE 15–4   Summary Tables for One-Way ANOVA Example

Model Summary

Source		d.f.	Sum of Squares	Mean Square	F-Value	P-Value
Model	Airline	2	11644.033	5822.017	28.304	.0001
Residual	Error	57	11724.550	205.694		
Total		59	23368.583			

Factor: Airline
Dependent: Flight Service Rating 1

Means Table

	Count	Mean	Std. Dev.	Std. Error
Delta	20	38.950	14.006	3.132
Lufthansa	20	58.900	15.089	3.374
KLM	20	72.900	13.902	3.108

Scheffé's S Multiple Comparison Procedure

	Vs.	Diff.	Crit. Diff.	P-Value	
Delta	Lufthansa	19.950	11.400	.0002	S
	KLM	33.950	11.400	.0001	S
Lufthansa	KLM	14.000	11.400	.0122	S

S = Significantly different at this level.
Significance level: .05
All data are hypothetical.

rejecting the null hypothesis is computed up to 100 percent α. That is, the probability value column reports the exact significance for the F ratio being tested.

A Priori Contrasts   When we computed a t test, it was not difficult to discover the reasons the null was rejected. But with one-way ANOVA, how do we determine which pairs are not equal? We could calculate a series of t tests, but they would not be independent of each other and the resulting Type I error would increase substantially. Obviously, this is not recommended. If we had decided in advance that a comparison of specific populations was important, a special class of tests known as *a priori* **contrasts** could be used after the null was rejected with the F test (*a priori* because the decision was made before the test.)[12]

A modification of the F test provides one approach for computing contrasts:

$$F = \frac{MS_{CON}}{MS_W}$$

The denominator, the within-groups mean square, is the same as the error term of the one-way's F ratio (recorded in the summary table, Table 15–4). We have previously referred to the denominator of the F ratio as the error variance estimator. The numerator of the contrast test is defined as

$$MS_{CON} = SS_{CON} = \frac{\left(\sum_j C_j \bar{X}_j\right)^2}{\sum_j \frac{C_j^2}{n}}$$

where
    C_j is the contrast coefficient for the group j.
    n_j is the number of observations recorded for group j.

A contrast is useful for experimental and quasi-experimental designs when the researcher is interested in answering specific questions about a subset of the factor. For example, in a comparison of coffee products, we have a factor with six levels. The levels, blends of coffee, are meaningfully ordered. Assume we are particularly interested in two Central American grown blends and one Columbian blend. Rather than looking at all possible combinations, we can channel the power of the test into fewer degrees of freedom by stating the comparisons of interest. This increases our likelihood of detecting differences if they really exist.

Multiple Comparison Tests   For the probabilities associated with the contrast test to be properly used in the report of our findings, it is important that the contrast strategy be devised ahead of the testing. In the airline study, we had no theoretical reason for an a priori contrast. However, after examining the means table (Table 15–4), it was apparent that the airline means were quite disparate. Comparisons after the results are compared require *post hoc* tests or **multiple comparison procedures.** Multiple comparison tests use group means and incorporate the MS_{error} term of the

F ratio. Together they produce confidence intervals for the population means and a criterion score. Differences between the mean values may be compared.

There are roughly a dozen such tests with different optimization goals: maximum number of comparisons, unequal cell size compensation, cell homogeneity, α or β error reduction, and so forth. The example in Table 15–4 is Scheffé's S. It is a conservative test that is robust to violations of assumptions.[13] The computer calculated the critical difference criterion as 11.4; all the differences between the pairs of means exceed this. The null hypothesis for the Scheffé was tested at the .05 level. Therefore, conclude that all combinations of flight service mean scores differ from each other.

While the table provides information for understanding the rejection of the one-way null hypothesis and the Scheffé null, in Figure 15–8 we use plots for the comparisons. The means plot shows relative differences among the three levels of the factor. The Means by Standard Deviations plot reveals lower variability in the opinions recorded by the hypothetical Delta and KLM passengers. Nevertheless, these two groups are sharply divided on the quality of in-flight service, and that is apparent in the upper plot.

Exploring the Findings with Two-Way ANOVA   Is the airline on which the passengers traveled the only factor influencing perceptions of in-flight service? By extending the one-way ANOVA, it is possible to learn more about the service ratings. There are many possible explanations. We have chosen to look at the fare class of the travelers in the interest of brevity.

Recall that in Table 15–3, data were entered for the variable fare class: economy and business-class travelers. Adding this factor to the model, we have a *two-way* analysis of variance. Now three questions may be considered with one model.

1. Are differences in flight service ratings attributable to airlines?
2. Are differences in flight service ratings attributable to fare class?
3. Do the airline and the fare class interact with respect to flight service ratings?

The third question reveals a distinct advantage of the two-way model. A separate one-way model on airlines averages out the effects of class. Similarly, a single factor test of class averages out the effects of the airline. But an interaction test of airline by class considers them *jointly*.

Table 15–5 reports a test of the hypotheses for these three questions. The significance level was established at the .01 level. We first inspect the interaction effect, airline by class, since the individual *main effects* cannot be considered separately if factors operate jointly. The interaction was not significant at the .01 level, and the null is accepted. Now the separate main effects, airline and class, can be verified. As with the one-way ANOVA, the null for the airline factor was rejected, and class was also found significant at .0001.

**FIGURE 15–8
One-Way
Analysis of
Variance Plots**

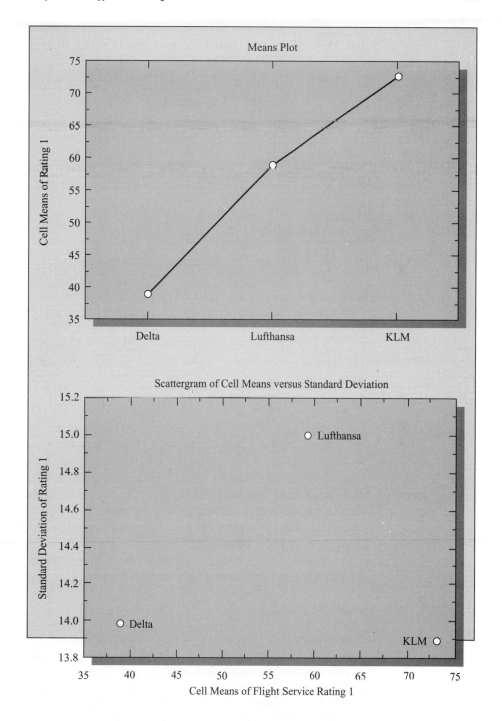

TABLE 15–5   Summary Tables for Two-Way ANOVA Example

Model Summary

Source	d.f.	Sum of Squares	Mean Square	F-Value	P-Value
Airline	2	11644.033	5822.017	39.178	.0001
Class	1	3182.817	3182.817	21.418	.0001
Airline * Class	2	517.033	258.517	1.740	.1853
Residual	54	8024.700	148.606		

Main Effects:
  Airline.
  Class.
Dependent: Flight Service Rating 1.

Means Table Effect: Airline * Class

	Count	Mean	Std. Dev.	Std. Error
Delta Economy	10	35.600	12.140	3.839
Delta Business	10	42.300	15.550	4.917
Lufthansa Economy	10	48.500	12.501	3.953
Lufthansa Business	10	69.300	9.166	2.898
KLM Economy	10	64.800	13.037	4.123
KLM Business	10	81.000	9.603	3.037

All data are hypothetical.

Means and standard deviations listed in the table are plotted in Figure 15–9 on p. 465. We note a band of similar deviations for economy-class travelers and a band of lower variability for business class—with the exception of one carrier. The plot of cell means confirms visually what we already know from the summary table: there is no interaction between airline and class ($p = .185$). If an interaction had occurred, the lines connecting the cell means would have crossed rather than displaying a parallel pattern.

Analysis of variance is an extremely versatile and powerful method that may be adapted to a wide range of testing applications. Discussions of further extensions in n-way and experimental designs may be found in the list of suggested readings.

Nonparametric Test   When there are k independent samples for which nominal data have been collected, the chi-square test is appropriate. It can also be used to classify data at higher measurement levels, but metric information is lost when reduced. The k sample χ^2 test is an extension of the two independent sample cases treated earlier. It is calculated and interpreted in the same way.

The Kruskal-Wallis test is appropriate for data that are collected on an ordinal scale or interval data that do not meet F-test assumptions, that cannot be

**FIGURE 15–9
Two-Way
Analysis of
Variance Plots**

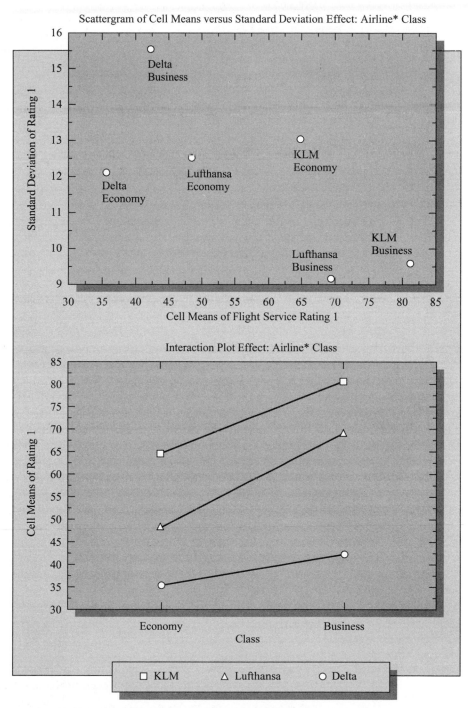

All data are hypothetical.

transformed, or for another reason prove to be unsuitable for a parametric test. Kruskal-Wallis is a one-way analysis of variance by ranks. It assumes random selection and independence of samples, and an underlying continuous distribution.

Data are prepared by converting ratings or scores to ranks for each observation being evaluated. The ranks range from the highest to lowest of all data points in the aggregated samples. The ranks are then tested to decide if they are samples from the same population. An application of this technique is provided in Appendix E.

k Related Samples Case

Parametric Test   A *k* **related samples test** is required for situations where (1) the grouping factor has more than two levels, (2) observations or subjects are matched or the same subject is measured more than once, and (3) the data are at least interval. In experimental or ex post facto designs with *k* samples, it is often necessary to measure subjects several times. These repeated measurements are called **trials.** For example, multiple measurements are taken in studies of stock prices, products evaluated by quality assurance, inventory, sales, and measures of human performance. Hypotheses for these situations may be tested with a univariate or multivariate general linear model. The latter is beyond the scope of this discussion.

The repeated measures ANOVA is a special type of *n*-way analysis of variance. In this design, the repeated measures of each subject are related just as they are in the related *t* test when only two measures are present. In this sense, each subject serves as its own control requiring a within-subjects variance effect to be assessed differently than the between-groups variance in a factor like airline or fare class. The effects of the correlated measures are removed before calculation of the *F* ratio.

This model is an appropriate solution for the data presented in Table 15–3. You will remember that the one-way and two-way examples considered only the first rating of in-flight service. Assume a second rating was obtained after a week by reinterviewing the same respondents. We now have two trials for the dependent variable, and we are interested in the same general question as with the one-way ANOVA with the addition of how the passage of time affects perceptions of in-flight service.

Following the testing procedure, we state:

1. *Null hypotheses.*
   (1) Airline: $H_0: \mu_{A1} = \mu_{A2} = \mu_{A3}.$
   (2) Ratings: $H_0: \mu_{R1} = \mu_{R2}.$
   (3) Ratings × Airline: $H_0: (\mu_{R1A1} - \mu_{R1A2} - \mu_{R1A3}) =$
                           $(\mu_{R2A1} - \mu_{R2A2} - \mu_{R2A3}).$

   For the alternative hypotheses, we will generalize to the statement that not all the groups have equal means for each of the three hypotheses.

2. *Statistical test.* The *F* test for repeated measures is chosen because we have related trials on the dependent variable for *k* samples, accept the assumptions of analysis of variance, and have interval data.

3. *Significance level.* Let $\alpha = .05$ and d.f. = [airline (2, 57), ratings (1, 57), ratings by airline (2, 57)].

4. *Calculated values.* See summary in Table 15–6.

5. *Critical test value.* Enter Appendix Table F–9 with d.f. (2, 57), $\alpha = .05$ and (1, 57), $\alpha = .05$. The critical values are 3.16 (2, 57) and 4.01 (1, 57).

6. *Decision.* The statistical results are grounds for rejecting all three null hypotheses and concluding there are statistically significant differences between means in all three instances. We conclude the perceptions of in-flight service were significantly affected by the different airlines, the interval between the two measures had a significant effect on the ratings, and the measures' time interval and the airlines interacted to a significant degree.

The ANOVA summary table found in Table 15–6 records the results of the tests. A means table provides the means and standard deviations for all combinations of ratings by airline. A second table of means reports the differences between flight service ratings 1 and 2. In Figure 15–10, there is an interaction plot for these

TABLE 15–6 Summary Tables for Repeated Measures ANOVA

Model Summary

Source	d.f.	Sum of Squares	Mean Square	F-Value	P-Value
Airline	2	35527.550	17763.775	67.199	.0001
Subject (Group)	57	15067.650	264.345		
Ratings	1	625.633	625.633	14.318	.0004
Ratings *Air. . .	2	2061.717	1030.858	23.592	.0001
Ratings * Subj. . .	57	2490.650	43.696		

Dependent: Flight Service Ratings 1 and 2.

Means Table Ratings * Airline

	Count	Mean	Std. Dev.	Std. Error
Rating 1, Delta	20	38.950	14.006	3.132
Rating 1, Lufthansa	20	58.900	15.089	3.374
Rating 1, KLM	20	72.900	13.902	3.108
Rating 2, Delta	20	32.400	8.268	1.849
Rating 2, Lufthansa	20	72.250	10.572	2.364
Rating 2, KLM	20	79.800	11.265	2.519

Means Table Effect: Ratings

	Count	Mean	St. Dev.	Std. Error
Rating 1	60	56.917	19.902	2.569
Rating 2	60	61.483	23.208	2.996

All data are hypothetical.

**FIGURE 15–10
Repeated Measures
ANOVA Plot**

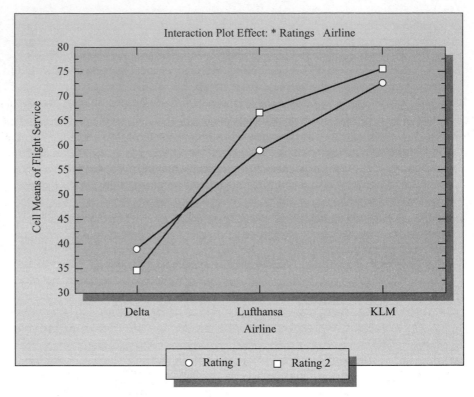

All data are hypothetical

data. Note that the second in-flight service rating was improved in two of the three groups after one week, and with the third carrier, there was a decrease in favorable response. The intersecting lines in the interaction plot reflect this finding.

Nonparametric Tests   When the k-related samples have been measured on a nominal scale, the Cochran Q test is a good choice.[14] This test extends the McNemar test, discussed earlier, for studies having more than two samples. It tests the hypothesis that the proportion of cases in a category is equal for several related categories.

When the data are at least ordinal, the Friedman two-way analysis of variance is appropriate. It tests matched samples, ranking each case and calculating the mean rank for each variable across all cases. It uses these ranks to compute a test statistic. The product is a two-way table where the rows represent subjects and the columns represent the treatment conditions.[15]

Summary

There are two approaches to hypothesis testing—classical or sampling theory statistics and the Bayesian approach. With classical statistics, we make inferences about a population based on evidence gathered from a sample. Although we cannot state unequivocally what is true about the entire population, representative samples allow us to make statements about what is probably true and how much error is likely to be encountered in arriving at a decision. The Bayesian approach also employs sampling statistics but has an additional element of prior information to improve the decision maker's judgment. With prudent use of prior probabilities, the Bayesian approach will also provide good results.

A difference between two or more sets of data is statistically significant if it actually occurs in a population. To have a statistically significant finding based on sampling evidence, we must be able to calculate the probability that some observed difference is large enough that there is little chance it could result from random sampling. Probability is the foundation for deciding on the acceptability of the null hypothesis, and sampling statistics facilitate acquiring the estimates.

Hypothesis testing can be viewed as a six-step procedure:

1. Establish a null hypothesis as well as the alternative hypothesis. It is a one-tailed test of significance if the alternative hypothesis states the direction of difference. If no direction of difference is given, it is a two-tailed test.

2. Choose the statistical test on the basis of the assumption about the population distribution and measurement level. The form of the data can also be a factor. In the light of these considerations, one typically chooses the test that has the greatest power efficiency or ability to reduce decision errors.

3. Select the desired level of confidence. While $\alpha = .05$ is the most frequently used, many others are also used. The α is the significance level that we desire and is typically set in advance of the study. Alpha is the risk of rejecting a true null hypothesis and represents a decision error. The β or Type II error is the decision error that results from accepting a false null hypothesis. Usually, one determines a level of acceptable α error then seeks to reduce the β error by increasing the size sample, shifting from a two-tailed to a one-tailed significance test, or both.

4. Compute the actual test value of the data.

5. Obtain the critical test value, usually by referring to a table for the appropriate type of distribution.

6. Make the decision by comparing the actual test value with the critical test value.

Parametric and nonparametric tests are applicable under the various conditions described in the chapter. They were also summarized in Figure 15–5. Parametric tests operate with interval and ratio data and are preferred when their assumptions can be met. Diagnostic tools examine the data for violations of those assumptions. Nonparametric tests do not require stringent assumptions about population distributions and are useful with less powerful nominal and ordinal measures.

In selecting a significance test, one needs to know, at a minimum, the number of samples, their independence or relatedness, and the measurement level of the data.

Statistical tests emphasized in the chapter were the Z and t tests, analysis of variance, and chi-square. The Z and t tests may be used to test for the difference between two means. The t test is chosen when the sample size is small. Variations on the t test are used for both independent and related samples.

One-way analysis of variance compares the means of several groups. It has a single grouping variable, called a factor, and a continuous dependent variable. Analysis of variance (ANOVA) partitions the total variation among scores into between-groups (treatment) and within-groups (error) variance. The F ratio, the test statistic, determines if the differences are sufficiently large to reject the null hypothesis. ANOVA may be extended to two-way, n-way, repeated measures, and multivariate applications.

Chi-square is a nonparametric statistic that is used frequently for crosstabulation or contingency tables. Its applications include testing for differences between proportions in populations and testing for independence. Corrections for chi-square were discussed.

KEY TERMS

a priori contrasts
alternative hypothesis
analysis of variance (ANOVA)
Bayesian statistics
chi-square test
classical statistics
critical value
F ratio
inferential statistics
k independent samples test
k related samples tests
level of significance
multiple comparison *(post hoc)* tests
nonparametric tests
normal probability plot
null hypothesis
one-sample tests

one-tailed test
parametric tests
power of the test
practical significance
regions of acceptance
regions of rejection
statistical significance
t distribution
t test
treatment (factor(s))
trials (repeated measures)
two independent samples tests
two related samples tests
two-tailed test
Type I error
Type II error
Z distribution
Z test

Discussion Questions

1. Distinguish between:
   a. Parametric and nonparametric tests.
   b. Type I and Type II errors.
   c. Null hypothesis and alternative hypothesis.
   d. Acceptance region and rejection region.
   e. One-tailed and two-tailed tests.
   f. Type II error and the power of the test.

2. Suggest situations where the researcher should be more concerned with Type II error than with Type I.

3. *a.* How can the probability of a Type I error be reduced? A Type II error?

   b. How does practical significance differ from statistical significance?

   c. Suppose you interview all members of the freshman and senior classes and find that 65 percent of the freshmen and 62 percent of the seniors favor a certain ecological proposal. Is this difference significant?

4. You conduct a survey of a sample of 25 members of this year's graduating class and find that their average GPA is 3.2. The standard deviation of the sample is 0.4. Over the last 10 years, the average has been 3.0. Is this year's class significantly different from the long-run average? At what alpha level would it be significant?

5. You are curious about whether the professors and students at your school are of different political persuasions. So you take a sample of 20 professors and 20 students drawn randomly from each population. You find that 10 professors say they are conservative while only 6 students claim they are conservative. Is this a statistically significant difference?

6. Summarize the steps of hypothesis testing. What is the virtue of this procedure?

7. In analysis of variance, what is the purpose of the mean square between and the mean square within? If the null hypothesis is accepted, what do these quantities look like?

8. Describe the assumptions for ANOVA and explain how they may be diagnosed.

9. You contact a random sample of 36 graduates of Western University and learn that their starting salaries were $18,000 last year. You then contact a random sample of 40 graduates from Eastern University and find that their average starting salary was $18,800. In each case, the standard deviation of the sample was $1,000.

   a. Test the null hypothesis that there is no difference between average salaries received by the graduates of the two schools.

   b. What assumptions are necessary for this test?

10. A random sample of students is interviewed to determine if there is an association between the class and attitudes toward corporations. With the following results, test the hypothesis that there is no difference among students on this attitude.

	Favorable	*Neutral*	*Unfavorable*
Freshman	100	50	70
Sophomore	80	60	70
Junior	50	50	80
Senior	40	60	90

11. You do a survey of business school students and liberal arts school students to find out how many times a week they read a daily newspaper. In each case, you interview 100 students. You find the following.

$$\overline{X}_b = 4.5 \text{ times per week}$$
$$s_b = 1.5$$
$$\overline{X}_{la} = 5.6 \text{ times per week}$$
$$s_{la} = 2.0$$

Test the hypothesis that there is no significant difference between these two samples.

Computer Problems

12. The management of the One-Koat Paint Company has developed a new type of porch paint that it hopes will be the most durable on the market. They test their product against the two leading competing products by using a machine that scrubs until it wears through the coating. One-Koat runs five trials with each product and secures the following results (in thousands of scrubs).

Trial	One-Koat	Competitor A	Competitor B
1	37	34	24
2	30	19	25
3	34	22	23
4	28	31	20
5	29	27	20

Test the hypothesis there are no differences between the means of these products ($\alpha = .05$).

13. Test the assumptions for ANOVA in the last problem using what graphical diagnostic checks may be available in your computer software.

14. Using the data in Table 15–3 for variables Flight Service Rating 2 and Airline (2, 3), test the hypothesis of no difference between means.

15. A computer manufacturer is introducing a new product specifically targeted at the home market and wishes to compare the effectiveness of three sales strategies: computer stores, home electronics stores, and department stores. The number of sales by 15 salespeople are recorded below:

Electronics store: 5, 4, 3, 3, 3

Department store: 9, 7, 8, 6, 5

Computer store: 7, 4, 8, 4, 3

a. Test the hypothesis that there is no difference between the means of the retailers ($\alpha = .05$).

b. Select a post hoc test, if necessary, to determine which groups differ in mean sales ($\alpha = .05$).

16. A financial analyst is interested in whether there was a significant change in profits for utilities from one period to another. A random sample of 11 companies from the Forbes 500 contributed the following data:

Company	Profits 1988	Profits 1989
Ohio Edison	218.9	361.0
Kentucky Utilities	79.4	82.3
PSI Holdings	99.1	125.2
Idaho Power	49.0	84.7
NY State E & G	171.5	157.8
Northeast Utilities	224.8	203.2
Southwestern Public Service	105.0	124.9
Pacific Corp.	446.8	465.6
Scana	120.7	122.6
Puget Sound Power & Light	128.2	117.7
Public Service Colorado	124.9	148.8

SOURCE: *Forbes,* April 30, 1990.

a. Should a test of independence or related samples be used?

b. Is there a difference in profits between the two years?

17. A consumer testing firm is interested in testing two competing antivirus products for personal computers. They want to know how many strains of virus will be removed.

The data are:

	Removed by Q-Cure?	
Removed by Anti-V?	*Yes*	*No*
Yes	45	33
No	58	20

Are Anti-V and Q-Cure equally effective ($\alpha = .05$)?

18. A researcher for an auto manufacturer is examining preferences for styling features of larger sedans. Buyers were classified as "first-time" and "repeat," resulting in the following table.

	Preference	
	European Styling	*Japanese Styling*
Repeat	40	20
First-time	8	32

a. Test the hypothesis that buying characteristic is independent of styling preference ($\alpha = .05$).

b. Should the statistic be adjusted?

Reference Notes

1. A more detailed example is found in Amir D. Aczel, *Complete Business Statistics,* 2nd ed. (Homewood, Ill.: Richard D. Irwin, 1993), pp. 235–38.
2. The standardized randomized variable, denoted by Z, is a deviation from expectancy and is expressed in terms of standard deviation units. The mean of the distribution of a standardized random variable is 0, and the standard deviation is 1. With this distribution, the deviation from the mean by any value of X can be expressed in standard deviation units.
3. Procedures for hypothesis testing are reasonably similar across authors. This outline was influenced by Sidney Siegel, *Nonparametric Statistics for the Behavioral Sciences* (New York: McGraw-Hill, 1956), chap. 2.
4. Marija J. Norusis/SPSS, Inc., *SPSS for Windows Base System User's Guide, Release 6.0* (Chicago: SPSS, Inc., 1993), pp. 601–6.
5. For further information on these tests, see ibid., pp. 187–88.
6. F. M. Andrews, L. Klem, T. N. Davidson, P. M. O'Malley, and W. L. Rodgers, *A Guide for Selecting Statistical Techniques for Analyzing Social Science Data* (Ann Arbor, Mich.: Institute for Social Research, 1976).
7. Statistical Navigator℠ is an IBM-PC/compatible product from The Idea Works, Inc., 100 West Briarwood, Columbia, Mo. 65203.
8. The figure is partially adapted from Siegel, *Nonparametric Statistics,* flyleaf.
9. See B. S. Everitt, *The Analysis of Contingency Tables* (London: Chapman and Hall, 1977).
10. The critiques are represented by: W. J. Conover, "Some Reasons for Not Using the Yates Continuity Correction on 2×2 Contingency Tables," *Journal of the American Statistical Association,* 69 (1974), pp. 374–76; and N. Mantel, "Comment and a Suggestion on the Yates Continuity Correction," *Journal of the American Statistical Association,* 69 (1974), pp. 378–80.
11. This data table and the analysis of variance tables and plots in this section were prepared with SuperANOVA℠.
12. See, for example, Roger E. Kirk, *Experimental Design: Procedures for the Behavioral Sciences* (Belmont, Calif.: Brooks/Cole, 1982), pp. 115–33. An exceptionally clear presentation for step-by-step hand computation is found in James L. Bruning and B. L. Kintz, *Computational Handbook of Statistics,* 2nd ed. (Glenview, Ill.: Scott, Foresman, 1977), pp. 143–68. Also, when using a computer program, the reference manual typically provides helpful advice in addition to the set-up instructions.
13. Kirk, *Experimental Design,* pp. 90–115. Alternatively, see Bruning and Kintz, *Computational Handbook of Statistics,* pp. 113–32.
14. For a discussion and example of the Cochran test, see Sidney Siegel and N. J. Castellan, Jr., *Nonparametric Statistics for the Behavioral Sciences,* 2nd ed. (New York: McGraw-Hill, 1988).
15. For further details, see ibid.; and Aczel, *Complete Business Statistics,* pp. 661–65.

Suggested Readings

1. Aczel, Amir D. *Complete Business Statistics,* 2nd ed. Homewood, Ill.: Richard D. Irwin, 1993. This excellent text is characterized by highly lucid explanations and numerous examples. It lives up to its title with comprehensive coverage of materials through advanced intermediate statistics.

2. deFinetti, Bruno. *Probability, Induction, and Statistics.* New York: John Wiley & Sons, 1972. A highly readable work on subjective probability and the Bayesian approach.

3. Kirk, Roger E. *Experimental Design: Procedures for the Behavioral Sciences.* Belmont, Calif.: Brooks/Cole, 1982. An excellent review of hypothesis testing and an authoritative source on analysis of variance and experimental design.

4. Berenson, Mark L.; David M. Levine; and David Rindskopf. *Applied Statistics: A First Course.* Englewood Cliffs, N.J.: Prentice Hall, 1988. For students or managers without recent statistical coursework, this text provides an excellent review.

5. Norusis, Marija J./SPSS Inc. *SPSS for Windows Base System User's Guide, Release 6.0.* Chicago: SPSS Inc., 1993. Application-oriented instruction of basic methods from one of the best documented software packages.

6. Siegel, Sidney, and N. J. Castellan, Jr. *Nonparametric Statistics for the Behavioral Sciences.* 2nd ed. New York: McGraw-Hill, 1988. The classic book on nonparametric statistics.

7. Winer, B. J. *Statistical Principles in Experimental Design.* 2nd ed. New York: McGraw-Hill, 1971. Another classic source. Thorough coverage of analysis of variance and experimental design.

CHAPTER 16 MEASURES OF ASSOCIATION

 FINDING
YOUR WAY

INTRODUCTION

Research questions in business frequently revolve around the study of relationships between two or more variables. Various objectives may be served by such analysis. The strength, direction, shape, and other features of the relationship may be discovered. Or tactical and strategic questions may be answered by predicting the values of one variable from those of another. Let's look at some typical management questions:

1. In the mail order business, excessive catalog costs quickly squeeze margins. Many mailings fail to reach receptive or active buyers. What is the relationship between various categories of mailings that delete inactive customers and the improvement in profit margins?

2. Medium-sized companies often have difficulty attracting the cream of the MBA crop, and when they are successful, they have trouble retaining them. What is the relationship between the ranking of candidates based on executive interviews and the ranking obtained from testing and assessment?

3. Retained cash flow, undistributed profits plus depreciation, is a critical source of funding for equipment investment. During a period of decline, capital spending suffers. What is the relationship between retained cash flow and equipment investment over the last year? Between cash flow and dividend growth?

4. Aggressive U.S. high-tech companies have invested heavily in the European chip market and their sales have grown 20 percent over the three largest European firms. Can we predict next year's sales based on present investment?

All these questions may be evaluated using measures of association. And all call for different techniques based on the level at which the variables were measured or the intent of the question. Problems one through three require nominal, ordinal, and interval measures, respectively. Problem four is answered through simple bivariate regression.

With correlation, one calculates an index to measure the nature of the relationship between variables. With regression, an equation is developed to predict the values of a dependent variable. Both are affected by the assumptions of measurement level and the distributions that underlie the data.

Table 16–1 lists some common measures and their uses. The chapter follows the progression of the table, first covering bivariate linear correlation, then simple regression, and concluding with nonparametric measures of association. Exploration of data through visual inspection and diagnostic evaluation of assumptions continue to be emphasized.

TABLE 16-1   **Commonly Used Measures of Association**

Measurement	Coefficient	Comments and Uses
Interval and Ratio	**Pearson product moment**	For continuous linearly related variables.
	Correlation ratio (eta)	For nonlinear data or relating a main effect to a continuous dependent variable.
	Biserial	One continuous and one dichotomous variable with an underlying normal distribution.
	Partial correlation	Three variables; relating two with the third's effect taken out.
	Multiple correlation	Three variables; relating one variable with two others
	Bivariate linear regression	Predicting one variable from another's scores.
Ordinal	**Gamma**	Based on concordant-discordant pairs: $(P - Q)$; proportional reduction in error (PRE) interpretation.
	Kendall's tau – b	$P - Q$ based; adjustment for tied ranks.
	Kendall's tau – c	$P - Q$ based; adjustment for table dimensions
	Somer's d	$P - Q$ based; asymmetrical extension of gamma.
	Spearman's rho	Product moment correlation for ranked data.
Nominal	**Phi**	Chi-square (CS) based for 2 x 2 tables.
	Cramer's V	CS based; adjustment when one table dimension > 2.
	Contingency Coefficient	CS based; flexible data and distribution assumptions.
	Lambda	PRE based interpretation
	Goodman & Kruskal's tau	PRE based with table marginals emphasis.
	Uncertainty Coefficient	Useful for multidimensional tables.
	Kappa	Agreement measure

Statistics covered are in **boldface.**

BIVARIATE CORRELATION ANALYSIS

Bivariate correlation analysis differs from nonparametric measures of association and regression analysis in two important ways. First, parametric correlation requires two continuous variables measured on an interval or ratio scale. Second, the coefficient does not distinguish between independent and dependent variables. It treats the variables symmetrically since the coefficient r_{xy} has the same interpretation as r_{yx}.

Pearson's Product Moment Coefficient *r*

The **Pearson** (product moment) **correlation coefficient** varies over a range of $+1$ through 0 to -1. The designation *r* symbolizes the coefficient's estimate of linear association based on sampling data. The coefficient ρ represents the population correlation.

Correlation coefficients reveal the magnitude and direction of relationships. The *magnitude* is the degree to which variables move in unison or opposition. The size of a correlation of $|.40$ is the same as one of $-.40$. The sign says nothing about size. The degree of correlation is modest. The coefficient's sign signifies the *direction* of the relationship. Direction tells us whether large values on one variable are associated with large values on the other (and small values with small values). When the values correspond in this way, the two variables have a positive relationship: As one increases, the other also increases. Family income, for example, is positively related to household food expenditures. As income increases, food expenditures increase. Other variables are inversely related. Large values on the first variable are associated with small values on the second (and vice versa). The prices of products and services are inversely related to their scarcity. In general, as products decrease in available quantity, their prices rise. The absence of a relationship is expressed by a coefficient of approximately zero.

Scatterplots for Exploring Relationships

Scatterplots are essential for understanding the relationships between variables. They provide a means for visual inspection of data that a list of values for two variables cannot. Both the direction and shape of a relationship are conveyed in a plot. With a little practice, the magnitude of the relationship can be seen.

Figure 16–1 contains a series of scatterplots that depict some relationships across the range *r*. The three plots on the left side of the figure have their points sloping from the upper left to the lower right of each *X-Y* plot.[1] They represent different magnitudes of negative relationships. On the right side of the figure, three plots have opposite patterns and show positive relationships.

When stronger relationships are apparent (for example, the $\pm.90$ correlations), the points cluster close to an imaginary straight line passing through the data. The weaker relationships ($\pm.40$) depict a more diffuse data cloud with points spread farther from the line.

The shape of linear relationships is characterized by a straight line, whereas nonlinear relationships have curvilinear, parabolic, and compound curves representing their shapes. Pearson's *r* measures relationships in variables that are linearly related. It cannot distinguish linear from nonlinear data. Summary statistics alone do not reveal the appropriateness of the data for the model, as the following example illustrates. One author constructed four small data sets possessing identical summary statistics but displaying strikingly different patterns.[2] Table 16–2 contains these data. Figure 16–2 on page 481 exhibits plots of the data. In the upper left panel of the figure, the variables are positively related. Their points follow a superimposed straight line through the data. This example is well suited to correlation analysis. In the second plot, the data are curvilinear in relation to the line, and *r* is an inappropriate measure of their relationship. The third plot shows the presence of an influential point that changed a coefficient that would have other-wise been a perfect +1.0. The last plot displays constant values of X (similar to what you might find in an animal or quality-control experiment). One leverage point establishes the fitted line for this data.

We will return to these concepts and the process of drawing the line when we discuss regression. For now, comparing plots 2 through 4 with 1 suggests the importance of visually inspecting correlation data for under-lying patterns. Careful analysts make scatterplots an integral part of the inspec-tion and exploration of their data. Although small samples may be plotted by hand, statistical software packages save time and offer a variety of plotting procedures.

FIGURE   16–1   Scatterplots of Correlations between Two Variables

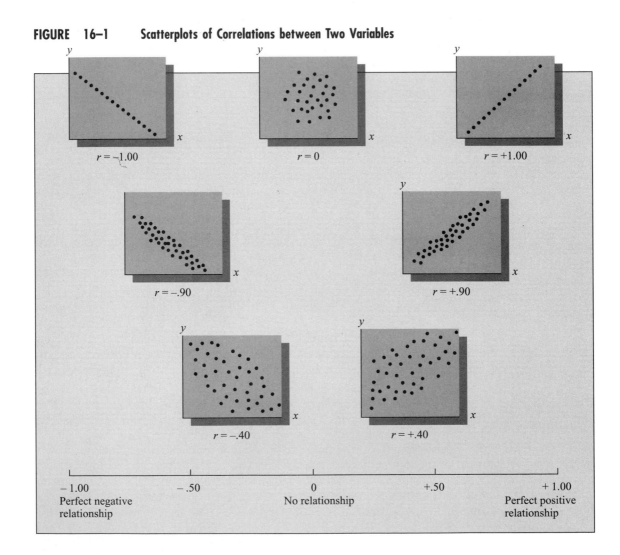

TABLE 16–2   **Four Data Sets with the Same Summary Statistics**

Ss	X_1	Y_1	X_2	Y_2	X_3	Y_3	X_4	Y_4
1	10	8.04	10	9.14	10	7.46	8	6.58
2	8	6.95	8	8.14	8	6.77	8	5.76
3	13	7.58	13	8.74	13	12.74	8	7.71
4	9	8.81	9	8.77	9	7.11	8	8.84
5	11	8.33	11	9.26	11	7.81	8	8.47
6	14	9.96	14	8.10	14	8.84	8	7.04
7	6	7.24	6	6.13	6	6.08	8	5.25
8	4	4.26	4	3.10	4	5.39	19	12.50
9	12	10.84	12	9.13	12	8.15	8	5.56
10	7	4.82	7	7.26	7	6.42	8	7.91
11	5	5.68	5	4.74	5	5.73	8	6.89
Pearson's r		.81642		.81624		.81629		.81652
r^2		.66654		.66624		.66632		.66671
Adjusted r^2		.62949		.62916		.62925		.62967
Standard error		1.23660		1.23721		1.23631		1.23570

FIGURE   16–2   Different Scatterplots for the Same Summary Statistics

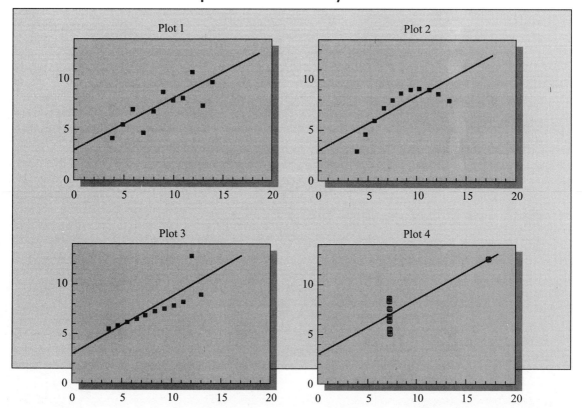

The Assumptions of r

Like other parametric techniques, correlation analysis makes certain assumptions of the data. Many of these assumptions are necessary to test hypotheses about the coefficient.

The first requirement for r is **linearity.** All of the examples in Figure 16–1 with the exception of $r = 0$ illustrate a relationship between variables that can be described by a straight line passing through the data cloud. When $r = 0$, no pattern is evident that could be described with a single line. Parenthetically, it is also possible to find coefficients of 0 where the variables are highly related but in a nonlinear form. As we have seen, plots make such findings evident.

The second assumption for correlation is a **bivariate normal distribution.** That is, the data are from a random sample of a population where the two variables are normally distributed in a joint manner.

Often these assumptions or the required measurement level cannot be met. Then the analyst should select a nonlinear or nonparametric measure of association, many of which are described later in the chapter.

Computation and Testing of r

The formula for calculating Pearson's r is

$$r = \frac{\Sigma(X - \overline{X})(Y - \overline{Y})}{(N - 1)s_x s_y} \tag{1}$$

where
   N is the number of pairs of cases.
   s_x, s_y are the standard deviations for X and Y.
   Alternatively,

$$r = \frac{\Sigma xy}{\sqrt{(\Sigma x^2)(\Sigma y^2)}} \tag{2}$$

since

$$s_x = \sqrt{\frac{\Sigma x^2}{N}} \quad s_y = \sqrt{\frac{\Sigma y^2}{N}}$$

If the numerator of equation (2) is divided by N, we have the *covariance,* the amount of deviation that the X and Y distributions have in common. With a positive covariance, the variables move in unison, and with a negative one, they move in opposition. When the covariance is 0, there is no relationship. The denominator for

TABLE 16-3   Computation of Pearson's Product Moment Correlation

Corporation	Net Profit ($ mil.) X	Cash Flow ($ mil.) Y	Deviations from Means $(X - \bar{X})\ x$	$(Y - \bar{Y})\ y$	xy	x^2	y^2
1	82.6	126.5	−93.84	−178.64	16763.58	8805.95	31912.25
2	89.0	191.2	−87.44	−113.94	9962.91	7645.75	12982.32
3	176.0	267.0	−0.44	−38.14	16.78	0.19	1454.66
4	82.3	137.1	−94.14	−168.04	15819.29	8862.34	28237.44
5	413.5	806.8	237.06	501.66	118923.52	56197.44	251602.56
6	18.1	35.2	158.34	−269.94	42742.30	25071.56	72867.60
7	337.3	425.5	160.86	120.36	19361.11	25875.94	14486.53
8	145.8	380.0	−30.64	74.86	−2293.71	938.81	5604.02
9	172.6	326.6	−3.84	21.36	−82.02	14.75	456.25
10	247.2	355.5	70.76	50.36	3563.47	5006.98	2536.13

$\bar{X} = 176.44 \quad \bar{Y} = 305.14 \qquad\qquad \Sigma xy = 224777.23$

$s_x = 216.59 \quad s_y = 124.01 \qquad\qquad\qquad\qquad \Sigma x^2 = 138419.71$

$$\Sigma y^2 = 422139.76$$

equation (2) represents the maximum potential variation that the two distributions share. Thus, correlation may be thought of as a ratio.

Table 16–3 contains a random subsample of 10 firms of the Forbes 500 sample described in Chapter 14. The variables chosen to illustrate computation of r are cash flow and net profits. Beneath each variable is its mean and standard deviation. In columns 4 and 5 we obtain the deviations of the X and Y values from their means, and in column 6 we find the product. Columns 7 and 8 are the squared deviation scores.

Substituting into the formula

$$r = \frac{224777.23}{\sqrt{138419.71} * \sqrt{422139.76}} = .9298$$

In this subsample, net profits and cash flow are positively related and have a very high coefficient. As net profits increase, cash flow increases; the opposite is also true. Linearity of the variables may be examined with a scatterplot such as the one shown in Figure 16–3. The data points fall along a straight line.

Common Variance as an Explanation   The amount of common variance in X (net profits) and Y (cash flow) may be summarized by r^2, the **coefficient of determination.**

As the diagram below shows, the overlap between the two variables is the proportion of their common or shared variance.

The shaded area represents the percentage of the total relationship accounted for by one or the other variables. So 86 percent of the variance in X is explained by Y, and vice versa.

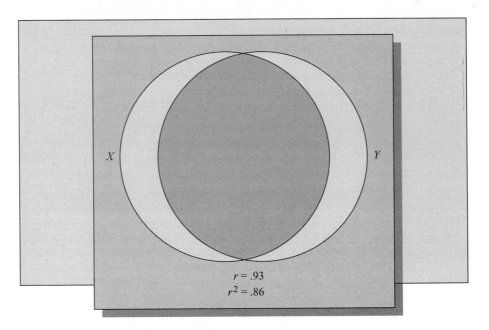

FIGURE 16–3
Plot of Net
Profits with
Cash Flow

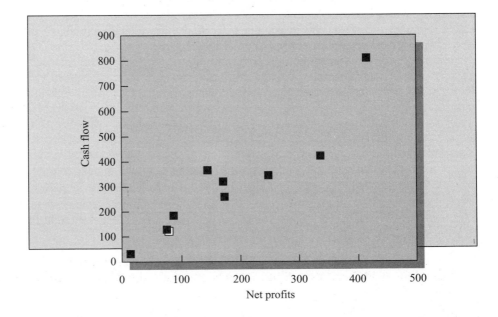

Testing the Significance of r   Is the coefficient representing the relationship between net profits and cash flow real or has it occurred by chance? This question tries to discover whether our r is a chance deviation from a population p of zero. In other situations, the researcher may wish to know if significant differences exist between two or more rs. In either case, r's significance should be checked before using it in other calculations or comparisons. For this test, we must have independent random samples from a bivariate normal distribution. Then the Z or t test may be used for the null hypothesis, $p = 0$.

The formula for small samples

$$t = \frac{r}{\sqrt{\dfrac{1 - r^2}{n - 2}}}$$

where

$r = .93$
$n = 10$

Substituting into the equation, t is calculated

$$t = \frac{.93}{\sqrt{\dfrac{1 - .86}{8}}} = 7.03$$

With $n - 2$ degrees of freedom, $p < .005$ for the one-tailed alternative, H_A: $\rho > 0$. We reject the hypothesis that there is no linear relationship between net profits and cash flow in the population. The above statistic is appropriate when the null hypothesis states a correlation of 0. It should be used only for a one-tailed test.[3] However, it is often difficult to know in advance whether the variables are positively or negatively related, particularly when a computer removes our contact with the raw data. Software programs produce two-tailed tests for this eventuality. The observed significance level for a one-tailed test is half of the printed two-tailed version in most programs.

Correlation Matrix

A **correlation matrix** is a table used to display coefficients for more than two variables. Table 16–4 shows the intercorrelations among six variables for the full Forbes 500 data set.[4]

It is conventional for a symmetrical matrix to report findings in the triangle below the diagonal. The diagonal contains coefficients of 1.00 that signify the relationship of each variable with itself. Journal articles and management reports often show matrices with coefficients at different probability levels. A symbol beside the coefficient keys the description of differences to a legend. The practice of reporting tests of the null hypothesis, $r = 0$, was followed in Table 16–4.

TABLE 16–4   Correlation Matrix for Forbes 500 Sample

	Assets ($ mil.)	Cash Flow ($ mil.)	Number Employed (thousands)	Market Value ($ mil.)	Net Profits ($ mil.)	Sales ($ mil.)
Assets	1.0000					
Cash flow	.3426	1.0000				
Employed	.3898	.8161	1.0000			
Market value	.3642	.9353	.8106	1.0000		
Net profits	.2747	.9537	.7467	.9101	1.0000	
Sales	.5921	.7990	.8831	.7485	.7267	1.0000

NOTES:

All coefficients are statistically significant, $p < .01$.

$n = 100$.

Correlation matrices have utility beyond bivariate correlation studies. Interdependence among variables is a common characteristic of most multivariate techniques. Matrices form the basis for computation and understanding the nature of relationships in multiple regression, discriminant analysis, factor analysis, and many others. Such applications call for variations on the standard matrix. Pooled within-groups covariance matrices average the separate covariances for several groups and array the results as coefficients. Total or overall correlation matrices treat coefficients as if they came from a single sample.

Interpretation of Correlations

A correlation coefficient of any magnitude or sign, whatever its statistical significance, does not imply causation. Increased net profits may cause an increase in market value, or improved satisfaction may cause improved performance in certain situations, but correlation provides no evidence of cause and effect. Several alternate explanations may be provided for correlation results: (1) X causes Y, (2) Y causes X, (3) X and Y are activated by one or more other variables, or (4) X and Y influence each other reciprocally. Ex post facto studies seldom possess sufficiently powerful designs to *demonstrate* which of these conditions could be true. By controlling variables under an experimental design, more rigorous evidence of causality may be obtained.

Take care to avoid so-called **artifact correlations** where distinct groups combine to give the impression of one. The upper panel of Figure 16–4 shows data from two sectors. If computed as a single group, the coefficient suggests a positive correlation. Calculations for separate sectors reveal no relationship between the X and Y variables. The lower panel contains a plot of Forbes 500 data on assets and sales. The narrow band enclosed by the ellipse are companies that score high on assets and low in sales—all are banks. Treated separately, the correlation is nearly perfect, but when returned to the sample, the overall relationship drops to the mid .80s.

Another issue affecting interpretation of coefficients concerns practical significance. Even when a coefficient is statistically significant, it must be practically

FIGURE 16–4
Artifact
Correlations

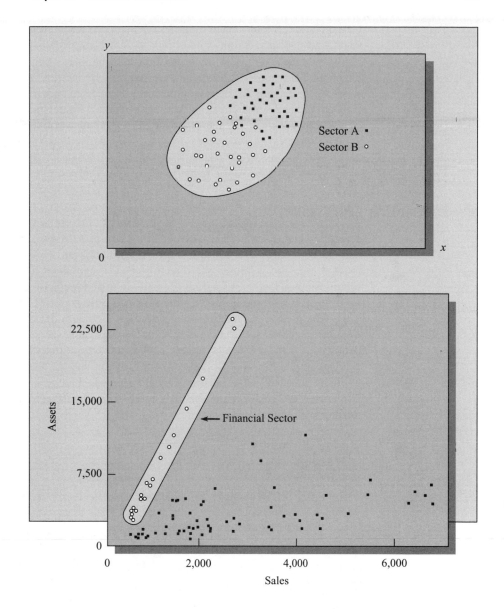

meaningful. In many relationships, other factors combine to make the coefficient's meaning misleading. For example, in nature we expect rainfall and the height of reservoirs to be positively correlated. But in states where water management and flood-control mechanisms are complex, an apparently simple relationship may not hold. Techniques like partial and multiple correlation or multiple regression are helpful in sorting out confounding effects.

With large samples, even exceedingly low coefficients can be statistically significant. This "significance" only reflects the likelihood of a linear relationship in the population. Should magnitudes less than .30 be reported when they are significant? It all depends. We might consider the correlations between variables such as cash flow, sales, market value, or net profits to be interesting revelations of a particular phenomenon whether they were high, moderate, or low. The nature of the study, the characteristics of the sample, or other reasons will be determining factors. But a coefficient is not remarkable simply because it is statistically significant.

By probing the evidence of direction, magnitude, statistical significance, and common variance together with the study's objectives and limitations, we reduce the chances of reporting trivial findings. Simultaneously, the communication of practical implications to the reader will be improved.

BIVARIATE LINEAR REGRESSION[5]

In the previous section, we focused on relationships between variables. The product moment correlation was found to represent an index of the magnitude of the relationship, the sign governed the direction, and r^2 explained the common variance. Relationships also serve as a basis for estimation and prediction.

When we take the observed values of X to estimate or predict corresponding Y values, the process is called simple prediction.[6] When more than one X variable is used, the outcome is a function of multiple predictors. Simple and multiple predictions are made using a technique called **regression analysis.**

The similarities and differences of regression and correlation are summarized in Figure 16–5. Their relatedness would suggest that beneath many correlation problems is a regression analysis that could provide further insight about the relationship of Y with X.

The Basic Model   A straight line is fundamentally the best way to model the relationship between two continuous variables. The bivariate linear regression may be expressed as

$$Y = \beta_0 + \beta_1 X_i$$

where the value of the dependent variable Y is a linear function of the corresponding value of the independent variable X_i in the ith observation. The slope, β_1, and the Y intercept, β_0, are known as **regression coefficients.** The **slope, β_1,** is the change in Y for a one-unit change in X. It is sometimes called the "rise over run." This is defined by the formula:

$$\beta_1 = \frac{\Delta Y}{\Delta X}$$

This is the ratio of change (Δ) in the rise of the line relative to the run or travel along the X axis. Figure 16–6 shows a few of the many possible slopes you may encounter.

The **intercept, β_0,** is the value for the linear function when it crosses the Y axis; it is the estimate of Y when $X = 0$. A formula for the intercept based on the mean scores of the X and Y variables is:

$$\beta_0 = \bar{Y} - \beta_1 \bar{X}$$

**FIGURE 16–5
Comparison of
Bivariate Linear
Correlation and
Regression**

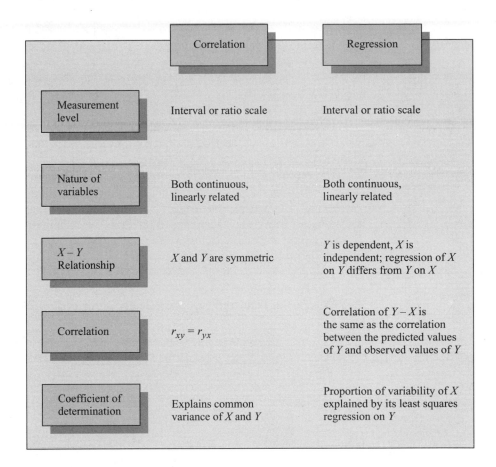

	Correlation	Regression
Measurement level	Interval or ratio scale	Interval or ratio scale
Nature of variables	Both continuous, linearly related	Both continuous, linearly related
$X - Y$ Relationship	X and Y are symmetric	Y is dependent, X is independent; regression of X on Y differs from Y on X
Correlation	$r_{xy} = r_{yx}$	Correlation of $Y - X$ is the same as the correlation between the predicted values of Y and observed values of Y
Coefficient of determination	Explains common variance of X and Y	Proportion of variability of X explained by its least squares regression on Y

**FIGURE 16–6
Examples of
Different Slopes**

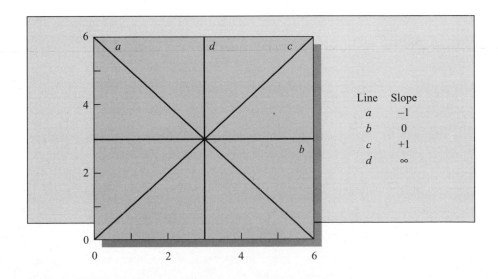

Line	Slope
a	-1
b	0
c	$+1$
d	∞

**Concept
Application**

The price of investment-grade wine is influenced in several ways, not the least of which is tasting. Tasting from the barrel is a major determinant of market *en primeur* or futures contracts, which represent about 60 percent of the harvest. After 18 to 24 months in oak casks, further tasting occurs, and the remaining stock is released.

Weather is widely regarded as responsible for pronouncements about wine quality. A Princeton economist has elaborated on that notion. He suggested that just a few facts about local weather conditions may be better predictors of vintage French red wines than the most refined palates and noses.[7]

The regression model developed predicts an auction price index for about 80 wines from winter and harvest rainfall and average growing-season temperatures. Interestingly, the calculations suggested that the 1989 Bordeaux would be one of the best since 1893. The "guardians of tradition" reacted hysterically to these methods yet agreed with the conclusion.

While this application of regression analysis requires multiple predictors, our first example will use one predictor with highly simplified data. Let X represent the average growing-season temperature in degrees Celsius and Y the price of a 12-bottle case in French francs. The data appear below.

X	Y
Average Temperature Celsius	*Price per Case (FF)*
12	2000
16	3000
20	4000
24	5000
$\overline{X} = 18$	$\overline{Y} = 3500$

The plotted data in Figure 16–7 show a linear relationship between the pairs of points and a perfect positive correlation, $r_{yx} = 1.0$. The slope of the line is calculated:

$$\beta_1 = \frac{Y_i - Y_j}{X_i - X_j} = \frac{4000 - 3000}{20 - 16} = \frac{1000}{4} = 250$$

where the $X_i Y_i$ values are the data points (20, 4000) and $X_j Y_j$ are points (16, 3000). The intercept β_0 is -1000, the point at which $X = 0$ in this plot. This area is off the graph and appears in an insert on the figure.

$$\beta_0 = \overline{Y} - \beta_1 \overline{X} = 3500 - 250(18) = -1000$$

Substituting into the formula, we have the simple regression equation

$$Y = -1000 + 250X_i$$

FIGURE   16–7   Plot of Wine Price by Average Growing Temperature

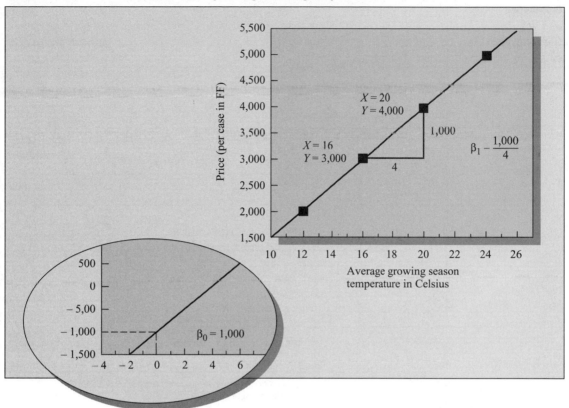

We could now predict that a warm growing season with 25.5°C temperatures would bring a case price of 5375 French francs. $\hat{Y}$ (called Y-hat) is the predicted value of Y.

$$\hat{Y} = -1000 + 250(25.5) = 5375$$

Unfortunately, one rarely comes across a data set composed of four paired values, a perfect correlation, and an easily drawn line. A model based on such data is *deterministic* in that for any value of X, there is only one possible corresponding value of Y. It is more likely that we will collect data where the values of Y vary for each X value. Considering Figure 16–8, we should expect a distribution of price values for the temperature $X = 16$, another for $X = 17$, and another for each value of X. The means of these Y distributions will also vary in some systematic way with X. These variabilities lead us to construct a *probabilistic* model that also uses a linear function.[8] This function is written

$$Y_i = \beta_0 + \beta_1 X_i + \epsilon_1$$

where ϵ symbolizes the deviation of the ith observation from the mean, $\beta_0 + \beta_1 X_i$.

FIGURE 16–8
Distribution
of Y for
Observations
of X

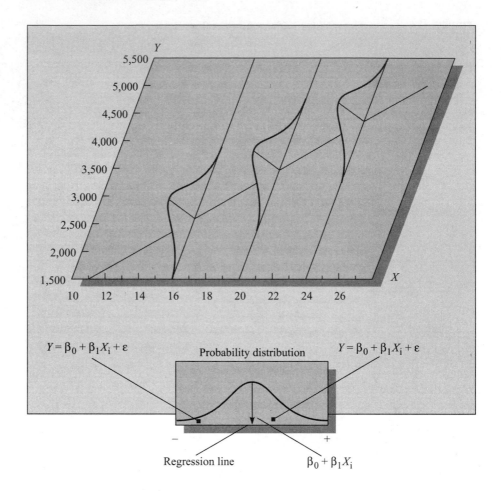

FIGURE 16–8 Distribution of Y for Observations of X

As shown in Figure 16–8, the actual values of Y may be found above or below the regression line represented by the mean value of Y ($\beta_0 + \beta_1 X_i$) for a particular value of X. These deviations are the error in fitting the line and are often called the **error term.**

Method of Least Squares

Table 16–5 contains a new data set for the wine price example. Our prediction of Y from X must now account for the fact that the X and Y pairs do not fall neatly along the line. Actually, the relationship could be summarized by several lines. Figure 16–9 suggests a few alternatives based on visual inspection—all of which produce errors, or vertical distances from the observed values to the line. The **method of least squares** allows us to find a regression line, or line of best fit, which will keep these errors to a minimum. It uses the criterion of minimizing the total squared errors of estimate. When we predict values of Y for each X_i, the difference between the actual Y_i and the predicted $\hat{Y}$ is the error. This error is squared

TABLE 16–5   Data for Wine Price Study

	Y Price (FF)	X Temperature (C°)	XY	Y²	X²	y²	x²
1	1813.00	11.80	21393.40	3286969.00	139.24	3186225.00	61.00
2	2558.00	15.70	40160.60	6543364.00	246.49	1081600.00	15.29
3	2628.00	14.00	36792.00	6906384.00	196.00	940900.00	31.47
4	3217.00	22.90	73669.30	10349089.00	524.41	145161.00	10.82
5	3228.00	20.00	64560.00	10419984.00	400.00	136900.00	0.15
6	3629.00	20.10	72942.90	13169641.00	404.01	961.00	0.24
7	3886.00	17.90	69559.40	15100996.00	320.41	82944.00	2.92
8	4897.00	23.40	114589.80	23980609.00	547.56	1687401.00	14.36
9	4933.00	24.60	121351.80	24334489.00	605.16	1782225.00	24.90
10	5199.00	25.70	133614.30	27029601.00	660.49	2563201.00	37.09
Σ	35988.00	196.10	748633.50	141121126.00	4043.77	11607518.00	198.25
Mean	3598.80	19.61					
s	1135.66	4.69					
Sum of squares (SS)	11607511.59	198.25	42908.82				

FIGURE 16–9
Scatterplot and
Possible
Regression Lines
Based on Visual
Inspection

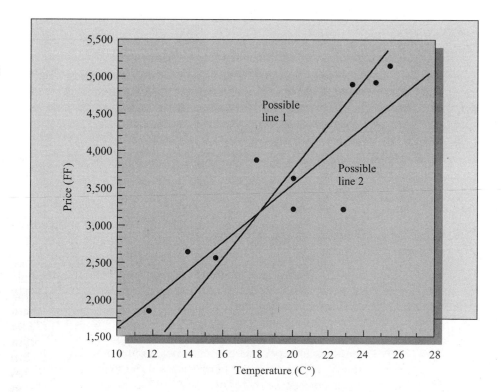

and then summed. The line of best fit is the one that minimizes the total squared errors of prediction.[9]

$$\sum_{i=1}^{n} e_i^2 \text{minimized}$$

Regression coefficients β_0 and β_1 are used to find the least squares solution. They are computed as follows:

$$\beta_1 = \frac{\Sigma XY - \dfrac{(\Sigma X)(\Sigma Y)}{n}}{\Sigma X^2 - \dfrac{(\Sigma X)^2}{n}}$$

$$\hat{\beta}0 = \overline{Y} - \hat{\beta}1\,\overline{X}$$

Substituting into both formulas with data from Table 16–5,

$$\beta_1 = \frac{748633.5 - \dfrac{(196.1)(35988)}{10}}{4043.77 - \dfrac{(196.1)^2}{10}} = 216.439$$

$$\hat{\beta}_0 = 3598.8 - (216.439)(19.61) = -645.569$$

The predictive equation is now $\hat{Y} = -645.57 + 216.44\ X_i$.

Drawing the Regression Line   Before drawing the regression line, we select two values of X to compute. Using values 13 and 24 for X_i, the points are

$$\hat{Y} = -645.57 + 216.44(13) = 2168.15$$

$$\hat{Y} = 645.57 + 216.44(24) = 4548.99$$

Comparing the line drawn in Figure 16–10 to the trial lines in Figure 16–9, one can readily see the success of the least squares method in minimizing the error of prediction.

Residuals   We now turn our attention to the plot of standardized residuals in Figure 16–11. A **residual** is what remains after the line is fit or $(Y_i - \hat{Y}_i)$. When standardized, they are comparable to Z scores with a mean of 0 and a standard deviation of 1. In this plot, the standardized residuals should fall between 2 and -2, be randomly distributed about zero, and show no discernible pattern. All these conditions say the model is applied correctly.

In our example, we have one residual at -2.2, a random distribution about zero, and few indications of a sequential pattern. It is important to apply other diagnostics to verify that the regression assumptions are met. Various software programs provide plots and other checks of normality, linearity, equality of variance, and independence of error.[10]

**FIGURE 16–10
Drawing the
Least Squares
Line**

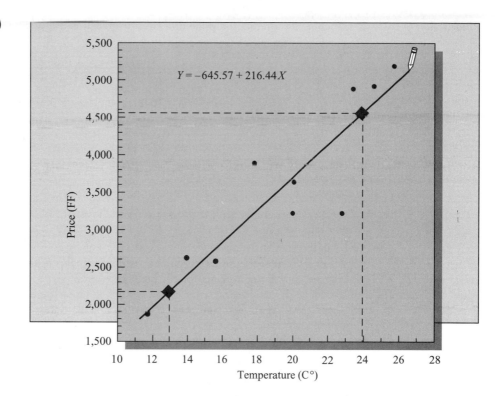

$Y = -645.57 + 216.44X$

**FIGURE 16–11
Plot of
Standardized
Residuals**

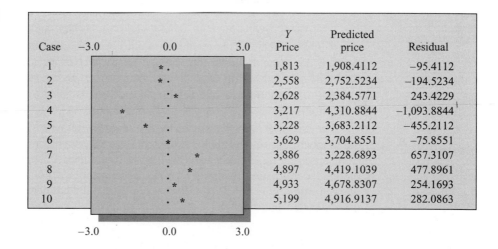

Case	−3.0	0.0	3.0	Y Price	Predicted price	Residual
1		* .		1,813	1,908.4112	−95.4112
2		* .		2,558	2,752.5234	−194.5234
3		. *		2,628	2,384.5771	243.4229
4	*	.		3,217	4,310.8844	−1,093.8844
5		* .		3,228	3,683.2112	−455.2112
6		*		3,629	3,704.8551	−75.8551
7		. *		3,886	3,228.6893	657.3107
8		. *		4,897	4,419.1039	477.8961
9		. *		4,933	4,678.8307	254.1693
10		. *		5,199	4,916.9137	282.0863

Predictions

If we wanted to predict the price of a case of investment-grade wine for a growing season that averages 21°C, our prediction would be

$$\hat{Y} = -645.57 + 216.44(21) = 3899.67$$

This is a *point prediction* of Y and should be corrected for greater precision. As with other confidence estimates, we establish the degree of confidence desired and substitute into the formula

$$\hat{Y} \pm t_{\alpha/2}\, s \sqrt{1 + \frac{1}{10} + \frac{(X - \overline{X})^2}{SS_x}}$$

where

$t_{\alpha/2}$ is the two-tailed critical value for t at the desired level (95 percent in this example).

s is the standard error of estimate (also the square root of the mean square error from the analysis of variance of the regression model) (Table 16–6).

SS_x is the sum of squares for X (Table 16–5).

$$3899.67 \pm (2.306)(538.559) \sqrt{1 + \frac{1}{10} + \frac{(21 - 19.61)^2}{198.25}}$$

$$3899.67 \pm 1308.29$$

We are 95 percent confident of our prediction that a case of investment-quality French red wine grown in a particular year at 21°C average temperatures will be initially priced at 3899.67 $\pm$ 1308.29, or from approximately 2591 to 5208 FF. The comparatively large band width results from the amount of error in the model (reflected by r^2), some peculiarities in the Y values, and the use of a single predictor.

It is more likely that we would want to predict the average price of *all* cases grown at 21°C. This prediction would use the same basic formula omitting the first digit (the 1) under the radical. A narrower *confidence* band is the result since the average of all Y values is being predicted from a given X. In our example, the confidence interval for 95 percent is 3899.67 $\pm$ 411.42, or from 3488 to 4311.

The predictor we selected, 21°C, was close to the mean of X (19.61). Because the **prediction and confidence bands** are shaped like a bow tie, predictors farther from the mean have larger band widths. For example, X values of 15, 20, and 25 produce confidence bands of ±565, ±397, and ±617, respectively. This is illustrated in Figure 16–12. The further one's selected predictor is from X, the wider the prediction interval.

Testing the Goodness of Fit

With the regression line plotted and a few illustrative predictions, we should now gather some evidence of how well the model fits the data, **goodness of fit.** The most important test in bivariate linear regression is whether the slope, β_1, is equal to zero.[11] We have already observed a slope of zero in Figure 16–6, line *b*. Zero slopes result from various conditions: (1) Y is completely unrelated to

FIGURE 16-12
Prediction and
Confidence Bands
Based on
Proximity to X

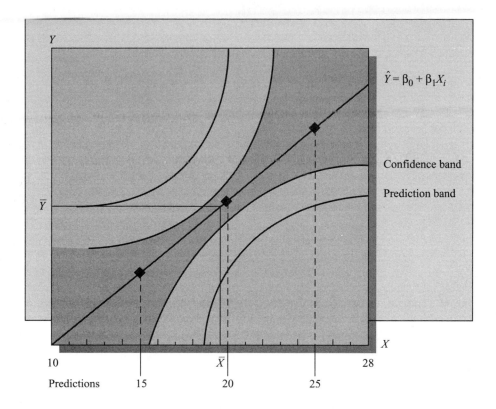

X, and no systematic pattern is evident; (2) there are constant values of Y for every value of X; or (3) the data are related but represented by a nonlinear function.

The t Test   To test whether $\beta_1 = 0$, we use a two-tailed test (since the actual relationship is positive, negative, or zero). The test follows the t distribution for $n - 2$ degrees of freedom.

$$t = \frac{b_1}{s(b_1)} = \frac{216.439}{38.249} = 5.659$$

where

b_1 was previously defined as the slope β_1.
$s(b_1)$ is the standard error of β_1.[12]

We reject the null, $\beta_1 = 0$ because the calculated t is greater than any t value for 8 degrees of freedom and $\alpha = .01$.

The F Test   Computer printouts generally contain an analysis of variance (ANOVA) table with an F test of the regression model. In bivariate regression, t and F tests produce the same results since t^2 is equal to F. In multiple regression, the F test has an overall role for the model, and each of the independent variables is

FIGURE   16–13   Components of Variation

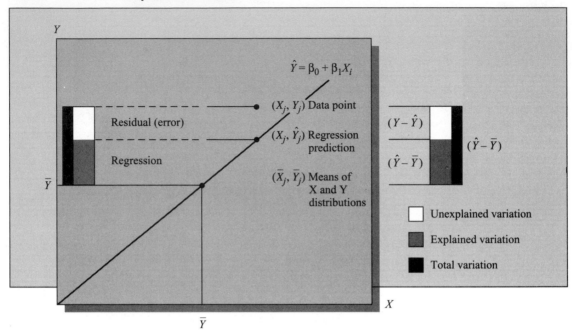

evaluated with a separate t test. From the last chapter, recall that ANOVA partitions variance into component parts. For regression, it comprises explained deviations, $\hat{Y} - \overline{Y}$, and unexplained deviations, $Y - \hat{Y}$. Together they constitute the total deviation, $Y - \overline{Y}$. This is shown graphically in Figure 16–13. These sources of deviation are squared for all observations and summed across the data points.

In Table 16–6, we develop this concept sequentially concluding with the F test of the regression model for the wine data. Based on the results presented in that table, we find statistical evidence of a linear relationship between variables. The alternative hypothesis, $r^2 \neq 0$, is accepted with $F = 32.02$, d.f., $(1,8)$, $p < .005$. The null hypothesis for the F test had the same effect as $\beta_1 = 0$ since we could select either test.

Coefficient of Determination   In predicting the values of Y without any knowledge of X, our best estimate would be Y, its mean. Each predicted value that does not fall on $\overline{Y}$ contributes to an error of estimate, $(Y - \overline{Y})$. The total squared error for several predictions would be $\Sigma(Y_i - \overline{Y})^2$. By introducing known values of X into a regression equation, we attempt to reduce this error even further. Naturally, this is an improvement over using $\overline{Y}$, and the result is $(\hat{Y} - \overline{Y})$. The total improvement based on several estimates is $\Sigma(\hat{Y}_i - Y)^2$, the amount of variation explained by the relationship between X and Y in the regression. Based on the formula, the *coefficient of determination* is the ratio of the line of best fit's error over that incurred

TABLE 16–6   Progressive Application of Partitioned Variance Concept

General Concept

$$(\hat{Y} - \bar{Y}) \qquad\qquad + \qquad\qquad (Y - \hat{Y}) \qquad\qquad = \qquad\qquad (Y - \bar{Y})$$

Explained Variation
(the regression relationship
between X and Y)

Unexplained Variation
(cannot be explained by
the regression relationship)

Total Variation

ANOVA Application

$$\sum_{i=1}^{n} (\hat{Y} - \bar{Y})^2 \qquad\qquad \sum_{i=1}^{n} (Y - \hat{Y})^2 \qquad\qquad \sum_{i=1}^{n} (Y - \bar{Y})^2$$

SSr
Sum of Squares Regression

SSe
Sum of Squares Error

SSt
Sum of Squares Total

Contents of Summary Table

Source	Degrees of Freedom	Sum of Squares	Mean Square	F ratio
Regression	1	SSr	$MSr = \dfrac{SSr}{1}$	$\dfrac{MSr}{MSe}$
Error	$n-2$	SSe	$MSe = \dfrac{SSe}{n-2}$	
Total		SSt		

ANOVA Summary Table: Test of Regression Model

Source	Degrees of Freedom	Sum of Squares	Mean Square	F ratio
Regression	1	9,287,143.11	9,287,143.11	32.02
Residual (error)	8	2,320368.49	290,046.06	
Total		11,607,511.60		

Significance of $F = .0005$

by using $\overline{Y}$. One purpose of testing, then, is to discover whether the regression equation is a more effective predictive device than the mean of the dependent variable.

As in correlation, the coefficient of determination is symbolized by r^2.[13] It has several purposes. As an index of fit, it is interpreted as the total proportion of variance in Y explained by X. As a measure of linear relationship, it tells us how well the regression line fits the data. It is also an important indicator of the predictive accuracy of the equation. Typically, we would like to have an r^2 that explains 80 percent or more of the variation. Lower than that, predictive accuracy begins to fall off. r^2 is calculated

$$r^2 = \frac{\sum_{i=1}^{n}(\hat{Y} - \overline{Y})^2}{\sum_{i=1}^{n}(Y - \overline{Y})^2} = \frac{SS_r}{SS_e} = 1 - \frac{SS_e}{SS_t}$$

For the wine price study, r^2 was found using the data from the bottom of Table 16–6.

$$r^2 = 1 - \frac{2320368.49}{11607511.61} = .80$$

Eighty percent of the variance in price may be explained by growing-season temperatures. With actual data and multiple predictors, our results would improve.

NONPARAMETRIC MEASURES OF ASSOCIATION[14]

Measures for Nominal Data

Nominal measures are used to assess the strength of relationships in cross-classification tables. They are often used with chi-square or may be used separately. In this section, we provide examples of three statistics based on chi-square and two that follow the proportional reduction in error approach.

There is no fully satisfactory all-purpose measure for categorical data. Some are adversely affected by table shape and number of cells while others are sensitive to sample size or marginals. It is perturbing to find similar statistics reporting different coefficients for the same data. This occurs because of a statistic's particular sensitivity or the way it was devised.

Technically, we would like to find two characteristics with nominal measures: (1) when there is no relationship at all, the coefficient should be 0 and (2) when there is a complete dependency, the coefficient should display unity or 1. This does not always happen. Coupled with the sensitivity problem, analysts should be alerted to the need for careful selection of tests.

Chi-Square-Based Measures   Table 16–7 reports a 2 × 2 variation of the data on smoking and job-related accidents from Chapter 15. In this example, the observed significance level is less than the testing level ($\alpha = .05$), and the null hypothesis is rejected. A correction to chi-square is provided. We now turn to measures of asso-

TABLE 16–7   Chi-Square-Based Measures of Association

On-the-Job Accident

		Count	Yes	No	Row Total
Smoker	Yes		21	10	31
	No		13	22	35
	Column Total		34	32	66

Chi-Square	Value	DF	Significance
Pearson	6.16257	1	.01305
Continuity Correction	4.99836	1	.02537

Minimum Expected Frequency 15.030

Statistic	Value	Approximate Significance
Phi	.30557	.01305*
Cramer's V	.30557	.01305*
Contingency Coefficient	.29223	.01305*

*Pearson chi-square probability.

ciation to detect the strength of the relationship. Notice that the table also provides an approximate significance of the coefficient based on the chi-square distribution. This is a test of the null hypothesis: no relationship between the variables of accidents and smoking.

The first **chi-square based measure** is applied to smoking and on-the-job accidents. It is called **phi.** Phi ranges from 0 to +1.0 and attempts to correct χ^2 proportionately to N. Phi is best employed with 2×2 tables like this one since its coefficient can exceed +1.0 when applied to larger tables. Phi is calculated

$$\phi = \sqrt{\frac{\chi^2}{N}} = \sqrt{\frac{6.616257}{66}} = .3056$$

Phi's coefficient shows a moderate relationship between smoking and job-related accidents. There is no suggestion in this interpretation that one variable causes the other nor is there an indication of the direction of the relationship.

Cramer's V is a modification of phi for larger tables and has a range up to 1.0 for tables of any shape. It is calculated

$$V = \sqrt{\frac{\chi^2}{N(k-1)}} = \sqrt{\frac{6.616257}{66(1)}} = .3056$$

where

k = the lesser number of rows or columns.

In this table, the coefficient is the same as phi.

The **contingency coefficient C** is reported last. It is not comparable to other measures and has a different upper limit for various table sizes. The upper limits are determined as

$$\sqrt{\frac{k - 1}{k}}$$

where

k = the number of columns.

For a 2 × 2 table, the upper limit is .71; for a 3 × 3, .82; and for a 4 × 4, .87. Although this statistic operates well with tables having the same number of rows as columns, its upper limit restriction is not consistent with a criterion of good association measurement. C is calculated as

$$C = \sqrt{\frac{\chi^2}{\chi^2 + N}} = \sqrt{\frac{6.616257}{6.61625 + 66}} = .2922$$

The chief advantage of C is its ability to accommodate data in almost every form: skewed or normal, discrete or continuous, and nominal or ordinal.

Proportional Reduction in Error (PRE)   PRE statistics are the second type used with contingency tables. *Lambda* and *tau* are the examples discussed here. The coefficient **lambda** (λ) is based on how well the frequencies of one nominal variable offer predictive evidence about the frequencies of another. Lambda is asymmetrical—allowing calculation for the direction of prediction—and symmetrical, predicting row and column variables equally.

The computation of lambda is straightforward. In Table 16–8, we have results from an opinion survey with a sample of 400 shareholders. Only 180 out of 400 (45 percent) favor capping executives' salaries while 220 (55 percent) do not favor it. With this information alone, if asked to predict the opinions of an individual in the sample, one would achieve the best prediction record by always choosing the modal category. Here it is "do not favor." By doing so, however, you would be wrong 180 out of 400 times. The probability estimate for an incorrect classification is .45, $P(1) = (1 - .55)$.

Now suppose one has prior information about the respondents' occupational status and was asked to predict opinion. Would it improve predictive ability? Yes, you would make the predictions by summing the probabilities of all cells that are not the modal value for their rows (for example, cell (2, 1) is 20/400 or .05):

$$P(2) = \text{cell } (1,2)\ .05 + \text{cell } (2,1)\ .15 + \text{cell } (3,1)\ .075 = .275$$

Lambda is then calculated:

$$\lambda = \frac{P(1) - P(2)}{P(1)} = \frac{.45 - .275}{.45} = .3889$$

TABLE 16–8   Proportional Reduction in Error Measures

What is your opinion about capping executives' salaries?

	Count Col. Pct.	Favor	Do not Favor	Row Total
	Managerial	90 22.5	20 5.0	110
Occupational Class	White collar	60 15.0	80 20.0	140
	Blue collar	30 7.5	120 30.0	150
	Column total	180 45.0%	220 55.0%	400 100.0%

Chi-Square	Value	DF	Significance
Pearson	98.38646	2	.00000
Likelihood Ratio	104.96542	2	.00000

Minimum Expected Frequency 49.500

Statistic	Value	ASE1	T-Value	Approximate Significance
Lambda:				
symmetric	.30233	.03955	6.77902	
with occupation dependent	.24000	.03820	5.69495	
with opinion dependent	.38889	.04555	7.08010	
Goodman & Kruskal Tau:				
with occupation dependent	.11669	.02076		.00000*
with opinion dependent	.24597	.03919		.00000*

*Based on chi-square approximation.

Note that the asymmetric lambda in Table 16–8, where opinion is the dependent variable, reflects this computation. As a result of knowing the respondents' occupational classification, we improved our prediction by 39 percent. If we wished to predict occupational classification from opinion instead of the opposite, a λ of .24 would be secured. This means that 24 percent of the error in predicting occupational class is eliminated by knowledge of opinion on the executives' salary question. Lambda varies between 0 and 1 corresponding with no ability to eliminate errors to elimination of all errors of prediction.

Goodman and Kruskal's **tau** statistic uses table marginals to reduce prediction errors. In predicting opinion on executives' salaries without any knowledge of occupational class, we would expect a 50.5 percent correct classification and a 49.5

percent probability of error. These are based on the column marginal percentages in Table 16–8.

Column Marginal		Column Percent		Correct Cases
180	*	45	=	81
220	*	55	=	$\frac{121}{202}$

Total correct classification

Correct classification of the opinion variable $= .505 = \dfrac{202}{400}$

Probability of error, $P(1) = (1 - .505) = .495$

When additional knowledge of occupational class is used, information for correct classification of the opinion variable is improved to 62.7 percent with a 37.3 percent probability of error. This is obtained using the cell counts and marginals for occupational class (refer to Table 16–8), as shown below:

Row 1	$\left(\dfrac{90}{110}\right)90 + \left(\dfrac{20}{110}\right)20$	$= 73.6364 + 3.6364$	$= 77.2727$
Row 2	$\left(\dfrac{60}{140}\right)60 + \left(\dfrac{80}{140}\right)80$	$= 25.7143 + 45.7142$	$= 71.4286$
Row 3	$\left(\dfrac{30}{150}\right)30 + \left(\dfrac{120}{150}\right)120$	$= 6.0 + 96.0$	$= \underline{102.0000}$

Total correct classification (with additional information on occupational class)   250.7013

Correct classification of opinion variable $= .627 = \dfrac{250.7}{400}$

Probability of error, $P(2) = (1 - .627) = .373$

Tau is then computed

$$\tau = \frac{P(1) - P(2)}{P(1)} = \frac{.495 - .373}{.495} = .246$$

Table 16–8 shows that the information about occupational class has reduced error in predicting opinion to approximately 25 percent.

The table also contains information on the test of the null hypothesis that tau = 0 with an approximate observed significance level and asymptotic error (for developing confidence intervals). Based on the small observed significance level, we would conclude that tau is significantly different from a coefficient of 0 and that there is an association between opinion on executives' salaries and occupational class in the population from which the sample was selected. We can also establish the confidence level for the coefficient at the 95 percent level as approximately .25 ± .04.

Measures for Ordinal Data

When data require **ordinal measures,** there are several statistical alternatives. We will illustrate *gamma,* Kendall's *tau b* and *tau c,* Somers's *d,* and Spearman's *rho.* All but Spearman's rank-order correlation are based on the concept of concordant and discordant pairs. None of these statistics requires the assumption of a bivariate normal distribution, yet by incorporating order, most produce a range from -1.0 (a perfect negative relationship) to $+1.0$ (a perfect positive one). Within this range, a coefficient with a larger magnitude (absolute value of the measure) is interpreted as having a stronger relationship. These characteristics allow the analyst to interpret both the direction and the strength of the relationship.

Table 16–9 presents data for 70 managerial employees of a large industrial design firm who have been evaluated for coronary risk by the firm's health insurer. The management levels are ranked as are the fitness assessments by the physicians. If we were to use a nominal measure of association with this data (such as Cramer's V), the computed value of the statistic would be positive since order is not present in nominal data. But by using ordinal measures of association, the actual nature of the relationship is revealed. In this example, all coefficients have negative signs.

The information in the table has been arranged so the number of concordant and discordant pairs of individual observations may be calculated. When a subject that ranks higher on one variable also ranks higher on the other variable, the pairs of observations are said to be **concordant.** If a higher ranking on one variable is accompanied by a lower ranking on the other variable, the pairs of observations are **discordant.** Let P stand for concordant pairs and Q stand for discordant. When concordant pairs exceed discordant pairs in a $P - Q$ relationship, the statistic reports

TABLE 16–9   Tabled Ranks for Management and Fitness Levels

		Management Level			
	Count	Lower	Middle	Upper	
Fitness	High	14	4	2	20
	Moderate	18	6	2	26
	Low	2	6	16	24
		34	16	20	70

Statistic	Value*
Gamma	−.70242
Kendall's tau *b*	−.51279
Kendall's tau *c*	−.49714
Somers's *d*	
Symmetric	−.51263
With fitness dependent	−.52591
With management-level dependent	−.50000

*The *t*-value for each coefficient is −5.86451.

a positive association between the variables under study. As discordant pairs increase over concordant pairs, the association becomes negative. A balance indicates no relationship between the variables. Table 16–10 summarizes the procedure for calculating the summary terms needed in all the statistics we are about to discuss.[15]

Goodman and Kruskal's **gamma** is a statistic that compares concordant and discordant pairs and then standardizes the outcome by maximizing the value of the denominator. It has a proportional reduction of error (PRE) interpretation that connects nicely with what we already know about PRE nominal measures. Gamma is defined as

$$\gamma = \frac{P - Q}{P + Q} = \frac{172 - 984}{172 + 984} = \frac{-812}{1156} = -.7024$$

For the fitness data, we conclude that as management level increases, fitness decreases. This is immediately apparent from the larger number of discordant pairs. A more precise explanation for gamma takes its absolute value (ignoring the sign) and relates it to PRE. Hypothetically, if one was trying to predict whether the pairs were concordant or discordant, one might flip a coin and classify the outcome. A better way is to make the prediction based on the preponderance of concordance or discordance; the absolute value of gamma is the proportional reduction in error when it is done the second way. For example, you would get a 50 percent hit ratio using the coin. A PRE of .70 improves your hit ratio to 85 percent ($.50 \times 70$) + ($.50$) = $.85$.

With a γ of $-.70$, 85 percent of the pairs are discordant and .15 percent are concordant.[16] There are almost six times as many discordant pairs as concordant pairs. In situations where the data call for a 2×2 table, the appropriate modification of gamma is Yule's Q.[17]

Kendall's **tau *b*** is a refinement of gamma that considers tied pairs. A tied pair occurs when subjects have the same value on the X variable, on the Y variable, or on both. For a given sample size, there are $n(n - 1)/2$ pairs of observations.[18] After removing concordant pairs and discordant pairs, the remainder are tied. Tau b does not have a PRE interpretation but does provide a range of -1.0 to $+1.0$ for square tables. Its compensation for ties uses the information found in Table 16–10. It may be calculated as

$$\tau_b = \frac{P - Q}{\sqrt{\left(\frac{n(n - 1)}{2} - T_x\right)\left(\frac{n(n - 1)}{2} - T_y\right)}}$$
$$= \frac{172 - 984}{\sqrt{(2415 - 871)(2415 - 791)}} = -.5128$$

Kendall's **tau *c*** is another adjustment to the basic $P - Q$ relationship of gamma. This approach to ordinal association is suitable for tables of any size. Although we illustrate tau c, we would select tau b since the cross-classification table for the fitness data is square. The adjustment for table shape is seen in the formula.

$$\tau_c = \frac{2m(P - Q)}{N^2(m - 1)} = \frac{2(3)(172 - 984)}{(70)^2(3 - 1)} - .4971$$

where m is the smaller number of rows or columns.

Somers's d rounds out our coverage of statistics employing the concept of concordant-discordant pairs. This statistic's utility comes from its ability to compensate for tied ranks and adjust for the direction of the dependent variable. Again, we refer to the preliminary calculations provided in Table 16–10 to compute the symmetric and asymmetric ds. As before, the symmetric coefficient (equation 1) takes the row and column variables into account equally. The second and third calculations show fitness as the dependent and management level as the dependent, respectively.

$$d_{sym} = \frac{(P - Q)}{n(n - 1) - T_x T_y/2} = \frac{-812}{1584} = -.5126 \tag{4}$$

$$d_{y-x} = \frac{(P - Q)}{\dfrac{n(n - 1)}{2} - T_x} = \frac{-812}{2415 - 871} = -.5259 \tag{5}$$

$$d_{x-y} = \frac{(P - Q)}{\dfrac{n(n - 1)}{2} - T_y} = \frac{-812}{2415 - 791} = -.5000 \tag{6}$$

The **Spearman's rho** correlation is a popular ordinal measure. Along with Kendall's tau, it is among the most widely used of ordinal techniques. Rho correlates ranks between two ordered variables. Occasionally, researchers find continuous variables with too many abnormalities to correct. Then, scores may be reduced to ranks and calculated with Spearman's rho.

As a special form of Pearson's product moment correlation, rho's strengths outweigh its weaknesses. When data are transformed by logs or squaring, rho remains unaffected. Second, outliers or extreme scores that were troublesome before ranking no longer pose a threat since the largest number in the distribution is equal to the sample size. Third, it is an easy statistic to compute. The major deficiency is its sensitivity to tied ranks. Too many ties distort the coefficient's size. However, there are rarely too many ties to justify the correction formulas available.

To illustrate the use of rho, consider a situation where a brokerage firm is recruiting account executive trainees. Assume the field has been narrowed to 10 applicants for final evaluation. They arrive at the company headquarters, go through a battery of tests, and are interviewed by a panel of three executives. The test results are evaluated by an industrial psychologist who then ranks the 10 candidates. The executives produce a composite ranking based on the interviews. Your task is

Table 16-10   Calculation of Concordant (P), Discordant (Q), Tied (T_x, T_y), and Total Paired Observations

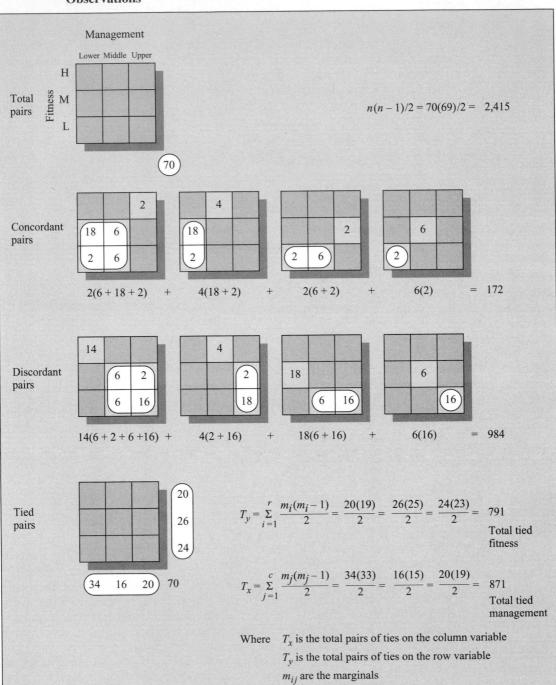

$n(n-1)/2 = 70(69)/2 = 2{,}415$

Concordant pairs

$2(6 + 18 + 2)$ + $4(18 + 2)$ + $2(6 + 2)$ + $6(2)$ = 172

Discordant pairs

$14(6 + 2 + 6 + 16)$ + $4(2 + 16)$ + $18(6 + 16)$ + $6(16)$ = 984

Tied pairs

$$T_y = \sum_{i=1}^{r} \frac{m_i(m_i - 1)}{2} = \frac{20(19)}{2} = \frac{26(25)}{2} = \frac{24(23)}{2} = 791$$

Total tied fitness

$$T_x = \sum_{j=1}^{c} \frac{m_j(m_j - 1)}{2} = \frac{34(33)}{2} = \frac{16(15)}{2} = \frac{20(19)}{2} = 871$$

Total tied management

Where T_x is the total pairs of ties on the column variable

T_y is the total pairs of ties on the row variable

m_{ij} are the marginals

TABLE 16-11   Data for Spearman's rho

| | Rank by | | | |
Applicant	Panel x	Psychologist y	d	d^2
1	3.5	6	−2.5	6.25
2	10	5	5	25.00
3	6.5	8	−1.5	2.25
4	2	1.5	0.5	0.25
5	1	3	−2	4.00
6	9	7	2	4.00
7	3.5	1.5	2	4.00
8	6.5	9	−2.5	6.25
9	8	10	−2	4.00
10	5	4	1	1.00
				57.0

NOTE: Tied ranks were assigned the average (of ranks) as if no ties had occurred.

to decide how well these two sets of ranking agree. Table 16–11 contains the data and preliminary calculations.

Substituting into the equation

$$r_s = 1 - \frac{6\Sigma d^2}{n^3 - n} = \frac{6(57)}{(10)^3 - 10} = .654$$

where n is the number of subjects being ranked.

The relationship between the panel's and the psychologist's ranking is moderately high, suggesting agreement between the two measures. The test of the null hypothesis that there is no relationship between the measures ($r_s = 0$) is rejected at the .05 level with $n - 2$ degrees of freedom.

$$t = r_s \sqrt{\frac{N - 2}{1 - r_s^2}} = \sqrt{\frac{8}{1 - .4277}} = 2.45$$

Summary

Research questions in business frequently involve relationships between two or more variables. Correlation analysis may be applied to study such relationships. Parametric correlation requires two continuous variables measured on an interval or ratio scale. The product moment correlation coefficient represents an index of the magnitude of the relationship, its sign governs the direction, and its square explains the common variance. Bivariate correlation treats X and Y variables symmetrically and is intended for use with variables that are linearly related.

Scatterplots allow the researcher to visually inspect relationship data for appropriateness of the selected statistic. Direction, magnitude, and shape of a relationship are conveyed in a plot. The shape of linear relationships is characterized by a straight line, whereas nonlinear relationships are curvilinear, parabolic, or have other curvature. The assumptions of linearity and bivariate normal distribution may be checked through plots and diagnostic tests.

A correlation matrix is a table used to display coefficients for more than two variables. Matrices form the basis for computation and understanding the nature of relationships in multiple regression, discriminant analysis, factor analysis, and many multivariate techniques.

A correlation coefficient of any magnitude or sign, regardless of statistical significance, does not imply causation. Similarly, a coefficient is not remarkable simply because it is statistically significant. Practical significance should be considered in interpreting and reporting findings.

Regression analysis is used to further our insight about the relationship of Y with X. When we take the observed values of X to estimate or predict corresponding Y values, the process is called simple prediction. When more than one X variable is used, the outcome is a function of multiple predictors. Simple and multiple predictions are made using regression analysis.

A straight line is fundamentally the best way to model the relationship between two continuous variables. The method of least squares allows us to find a regression line, or line of best fit, that minimizes errors in drawing the line. It uses the criterion of minimizing the total squared errors of estimate. Point predictions made from well-fitted data are subject to error. Prediction and confidence bands may be used to find a range of probable values for Y based on the chosen predictor. The bands are shaped in such a way that predictors further from the mean have larger band widths.

We test regression models for linearity and to discover whether the equation is effective in fitting the data. An important test in bivariate linear regression is whether the slope is equal to zero. In bivariate regression, t and F tests of the regression produce the same result since t^2 is equal to F.

Often the assumptions or the required measurement level for parametric techniques cannot be met. Nonparametric measure of association offer alternatives. Nominal measures of association are used to assess the strength of relationships in cross-classification tables. They are often used in conjunction with chi-square or may be based in the proportional reduction in error (PRE) approach.

Phi ranges from 0 to $+1.0$ and attempts to correct chi-square proportionately to N. Phi is best employed with 2×2 tables. Cramer's V is a modification of phi for larger tables and has a range up to 1.0 for tables of any configuration. Lambda, a PRE statistic, is based on how well the frequencies of one nominal variable offer predictive evidence about the frequencies of another. Goodman and Kruskal's tau uses table marginals to reduce prediction errors.

Measures for ordinal data include gamma, Kendall's tau b and tau c, Somers's d, and Spearman's rho. All but Spearman's rank-order correlation are based on the concept of concordant and discordant pairs. None of these statistics requires the assumption of a bivariate normal distribution, yet by incorporating order, most produce a range from -1 to $+1$.

Key Terms

artifact correlations
bivariate correlation analysis
bivariate normal distribution
chi-square-based measures
    contingency coefficient C
    Cramer's *V*
    phi
coefficient of determination
concordant (discordant)
    observations
correlation matrix
error term
goodness of fit
linearity
method of least squares

ordinal measures
    gamma
    Somers's *d*
    Spearman's *rho*
    tau *b*
    tau *c*
Pearson correlation coefficient
prediction and confidence bands
proportional reduction in error (PRE)
    lambda
    tau
regression analysis
regression coefficients
    intercept
    slope
residual
scatterplots

Discussion Questions

1. Distinguish between:
    a. Regression coefficient and correlation coefficient.
    b. $r = 0$ and $\rho = 0$.
    c. The test of the true slope, the test of the intercept, and $r^2 = 0$.
    d. r^2 and r.
    e. A slope of 0.
    f. F and r^2.

2. Describe the relationship between the two variables in the four plots.

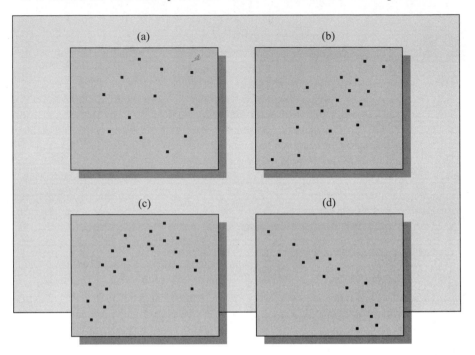

3. _____

X	Y
3	6
6	10
9	15
12	24
15	21
18	20

a. Create a scatter plot of the data.
b. Find the least squares line.
c. Plot the line on the diagram.
d. Predict: *Y* if *X* is 10.
          Y if *X* is 17.

4 _____

X	Y
2	1
3	3
5	5
6	6
8	5
10	3

   a. Create a scatter plot of the data.
   b. Which measure of association is appropriate for this data?

5. Fill in the missing blocks for the ANOVA summary table on net profits and market value used with regression analysis.
   a. What does the F tell you? $(\alpha.05)$
   b. What is the t value? Explain its meaning.

ANOVA Summary Table

	DF	Sum of Squares	Mean Square	F
Regression	1	11116995.47	☐	☐
Error	☐	☐	116104.63	
Total	9	12045832.50		

6. Using a computer program, produce a correlation matrix for the following data:

Forbes 500 Random Subsample (dollars in millions)

Assets	Sales	Market Value	Net Profit	Cash Flow	Number of Employees (thousands)
1034.00	1510.00	697.00	82.60	126.50	16.60
956.00	785.00	1271.00	89.00	191.20	5.00
1890.00	2533.00	1783.00	176.00	267.00	44.00
1133.00	532.00	752.00	82.30	137.10	2.10
11682.00	3790.00	4149.00	413.50	806.80	11.90
6080.00	635.00	291.00	18.10	35.20	3.70
31044.00	3296.00	2705.00	337.30	425.50	20.10
5878.00	3204.00	2100.00	145.80	380.00	10.80
1721.00	981.00	1573.00	172.60	326.60	1.90
2135.00	2268.00	2634.00	247.20	355.50	21.20

7. Secure Spearman rank-order correlations for the largest Pearson coefficient in the matrix. Explain the differences between the two findings.

8. A tax on the market value of stock and bond transactions has been proposed as one remedy for the budget deficit. The following data were collected on a sample of 60 registered voters by a polling organization.

	Education		
Opinion about Market Tax	*H.S.*	*College Grad.*	*MBA*
Favorable	15	5	0
Undecided	10	8	2
Unfavorable	0	2	18

    a. Compute gamma for the table.
    b. Compute tau *b* or tau *c* for the same data.
    c. What accounts for the differences?
    d. Which is more suitable for this data?

9. Using the tabled data in 8, compute Somers's *d* symmetric; and then use opinion as the dependent variable. Interpret your results.

10. _____

X	Y
25	5
19	7
17	12
14	23
12	20
9	25
8	26
7	28
3	20

    a. Calculate the correlation between *X* and *Y.*
    b. Interpret the sign of the correlation.
    c. Interpret the square of the correlation.
    d. Plot the least squares line.
    e. Test for a linear relationship:
        (1) $\beta_1 = 0$.
        (2) $r = 0$.
        (3) An *F* test.

11. A research team conducted a study of voting preferences among 130 registered Democrats and 130 registered Republicans before an election on a specific tax proposal. They secured the following results:

	Favor	Against
Democrats	50	80
Republicans	90	40

Calculate an appropriate measure of association.

12. Using the matrix data in 6, select a pair of variables and run a simple regression. Then investigate the appropriateness of the model for the data using diagnostic tools for evaluating assumptions.

Reference Notes

1. Typically, we plot the X (independent) variable on the horizontal axis and the Y (dependent) variable on the vertical axis. Although correlation does not distinguish between independent and dependent variables, the convention is useful for consistency in plotting and will be used later with regression.

2. F. J. Anscombe, "Graphs in Statistical Analysis," *American Statistician* 27 (1973), pp. 17–21. Cited in Samprit Chaterjee and Bertram Price, *Regression Analysis by Example* (New York: John Wiley & Sons, 1977), pp. 7–9.

3. Amir D. Aczel, *Complete Business Statistics,* 2nd ed. (Homewood, Ill.: Richard D. Irwin, 1993), p. 433.

4. The coefficient for net profits and cash flow in the example calculation used a subsample ($n = 10$) and was found to be .93. The matrix shows the coefficient as .95. The matrix calculation was based on the larger sample ($n = 100$).

5. This section is partially based on the concepts developed by Emanuel J. Mason and William J. Bramble, *Understanding and Conducting Research* (New York: McGraw-Hill, 1989), pp. 172–82; and elaborated in greater detail by Aczel, *Complete Business Statistics,* pp. 414–29.

6. Technically, estimation uses a concurrent criterion variable where prediction uses a future criterion. The statistical procedure is the same in either case.

7. Peter Passell, "Can Math Predict a Wine? An Economist Takes a Swipe at Some Noses," *International Herald Tribune,* March 5, 1990, p. 1; Jacques Neher, "Top Quality Bordeaux Cellar Is an Excellent Buy," *International Herald Tribune,* July 9, 1990, p. 8.

8. See Alan Agresti and Barbara Finlay, *Statistical Methods for the Social Sciences* (San Francisco: Dellen Publishing, 1986), pp. 248–49. Also see the discussion of basic regression models in John Neter, William Wasserman, and Michael H. Kutner, *Applied Linear Statistical Models* (Homewood, Ill.: Richard D. Irwin, 1990), pp. 23–49.

9. We distinguish between the error terms $\epsilon_1 = Y_i - E\{Y_i\}$ and the residual $e_i = (Y_i - \hat{Y}_i)$. The first is based on the vertical deviation of Y_i *from the true regression line. It is unknown and estimated. The second is the vertical deviation of* Y_i from the fitted $\hat{Y}$ on the estimated line. See Neter et al., *Applied Linear Statistical Models,* p. 47.

10. For further information on software-generated regression diagnostics, see Marija J. Norusis/SPSS, Inc., *SPSS for Windows Base System User's Guide, Release 6.0,* (Chicago: SPSS, Inc., 1993); Marija J. Norusis/SPSS, Inc., *SPSS Advanced Statistics User's Guide* (Chicago: SPSS, Inc., 1990); *MINITAB Reference Manual,* Release 7 (State College, Pa.: Minitab, Inc., 1989); W. J. Dixon, ed., *BMDP Statistical Software Manual,* vols. 1 and 2 (Berkeley, Calif.: University of California Press, 1988); *SAS User's Guide: Statistics,* Version 6 ed. (Cary, N.C.: SAS Institute, 1987).

11. Aczel, *Complete Business Statistics,* p. 434.

12. This calculation is normally listed as the standard error of the slope (SE B) on computer printouts. It is further defined as for this data:

$$s(b_1) = \frac{8}{\sqrt{SS_x}} = \frac{538.559}{\sqrt{198.249}} = 38.249$$

where

s = The standard error of estimate (and the square root of the mean square error of the regression).

SS_x = The sum of squares for the X variable.

13. Computer printouts use upper case (R^2) because most procedures are written to accept multiple and bivariate regression.

14. The table output for this section is modified from SPSS and described in Norusis/SPSS, Inc., *SPSS Base System User's Guide.* For further discussion and examples of nonparametric measures of association, see S. Siegel and N. J. Castellan, Jr., *Nonparametric Statistics for the Behavioral Sciences,* 2nd ed. (New York: McGraw-Hill, 1988).

15. Calculation of concordant and discordant pairs is adapted from Agresti and Finlay, *Statistical Methods for the Social Sciences,* pp. 221–23.

16. We know that the percentage of concordant plus the percentage of discordant pairs sums to 1.0. We also know their difference is $-.70$. The only numbers satisfying these two conditions are .85 and .15 (.85 + .15 = 1.0, .15 − .85 = −.70).

17. G.U. Yule and M. G. Kendall, *An Introduction to the Theory of Statistics* (New York: Hafner, 1950).

18. M. G. Kendall, *Rank Correlation Methods,* 4th ed. (London: Charles W. Griffin, 1970).

Suggested Readings

1. Aczel, Amir D. *Complete Business Statistics.* 2nd ed. Homewood, Ill.: Richard D. Irwin, 1993. Chapter 10 covers simple regression/correlation with impeccable exposition and examples. Highly recommended.

2. Agresti, Alan, and Barbara Finlay. *Statistical Methods for the Social Sciences.* San Francisco: Dellen Publishing, 1986. Highly readable coverage of nonparametric measures of association.

3. Chaterjee, Samprit, and Bertraum Price. *Regression Analysis by Example.* New York: John Wiley & Sons, 1977.

4. Draper, N. R., and H. Smith. *Applied Regression Analysis.* 2nd ed. New York: John Wiley & Sons, 1981. A more advanced test that requires familiarity with matrix algebra.

5. Neter, John; William Wasserman; and Michael H. Kutner. *Applied Linear Statistical Models*. Homewood, Ill.: Richard Irwin, 1990. Chapters 1 through 13 provide an excellent introduction to regression analysis.
6. Siegel, S., and N. J. Castellan, Jr. *Nonparametric Statistics for the Behavioral Sciences*. 2nd ed. New York: McGraw-Hill, 1988.

CHAPTER
17

MULTIVARIATE ANALYSIS: AN OVERVIEW

 **FINDING
YOUR WAY**

INTRODUCTION

In recent years, multivariate statistical tools have been applied with greater frequency to research problems. This is a recognition that many problems we encounter are more complex than bivariate models can explain. Simultaneously, computer programs have taken advantage of the complex mathematics needed to manage multiple variable relationships. Today, desktop computers and versatile software bring these powerful techniques to business researchers.

Throughout the functional areas of business, more and more management problems are being addressed by considering multiple independent and/or multiple dependent variables. Sales managers base forecasts on various product history variables; marketers consider the complex set of buyer preferences and preferred product options; financial analysts classify levels of credit risks based on a set of predictors; and human resource managers devise future wage and salary compensation plans with multivariate techniques.

Many of the illustrations presented in this text could be considered multivariate problems. The revenue improvements for a physicians' group who decided to join a different insurance program was based on multiple factors. In another example, the aviation industry was attempting to control radiation risks for passengers and crew by altering the proximity of air routes to the poles, aircraft shielding, altitude, and other variables. The price of investment-grade wine was forecast based on spring and harvest rainfall and growing-season temperatures.

One author defines **multivariate analysis** as "those statistical techniques which focus upon, and bring out in bold relief, the structure of simultaneous relationships among three or more phenomena."[1] Our overview of multivariate analysis seeks to illustrate the meaning of this definition while building on your understanding of bivariate statistics from the last few chapters. Several common multivariate techniques and examples will be discussed.

Because a complete treatment of this subject would require a thorough consideration of the mathematics, assumptions, and diagnostic tools appropriate for each technique, our coverage is necessarily limited. Readers needing greater detail are referred to the suggested readings at the end of the chapter.

SELECTING A MULTIVARIATE TECHNIQUE

Multivariate techniques may be classified according to **dependency** and **interdependency** characteristics. Selecting an appropriate technique starts with an understanding of this distinction. If criterion and predictor variables exist in the research question, then we will have an assumption of dependence. MANOVA, multiple regression, and discriminant analysis are examples where criterion or dependent variable(s) and predictor or independent variables are present. Alternatively, if the variables are interrelated without designating some dependent and others independent, then interdependence of the variables is assumed. Factor analysis, cluster analysis, and multidimensional scaling are examples of this situation.

Figure 17–1 provides a diagram to guide in the selection of techniques. Let's take an example to show how you might make a decision. Every other year since 1978, the Roper organization has tracked public opinion toward business by providing a list of items that are said to be the responsibility of business. The respondents are asked whether business fulfills these responsibilities "fully, fairly well, not too well, or not at all well." The following issues make up the list:[2]

- Developing new products and services.
- Producing good quality products and services.
- Making products that are safe to use.
- Hiring minorities.
- Providing jobs for people.
- Being good citizens of the communities in which they operate.
- Paying good salaries and benefits to employees.
- Charging reasonable prices for goods and services.
- Keeping profits at reasonable levels.
- Advertising honestly.
- Paying their fair share.
- Cleaning up their own air and water pollution.

You have access to data on these items and wish to know if they could be reduced to a smaller set of variables that would account for most of the variation among respondents. In response to the first question in Figure 17–1, you correctly determine there are no dependent variables in the data set. You then check to see if the variables are **metric** or **nonmetric.** In the figure, metric refers to ratio and interval measurements, and nonmetric refers to data that are nominal and ordinal. Based on the measurement scale, which appears to have equal intervals, and the preliminary findings that show a linear relationship between several variables, you decide the data are metric. This decision leads you to three options: multidimensional scaling, cluster analysis, or factor analysis. Multidimensional scaling develops a geometric picture or map of the locations of some objects relative to others. This map specifies how the objects differ. Cluster analysis identifies homogeneous subgroups or clusters. Factor analysis looks for patterns among the variables to discover if an underlying combination of the original variables (a factor) can summarize the original set. Based on your research objective, you select factor analysis.

Suppose you are interested in predicting family food expenditures from family income, family size, and whether the family's location is rural or urban. Returning to Figure 17–1, you conclude there is a singular dependent variable, family food expenditures. You decide this variable is metric since dollars are measured on a ratio scale. The independent variables, income and family size, also meet the criteria for metric data. However, you are not sure about the location variable since it appears to be a dichotomous nominal variable. According to the figure, your choices

FIGURE 17–1   Selecting from the Most Common Multivariate Techniques

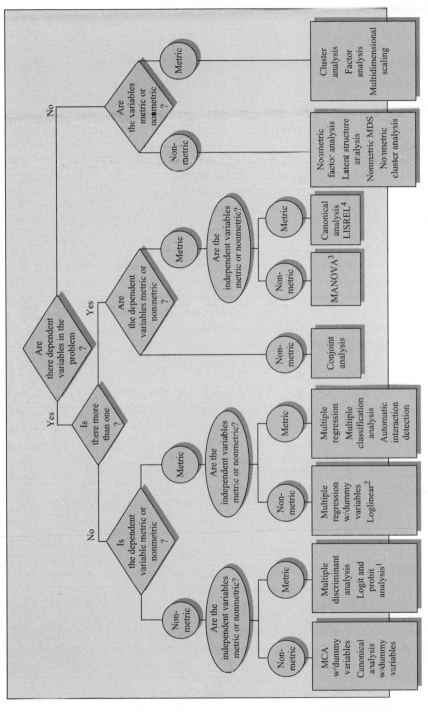

NOTES:

[1] The independent variable is metric only in the sense that a transformed proportion is used.

[2] The dependent variable is metric only when we consider that the number of cases in the crosstabulation cell are used to calculate the logs.

[3] Factors may be considered nonmetric independent variables in that they organize the data into groups. We do not classify MANOVA and other multivariate analysis of variance models.

[4] LISREL refers to a linear structural equations model for latent variables. It is a family of models appropriate for confirmatory factor analysis, path analysis, time series analysis, recursive and nonrecursive models, and covariance structure models. Because it may handle dependence and interdependence, metric and nonmetric, it is arbitrarily placed in this diagram.

SOURCE: Partially adapted from T. C. Kinnear and J. R. Taylor, "Multivariate Methods in Marketing: A Further Attempt at Classification," *Journal of Marketing*, October 1971, p. 57; and J. F. Hair, Jr., Rolph E. Anderson, Ronald L. Tatham, and Bernie J. Grablowsky, *Multivariate Data Analysis* (Tulsa, Okla.: Petroleum Publishing Co., 1979), pp. 10–14.

are automatic interaction detection (AID), multiple classification analysis (MCA), and multiple regression. You recall from Chapter 14 that AID was designed to locate the most important interaction effects and typically uses numerous independent variables in its sequential partitioning procedure. MCA handles weak predictors (including nominal variables), correlated predictors, and nonlinear relationships. Multiple regression is the extension of bivariate regression. You believe that your data exceed the assumptions for the first two techniques, and by treating the nominal variable's values as 0 or 1, it could be used as an independent variable in a multiple regression model. You prefer this to losing information from the other two variables—a certainty if you reduce them to nonmetric data.

In the next two sections, we will extend this discussion as we illustrate techniques in the categories of dependency and interdependency.

DEPENDENCY TECHNIQUES

Multiple Regression

Multiple regression is used as a descriptive tool in three types of situations. First, it is used often to develop a self-weighting estimating equation by which to predict values for a criterion variable (DV) from the values for several predictor variables (IVs). Thus, we might try to predict company sales on the basis of new housing starts, new marriage rates, annual disposable income, and a time factor. Another prediction study might be one in which we estimate a student's academic performance in college from the variables of rank in high school class, SAT verbal scores, SAT quantitative scores, and a rating scale reflecting impressions from an interview.

A descriptive application calls for controlling for confounding variables to better evaluate the contribution of other variables. For example, one might wish to control the brand of a product and the store in which it is bought to study the effects of price as an indicator of product quality.[3] A third use of multiple regression is to test and explain causal theories. In this approach, often referred to as **path analysis,** regression is used to describe an entire structure of linkages that have been advanced from a causal theory.[4] In addition to being a descriptive tool, a multiple regression is also used as an inference tool to test hypotheses and to estimate population values.

Method Multiple regression is an extension of the bivariate linear regression presented in Chapter 16. The terms defined in that chapter will not be repeated here. Although **dummy variables** (nominal variables coded 0, 1) may be used, all other variables must be interval or ratio. The generalized equation is

$$Y = \beta_0 + \beta_1 X_1 + \beta_2 X_2 + \ldots + \beta_n X_n + \epsilon$$

where

β_0 = a constant, the value of Y when all X values are zero.

β_i = the slope of the regression surface or the response surface. The β represents the regression coefficient associated with each X_i.

ϵ = an error term, normally distributed about a mean of 0. For purposes of computation, the ϵ is assumed to be 0.

The regression coefficients are stated either in raw score units (the actual X values) or as **standardized coefficients** (X values restated in terms of their standard deviations). In either case, the value of the regression coefficient states the amount that Y varies with each unit change of the associated X variable when the effects of all other X variables are being held constant. When the regression coefficients are standardized, they are called **beta weights** (β) and their values indicate the relative importance of the associated X values, particularly when the predictors are unrelated. For example, in an equation where $\beta_1 = .60$ and $\beta_2 = .20$, one concludes that X_1 has three times the influence on Y as does X_2.

Example   We will use a food expenditure problem to illustrate multiple regression. The equation includes the following variables:

Y = Annual family food expenditures
X_1 = Annual family income
X_2 = Family size
X_3 = Family location (0 = rural, 1 = urban)

A computer program is used to compute the correlation values and the regression coefficients. The standard elements in a printout are shown in Figure 17–2. The inclusion of the three independent variables correlates well with family food

FIGURE   17–2   Multiple Regression Analysis of Family Income, Family Size, and Location, on Family Food Expenditures

```
MULTIPLE REGRESSION

------------------------- MULTIPLE REGRESSION ------------------------- VARIABLE LIST 1
                                                                        REGRESSION LIST 1

DEPENDENT VARIABLE . .       V2     FOOD

VARIABLE(S) ENTERED ON STEP NUMBER 1 . .      X3     LOCATION
                                              X1     HOUSEHOLD INCOME
                                              X2     HOUSEHOLD SIZE

MULTIPLE R          0.87804    ANALYSIS OF VARIANCE   DF   SUM OF SQUARES  MEAN SQUARE       F
R SQUARE            0.77095    REGRESSION              3.        66.19259     22.06420   29.17050
ADJUSTED R SQUARE   0.74452    RESIDUAL               26.        19.66607      0.75639
STANDARD ERROR      0.86971

--------------VARIABLES IN THE EQUATION--------------    ---VARIABLES NOT IN THE EQUATION---
VARIABLE        B           BETA    STD ERROR B      F    VARIABLE BETA IN PARTIAL TOLERANCE F

X3         1.102366     0.27560      0.38594    8.159
X1         0.758286D-01 0.61723      0.01189   40.659
X2          .6076182    0.44860      0.12890   22.221
(CONSTANT) -.1899372

ALL VARIABLES ARE IN THE EQUATION

STATISTICS WHICH CANNOT BE COMPUTED ARE PRINTED AS ALL NINES.
```

SOURCE: Data are hypothetical.

expenditures ($R = .878$). The R^2 of .771 indicates that about 77 percent of the variation in family food expenditures for this sample of 30 families is explained by family income, family size, and whether families live in urban or rural areas.

The other reported statistics have the following interpretations.

1. Adjusted R square $= .7445$—R^2 is adjusted to reflect the model's goodness of fit for the population. The net effect of this adjustment is to reduce the R^2 slightly but to make it comparable to other R^2s from equations with a different number of independent variables.

2. Standard error $= .8697$—This is the standard deviation of actual values of Y about the regression line of estimated Y values.

3. Analysis of variance—This analysis measures whether or not the equation represents a set of regression coefficients that, in total, are statistically significant from zero. The critical value for F is found in Appendix Table F–9 with degrees of freedom for the numerator equaling k, the number of independent variables, and for the denominator, $n - k - 1$, where n for this problem is 30 observations. Thus, d.f. $= (3, 26)$. Appendix Table F–9 indicates a critical value of 2.98 for an $\alpha = .05$. The equation is statistically significant.

4. The column headed B indicates the regression coefficients for the equation:

$$Y = -.1899 + .0758X_1 + .6076X_2 + 1.1024X_3$$

5. The column headed Beta gives the regression coefficients expressed in standardized form. When these are used, the regression Y intercept is zero. The beta weights also show the relative contribution of the three independent variables to the explanatory power of this equation. Household income explains more than either of the other two variables.

6. Standard error of B is a measure of the sampling variability of each regression coefficient. That is, .01189 is the standard deviation of the sampling variability of .0758, the regression coefficient for family income.

7. Column F measures the statistical significance of each of the regression coefficients. Again compare these to the table of F values in Appendix Table F–9, using degrees of freedom for one independent variable, d.f. $= (1, 26)$. All three regression coefficients are judged to be significantly different from zero.

Therefore, the regression equation in 4 above shows the relationship between the dependent variable, food expenditures, and three independent variables: income, family size, and location. The regression coefficients are both individually and jointly statistically significant. The independent variable location influences food expenditures the most, followed by family size and then income.

One difficulty with multiple regression is that of **multicollinearity**—the situation where some or all of the independent variables are highly correlated. When this condition exists, the estimated regression coefficients can fluctuate widely from sample to sample, making it risky to use the coefficients as an indicator of the relative importance of predictor variables. Just how high can acceptable correlations be between independent variables? There is no definitive answer, but correlations at a .80 or greater level should be dealt with in one of two ways: (1) choose one of the variables and delete the other or (2) create a new variable that is a composite of the highly intercorrelated variables and use this new variable in place of its components. In the example just presented, the correlation matrix of simple correlations shows there is no correlation between any two independent variables greater than .20, indicating that multicollinearity is not a problem.

Another difficulty with regression occurs when researchers fail to evaluate the equation with data beyond those used originally to calculate it. A practical solution is to set aside a portion of the data (a fourth to a third) and use only the remainder to compute the estimating equation. This is called a **holdout sample.** One then uses the equation on the holdout data to calculate an R^2. This can then be compared to the original R^2 to determine how well the equation predicts beyond its database.

Discriminant Analysis

Researchers often wish to classify people or objects into two or more groups. One might need to classify persons as either buyers or nonbuyers, good or bad credit risks, or superior, average, or poor performers in some activity. The objective is to establish a procedure to find the predictors that best classify subjects.

Method   **Discriminant analysis** joins a nominally scaled criterion or dependent variable with one or more independent variables that are interval or ratio scaled. Once the discriminant equation is found, it can be used to predict the classification of a new observation. This is done by calculating a linear function of the form:

$$D_i = d_0 + d_1X_1 + d_2X_2 + \cdots + d_pX_p$$

where

D_i is the score on discriminant function i.
The d_is are weighting coefficients; d_o is a constant.
The Xs are the values of the discriminating variables used in the analysis.

A single discriminant equation is required if the categorization calls for two groups. If three groups are involved in the classification, it requires two discriminant equations. If more categories are called for in the dependent variable, it is necessary to calculate a separate discriminant function for each pair of classifications in the criterion group.

While the most common use for discriminant analysis is to classify persons or objects into various groups, it can also be used to analyze known groups to determine the relative influence of specific factors for deciding into which group various cases fall. Assume we have supervisory ratings that enable us to classify administrators as successful or unsuccessful on administrative performance. We might also be able to secure test results on three measures: ability to work with others (X_1), motivation for administrative work (X_2), and general professional skill (X_3). Suppose the discriminant equation is:

$$D = .06X_1 + .45X_2 + .30X_3$$

Since discriminant analysis uses standardized values for the discriminant variables, we conclude from the coefficients that ability to work with others is less important than the other two in classifying administrators.[5]

Example   An illustration of the method takes us back to the problem in the last chapter where a brokerage firm was hiring MBAs for its account executive program. Over the years the firm had indifferent success with the selection process. You are asked to develop a procedure to improve this. It appears that discriminant analysis is a perfect technique. You begin by gathering data on 30 MBAs who were hired in recent years. Fifteen of these have been successful employees while the other 15 were unsatisfactory. The personnel files provide the following information that can be used to conduct the analysis.

X_1 = Years of prior work experience
X_2 = GPA in graduate program
X_3 = Employment test scores

An algorithm determines how well these three independent variables will correctly classify those who are judged successful from those judged unsuccessful. The classification results are shown in Table 17–1. This indicates that 25 of the 30 cases were correctly classified using these three variables.

The standardized and unstandardized discriminant function coefficients are as follows:

	Unstandardized	*Standardized*
X_1	.36084	.65927
X_2	2.61192	.57958
X_3	.53028	.97505
(constant)	12.89685	

These results indicate that X_3 (the employment test) has the greatest discriminating power. Several significance tests are also computed. One, Wilk's lambda, has a chi-square transformation for testing the significance of the discriminant function.

TABLE 17–1   Discriminant Analysis Classification Results

Actual Group		Number of Cases	Predicted Group Membership	
			0	*1*
Group Unsuccessful	0	15	13 86.7%	2 13.3%
Group Successful	1	15	3 20.0%	12 80.0%
Percent of "grouped" cases correctly classified: 83.33%				

It indicates the equation is statistically significant at the $\alpha = .0004$ level. Using the discriminant equation,

$$D = .659X_1 + .580X_2 + .975X_3$$

you can now predict whether future candidates will likely be successful account executives.

MANOVA

Multivariate analysis of variance, or **MANOVA,** is a commonly used multivariate technique. MANOVA assesses the relationship between two or more dependent variables and classificatory variables or factors. In business research, MANOVA can be used to test differences among samples of employees, customers, manufactured items, production parts, and so forth.

Method   MANOVA is similar to the univariate ANOVA described earlier, with the added ability to handle several dependent variables. If ANOVA is applied consecutively to a set of interrelated dependent variables, erroneous conclusions may result. MANOVA can correct this by simultaneously testing all the variables and their interrelationships. MANOVA employs sums-of-squares and cross-products (SSCP) matrices to test for differences among groups. The variance between groups is determined by partitioning the total SSCP matrix and testing for significance. The *F* ratio, generalized to a ratio of the within-group variance and total-group variance matrices, tests for equality among treatment groups.

MANOVA examines similarities and differences among the multivariate mean scores of several populations. The null hypothesis for MANOVA is that all of the **centroids** (multivariate means) are equal, $H_0 : \mu_1 = \mu_2 = \mu_3 = \ldots \mu_n$. The alternative hypothesis is that the vector of centroids are unequal, $H_A : \mu_1 \neq \mu_2 \neq \mu_3 \neq \ldots \mu_n$. Figure 17–3 shows graphically three populations whose centroids are unequal, allowing the researcher to reject the null hypothesis. When the null hypothesis is rejected, additional tests are done to better understand the data. Several alternatives may be considered:

1. Univariate *F* tests can be run on the dependent variables.
2. Simultaneous confidence intervals can be produced for each variable.
3. Step-down analysis, like stepwise regression, can be run by computing *F* values successively. Each value is computed after eliminating the effects of the previous dependent variable.
4. Multiple discriminant analysis can be used on the SSCP matrices. This aids in the discovery of which variables contribute to the MANOVA's significance.[6]

Example   To illustrate, let's look at a firm that manufactures compact disk (CD) players. The plant manager is concerned about the quality of CD players coming off the manufacturing line. Two measures are used to assess quality in this example: adherence to product specifications and time before failure. Measured on a 0–100

**FIGURE 17–3
MANOVA
Techniques
Show These
Three Centroids
to Be Unequal**

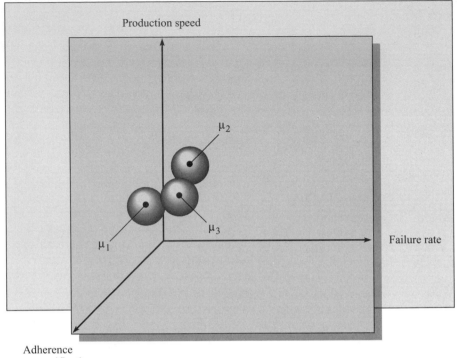

scale with 100 meeting all product specifications, the specification variable is averaging approximately 90. The mean time before failure is calculated in weeks; it is approximately 159 weeks, or three years.

The plant manager asks the industrial engineering department to devise a modified manufacturing procedure that will improve the quality measures but not change the production rate significantly. A new method is designed that includes more efficient parts handling and "burn-in" time where CD players are powered up and run at high temperatures.

Engineering takes a sample of 15 CD players made with the old manufacturing method and 15 made with the new method. The players are measured for their adherence to product specifications and stress tested to determine their time before failure. The stress test uses accelerated running conditions and adverse environmental conditions to simulate years of use in a short time.

Table 17–2 shows the mean and standard deviation of the dependent variables (failure, specifications, and manufacturing speed) for each level of method.[7] Level 1 represents the current manufacturing process, and level 2 is the new process. The new method extended the time before failure to 181 weeks, compared to 159 weeks for the existing method. The adherence to specifications is also improved, up to 95 from 90. But the manufacturing speed is slower by approximately 30 minutes (.473 hour).

Table 17-2   MANOVA Cell Means and Standard Deviations

VARIABLE	FACTOR	LEVEL	MEAN	STD. DEV.
FAILURE				
	METHOD	1	158.867	4.998
	METHOD	2	181.067	5.994
	For entire sample		169.967	12.524
SPECIFICATIONS				
	METHOD	1	89.800	2.077
	METHOD	2	94.800	2.178
	For entire sample		92.300	3.292
SPEED				
	METHOD	1	2.126	.061
	METHOD	2	2.599	.068
	For entire sample		2.362	.249

We have used diagnostics to check the assumptions of MANOVA except for equality of variance. Both levels of the manufacturing method variable produce a matrix, and the equality of these two matrices must be determined. Table 17–3 contains homogeneity of variance tests for separate dependent variables and a multivariate test. The former are known as univariate tests. The multivariate test is a comparable version that tests the variables simultaneously to determine whether MANOVA should proceed.

The significance levels of the Cochran and Bartlett-Box F do not allow us to reject any of the tests for the dependent variables considered separately. This means the two methods have equal variances in each dependent variable. This fulfills the univariate assumptions for homogeneity of variance. We then consider the variances and covariances simultaneously with Box's M, also found in Table 17–3. Again, we are unable to reject the homogeneity of variance assumption regarding the matrices. This satisfies the multivariate assumptions.

When MANOVA is applied properly, the dependent variables are correlated. If the dependent variables are unrelated, there would be no necessity for a multivariate test, and we could use separate F tests for failure, specifications, and speed much like the ANOVAs in Chapter 15. Bartlett's test of sphericity helps us decide if we should continue analyzing MANOVA results or return to separate univariate tests. In Table 17–4, we will look for a determinant value that is close to 0. This implies that one or more dependent variables is a linear function of another. The determinant has a chi-square transformation that simplifies testing for statistical significance. Since the observed significance is below that set for the model ($\alpha = .05$), we are able to reject the null hypothesis and conclude there are dependencies among the failure, specifications, and speed variables.

TABLE 17–3   MANOVA Homegeneity of Variance Tests

```
VARIABLE            TEST                    RESULTS

FAILURE

          Cochran's C (14,2) =      .58954, P = .506 (approx.)
          Bartlett-Box F (1,2352) = .44347, P = .506

SPECIFICATIONS

          Cochran's C (14,2) =      .52366, P = .862 (approx.)
          Bartlett-Box F (1,2352) = .03029, P = .862

SPEED

          Cochran's C (14,2) =      .55526, P = .684 (approx.)
          Bartlett-Box F (1,2352) = .16608, P = .684

     Multivariate Test for Homogeneity of Dispersion Matrices

          Box's M =                 6.07877
          F with (6,5680) DF =       .89446, P = .498 (approx.)
          Chi-Square with 6 DF =    5.37320, P = .497 (approx.)
```

TABLE 17–4   Bartlett's Test of Sphericity

```
Statistics for WITHIN CELLS correlations

Log (Determinant) =                 -3.92663
Bartlett's test of sphericity =    102.74687 with 3 D.F.
Significance =                          .000

F(max) criterion =                 7354.80161 with (3,28) D.F.
```

We now move to the test of equality of means that considers the three dependent variables for the two levels of manufacturing method. This test is analogous to a t or F test for multivariate data. The sums-of-squares and cross-products (SSCP) matrices are used. Table 17–5 shows three tests, including Hotelling's T^2. All the tests provided are compared to the F distribution for interpretation. Since the observed significance level is less than $\alpha = .05$ for the T^2 test, we reject the null hypothesis that said methods 1 and 2 provide equal results with respect to failure, specifications, and speed. Pillai's trace and Rao's statistic supply similar results.

Finally, to detect where the differences lie, we can examine the results of uni-

TABLE 17–5   Multivariate Tests of Significance

```
Multivariate Tests of Significance (S = 1, M = 1/2, N = 12)

Test Name       Value        Exact F    Hypoth. DF    Error DF    Sig. of F

Hotellings     51.33492     444.90268        3.00       26.00        .000
Pillais          .98089     444.90268        3.00       26.00        .000
Wilks            .01911     444.90268        3.00       26.00        .000
```

NOTE: *F* statistics are exact.

TABLE 17–6   Univariate Tests of Significance

```
Univariate F-tests with (1,28) D.F.

Variable    Hypoth. SS     Error SS    Hypoth. MS    Error MS        F      Sig. of F

FAILURE     3696.30000    852.66667    3696.30000    30.45238   121.37967     .000
SPECS        187.50000    126.80000     187.50000     4.52857    41.40379     .000
SPEED          1.67560       .11593       1.67560      .00414   404.68856     .000
```

NOTE: *F* statistics are exact.

variate F tests in Table 17–6. Since there are only two methods, the F is equivalent to t^2 for a two-sample t test. The significance levels for these tests do not reflect that several comparisons are being made, and we should use them principally for diagnostic purposes. This is similar to problems that require the use of multiple comparison tests in univariate analysis of variance. Note, however, that there are statistically significant differences in all three dependent variables resulting from the new manufacturing method. Techniques for further analysis of MANOVA results were listed at the beginning of this section.

Canonical Analysis[8]

A researcher interested in explaining one dependent variable from a set of several independent variables frequently selects multiple regression analysis. But what if the researcher is interested in explaining several dependent variables? And suppose there is a need to explain the set, not just one at a time.

Canonical analysis is used when we have two sets of variables and we are interested in explaining the effects of one set on the other. The independent variables are grouped into a weighted set, and the dependent variables are also weighted and grouped. We could explain the number of credit cards and average monthly charges on credit cards (dependent variables) because of family size and income (independent variables).

The analysis results in pairs of canonical variates that are similar to factors except that they account for maximum amount of relationship between the two sets of variables. The number of variates generated equals the smallest number of dependent or independent variables. Each pair of canonical variates is independent of other variates and explains successively lower correlation. Besides the canonical variates, the analysis provides canonical correlation between the variates, statistical significance, and a redundancy measure of shared variance.

LISREL[9]

LISREL, an acronym for linear structural relationships, was introduced by Karl Jöreskog in 1973. It is a complicated technique, well beyond the scope of this text, but is extremely useful in explaining causality among constructs that cannot be directly measured. It is used in various ways in the social and behavioral sciences; its application to business issues can be seen in macroeconomic policy formation, racial discrimination in employment, and consumer behavior, among others.

LISREL analyzes covariance structures. It has two parts, one is a *measurement model.* Since hypothetical constructs cannot be measured directly, the measurement model is used to relate the observed, recorded, or measured variables to the latent variables (constructs). For example, to understand an employee's performance, several variables may be used, including (1) the manager's observations, (2) recorded measures of work output, and (3) the number of requests for peer assistance from the employee. These variables can be combined to give the researcher an understanding of the employee's performance. Measurement models are important for modeling constructs such as attitude, feelings, and motivation that cannot be directly observed.

The second part of the LISREL is the *structural equation model.* This model shows the causal relationships among the latent variables. In addition, it describes the causal effects and the variance that are unexplained. The structural equation model is often diagramed for better understanding. This is a form of *path analysis,* and the resulting figure is a path diagram. Translated into mathematics, the model is described by a set of linear structural equations. A causal structure among the variables is assumed.

Figure 17–4 shows a path diagram of employee performance. In this example, the latent factors are training, motivation, and performance, shown within circles. The observable or measurable variables are shown within rectangles. Arrows signify influence. Since the latent factors affect the measurable variables (motivation affects the motivation test results, not vice versa), the arrows point from the construct to the measured variables. The figure also shows an interrelationship between motivation and training. The researchers believe motivation influences the effectiveness of training and training reciprocally influences motivation. Each of these independent variables has a causal effect on the employee's performance. A more complex representation of this model would show error variances influencing each of the measurable variables and the dependent factor.

**FIGURE 17–4
Path Diagram
for Employee
Performance**

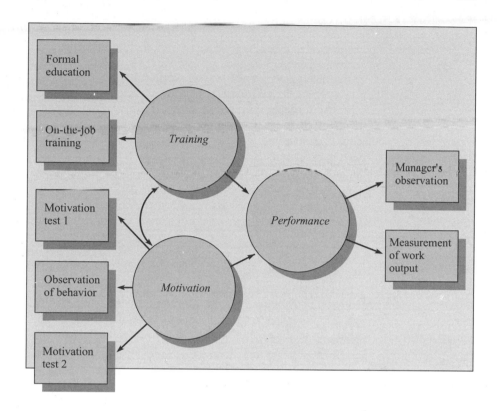

Although it is a complicated technique, LISREL allows researchers to analyze complex covariance structures. Latent, interdependent, and reciprocally causal variables are easily handled within the measurement and structural equation models.

Conjoint Analysis In business research, the most common applications for conjoint analysis are market research and product development. Consumers buying a home computer, for example, may evaluate a set of attributes to choose the product that best meets their needs. They may consider brand, speed, price, educational values, games, or capacity for work-related tasks. The attributes and their features require the buyer to make trade-offs in the final decision making.

Method   **Conjoint analysis** typically uses input from nonmetric independent variables. Normally, we would use cross-classification tables to handle such data, but even multiway tables become quickly overwhelmed by the complexity. If there were three prices, three brands, three speeds, two levels of educational values, two categories for games, and two categories for work assistance, the model would have 216 decision levels ($3 \times 3 \times 3 \times 2 \times 2 \times 2$). A choice structure this size poses enormous difficulties for respondents and analysts. Conjoint analysis solves this problem with various optimal scaling approaches, often with loglinear models, to provide researchers with reliable answers that could not be obtained otherwise.

The objective of conjoint analysis is to secure *part-worths* or **utility scores** that represent the importance of each aspect of a product or service in the subjects' overall preference ratings. Utility scores are computed from the subjects' rankings or ratings of a set of cards. Each card in the deck describes one possible configuration of combined product attributes.

The first step in a conjoint study is to select the attributes most pertinent to the purchase decision. This may require an exploratory study such as a focus group or could be done by an expert with thorough market knowledge. The attributes selected are the independent variables and are called *factors*. The possible values for an attribute are called *factor levels*. In the home computer example, the speed factor may have levels of 33 megahertz (MHz), 50MHz, and 66MHz. Speed, like price, approaches linear measurement characteristics since consumers typically choose higher speeds and lower prices. Other factors like brand are measured as discrete variables.

After selecting the factors and their levels, a computer program determines the number of product descriptions necessary to estimate the utilities. SPSS procedures ORTHOPLAN, PLANCARDS, and CONJOINT build a file structure for all possible combinations, generate the subset required for testing, produce the card descriptions, and analyze results. The command structure within these procedures provides for holdout sampling, simulations, and other requirements frequently used in commercial applications.[10]

Example   Water sports enthusiasts know the dangers of ultraviolet (UV) light. It fades paint and clothing; yellows surfboards, skis, and sailboards; and destroys sails. More important, UV damages the eye's retina and cornea. At the beginning of the 1990s, Americans were spending $1.3 billion on 189 million pairs of sunglasses, most of which failed to provide adequate UV protection. Manufacturers of sunglasses for specialty markets have improved their products to where all of the companies in our example advertised 100 percent UV protection. Many other features influence trends in this market. We chose four factors from information contained in a review of sun protection products.[11]

Brand		Style	Flotation	Price
Bolle	A	Multiple color choices for	Yes	$100
Hobbies		frames, lenses, and temples	No	72
Oakley	B	Multiple color choices for		60
Ski Optiks		frames, lenses, and straps		40
		(no hard temples)		
	C	Limited colors for frames,		
		lenses, and temples		

This is a $4 \times 4 \times 3 \times 2$ design or a 96-option full-concept study. The algorithm selected 16 cards to estimate the utilities for the full concept. Combinations of interest that were not selected can be estimated later from the utilities. In addition, four holdout cards were administered to subjects but evaluated separately. The cards shown in Figure 17–5 were administered to a small sample ($n = 10$). Subjects were asked to order their cards from most to least desirable. The data produced the results presented in Figures 17–6 and 17–7.

Figure 17–6 contains the results of the eighth subject's preferences. This individual was an avid boardsailor, and flotation was the most important attribute for

FIGURE 17–5
Concept Cards for Conjoint Example

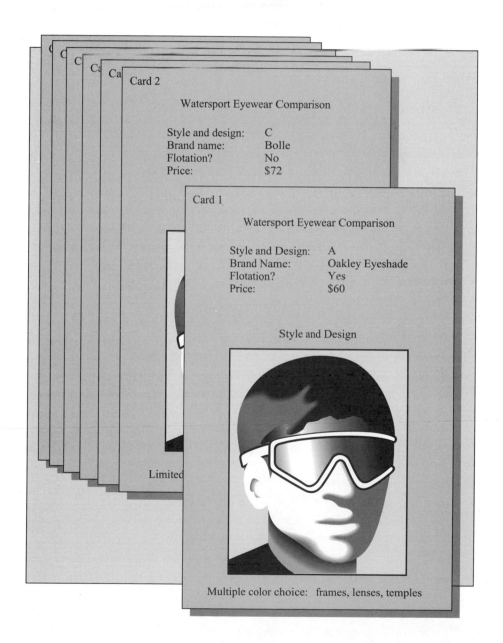

Card 2

Watersport Eyewear Comparison

Style and design: C
Brand name: Bolle
Flotation?   No
Price: $72

Card 1

Watersport Eyewear Comparison

Style and Design: A
Brand Name: Oakley Eyeshade
Flotation?   Yes
Price: $60

Style and Design

Multiple color choice: frames, lenses, temples

FIGURE   17–6   Conjoint Results for Subject 8

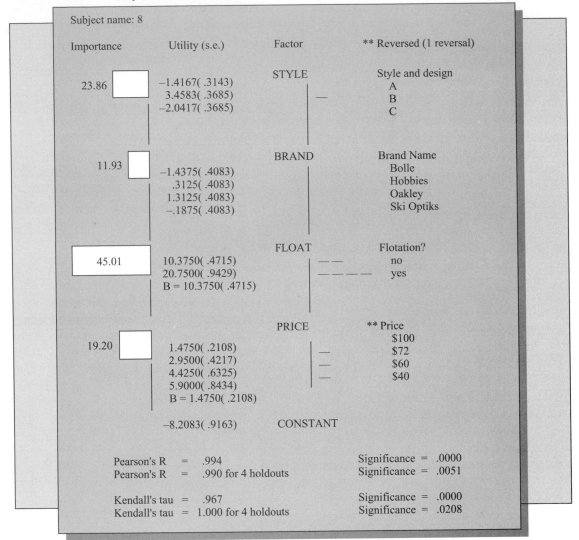

Subject name: 8

Importance	Utility (s.e.)	Factor	** Reversed (1 reversal)
		STYLE	Style and design
23.86	−1.4167(.3143)		A
	3.4583(.3685)		B
	−2.0417(.3685)		C
		BRAND	Brand Name
11.93	−1.4375(.4083)		Bolle
	.3125(.4083)		Hobbies
	1.3125(.4083)		Oakley
	−.1875(.4083)		Ski Optiks
		FLOAT	Flotation?
45.01	10.3750(.4715)		no
	20.7500(.9429)		yes
	B = 10.3750(.4715)		
		PRICE	** Price
19.20	1.4750(.2108)		$100
	2.9500(.4217)		$72
	4.4250(.6325)		$60
	5.9000(.8434)		$40
	B = 1.4750(.2108)		
	−8.2083(.9163)	CONSTANT	

Pearson's R = .994   Significance = .0000
Pearson's R = .990 for 4 holdouts   Significance = .0051

Kendall's tau = .967   Significance = .0000
Kendall's tau = 1.000 for 4 holdouts   Significance = .0208

her, followed by style and price and then brand. From her preferences, we can compute her total utility score:

(Style B) 3.46 + (Oakley brand) 1.31 + (flotation) 20.75
+ (price @ $40) 5.90 + (constant) − 8.21 = 23.21

If brand and price remain unchanged, a design that uses a hard temple with limited color choices (style c) and no flotation would produce a considerably lower total utility score for this respondent. For example:

(Style C) − 2.04 + (Oakley brand) 1.31 + (no float) 10.38
+ (price @ 40) 5.90 + (constant) − 8.21 = 7.34

FIGURE   17-7   Conjoint Results for Sample (N = 10)

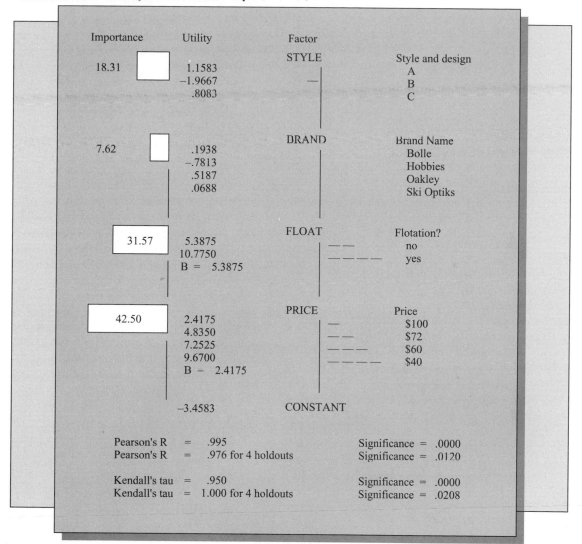

We could also calculate other combinations that would reveal the range of this individual's preferences. Our prediction that respondents would prefer less expensive prices did not hold for the eighth respondent as revealed by two asterisks next to the price factor in Figure 17–6. She reversed herself once on price to get flotation. Other subjects also reversed once on price to trade off for other factors.

The results for the sample are presented in Figure 17–7. In contrast to individuals, the sample placed price first in importance, followed by flotation, style, and brand. Group utilities may be calculated just as we did for the individual. At the bottom of the printout we find Pearson's *r* and Kendall's tau. Each was discussed in the last chapter. In this application, they measure the relationship between observed and estimated preferences. Since holdout samples (in conjoint, regression, discriminant, and other methods) are not used to construct the estimating equation, the coefficients for the holdouts are often a more realistic index of the model's fit.

Conjoint analysis is an effective tool for researchers to match preferences to known characteristics of market segments and design or target the product accordingly.

INTERDEPENDENCY TECHNIQUES

Factor Analysis

Factor analysis is a general description for several specific computational techniques. All have the objective of reducing many variables to a more manageable number that belong together and have overlapping measurement characteristics. The predictor-criterion relationship that was found in the dependence situation is replaced by a matrix of intercorrelations among several variables, none of which is viewed as being dependent upon another. For example, one may have data on 100 employees with scores on six attitude scale items.

Method   Factor analysis begins by constructing a new set of variables based on the relationships in the correlation matrix. While this can be done in a number of ways, the most frequently used approach is **principal components analysis.** This method transforms a set of variables into a new set of composite variables or principal components that are not correlated with each other. These linear combinations of variables, called **factors,** account for the variance in the data as a whole. The best combination makes up the first principal component and is the first factor. The second principal component is defined as the best linear combination of variables for explaining the variance *not* accounted for by the first factor. In turn, there may be a third, fourth, and *k*th component, each being the best linear combination of variables not accounted for by the previous factors.

FIGURE   17–8   Principal Components Analysis from a Three-Variable Data Set

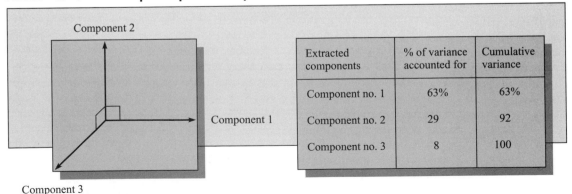

Extracted components	% of variance accounted for	Cumulative variance
Component no. 1	63%	63%
Component no. 2	29	92
Component no. 3	8	100

The process continues until all the variance is accounted for, but as a practical matter, it is usually stopped after a small number of factors have been extracted. The output of a principal components analysis might look like the hypothetical data shown in Figure 17–8.

Numerical results from a factor study are shown in Table 17–7. The values in this table are correlation coefficients between the factor and the variables (.70 is the *r* between variable *A* and factor I.) These correlation coefficients are called **loadings.** Two other elements in Table 17–7 need explanation. Eigenvalues are the sum of the variances of the factor values (for factor I the eigenvalue is $.70^2 + .60^2 + .50^2 + .60^2 + 60^2$). When divided by the number of variables, an eigenvalue yields an estimate of the amount of total variance explained by the factor. For example, factor I accounts for 36 percent of the total variance. The column headed h^2 gives the **communalities** or estimates of the variance in each variable that is explained by the two factors. With variable *A,* for example, the communality is $.70^2 + (-.40)^2 = .65$, indicating that 65 percent of the variance in variable *A* is statistically explained in terms of factors I and II.

In this case, the unrotated factor loadings are not enlightening. What one would like to find is some pattern in which factor I would be heavily loaded (have a high *r*) on some variables and factor II on others. Such a condition would suggest rather "pure" constructs underlying each factor. You attempt to secure this less ambiguous condition between factors and variables by **rotation.** This procedure can be carried out by either orthogonal or oblique methods, but only the former will be illustrated here.

To understand the rotation concept, consider that you are dealing only with simple two-dimensional rather than multidimensional space. The variables in Table 17–7 can be plotted in two-dimensional space as shown in Figure 17–9. Two axes divide this space, and the points are positioned relative to these axes. The location of these axes is arbitrary, and they represent only one of an infinite number of reference frames that could be used to reproduce the matrix. As long as you do not

TABLE 17–7   Factor Matrices

Variable	A Unrotated Factors			B Rotated Factors	
	I	*II*	h^2	*I*	*II*
A	.70	−.40	.65	**.79**	.15
B	.60	−.50	.61	**.75**	.03
C	.60	−.35	.48	**.68**	.10
D	.50	.50	.50	.06	**.70**
E	.60	.50	.61	.13	**.77**
F	.60	.60	.72	.07	**.85**
Eigenvalue	2.18	1.39			
Percent of variance	36.30	23.20			
Cumulative percent	36.30	59.50			

FIGURE 17–9
Orthogonal
Factor Rotations

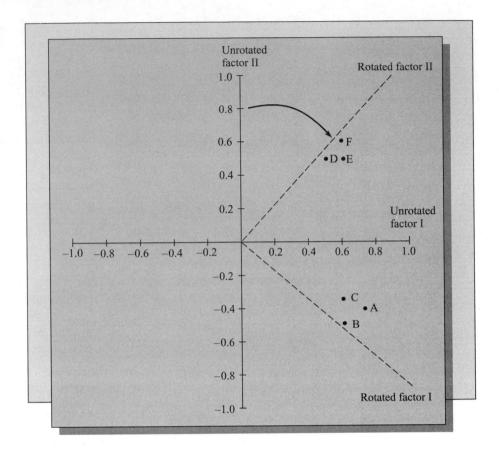

change the intersection points and keep the axes at right angles, when an orthogonal method is used, you can rotate them to find a better solution or position for the reference axes. "Better" in this case means a matrix that makes the factors as pure as possible (each variable loads onto as few factors as possible). From the rotation shown in Figure 17–9, it can be seen that the solution is improved substantially. Using the rotated solution suggests that the measurements from six scales may be summarized by two underlying factors (see the rotated factors section of Table 17–7).

The interpretation of factor loadings is largely subjective. There is no way to calculate the meanings of factors; they are what one sees in them. For this reason, factor analysis is largely used for exploration. One can detect patterns in latent variables, discover new concepts, and reduce data. Factor analysis is also used to test hypotheses, although the confirmatory models are beyond the scope of this discussion.

Example   Student grades make for an interesting example. The director of an MBA program has been reviewing grades for the first-year students and is struck by the

TABLE 17–8 **Correlation Coefficients, Student Grade Data**

Variable	Course	V1	V2	V3	V10
V1	Financial Accounting	1.00	.56	.17	−.01
V2	Managerial Accounting	.56	1.00	−.22	.06
V3	Finance	.17	−.22	1.00	.42
V4	Marketing	−.14	.05	−.48	−.10
V5	Human Behavior	−.19	−.26	−.05	−.23
V6	Organization Design	−.21	−.00	−.56	−.05
V7	Production	− 44	−.11	.04	−.08
V8	Probability	.30	.06	.07	.10
V9	Statistical Inference	−.05	.06	−.32	.06
V10	Quantitative Analysis	−.01	.06	.42	1.00

patterns in the data. His hunch is that distinct types of people are involved in the study of management, and he decides to gather evidence for this idea.

Suppose a sample of 21 grade reports is chosen for students in the middle of the GPA range. Three steps are followed:

1. Calculate a correlation matrix between the grades for all pairs of the 10 courses for which data exist.
2. Factor analyze the matrix by the principal components method.
3. Select a rotation procedure to clarify the factors and aid in interpretation.

Table 17–8 shows a portion of the correlation matrix. These data represent correlation coefficients between the 10 courses. For example, grades secured in V1 (Financial Accounting) correlated rather well (0.56) with grades received in course V2 (Managerial Accounting). The next best correlation with V1 grades is an inverse correlation (−.44) with grades in V7 (Production).

After the correlation matrix, the extraction of components is shown in Table 17–9. While the program will produce a table with as many as 10 factors, you choose, in this case, to stop the process after three factors have been extracted. Several features in this table are worth noting. Recall that the communalities indicated the amount of variance in each variable that is being "explained" by the factors. Thus, these three factors accounted for about 73 percent of the variance in grades in the Financial Accounting course. It should be apparent from these communality figures that some of the courses are not explained well by the factors selected.

The eigenvalue row in Table 17–9 is a measure of the explanatory power of each factor. For example, the eigenvalue for factor 1 is 1.83 and is computed as follows:

$$1.83 = (.41)^2 + (.01)^2 + \cdots + (.25)^2$$

The percent of variance accounted for by each factor in Table 17–9 is computed by dividing eigenvalues by the number of variables. When this is done, one sees that

TABLE 17-9　Factor Matrix Using Principal Factor with Iterations, Student Grade Data

Variable	Course	Factor 1	Factor 2	Factor 3	Communality
V1	Financial Accounting	.41	.71	.23	.73
V2	Managerial Accounting	.01	.53	−.16	.31
V3	Finance	.89	−.17	.37	.95
V4	Marketing	−.60	.21	.30	.49
V5	Human Behavior	.02	−.24	−.22	.11
V6	Organization Design	−.43	−.09	−.36	.32
V7	Production	−.11	−.58	−.03	.35
V8	Probability	.25	.25	−.31	.22
V9	Statistical Inference	−.43	.43	.50	.62
V10	Quantitative Analysis	.25	.04	.35	.19
	Eigenvalue	1.83	1.52	.95	
	Percent of variance	18.30	15.20	9.50	
	Cumulative percent	18.30	33.50	43.00	

the three factors accounted for about 43 percent of the total variance in course grades.

In an effort to further clarify the factors, a varimax rotation is used to secure the matrix shown in Table 17–10. The heavy factor loadings for the three factors are as follows:

Factor 1		Factor 2		Factor 3	
Financial Accounting	.84	Finance	.90	Marketing	.65
Managerial Accounting	.53	Organization Design	−.56	Statistical Inference	.79
Production	−.54				

Interpretation　The varimax rotation appears to clarify the relationship among course grades, but as pointed out earlier, the interpretation of the results is largely subjective. We might interpret the above results as showing three kinds of students, classified as the accounting, finance, and marketing types. Other interpretations could be made.

A number of problems affect the interpretation of these results. Among the major ones are:

1. The sample is small and any attempt at replication might produce a different pattern of factor loadings.
2. Using the same data, another number of factors rather than three can result in different patterns.
3. Even if the findings are replicated, the differences may be due to the varying influence of professors or the way they teach the courses rather than the subject content.

TABLE 17–10   **Varimax Rotated Factor Matrix, Student Grade Data**

Variable	Course	Factor 1	Factor 2	Factor 3
V1	Financial Accounting	.84	.16	−.06
V2	Managerial Accounting	.53	−.10	.14
V3	Finance	−.01	.90	−.37
V4	Marketing	−.11	−.24	.65
V5	Human Behavior	−.13	−.14	−.27
V6	Organization Design	−.08	−.56	−.02
V7	Production	−.54	.11	−.22
V8	Probability	.41	−.02	.24
V9	Statistical Inference	.07	.02	.79
V10	Quantitative Analysis	−.02	.42	.09

4. The labels may not truly reflect the latent construct that underlies any factors we extract.

This suggests that factor analysis can be a demanding tool to use. It is powerful, but the results achieved must be interpreted with great care.

Cluster Analysis

Unlike techniques for analyzing the relationships between variables, **cluster analysis** is a set of techniques for grouping similar objects or people. Originally developed as a classification device for taxonomy, its use has spread because of classification work in medicine, biology, and other sciences. Its visibility in those fields and the availability of high-speed computers to carry out the extensive calculations have sped its adoption in engineering, economics, marketing, and a host of other areas.

Cluster shares some similarities with factor analysis, especially when factor is applied to people (*Q*-analysis) instead of to variables. It differs from discriminant analysis in that discriminant begins with a well-defined group composed of two or more distinct sets of characteristics in search of a set of variables to separate them. Cluster starts with an undifferentiated group of people, events, or objects and attempts to reorganize them into homogeneous subgroups.

Method   Five steps are basic to the application of most cluster studies:

1. Selection of the sample to be clustered (e.g., buyers, medical patients, inventory, products, employees).
2. Definition of the variables on which to measure the objects, events, or people (e.g., financial status, political affiliation, market segment characteristics, symptom classes, product competition definitions, productivity attributes).
3. Computation of similarities among the entities through correlation, Euclidean distances, and other techniques.

**FIGURE 17–10
Cluster Analysis
on Three Dimensions**

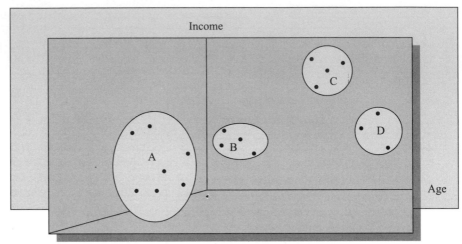

Family size

4. Selection of mutually exclusive clusters (maximization of within-cluster similarity and between-cluster differences) or hierarchically arranged clusters.
5. Cluster comparison and validation.

Different clustering methods can and do produce different solutions. It is important to have enough information about the data to know when the derived groups are real and not merely imposed on the data by the method.

The example shown in Figure 17–10 shows cluster analysis of individuals based on three dimensions: age, income, and family size. Cluster analysis could be used to segment the car-buying population into distinct markets. For example, cluster A may be targeted as potential minivan or sport-utility vehicle buyers. The market segment represented by cluster B would be a sports and performance car segment. Clusters C and D would both be targeted as buyers of sedans, but the C cluster would be the luxury buyer. This form of clustering or a hierarchical arrangement of the clusters may be used to plan marketing campaigns and develop strategies.

Example   Serious movie fans find that Paris offers one of the world's best selections of films. Residents of New York and Los Angeles are often surprised to discover they are eclipsed by Paris's average of 300 films per week shown in over 100 locations.

We selected ratings from 12 cinema reviewers using sources ranging from *Le Monde* to international publications sold in Paris. The reviews reputedly influence box-office receipts, and the entertainment business takes them seriously.

The object of this cluster example was to classify 19 films into homogeneous subgroups. The production companies were American, Canadian, French, Italian, Spanish, Finnish, Egyptian, and Japanese. Three genre of films were represented: comedy, dramatic comedy, and psychological drama. Table 17–11 shows the data

TABLE 17-11   Film, Country, Genre, and Cluster Membership

Film	Country	Genre	Case	Number of Clusters			
				5	4	3	2
Cyrano de Bergerac	France	DramaCom	1	1	1	1	1
Il y a des Jours	France	DramaCom	4	1	1	1	1
Nikita	France	DramaCom	5	1	1	1	1
Les Noces de Papier	Canada	DramaCom	6	1	1	1	1
Leningrad Cowboys . . .	Finland	Comedy	19	2	2	2	2
Storia de Ragazzi . . .	Italy	Comedy	13	2	2	2	2
Conte de Printemps	France	Comedy	2	2	2	2	2
Tatie Danielle	France	Comedy	3	2	2	2	2
Crimes and Misdem . . .	USA	DramaCom	7	3	3	3	2
Driving Miss Daisy	USA	DramaCom	9	3	3	3	2
La Voce della Luna	Italy	DramaCom	12	3	3	3	2
Che Hora e	Italy	DramaCom	14	3	3	3	2
Attache-Moi	Spain	DramaCom	15	3	3	3	2
White Hunter Black . . .	USA	PsyDrama	10	4	4	3	2
Music Box	USA	PsyDrama	8	4	4	3	2
Dead Poets Society	USA	PsyDrama	11	4	4	3	2
La Fille aux All . . .	Finland	PsyDrama	18	4	4	3	2
Alexandrie, Encore . . .	Egypt	DramaCom	16	5	3	3	2
Dreams	Japan	DramaCom	17	5	3	3	2

by film name, country of origin, and genre. The table also lists the clusters for each film using the *average linkage method*. This approach considers distances between all possible pairs rather than just the nearest or farthest neighbor.

The sequential development of the clusters and their relative distances is displayed in a diagram called a *dendogram*. Figure 17–11 shows that the clustering procedure begins with 19 films and continues until all the films are again an undifferentiated group. The solid vertical line shows the point at which the clustering solution best represents the data. This determination was guided by coefficients provided by the SPSS program for each stage of the procedure. Five clusters explain this data set.

The first cluster shown in Figure 17–11 has four French-language films, all of which are dramatic comedies. Cluster two consists of comedy films. Two French and two other European films joined at the first stage, and then these two groups came together at the second stage. Cluster three, composed of dramatic comedies, is otherwise diverse. It is made up of two American films with two Italian films adding to the group at the fourth stage. Late in the clustering process, cluster three is completed when a Spanish film is appended. In cluster four, we find three American psychological dramas combined with a Finnish film at the second stage. In cluster five, two very different dramatic comedies are joined in the third stage.

Cluster analysis classified these productions based on reviewers' ratings. The similarities and distances are influenced by film genre and culture (as defined by the translated language).

FIGURE   17–11   Dendogram Using Average Linkage

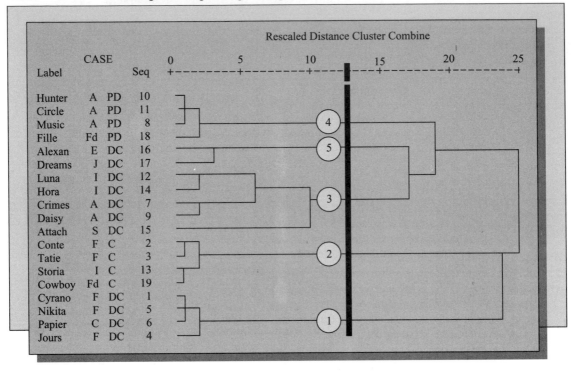

Multidimensional Scaling

Multidimensional scaling (MDS) creates a spacial description of a respondent's perception about a product, service, or other object of interest. This often helps the business researcher to understand difficult-to-measure constructs such as product quality or desirability. In contrast to variables that can be measured directly, many constructs are perceived and cognitively mapped in different ways by individuals. With MDS, items that are perceived to be similar will fall close together in multidimensional space, and items that are perceived to be dissimilar will be farther apart.

Method   We may think of three types of attribute space, each representing a multidimensional map. First, there is objective space in which an object can be positioned in terms of its measurable attributes; its flavor, weight, and nutritional value. Second, there is subjective space where perceptions of the object's flavor, weight, and nutritional value may be positioned. Objective and subjective attribute assessments may coincide, but often they do not. A comparison of the two allows us to judge how accurately an object is being perceived. Individuals may hold different perceptions of an object simultaneously, and these may be averaged to present a summary measure of perceptions. In addition, a person's perceptions may vary over time and in different circumstances; such measurements are valuable to gauge the impact of various perception-affecting actions, such as advertising programs.

TABLE 17–12   Similarities Matrix of 16 Companies

	1	2	3	4	5	6	7	8	9	10	11	12	13	14	15	16
1	0															
2	3.9	0														
3	4.7	6.7	0													
4	4.4	2.8	4.7	0												
5	14.0	12.4	18.5	15.2	0											
6	4.9	6.7	0.2	4.9	18.7	0										
7	0.8	3.7	4.1	3.7	14.5	4.3	0									
8	6.0	2.1	8.5	4.0	11.8	8.7	5.8	0								
9	4.3	6.9	1.1	5.3	18.3	1.2	3.8	8.9	0							
10	8.2	4.7	8.5	4.1	15.3	8.6	7.6	3.9	9.3	0						
11	8.6	8.7	4.7	5.9	21.1	4.5	7.8	9.7	5.7	7.7	0					
12	2.2	3.7	6.9	5.5	11.8	7.1	2.8	5.5	6.5	8.5	10.5	0				
13	8.4	9.8	3.7	7.2	22.0	3.5	7.8	11.2	4.5	10.0	2.9	10.6	0			
14	12.8	13.4	8.2	10.6	25.8	8.1	12.1	14.4	9.1	12.0	4.7	14.9	4.6	0		
15	19.1	18.2	23.8	21.0	6.2	24.0	19.7	17.8	23.4	21.5	26.9	16.9	27.4	31.5	0	
16	2.6	5.2	2.1	4.0	16.5	2.3	2.0	7.2	1.9	8.0	6.3	4.8	5.8	10.3	21.7	0

SOURCE: Similarities matrix based on data from "Executive Compensation Scoreboard," *International Business Week,* May 7, 1990, pp. 74–75.

With a third map we can describe respondents' preferences using the object's attributes. This represents their ideal; all objects close to this ideal point are interpreted as preferred by them to those that are more distant. Ideal points from many people can be positioned in this preference space to reveal the pattern and size of preference clusters. These can be compared to the subjective space to assess how well the preferences correspond to perception clusters. In this way, cluster analysis and MDS can be combined to map market segments and then examine products designed for those segments.

Example   We illustrate multidimensional scaling with a study of 16 companies from *Business Week's* "Executive Compensation Scoreboard."[12] The companies chosen are from the natural resources (fuel) segment of the scoreboard. *Business Week* reported data from 1989 including executive total compensation (salary, bonus, and long-term compensation for 1987–1989), shareholders' return (the 1989 year-end value based on $100 invested in corporate stock in 1987), and the company's return on common equity (ROE) for the three-year period, 1987–1989. We created a metric algorithm measuring the similarities among the 16 companies based on total executive compensation and the ROE. The matrix of similarities is shown in Table 17–12. Higher numbers reflect the items that are more dissimilar.

If we were using respondents and producing a matrix of similarities among the perception of objects, we might obtain ordinal data. Then the matrix would contain ranks with 1 representing the most similar pair and n indicating the most dissimilar pair.

A computer program is used to analyze the data matrix and generate a spatial map.[13] The objective is to find a multidimensional spatial pattern that best reproduces the original order of the data. For example, the most similar pair (companies 3,6) must be located in this multidimensional space closer together than any other pair. The least similar pair (companies 14,15) must be the farthest apart. The computer program presents these relationships as a geometric configuration so all distances between pairs of points closely correspond to the original matrix.

Determining how many dimensions to use is complex. The more dimensions of space we use, the more likely the results will closely match the input data. Any set of n points can be satisfied by a configuration of $n - 1$ dimensions. Our aim, however, is to secure a structure that provides a good fit for the data and has the fewest dimensions. MDS is best understood using two or at most three dimensions.

Most algorithms include the calculation of a **stress index** (*S*-stress or Kruskal's stress) that ranges from the worst fit (1) to the perfect fit (0). This study, for example, had a stress of .001. Another index, R^2, is interpreted as the proportion of variance of transformed data accounted for by distances in the model. A result close to 1.0 is desirable.

In the executive compensation example, we conclude that two dimensions represent an acceptable geometric configuration as shown in Figure 17–12. The distance between Anadarko and Chevron (3,6) is the shortest, while that between Texaco and Union Texas Petro Holdings (14,15) is the longest. As with factor analysis, there is no statistical solution to the definition of the dimensions represented by the X and Y axes. The labeling is judgmental and depends upon the insight of the researcher, analysis of information collected from respondents, or another basis. Respondents sometimes are asked to state the criteria they used for judging the similarities, or they are asked to judge a specific set of criteria. In this example, the horizontal dimension approximates the total executive compensation while the vertical dimension represents return on equity.

Consistent with raw data, Union Texas and Atlantic Richfield have high ROE but compensate their executives close to the sample mean. In contrast, Exxon and Mobil generated an ROE close to the sample's average while providing higher compensation for their executives. We could hypothesize that these latter two companies may be more difficult to run—are larger and more complex—but that would need to be confirmed with another study. The clustering of companies in attribute space shows that they are perceived to be similar along the dimensions measured.

MDS is most often used to assess perceived similarities and differences among objects. Using MDS allows the researcher to understand constructs that are not directly measurable. The process provides a spatial map that shows similarities in terms of relative distances. It is best understood when limited to two or three dimensions that can be graphically displayed.

FIGURE   17–12   Multidimensional Scaling Plot of Natural Resource Companies' Return on Equity and Executive Compensation

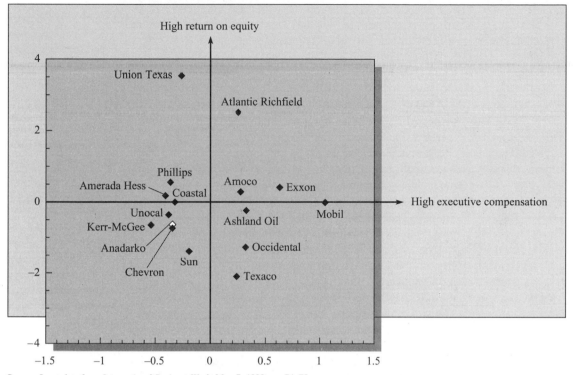

SOURCE: Input data from *International Business Week,* May 7, 1990, pp. 74–75.

Summary

The application of multivariate statistical tools to problems in business research has multiplied in recent years. Recognition of the complexities of business problems coupled with the computer revolution have been largely responsible.

Multivariate techniques are classified into two categories: dependency and interdependency. When the problem reveals the presence of criterion and predictor variables, we have an assumption of dependence. If the variables are interrelated without designating some dependent and others independent, then interdependence of the variables is assumed. The choice of techniques is guided by the number of dependent and independent variables involved and whether they are measured on metric or nonmetric scales.

Multiple regression is an extension of bivariate linear regression. When a researcher is interested in explaining or predicting a metric dependent variable from a set of metric independent variables (although dummy variables may also be used), multiple regression is often selected. Regression results provide information on the statistical significance of the independent variables, the strength of association between one or more of the predictors and the criterion, and a predictive equation for future use.

Discriminant analysis is used to classify people or objects into groups based on several predictor variables. The groups are defined by a categorical variable with two or more values whereas the predictors are metric. The effectiveness of the discriminant equation is not only based on its statistical significance but also on its success in correctly classifying cases to groups.

Multivariate analysis of variance, or MANOVA, is one of the more adaptive techniques for multivariate data. MANOVA assesses the relationship between two or more metric dependent variables and classificatory variables or factors. MANOVA is most commonly used to test differences among samples of people or objects. In contrast to ANOVA, MANOVA handles multiple dependent variables, thereby simultaneously testing all the variables and their interrelationships.

Canonical analysis is used when researchers have two sets of variables and are interested in explaining the effects of one set on the other. The independent and dependent variables are grouped into weighted sets so their linear combinations are optimally correlated. Like factor analysis, each successive pair of linear combinations, or canonical variates, extracted is uncorrelated with the next and explains progressively less and less of the relationship.

The LISREL technique is extremely useful in explaining causality among constructs that cannot be directly measured. LISREL has two parts, a measurement model and a structural equation model. The measurement model is used to relate the observed, recorded, or measured variables to the latent variables (constructs). The structural equation model specifies causal relationships, causal effects, and unexplained variance among the constructs.

Conjoint analysis is a technique that typically handles nonmetric independent variables. Conjoint analysis allows the researcher to determine the importance of product or service attributes and the levels or features that are most desirable. Respondents provide preference data by ranking or rating cards that describe products. These data became utility weights of product characteristics by means of optimal scaling and loglinear algorithms.

Interdependence techniques are used when there is no assumption of asymmetry, influence, or causality. Principal components analysis extracts uncorrelated factors that account for the largest portion of variance from an initial set of variables. Factor analysis goes one step further by attempting to reduce the number of variables and discover the underlying constructs that explain the variance. A correlation matrix is used to derive a factor matrix from which the best linear combination of variables may be extracted. In many applications, the factor matrix will be rotated to simplify the factor structure.

Unlike techniques for analyzing the relationships between variables, cluster analysis is a set of techniques for grouping similar objects or people. The cluster procedure starts with an undifferentiated group of people, events, or objects and attempts to reorganize them into homogeneous subgroups.

Multidimensional scaling (MDS) is often used in conjunction with cluster analysis or conjoint analysis. It allows a respondent's perception about a product, service, or other object of their attitude to be described in a spatial manner. MDS assists the business researcher to understand difficult-to-measure constructs such as product quality or desirability, which are perceived and cognitively mapped in different ways by individuals. Items judged to be similar will fall close together in multidimensional space and are revealed numerically and geometrically by spatial "maps."

Key Terms

beta weights	LISREL
canonical analysis	loadings
centroids	metric (nonmetric) measures
cluster analysis	multicollinearity
communalities	multidimensional scaling
conjoint analysis	multiple regression
dependency techniques	multivariate analysis
discriminant analysis	multivariate analysis of variance
dummy variables	(MANOVA)
factor analysis	path analysis
factors	principal components analysis
holdout sample	rotation
interdependency techniques	standardized coefficients
	stress index
	utility scores (part-worths)

Discussion Questions

1. Distinguish among:
   a. Multidimensional scaling.
   b. Cluster analysis.
   c. Factor analysis.
2. Describe the differences between dependence techniques and interdependence techniques. When would you choose a dependence technique?
3. How could discriminant analysis be used to provide insight to MANOVA results where the MANOVA has one independent variable (a factor with two levels)?
4. Describe how you would create a conjoint analysis study of off-road vehicles. Restrict your brands to three and suggest possible factors and levels. The full-concept description should not exceed 256 decision options.
5. An analyst sought to predict the annual sales for a home-furnishing manufacturer using the following predictor variables:

   X_1 = Marriages during the year
   X_2 = Housing starts during the year
   X_3 = Annual disposable personal income
   X_4 = Time trend (first year = 1, second year = 2, and so forth)

Using data for 24 years, the analyst calculated the following estimating equation:

$$Y = 49.85 - .068X_1 + .036X_2 + 1.22X_3 - 19.54X_4$$

The analyst also calculated an $R^2 = .92$ and a standard error of estimate of 11.9. Interpret the equation and the statistics above.

6. What type of multivariate methods do you recommend in each of the following and why?
   a. You want to develop an estimating equation that will be used to predict which applicants will come to your university as students.
   b. You would like to predict family income using such variables as education, stage in family life cycle, and so forth.
   c. You wish to estimate standard labor costs for manufacturing a new dress design.
   d. You have been studying a group of successful salespeople. You have given them a number of psychological tests. You want to bring meaning out of these test results.

7. A researcher was given the assignment of predicting which of three actions would be taken by the 280 employees in the Desota plant that was going to be sold to its employees. The alternatives were:
   a. Take severance pay and leave the company.
   b. Stay with the new company and give up severance pay.
   c. Take a transfer to the plant in Chicago.
   She gathered data on employee opinions, inspected personal files, and the like, and then did a discriminant analysis. Later, when the results were in, she found the following results:

	Predicted Decision		
Actual Decision	A	B	C
A	80	5	12
B	14	60	14
C	10	15	70

How successful was the researcher's analysis?

8. Referring to the example in this chapter concerning student grades, answer the following questions:
   a. How are the factor loadings interpreted?
   b. What is the meaning of a communality of .11 found in Table 17–9?
   c. Give another interpretation of the three factors extracted in Table 17–10.

Reference Notes

1. Jagdish N. Sheth, ed., *Multivariate Methods for Market and Survey Research* (Chicago: American Marketing Association, 1977), p. 3.
2. William Schneider, "Opinion Outlook," *National Journal,* July 1985.
3. Benson Shapiro, "Price Reliance: Existence and Sources," *Journal of Marketing Research,* August 1973, pp. 286–89.
4. For a discussion of path analysis, see Elazar J. Pedhazur, *Regression in Behavioral Research: Explanation and Prediction,* 2nd ed. (New York: Holt, Rinehart & Winston, 1982), chap. 15.
5. Fred Kerlinger, *Foundations of Behavioral Research,* 3rd ed. (New York: Holt, Rinehart & Winston, 1986), p. 562.
6. Joseph F. Hair, Jr., Rolph E. Anderson, Ronald L. Tatham, and William C. Black, *Multivariate Data Analysis with Readings* (New York: Macmillan, 1992), pp. 153–81.
7. This section was based on the SPSS procedure, MANOVA, described in Marija J. Norusis/SPSS, Inc., *SPSS Advanced Statistics Users Guide* (Chicago: SPSS, Inc., 1990), pp. 71–104.
8. Adapted from Hair et al., *Multivariate Data Analysis,* pp. 193–207.
9. This section is based on Karl G. Jörgeskog, Dag Sorbom/SPSS, Inc., *LISREL 7: A Guide to the Program and Applications,* 2nd ed. (Chicago: SPSS, Inc., 1989).
10. SPSS, Inc., *SPSS Categories* (Chicago: SPSS, Inc., 1990).
11. Product specifications adapted from Lewis Rothlein, "A Guide to Sun Protection Essentials," *Wind Rider,* June 1990, pp. 95–103.
12. "Executive Compensation Scoreboard," *International Business Week,* May 7, 1990, pp. 74–75.
13. See the ALSCAL Procedure in Marija J. Norusis/SPSS, Inc., *SPSS Base System User's Guide* (Chicago: SPSS, Inc., 1990), pp. 397–416.

Suggested Readings

1. Hair, Joseph F., Jr.; Rolph E. Anderson; Ronald L. Tatham; and William C. Black. *Multivariate Data Analysis with Readings.* 3rd ed. New York: Macmillan, 1992. A very readable book covering most multivariate statistics.
2. Myers, R. *Classical and Modern Regression with Applications.* 2nd ed. Boston: Duxbury Press, 1990. Excellent coverage of regression analysis.
3. Norusis, Marija J./SPSS Inc. *SPSS for Windows Base Systems User's Guide, Release 6.0.* Chicago: SPSS, Inc., 1993; and Marija J. Norusis./SPSS Inc. *SPSS Advanced Statistics User's Guide.* Chicago: SPSS, Inc., 1990. These two texts link computer program usage, sample problems, and coverage of most multivariate techniques in an understandable style.
4. Pedhazur, Elazar, and L. Schmelkin. *Measurement, Design, and Analysis.* Hillsdale, N.J.: Lawrence Erlbaum Associates, 1991. An excellent introduction to multivariate with LISREL and EQS examples.
5. Sage Series in Quantitative Applications in the Social Sciences. Thousand Oaks, Calif.: Sage Publishing. This monograph series includes papers on most multivariate methods.
6. Stevens, James. *Applied Multivariate Statistics for the Social Sciences.* 2nd ed. Hillsdale, N.J.: Lawrence Erlbaum Associates, 1992. Comprehensive coverage with excellent computer examples.

CHAPTER
18

PRESENTING RESULTS: WRITTEN AND ORAL REPORTS

 **FINDING
YOUR WAY**

BRINGING RESEARCH TO LIFE

"**H**as it occurred to you that your draft of the report to the MindWriter people has not been touched in the last two days? The stack of marked-up pages is right there on your desk, and you have been working all around it. I've been watching."

Jason frowned and momentarily flicked his eyes to the papers and immediately glanced away at his shoe tops.

But Myra plunged ahead with her complaint. "It's no big deal, you know. You promised to chop out three pages of methodology that nobody will care about but your fellow statistics jocks . . ." Jason shot her an aggrieved look. ". . . And to remove your recommendations and provide them in a separate, informal letter so that someone at MindWriter can issue them under her own name and claim credit for your 'brilliance.' "

"I think I have writer's block."

"No. Writer's block is when you can't write. You have already written. You can't unwrite; that's the problem. You have unwriter's block."

"Well, it isn't funny, Myra. That report might as well be a 15,000-volt power line. I know that if I touch it, I'll never be able to let go."

"OK, Jason. You are right. It isn't funny to have an emotional block against writing . . . or unwriting."

"It's not an emotional problem, Myra."

"Well, of course it is. It always is. Your brain has not deteriorated, has it? In the last week?

"Some people do great research and then panic when they have to decide what goes in the report and what doesn't. Or they can't take all the great ideas running around in their heads and express their abstractions in words. Or they don't believe they are smart enough to communicate with their clients, or vice versa. So they freeze up. There is some sort of emotional problem around this MindWriter report, Jason, and you have got to face it."

"But I love the MindWriter project."

"Ah, *there's* the problem," she said.

"What? That I love it? Loving it is a problem?"

"Jason, I have heard you say that you hated projects, and I have heard you say that you *liked* projects. But this is the first time I have heard you say you *loved* a project."

"I still don't see the problem."

"Then let me tell you a story. My son-in-law has been assigned to a submarine tender in Iceland. My daughter wants to bring the kids and move in with me. I think I am going to have to tell her no, and the decision is killing me."

"The decision."

"She is my only child. After Harry was gone I raised her alone. I would have been a network anchor, Jason, if I hadn't made it my number one priority to raise Janice. I had to be her father and mother. The week she married I stayed awake for three days and nights, just crying. Not because she married a bad person, but because I had to let go. There comes a time when, after you have nurtured something, you have to let go. Then it isn't yours. It is someone else's, or it is its own thing, but it is not yours.

"When something is not yours anymore . . . when someone is their own person . . . or some work is passed to someone else . . . you don't own it. You do not get to go back and change it. It is out of your hands."

She paused. "Take Janice. She is a delight. I love to have her and the kids for a visit. But she can't come back. I have my life. She has hers. I don't own her anymore. She is not mine the way she was, and it is very important that I accept that unconditionally."

"I think I know what you mean. This MindWriter project was my baby—yours and mine. If I chop five pages out of the report, it is finished. Then it belongs to the client. I don't own it anymore. I can't fix it. I can't change anything. I can't have second thoughts."

"Fix it, then. Send them an invoice. Write a proposal for follow-up work. Do *something*, Jason. Find another project you love just as much. Finish it. Let go and move on."

THE WRITTEN RESEARCH REPORT

It may seem unscientific and even unfair, but a study can be destroyed by a poor final report or presentation. Research technicians may appreciate the brilliance of badly reported content, but most will be influenced by the quality of the reporting. This fact should prompt researchers to make special efforts to communicate clearly and fully.

The research report contains findings, analysis of findings, interpretations, conclusions, and sometimes recommendations. The researcher is the expert on the topic and knows the specifics in a way no one else can. Because a research report is an authoritative one-way communication, it imposes a special obligation for maintaining objectivity. Even if your findings seem to point to an action, you should demonstrate restraint and caution when proposing that course.

Reports may be defined in terms of their degree of formality and design. The formal report follows a well-delineated and longer format. This contrasts to the more informal or short report.

Short Reports

Short reports are appropriate when the problem is well defined, of limited scope, and has a simple and straightforward methodology. Most informational, progress, and interim reports are of this kind: a report of cost-of-living changes for upcoming labor negotiations or an exploration of filing "dumping" charges against a foreign competitor.

Short reports are about five pages. At the beginning, there should be a brief statement on the authorization for the study, the problem examined, and its breadth and depth. Next are the conclusions and recommendations, followed by the findings that support them. Section headings should be used.

Short reports are produced by a memo or a letter of transmittal. A five-page report may be produced to track sales on a quarterly basis. The report would be direct, make ample use of graphics to show trends, and refer the reader to the research department for further information. Detailed information on the research method would be omitted, although an overview could appear in an appendix. The purpose of this type of report is to distribute information quickly in an easy-to-use format. Short reports are also produced for clients with small, relatively inexpensive research projects.

The letter is a form of a short report. Its tone should be informal. The format follows that of any good business letter and should not exceed a few pages. A letter report is often written in personal style (we, you), although this depends on the situation.

Memorandum reports are another variety and follow the *To, From, Subject* format. The following suggestions may be helpful for writing short reports:

1. Tell the reader why you are writing (it may be in response to a request).
2. If the memo is in response to a request for information, remind the reader of the exact point raised, answer it, and follow with any necessary details.
3. Write in an expository style with brevity and directness.

4. If time permits, write the report today and leave it for review tomorrow before sending it.

5. Attach detailed materials as appendices when needed.

Long Reports

Long reports are of two types, the technical or base report and the management report. The choice depends on the audience and the researcher's objectives.

Many projects will require both types of reports: a **technical report,** written for an audience of researchers, and a **management report,** written for the non-technically oriented client. While some researchers try to write a single report that satisfies both needs, this complicates the task and is seldom satisfactory. The two types of audiences have different technical training, interests, and goals.

The Technical Report   This report should include full documentation and detail. It will normally survive all working papers and original data files and so will become the major source document. It is the report that other researchers will want to see because it has the full story of what was done and how it was done.

While completeness is a goal, you must guard against including nonessential material. A good guide is that sufficient procedural information should be included to enable others to replicate the study. This includes sources of data, research procedures, sampling design, data gathering instruments, index construction, and data analysis methods. Most information should be attached in an appendix.

A technical report should also include a full presentation and analysis of significant data. Conclusions and recommendations should be clearly related to specific findings. Technical jargon should be minimized but defined when used. There can be brief references to other research, theories, and techniques. While you expect the reader to be familiar with these references, it is useful to include some short explanations, perhaps as footnotes or end notes.

The Management Report   Sometimes the client has no research background and is interested in results rather than methodology. The major communication medium in this case is the management report. It is still helpful to have a technical report if the client later wishes to have a technical appraisal of the study.

Because the management report is designed for a nontechnical audience, the researcher faces some special problems. Readers are less concerned with methodological details but more interested in learning quickly the major findings and conclusions. They want help in making decisions. Often the report is developed for a single person and needs to be written with that person's characteristics and needs in mind.

The style of the report should encourage rapid reading, quick comprehension of major findings, and prompt understanding of the implication and conclusions. The report tone is journalistic and must be accurate. Headlines and underlining for emphasis is helpful; pictures and graphs often replace tables. Sentences and paragraphs should be short and direct. Consider liberal use of white space and wide margins. It may be desirable to put a single finding on each page. It also helps to have a theme running through the report and even graphic or animated characters designed to vary the presentation.

RESEARCH REPORT COMPONENTS

Research reports, long and short, have a set of identifiable components. Usually the headings and subheadings divide the sections. Each report is individual; sections may be dropped or added, condensed or expanded to meet the needs of the audience. Figure 18–1 lists four types of reports, the sections that are typically included, and the general order of presentation.

The technical report follows the flow of the research. The prefatory materials, such as a letter of authorization and a table of contents, are first. An introduction covers the purpose of the study followed by a section on methodology. The findings are presented next, including tables and other graphics. The conclusions section includes recommendations. Finally, the appendices contain technical information, instruments, glossaries, and references.

In contrast to the technical report, the management report is for the nontechnical client. The reader has little time to absorb details and needs a prompt exposure to the most critical findings, thus the report's sections are in an inverted order. After the prefatory and introductory sections, the conclusions with accompanying

FIGURE   18–1   Research Report Sections and Their Order of Inclusion

Report Modules	Short Report		Long Report	
	Memo or Letter	*Short Technical*	*Management*	*Technical*
Prefatory information		1	1	1
Letter of transmittal		✔	✔	✔
Title page		✔	✔	✔
Authorization statement		✔	✔	✔
Executive summary		✔	✔	✔
Table of contents			✔	✔
Introduction	1	2	2	2
Problem statement	✔	✔	✔	✔
Research objectives	✔	✔	✔	✔
Background	✔	✔	✔	✔
Methodology		✔ (briefly)	✔ (briefly)	3
Sampling design				✔
Research design				✔
Data collection				✔
Data analysis				✔
Limitations		✔	✔	✔
Findings		3	4	4
Conclusions	2	4	3	5
Summary and conclusion	✔	✔	✔	✔
Recommendations	✔	✔	✔	✔
Appendices		5	5	6
Bibliography				7

recommendations are presented. Individual findings are presented next, supporting the conclusions already made. The appendices present any required methodological details.

The order of the management report allows clients to grasp the conclusions and recommendations quickly, without much reading. Then, if they wish to go further, they may read on into the findings. The management report should make liberal use of visual displays.

The short technical report covers the same items as the long technical report but in an abbreviated form. The methodology is included as part of the introduction and takes no more than a few paragraphs. Most of the emphasis is placed upon the findings and conclusions. A memo or letter format covers only the minimum: what the problem is and what the research conclusions are. Each of these formats can be modified to meet the needs of the audience.

Prefatory Items

Prefatory materials do not have direct bearing on the research itself. Instead, they assist the reader in using the research report.

Letter of Transmittal

When the relationship between the researcher and the client is formal, a **letter of transmittal** should be included. This is appropriate when a report is for a specific client (e.g., the company president) and when it is generated for an outside organization. The letter should refer to the authorization for the project and any specific instructions or limitations placed on the study. It should also state the purpose and the scope of the study. For many internal projects, it is not necessary to include a letter of transmittal.

Title Page

The title page should include four items: the title of the report, the date, and for whom and by whom it was prepared. The title should be brief but include the following three elements: (1) the variables included in the study, (2) the type of relationship among the variables, and (3) the population to which the results may be applied.[1]

Redundancies such as, "A Report of . . . , A Discussion of . . ." merely add length to the title but little else. Single-word titles are also of little value. Several acceptable ways of stating report titles are:

Descriptive study:	The Five-Year Demand Outlook for Plastic Pipe in the United States
Correlation study:	The Relationship between the Value of the Dollar in World Markets and Relative National Inflation Rates
Causal study:	The Effect of Various Motivation Methods on Worker Attitudes among Textile Workers

Authorization Letter   When the report is sent to a public organization, it is common to include a letter of authorization showing the authority for undertaking the research. This is especially true for reports to federal and state governments and nonprofit organizations. The letter not only shows who sponsored the research, but also delineates the original request.

Executive Summary   An **executive summary** can serve two purposes. It may be a report in miniature—covering all the aspects in the body of the report in abbreviated form. Or it could be a concise summary of the major findings and conclusions, including recommendations. Two pages are generally sufficient for executive summaries. Write this section after the rest of the report is finished. It should not include new information but may require graphics to present a particular conclusion. Expect the summary to contain a high density of significant terms since it is repeating the highlights of the report.

Table of Contents   As a rough guide, any report of several sections that totals more than 6 to 10 pages should have a table of contents. If there are many tables, charts, or other exhibits, they should also be listed after the table of contents in a table of illustrations.

Introduction

The introduction prepares the reader for the report by describing the parts of the project: the problem statement, research objectives, and background material.[2] In most projects, the introduction can be taken from the research proposal with minor editing.

Problem Statement   The problem statement contains the need for the research project. The problem is usually represented by a management question. It is followed by a more detailed set of objectives.

Research Objectives   The research objectives address the purpose of the project. These may be research question(s) and associated investigative questions. In correlational or causal studies, the hypothesis statements are included. As we discussed in Chapter 2, hypotheses are declarative statements describing the relationship between two or more variables. They state clearly the variables of concern, the relationships among them, and the target group being studied. Operational definitions of critical variables should be included.

Background   Background material may be of two types. It may be the preliminary results of exploration from an experience survey, focus group, or another source. Alternatively, it could be secondary data from the literature review. A traditional organizational scheme is to think of the concentric circles of a target. Starting with the outside ring, the writer works toward the center. The bull's-eye contains the material directly related to the problem. Sources and means for securing this information are presented in Chapter 9 and in Appendix A.

Previous research, theory, or situations that led to the management question are also discussed in this section. The literature should be organized, integrated, and presented in a way that it is connected logically to the problem. The background includes definitions, qualifications, and assumptions. It gives the reader the information needed to understand the remainder of the research report.[3]

Background material may be placed before the problem statement or after the research objectives. If it is composed primarily of literature review and related research, it should follow the objectives. If it contains information pertinent to the management problem or the situation that led to the study, it can be placed before the problem statement (where it is found in many applied studies).

Methodology

In short reports and management reports, the methodology should not have a separate section. Then it should be mentioned in the introduction with details placed in an appendix. However, for a technical report, the methodology is an important section. It contains at least five parts.

Sampling Design   The researcher explicitly defines the target population being studied and the sampling methods used. For example, was this a probability or nonprobability sample? If probability, was it simple random or complex random? How were the elements selected? How was the size determined? How much confidence do we have and how much error was allowed?

Explanations of the sampling methods, uniqueness of the chosen parameters, or other points that need explanation should be covered with brevity. Calculations should be placed in an appendix instead of in the body of the report.

Research Design   The coverage of the design must be adapted to the purpose. In an experimental study, the materials, tests, equipment, control conditions, and other devices should be described. In descriptive or ex post facto designs, it may be sufficient to cover the rationale for using one design over competing alternatives. Even with a sophisticated design, the strengths and weaknesses should be identified, and the instrumentation and materials discussed. Copies of materials are placed in an appendix.

Data Collection   This part of the report describes the specifics of gathering the data. Its contents depend on the selected design. Survey work generally uses a team with field and central supervision. How many were involved? What was their training? How were they managed? When were the data collected? How much time did it take? What were the conditions in the field? How were irregularities handled?

In an experiment, we would want to know about subject assignment to groups, the use of standardized procedures and protocols, the administration of tests or observational forms, manipulation of the variables, and so forth.

Typically, you would include a discussion on the relevance of secondary data that guided these decisions. Again, detailed materials such as field instructions should be included in an appendix.

Data Analysis   This section summarizes the methods used to analyze the data. Describe data handling, preliminary analysis, statistical tests, computer programs, and other technical information. The rationale for the choice of analysis approaches should be clear. A brief description or commentary on assumptions and appropriateness of use should be presented.

Limitations   This topic is often handled with ambivalence. Some people wish to ignore the matter, feeling that mentioning it detracts from the impact of the study. This attitude is unprofessional and possibly unethical. Others seem to adopt a masochistic approach of detailing everything. The section should be a thoughtful presentation of significant methodology or implementation problems. An even-handed approach is one of the hallmarks of an honest and competent investigator. All research studies have their limitations, and the sincere investigator recognizes that readers need aid in judging the study's validity.

Findings

This is generally the longest section of the report. The objective is to explain the data rather than draw interpretations or conclusions. When quantitative data can be presented, this should be done as simply as possible with charts, graphics, and tables.

The data need not include everything you have collected. The criterion for inclusion is, "Is this material important to the reader's understanding of the problem and the findings?" However, make sure to show findings unfavorable to your hypotheses and those that support them.

It is useful to present findings in numbered paragraphs or to present one finding per page with the quantitative data supporting the findings presented in a small table or chart on the same page (see Figure 18–2). While this practice adds to the bulk of the report, it is convenient for the reader.

**FIGURE 18–2
Example of a
Findings Page in a
Commercial Bank
Market Study**

Findings: 1. In this city, *commercial banks are not the preferred savings medium.* Banks are in a weak third place behind money market accounts.
           2. Customers of the Central City Bank have a *somewhat more favorable attitude towards bank savings* and less of a preference for government bonds.

Question: Suppose that you have just received an extra $1,000 and have decided to save it. Which of the savings methods listed would be your preferred way to save it?

Savings Method	*Total Replies*	*Central City Customers*	*Other Bank Customers*
Government bonds	24%	20%	29%
Savings and loan	43	45	42
Bank	13	18	8
Credit union	9	7	11
Stock	7	8	5
Other	4	2	5
Total	100%	100%	100%
	n = 216	105	111

Conclusions

Summary and Conclusions   The summary is a brief statement of the essential findings. Sectional summaries may be used if there are many specific findings. These may be combined into an overall summary. In simple descriptive research, a summary may complete the report, as conclusions and recommendations may not be required.

Findings state facts while conclusions represent inferences drawn from the findings. A writer is sometimes reluctant to make conclusions and leaves the task to the reader. Avoid this temptation when possible. As the researcher, you are the one best informed on the factors that critically influence the findings and conclusions.

Conclusions may be presented in a tabular form for easy reading and reference. Summary findings may be subordinated under the related conclusion statement. These may be numbered to refer the reader to pages or tables in the findings sections.

Recommendations   There are usually a few ideas about corrective actions. In academic research, the recommendations are often further study suggestions that broaden or test understanding of the subject area. In applied research the recommendations will usually be for managerial action rather than research action. The writer may offer several alternatives with justifications.

Appendices

The appendices are the place for complex tables, statistical tests, supporting documents, copies of forms and questionnaires, detailed descriptions of the methodology, instructions to field workers, and other evidence important for later support. The reader who wishes to learn about the technical aspects of the study and to look at statistical breakdowns will want a complete appendix.

Bibliography

The use of secondary data requires a bibliography. Proper citation, style, and formats are unique to the purpose of the report. Style requirements are often specified by the instructor, program, institution, or client. The end notes and references in this chapter provide only one example of many. As in the proposal, we recommend Kate L. Turabian, *A Manual for Writers of Term Papers, Theses, and Dissertations;* Joseph Gibaldi and Walter S. Achtert, *MLA Handbook for Writers of Research Papers;* and the *Publication Manual of the American Psychological Association.*

WRITING THE REPORT

Students often give inadequate attention to reporting their findings and conclusions. This is unfortunate. A well-presented study will often impress the reader more than a study with greater scientific quality but a weaker presentation. Report-writing skills are especially valuable to the junior executive or management trainee who aspires to rise in an organization. A well-written study frequently enhances career prospects.

Prewriting Concerns

Before writing, one should ask again, "What is the purpose of this report?" Writing a reply to this question is one way to crystalize the problem.

The second prewriting question is, "Who will read the report?" Thought should be given to the needs, temperament, and biases of the audience. You should not distort facts to meet these needs and biases but should consider them while developing the presentation. Knowing who reads the report may suggest its appropriate length. Generally, the higher the report goes in an organization, the shorter it should be.

Another consideration is technical background—the gap in subject knowledge between the reader and the writer. The greater the gap, the more difficult it is to convey the full findings meaningfully and concisely.

The third prewriting question is, "What are the circumstances and limitations under which you are writing?" Is the nature of the subject highly technical? Do you need statistics? Charts? What is the importance of the topic? A crucial subject justifies more effort than a minor one. What should be the scope of the report? How much time is available? Deadlines often impose limitations on the report.

Finally, "How will the report be used?" Try to visualize the reader using the report. How can the information be made more convenient? How much effort must be given to getting the attention and interest of the reader? Will the report be read by more than one person? If so, how many copies should be made? What will be the distribution of the report?

The Outline   Once the researcher has made the first analysis of the data, drawn tentative conclusions, and completed statistical significance tests, it is time to develop an outline. A useful system employs the following organization structure:

I. *Major Topic Heading*
   A. Major subtopic heading
      1. Subtopic
         a. Minor subtopic
            (1) Further detail
               (a) Even further detail

Software for developing outlines and visually connecting ideas simplifies this once onerous task. Two styles of outlining are widely used—the **topic outline** and the sentence outline. In the topic form, a key word or two is used. The assumption is that the writer knows its significance and will later remember the nature of the argument represented by that point. Alternatively, the outliner knows that a point should be made but is not yet sure how to do it.

The **sentence outline** expresses the essential thoughts associated with the specific topic. This approach leaves less development work for later writing, other than elaborations and explanations to improve readability. It has the obvious advantages of pushing the writer to make decisions on what to include and how to say it. It is probably the best outlining style for the inexperienced researcher because it divides the writing job into its two major components—what to say and how to say it. An example of the type of detail found with each of these outlining formats is:

Topic Outline	*Sentence Outline*

I. Demand
   A. How measured
      1. Voluntary error
      2. Shipping error
         a. Monthly variance
	I. Demand for refrigerators
	   A. Measured in terms of factory shipments as reported to the U.S. Department of Commerce
	      1. Error is introduced into year-to-year comparisons because reporting is voluntary.
	      2. A second factor is variations from month to month because of shipping and invoicing patterns.
	         a. Variations up to 30 percent this year depending upon whether shipments were measured by actual shipment date or invoice date

The Bibliography   Long reports, particularly technical ones, require a bibliography. A bibliography documents the sources used in writing the paper. Although bibliographies may contain entries used as background or for further study, it is preferable to include only sources used for preparing the report.

Chapter 9 describes a recording system for converting source notes to footnotes and bibliographies. Style manuals such as *The Publications Manual of the American Psychological Association, MLA Handbook for Writers of Research Papers,* and Turbian's *A Manual for Writers* provide guidelines on form, section and alphabetical arrangement, and annotation.

Bibliographic retrieval software allows researchers to locate and save references from online services and translate them into database records. Entries can be further searched, sorted, indexed, and formatted into bibliographies of any style. Many are network compatible and connect to popular word processors.

Writing the Draft   Once the outline is complete, decisions can be made on the placement of graphics, tables, and charts. Each should be matched to a particular section in the outline. It is helpful to make these decisions before your first draft. While additional graphics might be added later or tables changed into charts, it is still helpful to make a first approximation of the graphics before beginning to write. Choices for reporting statistics will be reviewed later in this chapter.

Each writer uses different mechanisms for getting thoughts into written form. Some will write longhand, relying on another to transcribe their prose into typewritten or word-processor format. Others are happiest in front of a word processor, able to add, delete, and move sections at will. Whichever works for you is the best approach to use.

Computer software packages check for spelling errors and provide a thesaurus for looking up alternative ways of expressing a thought. Writers with CD-ROM equipment can call up the 20-volume *Oxford English Dictionary,* believed to be the greatest dictionary in any language. Common word confusion (there for their, to for too, or effect for affect) will not be found by standard spelling checkers. Advanced programs will scrutinize your report for grammar, punctuation, capitalization, doubled words, transposed letters, homonyms, style problems, and readability level. The style checker will reveal misused words and indicate awkward phrasing. Figure 18–3 shows sample output from a commerical package used on one of this text's vignettes. The program shown writes comments to a text file, prepares a backup copy of the original, and generates a statistics report. The statistics summarize the program's evaluation of readability, grade level, and sentence structure. Comparisons to "reference" documents, or documents that you submit for comparisons, may be made. The software cannot guarantee an error-free report, but will greatly reduce your time in proofreading and enhance the style of the completed product.[4]

Readability   Sensitive writers consider the reading ability of their audience to assure high readership. You can achieve high readership more easily if the topic interests the readers and is in their field of expertise. In addition, you can show the usefulness of the report by pointing out how it will help the readers. Finally, you can write at a level that is appropriate to the readers' reading abilities. To test writing for difficulty level, there are standard **readability indices.** The Flesch Reading Ease Score gives a score between 0 and 100. The lower the score, the harder it is to read. The Flesch Kincaid Grade Level and Gunning's Fog Index both provide a score that corresponds with the grade level needed to easily read and understand the document. Although it is possible to calculate these indices by hand, some software packages will do it automatically. The most sophisticated packages allow you to specify the preferred reading level. Words that are above that level are highlighted to allow you to choose an alternate.

Advocates of readability measurement do not claim that all written material should be at the simplest level possible. They argue only that the level should be appropriate for the audience. They point out that comic books score about six on the Gunning scale (that is, a person with a sixth-grade education should be able to read that material). *Time* usually scores at about the 10 level, while *The Atlantic* is reported to have a score of 11 or 12. Material that scores much above 12 becomes difficult for the public to read comfortably.

Such measures obviously give only a rough idea of the true readability of a report. Good writing calls for a variety of other skills to assure reading comprehension.

Comprehensibility   Good writing varies with the writing objective. Research writing is designed to convey information of a precise nature. Avoid ambiguity, multiple meanings, and allusions. Take care to choose the right words—words that convey thoughts accurately, clearly, and efficiently. When concepts and constructs are used, they must be defined, either operationally or descriptively.

Words and sentences should be carefully organized and edited. Misplaced modifiers run rampant in carelessly written reports. Subordinate ideas mixed with major ideas make the report confusing to readers. Readers must sort out what is important and what is secondary when this should have been done for them.

FIGURE 18-3   Grammar and Style Proofreader Results

Statistics

Statistics for: Chapter 3 Vignette   Problems marked/detected: 8/8

Readability Statistics

Flesch Reading Ease: 66	Flesch-Kincaid Grade Level: 8
Gunning's Fog Index: 11	

Paragraph Statistics

Number of paragraphs: 25   Average length: 2.2 sentences

Sentence Statistics

Number of sentences: 55   Passive voice: 4
Average length: 13.8 words   Short (< 12 words) : 39
End with "?" :   2   Long (> 28 words) :   7
End with "!" :   0

Word Statistics

Number of words: 759   Average length: 4.58 letters

Document Summary for: Chapter 3 Vignette   Problems detected: 8

Readability Statistics	Interpretation
Grade level: 8 (Flesch-Kincaid)	Preferred level for most readers.
Reading ease score: 66 (Flesch)	This represents 6 to 10 years of schooling.
Passive voice: 331	Writing may be difficult to read or ambiguous for this writing style.
Average sentence length: 13.8 words	Most readers could easily understand sentences of this length.
Average word length: 1.50 syl.	Vocabulary used in this document is understandable for most readers.
Average paragraph length: 2.2 sentences	Most readers could easily follow paragraphs of this length.

Comparisons

Readability Comparison Chart

Flesch Reading Ease Score
Chapter 3 Vignette   66
Gettysburg Address   64
Hemingway short story   86
Life insurance policy   45

Flesch-Kincaid Grade Level
Chapter 3 Vignette   8
Gettysburg Address   1
Hemingway short story   5
Life insurance policy   13

Sentence Statistics Comparison Chart

Average Sentence per Paragraph
Chapter 3 Vignette   2.2
Gettysburg Address   4.1
Hemingway short story   2.8
Life insurance policy   3.2

Average Words per Sentence
Chapter 3 Vignette   13.8
Gettysburg Address   26.8
Hemingway short story   13.5
Life insurance policy   23.9

Word Statistics Comparison Chart

Average Letters per Word
Chapter 3 Vignette   4.5
Gettysburg Address   4.2
Hemingway short story   4.0
Life insurance policy   4.7

Finally, there is the matter of pace. Pace is defined as:

> The rate at which the printed page presents information to the reader . . . The proper pace in technical writing is one that enables the reader to keep his mind working just a fraction of a second behind his eye as he reads along. It logically would be slow when the information is complex or difficult to understand; fast when the information is straightforward and familiar. If the reader's mind lags behind his eye, the pace is too rapid; if his mind wanders ahead of his eye (or wants to) the pace is too slow.[5]

If the text is overcrowded with concepts, there is too much information per sentence. By contrast, sparse writing has too few significant ideas per sentence. Writers use a variety of methods to adjust the pace of their writings.

1. Use ample white space and wide margins to create a positive psychological effect on the reader.

2. Break large units of text into smaller units with headings to show organization of the topics.

3. Relieve difficult text with visual aids when possible.

4. Emphasize important material and deemphasize secondary material through sentence construction and judicious use of italicizing, underlining, capitalization, and parentheses.

5. Choose words carefully, opting for the known and the short rather than the unknown and long. Graduate students, in particular, seem to revel in using jargon, pompous constructions, and long or arcane words. Naturally, there are times when technical terms are appropriate. Scientists communicate efficiently with jargon, but in most applied business research, the audiences are not scientifically trained and need more help than many writers supply.

6. Repeat and summarize critical and difficult ideas so readers have time to absorb them.

7. Make strategic use of service words. These are words that "do not represent objects or ideas, but show relationship. Transitional words, such as the conjunctions, are service words. So are phrases such as 'on the other hand,' 'in summary,' and 'in contrast.' "[6]

Tone   Review the writing to ensure the tone is appropriate. The reader can, and should, be referred to, but researchers should avoid referring to themselves. One author notes that the "application of the 'you' attitude . . . makes the message sound like it is written to the reader, not sent by the author. A message prepared for the reader conveys sincerity, personalization, warmth, and involvement on the part of the author."[7] To accomplish this, remove negative phrasing and rewrite the thought positively. Do not change your recommendations or your findings to make them positive. Instead, review the phrasing. Which of the following sounds better?

1. End users do not want the Information Systems Department telling them what software to buy.

2. End users want more autonomy over their computer software choices.

The messages convey the same information, but the positive tone of the second message does not put readers from the Information Systems Department on the defensive.

Final Proof   It is helpful to put the draft away for a day before doing the final editing. Go to the beach, ride a bicycle in the park, see a movie—do anything that is unrelated to the research project. Then return to the report and read it with a critical eye. Does the writing flow smoothly? Are there transitions where they are needed? Is the organization apparent to the reader? Are the problem statement and the research objectives adequately met by the findings and conclusions? Are the tables and graphics displaying the proper information in an easy-to-read format? After assuring yourself that the draft is complete, write the executive summary.

Presentation Considerations

The final consideration in the report-writing process is production. Reports can be typed; printed on an ink jet, laser, color, or other printer; or sent out for typesetting. Most student and small research reports are typed or produced on a computer printer. The presentation of the report conveys to the readers the professional approach used throughout the project. Care should be taken to ensure compatible fonts are used for the entire report. The printer should produce consistent, easy-to-read letters on quality paper. When reports are photocopied for more than one reader, make sure the copies are clean with no black streaks or gray areas.

Overcrowding of text represents an appearance problem. Readers need the visual relief provided by ample white space. We define "ample" as one inch of white space at the top, bottom, and right-hand margins. On the left side, the margin should be at least one and one-fourth inches to provide room for binding or punched holes. Even greater margins will often improve report appearance and highlight key points on sections. Overcrowding also occurs when the report contains page after page of large blocks of unbroken text. This produces an unpleasant psychological effect on readers because of its formidable appearance. Overcrowded text may be avoided if writers will:

1. Use shorter paragraphs. As a rough guide, any paragraph longer than half of a page is suspect. Remember that each paragraph should represent a distinct thought.
2. Indent parts of text that represent listings, long quotations, or examples.
3. Use headings and subheadings to divide the report and its major sections into homogeneous topical parts.
4. Use vertical listings of points (such as this list).

Inadequate labeling is another physical problem. Each graph or table should contain enough information to be self-explanatory. Text headings and subheadings also help with labeling. They function as signs for the audience, describing the organization of the report and indicating the progress of discussion. They also help readers to skim the material and to return easily to particular sections of the report.

CLOSE-UP

A written report is the culmination of the MindWriter project, which has illustrated the research process throughout the book. Myra and Jason's contract for the CompleteCare project requires a report about the size of a student term project. Although repetitive portions have been omitted to conserve space, it should give the reader some ideas of how an applied project of this size is summarized. Descriptive statistics and simple graphics are used to analyze and present most of the data. References to chapters where specific details may be reviewed are shown in the marginal comments.

The presentation of findings follows the content specifications of Figure 18–1 for short reports. It falls between a memo/letter and a short technical report. The objective was to make it available quickly for feedback to the CompleteCare team. It was therefore set up as a fax document.

FAX Transmittal Memo

To:	Ms. Gracie Uhura	From:	M. Wines/J. Henry
Company:	MindWriter Corp.	**Company:**	Wines & Henry, Assoc.
Location:	Austin, TX Bldg 5	**Location:**	Palm Beach, FL
Telephone:	512.555.1234	**Telephone:**	407.555.4321
Fax:	512.555.1250	**Fax:**	407.555.4357

Total number of pages including this one: 10

March 7, 1994

Dear Gracie,

This fax contains the CompleteCare February report requested by Mr. Malraison. You may expect the plain paper copies tomorrow morning for distribution.

We hope that the Call Center will complete the nonrespondent survey so that we can discover the extent to which these results represent all CompleteCare customers.

This month's findings show improvements in the areas we discussed last week by telephone. The response rate is also up. You will be delighted to know that our preliminary analysis shows improvements in the courier's ratings.

Best regards,
Myra

The fax cover sheet acts as a temporary transmittal letter until the plain paper copies are sent.

It provides all necessary identification and contact information. The writer's and recipient's relationship makes using first names appropriate.

Authorization for the study. Scope of findings (month). Specific instructions for process issues.
Request for follow-up by the client to reduce the study's limitations.
Progress update and feedback on improvements.

**CompleteCare Customer
Survey Results
for February**

Title contains reference to a known survey and program. Descriptions of variables, relationships, and population are unnecessary.

**Prepared for Ms. Gracie Uhura
MindWriter Corporation
March 1994**

The recipient of the report, corporation, and date appear next.

**Wines and Henry Associates
Research Services
200 ShellPoint Tower
Palm Beach, Florida 33480**

407.555.4321

The report's preparer, location, telephone number facilitate contact for additional information.

MindWriter CONFIDENTIAL

The information level identifies this as a restricted circulation document for in-house use only.

Title repeated.

MindWriter CompleteCare February Results

Introduction

This report is based on the February data collected from the MindWriter CompleteCare Survey. The survey asks customers about their satisfaction with the CompleteCare repair and service system. Its secondary purpose is to iden- tify monthly improvement targets for management.

The findings are organized into the following sections: (1) an executive sum- mary, (2) the methods used, (3) the Service Improvement Grid, (4) detailed findings for each question, and (5) patterns in the open-ended questions.

Executive Summary

The highest degrees of satisfaction with CompleteCare were found in the cat- egories of "delivery speed" and "pickup speed." Average scores on these items were between 4.2 and 4.4 on a 5-point scale. "Speed of repair," "condition on arrival" and "overall impression of CompleteCare's effectiveness" also scored relatively well. They were above the *met all expectations* level (see appropri- ate charts).

Several questions were below the *met all expectations* level. From the lowest, "Call Center's responsiveness," to "Call Center's technical competence," and "courier service's arrangements," the average scores ranged from 2.0 to 3.9. In general, ratings have improved since January with exception of "condition on arrival."

The three items generating the most negative comments are (1) problems with the courier's arrangements, (2) long telephone waits, and (3) transfer among many people at the Call Center. These same comments carry over for the last two months.

CompleteCare's criteria for Dissatisfied Customers consists of negative com- ments in the Comments/Suggestions section or ratings of less than three (3.0) on questions one through eight. Forty-three percent of the sample met these criteria, down from 56% last month. By counting only customers' comments (negative or +/−), the percentage of Dissatisfied Customers would be 32%.

The ratio of negative to positive comments was 1.7 to 1, an improvement over January's ratio (2.3 to 1).

Title repeated.

Section headings are used.
Introduction contains period of coverage for report, management question, and second- ary research objec- tive.

An overview of the report's contents al- lows readers to turn to specific sections of interest.

The executive sum- mary provides a syn- opsis of essential find- ings. It is the report in miniature; six para- graphs.

Both positive and negative results are capsulized.

Criteria for indices are provided as re- minders.

When the expectation-based satisfaction scores are adjusted for perceived importance, "Call Center responsiveness," "Call Center technical competence," and "courier's arrangements" are identified as action items. "Repair speed" and "problem resolution" maintained high importance scores and are also rated above average.

Methodology

The data collection instrument is a postage-paid postcard that is packed with the repaired product at the time the unit is shipped back to the customer.

The survey consists of twelve satisfaction questions measured on 5-point scales. The questions record the degree to which the components of the CompleteCare process (arrangements for receiving the customer's computer through return of the repaired product) meet customers' *expectations.* A final categorical question asks whether customers will use CompleteCare again. Space for suggestions is provided.

Sample

The sample consisted of 175 customers who provided impressions of CompleteCare's effectiveness. For the four week-period, the response rate was 35% with no incentive given. Nothing is yet known about the differences between respondents and nonrespondents.

Service Improvement Grid

The grid on page 3 compares the degree to which expectations were met along with the *derived importance* of those expectations. The average scores for both axes determine the dividing lines for the four quadrants. The quadrants are labeled to identify actionable items or to highlight those that bear watching for improvement or deterioration.

The **Concentrate Efforts** quadrant is the area where customers are marginally satisfied with service but consider service issues important. Question 1a, "Call Center's responsiveness," Question 1b, "Call Center's technical competence," and Question 2a, "Courier arrangements" are found here. "Technical competence" was similarly rated last month. Its perceived importance was rated higher in previous months. "Courier arrangements" has increased in perceived importance over previous reports.

The methodology, reported in brief, reminds the reader of the data collection method, nature and format of the questionnaire, scales used, and target measurement issues.

The sample, a self-selecting non probability sample, and the response rate are shown. With respondents' data from the postcards and the Call Center's files on nonrespondents, a future study on nonresponse bias is planned.

This section begins the Findings section. Findings consist of the action planning grid and detailed results sections. The headings were specified by the client.

The method for creating the planning grid and the grid's contents are highlighted.

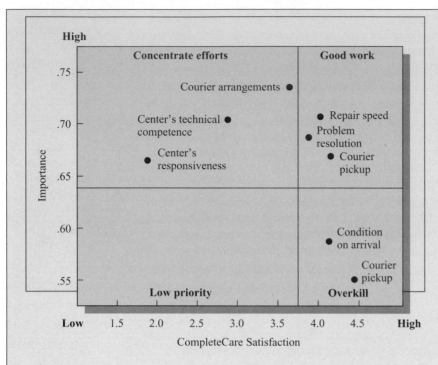

NOTE: Satisfaction scores are in the range of 1.0 to 5.0 and importance is in the range of 0 to 1.0

The statistical technique for producing the grid is correlation. A modification of scatterplots was used to create a plot with reference lines (see Chapter 16).

In the **Good Work** quadrant, CompleteCare has, on average, *met all expectations* with the "repair speed" and "courier pickup" questions. Their mean scores are greater than 4.0 and are considered important by respondents. "Problem resolution" has improved but remains a borderline concern.

There are no items in the **Low Priority** quadrant.

Over Kill, the last quadrant, contains two questions. Question 5, "condition on arrival" has improved its ratings over last month but has dropped slightly on the importance scale because the average of importance scores (horizontal line) moved upward. Question 2c, "courier delivery speed," has a high satisfaction rating, but respondents considered this item to have lower importance than most issues in CompleteCare.

The contents of each quadrant are described. Comparisons and connections to the next section are previewed.

Detailed Findings

The figures that follow provide: (1) a comparison of the mean scores for each of the questions for the last three months, and (2) individual question results. The latter contains frequencies for the scale values, percentages for each category, mean scores, standard deviations, and valid cases for each question. (See Appendix for question wording and placement).

The three-month comparison (December, January, and February) shows results for all scaled questions. February data bars (in black) reveal improvements on all average scores (vertical axis) except Question 5, "condition on arrival." Most aspects of the service/repair process have shown improvement over the three-month period.

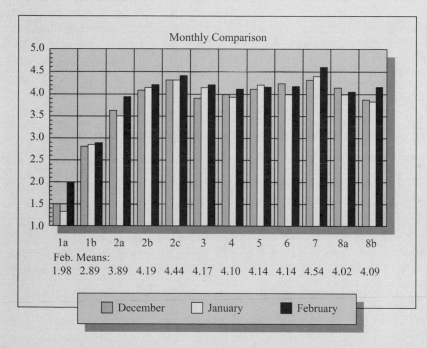

Detailed findings show the results of individual questions. This section announces the two-part content and presents, briefly and in a direct style, the most pertinent outcomes.

This graphic gives the reader a three-month view and all questions at a glance. Vertical bars are the simplest and easiest to read for the amount of space allocated. Horizontal grid lines guide the eye from the bar tops to the closest value on the mean score axis.

Charts similar to these may be produced by the same spreadsheet that handles data entry. Charting programs offer other options and will import the data from spreadsheets.

Question 1a. Call Center's Responsiveness. This question has the lowest mean score of the survey. Using a **top-box** method of reporting (combining the top two categories), 11% of the respondents felt that the Call Center met or exceeded their expectations for service responsiveness. This has improved only marginally since January and has significant implications for program targets. Based on our visit and recent results, we recommend that you begin immediately the contingency programs we discussed: additional training for Call Center operators and implementation of the proposed staffing plan.

The first individual item is reported with with means scores, percentages, and recommendations for improvement.

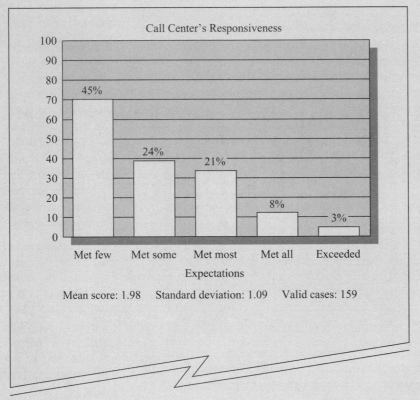

This chart conveys the message of low responsiveness rather well but does not have a label for the vertical axis. It is easy to confuse percentages with the number of respondents (which it is supposed to represent).

Similar reporting formats are skipped.

Question 6. Overall Impression of CompleteCare's effectiveness.
CompleteCare has increased the number of truly satisfied respondents with
46% (versus 43% in January) in the *exceeded* expectations category. The top-
box score has increased to 75% of respondents (against 70% in January).

Question 6 shows the respondents' overall impression of CompleteCare. It would be an ideal dependent variable for a regression study in which questions 1 through 5 were the independent variables (see Chapters 16 and 17).

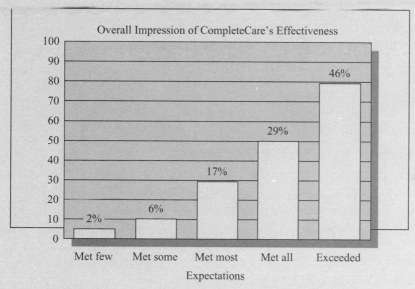

Mean score: 4.14   Standard deviation: 0.98   Valid cases: 169

**Question 8a. Likelihood of Repurchasing MindWriter Based on Service/
Repair Experience.**   Respondents' average scores (4.02) for this likelihood
scale are the highest this month since measurement began. Improvement of
the courier service's arrangements with customers and the resolution of the
problem that prompted service appear to be the best predictors of repurchase
at this time.

Question 8a is another question for more detailed research. It allows the researcher to connect the variables that describe the service/repair experience with repurchase intentions.

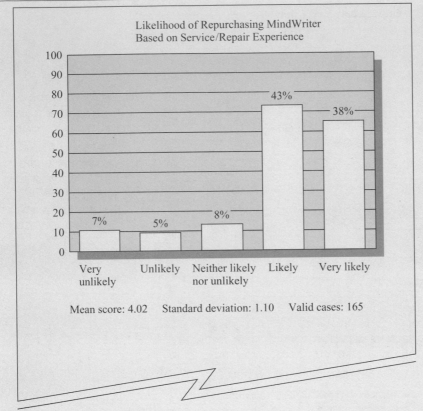

Likelihood of Repurchasing MindWriter
Based on Service/Repair Experience

Mean score: 4.02   Standard deviation: 1.10   Valid cases: 165

Using regression, it was possible to identify two key influences for this question.

Question 8b (not shown) is similar, asking about the relation of product performance with repurchase intention.

Patterns in the Open-Ended Questions

The following categories were found when the comments and suggestions were analyzed. The ratio of negative to positive comments was 1.7 to 1. Pick-up problems continue to be "courier only" problems and coordination between MindWriter's telephone support and the courier. Customers complain of holding on the phone for long periods and transfers between support people. Problems with service are split between large problems that have not been fixed and small, nuisance problems that customers are prepared to live with. Positive comments commend turnaround and service and also praise specific technical operators.

The questionnaire has one open-ended question that encourages respondents to make comments or suggestions.

Content Analysis is used to distill the responses (see Chapter 14).

Negative Comments	Count	Although Content
Shipping	19	Analysis produces

Pick-up problems (15)		more than frequency
Delivery problems (2)		counts of recurring
Box damage (1)		themes, it is a labor-
The courier charged customer (1)		intensive process. The
Call Center	19	project's restrictive
Too long on hold (9)		budget and the needs
Transferred call too frequently / Confusion (8)		of the audience made
Untrained / Hard to understand (2)		this section of the re-
Service	13	port adequate for its
Problem continues (5)		purpose.
Small things not fixed / damaged (6)		
Took too long (2-7 weeks) (2)		
Product	6	
Multiple repairs needed (3)		
Paint wears off (2)		
General dislike of product (1)		

Positive Comments

General positive comment about the process	13
Quick response	12
Great service	7
Helpful phone personnel	6

Other Comments

MindWriter shouldn't need to be repaired	4
Provide more information on what was done	2
Offer extended warranty	1
Won't use MindWriter Call Center again	1

Appendix Contents: Sample Questionnaire

The report's appendix contains a copy of the questionnaire (see Figure 11–1 in Chapter 11).

MindWriter personal computers offer you ease of use and maintenance. When you need service, we want you to rely on *CompeteCare,* wherever you may be. That's why we're asking you to take a moment to tell us how well we've served you.

	Met **few** expectations	Met **some** expectations	Met **most** expectations	Met **all** expectations	**Exceeded** expectations
	1	2	3	4	5

1. Telephone assistance with your problem: 1 2 3 4 5
    a. Responsiveness   1 2 3 4 5
    b. Technical competence   1 2 3 4 5
2. The courier service's effectiveness:
    a. Arrangements   1 2 3 4 5
    b. Pickup speed   1 2 3 4 5
    c. Delivery speed   1 2 3 4 5
3. Speed of the overall repair process.   1 2 3 4 5
4. Resolution of the problem that prompted service/repair.   1 2 3 4 5
5. Condition of your MindWriter on arrival.   1 2 3 4 5
6. Overall impression of CompleteCare's effectiveness.   1 2 3 4 5
7. Likelihood of using CompleteCare on another occasion.
    (1 = very unlikely   3 = neither likely nor unlikely   5 = very likely)   1 2 3 4 5
8. Likelihood of repurchasing a MindWriter based on:
    (1 = very unlikely   3 = neither likely nor unlikely   5 = very likely)
    a. Service/repair experience   1 2 3 4 5
    b. Product performance   1 2 3 4 5

Comments/Suggestions: _____

_____

How may we contact you to follow up on any problems you have experienced?

_____   (_____) _____
Last Name   First Name   Phone

_____
                                        City   State   Zip

Service Code

PRESENTATION OF STATISTICS[8]

The presentation of statistics in research reports is a special challenge for writers. Four basic ways to present such data are: (1) a text paragraph, (2) semitabular form, (3) tables, or (4) graphics.

Text Presentation

This is probably the most common when there are only a few statistics. The writer can direct the reader's attention to certain numbers or comparisons and emphasize specific points. The drawback is that the statistics are submerged in the text, requiring the reader to scan the entire paragraph to extract the meaning. The following material has a few simple comparisons but becomes more complicated when text and statistics are combined.

> A comparison of the three aerospace and defense companies from the high-tech stratum of the Forbes 500 sample show that Sundstrand had the best sales growth record over the years 1988–1989. Its growth was 8.0 percent—with sales significantly lower than the other two firms in the sample. This compares to sales growth for Rockwell International of 3.3 percent, and Allied-Signal was third at only 0.8 percent sales increase. Rockwell International generated the most profits in 1989 among the three companies. Rockwell's net profits were $720.7 million as compared to $528 million for Allied-Signal and $120.8 million for Sundstrand.

Semitabular Presentation

When there are just a few figures, they may be taken from the text and listed. Lists of quantitative comparisons are much easier to read and understand than embedded statistics. An example of semitabular presentation is shown below.

> A comparison of the 3 aerospace-defense companies in the Forbes 500 sample shows that Sundstrand showed the best sales growth between 1988 and 1989. Rockwell International generated the highest net profits for the year 1989.

	Annual Sales Growth	*1989 Net Profits ($ millions)*
Sundstrand	8.0%	$120.8
Rockwell	3.3	720.7
Allied-Signal	0.8	528.0

Tabular Presentation

Tables are generally superior to text for presenting statistics, although they should be accompanied by comments directing the reader's attention to important figures. Tables facilitate quantitative comparisons and provide a concise, efficient way to present numerical data.

Tables are either general or summary in nature. General tables tend to be large, complex, and detailed. They serve as the repository for the statistical findings of the study and are usually in the appendix of a research report.

Summary tables contain only a few key pieces of data closely related to a specific finding. To make them inviting to the reader (who often skips them), the table designer should omit unimportant details and collapse multiple classifications into composite measures that may be substituted for the original data.

Any table should contain enough information for the reader to understand its contents. The title should explain the subject of the table, how the data are classified, the time period, or other related matters. A subtitle is sometimes included under the title to explain something about the table; most often this is a statement of the measurement units in which the data are expressed. The contents of the columns should be clearly identified by the column heads, and the contents of the stub should do the same for the rows. The body of the table contains the data, while the footnotes contain any needed explanations. Footnotes should be identified by letters or symbols such as asterisks, rather than by numbers, to avoid confusion with data values. Finally, there should be a source note if the data do not come from your original research. Table 18–1 illustrates the various parts of a table.

Graphic Presentation

Compared with tables, graphs show less information and often only approximate values. However, they are more often read and remembered than tables. Their great advantage is that they convey quantitative values and comparisons more readily than tables. With personal computer charting programs, you can easily turn a set of numbers into a chart or graph.

There are many different graphic forms. Figure 18–4 shows the most common ones and how they should be used. Statistical explanation charts such as boxplots, stem-and-leaf displays, and histograms were discussed in Chapter 14. Line graphs, area, pie, and bar charts, and pictographs and 3-D receive additional attention here.

TABLE 18–1   **U.S. Production of Shoes and Slippers, by Class, 1965 and 1975 (millions of pairs)***   } Title

Class	1965	1975	} **Column heads**
Total	626.7	433.7	
Footwear, except slippers	536.0	365.2	
Men	118.2	104.8	
Youth and boys	25.6	17.7	
Women	280.0	173.5	
Misses	36.5	15.2	**Body**
Children	33.5	17.2	
Infants and babies	32.5	21.9	
Athletic shoes	7.0	11.4	
Other footwear	2.8	3.5	
Slippers	90.7	68.5	

(Stub)

Footnote {*Excludes Alaska and excludes rubber footwear.
Source note {Source: U.S. Bureau of Census, *Current Industrial Reports,* M31A.

FIGURE   18–4   Guide to Graphs

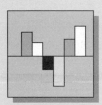

Column Compares sizes and amounts of categories usually for the same time. Places categories on X axis and values on Y axis.

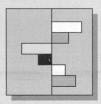

Bar Same as the column but positions categories on Y axis and values on X axis. Deviations, when used, distinguish positive from negative values.

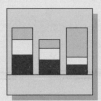

Stacked Bar In either bar or column, shows how components contribute to the total of the category.

Pie Shows relationship of parts to the whole. Wedges are row values of data.

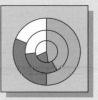

Stacked Pie Same as pie but displays two or more data series.

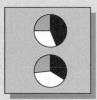

Multiple Pie Uses identical data as stacked pie but plots separate pies for each column of data without stacking.

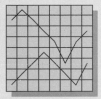

Line Compares values over time to show changes in trends.

Filled Line Similar to line chart but uses fill to highlight series.

Area (surface) Like line chart compares changing values but emphasizes relative value of each series.

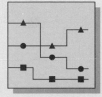

Step Compares discrete points on the value axis with vertical lines showing difference between points. Not for showing a trend.

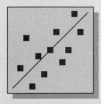

Scatter Shows if relationship between variables follows a pattern. May be used with one variable at different times.

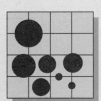

Bubble Used to introduce third variable (dots of different sizes). Axes could be sales, profits; bubbles are assets.

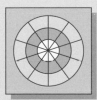

Spider (and Radar) Radiating lines are categories, values are distances from center (shows multiple variables (performance, ratings, progress).

Polar Shows relationship between a variable and angle measured in degrees (cyclical trends, pollution source vs. wind direction, etc.).

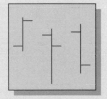

Open Hi Lo Close Shows fluctuating values in a given period (hour, day). Often used for investments.

Boxplots Displays distribution(s) and compares characteristics of shape (ch. 14).

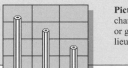

Pictographic Special chart that uses pictures or graphic elements in lieu of bars.

Line Graphs   Line graphs are used chiefly for time series and frequency distribution. There are several guidelines for designing a **line graph.**

1. Put the time units or the independent variable on the horizontal axis.
2. When showing more than one line, use different line types (solid, dashed, dotted, dash-dot) to enable the reader to easily distinguish among them.
3. Try not to put more than four lines on one chart.
4. Use a solid line for the primary data.

Beyond these suggestions, it is important to be aware of perceptual problems with line diagrams. The first is the use of a zero base line. Since the length of the bar or distance above the base line indicates the statistic, it is important that graphs give accurate visual impressions of values. A good way to achieve this is to include a zero base line on the scale on which the curves are plotted. To set the base at some other value is to introduce a visual bias. This can be seen by comparing the visual impressions in Parts A and B of Figure 18–5. Both are accurate plots of the gross national product of the United States from 1972 through 1977. In Part A, however, using the base line of zero places the curve well up on the chart and gives a better perception of the relation between the absolute size of GNP and the changes from year to year. The graph in Part B, with a base line at $1,000 billion,

FIGURE   18–5   U.S. Gross National Product, 1972–1977 (dollars in billions)

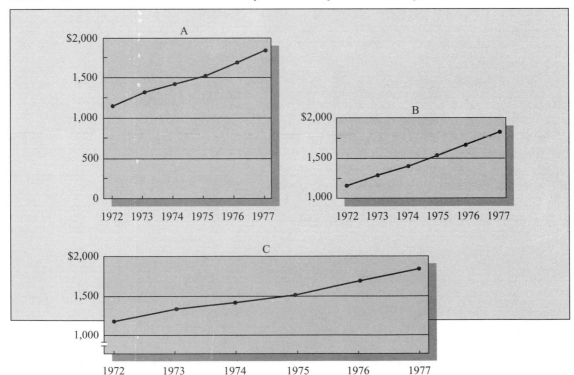

can easily give the impression that the growth was at a more rapid rate. When space or other reasons dictate using shortened scales, the zero base point should still be used but with an added break in the scale as shown in Part C of Figure 18–5. This will warn the reader that the scale has been reduced.

The balance of size between vertical and horizontal scales also affects the reader's impression of the data. There is no single solution to this problem, but the results can be seen by comparing Parts B and C in Figure 18–5. In Part C, the horizontal scale is twice that in Part B. This changes the slope of curve, creating a different perception of growth rate.

A third distortion with line diagrams occurs when relative and absolute changes among two or more sets of data are shown. In most charts, we use arithmetic scales where each space unit has identical value. This shows the absolute differences between variables, as in Part A of Figure 18–6, which presents the total U.S. population and that of the three Pacific states. This is an arithmetically correct way to present these data; but if we are interested in rates of growth, the visual impressions from a semilogarithmic scale are more accurate. A comparison of the line diagrams in Parts A and B of Figure 18–6 shows how much difference a semilogarithmic scale makes. Each is valuable and each can be misleading. In Part A, notice that both areas have been growing in population and that the population of the Pacific states is only a small portion of total U.S. population. One can even estimate what this proportion is. Part B gives insight into growth rates that are not clear from the arithmetic scale. Part B shows that the Pacific states' population has grown at a much faster rate than for the United States in total.

**FIGURE 18-6
Population of the United States and Pacific States Area, 1920-1970 (millions)**

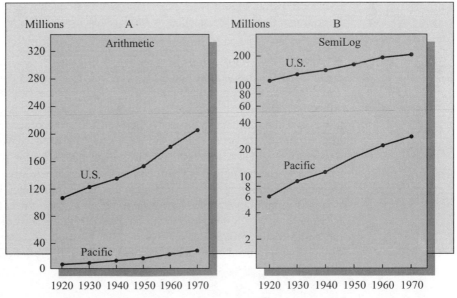

SOURCE: U.S. Department of Commerce.

Area (Stratum or Surface) Charts   An area chart is also used for a time series. Consisting of a line that has been divided into component parts, it is best used to show changes in patterns over time. The same rules apply to stratum charts as to line charts (see Figure 18-4).

Pie Charts   Pie charts are another form of an area chart. They are often used with business data. However, they can easily mislead the reader or be improperly prepared. Research shows that the reader's perception of the percentages represented by the pie slice is consistently inaccurate.[9] Consider the following suggestions when designing pie charts.

1. Show 100 percent of the subject being graphed.
2. Always label the slices with "call-outs" and with the percentage or amount that is represented. This allows you to dispense with the legend.
3. Put the largest slice at 12 o'clock and move clockwise in descending order.
4. Use light colors for large slices, darker colors for smaller slices.
5. In a pie chart of black and white slices, a single red one will command the most attention and be memorable. Use it to communicate your most important message.[10]
6. Do not show evolution over time with pie charts as the only medium. Since pie charts always represent 100 percent, growth of the overall whole will not be recognized. If you must use a series of pie charts, complement them with an area chart.

As shown in Figure 18–7, pie charts portray frequency data in interesting ways. In addition, they can be stacked to show relationships between two sets of data.

Bar Charts   Bar charts can be very effective if properly constructed. Use the horizontal axis to represent time and the vertical axis to represent units or growth-related variables. Vertical bars are generally used for time series and for quantitative classifications. Horizontal bars are less often used. If neither variable is time related, however, either format can be used. Charts are easily generated by a computer charting program.[11] If you are preparing a bar chart by hand, leave space between the bars equal to at least half the width of the bar. An exception to this is the specialized chart—the histogram—where continuous data are grouped into intervals for a frequency distribution. Histograms were discussed in Chapter 14. A second exception is the multiple variable chart, where more than one bar is located at a particular time segment. In this case, the space between the groups of bars is at least half the width of the group. Bar charts come in a variety of patterns. In Chapter 14, Figure 14–9 showed a standard vertical bar graph. Variations are illustrated in Figure 18–4.

Pictographs and Geographics   These graphics are used in popular magazines and newspapers because they are eye-catching and imaginative. *USA Today* and a host

FIGURE   18–7   Examples of Area Charts: A Stratum Chart and Two Pie Charts

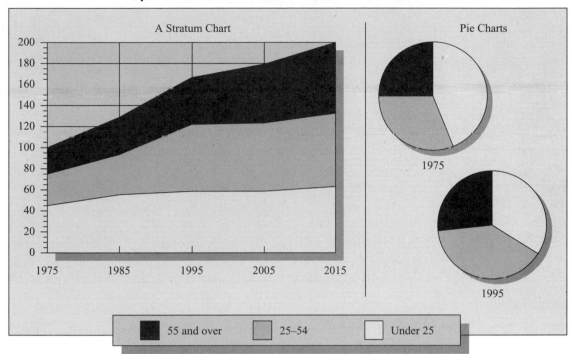

Notice the two pie charts seem to indicate a dramatic decrease in the number of "under 25" category. Now look at the stratum chart. The number of "under 25" never decreased, it only changed relative to the entire population. It is important not to use pie charts alone in a time series to avoid giving erroneous impressions.

of imitators are often guilty of taking this to the extreme by decorating graphs to where they are incomprehensible. A pictograph uses pictorial symbols (an oil drum for barrels of oil, a stick figure for numbers of employees, or a pine tree for amount of wood). The symbols represent data volume instead of a bar in a bar-type chart. It is proper to stack the same size image to express more of a quantity and to show fractions of a picture to show less. Altering the scale of the symbol produces problems. Since the pictures represent actual objects, doubling the size will increase the area of the symbol by four (and the volume by more). This misleads the reader into believing the increase is larger. The exception is a graphic that is easily substituted for a bar such as the pencils in Figure 18–4.

Geographic charts use a portion of the world's map, in pictorial form, to show differences in regions. This can be used for product production, per capita rates, demographics, or any of a number of other geographically specific variables.

3-D Graphics   With current charting techniques, virtually all charts can now be made three-dimensional. Although dimensional charts add interest, they can also obscure data. Care must be used in selecting the 3-D chart candidates (see Figure 18–8). Pie and bar charts achieve dimensionality simply by adding depth to the graphics; this is not 3-D. A 3-D column chart, however, allows you to compare three or more

FIGURE   18–8   3-D Charts

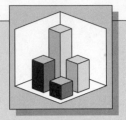  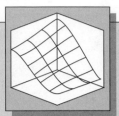 

3-D Column
A variation on column
charts, they compare
variables to each other
or over time. Axes:
X = categories,
Y = series, Z = values.
Other variations include
3-D area charts and
connect-the-dots
scatter charts.

3-D Ribbon This
example is a one-wall
plot showing columns
of data (series) as
ribbons. One or more
columns are used.
Axes: X = categories,
Y = series, Z = values.

3-D Wireframe
A variation of a contour
or response surface;
suitable for changes
time and multivariate
data. Axis: X = values,
Y = series, Z = values.

3-D Surface Line
Handles three columns
of data and plots XYZ
coordinates to show a
response surface.
Helpful for multivariate
applications.

variables from the sample in one bar-chart-type graph. If you want to display
several quarters of sales results for Hertz, Avis, Budget, and National, you have
3-D data. But be careful about converting line charts to ribbon charts, and area
charts to 3-D area charts.

Surface charts and 3-D scatter charts are helpful for displaying complex data
patterns if the underlying distributions are multivariate. Otherwise, do not enter the
third dimension unless your data are there.

ORAL PRESENTATIONS

Researchers often present their findings orally. These presentations, sometimes
called **briefings,** have some unique characteristics that distinguish them from most
other kinds of public speaking. Only a small group of people are involved; statistics
normally constitute an important portion of the topic; the audience members are usually managers with an interest in the topic, but they want to hear only the critical elements; speaking time will often be as short as 20 minutes but may run longer than an
hour; and the presentation is normally followed by questions and discussion.

Preparation   A successful briefing typically requires condensing a lengthy and complex body of
information. Since speaking rates should not exceed 100 to 150 words per minute,
a 20-minute presentation limits you to about 2,000 to 2,500 words. If you are to
communicate effectively under such conditions, you must plan carefully. Begin by
asking two questions. First, how long should you plan to talk? Usually there is an
indication of the acceptable presentation length. It may be the custom in an orga-

nization to take a given allotted time for a briefing. If the time is severely limited, then the need for topical priorities is obvious. This leads to the second question: What are the purposes of the briefing? Is it to raise concern about problems that have been uncovered? Is it to add to the knowledge of audience members? Is it to give them conclusions and recommendations for their decision making? Questions such as these illustrate the general objectives of the report. After answering these questions, you should develop a detailed outline of what you are going to say. Such an outline should contain the following major parts.

1. *Opening.* A brief statement, probably not more than 10 percent of the allotted time, designed to set the stage for the body of the report. The opening should be direct, get attention, and introduce the nature of the discussion that follows. It should explain the nature of the project, how it came about, and what it attempted to do.

2. *Findings and conclusions.* The conclusions may be stated immediately after the opening remarks, with each conclusion followed by the findings that support it.

3. *Recommendations.* Where appropriate, these are stated in the third stage; each recommendation may be followed by references to the conclusions leading to it. Presented in this manner, they provide a natural climax to the report. At the end of the presentation, it may be appropriate to call for questions from the audience.

Early in the planning stage you need to make two further decisions. The first concerns the type of audiovisuals (AV) that will be used and the role they will play in the presentation. AV decisions are important enough that they are often made *before* the briefing outline and text are developed. More will be said about AV later.

Then you must decide on the type of presentation. Will you give a memorized speech, read from your manuscript, or give an extemporaneous presentation? We rule out the impromptu briefing as an option because impromptu speaking does not involve preparation. Your reputation and the research effort should not be jeopardized by "winging it."

Memorization is a risky and time-consuming course to follow. Any memory slip during the presentation can be a catastrophe. It also sounds stilted and distant. Memorization virtually excludes establishing rapport with the audience and adapting to their reactions while you speak. It produces a self- or speaker-centered approach and is not recommended.

Reading a written manuscript is also not advised even though many professors seem indifferent to it by rewarding students who do it (perhaps because they get away with it themselves at professional meetings). It sounds dull and lifeless because most people are not trained to read aloud and therefore do it badly. They become focused on the manuscript to the exclusion of the audience. This head-down preoccupation with the manuscript is clearly inappropriate for business presentations.

The **extemporaneous** delivery is audience centered and presented from minimal notes or an outline. This mode permits the speaker to be natural, conversational, and flexible. Clearly, it is the best choice for the business presentation. Preparation consists of writing a draft along with a complete sentence outline and converting the main points to notes. In this way, you can try lines of argument, experiment with various ways of expressing thoughts, and develop phraseology. Along the way, the main points are fixed sequentially in your mind and supporting connections are made.

Audiences accept notes and their presence does wonders in allaying speaker fears. Even if you never use them, they are there for psychological support. Many prefer to use 5×8 inch cards for their briefing notes because they hold more information and so require less shuffling than the smaller 3×5 inch size. Card contents vary widely, but some general guides for their design are:

1. Place title and preliminary remarks on the first card.
2. Use each of the remaining cards to carry a major section of the presentation, with the amount of detail depending on the need for precision and the speaker's desire for supporting information.
3. Include key phrases, illustrations, statistics, dates, and pronunciation guides for difficult words. Include also quotations and ideas that bear repeating.
4. Along the margin place instructions and cues, such as SLOW, FAST, EMPHASIZE, TRANSPARENCY A, TURN CHART, and GO BACK TO CHART 3.

After the outline and the AV aids comes the final stage of preparation—the rehearsal. Rehearsal is a prerequisite to effective briefing but *it is too often slighted,* especially by inexperienced speakers. Giving a briefing is an artistic performance, and nothing improves it more than for the speaker to demonstrate mastery of the art. First rehearsal efforts should concentrate on those parts of the presentation that are awkward or poorly developed. After the problem areas have been worked out, there should be at least a few full-scale practices under simulated presentation conditions. All parts should be timed and edited until the time target is met. A videotape recorder is an excellent diagnostic tool.

Delivery

While the content of a report is the chief concern, the speaker's delivery is also important. A polished presentation adds to the receptiveness of the audience, but there is some danger that the presentation may overpower the message. Fortunately, the typical research audience knows why it is assembled, has a high level of interest, and does not need to be entertained. Even so, the speaker faces a real challenge in communicating effectively. The delivery should be restrained. Demeanor, posture, dress, and total appearance should be appropriate for the occasion. Speed of speech, clarity of enunciation, pauses, and gestures all play their part. Voice pitch, tone quality, and inflections are proper subjects for concern. There is little time for anecdotes and other rapport-developing techniques, yet the speaker must get and hold audience attention.

Speaker Problems   Inexperienced speakers have many difficulties in making presentations. They often are nervous at the start of a presentation and may even find breathing difficult. This is natural and should not be of undue concern. It may help to take a deep breath or two, holding each for a brief time before exhaling as fully as possible. This can be done inconspicuously on the way to the podium.

Several characteristics of inexperienced speakers may be summarized as questions. Even if you are an accomplished speaker, it is helpful to review them as you watch a videotape of your presentation.

1. Vocal characteristics:
   a. Do you speak so softly that someone cannot hear you well? It is helpful to have someone in the back of the room who can signal if your voice is not carrying far enough.
   b. Do you speak too rapidly? Remind yourself to slow down. Make deliberate pauses before sentences. Speak words with precision without exaggerating. However, some people talk too slowly, and this can make the audience restive.
   c. Do you vary volume, tone quality, and rate of speaking? Any of these can be used successfully to add interest to the message and engage audience attention. Speakers should not let their words trail off as they complete a sentence.
   d. Do you use overworked pet phrases, repeated "uhs," "you know," and "in other words?"

2. Physical characteristics:
   a. Do you rock back and forth or roll or twist from side to side or lean too much on the lectern?
   b. Do you hitch or tug on clothing, scratch, fiddle with pocket change, keys, pencils, or other devices?
   c. Do you stare into space? The lack of eye contact is particularly bothersome to listeners and is common with inexperienced speakers. Many seem to choose a spot above the heads of the audience and continue to stare at this spot except when looking at notes. *Eye contact is important.* Audience members need to feel that you are looking at them. It may be helpful to pick out three people in the audience (left, right, and center) and practice looking at them successively as you talk.
   d. Do you misuse visuals by fumbling, putting them on in incorrect order or upside down? Do you turn your back to the audience to read from visuals?

Audiovisuals

Researchers can use a variety of AV media with good results. While there is some need for computer-assisted media in many business applications, they will only be mentioned briefly. Our emphasis is on **visual aids** that are relatively simple and inexpensive to make.

1. Chalkboards and whiteboards—Chalkboards are flexible, inexpensive, and require little specific preparation. On the other hand, they are not novel and do not project a polished appearance. Whiteboards, both portable and

installed, provide visual relief, particularly when color markers are used. Both varieties reduce speaking time while the speaker is writing. If you use either, write legibly or print, leave space between lines, and do not talk to the board with the audience to your back. If you are in an unfamiliar room, it is best to arrive prepared with erasable markers (or chalk) and erasure materials.

2. Handout materials—These are inexpensive and can give a professional look if done carefully. Handouts can include pictures and graphic materials that might be difficult to display otherwise. The disadvantages include the time needed to produce them and their distracting impact if not properly used. You may distribute them when the audience leaves, but a better use is to refer to them during your talk. If you use them this way, *do not hand them out until you are ready to refer to them.*

3. Flip charts—You can show color, pictures, and large letters with these. They are easy and inexpensive to make; they can focus listener attention on a specific idea. If not well made, they can be distracting. Unless they are large, they should be restricted to small groups and to types of material that can be summarized in a few words.

4. Overhead transparencies—These may be of different sizes, but the most common is about the same as an $8\frac{1}{2} \times 11$ inch page. They are easily made with color markers or with a copy machine. Computer-graphics can be plotted or printed directly to transparencies for a more accurate and professional look. Multiple-color and single-color renditions are available. You can also show overlays and buildups. In using transparencies, be sure they are in correct order and right side up when you place them on the projector.

5. Slides—Most slides are 35mm, but larger sizes are sometimes used. They are relatively inexpensive and colorful and present a professional looking image if done well. They are somewhat more difficult to make but can be prepared with a personal computer and slide-construction software.

6. Computer-drawn visuals—For transparencies and slides, the draw and paint programs for personal computers provide the presenter with limitless options for illustrating the message. Stored visuals can be teamed with a device for projecting the computer output to a screen, or the briefer can use the software to create the image at the moment a question is asked or demonstration is appropriate. Be careful that the technology does not distract from the purpose of the message.

7. Computer animation—The development of larger and faster processors, memory chips, and disks has made it possible to store voice and image data in quantity in personal computers. Technology permits multimedia presentations using videotape, videodisk, and CD-ROM elements that are integrated for the ultimate in image reproduction. For proposals, large contracts, or other business applications, the preparation and expense may be justifiable.

The choice of visual aids is determined by your intended purpose, the size of the audience, meeting room conditions, time and budget constraints, and available equipment.

Visual aids serve the presenter of a research presentation in several ways. They present materials that cannot otherwise be communicated effectively. Statistical relationships are difficult to describe verbally, but a picture or graph communicates well. How better to describe some object or material than to show it or picture it?

Visual aids help the speaker to clarify major points. With visual reinforcement of a verbal statement, the speaker can stress the importance of points. In addition, the use of two channels of communication (hearing and sight) enhances the probability that the listener will understand and remember the message.

The continuity and memorability of the speaker's message are also improved with visual aids. Verbal information is so transient that any slight lapse of listener attention results in losing the information thread. The failure to fully comprehend a given point cannot be remedied by going back to hear it again for the speaker has gone on. With a visual aid, however, there is more opportunity to review this point, relate it to earlier comments by the speaker, and improve retention.

Summary

A quality presentation of research findings can have an inordinate effect on a reader's or listener's perceptions of a study's quality. Recognition of this fact should prompt a researcher to make a special effort to communicate skillfully and clearly.

Research reports contain findings, analysis, interpretation, conclusions, and sometimes recommendations. They may follow the short informal format typical of memoranda and letters, or they may be longer and more complex. Long reports are either of a technical or management type. In the former, the problem is presented followed by the findings, conclusions, and recommendations. In the management report, the conclusions and recommendations precede the findings. The technical report is targeted at the technically trained reader, and the management report is intended for the manager-client.

The writer of research reports should be guided by four questions: (1) What is the purpose of this report? (2) Who will read it? (3) What are the circumstances and limitations under which it is written? and (4) How will the report be used? Reports should also be clearly organized, physically inviting, and easy to read. Writers can achieve these goals if they are careful with mechanical details, writing style, and comprehensibility. There is a special challenge to presenting statistical data. While some may be incorporated in the text, most statistics should be placed in tables, charts, or graphs. The choice of a table, chart, or graph depends on the specific data and presentation purpose.

Oral presentations of research findings are common and should be developed with concern for the communication problems that are unique to such settings. Briefings are usually under time constraints; good briefings require careful organization and preparation. Visual aids are a particularly important aspect of briefings but are too often ignored or treated inadequately.

Whether written or oral, poor presentations do a grave injustice to what might otherwise be excellent research. Good presentations, on the other hand, add luster to both the research and the reputation of the researcher.

Key Terms

area charts	pictographs (geographics)
bar charts	pie charts
briefings	readability indices
executive summary	sentence outline
extemporaneous presentation	technical report
letter of transmittal	3-D graphics
line graphs	topic outline
management report	visual aids

Discussion Questions

1. Distinguish between:
   a. Speaker-centered and extemporaneous presentations.
   b. Technical and management reports.
   c. Topic and sentence outlines.
2. What should you do about:
   a. Putting information in a research report concerning the study's limitations?
   b. The size and complexity of tables in a research report?
   c. The physical presentation of a report?
   d. Pace in your writing?
3. What type of report would you suggest be written in each of the following cases:
   a. The president of the company has asked for a study of the company's pension plan and its comparison to those of other firms in the industry.
   b. You have been asked to write up a marketing experiment, which you recently completed, for submission to the *Journal of Marketing Research.*
   c. Your division manager has asked you to prepare a forecast of cash requirements for the division for the next three months.
   d. The National Institutes of Health has given you a grant to study the relation between industrial accidents and departmental employee morale.
4. Research reports often contain statistical materials of great importance that are presented poorly. Discuss ways to improve statistical presentation.
5. The typical student research report has many deficiencies in presentation in addition to its limitations in project design and content. Make a list of what you believe to be the major presentation problems with student written research reports. With student oral research reports.
6. What major problems do you personally have with writing good reports? What can you do about these problems?

7. Outline a set of visual aids that you might use in an oral briefing on:

   a. How to write a research report.

   b. The outlook for the economy over the next year.

   c. The major analytical article in the latest *Business Week.*

8. There are a number of graphic presentation forms. Which would you suggest using to show each of the following? Why?

   a. A comparison of changes in average annual per capita income for the United States and the Soviet Union from 1985 to 1995.

   b. The percentage composition of average family expenditure patterns, by the major types of expenditures, for families whose heads are under 35 years compared with families whose heads are 55 years or older.

   c. A comparison of the change between December 31, 1994, and December 31, 1993, of common stock of six major electronics firms.

Reference Notes

1. Paul E. Resta, *The Research Report* (New York: American Book Company, 1972), p. 5.

2. John M. Penrose, Jr., Robert W. Rasberry, and Robert J. Myers, *Advanced Business Communication* (Boston: PWS-Kent Publishing, 1989), p. 185.

3. Ibid., p. 185.

4. Most word processors contain dictionaries. All-purpose word processors such as WordPerfect, WriteNow, AmiPro, MacWritePro, or Word contain a spelling checker, table and graphing generators, and a thesaurus. For style and grammar checkers, programs such as Grammatik, RightWriter, Spelling Coach, Thunder, and Punctuation + Style are available. New programs are reviewed periodically in the business communication literature and in magazines devoted to personal computing. Figure 18–3 was prepared from GrammatikMac™ output.

5. Robert R. Rathbone, *Communicating Technical Information* (Reading, Mass.: Addison-Wesley Publishing Company, © 1966), p. 64. Reprinted with permission.

6. Ibid., p. 72.

7. Penrose, Rasberry, and Myers, *Advanced Business Communication,* p. 89.

8. The material in this section draws upon Stephen M. Kosslyn, *Elements of Graph Design* (San Francisco: W. H. Freeman, 1993); DeltaPoint, Inc., *DeltaGraph User's Guide* (Monterey, Calif.: DeltaPoint, Inc., 1993); Gene Zelazny, *Say It With Charts* (Homewood, Ill.: Business One Irwin, 1991); Jim Heid, "Graphs that Work," *MacWorld,* February 1994, pp. 155–56; and Penrose, Rasberry, and Myers, *Advanced Business Communication,* chap. 3.

9. Marilyn Stoll, "Charts Other than Pie Are Appealing to the Eye," *PC Week,* March 25, 1986, p. 138–39.

10. Stephen M. Kosslyn and Christopher Chabris, "The Mind is not a Camera, the Brain is not a VCR," *Aldus Magazine,* September/October 1993, p. 34.

Suggested Readings

Kosslyn, Stephen M. *Elements of Graph Design.* San Francisco: W. H. Freeman, 1993.

Lesikar, Raymond. *Basic Business Communication.* 6th ed. Burr Ridge, Ill.: Richard D. Irwin, 1993. Practical guidance for writing and presenting reports.

Moyer, Ruth; Eleanor Stevens; and Ralph Switzer. *The Research Handbook for Managers and Executives in Business, Industry, and Government.* New York: John Wiley & Sons, 1981. A comprehensive source on the preparation of reports, their documentation, sources of information, and writing style.

Penrose, John M.; Robert W. Rasberry; and Robert J. Myers. *Advanced Business Communication.* 2nd ed. Belmont, Calif.: Wadsworth Publishing, 1993. A presentation of all aspects of business communications from organization through final writing and oral presentation.

Strunk, William, Jr., and E. B. White. *The Elements of Style.* New York: Macmillan, 1959. A classic on the problems of writing style.

Tufte, Edward R. *The Visual Display of Quantitative Information.* New Haven, Conn.: Graphics Press, 1983. The book that started the revolution against gaudy, low-infographics.

APPENDICES

BUSINESS REFERENCE TOOLS

 FINDING
YOUR WAY

This appendix describes the most important bibliographies and reference works in the field of business. The reader will need to be familiar with these tools before writing a literature review, research paper, or thesis. The content is divided into four sections: (1) guides to reference materials, (2) guides to computerized sources, (3) bibliographies, and (4) other reference sources.

GENERAL GUIDES TO BUSINESS REFERENCE SOURCES

This list of reference tools describes the major works. Students should also examine one or more of the guides described below for alternate sources. They describe the varied sources of information available in the field of business, tell the purposes for which these sources may be used, and give directions on their use. There are also guides to more specialized topics, such as the guides to statistics listed in the section on that subject.

Daniells, Lorna M. *Business Information Sources.* 3rd ed. Berkeley, Calif.: University of California Press, 1993.

    This comprehensive list of business sources is organized by general subject area. It also includes a section on computerized sources.

Encyclopedia of Business Information Sources. 9th ed. Detroit: Gale Research, 1992.

    The sources of business information found here are arranged alphabetically by subject area in the first volume. The second volume is a geographical arrangement.

Freed, Melvyn N., and Virgil P. Diodato. *Business Information Desk Reference: Where to Find Answers to Business Questions.* New York: Maxwell Macmillan, International, 1991.

    This reference source provides answers to specific business questions.

Li, Tze-chung. *Social Science Reference Sources: A Practical Guide.* 2nd ed. New York: Greenwood Press, 1990.

    The sources listed are arranged by the various social science disciplines. Additional helpful sections include a title index and a listing of online databases in the appendices.

Philcox, Phil. *The Executive's Business Information Sourcebook.* Englewood Cliffs, N.J.: Prentice Hall, 1990.

    The references in this book lead the researcher to various types of information including references to professional associations, periodicals, and others.

Sheehy, Eugene P. *Guide to Reference Books.* 10th ed. Chicago: American Library Association, 1986.

    This standard bibliography of reference works includes many titles in business and related fields. This guide will refer to Sheehy occasionally as a source of additional references. The 10th edition is supplemented by *Guide to Reference Books: Covering Materials from 1985–1990.*

Smith, Robert V. *Graduate Research: A Guide for Students in the Sciences.* 2nd ed. New York: Plenum Publishing, 1990.

     Although aimed at graduate students in the sciences, this handbook is helpful for all students approaching a thesis or dissertation for the first time.

GUIDES TO COMPUTERIZED SOURCES OF INFORMATION

Computer-based searches for information allow the researcher to search an online database, a CD-ROM database, or the Internet. Generally, the information obtained from searching these three sources will include: bibliographic citations (references), abstracts (summaries), or the full text of the needed information.

Internet Sources

Access to the Internet is becoming more readily available to university students. However, finding information in the Internet, which is a vast network of computers around the world, can be frustrating and confusing. Listed below are a few citations that will help the researcher understand more about the Internet and how to access information through it.

Dern, Daniel P. *The Internet Guide for New Users.* New York: McGraw-Hill, 1994.

Engst, Adam C. *Internet Starter Kit for Macintosh.* Indianapolis, Ind. Hayden Books, 1993.

Estrada, Susan. *Connecting to the Internet: A Buyer's Guide.* Sebastopol, Calif.: O'Reilly & Associates, 1993.

Marine, April, et al., eds. *Internet—Getting Started.* Englewood Cliffs, N.J.: PTR Prentice Hall, 1994.

Parker, Tracy L., and Jeanne C. Ryer. *The Internet Companion: A Beginner's Guide to Global Networking.* Reading, Mass.: Addison-Wesley Publishing Co., 1993.

Rheingold, Howard. *The Virtual Community: Homesteading on the Electronic Frontier.* Reading, Mass.: Addison-Wesley Publishing Co., 1993.

Smith, Richard J., and Mark Gibbs. *Navigating the Internet.* Carmel, Ind.: Sams Publishing, 1993.

Tennant, Roy; John Ober; and Anne G. Lipow. *Crossing the Internet Threshold: An Instructional Handbook.* Berkeley, Calif.: Library Solutions Press, 1993.

Database Directories

The number and types of computerized databases are growing daily. Both CD-ROM databases and online computer retrieval databases are provided by many different publishers and vendors. The following list offers examples of available directories. These directories cover either CD-ROM databases, online sources, or a combination.

Cormack, Erin, ed. *The CD-ROM Directory 1989.* 3rd ed. London: TFPL Publishing, 1988.

Listing 390 CD-ROM titles, this directory includes information about the types of data, publisher, and purchase information on the listed CD-ROMs.

Database Directory. White Plains, N.Y.: Knowledge Industry, 1985–. Published semiannually.

Using a variety of indexing approaches, this directory contains complete information on each database covered including prices and the average cost of a typical online search.

Directory of Online Databases. New York: Cuadra/Elsevier Associates, 1979–. Published quarterly.

A major guide to databases, it is divided into three sections: (1) database descriptions, integrated reference lists of producer, online service, and gateway addresses, (2) indices by subject, producer, online service telecommunications, and (3) a master index. Prices are not included.

Hall, James L., and Marjorie J. Brown. *Online Bibliographic Databases: A Directory and Sourcebook.* 4th ed. London: Aslib, 1986.

Orenstein, Ruth M., ed. *Fulltext Sources Online.* Needham Heights, Mass.: BiblioData, 1989.

Over 180 pages of references and journals are listed with a compilation of databases that cover those sources. All of the databases covered are online, not CD-ROM. No price information is included.

Williams, Martha. *Computer Readable Databases.* Chicago: American Library Association, 1976–. Updated on an irregular basis.

This guide contains a comprehensive listing of both source and reference databases. Divided into two sections, coverage includes (1) business, law, humanities, and social sciences and (2) science, technology, and medicine.

Vendor Guides Each online vendor produces a manual with instructions for use. The guides include a description of the databases that are online. For instructions, check with the research librarian of a university library. Two such guides are:

BRS Reference Manual and Database Search Guide. Latham, N.Y.: BRS, 1979–. Updated regularly.

The guide lists and describes each database contained within BRS's service. Instructions for using BRS are included.

Guide to Dialog Databases. Palo Alto, Calif.: Lockheed, 1978–. Published regularly.

This vendor's publication includes a good beginner's guide. In addition, a comprehensive listing of vendor offerings is included.

Periodical Guides Several periodicals covering computerized databases have been started in the last decade. Since the field is experiencing explosive growth, more periodicals may appear in the near future. Check the following for the latest information on databases.

> *Database.* Weston, Conn.: Online, Inc. Published quarterly.
> This magazine reviews databases and can be used as a database reference guide.
>
> *Online.* Weston, Conn.: Online, Inc. Published quarterly.
> Containing general information, this periodical concentrates on online information systems.
>
> *Online Review.* Oxford, N.Y.: Learned Information. Published bimonthly.
> This international journal covers online and teletext information systems.

Online Databases   Online databases, accessible through telephone communications with a terminal or a personal computer, provide a method of obtaining bibliographic, abstract, and full-text information. Hundreds exist, and many are accessible through one of the general services listed below. Your library may have access to different online databases.

> *ABI/INFORM.* Louisville, Ky.: U.M.I./Data Courier, Inc.
> The service offers citations and abstracts from 800 major magazines and journals.
>
> *BRS.* Latham, N.Y.: Bibliographic Retrieval Services.
> Bibliographic and full-text retrieval with multiple databases are available.
>
> *Compuserve (CIS).* Columbus, Ohio: Compuserve, Inc., a subsidiary of H & R Block.
> One hundred and fifty databases are available for access, including ERIC, Educational Research Information Center.
>
> *DIALOG Information Services.* Palo Alto, Calif.: DIALOG Information Services, Inc., a subsidiary of Lockheed.
> Many databases can be accessed through this gateway, which includes bibliographic citations, abstracts, and the full text of many articles.
>
> *Dissertation Abstracts Online.* Ann Arbor, Mich.: University Microfilms International.
> Service provides subject, title, and author guide to dissertations accepted at accredited American colleges and universities since 1961.
>
> *Dow Jones News/Retrieval.* Princeton, N.J.: Dow Jones, Inc.
> Service offers database from national newspapers and the Dow Jones news wire.
>
> *Lexis.* Dayton, Ohio: Mead Data Central, Inc.
> Full-text legal database is offered.
>
> *Nexis.* Dayton, Ohio: Mead Data Central, Inc.
> Full text from 150 newspapers and abstracts from 1,600 publications and documents for the business reader are available.

ORBIT. Santa Monica, Calif.. System Development Corp.

Many of the 70 bibliographic and numeric databases from independent suppliers include citations and abstracts.

PAIS International. New York: Public Affairs Information Service, Inc.

Reference information from the social sciences is provided.

PTS Prompt (Predicasts Overview of Markets & Technology). Cleveland, Ohio: Predicasts, Inc.

This abstracts information from newspapers, business magazines, government reports, and other sources about trends in marketplaces and in technology.

The Source. MacLean, Va.: Reader's Digest Association.

Service offers a variety of business and other databases.

CD-ROM Databases

CD-ROMs provide the latest indexing information in a readily accessible format for personal computer users. The CD-ROM databases are quickly replacing traditional databases (book or periodical form) because more data can be stored in significantly less space. Many traditional indices, now being produced in CD-ROM form, are listed in the Database Directories section of this appendix. It is beyond our ability to list all available CDs. We do cover some so the researcher knows the type of databases that are available.

Just as there are new ways to publish information, there are new ways to obtain it. CDs come from vendors on a subscription basis. Therefore, no specific publication data arc listed. In addition, many vendors (publishers) have installed toll-free telephone lines, as shown.

ABI/INFORM ONDISC. U.M.I./Data Courier. (1-800-521-0600).

Abstracts and indexing to business articles from over 800 business and management journals extend from 1971 to present.

Book Review Digest. H. W. Wilson. (1-800-622-4002).

CD has access to book and periodicals reviews from more than 470 popular, professional, and academic publications. Coverage begins with 1983.

Business Dateline OnDisc. University Microfilms International. (1-800-521-0600).

Indexes articles by topic or company name (and other access points) from regional business journals, such as *Florida Trend* magazine.

Business Periodicals OnDisc. University Microfilms International. (1-800-521-0600).

This service combines the ABI/Inform database of article references and abstracts with viewing and printing complete articles from many periodicals. Coverage begins with July 1984.

CIRR OnDisc. Silver Platter. (1-800-284-8353).

Access to more than 100,000 research reports published by major Wall Street and international investment firms is provided.

CIS Congressional Masterfile I and II. Congressional Information Service. (1-800-638-8380).

Bibliographic records of congressional documents are recorded from the first Congress (1789) to the present one. Masterfile II covers 1970 to present. Citations refer researchers to microfiche collections of congressional hearings and reports.

CIS Statistical Masterfile. Congressional Information Service. (1-800-638-8380).

Search capabilities for the following databases are provided:

1. American Statistics Index, 1973–present. From statistical publications of the U.S. government.
2. Index to International Statistics, 1983–present. From statistical publications of international intergovernmental organizations.
3. Statistical Reference Index, 1980–present. Selective American statistical publications from private organizations and state government sources.

Disclosure. Disclosure Inc. (1-800-843-7747).

Financial and management information on over 12,000 public companies are contained. The vendor extracts company data from annual and periodic SEC-filed reports.

ERIC. DIALOG Information Services. (1-800-334-2564).

A database of educational materials collected by the Educational Resources Information Center of the U.S. Department of Education includes Resources in Education (RIE), covering documents, and the Current Index to Journals in Education (CIJE), covering approximately 750 journals and serial publications. Abstracts are contained for each citation. Coverage begins in 1966.

Government Documents Catalog Service. Auto-graphics, Inc. (1-800-325-7961).

CD provides an easy-to-use index for the U.S. Government Printing Office publications. Coverage begins in 1976 and is updated monthly.

Infotrac. Information Access Company. (1-800-227-8431).

Three separate files are included:

1. Business Index: references to articles on business topics.
2. General Business File: company and industry information.
3. Investext: financial information on companies.

New York Times OnDisc. University Microfilms OnDisc. (1-800-521-0600).

This index also includes the full text of the articles.

Newsbank. Newsbank. (1-203-966-1100).

CD contains over a million references to newspaper articles from over 500 U.S. newspapers. Coverage begins in 1981.

Psyclit. Silver Platter. (1-800-284-8353).

CD contains summaries of journal articles in psychology and related disciplines from 1,300 journals in 27 languages. Coverage begins in 1974.

Social Sciences Index. H. W. Wilson. (1-800-622-4002).

CD indexes 300 periodicals in the social sciences from the United States, Canada, and the United Kingdom. Other countries are included. Coverage begins in February 1983.

Sociofile. H. W. Wilson. (1-800-622-4002).

Sociology and related disciplines are covered, and bibliographic citations and abstracts from 1,600 journals in 30 languages are included. Dissertation citations are provided. Coverage begins in 1974.

UMI Dissertation Abstracts. University Microfilms International. (1-800-521-0600).

Bibliographic citations and abstracts for doctoral dissertations completed at accredited North American Colleges and Universities are listed. Coverage from 1861.

Wall Street Journal OnDisc. University Microfilms International. (1-800-521-0600).

This computerized index contains the full text of articles.

BIBLIOGRAPHIES AND OTHER REFERENCE SOURCES

A bibliography is a list of books or other printed materials. Most bibliographies are arranged either by author or subject. The card catalog, an important bibliography, lists books available in a given library or group of libraries, while other bibliographies list books that may not be in their collection. Some bibliographies list only certain types of publications, such as dissertations or government publications. To collect all the important references on a subject, it is necessary to use bibliographies.

Single-Subject Bibliographies

Unfortunately, there is no single comprehensive bibliography of business literature, but there are many bibliographies covering specific areas such as production, marketing, and accounting. It is advantageous to examine bibliographies on the specific subject. Books that are primarily bibliographies may be found in the public catalog under the appropriate subject heading, for example, Accounting—Bibliography.

General Bibliographies

If you cannot find a bibliography on your subject, or if you believe the bibliographies you have located are incomplete or out of date, you should consult the general bibliographies. This category includes the catalogs of the great national libraries and national and trade bibliographies. Here are the most important American general bibliographies with a subject orientation:

American Book Publishing Record, BPR. Vol. 1–. New York: R. R. Bowker, 1960–. Published monthly.

This periodical aims to be a complete record of American books published in the month preceding its date of issue. It is arranged by the Dewey decimal classification, with author and title indices. There is also an annual accumulation.

Association for University Business and Economic Research. *Bibliography of Publications of University Bureaus of Business and Economic Research,* AUBER bibliography. Vol. 22–. Morgantown, W.Va.: Bureau of Business Research, West Virginia University, 1977–.

This is a selective index to reports, bulletins, and monographs published by bureaus of business research associated with universities. The supplements also list some articles appearing in periodicals published by these bureaus. There is an author and subject index.

Bibliographic Index: A Cumulative Bibliography of Bibliographies. New York: H. W. Wilson, 1937–.

Separately published bibliographies and bibliographies printed in books and periodicals are listed by subject.

Cumulative Book Index: A World List of Books in the English Language. New York: H. W. Wilson, 1928–.

Books published in the English language are recorded by author, title, and subject in this comprehensive bibliography. After 1930, books from other parts of the world are included.

Subject Guide to Books in Print. New York: R. R. Bowker, 1957–.

Currently available American trade books are listed by subject.

Subject Guide to Forthcoming Books. Vol. 1–. New York: R. R. Bowker, 1967–.

This bimonthly publication attempts "to list all books expected to be published in the United States during the next five months."

Most general bibliographies are arranged by author. If you know authors who have written about your subject, these bibliographies will help you find the titles of other books they have written. General bibliographies can verify and complete references when you know the author's name but are not sure of the title, date, or publisher.

Books in Print. New York: R. R. Bowker, 1948–.

This is an annual author, title, and subject index to the collection of publishers' catalogs, *The Publishers' Trade List Annual.* It can be used for quick identification of recent book publications when only the author or title or subject is known. Also, it is used to find out whether a particular book is available for purchase. For information about books published after this annual appears (published semiannually), use *Forthcoming Books,* below, or the *Cumulative Book Index* and *American Book Publishing Record,* described above.

Forthcoming Books. Vol. 1–. New York: R. R. Bowker, 1966–.

This publication is an author-title-list, including new books in print.

The National Union Catalog, Pre-1956 Imprints: A Cumulative Author List Representing Library of Congress Printed Cards and Titles Reported by Other American Libraries. London: Mansell, 1968–1981. 754 vols.

The National Union Catalog: A Cumulative Author List Representing Library of Congress Printed Cards and Titles Reported by Other American Libraries. New York: Roman and Littlefield. Various sets from 1985.

These companion works and monumental bibliographical tools are especially valuable for providing locations of books in major American libraries.

Indices to Periodicals, Newspapers, and Serials

Current information on most subjects is found in periodicals and newspapers. Some information may never be published in any other form. To locate them, use indices designed for that purpose. Listed below are paper indices.

Applied Science and Technology Index (formerly *Industrial Arts Index*). New York: H. W. Wilson, 1913–.

This is a cumulative subject index to English-language periodicals with more than 300 periodicals on the applied sciences. Many periodicals indexed have a direct bearing upon business activity and carry business information in reports, articles, news notes, and special issues. Subject headings include Budget–United States, Business Management, Business Charts, Finance, and Stocks.

Business Periodicals Index. New York: H. W. Wilson, 1958–.

Approximately 260 business and economics periodicals in the English language are cumulatively indexed by subject. This index is particularly good for practical business operations and specific businesses, industries, and trades. For material before 1958, see the *Industrial Arts Index, 1913–57.*

Index to Legal Periodicals. New York: H. W. Wilson, 1908–.

These monthly indices, containing subject headings from areas of human activity, are published for the American Association of Law Libraries. Annual cumulation covers periodicals from the United States, Canada, Great Britain, Ireland, Australia, and New Zealand.

New York Times Index. New York: New York Times Co., 1851–.

This comprehensive newspaper index is also valuable for establishing dates of articles in other newspapers.

PAIS-Bulletin. New York: Public Affairs Information, Inc., 1915–.

Published monthly and cumulated annually, this index is also available on CD-ROM. Many English-language periodicals worldwide are selectively indexed. Books, government publications, and pamphlets are listed by subject in this bibliography covering business, banking, and economics, and public affairs. It is often cited as PAIS. Note the cumulative indices for 1915–74. *The Foreign Language Index* covers materials in French, German, Italian, Portuguese, and Spanish beginning with 1968.

Selected Rand Abstracts. Vol. 1–. Santa Monica, Calif.: Rand Corporation, 1963–.

The Rand Corporation, established in 1948 as an independent, nonprofit organization, is engaged in research concerned with the security and public welfare of the United States. This research is financed by the U.S. Air Force, by other government agencies, and by the corporation. *Selected Rand Abstracts,* a complete guide to current unclassified publications of the Rand Corporation, is published four times each year. The volume is cumulative through the year. Issue no. 4 (December) is the permanent record for the year. Documents issued during the period 1946–62 are listed in the Index of Selected Publications.

Social Sciences Citation Index: An International Interdisciplinary Index to the Literature of the Social Sciences. Philadelphia: Institute for Scientific Information, 1969–.

This lists references to publications cited during the period covered and the original articles. It is especially valuable for tracing a given author's influence in a specific field.

Social Sciences Index. New York: H. W. Wilson. Published quarterly.

Author and subject entries to periodicals cover a wide field, many directly affecting business. There is a separate listing of book reviews. A bound annual cumulation is published.

Vertical File Index: A Subject and Title Index to Selected Pamphlet Materials. New York: H. W. Wilson, 1935–. Monthly (except August).

This is a useful source for locating ephemeral material. *The Monthly Catalog* listed below should be consulted for references to pamphlets issued by the U.S. government. Most pamphlets are not cataloged.

The Wall Street Journal Index. Princeton, N.J.: Dow Jones Books, 1957–.

This monthly index is divided into two sections, one for corporate news (arranged by the name of the firm) and one for general news (arranged by subject).

Lists of Periodicals

Students working with periodicals often need information of the type found in the two kinds of periodicals in this section. The first type, represented by the first four directories, shows titles that are currently being published and gives their addresses, subscription prices, and similar information. The second, represented by the last three titles, is primarily intended to tell the user where the periodicals may be found.

Ayer Directory of Publications. Philadelphia: Ayer Press, 1880–.

This annual list of American newspapers and periodicals is arranged by state and city and gives detailed information (editor, publisher, address, circulation figures, subscription price) for each title. It has an alphabetical index of periodical titles and a classified list of trade, technical, and professional journals.

Business Marketing. "Guide to Special Issues." Chicago: Crain Communications, Inc. Published monthly.

The directory, included occasionally, includes the name of the special issue, date of publication, a brief description of the issue, and advertising closing date. This listing includes issues released up to three months before the advertising closing date.

National Trade and Professional Associations of the United States. 28th ed. Washington, D.C.: Columbia Books, 1993.

This directory lists trade and professional associations and their publications.

New Serial Titles. Washington, D.C.: Library of Congress, 1950–.

This supplement to the *Union List of Serials* is similar and used for the same purpose.

Standard Periodical Directory. New York: Oxbridge Publishing Company, 1964/65–.

This directory provides a subject arrangement of over 65,000 U.S. and Canadian periodicals, with an alphabetical title index. Entries include publisher, editor, address, frequency, price, circulation, and special features. It covers every type of periodical except suburban weekly and small daily newspapers.

Ulrich's International Periodicals Directory: A Classified Guide to Current Periodicals, Foreign and Domestic. New York: R. R. Bowker, 1932–.

This is a particularly useful bibliography for finding comprehensive lists of periodicals in various subject fields and for discovering the indices for periodicals. It also identifies periodicals containing bibliographies and book reviews.

Union List of Serials in Libraries of the United States and Canada. 3rd ed., 5 vols. New York: H. W. Wilson, 1965.

This is the most comprehensive list of periodicals available. It gives a brief bibliographical description of each title and shows holdings in American libraries. It is a basic tool for identifying periodical titles and for locating specific volumes.

Dissertations and Research in Progress

Dissertations are not systematically listed in any of the sources already described. The following bibliographies list both completed dissertations and research projects that are in progress. January issues of the *Journal of Business* include a list of recently completed doctoral dissertations in business.

American Doctoral Dissertations. Ann Arbor, Mich.: University Microfilms, 1955–56.

This annual publication provides "a complete listing of Ph.D. and other doctoral dissertations accepted by American and Canadian universities." Business-related topics may be found under Business Administration and Economics, Commerce–Business. The indexing titles vary.

Dissertation Abstracts International. Ann Arbor, Mich.: Xerox University Microfilms, 1938–.

Abstracts of doctoral dissertations that may be purchased in microform or xerographic copy are arranged by subject areas with an author index. Beginning with Volume 27 (1966), *Dissertation Abstracts* was divided into two sections: A, the Humanities and Social Sciences, and B, the Sciences and Engineering. Both sections have indices that are issued separately. In Volume 30 (1969), *Dissertation Abstracts* became *Dissertation Abstracts International.* It now includes section C, European Abstracts. Another comprehensive list of dissertations is the *Comprehensive Dissertation Index,* with annual supplements.

Library Catalog

The catalog is a bibliography of books in a library. Records for books are filed under author, title, and subject. When you are searching for material and are not sure of the correct subject heading, consult the following work:

U.S. Library of Congress. Cataloging Policy and Support Office. *Library of Congress Subject Headings.* 16th ed. Washington, D.C.: Cataloging Distribution Service, Library of Congress, 1993.

This list tells what headings are used in the catalog and provides cross-references from headings that are not used to ones that are. If you look for the subject "Business Arithmetic," this list will tell you that the subject heading used in the catalog is "Business Mathematics." The Library of Congress list also suggests related subjects to consult. Under "Office Management," you find the related headings "Business Records," "Credit Managers," and "Office Procedures." Similar cross-references are made in library catalogs.

Remember that subject headings are usually specific. When looking for material on marketing, try that subject first, not the more general subject of business. Cross-references usually will help lead you from the general headings to more specific ones. The cross-references under business refer to special fields of business, such as accounting, advertising, or marketing. If you do not find enough material under your specific topic, try the next broader topic that includes it.

Most computerized card catalogs allow the researcher to search for subject, title, or author through a computer terminal. Book lists, catalog information, and abstracts are all shown on the terminal screen when the search is successful.

A library's public catalog does not record every publication received by that library. Among the materials excluded from the catalog are the following:

1. Most U.S. government publications. (See the later sections of this guide that describe government document bibliographies.)
2. Most United Nations publications.
3. Reports from companies (for example, corporation annual reports).

U.S. Government Publications

Publications issued by the U.S. government contain vital information for business. Some bibliographies already described, such as the *National Union Catalogs,* list government publications, as does *PAIS,* described above with the periodical indices. To locate all relevant materials, you should use the special document bibliographies. The most important ones are listed below. Also consult *Sheehy's Guide to Reference Books.*

> *Guide to U.S. Government Publications.* McLean, Va.: Documents Index, 1973–.
> This is an invaluable tool for access to U.S. government serials and periodicals by issuing agency, title, or documents number.

> *Monthly Catalog of United States Government Publications.* Washington, D.C.: U.S. Government Printing Office, 1895–.
> Entries in the *Monthly Catalog* are indexed by author, title, subject, and series/report. Cumulative indices are published semiannually and annually. Titles in all indices are followed by the text entry number where more detailed information is available.
> A library catalog does not list most government publications. The *Monthly Catalog* serves as the catalog to the government documents collection. The call numbers, Superintendent of Documents numbers, are used to arrange and shelve these publications.

> *Congressional Informational Service.* CIS Index 1970–. Washington, D.C.: U.S. Government Printing Office.
> This index to publications of the U.S. Congress is published monthly with quarterly and annual accumulations. CIS provides current, comprehensive access to the contents of the entire spectrum of congressional working papers.

> U.S. Department of Commerce. *Publications Catalog of the U.S.* Washington, D.C.: U.S. Government Printing Office, 1979–.
> This catalog and subject index is based on the Commerce Department's biweekly *Commerce Publication Updates.* Represented are: the Office of Technical Services, the Area Redevelopment Administration, the Business and Defense Services Administration, the Bureau of International Commerce, the National Bureau of Standards, and the Bureau of the Census. The Census Bureau also issues its own catalog for its publications from 1790.

> U.S. Congress. *Congressional Record.* Washington, D.C.: U.S. Government Printing Office, 1873–.
> This is "the public proceedings of each House of Congress as reported by the Official Reporters thereof . . . . Published each day that one or both Houses are in session, excepting infrequent instances when two or more small consecutive issues are printed at one time." The weekly index has many subjects related to business; each indicates the possibilities of intended or accomplished congressional action, remarks, speeches, and discussion.

**United Nations
Publications**

United Nations Documents Index. UNDOC. New York: United Nations, Dag Hammarskjold Library, 1979–.

The UN publishes extensively in the field of international economic problems: finance, natural resources, technical development, and trade. Publications are listed in this index by issuing body and by subject. The monthly issues are superseded by an annual cumulation.

As with U.S. government documents, most UN publications are not listed in the public catalog.

ADDITIONAL REFERENCE SOURCES

In the preceding sections, the emphasis was bibliographical—most works cited help find information about published materials. The books described in this section, with a few exceptions, are compilations of facts arranged for ease of consultation. Some books will refer you to further, more detailed sources, but all contain explicit answers to questions. Following are samples of the type of questions answered by these works:

What was the gross national product (GNP) of the United States for the last five years?

What companies manufacture clay pipe?

What kind of measurement is the beta?

Atlases

Atlases are useful to executives concerned with marketing, exporting and importing, and transportation. Excellent general atlases are described in *Sheehy's Guide to Reference Books.* An atlas designed for business use is described below:

The Commercial Atlas and Marketing Guide. Chicago: Rand McNally, published annually.

This atlas contains reference maps for foreign countries, U.S. states, and Canadian provinces. Special maps cover transportation, communications, population distribution, retail trade and manufacturing, time zones, and airline distances. There are many tables of useful statistical facts.

**Biographical
Works**

American Assembly of Collegiate Schools of Business. *Faculty Personnel: A Directory of the Instructional Staffs of Member Schools.* St. Louis, Mo.: American Assembly of Collegiate Schools of Business, 1925–.

This listing of more than 16,200 faculty members from approximately 470 universities and colleges includes selected background information on full-time faculty with the rank of instructor and above at both accredited and nonaccredited schools. Faculty members are alphabetically grouped under their current university or college affiliation.

Dun & Bradstreet Reference Book of Corporate Managements. New York: Dun & Bradstreet, 1967–.

This book lists over 30,000 officers and directors in the 2,400 companies of greatest investor interest. The entries are arranged alphabetically by the name of the corporation, and there is an index to principal officers.

The International Who's Who. London: Europa Publications Ltd., 1935–.

Work includes biographies of people from almost every country in the world and in almost every sphere of human activity.

Standard & Poor's Register of Corporations, Directors, and Executives. New York: Standard & Poor's Corp., 1928–.

This publication lists the directors and executive personnel of over 38,000 industrial corporations. Biographical information for each person includes the following information: business affiliations, business address, home address, fraternal membership, education, and date of birth. This directory also provides the following data for the companies: address of the home office, the principal products, number of employees, and annual sales range. A geographical index lists the corporations by state and city.

Who's Who in Finance and Industry. Chicago: Marquis Who's Who, 1936–.

This complete summary of the backgrounds of distinguished commercial people includes more than found in *Who's Who in America* and gives more detail than *Standard & Poor's Register.* Business affiliations, education, clubs and organizations, and addresses for over 18,000 American and foreign leaders in business administration, production, technology, sales, and business-related professions are listed.

Business Services

Because business changes rapidly, most reference works become dated. The latest information on such subjects as commodity prices, foreign exchange, securities, and tax regulations is contained in business service publications, which are kept up-to-date by supplements or loose-leaf revisions.

Commodity Year Book. New York: Commodity Research Bureau, 1938–.

This annual volume is designed to help clarify changes in the world of commodities by means of graphs, charts, tables, and text. It is updated three times yearly by the Commodity Year Book Statistical Abstract Service.

Consumerism: New Developments for Business. Chicago: Commerce Clearing House, 1971–.

This weekly service briefly explains developments in consumer legislation and rulings by government agencies.

Daily Stock Price Record: New York Stock Exchange. New York: Standard & Poor's, 1961–.

This quarterly publication is divided into two parts. "Major Technical Indicators of the Stock Market" is devoted to market indicators widely followed as technical guides to the stock market. "Daily and Weekly Stock

Action" gives the daily and weekly record of stocks listed on the NYSE, the ASE, or the OTC market.

Directory of Business and Financial Services. New York: Special Libraries Association, 1924–.

This guide describes 1,051 services, including newsletters, bulletins, reports, and other publications, and represents 421 publishers.

Index of Publications of Bureaus of Business and Economic Research. Eugene, Ore.: Associated University Bureau of Business and Economic Research, 1957–. Published annually.

The publication indexes reports by university research groups.

Moody's Industrial Manual. New York: Moody's Investors Service, 1909–.

This annual book presents comprehensive company data including the company history, product description, principal locations, officers, directors, and financial data. It is updated by the semiweekly Moody's Industrial News Reports, a loose-leaf service with cumulative indices. Other Moody's Manuals are devoted to banks, investments, municipalities, public utilities, and transportation firms.

United States Tax Reporter. New York: Research Institute of America, 1992–.

This tax service gives detailed explanations of federal tax laws, regulations, rulings, decisions, and court cases.

Standard & Poor's Statistical Service. New York: Standard & Poor's, 1941–. Loose-leaf.

This service includes basic statistics: banking and finance, production and labor, price indices, income and trade, building, electric power and fuels, metals, transportation, textiles, chemicals, and paper, agricultural products, and a security price index.

Stock Reports, Over-the-Counter Regional Exchanges. New York: Standard & Poor's. Paper. Published regularly.

This report was changed from a loose-leaf service to a paper service. Separate volumes exist for the NYSE, OTC, ASE, and bonds. Comprehensive two-page reports on companies listed in the market are included.

The Value Line Investment Survey. New York: Arnold Bernhard. Weekly.

This publication is divided into four parts: (1) summary and index, (2) selection and opinion, (3) ratings and reports, and (4) miscellaneous. It is a valuable source for regularly updated financial information on hundreds of companies.

University libraries may have a microfiche file of annual business reports, 10K reports, and prospectuses of companies listed on the American and New York stock exchanges.

Dictionaries and Encyclopedias

For definitions of business terms not found in general dictionaries, consult the following specialized reference works.

Downes, John, and Jordan Elliot Goodman. *Dictionary of Finance and Investment Terms.* New York: Barron's, 1991.

This is a concise dictionary of financial and investment terms.

Heyel, Carl, ed. *The Encyclopedia of Management.* 3rd ed. New York: Van Nostrand Reinhold, 1982.

This work summarizes the major areas of management and provides references for further reading.

International Encyclopedia of the Social Sciences. 17 vols. New York: Macmillan, 1968.

This basic reference source for the social sciences includes such topics as economics, industrial organization, labor economics, money and banking, public finance, and certain aspects of business management. Bibliographies at the end of each article and a detailed index in the final volume lead to additional sources of information. Its predecessor, *The Encyclopedia of the Social Sciences,* 1930, is still valuable for historical and biographical material.

Johannsen, Hano, and G. Terry Page. *International Dictionary of Management.* 4th ed. East Brunswick, N.J.: Nichols Pub., 1990.

The appendix lists world currencies by country.

Munn, Glenn G. *Encyclopedia of Banking and Finance.* 9th ed. Rolling Meadows, Ill.: Bankers Publishing, 1991.

This one-volume encyclopedia includes definitions of words and phrases used in business and encyclopedic articles with bibliographies covering the fields of money, credit, and banking.

Directories

Business directories are lists of organizations or companies, systematically arranged to give addresses, officers, and other data. Many directories dealing with specific industries and trades contain factual and statistical data. Many are revised frequently, making them valuable sources of current information.

Darnay, Arsen J., ed. *Manufacturing USA.* Detroit: Gale Research, 1989–.

This comprehensive guide to economic activity in nearly 450 manufacturing industries provides analysis and synthesis of federal statistics and includes 17,000 of the largest U.S. manufacturing corporations.

Directories in Print. Detroit: Gale Research, 1978–.

The publication provides detailed and comprehensive information on nearly 10,000 directories, including (1) business and industrial, (2) professional and scientific, (3) online directory databases, and (4) other lists and guides. A companion volume, *International Directories in Print,* is available covering 50,000 directories published in over 100 countries.

Klein, Barry T., and Bernard Klein, eds. *Guide to American Directories: A Guide to the Major Directories of the United States Covering All Trade, Professional and Industrial Categories.* 12th ed. Coral Springs, Fla: G. Klein Publications, 1989.

Thomas Register of American Manufacturers and Thomas Register Catalog File. New York: Thomas Publishing, 1905–.

This directory lists approximately 75,000 different products with the companies that manufacture it. The main section groups company names by state and city under the product. One volume is an alphabetical list of companies; another contains a brand names index. The final volumes are devoted to catalogs of companies.

Consultants and Consulting Organizations Directory. 2nd ed., Detroit: Gale Research, 1973–.

This is a reference guide to firms and individuals engaged in consultation for business and industry.

Consumer Sourcebook. Detroit: Gale Research, 1974–.

The subtitle of this book provides a thorough description: "A Directory and Guide to Government Organizations; Associations; Centers and Institutes; Media Services; Publications Relating to Consumer Topics; Sources of Recourse and Advisory Information; and Company and Trade Name Information."

Encyclopedia of Associations. Detroit: Gale Research, 1959–. Now available on CD-ROM.

U.S. and selected international associations are listed in three volumes: (1) national organizations of the United States, (2) geographic and executive index, (3) new associations and projects. Brief descriptions of the associations, dates, addresses, officers, meetings size, and publications are among the details provided.

Statistical Works

Guides and Bibliographies   So many publications contain statistics that it is sometimes difficult to find precisely the data you need. *Sheehy's Guide to Reference Books, the Business Periodicals Index, PAIS,* and *The Wall Street Journal* are useful for locating sources for statistics. When U.S. government statistics are needed, the new *American Statistics Index* is especially helpful.

American Statistics Index. Washington, D.C.: Congressional Information Service, 1973–.

The cover of this regularly updated service reads, "A comprehensive guide and index to the statistical publications of the U.S. government."

Guide to U.S. Government Statistics. Arlington, Va.: Documents Index, 1956–.

This is an annotated guide to more than 13,000 U.S. government statistical publications.

Statistical Reference Index. 1980–. Washington, D.C.: Congressional Information Service. Published monthly with annual accumulation.

Darnay, Arsen J., ed. *Manufacturing USA.* Detroit: Gale Research, 1989–.

This comprehensive guide to economic activity in nearly 450 manufacturing industries provides analysis and synthesis of federal statistics and includes close to 17,000 of the largest U.S. manufacturing corporations.

Directories in Print. Detroit: Gale Research, 1978–.

The directory provides detailed and comprehensive information on nearly 10,000 directories, including (1) business and industrial, (2) professional and scientific, (3) online directory databases, and (4) other lists and guides. A companion volume, *International Directories in Print,* is available covering 50,000 directories published in over 100 countries.

Statistics Sources: A Subject Guide to Data on Industrial Business, Social, Educational, Financial, and Other Topics for the United States and Internationally. Detroit: Gale Research, 1962–.

U.S. Bureau of the Census. *Bureau of the Census Catalog and Guide.* Washington, D.C.: U.S. Department of Commerce, Bureau of the Census, 1985–.

This work is designed to give the user the means of locating needed data. It gives details of reports issued and other material that became available during the period covered. The catalog is kept up to date by monthly product announcements and data user news. It is cumulated periodically.

Compilations of Statistics   The following works are useful compilations of statistics.

U.S. Bureau of the Census. *Statistical Abstract of the United States.* 1878–. Washington, D.C.: U.S. Government Printing Office, 1879–.

This annual compendium of summary statistics on political, social, industrial, and economic organizations of the United States should be the starting point for gathering business statistics. Information is by federal, regional, state, and metropolitan areas. The tables' source notes and the appended sources of statistics bibliography lead to more detailed publications.

There are several supplements to the *Statistical Abstract. The County and City Data Book* provides recent figures for counties, cities, standard metropolitan statistical areas, and urbanized areas. *The Congressional District Data Book* presents a variety of statistical information for districts of the Congress. *Historical Statistics of the United States: Colonial Times to 1970,* 2 vols., has a broad range of data for historical research. This book also provides valuable leads to other sources.

U.S. Office of Business Economics. *Survey of Current Business.* Washington, D.C.: U.S. Government Printing Office, 1921–.

Each issue of this periodical contains statistical series on national income, personal income and expenditures, expenditures for new plants and equipment, production and prices of commodities, and similar information about the nation's economy. Historical data carried in the monthly issues are available in several supplements, the most important of which is *Business*

Statistics, published in odd-numbered years. For a list of other supplements to the *Survey of Current Business,* see *Statistical Services of the U.S. Government* or *Guide to U.S. Government Publications.*

Yearbooks, Reports, and Almanacs

Yearbooks are published annually and typically cover a single subject in depth. A yearbook concentrates on significant information from the year. Yearly trends are included. Many professional associations publish yearbooks. An example is:

Commodity Yearbook. New York: St. Martin's Press. Published annually.
Basic commodity information for all commodities on the market is provided in this complete and comprehensive source book.

Another single-topic source is the company report. Corporate annual reports and stockholder reports have useful information about specific companies and their industries. In addition, many companies issue regular employee newsletters, customer newsletters, and research or development newsletters. All are sources of information on the company. Often these reports can be obtained directly from the corporation. The annual and stockholder reports can be obtained from the corporation, from a library file, or through an online or CD-ROM database, such as *Disclosure.*

Some libraries also carry corporate microfiles that include copies of the annual reports on the major U.S. corporations.

Almanacs are another source of information and facts about a broad range of subjects. Based on the yearly cycle, many almanacs have a publication focus. One example of an almanac is:

Levine, Sumner N., ed. *Dow Jones-Irwin Business and Investment Almanac.* Homewood, Ill.: Dow Jones-Irwin, 1986–.
This almanac contains yearly information and data on business, investments, finance, and the U.S. economy.

B DECISION THEORY PROBLEM

DECISION THEORY PROBLEM

The value of research information can be assessed by several means, one of which is through decision theory. This example considers the case of a manager who is deciding on a change in production equipment. Research information will play a major role in this decision.

The new equipment can be leased for five years and will replace several old machines that require constant attention to operate. The problem facing the manager is, "Shall I lease the new machines with the attendant efficiencies, reduced labor, and higher lease charges, or shall I continue to use the old equipment?"

The decision situation has been prompted by news that the firm might secure several large orders from companies that have not been previous customers. With added volume, departmental profit contributions will increase substantially with the new equipment. For this decision, the manager adopts the decision variable "average annual departmental profit contribution."[1] The decision rule is, "Choose that course of action that will provide the highest average annual contribution to departmental profits."

Exhibit B–1 indicates the results of the evaluation of the two available actions. Under the conditions cited, it is obvious that course A_1 is preferred.

Conditions of Certainty

Exhibit B–1 presents the case with the assumption that the anticipated new business will materialize. It therefore represents, in decision theory terminology, *decision making under conditions of certainty*. It is assumed the payoffs are certain to occur if the particular action is chosen and the probability of the additional business being secured is 1.0.[2] The decision to choose action A_1 is obvious under these conditions with the given payoff data and decision rule.

Conditions of Uncertainty

In a more realistic situation, the outcome is less than certain. The new business may not materialize, and then the department might be left with costly excess capacity. The union may resist introduction of the new equipment because it replaces workers. The new equipment may not perform as anticipated. For these or other reasons, the decision maker may be uncertain about the consequences (for instance, that course A_1 will result in a $20,000 contribution).

Suppose the manager considers these other possible outcomes and concludes the one serious uncertainty is that the new business may not be forthcoming. For purposes of simplicity, one of two conditions will exist in the future—either the new business will be secured as expected (O_1) or the new business will not

Exhibit B–1   Payoff under Conditions of Certainty

Course of Action	Average Annual Department Profit Contribution
A_1—Lease new equipment	$20,000
A_2—Retain old equipment	12,000

Exhibit B-2　Payoff under Conditions of Uncertainty

	Average Annual Departmental Profit Contribution		
	New Business (O_1)	No New Business (O_2)	Expected Monetary Value
A_1—Lease new equipment	$20,000	$5,000	$14,000
A_2—Retain old equipment	12,000	9,000	10,800

materialize (O_2). In the first case, the expected payoffs would be the same as in Exhibit B–1; but if the new business is not secured, then the addition of the new equipment would give the department costly excess capacity, with fixed lease changes. The payoff table may now be revised as Exhibit B–2.

Under these conditions, the original decision rule does not apply. That rule said, "Choose that course of action which will provide the highest average annual departmental profit contribution." Under the conditions in Exhibit B–2, action A_1 would be better if the new business is secured, but A_2 would be the better choice if the new business is not secured. If the decision can be delayed until the new order question is resolved, the dilemma is escapable. However, because of lead times, the equipment decision may need to be made first.

When faced with two or more possible outcomes for each alternative, the manager can adopt one of two approaches. First, the likelihood that the company will receive the new business cannot be judged. Even so, a rational decision can be made by adopting an appropriate decision rule. For example, "Choose that course of action for which the minimum payoff is the highest." This is known as the *maximum criterion* because it calls for maximizing the minimum payoff. In Exhibit B–2, the minimum payoff for alternative A_1 is shown as $5,000, and the minimum payoff for A_2 is $9,000. According to the *maximum* rule, the choice would be A_2 because it is the best of the worst outcomes. This decision is a "cut your losses" strategy.

The second approach is to use subjective judgment to estimate the probability that either O_1 or O_2 will occur.[3] When the assumption was decision under certainty, only one event was possible (had a probability of 1.0). Now, however, with experience and information from other sources, there is a less-than-certain chance of the new business materializing and this doubt should be part of the decision.

One might estimate that there is a 0.6 chance the new business will be secured and a 0.4 chance it will not. With this or any other set of similar probabilities, an overall evaluation of the two courses of action is possible. One approach is to calculate an *expected monetary value (EMV)* for each alternative.[4]

The Decision Flow Diagram

The decision problem already has been summarized in a payoff table, but further illustration in the form of a decision flow diagram (or decision tree) may be helpful. The decision tree for the equipment problem is shown in Exhibit B–3. The

Exhibit B-3   **Decision Tree for Equipment Problem**

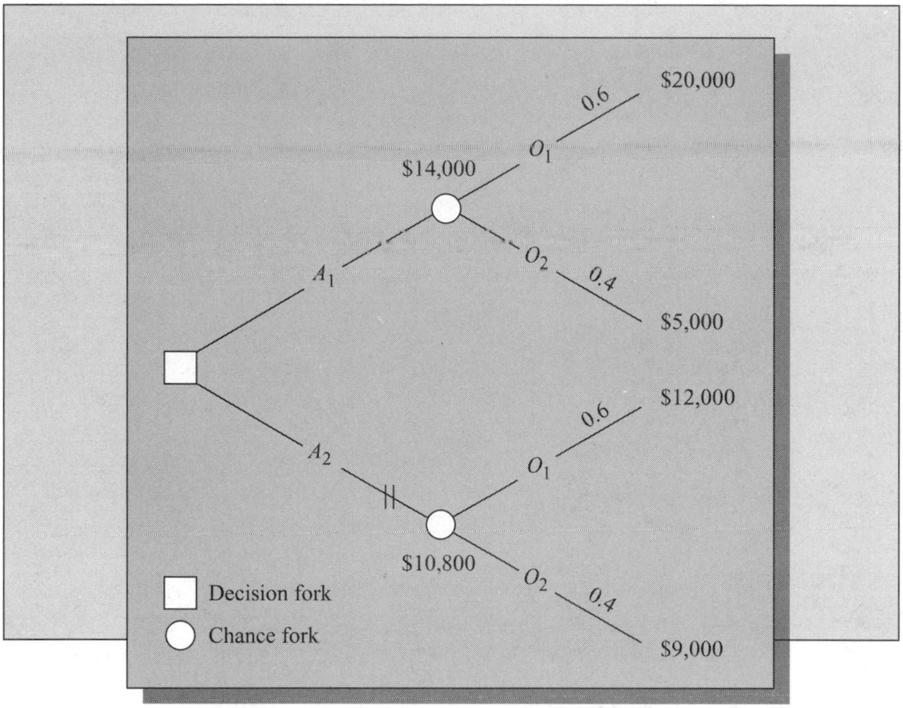

diagram may be seen as a sequential decision flow. At the square node on the left, the manager must choose between A_1 and A_2. After one of these actions, a chance event will occur—either the new business will be received by the company (O_1) or it will not be received (O_2). At the right extremity of the branches are listed the conditional payoffs that will occur for each combination of decision and chance event. On each chance branch is placed the expected probability of that chance event occurring. Keep in mind that these are subjective probability estimates by the manager that express a degree of belief that such a chance event will occur.

Having set up this series of relationships, one calculates back from right to left on the diagram by an *averaging out and folding back* process. At each decision juncture, the path that yields the best alternative for the decision rule is selected. Here the *EMV* for A_1 averages out to $14,000, while the *EMV* for A_2 is $10,800. The double slash line on the A_2 branch indicates it is the inferior alternative and should be dropped in favor of A_1.

The Contribution of Research

Now, the contribution of research can be assessed. Recall that the value of research may be judged as "the difference between the results of decisions made with the information and the results that would be made without it." In this example, the research need is to decide whether the new business will be secured. This is the

Exhibit B-4   **The Value of Perfect Information**

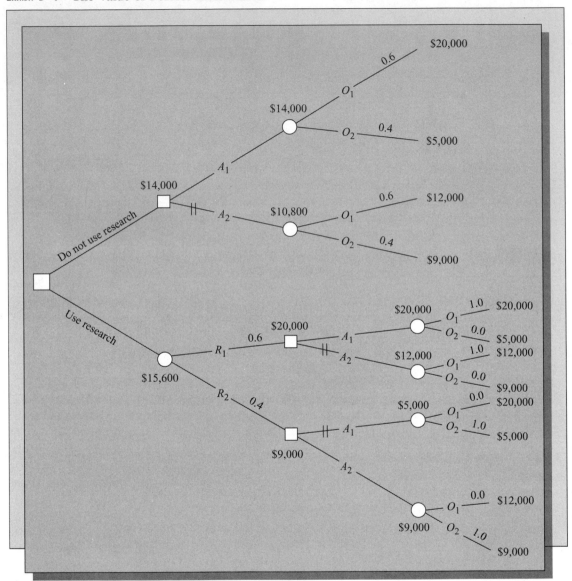

uncertainty that, if known, would make a perfect forecast possible. Just how much is a perfect forecast worth in this case?

Consider Exhibit B–3 once again. What would happen if the manager had information to accurately predict whether the new business orders would be secured? The choice would be A_1 if the research indicated the orders would be received, and A_2 if research indicated the orders would not be received. However, at the decision point (before the research is undertaken) the best estimate is that there is a 0.6 chance that the research will indicate the O_1 condition and 0.4 that the condition will be O_2. The decision flow implications of the use of research are illustrated in Exhibit B–4.

The decision sequence begins with the decision fork at the left. If the manager chooses to do research *(R)*, the first chance fork is reached where one of two things will occur. Research indicates either that the orders will be received *(R_1)* or the orders will not be received *(R_2)*. Before doing the research, the best estimate of the probability of R_1 taking place is the same as the estimate that O_1 will occur (0.6). Similarly, the best estimate that R_2 will occur is 0.4.

After the manager learns R_1 or R_2, there is a second decision fork; A_1 or A_2. After the A_1–A_2 decision, there is a second chance fork *(O_1 or O_2)* that indicates whether the orders were received. Note that the probabilities at O_1 and O_2 have now changed from 0.6 and 0.4, respectively, to 1.0 and 0.0, or to 0.0 and 1.0, depending upon what was learned from the research. This change occurs because we have evaluated the effect of the research information on our original O_1 and O_2 probability estimates by calculating *posterior probabilities*. These are revisions of our prior probabilities that result from the assumed research findings. The posterior probabilities (for example, $P(O_1 \mid R_i)$ and $P(O_2 \mid R_i)$ are calculated by using Bayes's theorem.[5]

Research Outcomes	States of Nature		Marginal Probabilities	Posterior Probabilities	
	O_1	O_2		$P(O_1 \mid R_i)$	$P(O_2 \mid R_i)$
R_1	0.6	0.0	0.6	1.0	0.0
R_2	0.0	0.4	0.4	0.0	1.0
Marginal probabilities	0.6	0.4			

The manager is now ready to average out and fold back the analysis from right to left to evaluate the research alternative. Clearly, if R_1 is found, A_1 is chosen with its EMV of \$20,000 over the A_2 alternative of \$12,000. If R_2 is reported, then A_2 is more attractive. However, before the research, the probabilities of R_1 and R_2 being secured must be incorporated by a second averaging out. The result is an EMV of \$15,600 for the research alternative versus an EMV of \$14,000 for the no research path. The conclusion then is this: Research that would enable the manager to make a perfect forecast regarding the potential new orders would be worth up to \$1,600. If the research costs more than \$1,600, decline to buy it because the net EMV of the research alternative would be less than the EMV of \$14,000 of the no-research alternative.

Imperfect Information

The analysis up to this point assumes that research on decision options will give a perfect prediction of the future states of nature, O_1 and O_2. Perfect prediction seldom occurs in practice. Sometimes research reveals one condition when later

Exhibit B–5   **The Value of Imperfect Information**

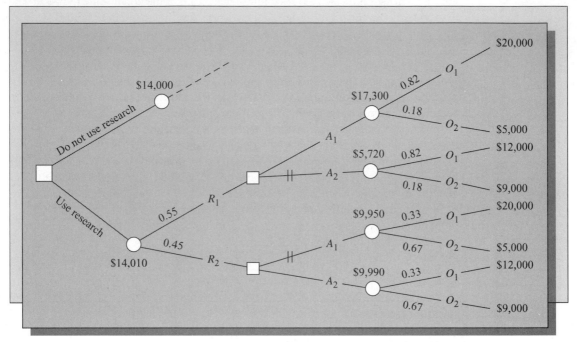

evidence shows something else to be true. Thus, we need to consider that the research in the machinery decision will provide less than perfect information and is, therefore, worth less than the $1,600 calculated in Exhibit B–4.

Suppose the research in that example involves interviews with the customers' key personnel and some customers' executives. They might all answer our questions to the best of their ability but still predict imperfectly what will happen. Consequently, we might judge that the chances of their predictions being correct are no better than 3 to 1, or 0.75. If we accept that our research results may provide imperfect information in this manner, we need to factor this into our evaluation decision. We do this by averaging out and folding back again. The results are shown in Exhibit B–5. The revised EMV, given research judged to be 75 percent reliable, is $14,010. This revised EMV is only $10 higher than the $14,000 EMV using no research and would seem to be hardly worth consideration.

Pragmatic Complications

This discussion, while simplified, contains the basic concepts for finding the value of research. Practical difficulties complicate the use of these concepts. First, the situation with two events and two alternatives is artificial. Problems with more choices and events are common, and the chief complication is the increased number of calculations.

Research Outcomes	States of Nature		Marginal Probabilities	Posterior Probabilities	
	O_1	O_2		$P(O_1 \mid R_i)$	$P(O_2 \mid R_i)$
R_1	0.45	0.10	0.55	0.82	0.18
R_2	0.15	0.30	0.45	0.33	0.67
Marginal probabilities	0.60	0.40			

A more serious problem is posed by the measurement of outcomes. We have assumed we could assess the various actions in terms of an unambiguous dollar value, but often we cannot. It is difficult to place a dollar value on outcomes related to morale or public image, for example.

An allied problem lies in the exclusive use of EMV as the criterion for decision. This is correct in an actuarial sense and implies that each decision maker has a linear system of evaluation. In truth, we often use another evaluation system. The person who accepts EMV as a criterion sees that an even bet of $20 between two people on the toss of a fair coin is a fair bet. Many people, however, may not be willing to make such a bet because they fear the loss of $20 more than they value the gain of $20. They may need to be offered a chance, say, to win $20 but to lose only $10 before they would be willing to bet. These persons have a nonlinear decision scale. The "utility" concept is more relevant here.

The development of more precise methods of evaluating the contribution of research continues. In the meantime, continued emphasis on improvement of our understanding of the researcher's task and the research process will make research more valuable when it is conducted.

References Notes

1. Recall that the decision variable is the unit of measurement used in the analysis. At this point, we need not be concerned with how this measure is calculated or whether it is the appropriate decision variable. Assume for purposes of this illustration that it is appropriate.

2. A probability is a measure between 1.0 and 0.0 that expresses the likelihood of an event occurring. For example, the probability of a "head" on a toss of a coin is 0.5. Under conditions of certainty, the forecasted outcome is assumed to have a probability of 1.0 even though we might agree that we normally cannot know the future with certainty. In most forecasting where a specific amount is named, there is an implicit assumption of certainty.

3. Concepts of probability enter into three types of situations. In the classical situation, each possible outcome has a known chance of occurrence. For example, a coin tossed in the air has a 0.5 chance of landing heads up; a spade card has a 0.25 chance of being drawn from a well-mixed deck.

   In the same type of situation, probabilities are thought of in terms of "relative frequency." Even if the probability is not known from the structure of the problem (as it is in the classical case), it can still be estimated if there is a body of empirical evidence. For example, experience may show that about 1 in 50 products produced is defective. From this statistic, one can estimate there is a 0.02 chance that any given product will be defective.

If there is no direct empirical evidence, one can still assess probability on the basis of opinion, intuition, and/or general experience. In such cases, uncertainty is expressed in terms of a subjectively felt "degree of confidence" or "degree of belief" that a given event will occur. The discussions in this chapter are cases in point. For more information on probability concepts, see any modern statistics text.

4. One calculates an *EMV* for an alternative by weighting each conditional value (for example, $20,000 and $5,000 for A_1) by the estimated probability of the occurrence of the associated event (0.6 probability of the $20,000 being made).

$$EMV = P_1(\$20,000) + P_2(\$5,000)$$
$$= 0.6(\$20,000) + 0.4(\$5,000)$$
$$= \$14,000$$

5. Bayes's theorem with two states of nature is:

$$P(O_1|R_i) = \frac{P(R_i|O_1) \times P(O_1)}{P(R_i|O_1) \times P(O_1) + P(R_i|O_2) \times P(O_2)}$$

$$= \frac{1.0 \times 0.6}{(1.0 \times 0.6) + (0.0 \times 0.4)}$$

$$= 1.0$$

REQUEST FOR PROPOSAL (RFP): ASSESSMENT AND CONTENTS

REQUEST FOR PROPOSAL (RFP): ASSESSMENT AND CONTENTS

Chapter 4 identified the RFP as a means to formalize the process of documenting, justifying, and authorizing a procurement of research. RFPs provide the opportunity to evaluate different solutions and offer a mechanism to establish, monitor, and control the performance of the winning supplier of research services.

SUMMARY OF RFP EFFECTIVENESS

In the literature (the *ABI/Inform* database from 1989 to 1993), 76 journal articles discussed the role of RFPs, ranging from the reasons to use them to specific industry applications. The emerging consensus is that, excepting government contracts and highly specialized industrial applications (e.g., engineering, manufacturing, construction, hospital systems), *traditional RFPs are not time and cost effective.* Commonly, the cost of preparing the RFP exceeds 15 percent of the final bid, the preparation can take as long as two years, and the document may run between several hundred and a thousand pages. A recent article in the *Journal of Business Communication* said this device has become virtually worthless for the procurement of services.

Several modifications or alternatives to RFPs are currently being considered:

- Send shorter RFPs by investing time up front to decide specific, desirable outcomes.
- Use site visits and demonstrations to be certain the suppliers' designs or systems can meet their claims.
- Automate the process to reduce time and cost of preparation (Strategic Systems Solutions International offers software called Product Analyzer to simplify objective supplier evaluation through various scoring algorithms).
- Replace the RFP with a request for application (RFA). The RFA would consist of the following:
  —An overview of the requesting firm's organizational structure.
  —Business objectives.
  —Basic operational procedures.
  —Problems that the supplier's bid should address.
- Replace the RFP with a request for recommendation (RFR). The RFR would contain a clear statement of the problem and be sent to small number of credible suppliers. The supplier's response would:
  —Be limited to a 10-page reply.
  —Contain ballpark prices for the information to be provided.
  —Include supplier recommendations with brief descriptions of solutions and support that can be offered.
  —Be due in three to four weeks (saving the cost of a consultant to prepare an RFP and leaving the firm with the flexibility to maintain control of the project's ultimate direction).

Suppliers (usually no more than six) would be invited to visit the firm and make a two-hour presentation. The firm's statement of work would then be refined and the supplier list narrowed.

- Similar to RFAs and RFRs, the request for information (RFI) is often the first step in overall RFP development. The RFI lets a supplier know you are gathering information but are not prepared to purchase a good or service. It provides the company with an opportunity to more carefully define its requirements and alerts suppliers to the opportunity to respond to its requirements. There are several advantages to RFIs. An RFI:
  —Is an accepted method for determining if the techniques and methods are available; if cost estimates are reasonable; and if solutions exist.
  —Requires in-house people to agree on the requirements and set minimal expectations.
  —Eliminates supplier surprise, thereby helping them to build a better response.
  —Requires a formal written response that may later be incorporated into the contract.
  —Provides a qualified list of suppliers and eliminates those who could not have responded to the RFP.

THE ORGANIZATION AND CONTENT OF AN RFP

The RFP process, properly modified, allows an organization to analyze its current operations, problems, and future challenges. Communications with potential suppliers can be clear and based on a mutual understanding of the problems being addressed and the proposed solutions. Proper planning and management commitment to the project are essential.

The first step in developing an RFP is to fully understand and define the problem being addressed. In a formal RFP process, an internal set of experts defines the problem. (One can hire an expert or a group of experts who specialize(s) in the problem area to help in defining the problem and writing the RFP.) Once the problem is defined, the technical section of the RFP can be written.

Besides defining the technical requirements, critical components of the RFP include project management, pricing, and contract administrations. These sections allow the supplier to understand and meet expectations of the management team for carrying out the contracted services. Also, a section on the proposal administration, including important dates, is included.

The components of an RFP are:

- Proposal administration information.
- Summary statement of the problem.
- Technical section.
- Management section.
- Pricing section.
- Contracts and license sections.

Proposal Administration

This section is an overview with important information on the administration of the proposal itself. It establishes the dates of the RFP process—when the RFP is released, the time when the RFP team is available for questions, the date the proposals are expected, and the dates of the evaluation and supplier selections. It includes all requirements for preparing the proposal and describes how the proposals will be evaluated. Contact names, addresses, and relevant telephone and fax information are listed.

Summary Statement of the Problem

This section can be an abstract of the technical section or it can be included as the first page of the technical section.

Technical Section

Technical information needed for the supplier to create the proposal comprises this section. It begins by describing the problems to be addressed and the technical detail of each requirement. It loosely describes the services to be performed, equipment, software, and documentation required. This should be neither too specific nor too general to allow the suppliers flexibility in design creativity but restrict them to meeting the needs of the corporation. Typically, the following would be included:

- Problem statement.
- Description of functional requirements.
- Identification of constraints.

Management Section

Each project requires some level of management. The extent to which the corporation expects schedules, plans, and reports is included in this section. The management section should include requirements for implementation schedules, training and reporting schedules, and other documentation requirements. If specific supplier qualifications are needed, they should be shown in this section. References from the supplier's customer should also be requested.

Pricing Section

To cost the proposal, all information needed by the supplier is contained in this section. By using a rigid format, proposals with different approaches can be compared on costs. The following list shows examples of items that should be included:

- Services.
- Data collection.
- Data analysis.
- Meetings with client.
- Travel.
- Respondent survey incentives.
- Mail and telephone costs.
- Design meetings.
- Pilot tests.
- Report preparations.
- Computer models.
- Project management.
- Deliverables.
  —Training.
  —Brochures/literature.
  —Videotapes.
  —Reports.

- Facilities and equipment.
- Extensions to work agreements.
- Questionnaire and reproduction costs.
- Manpower costs.

Contracts and License Section

This section includes the types of contracts the supplier is expected to sign and any nondisclosure agreements. The safeguarding of intellectual property and the use of copyright are discussed. Terms of payment and required benchmarks are set forth. Typically a sample purchase contract would be included.

CONCLUSION

A well-written RFP allows an organization to request state-of-the-art proposals for dealing with complex problems. When not done properly, the process will take longer, cost more, and not provide a complete long-term solution. Therefore, it is essential when an organization decides to put a project to bid using an RFP-type mechanism that time and effort are invested at the beginning of the process. Modifications to traditional RFP methods would also be beneficial. Clear communications with suppliers through a coherent RFP will result in a well-managed project with long-term benefits.

D SAMPLE STUDENT TERM PROJECT

Four members of a graduate research methods course formed a team to investigate career prospects in product management. Their stated research objectives were: (1) provide an inventory of major U.S. manufacturers that use the product management system, (2) gather descriptive data on the nature and degree of product management, and (3) collect information on how product managers are recruited, selected, and prepared for their responsibilities.

The research question was: What is the role and scope of product management in U.S. manufacturing companies? Since financial support from the student research fund was limited to *Fortune's* top 1,000 manufacturing companies, they further defined manufacturers according to this criterion. Their investigative questions were:

1. What is the incidence of use of the product manager system?
   a. To what degree is it presently in use?
   b. Has it been used in the past and discontinued?
   c. Was it considered and not adopted?
   d. What are future expectations regarding its use?
2. How are product managers recruited and selected?
3. What are the qualifications for employment as a product manager?
4. How does the product manager function in the company?
5. How can we classify the characteristics of individuals and companies to discern trends and differences?

They selected a mail survey as their data collection method. Their initial plan was to use a screening or qualifying question to establish which companies use product management.

The team members developed the following procedure for constructing their questionnaire. Having agreed upon the investigative questions, each member attempted to write measurement questions aimed at tapping the essence of each investigative question. Each measurement question was written on a 5 × 8 card to facilitate comparisons, revisions, additions, and deletions. At a meeting of the team, all questions were reviewed, duplicates were eliminated, and a general winnowing occurred. The remaining 31 questions were included in questionnaire draft 1, shown in Exhibit D–1. In this first draft, there was no effort to place questions in sequence or to present them graphically as they would eventually be seen by respondents.

After discussion, the team members concluded the questionnaire would probably need to be three pages long. In addition, the cover letter would require a page. They decided to use a printed cover letter and to incorporate it as the first page of the questionnaire. The combination would be printed on both sides of an 11 × 17 inch sheet of paper, folded in booklet form to 8½ × 11 size.

Each team member was assigned the task of translating draft 1 into a draft 2. In the new draft, the questions should be in planned sequence, have response formats chosen, and have graphic arrangements selected. Individual drafts were submitted to a subcommittee of the team who used them as the basis for developing questionnaire draft 2. This is shown in Exhibit D–2.

Exhibit D-1   Preliminary Questionnaire, Product Manager Study—Draft 1

---

1. What is your position in the company?
2. Is your company engaged primarily in industrial products, consumer products, or both?
3. Does your company use product managers?
4. How many product managers does the company have?
5. How many products are assigned to one PM?
6. Would you please give or include a job description of your company's PM position?
7. How many brands does your company have?
8. Approximately what percentage of your company's brands have product managers?
9. What percentage of sales volume do the brands in question 8 account for as a whole?
10. How long have product managers been used in your company?
11. Has a PM system been used and dropped in your company? If yes, why was it dropped?
12. Has a PM system ever been considered but never adopted in your company? If yes, why was it not adopted?
13. Are there any plans for the adoption of a PM system in the future?
14. What percentage of your product managers come *directly* from each of the following sources? Campuses, within the company, other companies, other (list).
15. If PMs come from within the company, what department or departments do they come from? Sales, marketing, production, advertising, other (list).
16. If PMs come from outside the company (other than campuses), what department or departments do they come from? Product manager, sales, marketing, production, advertising, other (list).
17. If PMs are recruited directly from campuses, what, if any, are typical degrees required?
18. Rank on a scale from 1 to 5 the relative importance of each of the following qualifications for a PM (1 denotes the greatest importance). Education, age, work experience, personality, creativity.
19. If PMs are recruited from within the company, what is the average age, length of work experience (with the company), and educational background?
20. If PMs are recruited from outside the company (not including campuses), what is the average age, length of work experience, and educational background?
21. What functions (e.g., advertising, pricing, etc.) does the PM actually perform in day-to-day activities, and what percentage of time is spent on each?
22. Of those functions listed in 21, which, if any, does the PM have *final* authority over?
23. To whom does the PM report?
24. Does your company have a structured training program for product management? If yes, please explain.
25. On the basis of which of the following is the PM evaluated? Market share, ROI, sales volume, profits, other (list)?
26. What were the objectives of the company in instituting the PM concept?
27. How successful has the PM concept been in fulfilling the objectives set for it?
28. What were the characteristics of the PM concept that contributed to the fulfillment of these objectives?
29. What elements, if any, of the PM system did not adequately contribute to the fulfillment of the objectives?
30. What specific actions, if any, have been taken to deal with the inadequacies listed in 29?
31. If your company is currently planning any broad revisions in the present PM program, please describe.

Draft 2 was reproduced and submitted to other members of the research class for critique. Comments and challenges were sought on (1) sources of confusion and vagueness; (2) question value (what useful information does the question provide? Not provide?); (3) appropriateness of the proposed response formats and suggestions for improvement; and (4) gaps in question coverage.

EXHIBIT D-2   Product Manager Questionnaire—Draft 2

---

1. Does your company now use product managers? yes ___ no ___ (If no, please go to question 17).
2. Would you please send a copy of your job description?
3. How many product managers does your company have? _____
4. What percentage of your total sales are accounted for by product managers? _____ %
5. How long have product managers been used by your company? _____ years
6. What percentage of your personnel enter the product management program from the following sources?
   Campuses _____ %
   Within the company _____ %
   From elsewhere _____ %
7. If product managers come from within the company or elsewhere, what department(s) do they come from?
   Sales _____ %
   Marketing _____ %
   Production _____ %
   Advertising _____ %
   Other product management programs _____ %
   Advertising agencies _____ %
   Elsewhere _____ %
8. If product managers are recruited directly from campuses, please rank the following degrees from 1 to 6, with 1 being the most desirable, 2 the next most desirable, and so forth.
   BS _____ areas _____
   AB _____ areas _____
   BSBA (BBA) ___ areas _____
   MA _____ areas _____
   MBA _____ areas _____
   PhD _____ areas _____
9. Briefly state what you consider to be an appropriate profile of a product manager recruited directly from the campus.
   Age

   Work experience (length and type)

   Personal traits (i.e., personality, creativity, aggressiveness, etc.)

   Education

After this critique, a second subcommittee revised the questionnaire. This resulted in questionnaire draft 3 (not presented here). The draft was again reviewed by the full team and modest changes were made to produce draft 4.

By this time, the team members were eager to test the questionnaire with respondents. Arrangements were made to have several local corporate executives complete the questionnaire. Team members picked up the completed questionnaires,

Exhibit D–2   Product Manager Questionnaire—Draft 2 *(concluded)*

10. What do you consider to be an appropriate profile for a product manager recruited from within or from another company?
    Age

    Work experience (length and type)

    Personal traits (i.e., personality, creativity, aggressiveness, etc.)

    Education

11. To whom does the product manager report? _____
12. What percentage of his time does the product manager spend in various functionary areas, such as production, advertising, pricing, etc.? Please list.
13. Please rank the following on a scale of 1 to 5 (1 is most important), the criteria used in evaluating a product manager.
    ___ Market share
    ___ Return on investment
    ___ Sales volume
    ___ Profits
    ___ Other (please explain) _____
14. Does the company have a structured training program?
    yes ___ no ___ If yes, please describe.
15. What prompted your firm to initiate the product manager system?
16. Is your company currently planning any future revisions in the product manager system?
    yes ___ no ___ If yes, please explain.
17. Is your company primarily engaged in:
    Industrial goods _____ %
    Food products _____ %
    Consumer package goods _____ %
    Consumer durable goods _____ %
    Automotive products _____ %
    Other (list)
    _____ _____ %
    _____ _____ %
18. What is your company's total sales volume? $ _____
    If you answered the first question yes, you have completed the questionnaire. If your answer was no, please answer question 19. Thank you for your cooperation.
19. Please check which of the following best describes your company's use of product managers.
    ___ Have never considered product managers
    ___ Have considered, but never adopted product management
    ___ Have used previously and discontinued
    ___ Presently considering adoption of the system in the future

interviewed the executives about their answers, and secured comments they had about the questions and the study. These experiences led to a revised draft 5. This was repeated twice more with other executives, finally ending with draft 7 shown here as Exhibit D–3. The limitations of time and money led the team to depend upon local product managers for testing rather than a full-scale dress rehearsal by mail. This decision limited the value of the pretesting but was accepted as a limitation of a student project.

The survey was sent to the top 1,000 manufacturing companies in the form described. Only one mailing was made because of time and money limitations. Usable returns numbered 192 at the cutoff point. Approximately 50 companies sent job descriptions of their product management positions.

Exhibit D–3   Product Manager Questionnaire—Final Draft

WASHINGTON UNIVERSITY

ST. LOUIS, MISSOURI 63130

GRADUATE SCHOOL
OF BUSINESS ADMINISTRATION

Inside Address

Dear Sir:

We at the Washington Business School are interested in learning more about the actual recruitment and use of product or brand managers. Our objective is to help expand the body of knowledge about this important area of marketing.

To do this, of course, means going to someone such as yourself who *knows*. Your help with the few questions on the attached pages will take only a few minutes and will make a real contribution to the accuracy and success of this study.

Your reply will be treated in strict confidence and will be available only to my research staff and myself. Any publication will be only of statistical totals for groups of companies.

Your assistance will be greatly appreciated and will help us to know more about product management and to teach about it in a more relevant and effective manner.

Sincerely,

William Emory
Professor of Marketing

EXHIBIT D–3   *(continued)*

We define a *product manager* (also called brand manager) as one who is responsible for the integration and planning of a broad range of marketing functions (e.g., pricing, distribution, and so forth) for a specific product, brand, or homogeneous group of products. The position usually has limited or no line authority, especially over the sales force.

1. Please indicate which of the following best describes your company/division's use of product managers.
   ___ We are currently using product managers.
   ___ We have previously used product managers, but discontinued.
   ___ We have considered the system, but never implemented it.
   ___ Presently considering adoption of the system in the future.
   ___ We have never considered product managers.

   If you are currently using product managers, please continue. If *you are not* currently using product managers you have completed the questionnaire. Thank you for your cooperation.

   (please check)
2. Will you be answering the following for: ___ your company
                                            ___ your division
3. How many product managers (include all levels such as group PM, PM, assoc. PM, and assistant PM) does your company/division employ?   ___
4. How long have product managers been used by your company/division?   ___ years
5. What percentage of your company/division total sales are accounted for by products controlled by product managers?   _____ %
6. From the following, please indicate whether the position exists in your company/division. Then indicate the source from which the personnel at the various levels were obtained to fill that position. If you have a similar position, but with a different name, please indicate that position in the blank.

	Do You Have?		(please check) Major Sources			
			Within Company			
	Yes	No	Campuses	Other PM Jobs	Other Jobs	Other Companies
Group PMs	___	___	___	___	___	___
PMs	___	___	___	___	___	___
Assoc. PMs	___	___	___	___	___	___
Asst. PMs	___	___	___	___	___	___
Other (specify)	___	___	___	___	___	___

Exhibit D-3   Product Manager Questionnaire—Final Draft *(continued)*

7. What is the typical age of your:
   Group product managers ___ years
   Product managers ___ years
   Associate PMs ___ years
   Assistant PMs ___ years

8. Of the following personal traits, would you please indicate the degree of importance in the evaluation of a candidate for a product management position.

(please check)

	Not Important	Desirable	Very Desirable	Essential
Leadership	___	___	___	___
Creativity	___	___	___	___
Aggressiveness	___	___	___	___
Analytical ability	___	___	___	___
Communications skill	___	___	___	___
Ability to work with others	___	___	___	___
Other _____	___	___	___	___

9. *(If you recruit directly from campus)* Please indicate the importance of the following traits of a product manager candidate.

(please check)

	Not Important	Desirable	Very Desirable	Essential
Business experience	___	___	___	___
High grade point avg.	___	___	___	___
Extra curricular activities	___	___	___	___
MBA	___	___	___	___
Master's, technical	___	___	___	___
Bachelor's, technical	___	___	___	___
Bachelor's, business	___	___	___	___
Other				
(specify) _____	___	___	___	___

Exhibit D-3   Product Manager Questionnaire—Final Draft *(continued)*

10. If you recruit into your PM group from other jobs (either from your company or other companies), please indicate the importance of the following experiences.

(please check)

Experience	Not Important	Desirable	Very Desirable	Essential
Sales	___	___	___	___
Other product manager programs	___	___	___	___
Other marketing positions	___	___	___	___
Production	___	___	___	___
Ad agencies	___	___	___	___
Undergraduate degree	___	___	___	___
Graduate degree	___	___	___	___
Other (specify) _____	___	___	___	___

11. Please indicate the percentage of time a typical product manager spends in the following activities:

Advertising	_____ %
Pricing	_____
Distribution	_____
Packaging	_____
Product Development	_____
Marketing Research	_____
Production Liaison	_____
Finance and Budgeting	_____
Other (specify) _____	_____
Other (specify) _____	_____
Total _____	100 %

12. Please indicate which of the following criteria are used in evaluating product managers in your company/division.
    a. _____ Market share
       _____ Return on investment
       _____ Sales volume
       _____ Dollar profits
       _____ Other (please specify) _____
    b. Which one is most important? _____

13. Does your company/division have a structured training program for product managers?
    yes ___ no ___ (If yes, please describe.)

    _____
    _____
    _____
    _____

14. Is your company/division currently planning any revision in its product manager system?
    yes ___ no ___ (If yes, please describe.)

    _____
    _____
    _____
    _____

Exhibit D-3   Product Manager Questionnaire—Final Draft *(concluded)*

15. Judging from your company's experience, what do you feel is the major problem facing the product management system?

    _____

    _____

    _____

16. It would be most valuable to our studies if you could supply a sample job description of your product manager positions.

    Are such available?

    ___ Yes, examples enclosed

    ___ Yes, examples sent under separate cover

    ___ Not available

    Thank you for your assistance

17. If you would like a summary of the results of this survey, please check here. ___

**FINDING
YOUR WAY**

This appendix contains additional nonparametric tests of hypotheses to augment those described in Chapter 15.

ONE-SAMPLE CASE

Kolmogorov-Smirnov (KS) Test

This test is appropriate when the data are at least ordinal and the research situation calls for a comparison of an observed sample distribution with a theoretical distribution. Under these conditions, the *KS* one-sample test is more powerful than the χ^2 test and can be used for small samples when the χ^2 test cannot. The *KS* is a test of goodness-of-fit in which we specify the *cumulative* frequency distribution that would occur under the theoretical distribution and compare that with the observed cumulative frequency distribution. The theoretical distribution represents our expectations under H_0. We determine the point of greatest divergence between the observed and theoretical distributions and identify this value as *D* (maximum deviation). From a table of critical values for *D*, we determine whether such a large divergence is likely on the basis of random sampling variations from the theoretical distribution. The value for *D* is calculated as follows:

$$D = \text{maximum}|F_O(X) - F_T(X)|$$

in which

$F_O(X)$ = The observed cumulative frequency distribution of a random
          sample of *n* observations. Where *X* is any possible score, $F_O(X) =$
          k/n, where *k* = the number of observations equal to or less than *X*.
$F_T(X)$ = The theoretical frequency distribution under H_0.

We illustrate the KS test, with an analysis of the results of the dining club study, in terms of various class levels. Take an equal number of interviews from each class but secure unequal numbers of people interested in joining. Assume class levels are ordinal measurements. The testing process is as follows: (See accompanying table.)

1. *Null hypothesis.* H_0: There is no difference among student classes as to
          their intention of joining the dining club.
          H_A: There is a difference among students in various
          classes as to their intention of joining the dining club.
2. *Statistical test.* Choose the KS one-sample test because the data are
          ordinal measured, and we are interested in comparing an observed
          distribution with a theoretical one.
3. *Significance level.* $\alpha = .05$, $n = 60$.
4. *Calculated value.* $D = \text{maximum } |F_O(X) - F_T(X)|$.

	Freshman	*Sophomore*	*Junior*	*Senior*	*Graduate*
Number in each class	5	9	11	16	19
$F_O(X)$	5/60	14/60	25/60	41/60	60/60
$F_T(X)$	12/60	24/60	36/60	48/60	60/60
$|F_O(X) - F_T(X)|$	7/60	10/60	11/60	7/60	0

$D = 11/60 = .183$;
  $n = 60$

5. *Critical test value.* We enter the table of critical values of D in the KS one-sample test (Appendix Table E–5) and learn that with $\alpha = .05$, the critical value for D is

$$D = \frac{1.36}{\sqrt{60}} = .175$$

6. *Decision.* The calculated value is greater than the critical value, indicating we should reject the null hypothesis.

TWO-SAMPLE CASE

Sign Test

The sign test is used with matched pairs when the only information is the identification of the pair member that is larger or smaller or has more or less of some characteristic. Under H_0, one would expect the number of cases in which $X_A > X_B$ to equal the number of pairs in which $X_B > X_A$. All ties are dropped from the analysis, and n is adjusted to allow for these eliminated pairs. This test is based on the binomial expansion and has a good power efficiency for small samples.

Wilcoxon Matched-Pairs Test

When you can determine both *direction* and *magnitude* of difference between carefully matched pairs, use the Wilcoxon matched-pairs test. This test has excellent efficiency and can be more powerful than the t test in cases where the latter is not particularly appropriate. The mechanics of calculation are also quite simple. Find the difference score (d_i) between each pair of values and rank order the differences from smallest to largest without regard to sign. The actual signs of each difference are then added to the rank values, and the test statistic T is calculated. T is the sum of the ranks with the less frequent sign. Typical of such research situations might be a study where husband and wife are matched, where twins are used, where a given subject is used in a before-after study, or where the output of two similar machines is compared.

Two types of ties may occur with this test. When two observations are equal, the d score becomes zero, and we drop this pair of observations from the calculation. When two or more pairs have the same d value, we average their rank positions. For example, if two pairs have a rank score of 1, we assign the rank of 1.5 to each and rank the next largest difference as third. When $n < 25$, use the table of critical values (Appendix Table F–4). When $n > 25$, the sampling distribution of T is approximately normal with:

$$\text{Mean} = \mu_T = \frac{n(n + 1)}{4}$$

$$\text{Standard deviation} = \sigma_T = \sqrt{\frac{n(n + 1)(2n + 1)}{24}}$$

$$\text{The formula for the test is } z = \frac{T - \mu_T}{\sigma_T}$$

Suppose you conduct an experiment on the effect of brand name on quality perception. Ten subjects are recruited and asked to taste and compare two samples of product, one identified as a well-known drink and the other as a new product being tested. In truth, however, the samples are identical. The subjects are then asked to rate the two samples on a set of scale items judged to be ordinal. Test these results for significance by the usual procedure.

1. *Null hypothesis.* H_0: There is no difference between the perceived qualities of the two samples.

   H_A: There is a difference in the perceived quality of the two samples.

2. *Statistical test.* The Wilcoxon matched-pairs test is used because the study is of related samples in which the differences can be ranked in magnitude.

3. *Significance level.* $\alpha = .05$, with $n = 10$ pairs of comparisons minus any pairs with a d of zero.

4. *Calculated value.* T equals the sum of the ranks with the less frequent sign. Assume we secure the following results:

Pair	Branded	Unbranded	d_i	Rank of d_i	Rank with Less Frequent Sign
1	52	48	4	4	
2	37	32	5	5.5*	
3	50	52	−2	−2	2
4	45	32	13	9	
5	56	59	−3	−3	3
6	51	50	1	1	
7	40	29	11	8	
8	59	54	5	5.5*	
9	38	38	0	*	
10	40	32	8	7	$T = 5$

*There are two types of tie situations. We drop out the pair with the type of tie shown by pair 9. Pairs 2 and 8 have a tie in rank of difference. In this case, we average the ranks and assign the average value to each.

5. *Critical test value.* Enter the table of critical values of T with $n = 9$ (Appendix Table F–4) and find that the critical value with $\alpha = .05$ is 6. Note that with this test, the calculated value must be smaller than the critical value to reject the null hypothesis.

6. *Decision.* Since the calculated value is less than the critical value, reject the null hypothesis.

Kolmogorov-Smirnov Two-Sample Test

When a researcher has two independent samples of ordinal data, the Kolmogorov-Smirnov two-sample test is useful. Like the one-sample test, this two-sample test is concerned with the agreement between two cumulative distributions, but both represent sample values. If the two samples have been drawn from the same population, the cumulative distributions of the samples should be fairly close to each other, showing only random deviations from the population distribution. If the cumulative distributions show a large enough maximum deviation D, it is evidence for rejecting the H_0. To secure the maximum deviation, one should use as many intervals as are available so as not to obscure the maximum cumulative difference. The two-sample KS formula is:

$$D = \text{maximum } |F_{N1}(X) - F_{N2}(X)| \text{ (two-tailed test)}$$

$$D = \text{maximum } |F_{N1}(X) - F_{N2}(X)| \text{ (one-tailed test)}$$

D is calculated in the same manner as before, but the table for critical values for the numerator of D, K_D (two-sample case) is presented in Appendix Table F–6 when $n_1 = n_2$ and is less than 40 observations. When n_1 and/or n_2 are larger than 40, D from Appendix Table E–7 should be used. With this larger sample, it is not necessary that $n_1 = n_2$.

Here we use a different sample from the smoking-accident study. (To make $n_1 = n_2$, we increased the sample size of no accidents to 34. Nonsmokers with no accidents is 24.) Suppose the smoking classifications represent an ordinal scale, and you test these data with the KS two-sample test. Proceed as follows:

1. *Null hypothesis.* H_0: There is no difference in on-the-job accident occurrences between smokers and nonsmokers.
   H_A: The more a person smokes, the more likely that person is to have an on-the-job accident.

2. *Statistical test.* The KS two-sample test is used because it is assumed the data are ordinal.

3. *Significance level.* $\alpha = .05$. $n_1 = n_2 = 34$.

4. *Calculated value* (see table, p. 653).

5. *Critical test value.* We enter Appendix Table F–6 with $n = 34$ to find that $K_D = 11$ when $p \leq .05$ for a one-tailed distribution.

	Heavy Smoker	Moderate Smoker	Nonsmoker
$F_{n1}(X)$	12/34	21/34	34/34
$F_{n2}(X)$	4/34	10/34	34/34
$d_i = K_{D/n}$	8/34	11/34	0

6. *Decision.* Since the critical value equals the largest calculated value, we reject the null hypothesis.

Mann-Whitney U Test

This test is also used with two independent samples if the data are at least ordinal; it is an alternative to the *t* test without the latter's limiting assumptions. When the larger of the two samples is 20 or less, there are special tables for interpreting *U;* when the larger sample exceeds 20, a normal curve approximation is used.

In calculating the *U* test, treat all observations in a combined fashion and rank them, algebraically, from smallest to largest. The largest negative score receives the lowest rank. In case of ties, assign the average rank as in other tests. With this test, you can also test samples that are unequal. After the ranking, the rank values for each sample are totaled. Compute the *U* statistic as follows:

$$U = n_1 n_2 + \frac{n_1(n_1 + 1)}{2} - R_1$$

or

$$U = n_1 n_2 + \frac{n_2(n_2 - 1)}{2} - R_2$$

in which

n_1 = Number in sample 1.
n_2 = Number in sample 2.
R_1 = Sum of ranks in sample 1.

With this equation, you can secure two *U* values, one using R_1 and the second using R_2. For testing purposes, use the smaller *U*.

An example may help to clarify the *U* statistic calculation procedure. Let's consider the sales training example with the *t* distribution discussion. Recall that salespeople with training method A averaged higher sales than salespeople with training method B. While these data are ratio measured, one still might not want to accept the other assumptions that underly the *t* test. What kind of a result could be secured with the *U* test? While the *U* test is designed for ordinal data, it can be used with interval and ratio measurements.

1. *Null hypothesis.* H_0: There is no difference in sales results produced by the two training methods.

    H_A: Training method A produces sales results superior to the results of method B.

2. *Statistical test.* The Mann-Whitney U test is chosen because the measurement is at least ordinal, and the assumptions under the parametric t test are rejected.

3. *Significance level.* $\alpha = .05$ (one-tailed test).

4. *Calculated value.*

Sales per Week per Salesperson

Training Method A	Rank	Training Method B	Rank
1,500	15	1,340	10
1,540	16	1,300	8.5
1,860	22	1,620	18
1,230	6	1,070	3
1,370	12	1,210	5
1,550	17	1,170	4
1,840	21	1,770	20
1,250	7	950	1
1,300	8.5	1,380	13
1,350	11	1,460	14
1,710	19	1,030	2
	$R_1 = 154.5$		$R_2 = 98.5$

$$U = (11)(11) + \frac{11(11+1)}{2} - 154.5 \qquad U = (11)(11) + \frac{11(11+1)}{2} - 98.5$$
$$= 32.5 \qquad\qquad\qquad\qquad\qquad = 88.5$$

5. *Critical test value.* Enter Appendix Table F–8 with $n_1 = n_2 = 11$, and find a critical value of 34 for $\alpha = .05$, one-tailed test. Note that with this test, the calculated value must be smaller than the critical value to reject the null hypothesis.

6. *Decision.* Since the calculated value is smaller than the critical value (34 > 32.5), reject the null hypothesis and conclude that training method A is probably superior.

Thus, one would reject the null hypothesis at $\alpha = .05$ in a one-tailed test using either the t or the U test. In this example, the U test has approximately the same power as the parametric test.

When $n > 20$ in one of the samples, the sampling distribution of U approaches the normal distribution with

$$\text{Mean} = \mu_U = \frac{n_1 n_2}{2}$$

$$\text{Standard deviation } \sigma_U = \sqrt{\frac{(n_1)(n_2)(n_1 + n_2 + 1)}{12}}$$

and

$$z = \frac{U - \mu_U}{\sigma_U}$$

Other Nonparametric Tests

Other tests are appropriate under certain conditions when testing two independent samples. When the measurement is only nominal, the Fisher exact probability test may be used. When the data are at least ordinal, use the median and Wald-Wolfowitz runs tests.

K SAMPLE CASE

You can use tests more powerful than χ^2 with data that are at least ordinal in nature. One such test is an extension of the median test mentioned earlier. We illustrate here the application of a second ordinal measurement test known as the Kruskal-Wallis one-way analysis of variance.

Kruskal-Wallis Test

This is a generalized version of the Mann-Whitney test. With it we rank all scores in the entire pool of observations from smallest to largest. The rank sum of each sample is then calculated, with ties being distributed as in other examples. We then compute the value of H as follows:

$$H = \frac{12}{N(N-1)} \sum_{j=1}^{k} \frac{T_j^2}{n_j} - 3(N+1)$$

where

T_j = Sum of ranks in column j.
n_j = Number of cases in jth sample.
$N = \Sigma w_j$ = Total number of cases.
k = Number of samples.

When there are a number of ties, it is recommended that a correction factor (C) be calculated and used to correct the H value as follows:

$$C = 1 - \left\{ \frac{\sum_{i}^{G}(t_i^3 - t_i)}{N^2 - N} \right\}$$

where

G = Number of sets of tied observations.
t_i = Number tied in any set i.
$H' = H/C$.

Exhibit E-1   **Kruskal-Wallis One-Way Analysis of Variance (price differentials)**

One Cent		Three Cents		Five Cents	
X_A	*Rank*	X_B	*Rank*	X_C	*Rank*
6	1	8	5	9	8.5
7	2.5	9	8.5	9	8.5
8	5	8	5	11	14
7	2.5	10	11.5	10	11.5
9	8.5	11	14	14	18
11	14	13	16.5	13	16.5
	$T_j = 33.5$		60.5		77

$T = 33.5 + 60.5 + 77$

$= 171$

$$H = \frac{12}{18(18-1)}\left[\frac{33.5^2 + 60.5^2 + 77^2}{6}\right] - 3(18+1)$$

$$= \frac{12}{342}\left[\frac{1{,}122.25 + 3{,}660.25 + 5{,}929}{6}\right] - 57$$

$$= 0.0351\left[\frac{10{,}711.5}{6}\right] - 57$$

$H = 5.66$

$$C = 1 - \left(\frac{3[(2)^3 - 2] + 2[(3)^3 - 3] + [(4)^3 - 4]}{18^3 + 18}\right)$$

$$= 1 - \frac{18 + 48 + 60}{5814}$$

$$= .978$$

$$H' = \frac{H}{C} = \frac{5.66}{.978} = 5.79$$

d.f. $= k - 1 = 2$

    $p > .05$

To secure the critical value for H', use the table for the distribution of χ^2 (Appendix Table F–3) and enter it with the value of H' and d.f. $= k - 1$.

    To illustrate the application of this test, use the price discount experiment problem. The data and calculations are shown in Exhibit E–1 and indicate that, by the Kruskal-Wallis test, one again barely fails to reject the null hypothesis with $\alpha = .05$.

SELECTED STATISTICAL TABLES

**FINDING
YOUR WAY**

TABLE F-1   Areas of the Standard Normal Distribution

				Second Decimal Place in z					
z	0.00	0.01	0.02	0.03	0.04	0.05	0.06	0.07	0.08	0.09
0.0	0.0000	0.0040	0.0080	0.0120	0.0160	0.0199	0.0239	0.0279	0.0319	0.0359
0.1	0.0398	0.0438	0.0478	0.0517	0.0557	0.0596	0.0636	0.0675	0.0714	0.0753
0.2	0.0793	0.0832	0.0871	0.0910	0.0948	0.0987	0.1026	0.1064	0.1103	0.1141
0.3	0.1179	0.1217	0.1255	0.1293	0.1331	0.1368	0.1406	0.1443	0.1480	0.1517
0.4	0.1554	0.1591	0.1628	0.1664	0.1700	0.1736	0.1772	0.1808	0.1844	0.1879
0.5	0.1915	0.1950	0.1985	0.2019	0.2054	0.2088	0.2123	0.2157	0.2190	0.2224
0.6	0.2257	0.2291	0.2324	0.2357	0.2389	0.2422	0.2454	0.2486	0.2517	0.2549
0.7	0.2580	0.2611	0.2642	0.2673	0.2704	0.2734	0.2764	0.2794	0.2823	0.2852
0.8	0.2881	0.2910	0.2939	0.2967	0.2995	0.3023	0.3051	0.3078	0.3106	0.3133
0.9	0.3159	0.3186	0.3212	0.3238	0.3264	0.3289	0.3315	0.3340	0.3365	0.3389
1.0	0.3413	0.3438	0.3461	0.3485	0.3508	0.3531	0.3554	0.3577	0.3599	0.3621
1.1	0.3643	0.3665	0.3686	0.3708	0.3729	0.3749	0.3770	0.3790	0.3810	0.3830
1.2	0.3849	0.3869	0.3888	0.3907	0.3925	0.3944	0.3962	0.3980	0.3997	0.4015
1.3	0.4032	0.4049	0.4066	0.4082	0.4099	0.4115	0.4131	0.4147	0.4162	0.4177
1.4	0.4192	0.4207	0.4222	0.4236	0.4251	0.4265	0.4279	0.4292	0.4306	0.4319
1.5	0.4332	0.4345	0.4357	0.4370	0.4382	0.4394	0.4406	0.4418	0.4429	0.4441
1.6	0.4452	0.4463	0.4474	0.4484	0.4495	0.4505	0.4515	0.4525	0.4535	0.4545
1.7	0.4554	0.4564	0.4573	0.4582	0.4591	0.4599	0.4608	0.4616	0.4625	0.4633
1.8	0.4641	0.4649	0.4656	0.4664	0.4671	0.4678	0.4686	0.4693	0.4699	0.4706
1.9	0.4713	0.4719	0.4726	0.4732	0.4738	0.4744	0.4750	0.4756	0.4761	0.4767
2.0	0.4772	0.4778	0.4783	0.4788	0.4793	0.4798	0.4803	0.4808	0.4812	0.4817
2.1	0.4821	0.4826	0.4830	0.4834	0.4838	0.4842	0.4846	0.4850	0.4854	0.4857
2.2	0.4861	0.4864	0.4868	0.4871	0.4875	0.4878	0.4881	0.4884	0.4887	0.4890
2.3	0.4893	0.4896	0.4898	0.4901	0.4904	0.4906	0.4909	0.4911	0.4913	0.4916
2.4	0.4918	0.4920	0.4922	0.4925	0.4927	0.4929	0.4931	0.4932	0.4934	0.4936
2.5	0.4938	0.4940	0.4941	0.4943	0.4945	0.4946	0.4948	0.4949	0.4951	0.4952
2.6	0.4953	0.4955	0.4956	0.4957	0.4959	0.4960	0.4961	0.4962	0.4963	0.4964
2.7	0.4965	0.4966	0.4967	0.4968	0.4969	0.4970	0.4971	0.4972	0.4973	0.4974
2.8	0.4974	0.4975	0.4976	0.4977	0.4977	0.4978	0.4979	0.4979	0.4980	0.4981
2.9	0.4981	0.4982	0.4982	0.4983	0.4984	0.4984	0.4985	0.4985	0.4986	0.4986
3.0	0.4987	0.4987	0.4987	0.4988	0.4988	0.4989	0.4989	0.4989	0.4990	0.4990
3.1	0.4990	0.4991	0.4991	0.4991	0.4992	0.4992	0.4992	0.4992	0.4993	0.4993
3.2	0.4993	0.4993	0.4994	0.4994	0.4994	0.4994	0.4994	0.4995	0.4995	0.4995
3.3	0.4995	0.4995	0.4995	0.4996	0.4996	0.4996	0.4996	0.4996	0.4996	0.4997
3.4	0.4997	0.4997	0.4997	0.4997	0.4997	0.4997	0.4997	0.4997	0.4997	0.4998
3.5	0.4998									
4.0	0.49997									
4.5	0.499997									
5.0	0.4999997									
6.0	0.499999999									

TABLE F-2 **Critical Values of *t* for Given Probability Levels**

df	Level of Significance for One-Tailed Test					
	.10	.05	.025	.01	.005	.0005
	Level of Significance for Two-Tailed Test					
	.20	.10	.05	.02	.01	.001
1	3.078	6.314	12.706	31.821	63.657	636.619
2	1.886	2.920	4.303	6.965	9.925	31.598
3	1.638	2.353	3.182	4.541	5.841	12.941
4	1.533	2.132	2.776	3.747	4.604	8.610
5	1.476	2.015	2.571	3.365	4.032	6.859
6	1.440	1.943	2.447	3.143	3.707	5.959
7	1.415	1.895	2.365	2.998	3.499	5.405
8	1.397	1.860	2.306	2.896	3.355	5.041
9	1.383	1.833	2.262	2.821	3.250	4.781
10	1.372	1.812	2.228	2.764	3.169	4.587
11	1.363	1.796	2.201	2.718	3.106	4.437
12	1.356	1.782	2.179	2.681	3.055	4.318
13	1.350	1.771	2.160	2.650	3.012	4.221
14	1.345	1.761	2.145	2.624	2.977	4.140
15	1.341	1.753	2.131	2.602	2.947	4.073
16	1.337	1.746	2.120	2.583	2.921	4.015
17	1.333	1.740	2.110	2.567	2.898	3.965
18	1.330	1.734	2.101	2.552	2.878	3.922
19	1.328	1.729	2.093	2.539	2.861	3.883
20	1.325	1.725	2.086	2.528	2.845	3.850
21	1.323	1.721	2.080	2.518	2.831	3.819
22	1.321	1.717	2.074	2.508	2.819	3.792
23	1.319	1.714	2.069	2.500	2.807	3.767
24	1.318	1.711	2.064	2.492	2.797	3.745
25	1.316	1.708	2.060	2.485	2.787	3.725
26	1.315	1.706	2.056	2.479	2.779	3.707
27	1.314	1.703	2.052	2.473	2.771	3.690
28	1.313	1.701	2.048	2.467	2.763	3.674
29	1.311	1.699	2.045	2.462	2.756	3.659
30	1.310	1.697	2.042	2.457	2.750	3.646
40	1.303	1.684	2.021	2.423	2.704	3.551
60	1.296	1.671	2.000	2.390	2.660	3.460
120	1.289	1.658	1.980	2.358	2.617	3.373
∞	1.282	1.645	1.960	2.326	2.576	3.291

Source: Abridged from Table III of Fisher and Yates, *Statistical Tables for Biological, Agricultural, and Medical Research*, 6th ed., published by Oliver and Boyd Ltd., Edinburgh, 1963. By permission of the publishers.

TABLE F–3   Critical Values of the Chi-Square Distribution

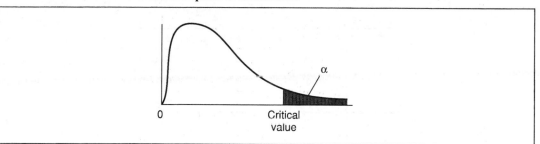

df	Probability under H_0 that $\chi^2 \geqq$ Chi Square				
	.10	.05	.02	.01	.001
1	2.71	3.84	5.41	6.64	10.83
2	4.60	5.99	7.82	9.21	13.82
3	6.25	7.82	9.84	11.34	16.27
4	7.78	9.49	11.67	13.28	18.46
5	9.24	11.07	13.39	15.09	20.52
6	10.64	12.59	15.03	16.81	22.46
7	12.02	14.07	16.62	18.48	24.32
8	13.36	15.51	18.17	20.09	26.12
9	14.68	16.92	19.68	21.67	27.88
10	15.99	18.31	21.16	23.21	29.59
11	17.28	19.68	22.62	24.72	31.26
12	18.55	21.03	24.05	26.22	32.91
13	19.81	22.36	25.47	27.69	34.53
14	21.06	23.68	26.87	29.14	36.12
15	22.31	25.00	28.26	30.58	37.70
16	23.54	26.30	29.63	32.00	39.29
17	24.77	27.59	31.00	33.41	40.75
18	25.99	28.87	32.35	34.80	42.31
19	27.20	30.14	33.69	36.19	43.82
20	28.41	31.41	35.02	37.57	45.32
21	29.62	32.67	36.34	38.93	46.80
22	30.81	33.92	37.66	40.29	48.27
23	32.01	35.17	38.97	41.64	49.73
24	33.20	36.42	40.27	42.98	51.18
25	34.38	37.65	41.57	44.31	52.62
26	35.56	38.88	42.86	45.64	54.05
27	36.74	40.11	44.14	46.96	55.48
28	37.92	41.34	45.42	48.28	56.89
29	39.09	42.56	46.69	49.59	58.30
30	40.26	43.77	47.96	50.89	59.70

Source: Abridged from Table IV of Fisher and Yates, *Statistics for Biological, Agricultural, and Medical Research,* published by Oliver and Boyd Ltd., Edinburgh, 1963. By permission of the publishers.

TABLE F–4   Critical Values of T in the Wilcoxon Matched-Pairs Test

N	Level of Significance for One-Tailed Test		
	.025	.01	.005
	Level of Significance for Two-Tailed Test		
	.05	.02	.01
6	0	—	—
7	2	0	—
8	4	2	0
9	6	3	2
10	8	5	3
11	11	7	5
12	14	10	7
13	17	13	10
14	21	16	13
15	25	20	16
16	30	24	20
17	35	28	23
18	40	33	28
19	46	38	32
20	52	43	38
21	59	49	43
22	66	56	49
23	73	62	55
24	81	69	61
25	89	77	68

Source: Adapted from Table I of F. Wilcoxon, *Some Rapid Approximate Statistical Procedures* (New York: American Cyanamid Company, 1949), p. 13, with the kind permission of the publisher.

TABLE F–5   Critical Values of D in the Kolmogorov-Smirnov One-Sample Test

Sample Size N	Level of Significance for $D = Maximum \, |F_0(X) - S_N(X)|$				
	.20	.15	.10	.05	.01
1	.900	.925	.950	.975	.995
2	.684	.726	.776	.842	.929
3	.565	.597	.642	.708	.828
4	.494	.525	.564	.624	.733
5	.446	.474	.510	.565	.669
6	.410	.436	.470	.521	.618
7	.381	.405	.438	.486	.577
8	.358	.381	.411	.457	.543
9	.339	.360	.388	.432	.514
10	.322	.342	.368	.410	.490
11	.307	.326	.352	.391	.468
12	.295	.313	.338	.375	.450
13	.284	.302	.325	.361	.433
14	.274	.292	.314	.349	.418
15	.266	.283	.304	.338	.404
16	.258	.274	.295	.328	.392
17	.250	.266	.286	.318	.381
18	.244	.259	.278	.309	.371
19	.237	.252	.272	.301	.363
20	.231	.246	.264	.294	.356
25	.21	.22	.24	.27	.32
30	.19	.20	.22	.24	.29
35	.18	.19	.21	.23	.27
Over 35	$\dfrac{1.07}{\sqrt{N}}$	$\dfrac{1.14}{\sqrt{N}}$	$\dfrac{1.22}{\sqrt{N}}$	$\dfrac{1.36}{\sqrt{N}}$	$\dfrac{1.63}{\sqrt{N}}$

Source: F. J. Massey, Jr., "The Kolmogorov-Smirnov Test for Goodness of Fit," *Journal of the American Statistical Association*, 46, p. 70. Adapted with the kind permission of the publisher.

TABLE F–6   Critical Values of K_D in the Kolmogorov-Smirnov Two-Sample Test (small samples)

N	One-Tailed Test*		Two-Tailed Test†	
	$\alpha = .05$	$\alpha = .01$	$\alpha = .05$	$\alpha = .01$
3	3	—	—	—
4	4	—	4	—
5	4	5	5	5
6	5	6	5	6
7	5	6	6	6
8	5	6	6	7
9	6	7	6	7
10	6	7	7	8
11	6	8	7	8
12	6	8	7	8
13	7	8	7	9
14	7	8	8	9
15	7	9	8	9
16	7	9	8	10
17	8	9	8	10
18	8	10	9	10
19	8	10	9	10
20	8	10	9	11
21	8	10	9	11
22	9	11	9	11
23	9	11	10	11
24	9	11	10	12
25	9	11	10	12
26	9	11	10	12
27	9	12	10	12
28	10	12	11	13
29	10	12	11	13
30	10	12	11	13
35	11	13	12	
40	11	14	13	

*Source: Abridged from I. A. Goodman, "Kolmogorov-Smirnov Tests for Psychological Research," *Psychological Bulletin* 51, 1951, p. 167, copyright (1951) by the American Psychological Association. Reprinted by permission.
†Source: Derived from Table 1 of F. J. Massey, Jr., "The Distribution of the Maximum Deviation between Two Sample Cumulative Step Functions," *Annals of Mathematical Statistics* 23, 1951, pp. 126–27, with the kind permission of the publisher.

TABLE F–7 Critical Values of D in the Kolmogorov-Smirnov Two-Sample Test for Large Samples (two-tailed)

Level of Significance	Value of D So Large As To Call for Rejection of H_0 at the Indicated Level of Significance, Where $D = Maximum \|S_{n_1}(X) - S_2(X)\|$
.10	$1.22 \sqrt{\dfrac{n_1 + n_2}{n_1 n_2}}$
.05	$1.36 \sqrt{\dfrac{n_1 + n_2}{n_1 n_2}}$
.025	$1.48 \sqrt{\dfrac{n_1 + n_2}{n_1 n_2}}$
.01	$1.63 \sqrt{\dfrac{n_1 + n_2}{n_1 n_2}}$
.005	$1.73 \sqrt{\dfrac{n_1 + n_2}{n_1 n_2}}$
.001	$1.95 \sqrt{\dfrac{n_1 + n_2}{n_1 n_2}}$

*Adapted from N. Smirnov, "Table for Estimating the Goodness of Fit of Empirical Distribution," *Annals of Mathematical Statistics* 18, 1948, pp. 280–81, with the kind permission of the publisher.

TABLE F-8 **Partial Table of Critical Values of *U* in the Mann-Whitney Test**

Critical Values for One-Tailed Test at α = .025 or a Two-Tailed Test at α = .05

n_1 \ n_2	9	10	11	12	13	14	15	16	17	18	19	20
1												
2	0	0	0	1	1	1	1	1	2	2	2	2
3	2	3	3	4	4	5	5	6	6	7	7	8
4	4	5	6	7	8	9	10	11	11	12	13	13
5	7	8	9	11	12	13	14	15	17	18	19	20
6	10	11	13	14	16	17	19	21	22	24	25	27
7	12	14	16	18	20	22	24	26	28	30	32	34
8	15	17	19	22	24	26	29	31	34	36	38	41
9	17	20	23	26	28	31	34	37	39	42	45	48
10	20	23	26	29	33	36	39	42	45	48	52	55
11	23	26	30	33	37	40	44	47	51	55	58	62
12	26	29	33	37	41	45	49	53	57	61	66	69
13	28	33	37	41	45	50	54	59	63	67	72	76
14	31	36	40	45	50	55	59	64	67	74	78	83
15	34	39	44	49	54	59	64	70	75	80	85	90
16	37	42	47	53	59	64	70	75	81	86	92	98
17	39	45	51	57	63	67	75	81	87	93	99	105
18	42	48	55	61	67	74	80	86	93	99	106	112
19	45	52	58	65	72	78	85	92	99	106	113	119
20	48	55	62	69	76	83	90	98	105	112	119	127

Critical Values for One-Tailed Test at α = .05 or a Two-Tailed Test at α = .10

n_2 \ n_1	9	10	11	12	13	14	15	16	17	18	19	20
1											0	0
2	1	1	1	2	2	2	3	3	3	4	4	4
3	3	4	5	5	6	7	7	8	9	9	10	11
4	6	7	8	9	10	11	12	14	15	16	17	18
5	9	11	12	13	15	16	18	19	20	22	23	25
6	12	14	16	17	19	21	23	25	26	28	30	32
7	15	17	19	21	24	26	28	30	33	35	37	39
8	18	20	23	26	28	31	33	36	39	41	44	47
9	21	24	27	30	33	36	39	42	45	48	51	54
10	24	27	31	34	37	41	44	48	51	55	58	62
11	27	31	34	38	42	46	50	54	57	61	65	69
12	30	34	38	42	47	51	55	60	64	68	72	77
13	33	37	42	47	51	56	61	65	70	75	80	84
14	36	41	46	51	56	61	66	71	77	82	87	92
15	39	44	50	55	61	66	72	77	83	88	94	100
16	42	48	54	60	65	71	77	83	89	95	101	107
17	45	51	57	64	70	77	83	89	96	102	109	115
18	48	55	61	68	75	82	88	95	102	109	116	123
19	51	58	65	72	80	87	94	101	109	116	123	130
20	54	62	69	77	84	92	100	107	115	123	130	138

Source: Abridged from D. Auble, "Extended Tables from the Mann-Whitney Statistic," *Bulletin of the Institute of Educational Research* at Indiana University 1, no. 2, reprinted with permission. For tables for other size samples consult this source.

TABLE F–9 Critical Values of the F Distribution for $\alpha = .05$

.05

F

Degrees of Freedom for Numerator

n_2	1	2	3	4	5	6	7	8	9	10	12	15	20	24	30	40	60	120	∞
1	161.4	199.5	215.7	224.6	230.2	234.0	236.8	238.9	240.5	241.9	243.9	245.9	248.0	249.1	250.1	251.1	252.2	253.3	243.3
2	18.51	19.00	19.16	19.25	19.30	19.33	19.35	19.37	19.38	19.40	19.41	19.43	19.45	19.45	19.46	19.47	19.48	19.49	19.50
3	10.13	9.55	9.28	9.12	9.01	8.94	8.89	8.85	8.81	8.79	8.74	8.70	8.66	8.64	8.62	8.59	8.57	8.55	8.53
4	7.71	6.94	6.59	6.39	6.26	6.16	6.09	6.04	6.00	5.96	5.91	5.86	5.80	5.77	5.75	5.72	5.69	5.66	5.63
5	6.61	5.79	5.41	5.19	5.05	4.95	4.88	4.82	4.77	4.74	4.68	4.62	4.56	4.53	4.50	4.46	4.43	4.40	4.35
6	5.99	5.14	4.76	4.53	4.39	4.28	4.21	4.15	4.10	4.06	4.00	3.94	3.87	3.84	3.81	3.77	3.74	3.70	3.67
7	5.59	4.74	4.35	4.12	3.97	3.87	3.79	3.73	3.68	3.64	3.57	3.51	3.44	3.41	3.38	3.34	3.30	3.27	3.23
8	5.32	4.46	4.07	3.84	3.69	3.58	3.50	3.44	3.39	3.35	3.28	3.22	3.15	3.12	3.08	3.04	3.01	2.97	2.93
9	5.12	4.26	3.86	3.63	3.48	3.37	3.29	3.23	3.18	3.14	3.07	3.01	2.94	2.90	2.86	2.83	2.79	2.75	2.71
10	4.96	4.10	3.71	3.48	3.33	3.22	3.14	3.07	3.02	2.98	2.91	2.85	2.77	2.74	2.70	2.66	2.62	2.58	2.54
11	4.84	3.98	3.59	3.36	3.20	3.09	3.01	2.95	2.90	2.85	2.79	2.72	2.65	2.61	2.57	2.53	2.49	2.45	2.40
12	4.75	3.89	3.49	3.26	3.11	3.00	2.91	2.85	2.80	2.75	2.69	2.62	2.54	2.51	2.47	2.43	2.38	2.34	2.30
13	4.67	3.81	3.41	3.18	3.03	2.92	2.83	2.77	2.71	2.67	2.60	2.53	2.46	2.42	2.38	2.34	2.30	2.25	2.21
14	4.60	3.74	3.34	3.11	2.96	2.85	2.76	2.70	2.65	2.60	2.53	2.46	2.39	2.35	2.31	2.27	2.22	2.18	2.13
15	4.54	3.68	3.29	3.06	2.90	2.79	2.71	2.64	2.59	2.54	2.48	2.40	2.33	2.29	2.25	2.20	2.16	2.11	2.07
16	4.49	3.63	3.24	3.01	2.85	2.74	2.66	2.59	2.54	2.49	2.42	2.35	2.28	2.24	2.19	2.15	2.11	2.06	2.01
17	4.45	3.59	3.20	2.96	2.81	2.70	2.61	2.55	2.49	2.45	2.38	2.31	2.23	2.19	2.15	2.10	2.06	2.01	1.96
18	4.41	3.55	3.16	2.93	2.77	2.66	2.58	2.51	2.46	2.41	2.34	2.27	2.19	2.15	2.11	2.06	2.02	1.97	1.92
19	4.38	3.52	3.13	2.90	2.74	2.63	2.54	2.48	2.42	2.38	2.31	2.23	2.16	2.11	2.07	2.03	1.98	1.93	1.88
20	4.35	3.49	3.10	2.87	2.71	2.60	2.51	2.45	2.39	2.35	2.28	2.20	2.12	2.08	2.04	1.99	1.95	1.90	1.84
21	4.32	3.47	3.07	2.84	2.68	2.57	2.49	2.42	2.37	2.32	2.25	2.18	2.10	2.05	2.01	1.96	1.92	1.87	1.81
22	4.30	3.44	3.05	2.82	2.66	2.55	2.46	2.40	2.34	2.30	2.23	2.15	2.07	2.03	1.98	1.94	1.89	1.84	1.78
23	4.28	3.42	3.03	2.80	2.64	2.53	2.44	2.37	2.32	2.27	2.20	2.13	2.05	2.01	1.96	1.91	1.86	1.81	1.76
24	4.26	3.40	3.01	2.78	2.62	2.51	2.42	2.36	2.30	2.25	2.18	2.11	2.03	1.98	1.94	1.89	1.84	1.79	1.73
25	4.24	3.39	2.99	2.76	2.60	2.49	2.40	2.34	2.28	2.24	2.16	2.09	2.01	1.96	1.92	1.87	1.82	1.77	1.71
26	4.23	3.37	2.98	2.74	2.59	2.47	2.39	2.32	2.27	2.22	2.15	2.07	1.99	1.95	1.90	1.85	1.80	1.75	1.69
27	4.21	3.35	2.96	2.73	2.57	2.46	2.37	2.31	2.25	2.20	2.13	2.06	1.97	1.93	1.88	1.84	1.79	1.73	1.67
28	4.20	3.34	2.95	2.71	2.56	2.45	2.36	2.29	2.24	2.19	2.12	2.04	1.96	1.91	1.87	1.82	1.77	1.71	1.65
29	4.18	3.33	2.93	2.70	2.55	2.43	2.35	2.28	2.22	2.18	2.10	2.03	1.94	1.90	1.85	1.81	1.75	1.70	1.64
30	4.17	3.32	2.92	2.69	2.53	2.42	2.33	2.27	2.21	2.16	2.09	2.01	1.93	1.89	1.84	1.79	1.74	1.68	1.62
40	4.08	3.23	2.84	2.61	2.45	2.34	2.25	2.18	2.12	2.08	2.00	1.92	1.84	1.79	1.74	1.69	1.64	1.58	1.51
60	4.00	3.15	2.76	2.53	2.37	2.25	2.17	2.10	2.04	1.99	1.92	1.84	1.75	1.70	1.65	1.59	1.53	1.47	1.39
120	3.92	3.07	2.68	2.45	2.29	2.17	2.09	2.02	1.96	1.91	1.83	1.75	1.66	1.61	1.55	1.50	1.43	1.35	1.25
∞	3.84	3.00	2.60	2.37	2.21	2.10	2.01	1.94	1.88	1.83	1.75	1.67	1.57	1.52	1.46	1.39	1.32	1.22	1.00

Degrees of Freedom for Denominator

Reprinted by permission from *Statistical Methods* by George W. Snedecor and William G. Cochran, sixth edition © 1967 by Iowa State University Press, Ames, Iowa.

TABLE F–10   **Random Numbers**

97446	30328	05262	77371	13523	62057	44349	85884	94555	23288
15453	75591	60540	77137	09485	27632	05477	99154	78720	10323
69995	77086	55217	53721	85713	27854	41981	88981	90041	20878
69726	58696	27272	38148	52521	73807	29685	49152	20309	58734
23604	31948	16926	26360	76957	99925	86045	11617	32777	38670
13640	17233	58650	47819	24935	28670	33415	77202	92492	40290
90779	09199	51169	94892	34271	22068	13923	53535	56358	50258
71068	19459	32339	10124	13012	79706	07611	52600	83088	26829
55019	79001	34442	16335	06428	52873	65316	01480	72204	39494
20879	50235	17389	25260	34039	99967	48044	05067	69284	53867
00380	11595	49372	95214	98529	46593	77046	27176	39668	20566
68142	40800	20527	79212	14166	84948	11748	69540	84288	37211
42667	89566	20440	57230	35356	01884	79921	94772	29882	24695
07756	78430	45576	86596	56720	65529	44211	18447	53921	92722
45221	31130	44312	63534	47741	02465	50629	94983	05984	88375
20140	77481	61686	82836	41058	41331	04290	61212	60294	95954
54922	25436	33804	51907	73223	66423	68706	36589	45267	35327
48340	30832	72209	07644	52747	40751	06808	85349	18005	52323
23603	84387	20416	88084	33103	41511	59391	71600	35091	52722
12548	01033	22974	59596	92087	02116	63524	00627	41778	24392
15251	87584	12942	03771	91413	75652	19468	83889	98531	91529
65548	59670	57355	18874	63601	55111	07278	32560	40028	36079
48488	76170	46282	76427	41693	04506	80979	26654	62159	83017
02862	15665	62159	15159	69576	20328	68873	28152	66087	39405
67929	06754	45842	66365	80848	15262	55144	37816	08421	30071
73237	07607	31615	04892	50989	87347	14393	21165	68169	70788
13788	20327	07960	95917	75112	01398	26381	41377	33549	19754
43877	66485	40825	45923	74410	69693	76959	70973	26343	63781
14047	08369	56414	78533	76378	44204	71493	68861	31042	81873
88383	46755	51342	13505	55324	52950	22244	28028	73486	98797
29567	16379	41994	65947	58926	50953	09388	00405	29874	44954
20508	60995	41539	26396	99825	25652	28089	57224	35222	58922
64178	76768	75747	32854	32893	61152	58565	33128	33354	16056
26373	51147	90362	93309	13175	66385	57822	31138	12893	68607
10083	47656	59241	73630	99200	94672	59785	95449	99279	25488
11683	14347	04369	98719	75005	43633	24125	30532	54830	95387
56548	76293	50904	88579	24621	94291	56881	35062	48765	22078
35292	47291	82610	27777	43965	31802	98444	88929	54383	93141
51329	87645	51623	08971	50704	82395	33916	95859	99788	97885
51860	19180	39324	68483	78650	74750	64893	58042	82878	20619
23886	01257	07945	71175	31243	87167	42829	44601	08769	26417
80028	82310	43989	09242	15056	48250	04529	96941	48190	69644
83946	46858	09164	18858	12672	55190	02820	45861	29104	75386
00000	41586	25972	25356	54260	95691	99431	89903	22306	43863
90615	12848	23376	29458	48239	37628	59265	50152	30340	40713
42003	10738	55835	48218	23204	19188	13556	06610	77667	88068
86135	26174	07834	17007	97938	96728	15689	77544	891P6	41252
54436	10828	41212	19836	89476	53685	28085	22878	71868	35048
14545	72034	32131	38783	58588	47499	50945	97045	42357	53536
43925	49879	13339	78773	95626	67119	93023	96832	09757	98545

Source: The Rand Corporation, *A Million Random Digits with 100,000 Normal Deviates* (Glencoe, Ill.: The Free Press, 1955), p. 225.

INDEX